DONALD W. PATTEN

JOHN REMLING

AUTOMOTIVE SERVICE BASICS

Fourth Edition

D1361427

Upper Saddle River, New Jersey
Columbus, Ohio

Library of Congress Cataloging-in-Publication Data

Patten, Donald W.
   Automotive service basics / Donald W. Patten.—4th ed.
      p.   cm.
   Rev. ed. of: Automotive service basics / John Remling, Donald W. Patten. c1997.
   Includes index.
   ISBN 0-13-089868-6
   1. Automobiles—Maintenance and repair.   I. Remling, John—Automotive service
basics. II. Title.
   TL152 .P334   2002
   629.28′72—dc21   2001021504

Editor in Chief: Stephen Helba
Executive Editor: Ed Francis
Production Editor: Stephen C. Robb
Production Supervision: TechBooks
Design Coordinator: Robin G. Chukes
Cover Designer: Rod Harris
Cover art: Neal Moss
Production Manager: Brian Fox
Marketing Manager: Jamie Van Voorhis

This book was set New Baskerville and Swiss by TechBooks. It was printed and bound by Banta Book Group.
The cover was printed by Phoenix Color Corp.

Earlier edition © 1981 by John Wiley & Sons, Inc.

Pearson Education Ltd., *London*
Pearson Education Australia Pty. Limited, *Sydney*
Pearson Education Singapore, Pte. Ltd.
Pearson Education North Asia Ltd., *Hong Kong*
Pearson Education Canada, Ltd. *Toronto*
Pearson Educación de Mexico, S.A. de C.V.
Pearson Education—Japan, *Tokyo*
Pearson Education Malaysia Pte. Ltd.
Pearson Education, *Upper Saddle River, New Jersey*

10 9 8 7 6 5 4 3
ISBN 0-13-089868-6

Preface

Environmental concerns and energy conservation continue to bring about revolutionary technical changes in automotive design and construction. Meanwhile, the role of computers is growing. Computers now monitor or control the brake systems, fuel systems, dash gauges, air-conditioning systems, and more, and the automotive industry plans to expand further the use of computers and sensors.

All of this means that technicians must know how to test these complicated systems using sophisticated diagnostic and repair procedures. This edition of *Automotive Service Basics* provides the means for readers to gain the required knowledge and develop the diagnostic and repair skills necessary to perform basic maintenance on vehicles in current production, as well as older vehicles.

This text is intended for use in *any* basic automotive course, regardless of academic level. The format for presentation of the material is individual lessons. The instructor can select a particular lesson, and the students can do as much work as class time permits. Any automotive service topic can be explored in greater depth through additional lessons.

Familiar features from past editions that have worked well remain relatively unchanged. However, advances in automotive technology since the last edition are thoroughly covered. Other changes focus on the reorganization of material by chapter and on content additions. All chapters include the following revisions:

- New chapter introductions more effectively preview the material to be covered in that chapter.
- Chapters have been re-sequenced to group more logically the related sections based on ASE areas.

- Sidebars and safety tips appear more frequently, highlighting important facts that students need to know.
- New photos and illustrations depict the latest and best products and procedures in the industry.
- New off-the-shelf products are covered.
- Component service is examined in greater detail.
- The role and importance of used parts are discussed.
- All chapter vocabulary questions have been revised.
- All review questions and SAE questions are new.

In specific chapters, there is new or expanded coverage of extended-life engine coolant, the latest engine oils and other lubricants, retrofitting with R-134a air-conditioner coolant and new compressor lubricants, and much more.

An instructor's manual is available and covers the major systems for each chapter. Features of the instructor's manual include the following:

- Lesson plans for each lesson
- A new feature called *focus* that helps direct the attention of the students to the chapter materials
- Additional questions on each lesson that can be used for pop tests or given to the students to help direct them to lesson details
- Answers to the vocabulary questions and the review questions

Many readers might not know that John Remling passed away after completion of the second edition. His efforts are still appreciated, but time marches on and it has been necessary to make many revisions. I am sure that John would have been proud to know that his basic efforts still live on in yet another edition.

Brief Contents

Table of Contents

What is Basic Automotive Maintenance?

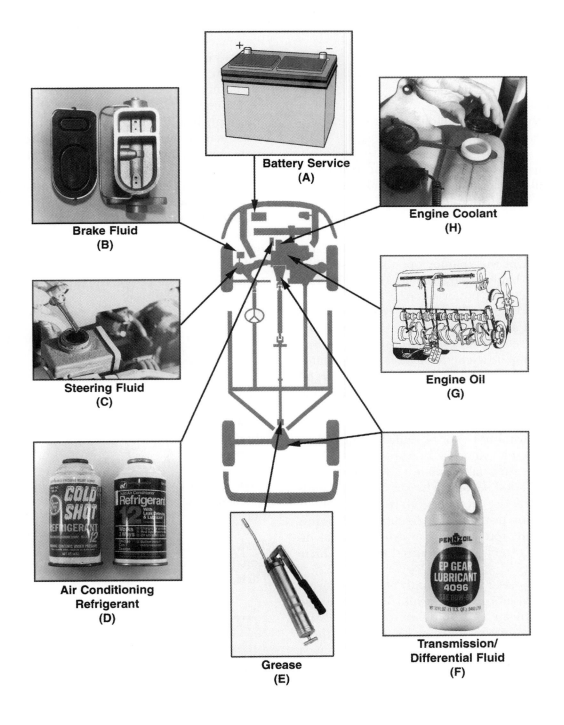

Battery Service (A)

Brake Fluid (B)

Engine Coolant (H)

Steering Fluid (C)

Engine Oil (G)

Air Conditioning Refrigerant (D)

Grease (E)

Transmission/ Differential Fluid (F)

Proper maintenance of an automobile is important in these areas:

1. *Safety.* If the various systems of an automobile are kept in good working order, accidents caused by system failures are minimized.
2. *Economy.* The advantages of properly maintaining an automobile are apparent not only in low operating costs but in high resale value.
3. *Fuel conservation.* A well-maintained automobile uses less fuel. The importance of fuel conservation cannot be overstated.
4. *Air pollution.* A properly maintained automobile emits fewer pollutants into the atmosphere.

Basic automotive maintenance is the process of keeping all the working parts of an automobile in good condition, to reduce wear and friction to a minimum. It also means replacing materials that are dirty or worn out.

Basic maintenance should include all of the items shown in the chapter opening illustration: servicing the battery (part A), checking brake fluid (part B), checking power steering fluid (see part C), and checking engine coolant (see part H). To prevent wear damage to the suspension parts, use a grease gun (see part E) to force grease into all suspension fittings on a scheduled basis. Check engine oil (see part F) and transmission fluid (see part G) and change on a schedule. The transmission and the engine are two of the most expensive parts in a vehicle and with some care can last the life of the automobile without repair or replacement. An automobile is a very expensive machine. Most vehicle owners want their automobile to be dependable and to give good service. The customer depends on the automotive technician to find and correct any lubrication problems and to change lubricants when needed. You should know the servicing intervals and correct fluids required for any vehicle serviced.

Oils and greases are constantly being improved. The specified lubricant for a vehicle today can be replaced with an improved lubricant tomorrow. As an automotive technician, be aware of these changes and ready to put the newest and latest materials to work when they are available. Engine oils and brake fluids are two products that have changed often through the years. Using obsolete American Petroleum Institute (API) rated engine oils in a new vehicle could destroy the engine, especially if these newer oils were created to solve past engine damage problems.

The vehicle owner's manual is the first place to look for the right maintenance products. Be alert for any improved lubrication materials made after the manual was printed. Manufacturers have important update bulletins, and parts suppliers have additional information. Be sure to consult these sources to keep up with the new technology.

The automobile contains thousands of parts connected and fitted so that they all work together. In many instances, the failure of one part will cause the failure of one or more other parts. Extensive repairs are then required. Not all parts failures can be blamed on defects in the parts. Improper adjustment, insufficient lubrication, and corrosion cause many failures. Proper maintenance will eliminate many of these causes, and thus minimize part failure.

The most efficient type of maintenance is preventive maintenance. Preventive maintenance emphasizes the simple jobs. Checking and adjusting the level of oil in an engine is a simple job. Yet if the oil level drops too low, extensive engine damage will result. Checking and adjusting air pressure in tires is another simple job. Yet underinflation is the most common cause of excessive tire wear. Many times the simple jobs are the most important.

TASKS

The following are three tasks to master before leaving this chapter:

Task 1-1. Learn how to identify and accurately check fluids and lubricants used in automotive maintenance.

Task 1-2. Learn how to identify failed, damaged, or missing vehicle parts and make correct repair decisions.

Task 1-3. Learn how to use vehicle identification information to obtain the correct replacement parts.

LESSON 1-1   Identification of Lubricants and Maintenance Materials

The specific purpose of this lesson is to identify and check some of the lubricants and maintenance materials found in a vehicle. These products are the heart of any maintenance plan. After studying this lesson material, select a vehicle and check these lubrication products. Check whether these fluids are dirty or low. If so, correct the problem or alert the owner to have it corrected. Before putting any fluids in a vehicle, consult the owner's manual or manufacturer's repair manuals to get the correct fluid recommendation. Research and study correct fluids while working toward becoming a lubrication specialist.

Never put any fluid anywhere in an automobile until absolutely sure it is correct for that particular vehicle, and you know where to add the fluid. Also be sure of the correct quantity to add and how to check the fluid level accurately. Overfilling can cause as many problems as not enough lubricant.

Engine Coolant

The primary purpose of a coolant (antifreeze) is to prevent internal engine freezing in winter temperatures and provide better heat–to–engine block transfer in summer temperatures. (see safety message 1).

Engine Coolant Maintenance List

- Check coolant level at radiator
- Check coolant level at recovery reservoir
- Test the coolant specific gravity with a hydrometer
- Check the coolant for contamination and rust

Note: Additional checks to the cooling system are covered in Chapter 10.

Coolant can be found inside the engine, heater system, and radiator (see Figure 1.1). The new generation of coolants are nitrite, phosphate, and silicate free. Coolants of this type meet the Japanese and European automotive manufacturers' standards where these chemicals are not to be used. The shelf life of coolants has increased from eighteen months to about eight years.

One type of coolant has a propylene glycol base, and the other still uses the conventional ethylene glycol. Both coolants provide superior protection for aluminum, brass, cast iron, steel, solder, and copper. This means the life of the coolant is extended and water pump life is improved because the pump seals last longer. Heat transfer between the engine and coolant is improved, which reduces summer boil-over. These products both provide superior winter freeze protection. They are 100% biodegradable if never used, but the percentage falls slightly when used in a vehicle. This means they should not be poured out on the ground but disposed of properly.

If the older conventional ethylene glycol coolant is added during service to this new extended-life coolant, a dilution of over 10% will decrease the extended-life protection. When adding coolant, use the same product. Use extended-life ethylene glycol if that is in the cooling system and extended-life propylene glycol where that is found. The best maintenance plan is to always add the same base extended-life coolant to the radiator system during service and change the coolant at the maximum

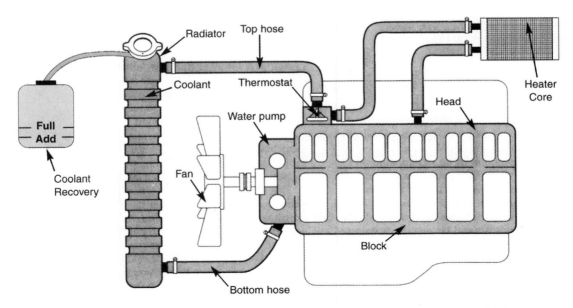

Figure 1.1 Engine coolant system. Engine coolant can be found in these places in an engine (courtesy of Training Enterprises Company).

recommended vehicle mileage and years. This can be as long as five years and 150,000 miles, which is longer than a great many owners drive their automobiles before trading.

A chemical coolant system flush is not recommended as a service procedure unless there are visible deposits inside the radiator and the tubes are restricted. But if a flush is used, be sure to neutralize the cleaner by running at least two clear water flushes before adding the nitrite-free extended-life coolant. Be sure the cleaner is out of the heater system as well. Use at least two water flushes when changing from conventional coolants to the extended-life coolants to reduce the possibility of contamination and shortening the coolant life.

In extreme cold weather temperatures the ratio of extended-life coolant to water can be changed up to 60% coolant and 40% water from the normal 50% water and antifreeze mix. Do not mix the antifreeze level to over 67% or under 40% for maximum benefits and protection.

> **!** **Safety Message 1:** All coolants should be handled carefully. They taste good to pets and small children but are a deadly poison. Don't let coolant drain out on the ground because dogs, cats, or other animals may swallow it. Do not store it in a commercial drink carton: small children may mistake it for a drinkable liquid. Do not let it get into your groundwater system—it could poison anyone getting water from the area.

Another important reason to use coolant instead of plain water in a vehicle is for temperature sensor accuracy. Coolant provides the right specific gravity and is the only correct fluid for any vehicle with an electronic computer, which depends on accurate sensor information.

When adjusting the coolant level, be careful not to overfill the radiator (see Figure 1.2). Coolant recovery systems are filled at the recovery tank. Fill these to the full mark with coolant only, not water. (see Figure 1.3).

The cooling system is a closed system and will develop pressures in excess of fifteen pounds per square inch (psi). The actual pressure depends on the pressure limit of the cap. It is not normal to find the coolant level below the top of the radiator in any system that has a coolant recovery system. There is a leak somewhere in the cooling system if the level has to be constantly adjusted. Leaks can occur either under pressure or when the system is cold and not pressurized. Common areas for leaks

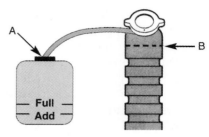

A. Fill point for coolant recovery systems.
B. Fill level for conventional systems.

Figure 1.2   Coolant level. When filling radiators without coolant recovery systems, leave expansion room at the top. Radiators with coolant recovery systems are filled to the maximum or cold coolant level at the recovery reservoir. Always check and adjust the radiator coolant level if the recovery reservoir is found empty (courtesy of Ford Motor Company).

to occur are the upper and lower radiator hose, radiator, cap, heater hoses, and coolant recovery tank. Coolant can leak inside the motor from a damaged cylinder head gasket and mix with the engine oil. When this happens, the oil will change to a heavy dark sludge. This is a very serious problem and must be corrected immediately. Coolant that enters the combustion chamber of the engine will cause a white exhaust smoke.

The radiator level can be maintained in a normal system by adding a 50/50 mix to the coolant recovery reservoir up to the "full" mark. If the reservoir level keeps dropping, follow these steps:

1. Wait for the radiator to cool down (at least fifteen minutes or more). When the system is warm to the touch, go to step 2.
2. Place a shop towel over the radiator cap and move it to the pressure release position

Figure 1.3   Coolant. A mixture of 50% water and 50% antifreeze is called *coolant*. For very cold climates this can be adjusted up to 70% antifreeze and 30% water.

(first position). Release all pressure before completely removing the cap. Keep the shop towel in place to avoid burning your hand.

3. Look at the level of the coolant in the radiator. It should be full.

4. Check the quality of the coolant and make a radiator cap inspection.

5. Adjust the coolant level in any low radiator. Since you may be adding coolant or water to a hot engine, it is safer to let the engine cool. Pouring cold fluid into a hot engine could result in a cracked engine block or head. To be even safer, start the engine if you need to add large amounts of coolant. This mixes the cold and hot liquids and reduces the chance of engine damage. The best and safest plan is to let the engine cool. If possible, use a coolant mix to fill a radiator, not water. As noted, water will dilute the coolant strength and change the ratio of water to antifreeze.

6. Install and lock the cap by turning it as far as it will go clockwise.

7. Check and fill the coolant recovery reservoir to the "full" mark (use only coolant). See Figures 1.2 and 1.4.

8. Have the customer drive the vehicle and monitor the cooling system to see how rapidly the reservoir drops to the "add" mark or if the coolant level is dropping in the radiator without dropping in the coolant reservoir. Any

rapid coolant loss will require further testing to find the source of the leak or leaks. Immediately correct all leaks. A low coolant level usually leads to overheated engines and engine damage.

For more information about the cooling system, see Chapter 10.

Automatic Transmission Fluid

Many cars have automatic transmissions. These transmissions are hydraulically operated, and the maintenance of the fluid level is very important.

Automatic Transmission Fluid Maintenance List

- Check fluid level and quality
- Check for fluid leaks
- Add the correct fluid to maintain the right level
- Monitor the fluid and filter change frequency
- Change fluid and filter when required

Note: Additional checks to the automatic transmission are covered in Chapter 13.

Different types of fluid are required for different types of transmissions. The use of the wrong fluid can affect the operation of a transmission and can result in damage to certain components. By

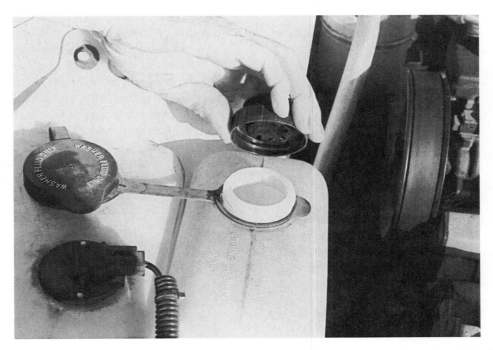

Figure 1.4 Filling recovery system. Fill the coolant recovery tank with antifreeze, water, or coolant only until the fluid reaches the "full" mark. Use coolant or antifreeze only in the winter to reduce freeze damage to the tank (courtesy of Training Enterprises Company).

Figure 1.5 Automatic transmission dipstick. The measurement is accurate only when the fluid is at normal temperature and when the engine is running (courtesy of Training Enterprises Company).

performing the jobs in this text, you will learn how to check the fluid level in automatic transmissions (see Figure 1.5). You will also learn how to select the correct fluid. Automatic transmission fluid lubricates all the gears, clutches, bands, and bearings in the transmission. It is a gold or red color when new, becoming darker when used. This fluid is pumped throughout the automatic transmission, torque converter, and transmission cooler system (see Figure 1.6).

Early Ford vehicles used a special transmission fluid type (type F) and General Motors used another (type A). A newer fluid called DEXTRON II-e/MERCON has replaced the type "A" and "F" fluids. The next generation of automatic transmission fluid, called DEXTRON III/MERCON, has

Figure 1.6 Automatic transmission fluid. Fluid like this is usually bought by the quart or liter for use in automatic transmissions. Be sure to use the right fluid for the vehicle being serviced, and never overfill the unit (courtesy Training Enterprises Company).

been on the market since 1994. This new fluid can be used in the older vehicles where a friction-modifying fluid is recommended.

In 1997 some Chrysler products required an automatic transmission fluid that meets their MS-7176D specifications. Use this fluid in the place of DEXTRON III/MERCON fluid. An improved DEXTRON III/MERCON fluid has been marketed that is semisynthetic. This fluid is especially formulated to have improved qualities over a base stock fluid. This new fluid superseded and replaces all General Motors and Ford specifications. This is an improvement over the regular 1994 DEXTRON III/MERCON automatic transmission fluid and can be used in any vehicle that requires the regular fluid.

> When checking the fluid level of any automatic transmission system, always inspect the fluid for dirt and contamination. Water contamination will show up as a white sludge.

Transmission fluid gets very hot. To prevent it from a thermal breakdown (overheating), it is circulated to the radiator where a heat exchanger cools the fluid.

There is a filter in the transmission located on the end of the oil pickup tube. This filter requires periodic replacement to keep the oil clean and to ensure normal oil flow. Vehicle mileage and use decide filter replacement intervals. Severe use requires more frequent filter changes.

Transmission fluid, like that shown in Figure 1.6, can leak out of the front and rear seal of the transmission, the pan gasket, at the speedometer cable, shift linkage, cooler lines, and cooler. Transmission fluid can enter the fuel intake system through a ruptured vacuum modulator diaphragm and can enter the radiator from a leak in the cooler heat exchanger. Transmission fluid burned in the engine will produce blue smoke at the exhaust pipe. Transmission fluid in the radiator coolant will turn the coolant into a white milky sludge. Correct all problems of this kind immediately.

To check automatic transmission fluid, follow these steps:

1. Warm the transmission by driving the vehicle (5 to 10 minutes).
2. Place the vehicle in park on a level surface with the engine running.
3. Remove the transmission dipstick and examine the fluid for dirt and contamination. Place

some fluid between your thumb and finger. Feel for any hard particles or metal shavings. Smell the fluid for a burned odor. Clutches and bands burn up from lack of pressure and from dirty fluid. Wipe the fluid from the stick with a clean cloth.

4. Insert the dipstick back into the transmission until it stops.
5. Pull the dipstick out and find the fluid level. It requires one pint (0.47 liters) of transmission fluid to bring the level from the "add" mark up to the "full" mark on most dipsticks. (refer to Figure 1.5). If this is not true for a particular vehicle, be sure you know how to read the dipstick you are using. Use the correct viscosity and type of fluid when adding any new fluid to a transmission (see Figure 1.6.).

For more automatic transmission information, see Chapter 13.

Manual Transmission Fluid

Manual transmissions use a variety of lubrication fluids (see Figure 1.7) to lubricate bearings, gears, shafts, shift levers, and synchronizers. The American Petroleum Institute (API) rates the quality of gear lubricant on a scale of one to five, with GL-5 being the best quality. In most of these classifications there are multiviscosity and single viscosity grades. SAE 80W-90 or 75W-90 are typical multiviscosity ranges, and SAE 90W a typical single one. As a rule, the temperature and climate decide the need for selecting the right viscosity. A multiviscosity oil will flow better when cold and will thicken when hot. Extreme heat would require the use of a thicker oil. A cold operating temperature would require a thinner oil or one with a lower multiviscosity starting range. Always consult the manufacturer's recommendations for the correct viscosity, quality, and type of lubricant to use. Some manufacturers have even started using motor oils in their manual transmissions, so always check before using any type of fluid in a manual transmission.

Manual Transmission Fluid Maintenance List

• Check fluid level and quality
• Check for fluid leaks
• Add the correct quality and viscosity fluid when needed
• Monitor the fluid change frequency intervals
• Change fluid when required

Figure 1.7 Gear lubricant. This fluid is usually bought in a quart or .947 ml squeeze bottle. Notice that limited-slip differentials have a special lubricant that should not be used in transmissions. The regular transmission and differential lubricant is not used in limited-slip differentials (courtesy Training Enterprises Company).

Note: Additional checks to manual transmissions are covered in Chapter 13.

New manual transmission fluid is light brown in color, turning darker with use. If a manual transmission has fluid leaks, inspect the front and rear seals of the transmission, the drain plug, the shift lever seals, the rear extension housing gasket, the cover bolts, and cover gasket. Tighten any lose bolts to the correct torque and wipe the transmission clean of any leaking fluid. Monitor this area to see if the leaks stop.

To check manual transmission fluid, follow these steps:

1. Raise the vehicle, using a lift or floor jack. Be sure to place jack stands under any vehicle raised by a floor jack. Also be sure the vehicle is level by jacking up both front and rear.

2. Remove the transmission filler plug, located on the side of the transmission.
3. Place your little finger inside the filler plug hole and try to reach the transmission gear lubricant. If you cannot touch any fluid, the level is too low.
4. Fill the transmission, using the correct viscosity and type of fluid, until the fluid reaches the bottom of the filler plug threads.
5. Install the filler plug. These have tapered pipe threads, which seal as the plug tightens. Use the correct torque to avoid plug or casting damage.
6. Lower the vehicle and make a record for the customer. Record the type and amount of fluid used and the transmission fluid level (which should be full). Use the current date and mileage in your record.

For additional information about servicing manual transmissions, see Chapter 13.

Brake/Hydraulic Clutch System Fluid

Cars and light trucks have hydraulically operated brake systems (see Figure 1.8). Hydraulic systems transmit pressure by means of fluids. This means that the only link between the driver and the brakes at each wheel is the fluid in the system. Not only must the correct fluid level be maintained, but the correct fluid must be used. The use of an incorrect

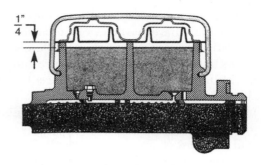

Figure 1.9   Master cylinder fluid level. The fluid in a master cylinder should be maintained at 1/4 in. (about 6 mm) below the reservoir top (courtesy of General Motors Corporation).

fluid in the system can result in brake failure. This text will show you how to check and adjust the level of fluid in brake systems (see Figure 1.9) and how to identify the correct fluid (see Figure 1.10).

Brake Fluid Maintenance List

• Check fluid level at the master cylinder for correct level and quality

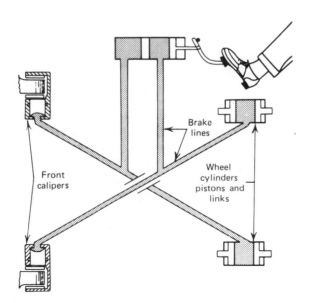

Figure 1.8   Typical hydraulic brake system. All cars of recent production have a dual hydraulic brake system. The effort exerted by the driver on the brake pedal is transmitted to the brake at each wheel by hydraulic fluid.

Figure 1.10   Brake fluid. It can be purchased by the quart (.946 liter), pint, gallon, or larger quantities. DOT 3 is still the most widely recommended quality even though DOT 4 and 5 are available (courtesy Training Enterprises Company).

- Add the correct Department of Transportation (DOT) classification brake fluid when needed
- Check for brake fluid leaks
- Change and flush brake system when contaminated
- Check condition of the low fluid warning light system (if equipped)

Note: Additional brake maintenance is covered in Chapter 17.

> **! Safety Message 2:** Brake fluid will remove the paint from your vehicle if it is spilled on any painted area. It will blind you if it gets into your eye. It is a poison if swallowed. It irritates the hands and skin if left on for long periods of time. Handle it carefully and safely. Wear safety glasses when bleeding a brake system.

> It is normal for the disc brake side of the master cylinder to require brake fluid as the disc brake pads wear. Do a pad inspection after one complete reservoir filling. They may need replacing.

The purpose of brake fluid is to provide a hydraulic fluid that will lubricate all brake parts, will not freeze in the winter, and will withstand the high heat found around the calipers and brake cylinders. Brake fluid is amber in color when new, and turns darker with use. The DOT (Department of Transportation) system measures brake fluid quality. DOT 3 is the highest quality brake fluid recommended for disc and drum brake systems (see Figure 1.10).

Hydraulic clutches also use DOT 3 brake fluid.

Not all DOT 3 brake fluids are the same. Some have a higher boiling point. Society of Automotive Engineers (SAE) recommendations require a minimum boiling point for DOT 3 fluid of 401°F. Some DOT 3 brake fluids can withstand temperatures of 450°F. DOT 4 brake fluid is manufactured. It is used in vehicles that produce very high temperatures at the calipers or wheel cylinders. DOT 4 brake fluid can withstand temperatures of 446°F and fights internal corrosion of critical brake parts. DOT 5 brake fluid has a silicone base and can be found in some import vehicles. Currently DOT 5 brake fluid is not recommended for use in antilock brake systems.

All brake fluids, except silicone (DOT 5), absorb moisture easily. Replace caps on containers and reservoirs immediately to prevent moisture contamination. Moisture in a brake system lowers the boiling point of the brake fluid and causes component failure. When brake fluid boils, it creates air bubbles in the system; the system then loses hydraulic power to apply to the calipers and pistons. Brake fluid leaks may occur at each wheel cylinder, along brake lines, and around the master cylinder. Look for damp spots anywhere on the brake or clutch system parts. If a brake or clutch master cylinder reservoir has to be filled frequently, it is a warning to inspect for a leak. Find it and repair it immediately because any brake fluid loss can result in a total system failure.

To check brake master cylinder and/or hydraulic clutch fluid, follow these steps:

1. Remove the master cylinder reservoir cover.
2. Check the front and rear sections of the reservoir. Also inspect the fluid for dirt or moisture. Contaminated fluid requires a complete system flush to correct the problem.
3. Add the correct DOT brake fluid specified for the vehicle. Add fluid until it gets to the full mark, or no more than 1/4 in. from the reservoir edge. Some master cylinders have a sight glass on the side with a mark for the maximum level. Do not exceed this level.
4. Replace the reservoir cover and make sure it is tight.

Refer to Chapter 17 for more brake servicing information.

Power Steering Fluid

Hydraulic fluid operates the power steering system. This fluid must work under high temperatures, yet flow well when cold. It should not thin out when hot and should not attack any hoses or seals. Figure 1.11 illustrates how a typical power steering system reservoir is checked for the correct fluid level. Three kinds of power steering fluid power are recommended, depending on the vehicle and the manufacturer. They are power steering fluid (see Figure 1.12), automatic transmission fluid, and special fluids developed by the manufacturer. Using an incorrect fluid or mixing one with the correct fluid will result in damage to seals, hoses, and other parts. It is very important to take the time to find the correct recommendation for each year, model, and make vehicle to be serviced.

Figure 1.11   Power steering reservoir. This is the method used to store excess fluid level in a typical power steering unit (courtesy of Training Enterprises Company).

Power Steering Fluid Maintenance List

- Check fluid level and quality
- Add the correct fluid for the system being serviced
- Check for leaks and for air in the system
- Change and flush system when contaminated or required

   Note: Additional power steering maintenance is covered in Chapter 15.

Avoid mixing power steering fluids or using a fluid that is not recommended. See Figure 1.12. To check power steering fluid, follow these steps:
   When the system is "cold":

1. Leave the engine "off" and remove the power steering dipstick. Some pull straight out and others have to be turned counterclockwise.
2. Wipe the dipstick clean and find the "cold" fluid level mark. (If there is not a "cold" mark, skip down to step one under "hot" checking.) See Figure 1.12.
3. Fully install the dipstick and remove it again.
4. Check the fluid level on the dipstick. If it does not reach the "cold" mark, or if it is above that mark, adjust the fluid level to the "cold" mark.

Figure 1.12   Power steering fluid. This type of lubricant can be used in all vehicle applications where power steering fluid is recommended (courtesy Training Enterprises Company).

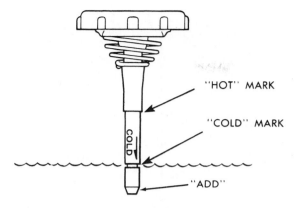

Figure 1.13 Power steering fluid dipstick. "Hot," "cold," and "add" marks allow fluid checks when the unit is either hot or cold (courtesy of Chevrolet Motor Division, General Motors Corporation).

When the system is "hot":

1. Start the vehicle and move the steering full left and back full right several times. Leave the wheels straight ahead and shut the engine off.
2. Check the fluid level using the "hot" mark on the dipstick. If the level is low, fill to the "hot" mark on the stick.

Never overfill the power steering reservoir, especially when the system is "cold." There has to be room at the top of the reservoir to allow for fluid expansion when the system reaches operating temperature. If the system is too low to check either "cold" or "hot," fill the reservoir up to the "cold" mark and start the engine. Move the steering full left and right several times to remove air from the system. After this, top the fluid to the correct mark on the dipstick. Refer to Figure 1.13.

For additional steering system service coverage, see Chapter 15.

> Power steering fluid can become contaminated over time. Thick dirty fluid should be replaced. This is an often overlooked service but necessary to prolong the life of the power steering system.

Engine Oil

Oil quality is measured by its service classification (Society of Automotive Engineers [SAE] rating) and viscosity (American Petroleum Institute [API] rating) (see Figure 1.14). The API uses two identifying marks, the API service symbol and the

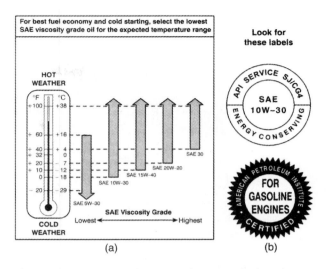

Figure 1.14 Viscosity recommendations and oil product markings. The chart (a) is used to select the correct viscosity motor oil. The SAE and API markings (b) help select the right quality and viscosity (courtesy Chrysler Corporation and Chevrolet Motor Division, General Motors Corporation).

ILSAC (International Lubricant Standardization & Approval Committee) symbol.

Engine Oil Maintenance List

- Check oil level and quality
- Select the correct viscosity and quality when adding or changing the oil
- Monitor the oil change frequency and change oil when required
- Check for leaks or loss through the engine
- Make viscosity changes when ambient (outside) air requires it

Note: Additional engine maintenance is covered in Chapter 5.

Currently the best classification of motor oil is SJ. This was introduced in 1996 and replaces the old SH rated oils. An oil in this classification will reduce engine sludge, engine varnish, cam wear, engine bearing loss, and engine rust. In the diesel and commercial category the best classification is CG-4.

Oil is a golden color when new and turns black when used. Look for oil leaks anywhere around the engine. Oil can leak out of every gasket and outside opening on the engine if the positive crankcase ventilation (PCV) valve becomes clogged (see Figure 1.15), and pressure builds up in the engine crankcase. This is another reason why regular engine maintenance is important. Recommended oil change intervals range from 3000 miles (5000 kilometers) to 7500 miles

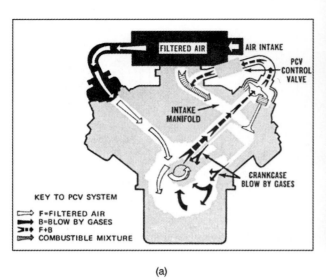

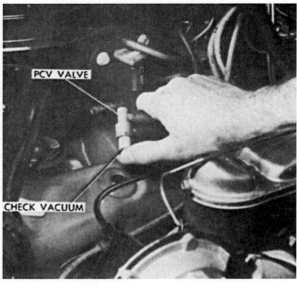

(a)   (b)

Figure 1.15 Operation and testing of a typical PCV system. Notice in part (a) how the gasses flow in a PCV system. To test a system, close off the end of the PCV valve (b) and feel for a strong vacuum (courtesy of Chrysler Corporation).

(12,000 kilometers) depending on the type of duty and vehicle operation conditions, such as extreme heat, dust, or stop-and-go driving.

> **!** *Safety Message 3:* Used motor oil can cause skin cancer as a result of constant contact. If it soaks into your clothes, change clothing and rinse the oil off as quickly as possible. Avoid handling parts and tools soaked in used motor oil. Keep your hands clean and wear rubber gloves if involved in many oil changes. Do not let motor oil get into any well or drinking water system. Don't pour used oil on the property. Instead, pour the old oil into the new empty containers (when you change the oil) and recycle them.

To check engine oil, follow these steps:

1. Make sure the vehicle is level.
2. If the engine has been running, turn if off and wait several minutes for all the oil to drain back into the engine base pan.
3. Remove the dipstick and wipe it clean. Examine the dipstick to find the "full" and "add" marks on the stick. The location of these marks can vary widely depending on the vehicle. It usually takes one quart (0.95 liters) to go from the "add" mark to the "full" mark.

If the dipstick has a "safe" range, do not fill the crankcase with oil above the top mark on this range. Sometimes you will find a "max" (maximum) mark above the "full" mark. These engines should be filled to the "full" mark, but never above the "max" mark.

4. Insert the dipstick back into the engine as far as it will go. Remove the dipstick and read the maximum level of the oil. Add oil if the level is below the "add" mark. If it is in the safe range, no action is required.

When an engine is run with an overfilled crankcase, the crankshaft will agitate the oil and create air bubbles. This can cause the oil pump to reduce oil flow to the critical parts in the engine. The result could be internal engine part failure. If you find an overfilled crankcase when checking the oil level of any engine, be sure to remove some oil to adjust the level down to the correct mark on the dipstick.

Chapter 5 provides an in-depth study of engine oil.

Air Conditioner R-12/R-134a Refrigerant and Refrigerant Oil

Refrigerant is used in an air conditioning system to absorb heat from the passenger compartment and release it outside the vehicle. Figure 1.16 shows standard containers in which R-12 or R-134a is sold.

Figure 1.16 Refrigerant containers. R-12 and R-134a are sold in these cans and in pressurized bottles. Avoid exposing them to excess heat (courtesy of Training Enterprises Company).

Refrigerant is either a liquid or a gas, depending on the temperature and pressure at any point in the system. R-12 is an ideal material for air conditioner use because it absorbs large amounts of heat, compresses easily, and is compatible with seals and hoses. However, because of scientific evidence that chlorofluorocarbons (CFCs) act to destroy the earth's ozone layer (see safety message 4), recent government laws halted the production of R-12 at the end of 1995.

> **! Safety Message 4:** Air conditioning freon has been proven to be one of the major causes of ozone damage. The ozone layer is what protects us from the ultraviolet rays of the sun. Too much exposure to these rays will result in skin cancer. It is now illegal to exhaust old freon out into the air. They now make machines that recover the freon and reuse it. Technicians must be licensed to handle freon. If your air conditioner system needs repair it should be taken to a licensed technician.

R-134a is R-12's replacement. It has a higher boiling point and is not compatible with older R-12 system parts. R-134a systems have special hoses and seals and use a synthetic polyalkylene glycol (PAG) oil to lubricate the internal parts. R-12 systems use a mineral-based oil that cannot be used in the R-134a systems.

Air Conditioner R-12/R-134a Refrigerant and Oil Maintenance List

- Temperature test air at inside ducts
- Check sight glass (if equipped)
- Check for leaks (use electronic leak detector)
- Use gauges and check both high and low side pressures
- Add refrigerant when needed
- Add refrigerant oil when needed

Note: Additional air conditioner maintenance is covered in Chapter 19.

Always follow the manufacturer's recommendations when selecting and using any refrigerant oil. Parts to each system do the same job but are not interchangeable. A separate set of service equipment for each system is required. Do not interchange them.

Since R-12 has been recently taken out of production most systems are now changed to the new R-134a by installing a change-over kit (see Figure 1.17). The system has to be completely flushed, new parts installed, and the new PAG, new compressor oil installed. This new oil is comparable

Figure 1.17 R-134a retro kit. A kit such as this is used to change the old R-12 systems over so they can use the new R-134a refrigerant. Notice that all the old refrigerant oil must be removed and new PAG oil placed in the system (courtesy Training Enterprises Company).

with the R-134a refrigerant. Different manufacturers require a PAG oil that is made for their system. The viscosity of the PAG oil varies by compressor manufacturer. Purchase a PAG oil by system manufacturer and do not pick any oil viscosity off the shelf. There is a synthetic oil sold called **ESTER Compressor Oil.** This too has viscosity differences and should be bought by compressor manufacturer. The viscosity for both type oils is rated at how well it flows at 40°C and how thin it gets at 100°C. The wrong compressor viscosity can cause compressor damage.

> R-12 and R-134a should not be mixed. This often means separate machines and gauges for each. The R-12 systems are slowly being replaced. Soon there will be only the R-134a systems left to service.

Refrigerant oil flows throughout both systems and sprays out when either R-12 or R-134a escapes from a leak. When the refrigerant in a system is constantly low, look for oil spots along the air conditioning hoses, compressor, evaporator, and condenser. Some, leaks can be found by mixing water with soap and applying it along an air conditioning system. The area around the leak will cause the soapy water to bubble.

Never attempt to replace air conditioning refrigerant without the right equipment. Environmental regulations now require that anyone working on an air conditioner obtain a license and know how to use a refrigerant recovery system. Obtain a license before attempting air conditioner service.

A license is not needed to performance test an air conditioner. Follow these steps:

1. Place a large fan in front of the vehicle to force air over the condenser.
2. Open both doors and insert a test thermometer into the center air conditioning duct.
3. Run the vehicle at a fast idle for 5 to 10 minutes with the air conditioner set on "maximum" and the blower speed set on "high." The fan should also be running at the front of the vehicle. Close the vehicle doors. *Note: NEVER* run a vehicle inside an enclosed area. Be certain that any place you operate a motor vehicle has good outside ventilation.
4. If the vehicle has a sight glass, look for bubbles (see Figure 1.18). Bubbles, oil streaks, and cloudiness along with a high temperature reading at the air conditioner duct mean the system needs servicing. A clear sight glass and a low

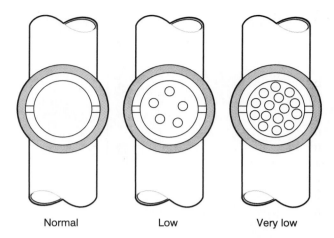

| Normal | Low | Very low |

Figure 1.18 Air conditioning sight glass. Bubbles in the sight glass are an indication the refrigerant is getting low. Learn to read a sight glass to help troubleshoot the system (courtesy of Training Enterprises Company).

temperature reading mean the system is operating properly.

> If an air conditioning system does not have a sight glass, high and low pressure is measured with a gauge set. When the results are compensated for humidity and ambient temperature the system condition can be evaluated. A thermometer placed in the inside air duct can also determine the system condition. Abnormal readings require further tests. The sight glass systems should have no bubbles inside the glass when normal.

5. Read the thermometer. A temperature reading at the duct at or below 50°F is normal. This reading will be affected by ambient temperature and high humidity. Duct temperature readings will get higher as the outside temperature and humidity increase.

For more information about air conditioning service, refer to Chapter 19.

Manual Steering Sector Lubricant

Heavy gear oil (refer to Figure 1.7) is used in the steering sector with some exceptions, such as rack and pinion systems. This is the same oil used in most standard transmissions. Two popular weights of gear oil are SAE 80W and 90W.

Manual Steering Sector Maintenance List

• Check lubricant level and quality
• Add the correct lubricant when required
• Check for leaks

Note: Additional steering sector maintenance is covered in Chapter 15.

Most owners never check the steering sector lubricant level. Frequently, the only time a sector gets checked is when it is too late and it has run out of lubricant. This is becoming less of a problem as more vehicles are equipped with power steering systems. Inspect steering sectors for leaks by checking around shaft seals and the cover gasket. If a vehicle with manual steering becomes hard to steer, check for the correct lubricant level and add lubricant if needed.

To check the fluid, remove a cover bolt or a plug on the top of the steering gear. Avoid overfilling any manual gear system because this can cause a pressure buildup and may damage the seals. Refer to the manufacturer's specifications if a complete lubricant change is necessary and use the correct amount, type, and weight (viscosity).

Grease

Grease is used in many areas, such as wheel bearings, constant velocity joints, suspension systems, steering linkage, and manual clutch linkage. Grease can either be soap or synthetic based. Lithium is used as an additive to reduce wear and friction. Disc brake grease must withstand high temperatures, and only products marked suitable for disc brakes should be used in these systems. Greases marked EP (extreme pressure) are recommended in areas where parts are under a heavy load, such as a suspension ball joint.

Suspension Lubrication Maintenance List

- Apply grease to all grease fittings
- Repair or replace those that do not accept grease
- Replace all plugs with the correct grease fitting
- Check for damaged or worn parts as the grease is applied
- Look for damaged grease seals

Note: Additional suspension lubrication is covered in Chapter 15.

Molybdenum disulfide is one additive that helps grease withstand heavy loads and high temperatures. A pressure grease gun (see Figure 1.19) lubricates any parts that have grease fittings. A recent trend is to reduce the number of places in suspension parts that have grease fittings or that require grease. In those parts that require grease, a plug may have to be removed and grease fittings

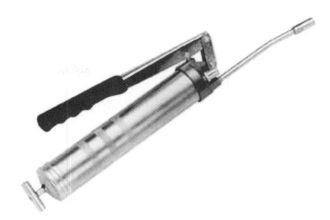

Figure 1.19 Pressure grease gun. This is used to force grease into front suspension parts using grease fittings (courtesy of Training Enterprises Company).

installed for the first grease job. Follow these steps to grease a front suspension system:

1. Jack up or lift the vehicle. Use jack stands when required and always use safety glasses.
2. Locate each fitting or plug. Replace any plugs with the correct grease fitting.
3. Wipe each fitting clean and check the condition of the grease seal. A flat seal means the part lacks grease. A torn seal may mean the part must be replaced.
4. Push the end of the grease gun onto the grease fitting. Squeeze the trigger on air-operated guns, or move the handle on hydraulic guns and watch the part and seal closely. There should not be any movement of the part as the grease fills the seal. Stop the grease flow when the seal fills out. Never keep going until grease starts flowing out the edges of the seal, as this may cause damage to the seal.

> Avoid mixing different brands of chassis grease. Not all greases are compatible with each other. The result can be a mixture that will not provide the proper lubrication, and the part can fail.

5. Some fittings can only be reached if the wheel is turned to the left or the right. Be sure to check for fittings on clutch linkage, drive shafts, and rear suspension areas.
6. Lower the vehicle and make a record of the mileage and date for the vehicle owner (usually placed on a sticker under the hood or on the side of the door).

For more details about chassis lubrication, see Chapter 15.

Battery Electrolyte

The battery contains a solution of 64% distilled water and 36% concentrated sulfuric acid. When a battery has removable caps, use only distilled water (water with impurities removed, Figure 1.20) to maintain the electrolyte level. Examine the sides of the battery case for cracks if the electrolyte level drops rapidly in any single cell. Also check for a high charging voltage, if all cells use too much water. A higher than normal charging voltage will produce enough battery heat to cause the water in the electrolyte to boil or to evaporate.

Battery Maintenance List

• Fill all battery cells to the split ring with distilled water (if cell covers are removable)
• Check for leaks or a cracked case

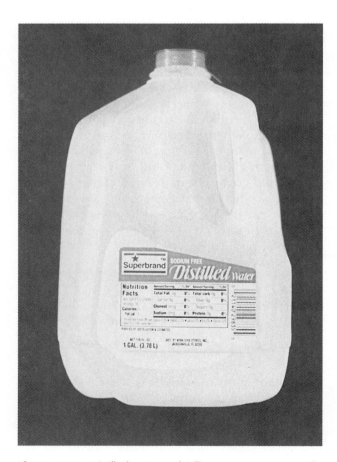

Figure 1.20 Distilled water. A distilling process removes all the impurities from water and makes it an ideal fluid to use in batteries (courtesy of Training Enterprises Company).

• Check built-in hydrometer (if battery has one)
• Make a standing voltage test of the battery with a voltmeter
• Make a load test on the battery
• Charge any battery (if it needs it)

Note: Additional battery maintenance is covered in Chapter 6.

> **!** ***Safety Message 5:*** Battery electrolyte is an acid that will cause severe damage to clothes, skin, eyes, concrete, car finishes, and many other items. Do not leave acid spills on anything of value. If a spill occurs, rinse and flush the area at once with clean water. Wash the acid off your skin immediately and remove soaked clothing at once. The acid will eat holes in any clothing if left without rinsing or neutralizing the area with water. Recycle used batteries; do not simply throw them away.

To service a battery with movable caps, follow these steps:

1. Put on safety glasses and rubber gloves before cleaning the top of the battery with a solution of baking soda and water. Brush it on and rinse it off.
2. Inspect the top and sides of the battery for cracks. Look for corrosion on the cables and terminals. Check for loose terminals and tighten them if necessary.
3. Remove the battery caps. Some turn counterclockwise; others pry off.
4. Fill each cell to the bottom of the split ring with distilled water.
5. Carefully dispose of any cleaning cloths used around a battery. Any electrolyte on the cloth contains sulfuric acid. Anyone picking up and using a cloth that has sulfuric acid on it could receive a chemical burn. See Safety Message 5.
6. Replace the battery caps.

For more details on battery servicing, see Chapter 6.

Windshield Washer Solvent

This is a menthol alcohol–based fluid with additives to cut road film and reduce streaking of the glass. The older fluid was colored blue; the newer fluid is tan. Tan-colored windshield washer fluid has a de-icer added to clear ice from the

Figure 1.21 Windshield washer solvent. This fluid contains alcohol, which reduces the chance of system freeze-ups and damage to the washer reservoir. It should always be used in the winter where the temperature drops below freezing (courtesy of Training Enterprises Company).

windshield. Windshield washer solvent (see Figure 1.21) is stored in a reservoir located under the hood. The alcohol in the fluid keeps the washer nozzles clear and prevents winter freezing. Not using washer fluid in cold weather could result in a destroyed washer pump or a cracked reservoir.

Windshield Wiper Maintenance List

- Fill the wiper reservoir to the correct level with the right fluid
- Change from regular fluid to a de-icer type in winter weather
- Check the pump pickup screen for obstructions
- Check the fluid flow from the wiper nozzles
- Check for damaged tubing or defective wiper blades
- Check the wiper nozzle aim

Sometimes the reservoir can be repaired, but often it has to be replaced. It is safest and cheapest to keep the right fluid in the washer system. Each

time the reservoir is filled, check the bottom of the intake strainer. Remove any dirt and debris. Follow these steps to service a windshield washer:

1. In cold weather, remove all the water in the reservoir with a sponge or cloth.
2. Check for any dirt or debris in the washer reservoir and remove it.
3. Check the pump inlet strainer and be sure it is open and clean.
4. Fill the reservoir to about 1/2 in. from the top. This space is necessary to allow for heat expansion in hot weather.
5. Check the system for correct operation by turning on the washer and observing the nozzle spray patterns. Both the left and right sides should have the right quantity of spray and the spray pattern should be directed correctly on the windshield. *Caution:* Be sure to keep the windshield wet with water or washer fluid while making this test. A wiper blade on a dry windshield could scratch the glass. If a wiper blade is worn or cut, replace it at this time.

> When you fill the windshield washer reservoir, always check the condition of the windshield wiper blade. A worn blade can damage the surface of the windshield and should be replaced.

6. If the spray pattern is not normal, inspect the entire system for missing, split, or clogged hoses. Replace any damaged, worn, or clogged parts. Open the ends of the nozzles if they are clogged.
7. If both sides are spraying a good pattern, test drive the vehicle and check the spray pattern when the vehicle is moving. The pattern will be different when air is moving across the windshield. Adjust the direction of each spray nozzle if the pattern is not right.
8. Don't forget to check rear window washers on those vehicles equipped with them. Check these systems in the same way as the front windshield washers.

Gasoline, Diesel Fuel, and Propane Gas

Gasoline is the most common automotive fuel. It is refined from crude oil or petroleum and is a hydrocarbon. Gasoline is very volatile (burns quickly) and should be handled with extreme care. The octane rating of gasoline, the measure of how well the fuel reacts in the engine, is an important consideration when purchasing gasoline. The higher the octane rating, the slower the fuel burns. If an engine "knocks" (uncontrolled combustion) a higher octane fuel usually corrects the problem. Some common octane ratings of gasoline are 87, 89, and 92.

Gasoline, Diesel Fuel, and Propane Gas Maintenance List

- Check for leaks in all system types
- Monitor the changing of diesel fuel filters
- Monitor the changing of gasoline filters
- Use additives when the system requires them
- Monitor for fuel contamination

> **! Safety Message 6:** Gasoline is a highly flammable, very dangerous product. If ignited, it can cause a powerful explosion. Gasoline leaks around a motor are a potential fire hazard. Repair any leaks immediately. Keep all flames away from open containers of gasoline. Store gasoline properly in clearly marked containers. Never clean parts in gasoline. Use appropriate cleaners that have a low flash point.

Most fuels in use today are "unleaded." These fuels were developed to reduce the amount of lead in the environment. Vehicles have been equipped with catalytic converters for a number of years to filter out and reduce the amount of hydrocarbons in the exhaust. "Leaded" fuels destroy the catalyst in the converters (see Figure 1.22), so unleaded fuels are required and necessary in automobiles to keep the converters working properly.

> Motor fuel can become contaminated by water and dirt. If you suspect there is dirt in the fuel, change the fuel filter more often. Water can be solved by using a fuel additive in the tank.

Gasolines contain additives such as detergents, manganese, and rust preventatives. In the winter, de-icers are added to keep any moisture in the fuel tank, pump, and lines from freezing. Detergents help keep injectors clean, and manganese is used to reduce engine knock.

When pumping gasoline, remember that it has a very low flash point (explodes easily) and always avoid pumping gasoline around any sparks or flames. Prolonged breathing of gasoline fumes can cause lung damage. Any fuel leaks can be very dangerous and should be corrected immediately. Look for leaks at the fuel tank, fuel lines, fuel pump, or fuel injector system. Usually a leak can be detected by smell or a visual inspection.

Diesel fuel used in automobiles comes in two grades, number one and number two. Number one is used for engines where the speed and load constantly changes; number two is for those engines where the speed stays uniform and the load is high. Diesel fuel is rated by its cetane number. If the cetane number is high, the fuel will ignite

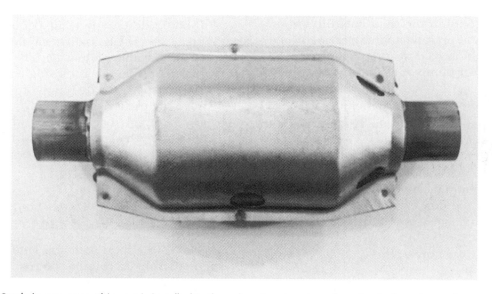

Figure 1.22 Catalytic converter. This part is installed in the exhaust system to reduce the hydrocarbon exhaust emissions (courtesy of Training Enterprises Company).

easier than the lower numbers. Diesel fuel has cetane numbers from 35 to 65, with number one fuel rated at about 50 cetane and number two about 45. Diesel fuel viscosity (ability to flow) is important. The higher the viscosity, the better the fuel will lubricate the internal engine parts. Number one diesel fuel has a lower viscosity than number two. Number two diesel fuel, with a cetane rating of 45 and a high viscosity, is a poorer choice in cold weather. Never let diesel fuel become contaminated with gasoline. This could severely damage the engine or result in an explosion.

Propane gas is another fuel gaining in favor with some types of vehicles, such as fork lifts and delivery trucks. It is a clean-burning fuel and reduces wear on the inside of the engine by reducing sludge buildup. The problem for automobiles is the uncertain availability of propane when needed. Also, some restrictions apply when going through tunnels. Propane is kept under pressure and used in vapor form rather than as a liquid. A damaged compressed gas cylinder would be as dangerous as gasoline in an accident.

Differential and Transaxle Lubricant

Most rear wheel drive differentials use gear oil. This is the same product discussed in the manual transmission section of this chapter. A high-performance synthetic or natural gear oil rated at GL-5 with a multiviscosity of 75W–90 would be suitable for most areas of the country, summer or winter. It would flow well when cold and thicken up to a 90 weight when hot. Gear oils can be purchased in single weights, but weather may be a factor if these are to be used year round. Three common multiviscosity selections are 75W–90, 80W–90, and 85W–140.

Positive-traction differentials use either a special lubricant or one that can be used for both standard and limited-slip applications. Never use a gear lubricant in a limited-slip differential that is not recommended for that application. Damage will result to the internal parts and friction materials.

Differentials are checked by removing a plug, placed at the full mark, on the cover or housing. Look for rear wheel differential leaks at either wheel, around the drain plug, drive shaft seal, and the cover gasket. When differential fluid leaks at the wheels, it will streak down the inside of the wheels. Usually, when the differential seals leak, the bearings are worn. Worn bearings cause the axle to wobble, and this destroys the seal. You must replace

a damaged seal. When you see streaks of lubricant running down the inside edges of the tires, check to see if the differential was overfilled or if the axle seals are damaged. Differential fluid can leak into the rear brake drums and destroy the brake lining.

To check differential fluid, follow these steps:

1. Jack or lift the vehicle. Make sure it is level and use jack safety stands when using a floor jack. Since you will be under the vehicle, be sure to wear safety glasses.
2. Remove the filler plug. Some plugs are located on the rear cover, and others are found in the front of the housing near the pinion.
3. Use your little finger to find the fluid level if it is not up to the filler plug hole. You should be able to touch fluid within 1/4 in. of the hole.
4. You may find a differential that was overfilled, and fluid may run out immediately when you remove the plug. Let the fluid drain until the level drops even with the lower edge of the filler plug hole.
5. If the fluid is low, select the correct quality and viscosity replacement fluid. Fill the differential until the level is up to the bottom of the plug hole threads. *Note:* When checking for the correct fluid, always identify limited-slip differentials and use only fluid recommended for this type of differential.

> Always check the quality of any differential or transaxle lubricant when checking the level. Contaminants in the fluid require a complete fluid change to prevent gear and bearing damage. Extreme cold weather conditions require a viscosity change.

6. Transaxles may use either gear oil, automatic transmission oil, or factory-recommended gear lubricant. Automatic transmission transaxles most often have the same fluid in both the automatic transmission and the transaxle. Identify the unit being serviced as manual, standard automatic, or limited-slip. Use only the recommended fluid in each type. To check fluid in a transaxle you may need to remove a plug or use a dipstick. Check and fill transaxles in the same manner as differentials. Use only the specified fluid and be sure it is at the right level when you are through.
7. Inspect and replace the filler plug. If the filler plug has a gasket, check it for damage. If the plug has pipe threads only, tighten it to the specified torque using a torque wrench.

8. Record the amount and type fluid used on a date/mileage sticker placed either on the driver's side door edge or under the hood by the radiator.

For more information about transaxles and differentials, see Chapter 14.

LESSON 1-2   Evaluation of Failed Parts

The purpose of this lesson is to go over some of the specific problems associated with vehicle maintenance and lubrication. When parts wear beyond the point where they are safe to keep in operation, repairs are necessary. Pay special attention to the warning signs. The lubrication specialist should always use the correct lubricants to reduce parts wear and save money. After you have read this lesson, make several vehicle inspections to be sure all fluids are at the correct level. Look for worn parts and fluid leaks. Fluids should always be checked even if the automobile is new.

There have been cases where fluids were never installed or they leaked out before the vehicle was sold. Remember that a unit will stop leaking if there is no fluid left in it to drain out.

Worn Parts

Everything on and in a vehicle begins to wear as soon as the owner uses the vehicle. Every time a switch is turned, the brakes applied, or the engine started, parts wear. To avoid premature wear, the parts of the automobile that run in grease and oil must be regularly serviced. Sometimes these materials either get low or are neglected. The following warning signs should cause you to inspect further to determine the cause:

1. Sticking parts
2. Unusual movement between normally stationary parts
3. Unusual noises
4. Puddles and leaks on car parts or under the car
5. Extreme heat in any moving part
6. Unusual vibrations
7. Anything that will not operate properly when you try to use it
8. Anything that will not hold the required fluid level
9. Blown fuses
10. Unusual smells

11. Smoking of any moving part or a rough running engine
12. Sluggish reaction when something is supposed to work quickly
13. Low, spongy, or soft brake pedal action before the brakes apply
14. Any red warning light that comes on and stays on
15. Any gauge that does not read in its normal range
16. When any trouble code is set in the vehicle computers

When any of the danger signs just listed appear, immediately determine the cause.

Check sheets are very useful when performing inspections. They act as reminders so that every item of importance is checked each time an inspection is performed. These can be modified to include items that pertain to specific vehicles. Use owner's manuals and shop manuals to get specific information.

Lack of Lubrication

Every spot on a vehicle designed to be lubricated should receive the correct lubrication when required. How frequently should a vehicle be lubricated or serviced? It should be done often enough to maintain the correct quality and level of lubrication materials. Consult each owner's manual or repair manuals for the correct lubrication product for each spot on a particular vehicle.

Damaged Parts

Sometimes parts will not operate properly because they are damaged. A torn wiper blade will not remove water from the windshield well even though the wiper arm is working. Brakes, tires, filters, and belts are just a few parts often found worn out or damaged. Suspension parts can become damaged or bent by running over something in the road. Wheels can become damaged the same way. Most of the time a damaged part will not operate normally.

When any part on the vehicle does not work right, visually inspect the area, and try to determine if there is damage. Jack up tires and spin them. A bent rim should be easily discovered by looking at the edge of the tire as it spins. It is the job of the lubrication specialist to develop a system to inspect and investigate everything on an automobile, to discover any damage. Many times the owner will

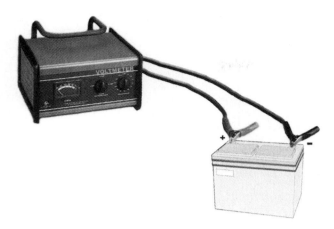

Figure 1.23 Voltage test. Electrical parts can be evaluated with a voltmeter to see if there is voltage in the circuit (courtesy of Chrysler Corporation).

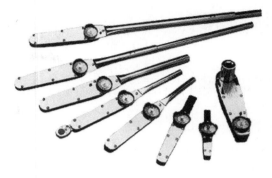

Figure 1.24 Torque wrenches. Tools such as this are used to make sure a bolt or nut is tightened properly. Using them prevents broken bolts or loose parts (courtesy of Training Enterprises Company).

not be aware of problems that have not yet become severe. If the owner does have a complaint, check these areas first.

Broken or Burned-Out Parts

If a unit will not operate, inspect it to determine if parts are broken. If it is an electrical part, check to see if voltage is getting to it (see Figure 1.23). Turn on lights and check for burned-out bulbs. Check fuses. It is the fuse's job to burn out before the wiring if a short occurs in the circuit. To order replacement bulbs, bring the old bulb to the parts store or supply the following information:

1. The name of the part where the bulb is to be installed
2. Vehicle identification information
3. Double or single contact
4. Type of socket or bulb base

Loose or Missing Parts

Many parts on an automobile use fasteners. These can become loose or drop out. Inspect for loose or missing fasteners on a regular basis. Tighten all loose fasteners and replace any that are missing. Tighten bolts with a torque wrench to get them tight enough so they will not vibrate out. A torque wrench such as the one being used in Figure 1.24 has an indicator that measures the exact amount of force being applied to the fastener. Engine head bolts and lug nuts are two places where a torque wrench should always be used. Consult the owner's

manual or repair manuals for torque specifications for all fasteners on any vehicle being repaired.

LESSON 1–3 Parts Ordering, Specifications, and Repair Procedures

Ordering parts to replace or repair worn parts can be a difficult task. Millions of parts are on the market, but in many cases there may be only one that will replace the one you need. To get the right parts, write down the identification numbers, model, year, manufacturer, and tag numbers of all items pertaining to the vehicle you are servicing, and take these numbers with you when you attempt to order parts. Vehicles use different parts depending on the kind of accessories in the vehicle and the vehicle model. Some manufacturers have placed a sticker in their vehicles that contains a code for every part on the vehicle. This code has become so important, it is recommended that you make a copy of the sticker and use it when going to the dealer to order parts. You will need this same information later to get the right adjustment specifications when installing the parts.

Vehicle Identification

VIN. Each vehicle made today is given a vehicle identification number (VIN), such as the one in Figure 1.25. This number is found by looking through the windshield glass on the driver's side, where there will be a plate with as many as seventeen numbers and letters in combination. Each letter and number means something to the manufacturer. The most used parts of the code are the

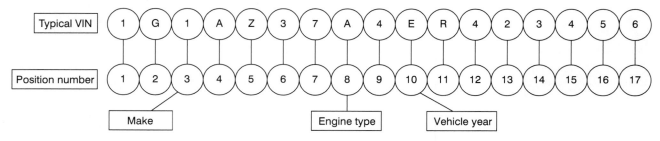

Figure 1.25 VIN. This chart shows a typical vehicle identification number and what the numbers represent. This number is used to identify the vehicle so replacement parts can be ordered correctly (courtesy of Training Enterprises Company).

engine size, the year of manufacture, and the body style. One word of caution: Sometimes parts will be changed and the code will then be incorrect. Transaxles, starters, alternators, manual transmissions, and differentials are some units that have their own identification tags or plates. If you are having trouble getting the correct part, it is a good practice to bring the old part to match with the new one at the parts counter before you leave. Bring all the identification available on a part being repaired or replaced.

Sometimes the parts suppliers will have updated parts when defects are found in the older original equipment parts and the manufacturer has corrected the problem. New materials are constantly being produced and these materials are used to make items stronger and better. The parts supplier should have this information and should be able to make the changes for you.

> Ordering information should include the VIN number, engine type, year, model, manufacturer, transmission type, and so on. The most important of these is the VIN number and the production options code if ordering from the factory. Parts places are used to dealing in specifics such as the type of engine.

Manufacturer. Each vehicle manufacturer is required to supply parts for the vehicles they sell. There is an age limitation. After a set number of years they may no longer have the parts in stock. There is a growing market for classic and antique automobiles and this can be a source of parts for older models. Don't overlook the used parts market. Many of those parts are in excellent condition, especially if the vehicle was in an accident when it was new and the used part has low mileage.

Model. Parts may vary from model to model in a vehicle line. Some parts are designed just for that model, such as taillights, and certain body parts.

Know the exact body style and model when ordering parts. Many units on General Motors vehicles, for example, are identical between models, but some items, such as engines, can be very different between manufacturer models. Since 1984, a sticker containing the production options code is placed in the trunk, glove box door, or engine compartment of General Motors vehicles. All General Motors parts departments are using this code to look up specific parts. A parts list and picture can be brought up on microfilm to order any specific piece for any option placed in the vehicle. Other useful information also is on this sticker, such as paint type, axle ratios, tires, and wheel covers.

Other manufacturers have similar systems. Chrysler has a body code plate located on the left front fender side shield, wheel housing, or left side of the radiator support. Each major part, such as an engine or transaxle, has an identification number and a serial number.

> Some manufacturers put the production options code on a sticker in the trunk. It can be removed and placed on a copy machine. Place the copy with other parts ordering information and use it when parts are needed. Note any changes from the original assembly line equipment.

Parts marking, tags, serial numbers, models, and so on, all differ from manufacturer to manufacturer. Parts must be identified correctly so that the right lubrication products will be placed in the right vehicle part. If, for example, you cannot identify a differential as either standard or limited-slip, then do not place lubricant in it until the correct identification can be established.

Year. Many changes are made in vehicle models from year to year. This is especially true when problems occur and have to be solved for the next model year. Sometimes the beginning and the end of the year will see many changes. The tenth number in the VIN code can tell the technician the year the vehicle was manufactured. This information may be needed to make repairs and order parts. Vehicle identification numbers are used by the manufacturer to issue a recall and to make changes to every vehicle manufactured during a certain time period. The police use the VIN to trace stolen vehicles.

Specifications, Changes, and Training

Auto Repair Manuals.   There are many sources of good material that will have the information needed to correctly adjust parts on automobiles. Figure 1.26 shows a specialized book for a particular vehicle. For simple items, always check the owner's manual. Today's vehicles have many electronic devices. Just setting the clock can be an experience if you don't have the instructions. If the owner's manual does not have the desired

information, consult one of the general repair manuals that are published for anyone trying simple repairs. There will be good sections on such things as engine tune-up, capacities, valve specifications, engine measurements, torque specifications, and wheel alignment specifications. There will be general directions on how to accomplish some of the easier operations.

Make sure the shop has an up-to-date library of factory repair manuals for the vehicles they repair. This information is one of the best resource tools that the manufacturer can offer to the technician. Revisions are provided as the need arises. Keep these manuals updated, and post the revisions. These manuals have a detailed section on vehicle component servicing along with the recommended maintenance materials to use.

Some of these manuals also have sections on heavier maintenance, such as engine and brake rebuilding. Use caution if you have never tried to do the more complicated operations. Many times, expensive special tools are needed. Sometimes there will be hundreds of complicated steps from start to finish, with the success of the repair depending on each step being accurately carried out. There may be a lack of detail in the repair descriptions. The steps may start with a statement such as, "after the engine is removed." Removal of an engine in the newer vehicles can be very complicated. This repair would not fall under general maintenance and should be avoided by maintenance technicians.

Factory Service Manual.   Every major vehicle dealership has a repair department. This department has a responsibility to prepare the new vehicles for sale. The technicians spend a lot of time keeping up with new technology changes. They help themselves do this by maintaining a good reference library. They have available to them repair manuals on each make and model of vehicle sold for each year that particular model is produced. These manuals are very detailed, sometimes several inches thick for one specific model. In addition, many dealerships maintain a file of all parts changes and revisions, including all the parts changes that have been made to solve specific problems. Without this information, mechanics would not be able to solve problems that are a result of manufacturing defects. It is possible to purchase these manuals and have them in your professional library. A good selection of factory service manuals or factory unit repair manuals would be the best

Figure 1.26 Automotive repair manuals. Shown here is a typical manual used to find specifications and adjustment information (courtesy of Training Enterprises Company).

repair item you could purchase in addition to your technician's tools.

Before doing any advanced maintenance on a particular vehicle, do some research and see if any changes have occurred since the vehicle came off the assembly line. Many complicated problems can be solved with the installation of the newer parts. Recently, information has become available on computer discs from companies that deal in supplying repair information. These are an excellent source of recent changes.

With the increase of computer products, what was in written form can now be purchased on CDs for most vehicles. This data is constantly being revised and is an excellent source of repair or service information. Hard copies can be printed on demand.

Owner's Manual. The owner's manual explains how to use all the special items on one specific automobile and how to service and maintain the vehicle. This material may cover several options, such as how to use all the types of radios and tape players offered on the particular line of vehicles. One of the items covered is how to use the exact factory-installed radio or tape player in this particular automobile.

Along with all the other wealth of information, the manual has a section on service and gives the quantities and quality of the fluids and parts needed to carry out the service. Remember this material is dated, and there may be new materials developed after the manual was printed. Do not get fooled into using obsolete maintenance materials. The manual suggests the latest and best materials to use up to the date it was printed. Use the owner's manual as a resource along with any other materials at your disposal. When corrections need to be made, point them out to the owner and correct the manual when necessary. Motor oil quality is a good example. Older motor oils should not be used when newer ones have been developed that do a better job protecting an engine.

Keep the owner's manual in the vehicle at all times and if the automobile does not have a manual, convince the owner to purchase a new one. Because owners do not read their manuals they often do not get the full value of all the features built into their vehicle. Good examples of this are how to increase speed on the cruise control or how to set stations on the radio. Some owners have never used a vehicle jack and cannot change a tire.

Parts Supplier Information. Each parts manufacturer has to keep up with the changes and improvements in each vehicle so their parts will work. Always read the instructions that come in the new parts boxes to identify any recent changes. If you do not know what specification to use when setting a part, ask your parts supplier. Most of this information is supplied to them by the parts manufacturer, and they will be glad to pass it on to you so the repair will be a success. Many times repair work is unsuccessful because the parts installer did not make the necessary adjustments. Adjustments can be critical in fuel system, electrical system, brake repair work, and other important areas.

Factory Recalls. The public is the best testing ground for the automobile. No matter how much engineering goes into the development of the vehicle, some parts may not last. Failure of some types of parts could result in danger. Brakes are a good example. When manufacturers determine that their product needs to be changed, they issue a recall. They usually notify the owner by mail and set up an appointment to bring the vehicle to the dealership and have the new parts replaced. When you are working on any vehicle, check to see if all the recalls were made, especially on items of safety. Recall repairs should be kept with the owner's manual and made part of the historical record of the vehicle.

Automotive Training

Factory Training Schools. You should constantly be in training to handle the new technology that is being developed. Factory training schools are one method manufacturers use to keep their technicians current. These schools have highly competent instructors that show the new technology to all the dealership mechanics. The technicians in the field are the first line in the battle to keep the vehicles repaired. If they can do their job better, the owners will be more satisfied with the product.

Community Colleges. Community colleges are used to train many beginning technicians. Courses range from one to two years. Each course is designed to take a specific area of the automobile and concentrate on how it works, how to repair it, and how to service it.

Speciality Clinics. Speciality clinics are used by suppliers of materials and equipment to acquaint technicians with products that can help them do their job more efficiently. The suppliers of these materials often do a one- or two-day training clinic. The product is introduced to the technicians and they can decide whether they need the materials. Some excellent products and tools have been developed and are often superior to anything being currently produced. It may be money saved if the technician buys the product and uses it. Anything that is faster and better is worth consideration, especially if the technician is working on a commission basis. Test equipment, maintenance products, and tools are some of the items offered by companies other than vehicle manufacturers.

Parts Purchasing

Parts Stores. Almost every town in the United States has at least one auto parts store similar to the one in Figure 1.27. Their purpose is to supply automotive repair parts. Remember to have the right parts identification numbers and all the necessary vehicle identification numbers when ready to purchase any parts. Bring in the old part for comparison when possible. Parts stores are very skilled in getting what you need. If they do not have a part in stock, they can usually get it overnight.

When ordering parts long distance, the correct initial identification of the broken part becomes important. Those taking the order must have enough information to supply the correct part. Most parts personnel will ask the right questions until they have all the facts they need.

Automotive Dealerships. Every dealership that sells automobiles has a parts department (see Figure 1.28). They are specialists in supplying parts for the cars they sell. First, go to a dealership that sells the particular model you are repairing. For a General Motors Buick, go to any General Motors dealer to order your part. They now have parts listings for all General Motors vehicles. A Ford dealership probably will not have your part unless looking for something like a light bulb. Remember to ask for special information such as repair bulletins that will supply the latest specifications and repair advice.

Chain Stores. Stores of this type have a lot of common repair items that most inexperienced vehicle owners use and install themselves. In a section of the store marked "Automotive" are items such as spark plugs, filters, motor oil, greases, waxes, floor mats, radios, tires, and batteries. Most of these stores have an area where they can install the items they sell. In many cases they have books and charts where you have to look up the item you need. Without the correct vehicle information you will

Figure 1.27 Parts supply store. Pictured here is a typical parts store. These stores supply replacement parts for all makes and models of vehicles (courtesy of Training Enterprises Company).

Figure 1.28 Dealership parts department. Each dealer must supply replacement parts so the technicians in the dealership can repair the vehicles sold at the dealership. The supply of parts is usually restricted to the manufacturer of the vehicles being sold (courtesy of Training Enterprises Company).

not be able to get the correct part. Look through some of these books to see what information is needed to get the right part. Be sure you have all the correct information before buying and installing a part that you select yourself. With spark plugs, for example, the heat range of the plug is critical. The plug may fit and install correctly, but never run right in the engine if the plug heat range is wrong for the particular vehicle being serviced.

Used Parts. An excellent source of parts is a used parts supplier. Anything on the automobile can be purchased used, and if care is taken in the selection, the part will be every bit as good as the part that failed in many cases it is better than those in the rest of the vehicle. Large items such as transmissions, motors, differentials, and brake parts are purchased through the used parts market every day. Used parts suppliers are linked together by phone and computer. If the local business does not have the part, use this network to find it from all the other used parts places in the country. Everyone drives used parts, but take care to make sure that the part being considered is not worn out. Many times the vehicle mileage is written on parts such as transmissions and engines. This helps determine the amount of wear to expect on the part. Most used parts suppliers offer a warranty and replace a part if it fails before the warranty period has expired.

VOCABULARY

Use the listed words in the blanks beside the following sentences to complete the definitions. Either write out the words or place the letters in the blanks.

A. Grease

B. Underinflation

C. Propylene glycol

D. Flush

E. "Full" mark

F. Dextron III/Mercon

G. Semisynthetic

H. GL-5

I. SAE

J. DOT

K. SJ

L. API service

M. PAG

N. Sight glass

O. EP

P. Molybdenum disulfide

Q. Electrolyte

R. Reservoir

S. Volatile

T. Cetane number

U. Multiviscosity

V. Production options code

W. Owner's manual

X. Factory recall

Y. Speciality clinic

_____ 1. Rating for brake fluid

_____ 2. Latest ATF fluid for Ford and GM

_____ 3. Used to reduce wheel bearing friction

_____ 4. Where refrigerant flow can be observed

_____ 5. Storage area for fluid

_____ 6. GM sticker for parts identification

_____ 7. Rating for grease, meaning extreme pressure

_____ 8. Means for suppliers to show their products

_____ 9. Part natural and part manufactured

_____ 10. Repair of a vehicle when factory defects are found

_____ 11. Maximum level to fill any fluid

_____ 12. Grease additive that helps it withstand loads

_____ 13. A product that changes ability to flow with heat

_____ 14. Society of American Engineers

_____ 15. How-to-use guide kept with the vehicle

_____ 16. Agency that determines oil quality

_____ 17. When there is too little air in a tire

_____ 18. A diesel fuel rating system

_____ 19. Best quality manual transmission fluid

_____ 20. Battery fluid made up of acid and water

_____ 21. Newest base for engine coolant

_____ 22. The ability of a fluid to burn rapidly

_____ 23. Removing rust and dirt from a radiator

_____ 24. Newest classification for engine oil

_____ 25. Air conditioning oil

REVIEW QUESTIONS

The following questions will help you determine if you have accomplished the tasks stated at the beginning of this chapter. If you don't know many of the answers, go back and review the material before proceeding to the next chapter.

Lesson 1–1

1. What does transmission fluid look like when it gets into the coolant?
2. What is the highest DOT rating for automotive brake fluid at this time?
3. What will be the result if the wrong fluid is used in a power steering system?
4. Name the highest classification of engine oil sold at this time?
5. What is the name of the new air conditioner refrigerant?
6. What does EP mean when referring to grease?
7. What chemical is added to distilled water to make electrolyte?
8. What chemical is in windshield washer fluid that prevents freezing?
9. What is the expected shelf life for the new coolants?
10. Name the new base for the extended-life coolants.
11. What is the highest allowed percentage of coolant-to-water ratio that can be allowed and still give maximum protection?
12. Under what two conditions do cooling system leaks occur?
13. Explain why a full coolant recovery reservoir does not always mean a full radiator.
14. Why should you let the radiator cool before checking the coolant level at the radiator cap?
15. Why is it important for the vehicle to be level before checking the automatic transmission fluid?
16. How is the automatic transmission fluid kept from getting too hot?
17. What factors determine the need for selecting a multiviscosity manual transmission fluid?
18. How does DOT 5 brake fluid differ from DOT 3 or 4?
19. Name the three kinds of power steering fluid used today.
20. When is the highest mark on the power steering dipstick used to determine fluid level?
21. What color is motor oil when new?
22. What is the advantage of the tan-colored windshield wiper fluid?
23. The octane system is used to rate gasoline. Name the system used to rate diesel fuel.
24. What is the highest GL number used to rate the best gear oil?
25. Name the two most common methods used to check transaxle lubricants.

Lesson 1–2

26. Name two parts that do not work well when damaged.
27. How do you detect if a wheel is bent?
28. How do you check for burned-out bulbs?
29. What is the job of the fuse?
30. What is the name of the tool used to torque fasteners?
31. Name some fluids that form puddles under a vehicle when there is a leak.
32. How frequently should a vehicle be lubricated or serviced?
33. Why is a check sheet a valuable lubrication item?
34. What is the best method to check a bulb or the bulb circuit?
35. What tool is used to make sure a bolt is tight?

Lesson 1–3

36. Name some information besides the VIN code that is usually needed to obtain the correct parts.
37. What information is provided by a GM production option sticker?
38. In what book can most simple adjustments be found?
39. Name one problem with auto repair manual information.
40. What are two reasons for using a parts store?
41. Which number represents the vehicle year in the VIN number?
42. What is the product options code?
43. When will the product options code be inaccurate?
44. What manual should be checked first to find basic lubrication about a specific vehicle?
45. Name three places where a technician can receive basic or additional training.
46. How do used parts suppliers communicate with each other?

ASE QUESTIONS

Each question or incomplete statement in this test is followed by four suggested answers or completions. In each case select the *one* that best answers the question or completes the statement.

1. Technician A says the new coolants can be mixed with the older types of coolant without any adverse effects. Technician B says that the new and old should not be mixed because the flush and change intervals will be shorter. Who is right?
   a. A only   b. B only
   c. Both A and B   d. Neither A nor B

2. Technician A says to check the coolant level at the radiator. Technician B says to check the coolant level at the coolant recovery reservoir. Who is right?
   a. A only   b. B only
   c. Both A and B   d. Neither A nor B

3. Technician A says that during periods of extreme cold, the ratio of coolant to water can be increased to 70% coolant and 30% water for maximum protection. Technician B says in the summer the ratio can be lowered to less than 30% coolant to 70% water and still have maximum effect. Who is right?
   a. A only   b. B only
   c. Both A and B   d. Neither A nor B

4. Technician A says the shelf life of the new coolant can be up to eight years. Technician B says the shelf life has not increased for either the new or old coolants and it is still eighteen months. Who is right?
   a. A only   b. B only
   c. Both A and B   d. Neither A nor B

5. Technician A says the radiator system goes into a vacuum when hot. Technician B says the radiator system goes under pressure when hot. Who is right?
   a. A only   b. B only
   c. Both A and B   d. Neither A nor B

6. Technician A says that Dextron III/Mercon fluid can be used in any type of older vehicle. Technician B says that this fluid should only be used where a friction-modifying fluid is recommended. Who is right?
   a. A only   b. B only
   c. Both A and B   d. Neither A nor B

7. Technician A says that DOT 4 brake fluid is the highest quality brake fluid currently recommended for general use. Technician B says DOT 5 is the highest quality brake fluid recommended for general use. Who is right?
   a. A only   b. B only
   c. Both A and B   d. Neither A nor B

8. Technician A says the best classification of motor oil is SJ. Technician B says the best commercial classification of motor oil is CG4. Who is right?
   a. A only   b. B only
   c. Both A and B   d. Neither A nor B

2 Basic Automotive Maintenance Safety

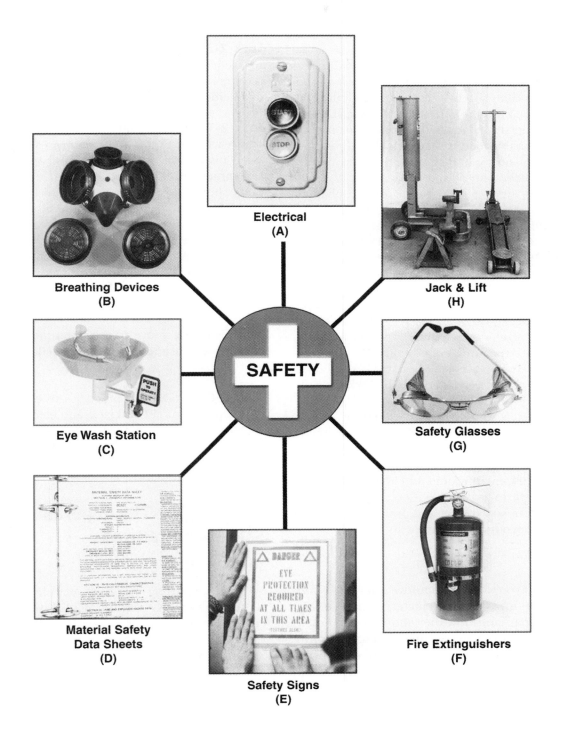

Electrical
(A)

Breathing Devices
(B)

Jack & Lift
(H)

Eye Wash Station
(C)

SAFETY

Safety Glasses
(G)

Material Safety
Data Sheets
(D)

Safety Signs
(E)

Fire Extinguishers
(F)

S afety is the direct responsibility of the technician and the owner of the business. Develop safety awareness early. The automotive occupation can be very dangerous for those who do not know how to take the necessary precautions. Make periodic inspections of the shop area and of all equipment. Conduct safety training immediately after the purchase of new machines and equipment. Color code marking should be done throughout the work area. Automotive technicians should know of any safety hazard materials found at the job and how to handle them correctly. The owners of the business and the technicians should form a partnership to make the work environment as safe as possible. Safety materials should be purchased when needed, and the technician should always use these materials.

Breathing devices (see part B of the chapter opening illustration) are extremely important to protect the lungs. An eye wash station (see part C) can prevent blindness if acid or other chemicals enter the eyes. MSDS sheets (see part D) should be on file in the shop where they can be used for reference when needed. Safety posters and signs (see part E) are a constant reminder to practice good safety. Fire extinguishers (see part F) should be inspected on a regular schedule, and they should be the right type for common fires in automotive settings. Safety glasses (see part G) should be worn at all times, especially when working with machines.

It is always wise to have knowledge of unsafe conditions and correct them before an accident occurs. We cover many safety procedures in this chapter. Add to this list when necessary. Look at your own work environment and apply as many of these procedures as possible. Look for unique situations at your workplace, and put into operation any safety procedures necessary.

TASKS

How well do you know automotive safety? Are you aware of the many types of materials used in automotive repair and how they should be handled safely? If you cannot answer these questions confidently, this may be the most important chapter in this textbook. When unsafe practices are followed there may not be a second chance to do the operation correctly. A good example is the handling of asbestos around automotive brakes. To use an air hose and blow off the dirt on a brake system could fill the air with asbestos particles. Breathing them could result in damaged lungs. There are six

lessons in this chapter. All of them have to do with safety. We suggest that you do not skip any of them.

The following are six tasks to master before leaving this chapter:

Task 2-1. Study and practice safe shop procedures to avoid injury and property damage.

Task 2-2. Train until the skills are obtained to react correctly when faced with an emergency. This requires the identification and correct application of all emergency equipment and supplies.

Task 2-3. Ensure that universal shop safety colors are used and know what they represent. Routine safety inspections should be carried out and safety recommendations should be acted on. Safety reports should be made out when accidents occur and these should be kept on file along with the recommendations to correct any safety problems.

Task 2-4. Always use personal protective equipment and make sure this equipment is the right type. Safety equipment should always be in place or available when needed.

Task 2-5. Be aware of the potential dangers of compressed air and follow the posted compressed air rules.

Task 2-6. Know and practice the correct hand tool, equipment, lift and jack, and electrical safety. All environmentally hazardous materials should be properly handled and disposed of using correct procedures.

LESSON 2-1   The Importance of Safe Shop Practices

To Yourself

Safety is something that each technician must assume as a personal responsibility. Today's technicians have to deal with materials unknown just a short time ago. Many of these materials are toxic and have to be handled in special ways. Often, special clothing must be used and skin contact avoided. Sometimes special breathing devices (see Figure 2.1) must be used. When finished with toxic materials, dispose of them so that the environment will not be harmed. How should a technician avoid using unsafe practices and comply with all the regulations? Here are some answers:

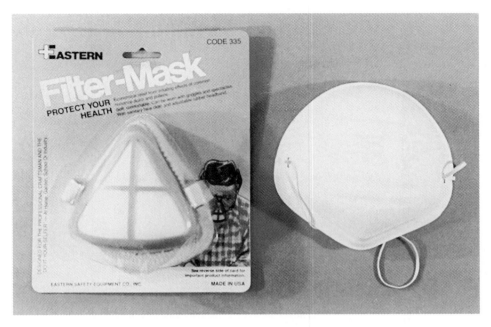

Figure 2.1 Breathing devices. Such safety equipment protects against breathing toxic materials (courtesy of Training Enterprises Company).

1. Read all labels on the products used in the shop (see Figure 2.2).
2. Purchase and wear all safety clothing and protection devices recommended.
3. Take out of service and mark all defective pieces of equipment. Repair them before attempting to reuse them.
4. Get the shop owners to install guards on all pieces of equipment that require guards. Make guards for all pieces of equipment that do not have guards.
5. Locate and inspect all emergency equipment. Be sure it is the right equipment for the job. Submit purchase orders for any equipment needed but not in stock.
6. Attend all safety meetings and follow all recommendations.
7. Report all dangerous situations immediately. Follow up to see that corrective measures are in place.
8. Take cardiopulmonary resuscitation (CPR) training and Heimlich maneuver training (for choking) at your local Red Cross.
9. Keep all material safety data sheets (MSDS) on file concerning any chemicals in the shop. These sheets have both emergency information and information about the handling of the materials (see Figure 2.3).
10. Conduct regular shop safety inspections. Correct any problems immediately.
11. Convince the shop owners to install environmentally safe disposal systems in the shop that will protect the groundwater, air, and those handling the materials. Recycle any materials such as used motor oil.

Safety requires a commitment. Safety also has a price tag. The technician must be able to convince others that an investment in safety is worth the cost.

WARNING: HARMFUL IF SWALLOWED. CONTAINS POISONS. EYE IRRITANT. KEEP OUT OF REACH OF CHILDREN. IF TAKEN INTERNALLY, CONTACT PHYSICIAN IMMEDIATELY.

Figure 2.2 Product label. Labels contain information about how to use the product properly and will have some safety tips about what to do if the product is misused (such as swallowed and is a poison) (courtesy of Training Enterprises Company).

A fast way to get MSDS sheets is to find those that pertain to the materials being used on the Internet and print them. At least you can order a copy for the shop records. Be sure to review them and follow any special materials handling instructions. Also pay attention to any special protective devices needed to keep all workers safe.

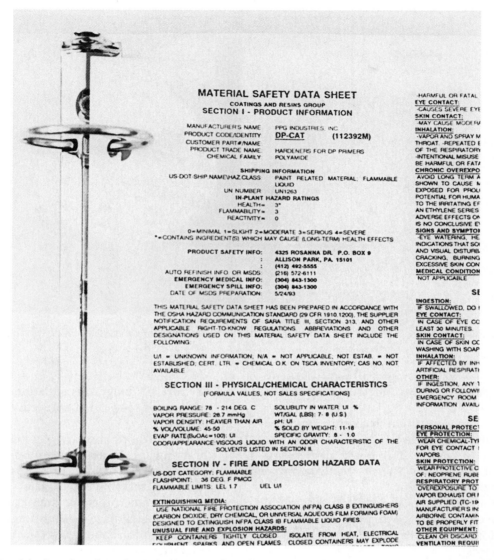

MATERIAL SAFETY DATA SHEET
COATINGS AND RESINS GROUP
SECTION I - PRODUCT INFORMATION

MANUFACTURER'S NAME   PPG INDUSTRIES, INC.
PRODUCT CODE/IDENTITY   **DP-CAT**   (112392M)
CUSTOMER PART#/NAME
PRODUCT TRADE NAME: HARDENERS FOR DP PRIMERS
CHEMICAL FAMILY: POLYAMIDE

SHIPPING INFORMATION
US-DOT-SHIP NAME\HAZ CLASS: PAINT RELATED MATERIAL, FLAMMABLE
                              LIQUID
UN NUMBER: UN1263
IN-PLANT HAZARD RATINGS
HEALTH =   3*
FLAMMABILITY = 3
REACTIVITY =   0

0 = MINIMAL 1 = SLIGHT 2 = MODERATE 3 = SERIOUS 4 = SEVERE
* = CONTAINS INGREDIENT(S) WHICH MAY CAUSE (LONG-TERM) HEALTH EFFECTS

PRODUCT SAFETY INFO: 4325 ROSANNA DR. P.O. BOX 9
        :   ALLISON PARK, PA. 15101
        :   (412) 492-5555
AUTO REFINISH INFO OR MSDS: (216) 572-6111
EMERGENCY MEDICAL INFO: (304) 843-1300
EMERGENCY SPILL INFO: (304) 843-1300
DATE OF MSDS PREPARATION: 5/24/93

THIS MATERIAL SAFETY DATA SHEET HAS BEEN PREPARED IN ACCORDANCE WITH
THE OSHA HAZARD COMMUNICATION STANDARD (29 CFR 1910.1200). THE SUPPLIER
NOTIFICATION REQUIREMENTS OF SARA TITLE III, SECTION 313, AND OTHER
APPLICABLE RIGHT-TO-KNOW REGULATIONS. ABBREVIATIONS AND OTHER
DESIGNATIONS USED ON THIS MATERIAL SAFETY DATA SHEET INCLUDE THE
FOLLOWING:

U/I = UNKNOWN INFORMATION; N/A = NOT APPLICABLE, NOT ESTAB. = NOT
ESTABLISHED; CERT. LTR. = CHEMICAL O.K. ON TSCA INVENTORY; CAS NO. NOT
AVAILABLE

SECTION III - PHYSICAL/CHEMICAL CHARACTERISTICS
[FORMULA VALUES, NOT SALES SPECIFICATIONS]

BOILING RANGE: 78 - 214 DEG. C   SOLUBILITY IN WATER: U/I %
VAPOR PRESSURE: 28.7 mmHg   WT/GAL (LBS): 7-8 (U.S.)
VAPOR DENSITY: HEAVIER THAN AIR   pH: U/I
% VOL/VOLUME: 45-50   % SOLID BY WEIGHT: 11-18
EVAP RATE (BuOAc = 100): U/I   SPECIFIC GRAVITY: .8 - 1.0
ODOR/APPEARANCE VISCOUS LIQUID WITH AN ODOR CHARACTERISTIC OF THE
                 SOLVENTS LISTED IN SECTION II.

SECTION IV - FIRE AND EXPLOSION HAZARD DATA
US-DOT CATEGORY: FLAMMABLE
FLASHPOINT: 36 DEG. F PMCC
FLAMMABLE LIMITS: LEL 1.7   UEL U/I

EXTINGUISHING MEDIA:
USE NATIONAL FIRE PROTECTION ASSOCIATION (NFPA) CLASS B EXTINGUISHERS
(CARBON DIOXIDE, DRY CHEMICAL, OR UNIVERSAL AQUEOUS FILM FORMING FOAM)
DESIGNED TO EXTINGUISH NFPA CLASS IB FLAMMABLE LIQUID FIRES.
UNUSUAL FIRE AND EXPLOSION HAZARDS:
KEEP CONTAINERS TIGHTLY CLOSED   ISOLATE FROM HEAT, ELECTRICAL

[Right column partially cut off:]
HARMFUL OR FATAL
EYE CONTACT:
CAUSES SEVERE EYE
SKIN CONTACT:
MAY CAUSE MODERA
INHALATION:
VAPOR AND SPRAY M
THROAT. REPEATED E
OF THE RESPIRATORY
INTENTIONAL MISUSE
BE HARMFUL OR FATA
CHRONIC OVEREXPO
AVOID LONG TERM A
SHOWN TO CAUSE M
EXPOSED FOR PROL
POTENTIAL FOR HUMA
TO THE IRRITATING EF
AN ETHYLENE SERIES
ADVERSE EFFECTS ON
IS NO CONCLUSIVE EV
SIGNS AND SYMPTOM
EYE WATERING, THE
INDICATIONS THAT SO
AND VISUAL DISTURB
CRACKING, BURNING
EXCESSIVE SKIN CON
MEDICAL CONDITION
NOT APPLICABLE

SE
INGESTION:
IF SWALLOWED, DO
EYE CONTACT:
IN CASE OF EYE CO
LEAST 30 MINUTES.
SKIN CONTACT:
IN CASE OF SKIN CO
WASHING WITH SOAP
INHALATION:
IF AFFECTED BY INH
ARTIFICIAL RESPIRATI
OTHER:
IF INGESTION, ANY T
DURING OR FOLLOWI
EMERGENCY ROOM
INFORMATION AVAIL

SE
PERSONAL PROTECT
EYE PROTECTION:
WEAR CHEMICAL-TY
FOR EYE CONTACT
VAPORS.
SKIN PROTECTION:
WEAR PROTECTIVE C
OF: NEOPRENE RUBE
RESPIRATORY PROT
OVEREXPOSURE TO
VAPOR EXHAUST OR
AIR SUPPLIED (TC-19
MANUFACTURER'S IN
AIRBORNE CONTAMIN
TO BE PROPERLY FIT
OTHER EQUIPMENT:
CLEAN OR DISCARD
VENTILATION REQUI

Figure 2.3   Material safety data sheet (MSDS). Sheets such as this contain vital information about how to work with a product. Important safety and recycling information can be found on these sheets, along with first aid procedures (courtesy of Training Enterprises Company).

To Others

Many technicians are hurt by those they work with. While following correct safety practices, others may not. One person who does not have good safety habits can make the shop dangerous for all. The following safety practices involve all workers in a shop:

1. *Running engines.* If the shop exhaust system is not hooked up when engines are being tested, carbon monoxide will fill the shop. All technicians in the shop could be overcome by the fumes.
2. *Running machines.* When a machine operator leaves any machine, it should be turned off. Unattended machines can endanger all who are around them.
3. *Hoists, jacks, and lifts.* All vehicles on a hoist should be positioned correctly so there will not be a chance they can slip off. Always place jack stands under any vehicle that has been jacked up. Do this before anyone goes under the vehicle.
4. *Flammable materials.* These should be stored properly. Never leave them in open containers around the shop. There will be many chances for materials of this type to come in contact with an open flame. If it explodes, one pail of gasoline could level the building. Use flame-proof cabinets to store flammable materials.

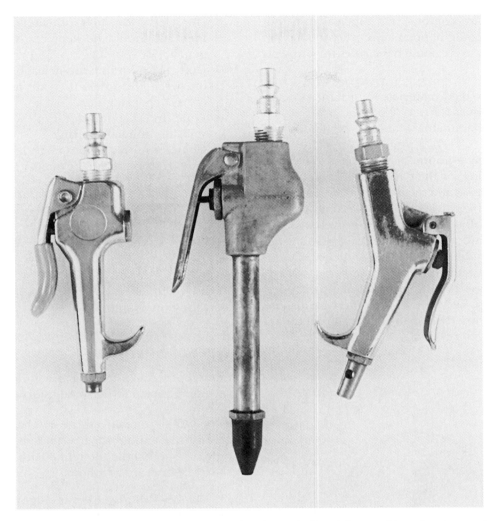

Figure 2.4 Air blow nozzles. Parts such as these are attached to the end of an air hose to blow air onto parts being cleaned (courtesy of Training Enterprises Company).

5. *Battery charging.* Sparks can ignite the gases produced when charging a battery. These gases are also toxic and, if produced in a nonventilated area, could overcome all personnel in the area. Always charge batteries in a spark-free, ventilated place.

6. *Acids and corrosive materials.* Materials of this type should be stored in appropriately constructed, clearly marked containers. Spilled acids can damage floors, car finishes, and clothing and are a danger to living organisms.

7. *Compressed air.* High-pressure compressed air can cause instant death if improperly used. We discuss compressed air later in this chapter. Be sure that compressed air hoses are in good shape and **never** allow anyone to play with the air blow nozzles (see Figure 2.4).

8. *Air conditioner refrigerant.* R-12 and R-234a are gases that can become deadly if they contact an open flame. It is against the law to discharge refrigerant into the air. It should be placed in a recovery system, dried, and reused.

9. *Vehicle movement.* In an automotive area, many vehicles move in for repair and go out for testing. Some of these vehicles may have faulty brake systems, which could be the reason they are in for repair. Be very careful when driving vehicles in and out of a shop. Defective brakes, sticking accelerator pedals, gasoline leaks, and other problems make normal movement of the vehicles very difficult. Don't be taken by surprise and trapped into a situation where personnel are hurt or property is damaged.

To Property

Develop good housekeeping habits. Gasoline-soaked rags stuffed into a wastebasket often ignite by spontaneous combustion, especially in hot weather. This could happen after everyone has left for the day. Here are some basic rules for property protection:

1. Store oil-soaked materials in airtight containers (see Figure 2.5).
2. Store all flammable materials in flameproof cabinets.
3. Unplug any equipment with electronic parts when leaving for the day.
4. Close windows and secure the work area before leaving.
5. Sweep up all trash, and empty wastebaskets.
6. Do not leave any vehicle leaking gasoline on the shop floor. Stop the leak and clean up the gasoline immediately.
7. Do not leave hazardous waste materials open in the shop. Recycle them or otherwise dispose of them properly (use the materials safety data sheet for that product).

Figure 2.5 Oily waste cans. Cans like this have a sealed lid that automatically closes each time it is used. This prevents oily rags from creating a fire due to spontaneous combustion (courtesy of Training Enterprises Company).

8. Don't let anyone play with safety and fire equipment. It should be kept ready for an emergency.
9. Don't leave equipment such as battery chargers on overnight unless they are adjusted to the correct charging rate.
10. Wipe up oil spills, and don't leave antifreeze spills for animals to drink.
11. Do not pour hazardous materials into any sanitary or storm drain, or on any open ground.

LESSON 2–2 How to React in an Emergency

The First Step

In case of an emergency, the first step is to always alert those in charge.

Types of Emergency

Emergencies fall into these categories: fire, electrical emergency, and personal injury accident.

Fire. After notifying those in charge, go to the nearest fire extinguisher. Check to see if it is the right class to handle the immediate fire. Common classes of fires are as follows:

1. Class A—wood, paper, and light combustibles
2. Class B—oil and grease–type fires
3. Class C—electrical fire

Note: Always try to make a class C fire a class A or B fire by shutting off the electrical power. Electricity is a danger in any fire. Many types of extinguisher are not safe for the operator in a class C fire. Shut off the power at the fire scene, if possible, to avoid electricity problems.

4. Class D—Burning metal. Some of the new wheel rims are made from magnesium. This metal will burn with a very hot flame. A regular A, B, or C extinguisher will not put out a class D fire. This requires special powdered chemicals.

A *multiclass fire extinguisher* is made for more than one class of fire. A common type is the ABC dry chemical extinguisher (see Figure 2.6). If a fire gets larger after using an extinguisher, you may have to evacuate the area and send someone to call the fire department. There is always the possibility of toxic smoke in automotive fires. Never stand in front of a vehicle to fight an engine fire. Some bumpers are

Figure 2.6 ABC dry extinguisher. This type of extinguisher can be used for all three types of fires: electrical, wood, and grease (courtesy of Training Enterprises Company).

shock mounted and will explode when exposed to fire. Anyone in the path of the bumper is at risk.

Electrical Emergency. Never touch anyone in contact with AC or regular "house" electricity unless the circuit is shut off. If the person is breathing, get him or her to the hospital as quickly as possible. If not breathing, start CPR (cardiopulmonary resuscitation) and have someone call the rescue squad. Help prevent lowered body temperature by covering the victim with a blanket. Take the piece of equipment out of service and place a "blue tag" on it until the electrical problem is repaired.

CPR and the Heimlich maneuver are advanced emergency procedures. If you do not know how to do any emergency procedure, find someone who does or wait until professional help arrives. The important emergency procedure to use first is to alert those that can help. It is always wise to learn any emergency techniques such as CPR. This knowledge could save the life of your family or friends.

Personal Injury Accident. Determine the type of injury and the extent of the damage. Look for internal damage, broken bones, and puncture wounds. Do not attempt to move anyone that appears to have a neck or back injury. Stop bleeding by applying pressure to the pressure points on arms and legs. Prevent lowered body temperature by covering the person with clothing or a blanket. Start CPR if the person is not breathing or if the heart stops. Call the rescue squad and try to prevent any movement of the body, arms, or legs if the person is having convulsions.

If a person is *choking*, ask if he (or she) can speak. If he can make any noise, stay with him and encourage him to cough it out. Do not slap the person on the back. If the person cannot make a sound, use abdominal thrusts (Heimlich maneuver) to force the air in the lungs to expel the blockage in the airway. Attempt to clear the airway so the person can breathe on his own. Have someone call the rescue squad. Start CPR if the airway becomes clear and the victim still is not breathing. Continue CPR until medical help arrives.

Location of Emergency Items

Know the location of all emergency items where you work. Locate all fire extinguishers and determine the types and sizes. Determine whether the right type of extinguisher is at the correct location. Know a telephone location and the code for getting an outside line. Keep a list of emergency numbers beside the phone, if they are different from 911. Find all fire alarm switches and first aid stations. Inspect any first aid supplies available and make certain all first aid kits are stocked. Locate all water and water hoses. In large buildings, know where the stairs and exits are located. Look to see if the exits are clearly marked. Check that the shop is color coded and periodic safety inspections are made to correct safety problems. Place safety signs where needed. "No smoking," "caution," and "danger" signs, like that shown in Figure 2.7, are needed in places around an automotive shop. Know the personnel in the building that can administer CPR and first aid. Know where the nearest hospital is located and if they have a trauma center and a burn unit.

The most important emergency work is done before the emergency. If correct safety practices are used, emergencies seldom happen. The two most important things a person can do during an emergency are to stay calm and give informed, accurate information.

Figure 2.7   Safety signs. These alert anyone in an area about activity that is not permitted or dangerous, or about required safety precautions, as in the example (courtesy of Training Enterprises Company).

LESSON 2–3   Shop Safety Procedures

Color Code

The American National Standards Institute (ANSI) has designated nine colors as safety colors:

1. **Safety red**—represents danger. Use for signs and around fire extinguishers. Red should be used on machines' "stop" buttons. Paint safety red on anything that poses an immediate danger.
2. **Safety orange**—represents warning. Use this color around machines with a cutting edge. Orange can be used on electrical control boxes. Paint the inside of equipment doors as a warning if the door is left open. Use this color on the edges of any machine where hands or figers could be injured.
3. **Safety yellow**—represents caution. Use on the controls of machines such as knobs and wheels. Yellow used with a black stripe outlines the edges of stationary hazards that could cause tripping. Solid yellow stripes can be used for lines to define walkways and paths. Black and yellow signs can be made for caution messages.
4. **Safety blue**—represents information. If a machine is out of order, place a blue sign on it. This shows others there is important information on the tag. Write all information in white letters so others may read it easily. Common tags are *Out of Order, Do Not Use*, and *Broken.*
5. **Safety green**—represents first aid or medical information. Place a green cross on first aid equipment, doors to first aid stations, eye wash stations, and emergency showers. Write any necessary information in white letters.
6. **Safety purple**—represents radiation hazards. Black and yellow is a substitute color combination for radiation hazards. Mark with this color code any containers, equipment, and radiation materials.
7. **Safety black** and **safety white**—represent traffic control. Black and white stripes are used in

Figure 2.8 Labeled pipe. This is an example of how pipes are labeled when they contain special fluids or liquids (courtesy of Training Enterprises Company).

parking areas. White arrows indicate direction of traffic movement. Use white in the place of yellow under trash cans, around stationary machines, and in storage areas.

8. **Safety gray**—represents machine body color and table top color. Gray is used on floors, the body areas of machines, and table tops. (Some machines also use "vista green," which is not considered a safety color.)

9. **Focal colors**—represented by vista green, ivory, and aluminum. Use vista green on machines and tool cabinets. Ivory is used to paint the edges of tables and machines so they stand out and help the technicians recognize the edges. An all-gray floor and table would blend together and the table might not be seen in reduced light. Aluminum is used to paint waste cans and shop containers. White lettering is used with the aluminum to indicate what is in the container.

10. **Pipe colors**—represented by color and writing. Paint all pipes the same color as the walls. Identify all pipes, with labels, such as those in Figure 2.8, telling the kind of fluids and gases they carry, using the following pipe codes and labels:
    a. Acetylene—red with black lettering
    b. Oxygen—green with black lettering
    c. Natural gas, steam, and high-pressure fluids—yellow with red letters
    d. Compressed air and inert low-pressure gases—blue with white lettering
    e. Vent lines—black with white lettering
    f. Service water and sprinkler pipes—gray bands with white lettering

Check to see how well the shop and work areas measure up on safety color coding. See if management will improve all areas if they are not compliant.

Equipment Inspections

All pieces of equipment being used in a shop should be inspected on a regular basis. The frequency of the inspections depends on the amount of use the equipment receives and how roughly it is used. The inspection should include lubrication and checking of fluids. A check sheet only takes a few minutes to prepare and can be used as a guide to cover all check points. Create forms for all pieces of equipment owned by a shop. A reminder file is helpful to indicate which equipment is due for inspection each month. Be sure to keep these reports filed for future reference.

Fire Procedures and Evacuation Routes

Give considerable thought to fire emergency procedures. Every shop should have a method to notify others of a fire in progress. Evacuation routes should be posted on the walls (see Figure 2.9). Plan alternate routes in case the primary route is blocked. Someone should be responsible to see that everyone is accounted for after the evacuation. Significant loss of life has occurred because no thought was given to these details. List any new materials stored in shop areas so the fire department will know what problems they face when fighting the fire. Experts say that in many work situations, a difference of several seconds can mean the difference between living and dying. Some shops have never had a fire drill. With much flammable material present, such places need to plan fire emergency procedures.

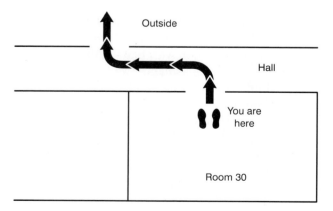

Figure 2.9 Evacuation route. These contain sketches of the building floor plan with arrows showing the routes to take when the building must be evacuated (courtesy of Training Enterprises Company).

Are there marked evacuation routes and are exit signs in place? If they are missing make a note of it and see if management will purchase and install them. Failure to mark these areas may be a violation of state and federal laws.

LESSON 2–4   Personal Protective Equipment

Eye Protection

Figure 2.10 shows two types of eye protection. Standards are set for safety glasses. They have to resist a certain amount of impact and they should have side protection. Side shields must be solid to resist chemical accidents. Select wire mesh when dealing with flying particles. Safety goggles offer more eye protection when dealing with liquids, but neither glasses nor goggles will protect the face. The full face shield protects both the eyes and the face. To keep the eye protection clean, use a liquid cleaner. When cleaning the lens of the glasses, face shield, and goggles, use lens tissue. This will prevent scratching. Store goggles and safety glasses in a sanitizing cabinet, which has special lights to kill bacteria. If you wear regular prescription glasses, plan to have one pair made with safety lenses and side shields to use for work.

Clothing

Protective clothing varies depending on the type of materials being used and the degree of protection needed. Bench work can be done in a shop apron, lab coat, or regular work clothes (shirt and pants). When working around chemicals, use rubber gloves and vinyl aprons or coveralls. Most technicians will put on a pair of coveralls when the work is dirty. For regular shop work, most technicians use work shirts and pants. These may be supplied by a uniform service and may have the company name and worker name on the shirt. Each week the uniform company delivers clean clothes and gathers the dirty clothes to be cleaned. Welding clothes are made of leather to resist burns. The gloves have large cuffs, which prevent welding sparks from getting on the hands. If you are doing heavy lifting, wear a safety belt and safety shoes with toe protection. Regular work shoes should have soles that resist grease and chemicals. Soft shoes are not suitable for automotive work.

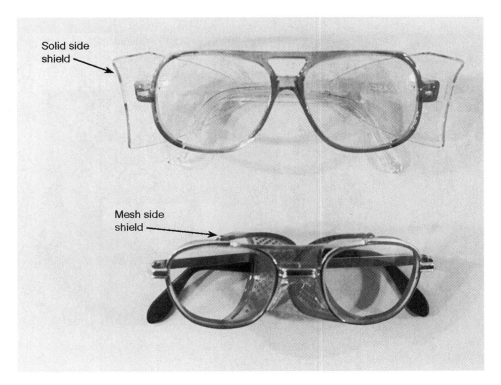

Solid side shield

Mesh side shield

Figure 2.10 Eye protection. Several types of eye protection are used by technicians when working on projects where protection is a necessity (courtesy of Training Enterprises Company).

Ear Protection

Any sound in a shop that goes above 100 decibels (*decibels* are units of sound measurement) can cause severe hearing damage over short periods of time. Sound over 80 decibels for long periods of time also damage the hearing. Hearing protection is not required for any sounds from 20 to 70 decibels. Use hearing protection when exposed to sounds above 80 decibels. When sound levels exceed 120 decibels, using just hearing protection is not enough. At this point, limit the amount of exposure time to 30 minutes and then rest for 5 minutes.

Conduct sound level tests by acquiring a decibel meter and checking the decibel level of the machines used in the shop. Don't forget to check the sound level of any car audio systems being used. It has been reported that many young people are experiencing permanent hearing loss as result of systems that are at too high a level for too long a period.

The important fact to remember is that standard hearing protection will not make you completely safe from hearing damage when exposed to high-decibel sounds (above 120) for long periods of time. Hearing protection is available in the form of

ear plugs and ear muffs (see Figure 2.11). Air impact wrenches and some engines reach sounds well above 100 decibels. Today some people play their car stereos loud enough to cause hearing damage. Take loud noise seriously and protect your hearing.

Breathing Protection

The automotive technician is exposed to many gases and vapors in the shop. The fumes from gasoline can be harmful if breathed long enough. Two of the most deadly materials found around an automotive shop are asbestos and R-12. Brake lining and clutch facings are the most common ways asbestos finds its way onto the shop floor. Sweeping up after the job releases asbestos into the air. Any level of exposure to asbestos is a health risk. Asbestos can be carried on work clothing, contaminating customers, the technician's family, and even pets. Asbestos causes mesothelioma (a fatal cancer of the lining of the chest or abdominal cavity). Asbestos can increase the risk of lung cancer at least 10 times for nonsmokers and 50 times for smokers. Cancer of the voice box, stomach, and large intestine may result if asbestos is swallowed. An important fact to remember about asbestos is how slowly it acts: it may take from 10 to 15 years to affect

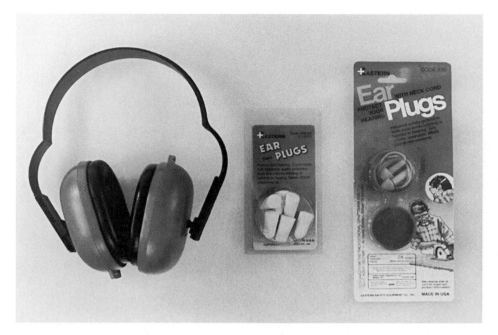

Figure 2.11   Hearing protection. Protective devices such as these are used to prevent hearing damage from high-decibel noise (courtesy of Training Enterprises Company).

an individual. This makes it hard to convince the technician to take this threat seriously.

A brake asbestos recovery system should be purchased and used in every shop that does brake work. The materials caught in the recovery system should be handled as a hazardous material and disposed of correctly. Asbestos *cannot* be dumped into a trash can.

Breathing protection falls into these categories:

1. Light—dust and mist
2. Medium—gas and vapor
3. Heavy—organic vapor
4. Very heavy—paint and pesticide

Figure 2.12 shows a type of breathing protection used for category two. The use of breathing equipment has to be stressed because so few technicians invest in it. Years of unprotected exposure may severely damage the lungs.

> Special breathing protection is needed for brake dust. Normal breathing protection as illustrated in Figure 2.12 is not adequate for exposure to asbestos. Asbestos can cause lung damage if breathed.

Refrigerant (R-12) when exposed to an open flame produces a deadly poison gas. It is a phosgene gas and was available to the military as a weapon. Always remember the danger of refriger-

ant when there is a fire in the engine compartment of a vehicle equipped with air conditioning. When the air conditioner lines burn through and the refrigerant ignites, you can no longer stay to put out the fire. You should immediately evacuate the area and warn all others to follow. There have been documented cases where workers were playing with refrigerant and sprayed it into an electric fan. When the refrigerant flowed over the hot fan motor, a poison gas was formed and killed a worker on the other side. Today, it is illegal to exhaust refrigerant into the air because it has been proven to damage the earth's ozone layer, increasing the risk to humans of getting skin cancer.

First Aid Equipment

An eye wash station should be installed in any shop where chemicals are being used. When anyone gets chemicals into the eye, the eye wash station can provide clean distilled water to neutralize and dilute the chemical. A typical eye wash station is pictured in Figure 2.13.

> All shops should have an eye wash station and a first aid kit. The eye wash station contains distilled water, which reduces eye infection. The first aid kit should stock items to cover the most common shop emergencies such as cuts, burns, and so on.

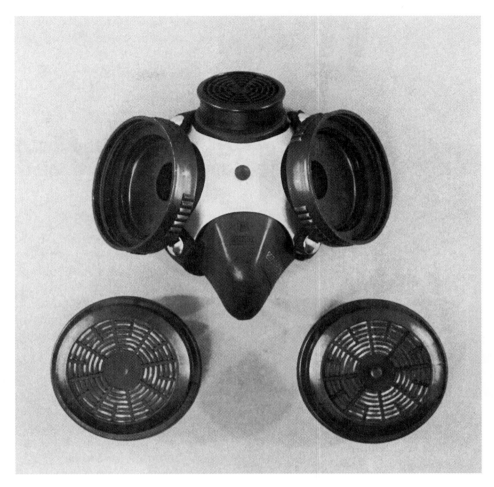

Figure 2.12 Breathing protection. Lungs and air passages are protected by equipment such as these. Breathing equipment is used where there are toxic chemicals or airborne dust (courtesy of Training Enterprises Company).

A first aid kit should be installed on the wall in each automotive laboratory and stocked to treat minor burns, cuts, and liquids in the eye.

LESSON 2-5   Compressed Air

High Pressure

A blast of compressed air at 40 psig (pounds per square inch gage) can rupture an ear drum at a distance of four inches. It can also cause a fatal brain hemorrhage. This same pressure can drive metal chips at speeds of 70 miles per hour or more. Usual shop pressure is around 120 psig—three times more powerful. Placing a shop air nozzle, with its higher air pressure, twelve inches away from a person would do the same damage as a 40 psig air jet. A 40 psig jet of air directed into the mouth can rupture lungs and intestines. A 4 psig jet can rupture the bowels. When directed against the skin,

compressed air can damage the tissues. This damage resembles a burn. A slight scratch or puncture can let the air enter the bloodstream and could be fatal.

No one should play with compressed air or let others play with it. Many people who are not informed feel that compressed air is harmless. High-pressure compressed air is used for inflating car and truck tires and to operate air jacks and lifts. It should *never* be used for blowing off parts.

Regulated Pressure

When compressed air is used to blow off parts, the pressure should be regulated from the regular line pressure of 120 psig down to about 30 (see Figure 2.14a). Safety air blow nozzles have pressure-reducing holes drilled into them on the side of the tip (see Figure 2.14b). These holes release the full pressure when the nozzle is placed directly on

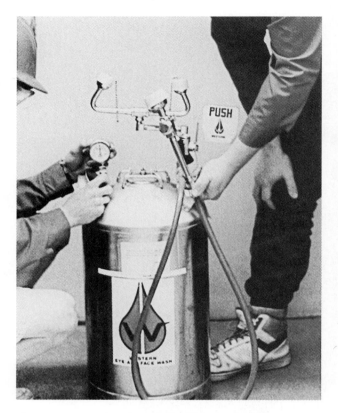

Figure 2.13 Eye wash station. Stations such as these contain clean distilled water to be used in case a technician gets dirt or chemicals into an eye (courtesy of Training Enterprises Company).

an object or the skin. The regulated pressure outlets should be marked and the air blow nozzle connected to only this lower pressure.

Does the shop have a set of compressed air rules posted in the work area? Is the pressure used to blow off parts regulated? These are some questions every technician should ask, and if the answer is no, develop rules and convince management to install regulators.

Compressed Air Rules

Compressed air is dangerous. Everyone working around it should obey the following rules:

1. Always use safety glasses or a full face shield when using compressed air.
2. Never direct the air nozzle at anyone at any time.
3. Never use compressed air to clean dust from you or your clothes.
4. Never spin bearings with compressed air.

5. Never blow compressed air directly on your hands while holding parts. Use parts holders.
6. Use only regulated pressure for parts cleaning.
7. Don't allow anyone to play with compressed air. Be sure everyone is informed about the safety problems.

LESSON 2-6   Hand Tool, Equipment, and Environmental Safety

Hand Tool Safety

Thousands of different tools are used in automotive maintenance and repair. We discuss here some general safety rules. Add to this list yourself as you add tools to your personal tool box.

Hand tools are made of many different materials; steel and plastic are the most common. In many cases the steel is case hardened on the outside to give added strength and durability. General hand tool safety rules follow:

1. Never use a dull cutting tool. Sharpen it.
2. Don't pry with tools that are not made for prying. Many times tools not made for prying are brittle and will fracture if used for this purpose.
3. Use only files that have handles. Put handles on those that have none.
4. Be sure that hammer heads are secure on the handles before using them.
5. Discard or repair broken ratchets and sockets. Push away rather than pull on wrench and ratchet handles.
6. Keep file teeth clean by using a file card.
7. Remove the mushroom edges that develop on chisels and punches. This edge will break off and could injure an eye (see Figure 2.15).
8. Never strike two hardened hammers together. Case hardened steel is very brittle and will shatter.
9. Use tool holders for chisels and other cutting tools. This reduces the chance of injury to your hand if you should miss when trying to strike the tool.
10. Always use safety glasses when using cutting tools.

Check to see how many dull tools are being used in the shop. Replace or sharpen each. It is dangerous to use tools that are not in good condition. It also wastes time.

11. Electrical hand tools should always be double insulated (to protect the operator from

(a)

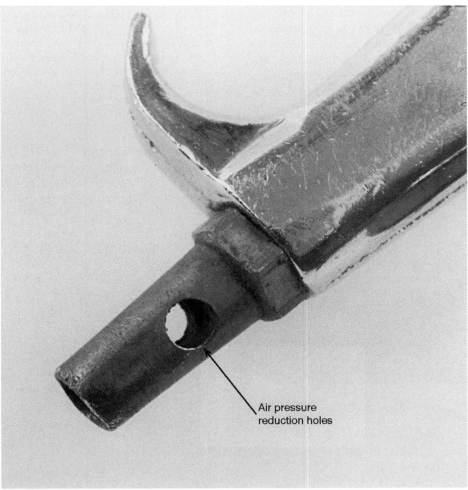

Air pressure
reduction holes

(b)

Figure 2.14 (a) Pressure Regulator. Reduces line pressure to a lower limit. (b) Pressure-reducing holes. Holes like these help reduce the air blow nozzle pressure. They divert the air from the end and make the nozzle safer to use (courtesy of Training Enterprises Company).

Figure 2.15 Mushroomed tool edge. A tool in this condition is not safe to use and should be repaired. Standard repair is to grind off the mushroom edge on a grinder (courtesy of Training Enterprises Company).

accidental grounding) or should have a separate ground connection. Never use an electrical tool if it appears to have an electrical defect, such as if it is emitting sparks or is slow to turn. Place a blue tag on it and either repair it or send it off for repair.

Equipment Safety

Automotive technicians are faced with learning how to use many different pieces of equipment to accomplish their work. Generally, this equipment is either mechanical, electrical, or hydraulic. Machines often use tremendous pressure. Many machines have controls that must be accurately set. Before anyone attempts to use any automotive equipment he or she should receive training on the equipment. Equipment safety is a two-part operation:

1. Receive the proper training or read the instructions.

2. Give each piece of equipment a regular inspection to check out the electrical, mechanical, and hydraulic parts.

Lubricate the machines according to the manufacturer's recommendations. Be sure all safety guards are in place. Know the standard color code for safety. Be sure that each electrically driven piece of equipment is grounded properly and there is a stop button at the machine. Never leave a machine running if you are going to leave the area—shut it off. Ventilate all machines that require it. Be sure that full face shields, safety goggles, safety glasses, rubber gloves, and hearing protection are where they can be used. Each technician should take the responsibility to wear furnished protective equipment. If it is needed but not furnished, technicians should consider getting their own.

Look to see if there are records of regular inspections made on each piece of equipment used in the shop. The inspections should include regular maintenance and lubrication. If there are not any inspections being carried out, make out inspection sheets and use them. Keep these sheets in a file for future reference. Machines can become dangerous to use if they are not lubricated and serviced when needed.

Lift Safety. A hydraulic lift (see Figure 2.16) can be a very dangerous piece of equipment if the operator is not properly trained. Automobiles will be lifted at least four or more feet off the ground and

Figure 2.16 Hydraulic lift. Equipment such as this is used to raise vehicles off the floor so technicians can work under them. Lifts have safety devices that should be in place and working (courtesy of Training Enterprises Company).

the technician will be working under them. Many times the technician will be doing a lot of prying and moving of parts. The lifting arms of the lift should be placed in spots where the vehicle will not break loose and fall. Here are some general lift safety rules:

1. Be sure the vehicle is balanced on the lift.
2. Be sure lift arms are placed correctly on the frame of the vehicle and not on a place that will not support the weight of the vehicle. Know where the lift points are on each vehicle.
3. Be sure the safety catches are working on the lift.
4. Always be sure everything is out from under the lift before attempting to lower any vehicle.
5. Avoid stopping and starting suddenly when either lowering or raising a vehicle on a lift.

Jack Safety. Floor jacks, bumper jacks, vehicle jacks, and safety stands (see Figure 2.17) all require that the vehicle be correctly prepared before

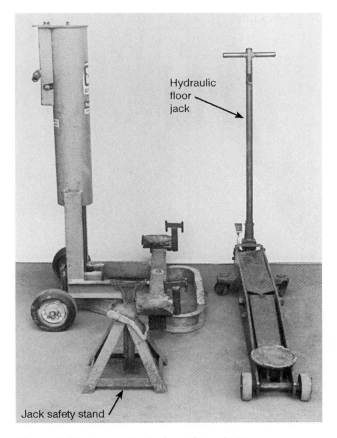

Figure 2.17 Automotive jacks and stands. Two common vehicle jacks are the floor and bumper. Always use jack stands after the vehicle is in the air (courtesy of Training Enterprises Company).

use. Follow these safety precautions when using jacks:

1. Be sure the vehicle is free to move before using a floor or hydraulic bumper jack. Take the transmission out of park or gear. Release the parking brake. Make sure the wheels are not blocked. The vehicle jack is different—when using such a jack, the vehicle should *not* be free to move. Block the wheels either in front or the rear depending on which end you are attempting to raise. Keep the transmission in gear and keep the parking brake on.
2. Check to make sure the jack is placed under the vehicle in the correct spot. Never jack up a vehicle by the radiator, gas tank, oil pan, or transmission pan. Use the correct places on the frame of the vehicle.
3. Always finish by placing jack stands under the vehicle frame. Never depend on the jack alone to keep the vehicle in the air. Hydraulic jacks can fail in an instant, letting the vehicle down quickly and unexpectedly.
4. Place the jack handle in the raised position. This reduces the chance of someone tripping over the handle.

Electrical Safety. All shops have several 110 volt electrical outlets. Heavy-duty electric motors require 220 volts. In each outlet, whether 220 or 110 volts, there will be a separate ground circuit. The 110 volt outlets have one "hot" wire and two ground wires. The 220 volt outlets have two "hot" wires and one ground. The ground wires give the most trouble. Check the ground circuit going from the plug to the equipment with an ohmmeter. Place one test prod on the ground prong of the plug and the other on the frame of the equipment. There should be a resistance reading indicating there is a path or closed wire.

Some pieces of electrical equipment may be double insulated. The plug will not have a ground wire or prong on the plug. The tool has internal insulation that keeps the electrical parts from grounding to the handle of the tool. On all other tools there should be a ground wire and it should *not* be "open." Always perform periodic ground wire inspections on all tools and equipment (see Figure 2.18).

Emergency Disconnect. Every shop should have one power box switch that will shut off all the outlets and major pieces of equipment in the shop. If any automotive technician gets involved

Ground
connection

Figure 2.18 Tool ground. The third wire is used to connect the equipment to a ground path. If it is not in place when a tool shorts out, the operator could become the ground path and may be hurt (courtesy of Training Enterprises Company).

with a shorted tool or machine, this switch can be pulled and the current shut off.

> Examine the plug on everything electrical used in the shop. Especially examine hand-held tools. Never operate anything unless it has a proper ground. *Note:* Double-insulated pieces of electrical equipment do not always have a ground plug. To be really safe have management install ground fault interrupter receptacles in each line of receptacles.

All stationary machines should have individual operation switches within reach of the operator (see Figure 2.19). The switches should be coded with an orange background and a red "stop" switch. The "on" switch should be black. Very dangerous machines should have magnetic switches that will keep the machine off after a power failure. Such machines must be reset after the power returns.

It is part of machine safety to regularly inspect all electrical, mechanical, and hydraulic parts of each machine. Motors, switches, and cords should be a part of this inspection.

Hand-Held Tools. All hand-held electrical tools should be checked for speed of operation and motor condition. Examine the power cord for bad insulation, bare wires, broken plugs, and bent prongs. Check the ground prong on the plug to see that it has not been broken or cut off. The tool would still run if this prong were missing. You would not be protected and could have all the current flow through you to ground if the motor were to become shorted. Any tool that sparks, smokes, or doesn't run up to

speed should be blue tagged and sent out for repair.

Electrical First Aid. *First aid* is the immediate assistance and care that is given to anyone that has been involved in an accident. If you are the

Figure 2.19 Machine switches. Each machine should have a switch that the operator can reach in case of emergency (courtesy of Training Enterprises Company).

one giving first aid, never touch anyone connected or involved with electrical current. The current can pass through the victim and electrocute you. Turn the current off *first* and then move the victim. If you cannot turn off the current, find an insulated piece of material and separate the person from the electrical contact. Immediately start to stabilize the body temperature by wrapping the victim in a blanket, and administer CPR if the heart stops beating. Clean any wounds and put on bandages. Stop any bleeding by using pressure points when necessary. Splint any broken limbs. Rinse chemicals out of eyes and remove dirt. Anyone untrained should never move a victim who has a spinal cord injury. Do as much as you can to immediately reduce any further damage. The first few minutes after an accident are critical. Make sure that medical help is called immediately. Controlling shock and administering CPR are the two most important things to do before help arrives.

Environmental Safety

Material safety data sheets (MSDS) are available for all chemicals used in an automotive shop (refer to Figure 2.3). There are eight important categories of information on these sheets.

1. *Ingredients.* This lists the percentage of each chemical in the material and the exposure limit index.
2. *Physical data.* Some typical items in this category are boiling point, vapor pressure, vapor density, solubility in water, specific gravity, viscosity, evaporation rate, and percent of volatility.
3. *Fire and explosion hazard data.* This lists the flash point, flammable limits, extinguishing limits, special firefighting procedures, and unusual fire and explosion hazards.
4. *Reactivity data.* This gives the stability, incompatibility (materials to avoid), hazardous polymerization, and hazardous decomposition products.
5. *Environmental information.* This category gives the spill response, recommended disposal method, and other environmental data.
6. *Suggested first aid.* Provides directions for immediate help if there is eye contact, skin contact, inhalation, or swallowing of the material.
7. *Precautionary information.* Gives directions for working with the materials—what to avoid, what eye protection to wear, special clothing,

type of ventilation, how to store containers, and special warnings.
8. *Health hazard data.* Provides known data about eye contact, skin contact, inhalation, and ingestion. The ingredients may be listed individually with a brief explanation on how the body will react if exposed to these materials. Liver damage, dizziness, nausea, vomiting, drowsiness, and respiratory irritation are some of the typical problems listed.

When any chemical is used, refer to these sheets and make sure the chemical is handled properly. Engine oil should never be poured down the drain or spread on the ground. Place used engine oil back into the containers the new oil was in, and make sure the oil is recycled (purified and reused). Many service stations put used oil in large containers and have it picked up by specialty firms that reclaim used oil. Oil filters should also be saved and recycled.

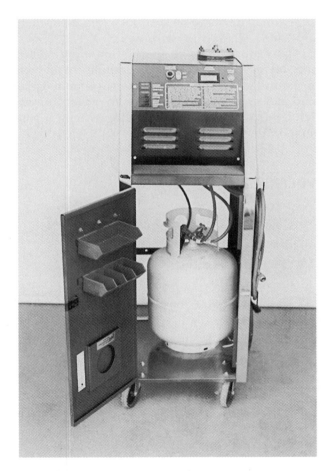

Figure 2.20 Air conditioner recycling equipment. Equipment such as this is used to remove refrigerant, clean it, and place it back into the system (courtesy of Training Enterprises Company).

Does the company you work for have an environmental safety plan? Are MSDS sheets kept on each product? If the answer is no, help develop a plan and order the sheets. Violation of environmental laws can be very costly in fines, lawyer fees, and workers' compensation.

Never pour chemicals onto the ground or down the drain. Place used antifreeze, brake fluid, and battery electrolyte in containers that will hold them and send them to a recycling plant.

Batteries contain lead, plastic, and sulfuric acid. Battery manufacturers take used batteries and reclaim these materials for use in new ones.

Refrigerant is harmful to the ozone layer of the earth. Handling air conditioning refrigerant requires special recycling equipment, such as that shown in Figure 2.20. These machines save the used refrigerant, remove the moisture, and make it pure enough to be reused in the original system. Technicians must be licensed to purchase and use refrigerant. They have to have recycling equipment available to them and must use it.

Many more items around an automotive shop may be recycled. It is the responsibility of all technicians to set up and follow an environmental plan and make sure that we continue to protect our water, land, and air. Start a recycling system in your shop if there is not one already.

VOCABULARY

A. Toxic

B. Guards

C. Product label

D. Carbon monoxide

E. Corrosive

F. Spontaneous combustion

G. Class A fire

H. AC

I. 911

J. Safety orange

K. Lubrication check sheet

L. Evacuation route

M. Eye protection

N. Coveralls

O. Hearing protection

P. Phosgene gas

Q. Eye wash station

R. Neutralize

S. Distilled water

T. File card

U. Double insulated

V. Lift point

W. Physical data

X. Environmental information

Y. Sulfuric acid

_____ 1. Alternating current

_____ 2. Chemical found in a storage battery

_____ 3. To dilute and change from an acid to water

_____ 4. Used to list all lubrication tasks

_____ 5. Means *warning* when on a machine

_____ 6. When a soaked item catches on fire by heating up

_____ 7. Placed on machines to avoid contact

_____ 8. Protects hearing by reducing noise

_____ 9. Used to clean file teeth

_____ 10. Places on a vehicle where a lift can be installed

_____ 11. Safety glasses made to resist impact

_____ 12. When wood and paper are burning

_____ 13. Chemicals that cause rust and deterioration

_____ 14. Harmful chemicals if swallowed or breathed

_____ 15. Prevents an electrical tool from accidentally grounding

_____ 16. Pure water where the chemicals and minerals have been removed

_____ 17. A poisonous gas when inhaled

_____ 18. Protection worn over regular clothes

_____ 19. Emergency telephone number

_____ 20. A poster showing the quickest exits in a building

_____ 21. An engine exhaust gas

_____ 22. Used to remove any chemicals in the eyes

_____ 23. Explains how to dispose of a material safely

_____ 24. Explains how to use a product correctly

_____ 25. Explains about the specific gravity and viscosity of a material

REVIEW QUESTIONS

The following questions will help you determine if you have accomplished the tasks stated at the beginning of this chapter. If you don't know many of the answers, go back and review the material before proceeding to the next chapter.

LESSON 2–1

1. What method should be used to help a person who is choking?
2. What is the advantage to recycling?
3. Name a material that should be recycled.
4. What piece of equipment should always be used with a jack?
5. What happens when freon comes in contact with an open flame?
6. Name one fluid spill that should always be removed immediately.

LESSON 2–2

7. What is the first step to take when there is an emergency?
8. What can be done to change a class C fire to either a class A or B?
9. Why should you never stand in front of a burning car?
10. What should you do when someone is caught by an electrical current?
11. Should you slap a choking victim on the back?
12. What number is universally used for the emergency number?
13. Name several emergency items that should be inspected by someone before an accident happens.

LESSON 2–3

14. Which safety color represents warning?
15. What safety color should an equipment control knob be painted?
16. What color would be on a sign attached to a piece of equipment just painted?
17. What color would the directional arrow on a shop floor be colored?
18. A natural gas pipe would be coded with a yellow patch and what color letters?
19. Why would a local automotive shop keep a list of all the stored materials and their location?

LESSON 2–4

20. High-impact lens and what other feature are on safety glasses?
21. Welding clothes are made with what type of materials?

22. At what decibel level is hearing protection no longer effective?
23. When sounds reach over 120 decibels, how long should you be exposed before taking a break?
24. Name a tool that will reach sounds of over 100 decibels.
25. Has an acceptable level of exposure to asbestos been determined?
26. How long does asbestos exposure take to show adverse effects?
27. What is the problem when freon contacts an open flame?

LESSON 2–5

28. At what speed would a 40 psig compressed air blast drive chips?
29. What size air pressure does it take to rupture the bowels?
30. What can be the result if compressed air is blown directly into a cut?
31. What is unregulated air pressure used for in the shop?
32. What safety item should always be used when working with compressed air?

LESSON 2–6

33. What should be on the file before you attempt to use it?
34. What is used to keep a file clean?
35. What is a mushroom on a hand tool?
36. What parts on a lift prevent it from coming down by accident?
37. Should the car be free to roll with a bumper jack?
38. Name several spots where a vehicle should never be lifted.
39. What two voltage sizes are used in a shop?
40. Which wire circuits give the most trouble?
41. What type of electrical shutoff should every shop have?

ASE QUESTIONS

Each question or incomplete statement in this test is followed by four suggested answers or completions. In each case select the *one* that best answers the question or completes the statement.

1. Technician A says that anytime a floor jack is used, jack stands should be placed under the vehicle. Technician B says that jack stands should also be used with a hydraulic lift. Who is right?

a. A only   b. B only
c. Both A and B   d. Neither A nor B

2. Technician A says the product label contains all the information needed to handle a product safely. Technician B says that the material safety data sheet contains all the information needed to handle a product safely. Who is right?
   a. A only   b. B only
   c. Both A and B   d. Neither A nor B

3. Technician A says that battery chargers can be left on overnight on batteries that are completely discharged. Technician B says that batteries left to charge overnight should only be on the correct charging rate. Who is right?
   a. A only   b. B only
   c. Both A and B   d. Neither A nor B

4. Technician A says that a class C fire can be turned into a class A fire by shutting off the electricity. Technician B says that a class C fire can be turned into a class B fire by shutting off the electricity. Who is right?
   a. A only   b. B only
   c. Both A and B   d. Neither A nor B

5. Technician A says an A or B fire extinguisher can be used for a class D fire. Technician B says it takes an ABC fire extinguisher to put out a class D fire. Who is right?
   a. A only   b. B only
   c. Both A and B   d. Neither A nor B

6. Technician A says a pipe colored green with black lettering contains acetylene. Technician B says a red-colored pipe with black lettering contains oxygen. Who is right?
   a. A only   b. B only
   c. Both A and B   d. Neither A nor B

7. Technician A says that hearing protection for sounds over 120 decibels is not adequate. Technician B says that sounds at 80 decibels over long periods of time can damage unprotected hearing. Who is right?
   a. A only   b. B only
   c. Both A and B   d. Neither A nor B

8. Technician A says that organic vapor requires medium breathing protection. Technician B says that gas and vapor require medium breathing protection. Who is right?
   a. A only   b. B only
   c. Both A and B   d. Neither A nor B

9. Technician A says that distilled water should always be used in an eye wash station. Technician B says that regular tap drinking water should be used. Who is right?
   a. A only   b. B only
   c. Both A and B   d. Neither A nor B

10. Technician A says that reactivity data is found on a material safety data sheet. Technician B says that environmental data is found on a MSDS sheet. Who is right?
    a. A only   b. B only
    c. Both A and B   d. Neither A nor B

3 Basic Automotive Maintenance Tools

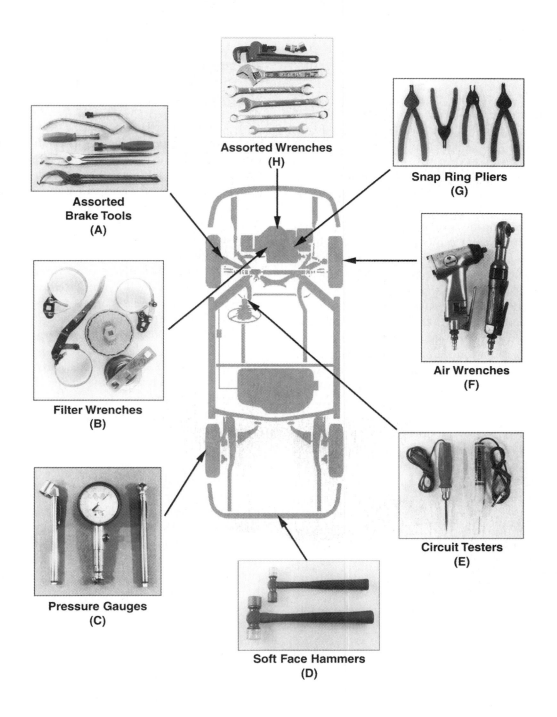

Assorted Brake Tools
(A)

Assorted Wrenches
(H)

Snap Ring Pliers
(G)

Filter Wrenches
(B)

Air Wrenches
(F)

Pressure Gauges
(C)

Circuit Testers
(E)

Soft Face Hammers
(D)

Automotive technicians are not able to perform their work without a large assortment of tools. Most places of employment require a technician to have a personal set of tools. After studying this chapter, you should know many of the tools essential for your own starter kit. Begin acquiring your personal tool set as soon as possible so this will not be a large expense when you graduate from your automotive training program.

TASKS

Beginning automotive technicians sometimes feel that a discussion of hand tools is too basic and unimportant. This is untrue. A wrong tool used at the wrong time can cause hours of additional work correcting a problem that could have been avoided with the correct tool selection. Imagine, for example, the problems experienced if you strip the edges of an engine head bolt with a twelve-point socket. You must then remove the bolt, which is a difficult job. Using a six-point socket would have made the job easy. Technicians should know the best tool to use in every situation.

The correct tool can save time, and time is money to a technician. Brake tools (see Figure 3a) are specialized and designed to remove and replace brake parts. Even a simple job like changing an oil filter requires special tools (see Figure 3b) to remove the old filter. When adjusting tire pressure on a vehicle, a gauge (see Figure 3c) is required. Air wrenches (see Figure 3f) are faster and superior to a hand wrench if this type of tool can be used.

New tools are designed and produced every day to meet the demands of the new vehicles. A technician is always in the market for tools and over a period of time will have an extensive personal inventory.

The following are five tasks to master before leaving this chapter:

Task 3-1. Learn to identify and use general hand tools. This list is not complete and it will be up to you to study all tools needed to accomplish the job.

Task 3-2. Be able to use specialized tools for use on engines and engine accessories to gain speed and accuracy.

Task 3-3. Be proficient in the use of automotive under-the-vehicle tools.

Task 3-4. Learn to use the tools and equipment necessary to repair tires, wheels, hubs, and brakes to factory standards.

Task 3-5. Learn to use electrical circuit and light system tools and equipment, which may require mastering the use of ohmmeters, voltmeters, and ammeters. Study and use the automotive oscilloscope, one of the more complicated pieces of equipment, which requires a combination of theory and equipment skills.

LESSON 3-1   General Hand Tools
Hand and Air Wrenches

Every mechanic should have a good assortment of hand wrenches. This should include the open end, box, combination, flare nut, adjustable, pipe wrench, and swivel socket wrench (see Figure 3.1). The open end wrench is the most common wrench. Wrenches are designed to hold or remove bolts and nuts. For automotive work the standard sizes start at 1/4 in. and run up to $1\frac{5}{8}$ in. The metric sizes range from 6 mm to 32 mm. The adjustable and pipe wrench are not recommended for use when the head of the bolt is not stripped. These two wrenches can cause damage to a bolt head or nut. After a bolt or nut is stripped, use a pipe wrench or vice grip plier to remove the stripped parts. The flare nut wrench is designed to be used on tubing nuts (see Figure 3.2). These parts are usually made of soft metal, such as brass or copper. The tubing nut wrench is the best tool to prevent rounding over the edges of the tubing nuts.

Air wrenches are the most popular tools used in an automotive shop (see Figure 3.3). The 1/2 in. drive is used for the larger size bolts and the 3/8 in. drive for the smaller sizes. Both the standard and metric size sockets should be purchased for each size drive. Air wrench sockets are designed to take the added stress of the air wrench hammer action. Additional sockets that can be purchased for air wrenches include screwdriver bits and universal style sockets. These sockets are specially made to handle the torque of an air wrench. Regular non–air operated 1/2, 3/8, and 1/4 in. ratchet sets are still used where an air wrench cannot reach. The technician still needs a set of these for use away from an air supply. Do *not* try to use these sockets and adapters with an air wrench.

Air wrenches require stronger walled sockets than regular socket sets. Regular sockets will be stripped and can crack at the sidewall and gripping surface. Air wrench sockets may be used with regular socket sets when additional socket strength is required.

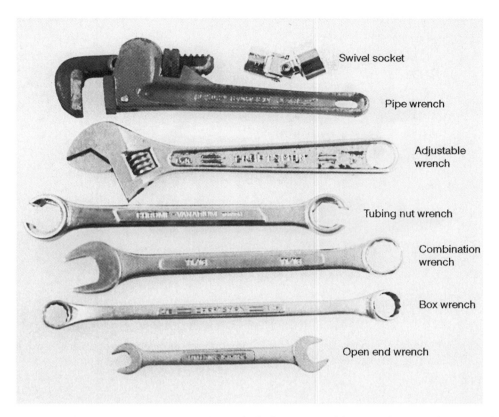

Figure 3.1 Assorted wrenches. Some common wrenches include the open end, box, combination, flare nut, adjustable, pipe, and swivel socket wrench (courtesy of Training Enterprises Company).

Pliers

Pliers are used to hold, cut, twist, and pull. Basic types of pliers are the slip joint, channel lock, cutting, and needle nose (see Figure 3.4). Some specialty pliers are locking (vice grip), battery, hose clamp, brake spring, snap ring, and wire stripper. These pliers help remove battery cables, hose clamps, brake springs, and snap rings. Wire strippers remove the insulation from the end of

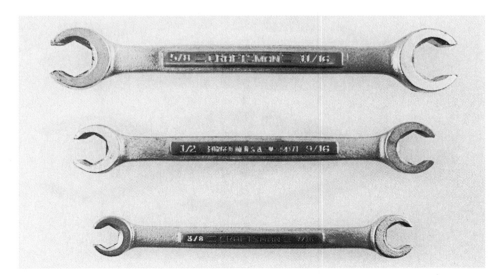

Figure 3.2 Flare nut wrench. Notice that this wrench is slit or open on the end to enable it to fit over tubing (courtesy of Training Enterprises Company).

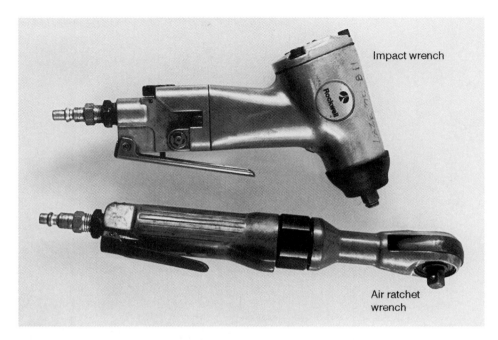

Figure 3.3   Air wrenches. Air-driven wrenches are used for fast removal and replacements of fasteners such as nuts and bolts. Common air wrench sizes are 1/2 in. drive and 3/8 in. drive (courtesy of Training Enterprises Company).

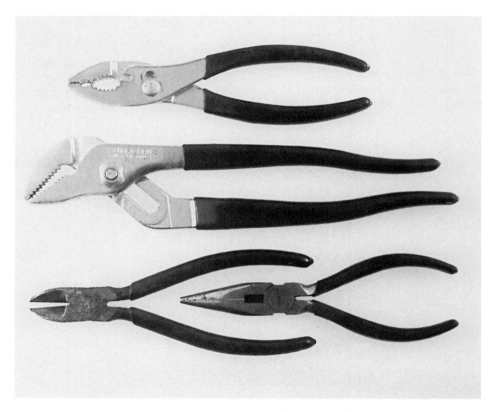

Figure 3.4   Pliers. Common pliers are the slip joint, channel lock, cutting, and needle nose (courtesy of Training Enterprises Company).

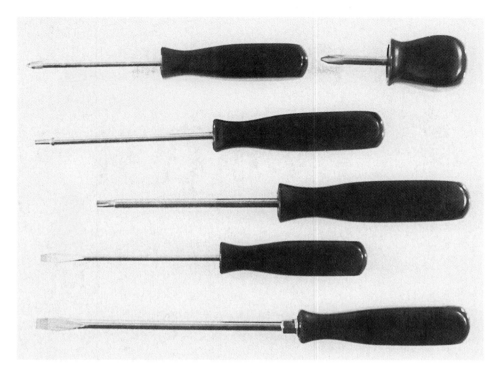

Figure 3.5 Screwdrivers. Three common types of screwdrivers are the Phillips, standard, and torx. These come in different sizes and shank length (courtesy of Training Enterprises Company).

protected electrical wire. Locking pliers have jaws that clamp together and lock. This is useful to hold two parts together while cutting or drilling them.

Screwdrivers, Screw Holders, and Nut Drivers

Screwdrivers come in many styles. The automotive technician should have standard, Phillips, and torx styles in all common sizes and lengths (see Figure 3.5). Screwdrivers are designed to remove slotted, Phillips and torx type fasteners. A special screwdriver, called a screw holder, locks the screw on the tool so it can be started easier. It also prevents dropping the screw down into a part from lack of room. Nut drivers are shaped like a screwdriver but have built-in sockets on the end. They are used for small nuts and bolts where a lot of turning force is not needed. They come in standard and metric sizes. The major advantage of a nut driver is speed.

Hammers

The ball peen hammer is the most common automotive hammer (see Figure 3.6). One end is very slightly rounded for striking tools such as chisels and punches, and the other end is shaped like a ball for hammering metal. An obsolete use for the ball part was to stretch metal. Today it is used to cut gaskets. Ball peen hammers come in sizes according to the weight of the head. Common sizes for ball peen hammers range from 2 ounces to 48 ounces. The 12, 16, and 20 ounce sizes are the most common for automotive use. Handles are made of hickory wood or fiberglass. Ball peen hammers are made of hardened steel.

Never strike two hammers against each other because the heads can shatter, sending metal fragments flying all over the shop. Always wear safety glasses when using hammers. Both the hammer and the tools can release metal chips. Holding tools with the hands while striking them can be risky. Tool holders are made to keep your hands out of striking range.

Soft Face Hammers. Soft face hammers (see Figure 3.7) are made for use where the hammer is expected to give rather than dent or chip the part being struck. Common tips are bronze, wood, soft plastic, and rubber; nylon is sometimes used when a harder tip is desired. The tips can be replaced when they have been worn or damaged.

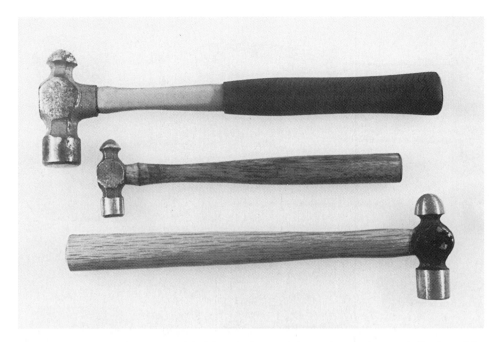

Figure 3.6   Hammers. The ball peen hammer is the common type used to strike punches and chisels and for general shop work (courtesy of Training Enterprises Company).

LESSON 3–2 Engine and Engine Accessory Tools

Engine Lubrication Tools

The filter wrench (see Figure 3.8) is a basic engine lubrication tool. There are many designs on the market to fit the various diameter filters and to remove those in hard-to-reach places. Some fit on the end of the filter like a socket; others go around the center of the filter. One type is designed to be used with an extension and ratchet. No matter how the wrench is designed, its purpose is to remove the oil filter. Slip the wrench on the end

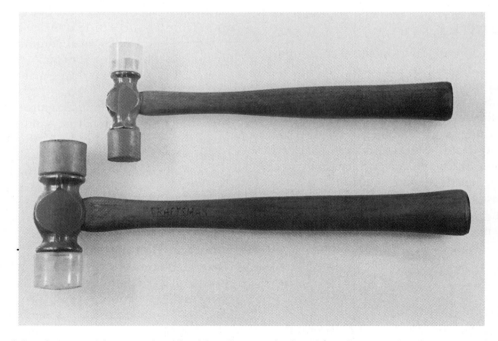

Figure 3.7   Soft face hammer. When a surface should not be scratched or chipped, use a nylon, bronze, wood, soft plastic, or rubber tipped soft hammer (courtesy of Training Enterprises Company).

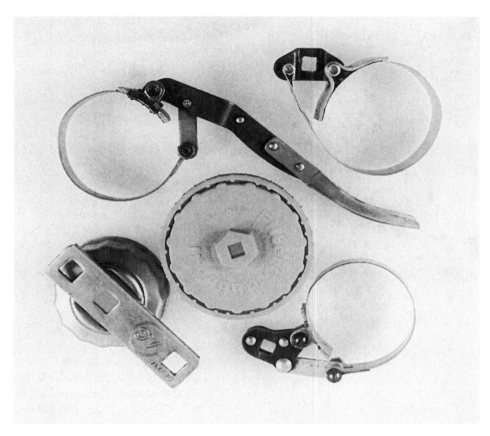

Figure 3.8 Filter wrenches. Pictured here are some of the different types of filter wrenches. They are all used for one purpose, to remove an engine oil filter (courtesy of Training Enterprises Company).

or over the filter and turn counterclockwise to remove. You should not need to use a tool to install a new filter. Just lubricate the filter seal with motor oil and tighten by hand at least 3/4 of a turn but no more than one full turn. The filter gasket should be compressed enough to seal without leaking and the filter should be tight enough to not vibrate loose. For additional information about engine lubrication, see Chapter 5.

Air Conditioning Tools

Service gauges (see Figure 3.9) are used to check the low- and high-side pressures of an air conditioning system. A separate set of gauges is needed for use with the new R-134a refrigerant systems. This avoids contamination from one system to the other. By looking at both the high-side and low-side pressure, any problems can be detected. High-side pressures can be from 100 pounds per square inch (psi) to 400 psi. The low side can range from 22 psi to 40 psi. The new R-134a system runs higher on

Figure 3.9 Air conditioner service gauges. Gauges such as these are used to check the low- and high-side refrigerant pressure on an air conditioning system (courtesy of Training Enterprises Company).

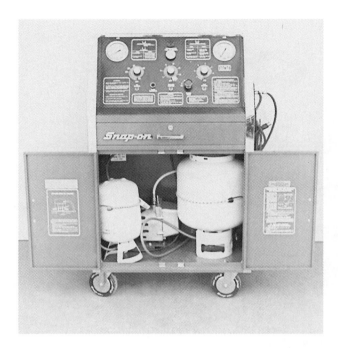

Figure 3.10 Air conditioner recovery station. This machine captures, cleans, and reuses the refrigerant in either the R-12 or the R-134a air conditioning system (courtesy of Training Enterprises Company).

the high-side and lower on the low-side pressures. Hot outside temperature and high humidity causes high-side gauge pressures to increase on both the old (R-12) and the new (R-134a) systems.

You must use a recovery system if you need to repair either system (see Figure 3.10). This equipment removes the R-12 or R-134a refrigerant, filters it, removes the moisture, and prepares it to be reused. The technician must have a license to repair air conditioners and buy refrigerant. A license is not needed to make routine inspections and check system pressures.

For more information about air conditioning service, refer to Chapter 19.

Battery and Charging System Tools

A special brush is used when the battery terminals and posts need to be cleaned on top post batteries (see Figure 3.11). One end of the brush cleans the terminal and the other end cleans the cable. As shown in Figure 3.11, another special brush is made to clean side post batteries. Both brushes have hard bristles and remove the corrosion down to the bare

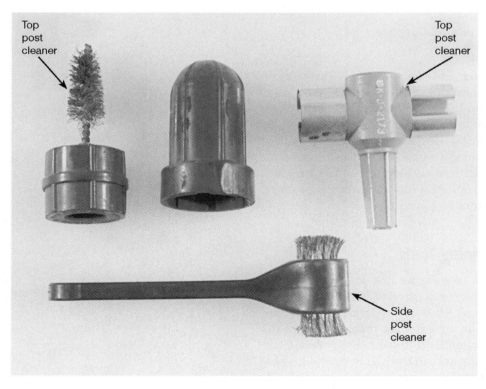

Figure 3.11 Battery post brushes. These brushes are made to clean the posts and cables on a battery (courtesy of Training Enterprises Company).

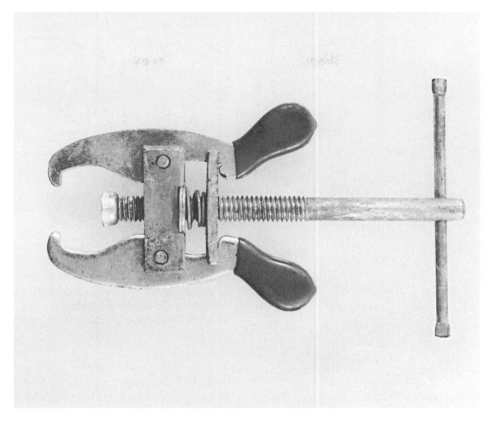

Figure 3.12 Battery puller. When a battery terminal bolt is rounded, the terminal can be removed with this puller. Replace the bolt before installing the terminal (courtesy of Training Enterprises Company).

metal. When both the cable and the terminal are a bright color, stop. Some metal is removed in the cleaning and the terminals are reduced in size but the cable clamp can still be tightened. Removing the corrosion allows a good electrical contact between the post and the terminal. Some technicians use a little chassis grease to seal off the battery terminals from the outside air and retard the formation of new corrosion.

> **❗ Safety Message:** When working around a battery, avoid shorting across the terminals or creating a spark. A fire or explosion could result.

Battery cable pullers (see Figure 3.12) are made especially to remove battery clamps that have been corroded by battery acid so a wrench will not work. The puller is made strong enough to clamp onto what is left of the cable to remove it. Turn the puller bolt to force the cable off the end of the post. If the battery puller cannot remove the corroded cable, use a hacksaw to cut the bolt in half. You can then

pull both ends out of the clamp by using pliers. Install a new battery cable bolt and nut so the clamp can be closed around the battery terminal. Remember to clean the battery posts and the cable clamps before reassembly.

When battery voltage is low (below 12.6 volts), use a battery charger (see Figure 3.13) to bring the voltage back to normal. The red charger lead goes to the positive battery terminal and the black charger lead clamps onto the negative battery terminal. The charger is set to the right amperage charge and left on until the specific gravity (weight of a fluid when compared to an equal volume of water) of the battery electrolyte and the voltage return to normal (12.6 volts).

A hydrometer is used to test the specific gravity of batteries with removable cell covers. A temperature-adjusted reading of 1.270 means that the battery charging is completed.

When the charging system needs to be tested, use a voltmeter. Observe correct test polarity by clamping the red tester lead on the positive battery terminal and the black tester lead on the negative battery terminal (see Figure 3.14). Start the engine. The voltmeter should indicate a test

Figure 3.13 Battery charger. This machine is used to recharge a discharged battery (courtesy of Century Manufacturing Company).

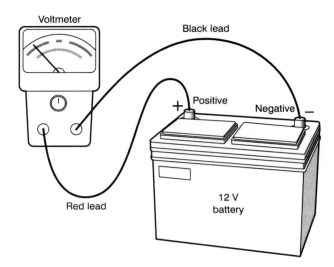

Figure 3.14 Voltmeter testing. A voltmeter hooked in parallel across the battery reads battery voltage and helps the technician determine if the battery and/or charging system are within specifications (courtesy of Training Enterprises Company).

voltage between 13.1 to 16 volts. If the charging system is defective, the voltmeter will indicate less than 12.6 volts, which is the normal standing or no-load voltage output of a fully charged automotive battery. There are some cases where the charging rate could be excessive or over 16 volts. At this point either the alternator or the regulator could be defective. Further testing or disassembly is needed to determine which unit needs further service or repair. For more information about batteries and charging systems, refer to Chapters 6 and 7.

Starter Tools

The voltmeter and ammeter are used to check starter voltage drop and current draw. As the starter begins to fail, it takes more battery power or amperage to operate. When amperage is drawn from a battery the voltage drops. If the voltmeter drops below 9.6 volts on a fully charged battery during starter use, the load on the battery is larger than normal. This can be caused by either a defective starter or an engine that has defective bearings.

Defective accessory bearings also can cause the starter to work harder. If the problem is the starter, look for worn bearings, burned field coils, worn-out brushes, or a defective armature.

When an ammeter is connected to a battery to find starter problems, the amperage draw reading will give you an indication of how much load the starter is placing on the battery. This can range from 150 amps to 250 amps depending on the size of the engine and the type of accessories being used. There should never be a load so large that it drops the battery voltage below 9.6 volts. Refer to Figure 3.14 to see how to hook a voltmeter to the battery. Figure 3.15 shows how to hook up an ammeter. The voltmeter is hooked in parallel and an ammeter is hooked in series.

Ignition Tools

A timing light (see Figure 3.16) is used to time the spark plug ignition to the operation of the pistons. If the timing is too early or late, there will be a loss of engine power. This results in poor fuel economy. Connect the timing light to the number one spark plug wire. When the engine is started and the timing light turned on, it freezes the movement of the timing pulley. Degree marks on either the moving or stationary parts show the technician how accurately the timing is set. If the timing needs to be adjusted, loosen the distributor and turn it until the timing is correct. Engine speed (revolutions per

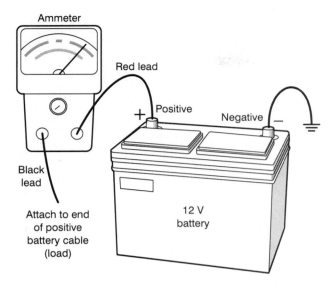

Figure 3.15 Ammeter testing. An ammeter tests the battery load when anything in the vehicle, such as the starter, is operating (courtesy of Training Enterprises Company).

minute) should be right before timing is set. Any vacuum or electronic spark advance systems have to be disabled before the timing can be set accurately. Refer to the manufacturer's specifications and timing procedures before you attempt to set any timing. For more information about ignition and starter servicing, refer to Chapters 8 and 9.

Cooling System Tools

The cooling system pressure tester is used to detect cooling system leak problems. There are two types of cooling system leaks: the pressure leak and the no-pressure leak. Pressure leaks occur when the system is hot. Both pressure and no-pressure leaks can be inside the engine where they are not easily detected. The pressure tester (see Figure 3.17) is designed to help detect cooling system leaks. Be sure the system is full and connect the tester to the radiator filler neck. Use the pump on the tester to

Figure 3.16 Timing light. This is used when the ignition timing needs to be checked or set (courtesy of Training Enterprises Company).

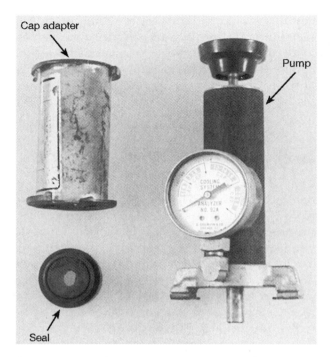

Figure 3.17 Cooling system pressure tester. When the cooling system is placed under pressure, leaks can be traced and corrected (courtesy of Training Enterprises Company).

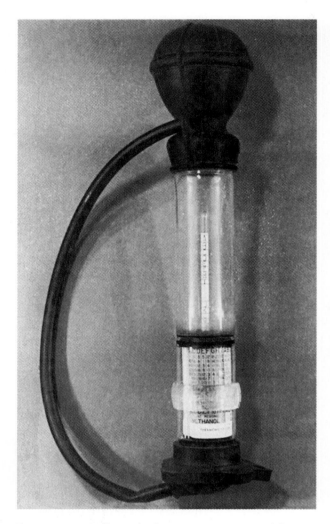

Figure 3.18 Antifreeze hydrometer tester. A test of the coolant specific gravity will determine if the antifreeze-to-water ratio is correct (courtesy of Training Enterprises Company).

place the system under pressure just as it would be when the system is hot. If the system has a pressure leak, the coolant will begin to run out at the leak point and the pressure gauge on the tester will drop to zero. A normal cooling system should not have a drop in pressure. If the leak is inside the engine, remove the spark plugs and turn the engine over with the starter. Coolant leaking into a cylinder will spray out the spark plug hole as the piston movement places the cylinder under pressure. Any cylinder that sprays coolant has a problem and needs to be checked further. Look for a crack or for head gasket failure.

When the cooling system is under pressure, look for ballooning or cracked hoses, loose hose clamps, radiator leaks, and leaking water pump seals.

Another tool used in cooling systems is the antifreeze protection hydrometer (see Figure 3.18). The specific gravity of the coolant changes when antifreeze is added to the cooling system. This change can be read by a hydrometer. Coolant is drawn up into a glass chamber until a float is suspended in the coolant. The hydrometer is read where the top of the coolant touches the float. Determine the freeze protection level by comparing the scale reading to a chart. This reading has to be temperature compensated (adjusted for hot or cold fluid temperatures) for accuracy.

The new extended life coolants require a specialized tester for accurate protection level checks. The old-style hydrometers can be used, but it must be understood that the test will not be as good as the new refraction testers produce. If there is some doubt, add coolant rather than water to the system.

General Motors Corporation, on most of their vehicles, uses a spring type clamp, such as the one in Figure 3.19. This clamp requires a special pair of pliers for installation and removal. The pliers are used in two positions, from the end or from the side. It is possible with great effort to use regular pliers to expand the clamp. However, if you are going to be working daily with vehicles having these clamps, you will find hose clamp pliers worth

Figure 3.19 Spring clamps. An important feature of this clamp is its ability to tighten when being used (courtesy of Training Enterprises Company).

the expense. This clamp tends to twist and rotate rather than expand unless it is held firmly. Often the clamp is located where only the special pliers can reach to remove it. The hose clamp is special. It is the only clamp that tightens itself as the material stretches. All the other clamps have to be checked or tightened on a periodic basis. This clamp should be reused if it is not damaged.

Fuel System Tools

Fuel is pumped from the fuel tank to the injector system or the carburetor by a mechanical or electrical fuel pump. Fuel line restrictions, clogged filters, and worn pumps give two types of problems: both pump pressure and fuel flow will be reduced. A fuel pressure gauge is used to check the condition of the pump (see Figure 3.20). Check fuel flow by letting fuel run into a measured cup for a short period of time. Refer to the manufacturer's specifications for fuel flow and pressure specifications. Replace any pump or repair any problem that causes fuel pressure to be above or below normal pressure.

A vacuum gauge is used to detect intake and mechanical problems in the valve and piston area of the engine (refer to Figure 3.20). A normal engine with no intake leaks has a high steady vacuum read-

ing at idle and a reduced reading under acceleration. Low readings or a gauge needle that vibrates means that intake leaks or engine mechanical problems are present. A burned valve causes the gauge to indicate a pressure loss on that cylinder. The engine should skip and the gauge reading should drop or the needle will vibrate. Low readings at idle and all speeds, plus a power loss, indicate engine timing problems such as a defective timing chain.

Check fuel injectors by installing a pressure gauge on the fuel rail. The injector is fired by installing a special tester on the wires controlling the injector (see Figure 3.21). As the injector is fired, the duration of the firing and the amount of pressure drop are recorded. Remove for further testing and cleaning any injector that does not fire, or one that does not allow a pressure drop. An off-the-car injector tester is used to determine if the injector is leaking or firing with an incorrect pattern. The injector is installed in the tester and fired just as it would be in the engine. Observe the pattern. A normal pattern would be a cone shape and the injector should shut completely off after firing. Clean and retest injectors with abnormal patterns or those that refuse to shut off. If a normal pattern cannot be obtained, replace the injector. Be sure to install new seals around the injectors when they are placed back into the engine.

LESSON 3–3 Under-the-Vehicle Tools

Drive Shaft Tools

Some drive shafts have grease fittings on the universal joints. Some grease guns will not have enough space between the parts to fit the end of the gun on the fitting. Use an adapter, such as those shown in Figure 3.22. These tools fit on the end of the grease gun and allow the gun to lubricate any difficult areas.

When you need to replace universal joints, use a set of special tools made to remove the old joints and install the new ones. These tools are made to be used with a press or vise.

Differential Tools

A dial indicator is used to check the ring and pinion gear backlash (see Figure 3.23). Backlash can be set in some differentials by making a bearing adjustment. Loosen the bearing caps and move the ring gear closer to the pinion gear when the

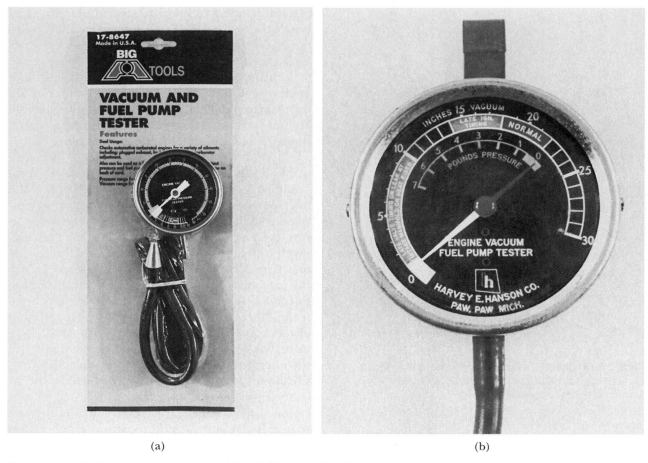

(a)   (b)

Figure 3.20 Fuel pressure tester. Guages (a) and (b) are used to check fuel pump pressure and also to check engine vacuum (courtesy of Training Enterprises Company).

Figure 3.21 Fuel injector tester. This tool allows the technician to test injectors suspected of being defective (courtesy of Training Enterprises Company).

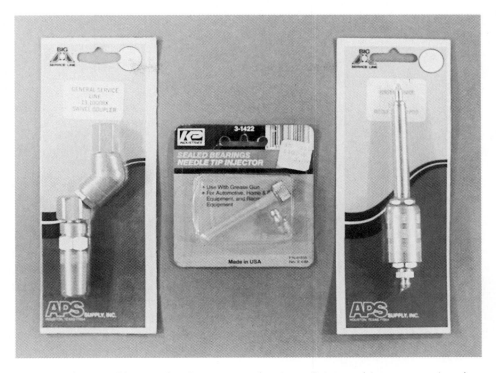

Figure 3.22 Grease gun adapters. This type of tool connects to the grease fittings and forces grease into the parts (courtesy of Training Enterprises Company).

clearance between the teeth needs to be reduced. Moving it away increases the clearance. The dial indicator is used to tell if the correct setting has been reached. Most clearances are set between .008 and .010 thousandths of an inch. For greater accuracy, always look up this setting for the specific differential being serviced. The setting is determined by the amount of heat expansion between the two gears. Some differentials run hotter than others and require a larger clearance. A hydraulic press is used to remove certain types of axle bearings that are press fitted to the axle shaft. Special tools are used to clamp around the bearing to enable the press to force it off the shaft. The same tools and press are used to install the new bearing.

Exhaust System Tools

Use a pipe cutter to cut through the old muffler or tail pipes when they need to be replaced (see Figure 3.24). The cutter is placed over the pipe and the handle turned to adjust the cutters. This adjustment should be tight enough so that pressure can be placed on the cutters when turning the handles. After placing pressure on the cutters, rotate the tool around the pipe. Constant rotation

and cutter pressure should result in the pipe being separated. The cut should be clean and smooth, which is one advantage to using this type of cutting tool.

To put a new section of pipe into a section of tail pipe or exhaust, use a pipe expander to expand the end of the pipe enough to put the new pipe into the expanded area (see Figure 3.25). To use the expander, place it into the end of the pipe and tighten. When the tool is tightened it places pressure inside the pipe and stretches it. Use the tool until the pipe is expanded enough to let the new pipe fit inside the old pipe. Finish the installation by using a clamp at the new joint.

A hydraulic bending and expansion machine is used in muffler shops to custom-make exhaust and tail pipes (see Figure 3.26). This machine will allow the operator to duplicate the old system by bending the new material in the same shape. The main advantage of this machine is that it reduces the amount of commercially made exhaust and tail pipes needed to be kept in stock to do repair operations. Technicians never have to wait for a part, but make their own. Another advantage is that rusted-out sections can be cut out and repair sections made for that special job.

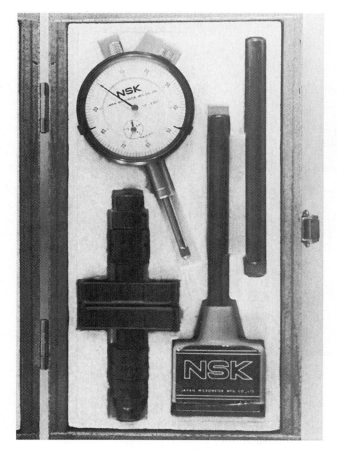

Figure 3.23   Dial indicator. This tool is used to measure and check the exact movement between parts to the nearest thousandth of an inch (courtesy of Training Enterprises Company).

Steering and Suspension Tools

Tie rods are tapered and forced together by tightening a nut on the end. It is very difficult to separate these tapered parts and special tools are made for this purpose (see Figure 3.27).

MacPherson struts require a coil spring compressor. After the old strut is removed, the new one has to be spring loaded before it is installed (see Figure 3.28).

Toe is the measurement between the front of the tire and one taken at the back. Toe is usually set in at the front, which means the tires are pointing toward each other when viewed at the front. *Camber* is the tilt of the tire at the top either toward or away from the vehicle. *Negative camber* is when the tire is tilted in at the top.

Alignment machines are used to check and set angles in the suspension system that help steering, avoid tire wear, and return the steering wheel after a trun (see Figure 3.29). A vehicle is driven on the machine so it will be perfectly level. Each front wheel is placed on turntables, which makes turning the wheel from side to side easier. The alignment technician can move under the vehicle and set the alignment angles if needed. Sensors attached to the vehicle tell the technician the preset alignment settings. After making the adjustments, the machine is used to check the final results. Learning how to operate an alignment machine and setting alignment angles is a maintenance skill speciality that technicians should learn. *Camber, caster,* and *toe* are three common alignment angles technicians change to reduce tire wear and make steering easier.

A suspension system is lubricated by a pressure grease gun (refer to Figure 1.19). Each grease fitting is cleaned and the tip of the gun placed over it. When the trigger is pulled, pressurized grease is forced into the part through the opening in the fitting.

A special tool is made to remove shock absorbers that will hold the end of the shock rod while the nut is removed (see Figure 3.30). The lower end of the shock absorber has two bolts that do not require any special tools. Remove the upper nut and both

Figure 3.24   Muffler and pipe cutter. This tool is made to remove the old muffler or tail pipe by cutting the pipe. This makes a smooth straight cut and makes installation of the new parts easier (courtesy of Training Enterprises Company).

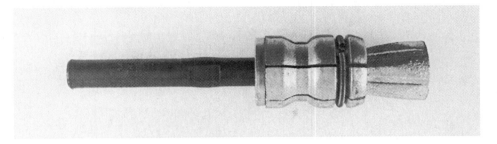

Figure 3.25 Tail pipe expander. This tool is used when two pipes of the same size need to be joined. One pipe is expanded so the other will fit inside it (courtesy of Training Enterprises Company).

bolts. You may then remove the shock absorber by pulling the rod out of the frame.

Transmission Tools

To evaluate an automatic transmission, a fluid pressure gauge is installed in the hydraulic passages of the transmission (see Figure 3.31). There are plugs, which have to be removed. The gauge is installed in the plug openings. The engine is run and the pressure checked as the transmission is shifted. For additional tests, the drive wheels can be jacked up and the vehicle driven. Low pressure or no pressure means the transmission should be checked further. Sometimes the problem can be corrected by a fluid and filter change or by cleaning the valve body. Other times if this does not help, the transmission has to be removed and overhauled. The gauge will make it easier to determine what repairs are needed. Consult the manufacturer's pressure charts for the normal pressures at each check point.

When the rear transmission seal needs to be replaced, there is a tool made to remove the old seal and one to replace the new seal (see Figure 3.32). Removing the old seal is done with a seal puller. The seal puller expands on the inside of the seal and locks in place. A slide hammer is used to remove the seal. Select the right size seal installation tool. It should be small enough to go inside the seal opening and large enough to support the metal around the seal. Use a ball peen hammer and seal driver to install a new seal.

Figure 3.26 Hydraulic pipe bender. A machine like this is used when mufflers and tail pipes need to be custom fitted to a vehicle. It also can bend and expand straight pipe to match the original (courtesy of Training Enterprises Company).

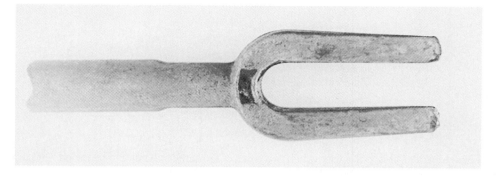

Figure 3.27 Tie rod removing tool. These tools are made to separate tapered steering linkage parts from each other so worn-out parts can be replaced (courtesy of Training Enterprises Company).

Snap ring pliers are made for two types of snap rings, internal and external. Transmissions contain some of each, and pliers are designed differently for each. For removal, internal snap rings have to be compressed and external rings have to be expanded. One type of snap ring plier is designed to be assembled and works with both types of rings. Another type handles rings that do not have holes in the ends. Figure 3.33 shows several types of snap ring pliers. To use snap ring pliers, follow these directions:

1. Select the snap ring pliers that has the correct tip for the type of ring being removed.
2. If you are using the type of plier that has to be assembled, put it together to handle external or internal rings according to the type of ring you are removing.
3. Select and install the correct size tip to fit the end holes of the snap ring.
4. Place the tip of the pliers into the snap ring holes. Squeeze the handles of the pliers together. After the ring is fully compressed or expanded, remove it from the part.
5. Repeat these steps to remove or install any additional rings.
6. When installing snap rings, place the correct side of the ring toward the direction of force. Don't reverse the rings because they may fail to hold.

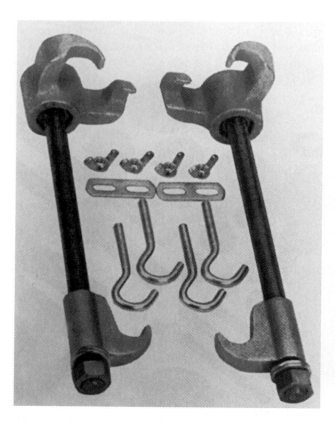

Figure 3.28 MacPherson strut spring compressor. This tool compresses MacPherson struts for removal and installation (courtesy of Training Enterprises Company).

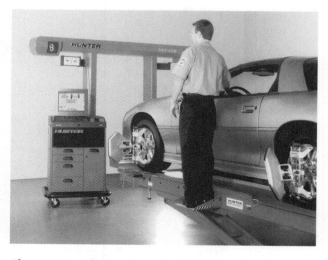

Figure 3.29 Alignment machine. Machines like this are used when alignment angles such as toe, camber, and caster need to be checked or set on each wheel (courtesy of Hunter Engineering Company).

Figure 3.32 Oil seal installers. Old grease seals can be removed and new ones installed by using these tools. Seal installation damage is reduced (courtesy of Training Enterprises Company).

Figure 3.30 Shock absorber tools. This is a special tool used to remove and install shock absorbers. The absorber shaft is held while the end nut is removed or replaced (courtesy of Training Enterprises Company).

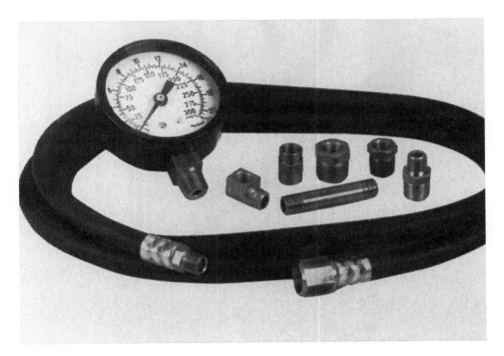

Figure 3.31 Transmission pressure tester. Measuring fluid pressure is an important transmission test. Problems can be diagnosed before removal of the transmission (courtesy of Training Enterprises Company).

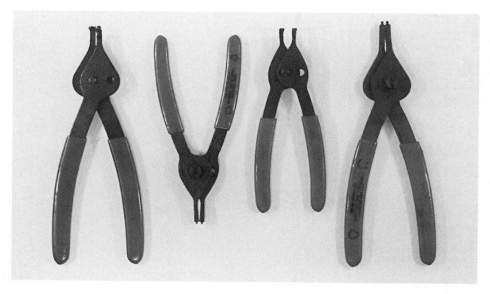

Figure 3.33 Snap ring pliers. Special pliers such as these are used to remove and install snap rings (courtesy of Training Enterprises Company).

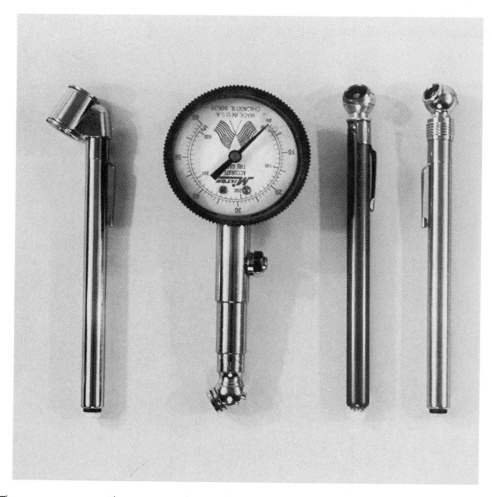

Figure 3.34 Tire pressure gauges. These gauges measure the air pressure in a tire and help the technician keep the right air pressure in each tire (courtesy of Training Enterprises Company).

LESSON 3-4 Tire, Wheel, Hub, and Brake Tools

Tire, Wheel, and Hub Tools

There are several types of tire pressure gauges in common use (see Figure 3.34). One type is an electronic or needle dial gauge; the other uses a sliding scale. The dial type is a little easier to read. Place the gauge over the tire stem and push down. The valve core releases the pressure and the gauge is ready to be read. Adjust the tire pressure according to the recommended pressures found on the inside of the front door panel or in the owner's manual.

An out-of-balance tire causes a vibration that can be felt on the steering wheel or the seat. A tire balancer is used to correct this problem. There are two types, on-the-car and off-the-car. Either type tells where to place the balance weights and how much weight to use (see Figure 3.35).

When a nail or other object is driven into a tire, the tire must be repaired. A string type tire patch is placed in the hole (see Figure 3.36).

Worn tires are removed and replaced with new ones on a tire changer. The tire is placed on the

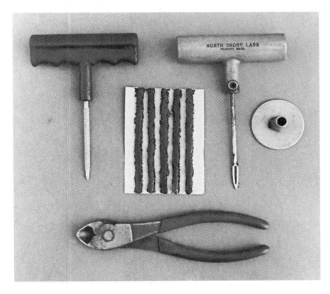

Figure 3.36 The patching tools. These tools are used to patch tire punctures. The patch seals the hole (courtesy of Training Enterprises Company).

changer and the air removed. One part of the changer breaks the tire bead from the rim. Another part of the changer lifts the tire over the rim. If a new valve stem is needed, remove the old one and

Figure 3.35 Tire balancer. This machine is used to correct static and dynamic tire imbalance. Weight is added to the rim of the tire where needed (courtesy of Hunter Engineering Company).

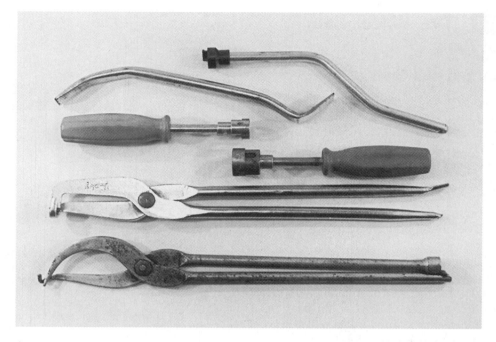

Figure 3.37 Brake spring pliers and other tools. These tools are made to be used when brake systems are being rebuilt. Spring pliers are used to remove and install brake shoe return springs (courtesy of Training Enterprises Company).

install another. The new tire is then placed on the rim and inflated.

When a stud becomes stripped or broken, it is replaced by a special tool used on a hydraulic press. The broken stud is pressed out and a new one pressed into place. Special tools expand the stud and lock it into place. This keeps it rigid in the drum or rotor.

Brake Tools

Shoe type brakes have several springs that have to be removed and installed during a brake shoe replacement job. Special tools such as those shown in Figure 3.37 are used to work with these springs. Follow these directions to use brake spring pliers:

Removal

1. Use the special part of the plier handle to remove springs.
2. Place the handle over the end of the shoe anchor and turn the handle clockwise. The spring end will slide up onto the plier handle. Pull out on the handle to let the spring clear the end of the anchor.
3. Repeat this process for each spring.

Assembly

1. Hook the bottom end of the spring in place on the brake shoe. Hook the pliers on the opposite end of the spring.
2. Place the other part of the plier jaw against something, such as the other brake shoe.
3. Force the plier handles closed and stretch the spring until the spring hook goes over the end of the anchor bolt.
4. Relax the pliers and free them from the end of the spring. The spring should now be hooked in place.
5. Use a regular pair of pliers to bend the spring hook around the post so it will not come off during brake operation.
6. Repeat this process for the other springs.

When wheel cylinders are to be rebuilt, a wheel cylinder hone is used to clean out the old cylinder bore before installing new parts. The hone is operated by a hand drill and rapidly moved from one edge of the wheel cylinder bore to the other until it is clean (see Figure 3.38).

A drum gauge is used to adjust the brake shoes before installing the brake drum. The gauge is set to the brake drum diameter. This measurement is transferred over to the outside of the brake

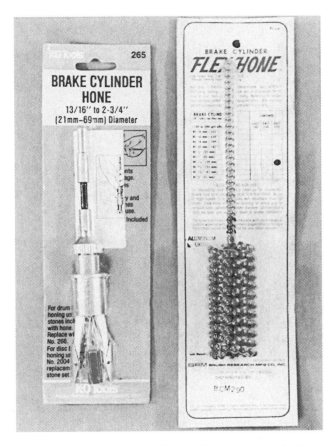

Figure 3.38 Brake cylinder hones. The hone smooths the inside of the brake cylinder by removing all the rust and scale. This prepares the cylinder for the new brake parts (courtesy of Training Enterprises Company).

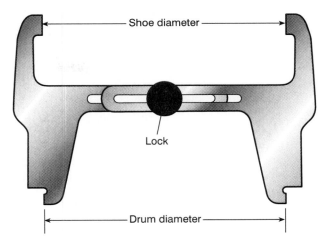

Figure 3.39 Brake shoe-to-drum gauge. The technician uses this gauge to set the brake shoe to drum clearance prior to installing the brake drum (courtesy of Training Enterprises Company).

shoes. The shoes are adjusted to this diameter (see Figure 3.39).

LESSON 3-5 Electrical Circuit and Light System Tools

Electrical Circuit Tools

A continuity tester is used to check the wires for a broken connection (see Figure 3.40). The tester contains a battery and bulb. When connected on each end of the wire to be tested, the tester lights if the wire is unbroken. Another version of this tester has a 12-volt bulb and two leads. Current is turned on to the wire that needs to be checked. The continuity tester is connected to the end of the wire and any good connection at the vehicle frame. If the tester does not light, either the ground circuit or the wire need to be tested for an "open" or no path.

Voltmeters and ammeters were discussed earlier in this chapter, but the new digital multimeters should always be used when checking electronic sensors. The old inductive analog-type multimeters can still be used to check electrical circuits such as lights and battery cables. The digital meters can check both electronic parts and electrical parts. An ohmmeter (see Figure 3.41) is used to check the amount of resistance to current flow in a wire or circuit. The current should be off when using an ohmmeter. Place one lead at one end of the wire and the other at the opposite end. A complete circuit is read in ohms. Many times there is a complete circuit in a system but rust and corrosion make it difficult for the current to flow. The ohmmeter helps solve these problems by indicating where the resistance is too high.

Most headlights (both high and low beams) are set by machine for the light pattern to drop two inches over a distance of twenty feet. They are set horizontally straight ahead. The low beam pattern automatically drops lower and to the right. Don't forget that loads in the trunk can raise the light pattern. The lights have to be adjusted for your particular vehicle conditions.

Light System Tools

Headlights need to be adjusted so the high beams of light show a maximum view of the road and the low beam position does not blind another driver. A headlight aimer, such as the one shown in

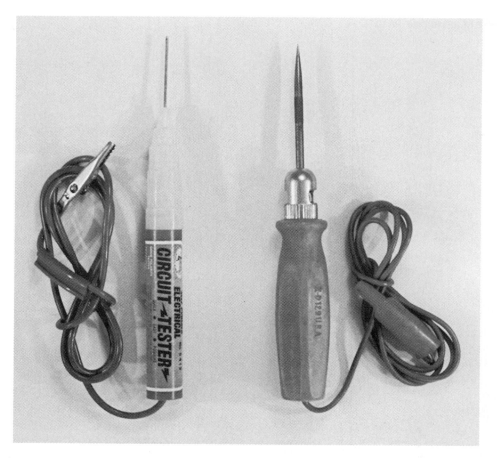

Figure 3.40 Circuit continuity tester. This tester determines if the electrical circuit has a complete path (courtesy of Training Enterprises Company).

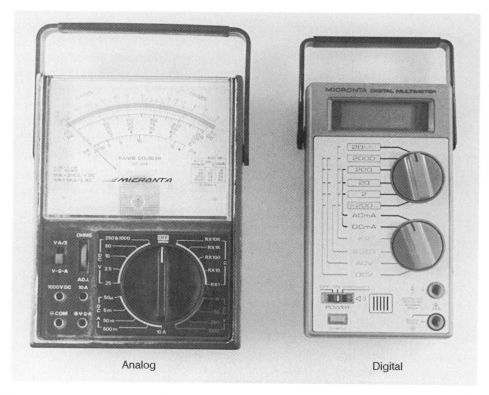

Analog   Digital

Figure 3.41 Ohmmeter and multi-tester. This tester will check circuit resistance and voltage (courtesy of Training Enterprises Company).

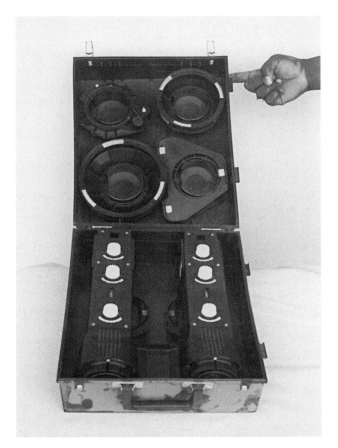

Figure 3.42 Headlight aimer. This machine is used to set the direction of the headlight beams. This allows maximum night vision and reduces beam glare to oncoming drivers (courtesy of Training Enterprises Company).

Figure 3.42, is used to set the lights and direct the beams for maximum night vision. The lights are not turned on when they are adjusted. Built-in pads are used to position the aimer. The lights are set by turning adjustment screws at the top, bottom, and sides of the bulb.

> The current carrying capacity of a wire is determined by the diameter of the wire measured by the gauge such as 8, 12, 14. The lower the gauge number, the larger the diameter of the wire conductor.

There are two types of wire strippers, pictured in Figure 3.43. Wire strippers remove the insulation from a piece of electrical wire so a connection can be made to the conducting material of the wire. One type of wire stripper automatically removes the insulation to the correct length. A great advantage of a wire stripper is removal of insulation quickly and accurately without damage to the wire. To use wire strippers, follow these directions:

1. Select the correct wire gauge slot in the pliers. Use a wire gauge to test a piece of wire if you are not certain of the size.
2. Clamp the pliers on the wire at a point to strip the right amount of insulation.
3. With the automatic strippers, all you have to do is clamp and squeeze the handles. With the

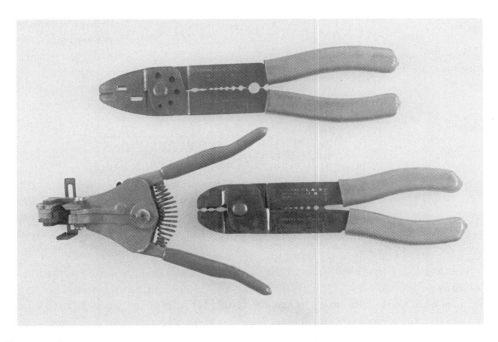

Figure 3.43 Figure caption to come

regular pliers, the handles have to be squeezed
and you have to hold the wire while pulling the
pliers off the end of the wire.

4. Check to see if the right amount of insulation
was removed, and inspect the wire to make sure
it was not cut.

VOCABULARY

Use the listed words in the blanks beside the sentences to complete the definitions. Either write out
the words or place the letters in the blanks.

A. Flare nut wrench
B. Snap ring
C. Wire stripper
D. Torx
E. Screw holder
F. Ball peen
G. Service gauge
H. R-134a
I. License
J. Battery voltage
K. Amperage
L. Hydrometer
M. Voltage drop
N. Parallel
O. Degree marks
P. Pressure leak
Q. Specific gravity
R. Antifreeze
S. Grease fitting
T. Backlash
U. Tie rod
V. MacPherson strut
W. Fluid pressure gauge
X. Toe
Y. Wheel balancer

_____ 1. Used to set ignition timing and
check spark advance
_____ 2. The inward and outward distance
between the front and rear of the
tires
_____ 3. Circular part that goes into a
groove on a shaft to retain parts
_____ 4. Holds screws so they can be installed in tight places

_____ 5. Refrigerant used in an air conditioner system
_____ 6. Fluid weight when compared to
water
_____ 7. Machine used to determine
where weight needs to be added
to a wheel
_____ 8. Used to cut gaskets from gasket
paper
_____ 9. Used to install and remove tubing
fittings
_____ 10. Clearance between differential
ring and pinion gears
_____ 11. 12.6 standing volts
_____ 12. Place where grease is forced by
pressure into a part
_____ 13. Used to measure specific gravity
_____ 14. Current flowing in a circuit
_____ 15. Front suspension part and part of
the vehicle steer system
_____ 16. Required to work on air conditioning systems
_____ 17. Special style of screwdriver
_____ 18. Occurs when a radiator is hot
_____ 19. Used with water to make a coolant
_____ 20. Used to check coolant pressure in
an air conditioner
_____ 21. Used to trim the insulation back
on the end of a wire
_____ 22. The measure of voltage lost in a
circuit
_____ 23. Used to check the internal condition of an automatic transmission
hydraulic system
_____ 24. Two wires starting at a point and
ending at another point making
two paths
_____ 25. A suspension system used in front
wheel drive vehicles

REVIEW QUESTIONS

The following questions will help you determine
if you have accomplished the tasks stated at the
beginning of this chapter. If you do not know many
of the answers, go back and review the material
before proceeding to the next chapter.

Lesson 3–1

1. What is the size range of metric hand wrenches
used in automotive work?
2. What type of wrench is the fastest and most
popular?
3. What is the disadvantage of a combination
wrench set?

4. What tools are used to remove a stripped nut or bolt?
5. How are air wrench sockets different from regular sockets?
6. What are four jobs that pliers are designed for?
7. What are locking pliers designed for?
8. What are nut drivers used for?
9. What materials are used to make soft-faced hammer tips?

Lesson 3–2
10. Name two types of filter wrench.
11. Which direction is a filter turned to be removed?
12. How tight should an oil filter be when installed properly?
13. Can the same service gauges be used for either R-134a or R-12?
14. What is the normal high side air conditioner system pressure range?
15. What is the normal low side air conditioner system pressure range?
16. Which system will run the higher pressures for the same temperature and humidity?
17. Name two conditions that will cause the high side pressure to rise.
18. What machine must be used to evacuate an air conditioner system?
19. To do a good job cleaning battery terminals, what parts must be clean?
20. What tool can be used to remove a stripped battery cable bolt?
21. Battery voltage is considered low when it measures below what value?
22. What is the correct voltage range to use when charging a battery?
23. What should be the normal voltage drop on a battery when cranking the engine?
24. Which tester is hooked in parallel and which is hooked in series to make tests?
25. What piece of equipment is needed when timing the spark ignition to the piston movement?
26. What should be set right before the ignition timing is set?
27. Name two times cooling system leaks occur.
28. Name some items to check when a cooling system is under pressure.
29. What is special about a General Motors Corbin clamp?
30. What would be the correct vacuum gauge reading of an engine at idle?

Lesson 3–3
31. What part must be used with a grease gun so difficult areas can be lubricated?

32. What tool is used to check differential ring and pinion gear backlash?
33. What is the normal clearance range for most ring and pinion gear backlash?
34. What determines the amount of backlash needed?

Lesson 3–4
35. What has to be done to the tire bead before the old tire can be removed?
36. Name two types of tire balancers.
37. What are two types of tire pressure gauges in use today?
38. What tool is used to remove shoe type brakes?
39. What is the name of the tool used to clean out brake wheel cylinder bores?

Lesson 3–5
40. What tool is used to check wire for opens?
41. What is the unit of resistance in a wire called?
42. Where is a headlight aimer placed on the bulb to be set?
43. Correct headlight aim is set to drop ___ inches over a distance of ___ feet.
44. What is an "open" wire?

ASE QUESTIONS

Each question or incomplete statement in this test is followed by four suggested answers or completions. In each case select the *one* that best answers the question or completes the statement.

1. Technician A says the adjustable and pipe wrench are commonly used automotive tools. Technician B says that an adjustable or pipe wrench should be used only in an emergency when the head of a bolt is stripped. Who is right?
   a. A only   b. B only
   c. Both A and B   d. Neither A nor B

2. Technician A says a flare nut wrench is used to loosen brass fittings. Technician B says that only a six-point box wrench should be used on brass fittings. Who is right?
   a. A only   b. B only
   c. Both A and B   d. Neither A nor B

3. Technician A says that snap ring pliers can be used in the place of needle nose pliers. Technician B says that diagonal cutting pliers can be used in the place of needle nose pliers. Who is right?
   a. A only   b. B only
   c. Both A and B   d. Neither A nor B

4. Technician A says a ball peen hammer can be used to make a gasket. Technician B says that a ball peen hammer can be used to strike a chisel or punch. Who is right?
   a. A only
   b. B only
   c. Both A and B
   d. Neither A nor B

5. Technician A says either pressure gauge on an air conditioner service unit can be used for either side of the system. Technician B says that only the right-hand gauge should be used for the high side. Who is right?
   a. A only
   b. B only
   c. Both A and B
   d. Neither A nor B

6. Technician A says it requires only a licensed person to service an automotive air conditioning system. Technician B says that the license is needed only when adding refrigerant to a system. Who is right?
   a. A only
   b. B only
   c. Both A and B
   d. Neither A nor B

7. Technician A says that either battery charger lead can be connected to either battery post when getting ready to use the charger. Technician B says that polarity must be observed. Who is right?
   a. A only
   b. B only
   c. Both A and B
   d. Neither A nor B

8. Technician A says that when using the starter, the battery voltage should not drop below 9.6 volts. Technician B says the battery voltage can go as low as 8.6 volts on a good system. Who is right?
   a. A only
   b. B only
   c. Both A and B
   d. Neither A nor B

9. Technician A says a voltmeter is hooked in parallel when used. Technician B says an ammeter is hooked in series when used. Who is right?
   a. A only
   b. B only
   c. Both A and B
   d. Neither A nor B

10. Technician A says a regular antifreeze hydrometer will be accurate when testing the new coolants. Technician B says the new coolants have a different specific gravity from previous coolants. Who is right?
    a. A only
    b. B only
    c. Both A and B
    d. Neither A nor B

11. Technician A says that a road test should be used to determine problems with an automatic transmission. Technician B says a pressure gauge will show up problems with an automatic transmission. Who is right?
    a. A only
    b. B only
    c. Both A and B
    d. Neither A nor B

12. Technician A says improper toe adjustments cause tire wear. Technician B says improper camber adjustments cause tire wear. Who is right?
    a. A only
    b. B only
    c. Both A and B
    d. Neither A nor B

13. Technician A says a tire pressure gauge is the only sure way to tell if the tire is inflated correctly. Technician B says tire wear is the only sure way to tell if the tire is inflated correctly. Who is right?
    a. A only
    b. B only
    c. Both A and B
    d. Neither A nor B

4 Basic Maintenance Service

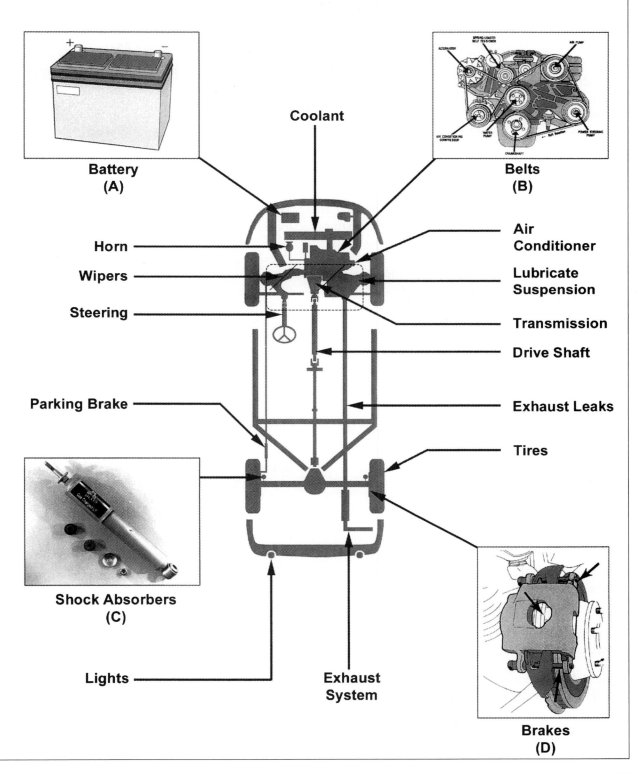

Battery
(A)

Coolant

Belts
(B)

Horn

Wipers

Steering

Air
Conditioner

Lubricate
Suspension

Transmission

Drive Shaft

Parking Brake

Exhaust Leaks

Tires

Shock Absorbers
(C)

Lights

Exhaust
System

Brakes
(D)

Many factors determine when to perform basic maintenance. The major factors are vehicle use, amount of time passed since service was last performed, and the mileage driven. Basic maintenance is also performed when there is fluid contamination or premature breakdown. Sometimes we forget that the automobile is a complex machine that takes a tremendous amount of abuse from normal daily travel. Daily, monthly, seasonal, and yearly maintenance has to be planned and performed. The plan depends on weather conditions, miles driven, elapsed time, type vehicle, manufacturer's recommendations, and driving conditions. We cover general plans for preventive and regular maintenance. You should take this one step further and develop a specific plan for each customer based on his or her particular needs. A vehicle that is subjected to temperatures down to −30°F would have very different coolant problems than a vehicle driven in weather that doesn't get below 30°F.

Make testing and inspections the center of your maintenance plans. The customer likes to be informed if there is a problem. To sell parts and solve problems, check and inspect each vehicle when it is brought to you. Some of the inspection areas are listed in Figure 4, although this list does not include everything.

TASKS

The following are five tasks to master before leaving this chapter:

Task 4-1.   Learn to perform all the service steps in a 3000 mile/5000 km or three-month vehicle maintenance service.

Task 4-2.   Learn to perform all the service steps in a 6000 mile/10,000 km or six-month vehicle maintenance service.

Task 4-3.   Learn to perform all the steps in a 9000 mile/15,000 km or nine-month vehicle maintenance service.

Task 4-4.   Learn to perform all the steps in a 12,000 mile/20,000 km or twelve-month vehicle maintenance service.

Task 4-5.   Learn to perform special and additional maintenance service when needed.

> *Note:* This list is not meant to be exhaustive and should be added to or subtracted from based on the individual needs of each vehicle be-

ing serviced. Some of these tasks are too advanced to perform at this time. Other chapters go into detail on how to perform these tasks. Come back and do these tasks after having studied the advanced material. This chapter is a guide designed to be used with all chapters.

LESSON 4-1   3000 Mile/5000 Km or Three-Month Maintenance Service

Wear increases each time the vehicle is driven. Each vehicle owner, with the help of an automotive technician, must start a maintenance program that will keep all the fluids at the right level. This plan will help discover and replace the fluids, lubricants, and parts that either need periodic replacement or have worn out. Some items need to be checked or replaced on a seasonal basis; others need to be looked at on a basis of mileage or hours of driving. We investigate both the time and mileage plans in this lesson and give you enough information to create good customer maintenance programs. The following changes, inspections, and checks are performed every 3000 miles or 5000 kilometers for the life of the vehicle. We have based this plan on the normal life of fluids, oils, and other lubrication materials. Reduce the time and mileage interval if the vehicle is being used in severe service (dusty, dirty conditions, or for short distances). Some manufacturers recommend a longer period of time or mileage between oil changes. For that plan, use the same checks and procedures but increase the time and mileage interval. The time and mileage recommendations are optional so a plan can be fitted to any situation. The checks, changes, and service discussed here are be performed at the 3000 mile/5000 km, 6000 mile/10,000 km, 9000 mile/15,000 km, and 12,000 mile/20,000 km intervals. When the vehicle has reached these intervals, be sure to perform the additional service operations in addition to this regular maintenance.

Under-the-Vehicle Service

Jack or lift the vehicle using the methods taught in Chapter 5. Perform the following operations:

- Remove the engine oil and change the oil filter (see Chapter 5). Follow the proper steps and procedures to perform this task. Be sure to install the drain plug and filter correctly before lowering the vehicle.

- Check for leaks from any area of the vehicle. Look for brake fluid, radiator coolant, engine oil, automatic transmission fluid, differential fluid, standard transmission fluid, shock absorber fluid, gasoline, transfer case fluid (four-wheel drive only), and grease leaks. When leaks are found, make a note of what is leaking and how much fluid is being lost. These units may have to be checked more often than the routine maintenance checks. Repair all leaks. Some leaks require immediate repair, such as those involving the fuel system, hydraulic clutch, power steering, coolant, and brakes. Do not let anything run out of lubricant. Keep fluid at the right level until the leak can be fixed.

- Check the fluid level. Check standard transmissions and transfer case fluid levels. Check rear wheel drive differentials and front wheel drive manual transmission transaxles for the right fluid level. In most cases the level can be checked by removing the filler plug on the side of the unit (refer to Figure 1.24). The fluid level should be even with the bottom threads of the filler plug hole when the vehicle is level. Some units have a dipstick. Remove it clean, and check the level. Add fluid to the unit that needs it.

- Check the exhaust system. Look for broken holders, marking clamps, and rusted out dented, or separated parts. Check inside the end of the exhaust pipe to see how well the fuel has burned. A black sooty deposit indicates too much unburned fuel. An oily deposit indicates oil in the combustion chamber. Both problems require additional repair and service.

- Check the tires. Check each tire with a pressure gauge. Inflate any tire that is low and reduce the pressure in any tire that is too high. Maximum tire pressures are stamped on the sidewall of the tire (see Figure 4.1 and refer to Figure 16.8). Cold inflation pressures are placed on stickers located on the passenger door edge or in the glove compartment. Information such as the minimum cold inflation pressure and the maximum cold pressure in relation to vehicle load are written on the sticker. Never exceed the maximum pressure placed on the tire. Use the chart in Figure 4.2 to inspect tires.

- Check the shock absorbers. Look for leaking fluid around the piston rod and down the outside. Check the upper rubber mounts and lower mounting bracket (see Figure 4.3). Inspect for bent or broken parts. Shocks also can be worn out internally, but this condition cannot be checked by an inspection. This will show up through abnormal tire wear and vehicle handling.

- Lubricate the suspension system. Locate all suspension system grease fittings and wipe off any

Figure 4.1 Sidewall maximum pressure stamp. Look at the markings on the sidewall of a tire. One of these is the maximum recommended tire inflation pressure for the tire. Do not exceed this pressure (courtesy of Training Enterprises Company).

TIRE INSPECTION CHART

WEAR PATTERNS AND CHECKS	RECOMMENDATIONS
1. Uneven wear between tires	Rotate the tires
2. Inside or outside tread edge wear	Check wheel alignment and toe setting
3. Center tread wear	Reduce inflation pressure
4. Inside and outside tread wear	Increase inflation pressure
5. Cupping wear on the tread	Worn suspension or tire balance
6. Sawtooth tread wear	Adjust toe or cornering wear
7. Nails or glass in tread	Remove and repair
8. Stem and core leaks	Replace with new parts
9. Lug nut torque	Check with a torque wrench
10. Bent rim check	Replace if bent
11. Tire separations and defects	Replace the tire
12. Sidewall cuts and defects	Replace the tire

Figure 4.2   Tire inspection chart. Look at the tire wear and compare it with the wear patterns on this chart. This should give a starting point to correct any abnormal tire wear (courtesy of Training Enterprises Company).

dirt on each one. Use a quality extreme pressure grease rated at least an NLGI (National Lubricating Grease Institute) GB/LB or GC/LB number two. Place the grease gun tip over the fitting and squeeze the trigger. Watch the grease seals on the part being greased. The seal should start to expand (see Figure 4.4). Stop

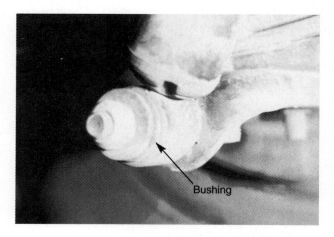

Figure 4.3   Shock absorber inspection. (a) Inspect for a bent shaft, worn bushings, and leaks. (b) Replace damaged or worn shock absorbers (courtesy of Training Enterprises Company).

when the seal looks full and slightly rounded. Never force grease into a part until the seal starts to leak. There should never be a movement between the two parts being greased. Parts movement as the grease is applied means the parts are worn out and should be replaced. Replace any parts that do not have a grease seal. Grease all suspension parts, steering linkage, and manual clutch linkage.

- Lubricate the drive shaft universals. Factory universal joints may not have lubrication fittings. Replacement universal joints will have grease fittings (see Figure 4.5). Since this maintenance schedule is to be followed every 3000 miles, grease any universal joints that have grease fittings and check the rest. Replacement joints should be greased on a regular basis. On front wheel drive vehicles, inspect the front drive axle boots and seals (see Figure 4.6). Rotate each wheel and look for damage on both right front and left front inner and outer boots. Check for looseness and clicking noises as the wheels rotate.
- Lubricate the parking brake cable guides. Use some chassis grease around any parking brake cable guides to reduce wear and prevent sticking.

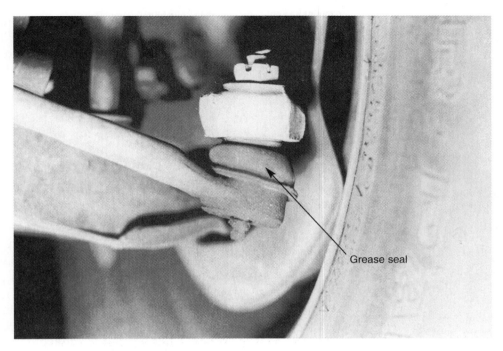

Grease seal

Figure 4.4 Grease seals. The grease seal should be expanded after lubrication. There should never be grease forced out the sides of the seal. This would be improper lubrication and service (courtesy of Training Enterprises Company).

Grease fitting

Figure 4.5 Universal joint grease fittings. Notice that a replacement universal joint has grease fittings. This joint should be serviced on a regular basis (courtesy of Training Enterprises Company).

Figure 4.6 Front wheel drive boots. Inspect the inner and outer front drive axle boots and seals for cracks or tears. Clean the parts, lubricate, and install a new boot immediately if any damage is found (courtesy of Training Enterprises Company).

- Lubricate the rear suspension. Some vehicles have grease fittings on moving parts in the rear suspension. Clean these fittings and grease them just like the front suspension parts.
  Not all greases are compatible (can be used together). It is always a good policy to stay with the grease you started with for the life of the vehicle.

This finishes the regular 3000 mile/5000 km or three-month under-the-vehicle maintenance service. If you are doing other mileage service maintenance, turn to the under-the-vehicle section in that lesson and continue the maintenance. Come back to this place in the text when the vehicle is ready to be lowered and perform the following under-the-hood maintenance.

Under-the-Hood Service

Lower the vehicle. Raise the hood and put two fender covers in place on each fender. You are now ready to do the under-the-hood servicing. Follow these steps:

- If the oil is removed in the under-the-vehicle service, be sure to fill the crankcase with the cor-

rect amount, viscosity, and quality engine oil. Engine oil was introduced in Chapter 1 and is covered in great detail in Chapter 5. Refer to these chapters if you have questions about engine oil.
After the correct amount of oil has been placed in the engine, start the engine. Let it idle until the oil light goes off or the gauge reaches the normal idle pressure. Leave the engine running and inspect for leaks at the pan plug and oil filter. Be sure to correct any leak problems.

- Check the transmission fluid. Most automatic transmissions are checked with the engine running and the transmission in park. Others require turning the engine off. Follow the manufacturer's recommendations and prepare the vehicle before checking the fluid level. Before wiping off the transmission dipstick, inspect the quality of the fluid. Look at the color and smell for any burned clutch and band material. If the fluid is thick, black, smells burned, or is contaminated, it should be changed. Be sure to fill the transmission to the correct level with the correct fluid. Transmission fluid was covered in Chapter 1.

- Check the power steering fluid. Most power steering units use the dipstick method. Start the engine and cycle the power steering by moving the steering wheel to the full stop position in both directions. Straighten out the wheels and stop the engine. Check for the correct level and the quality of the fluid (see Figure 4.7). Dirty, thick, or contaminated fluid should be changed. If the vehicle is cold, do not fill the power steering reservoir above the "cold" mark on the dipstick. Inspect the power steering belt. Check the belt for the correct tension and check the condition. Look for glazing, cracks, wrong width, separated plies, and ragged edges. Start the engine and move the steering wheel in one direction until it stops. Keep the wheel in this position. The power steering pump will sound louder because it is under maximum load. If the belt is too loose, it will make a loud squealing sound. Repair this condition by placing more tension on the belt.

Let the engine cool at this point (there will be a coolant inspection later) and do the following checks:

- Check the brake fluid and hydraulic clutch fluid (if equipped). Remove the brake/clutch master

Figure 4.7 Power steering fluid level check. Check the level with the dipstick and inspect the fluid quality. Drain and refill with clean fluid if needed (courtesy of Training Enterprises Company).

cylinder cover even if it has a fluid sight glass on the side. Look at the color and the quality of the fluid. Fill both front and rear reservoir chambers up to 1/4 in. from the top (see Figure 4.8). Some master cylinders are installed at an angle. Use care not to overfill this type. Measure from the highest fluid point to the top edge of the cylinder. It is normal for the disc brake side of the master cylinder to drop in level. As the disc

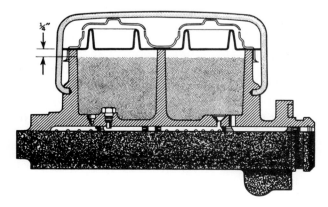

Figure 4.8 A sectional view of a dual master cylinder showing the correct level of fluid (courtesy of Chevrolet Motor Division, General Motors Corporation).

brake pads wear, the piston moves to compensate and some additional fluid from the reservoir stays in the brake caliper. The rear drum brake side should not need frequent filling to maintain the correct level. The disc brake side of the reservoir can be a monitor on brake pad wear. With no leaks in the system, the pads will be worn out if the reservoir fluid level drops until it is almost empty. Almost no one lets this happen. There is a warning light on the dash on most systems indicating low brake fluid. Be sure to use the right DOT brake fluid when filling the master cylinder. Brake fluid was discussed in Chapter 1.

• Check the battery. Maintenance-free batteries need service. Look to see if the terminals are tight or need cleaning. Most of these batteries have a built-in hydrometer. To read this type of hydrometer, clean off the top and look directly down into the plastic "eye" (see Figure 4.9). If you see a green dot, the battery has from a 65% to a full charge and should perform well. A completely dark or red dot indicates the battery is below 65% of charge and may not supply the needed power to operate the starter and be dependable. Use a battery charger and place a charge on the battery. If this doesn't correct the battery problem, test further to determine if either the battery or the charging system is defective. A clear or light yellow dot means the battery has lost enough electrolyte for the level to drop below the bottom of the eye. Look for a cracked case. Do not attempt to charge a battery in this condition. Replace the battery, since there is no way to restore the electrolyte level. Batteries with removable caps should be checked for the correct electrolyte level. Inspect each cell. You should not see the top of the plates. Add distilled water to bring the electrolyte level up to the split rings in the cell openings. Clean the battery terminals and cable clamps when they are corroded (refer to Figure 6.32). Tighten any battery cable clamps that are loose. Check the battery holddown brackets or clamps for tightness and condition. Complaints that appear to be battery related require additional testing. A battery hydrometer, voltmeter, and ammeter are used to test batteries. For a more detailed explanation of these tests, see Chapter 6.

• Check or fill the engine coolant. Maintain the coolant level up to the full mark in the coolant recovery reservoir. When the vehicle is cool, remove the radiator cap and see if the radiator is

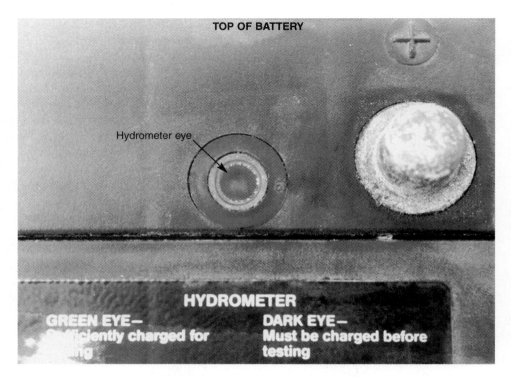

Figure 4.9 Built-in battery hydrometer. A "green" dot means the battery has at least a 65% charge, up to a full charge (courtesy of Training Enterprises Company).

full. Fill the radiator and fill the coolant recovery reservoir. Use coolant, which is a 50/50 mix of water and antifreeze. If the radiator is low but the coolant recovery reservoir stays full, replace the coolant recovery hoses and radiator cap. Make sure there are no leaks in any part of the cooling system. Coolant will not move from the recovery reservoir to the radiator and back again if there is either a pressure leak or a vacuum leak.

> Always use extended-life coolant in systems already using it. The color of the coolant and a sticker on the radiator should indicate which is being used. Do not mix extended-life coolant and regular coolant if the change interval of the new extended-life coolant is to be maintained. Mixing with older style coolants will reduce the life back to that of regular coolant and the system will have to be flushed and changed yearly.

- Check all vehicle lights and horn. Headlights, running lights, stop lights, turn signals, backup lights, and parking lights should all be tested to see if any fail to light. Turn the emergency flashers on to see if they operate correctly. Turn

on the headlights and switch from low beam to high beam. See if all headlights light when they should. The high-beam indicator light should burn when the light dimmer switch is turned to the high-beam position.

Check the horn by pushing on the horn button. Try several positions of the horn button to see if the horn will blow in any position. In the case of dual horns, make sure both horns are operating.

- Lubricate hinges, latches, and other parts. Lubricate hinges on doors, hood, and trunk lid with a 30W weight engine oil. Lock cylinders use several products, including light oil, silicone lubricant, and liquid graphite. Use the kind recommended by the manufacturer. The door locks and striker plate requires lubriplate (a stick form of lubricant). Put the lubriplate on the door lock where it contacts the striker plate. Keep it off the striker plate so it will not soil any clothing as people enter and leave the vehicle. Hood and trunk striker plates and locks can be lubricated with lubriplate on both parts. Wipe all weatherstripping around the doors, hood, and trunk with a thin layer of silicone paste lubricant or some silicone spray on a cloth.

After you have finished this maintenance, if you are doing other mileage service, turn to the under-the-hood section of that lesson and continue. If you are making other checks such as the 6000, 9000, and 12,000 mile checks, turn to those lessons and perform the operations.

LESSON 4–2 6000 Mile/10,000 Km or Six-Month Maintenance Service

This 6000 mile/10,000 kilometer or six-month inspection should be in addition to the regular 3000 mile/5000 kilometer or three-month service. Many service operations are not needed every 3000 miles and can be delayed until now.

Under-the-Vehicle Service

Do the following operations in addition to the regular scheduled under-the-vehicle service described in the last lesson. The vehicle should already be jacked or lifted while the 3000 mile maintenance is being performed.

- Rotate the tires and balance (if needed). Follow strict rotation plans depending on the kind of tires and vehicle type (refer to Figure 16.24). Tire rotation should be performed every 6000 miles. Use this same plan for the 12,000 mile rotation and every 6000 miles from that point on. Front wheel drive rotation plans are different from those used with rear wheel drive vehicles. If a regular tire (not space saver) is used as a spare, include it in the rotation plan. Adjust the tire pressure on all tires because the tires have been rotated to new positions and the weight on them will be different. Some types of tires cannot be rotated so they turn in a different direction from the original position. These tires must stay on the same side of the vehicle and are rotated from front to rear but not rotated to the other side. Follow correct lug nut patterns (refer to Figures 16.28 and 16.29) to tighten the lug nuts. Always use a torque wrench to avoid warping the brake rotors and brake drums. While the tires are off the vehicle, inspect the thickness of the disc brake pads and the condition of each brake rotor.

Go back to the 3000 mile/5000 km lesson and continue with the under-the-hood service. Come back to this spot and do the checks that follow to finish up the service.

Space saver tires cannot be used in a tire rotation plan. Some owners buy a regular tire and rim that can be kept on the ground in an emergency or until the regular tire is repaired. Space saver tires should not be driven long distances or at a high rate of speed. They do not have the braking surface needed to stop safely in an emergency high-speed stop and were never intended to be used full time.

Under-the-Hood Service

At this point, all the 3000 mile/5000 km service should be completed. The following checks will complete the 6000 mile/10,000 km maintenance. Be sure you replace the oil that was drained out in the under-the-vehicle maintenance.

- Check the engine air filter. Remove the top from the air cleaner housing and remove the air filter (see Figure 4.10). Place a service light inside the filter and check for dust and dirt blocking the light. If you cannot see any light, replace the filter. Round filters should be turned 1/4 turn from their original position. This allows incoming air to strike a new section of the filter. Repeat this each time the filter is checked. After four checks, the filter will have 24,000 miles/40,000 km of use and should be replaced.
- Service the cooling system. Inspect both the upper and lower radiator hose. Check and tighten all loose clamps. Inspect the heater hoses. Look for cracks, ballooning, and hardened material. When the system is cool, remove the pressure cap. Inspect the cap for a torn or cracked gasket. Pressure check the cap and the radiator using a pressure tester (see Figure 4.11). Look for leaks at the water pump and check for leaks at all the expansion plugs in the cylinder head or engine block.
  When a cooling system is under pressure, there should never be a pressure loss. This would indicate a serious leak. Find and repair all leaks. Look at the color and condition of the coolant. It should be a clear color (usually green), not a dirty brown color. Dirty or contaminated coolant must be replaced. The system should also be cleaned. Check the protection level with a hydrometer. Look for rust and contamination as the coolant is drawn into the hydrometer.

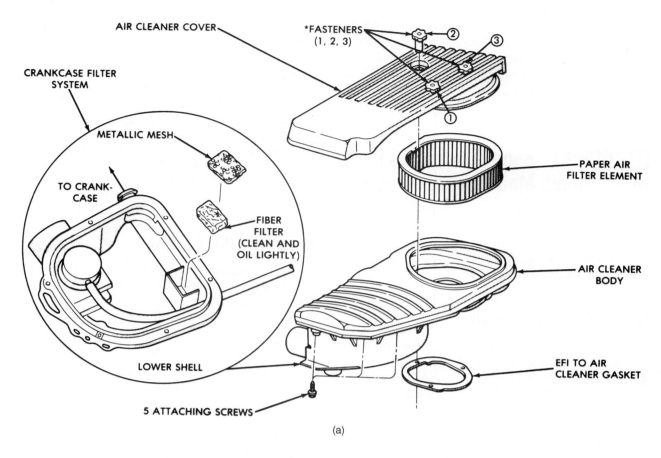

(a)

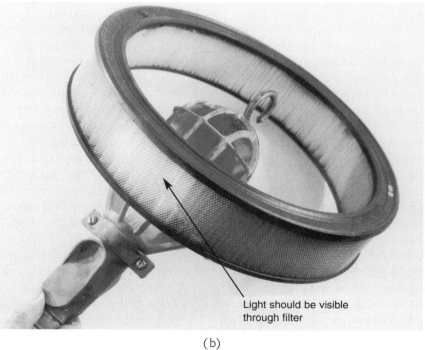

Light should be visible
through filter

(b)

Figure 4.10   (a) Removing and checking air cleaner housing. A service light placed inside an air filter element will determine its condition. (b) Replace air filters when dirty or on a regular maintenance plan based on use (courtesy of Training Enterprises Company).

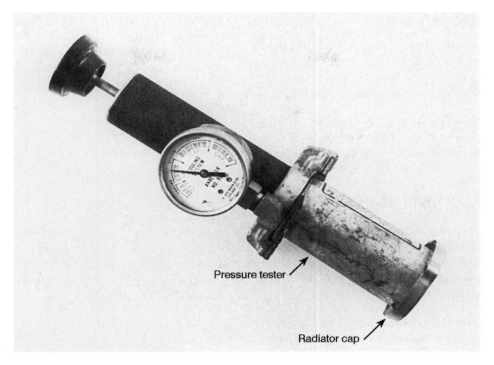

Pressure tester

Radiator cap

Figure 4.11 Radiator cap testing. This tester places pressure on the cap and radiator to test for damage or leaks (courtesy of Training Enterprises Company).

Correct the protection level in the winter to protect the engine from freezing. Transmission oil can enter the radiator if there is a leak in the radiator transmission heat exchanger. Inspect the coolant recovery reservoir for leaks or cracked hose. Fill the reservoir to the full level. Schedule additional maintenance to correct any cooling system problem.

> When the coolant is at the correct strength it will protect down to −34°F. Diluted coolant should be corrected by adding more antifreeze. Coolant should be kept at the right strength for the computer sensors to operate correctly.

• Check air conditioner and heater systems. Turn the air conditioner on and see if the compressor clutch engages. If the system has a sight glass, it should be clear after the system has stabilized. A milky or streaked sight glass reading coupled with insufficient cooling indicates a problem and repair should be scheduled. Use a thermometer in the center duct. Leave it there for several minutes with the air conditioner placed on "maximum" and a fan in front of the radiator. The temperature should drop down to the normal range for the type of system being checked. Switch the system over to the heater. When the radiator is at operating temperature, the heater should blow hot air. If either system does not respond normally, schedule further tests.

> The air conditioner condition can be checked by using a thermometer in the center duct while driving the vehicle. The temperature should be from 40° to 50°F. Outside temperature and humidity will also affect the temperature.

LESSON 4-3 9000 Mile/15,000 Km or Nine-Month Maintenance Service

The regular 3000 mile/5000 kilometer or three-month service should be done as well as the following. Do all the 3000 mile/5000 km or three-month under-the-vehicle maintenance first, and then continue with the following checks.

Under-the-Vehicle Service

- Adjust the parking brake cable. Adjust the cable when the rear brake shoes wear and the parking brake will no longer hold the vehicle when fully applied. Make the cable shorter to adjust it.

Go back and do the regular under-the-hood maintenance checks in the 3000 mile section first before returning to do the following:

Under-the-Hood and Other Service

The following steps are a continuation of the maintenance service from the 3000 mile regular checks in Lesson 4–1. Did you fill the engine with engine oil? Do that now and then continue on with these maintenance steps.

- Adjust the valves (on those engines that adjust). Refer to the repair manuals on each engine to determine when and how the valves are adjusted. Solid lifter systems require a gap between the valve stem and the lifter or push rod. Hydraulic lifters should be set so the lifter is halfway along its total travel path. These lifters automatically adjust for valve stem and metal expansion due to heat. Adjusting lifters requires removal of the valve cover. Use a new gasket when installing the cover.
- Adjust headlights. Headlights should be checked and set if needed. Burned-out bulbs should be replaced before setting the lights. Headlight aimers, such as the one in Figure 4.12, are used to set the horizontal and vertical position of the beam. Pads are used on the headlight bulbs for the adjuster to rest on and the lights do not have to be burning when using this type of machine (refer to Figure 18.76). Headlight horizontal settings are straight ahead. The vertical light beam pattern should drop about 2 in., measured 20 feet from the front of the bulb. Low-beam light patterns are designed to move down and to the right so as not to blind oncoming traffic.
- Check all instrument panel gauges and warning lights. Some lights are checked in the ON position, with the engine "off." Others are checked when the key is turned to the START position just before the engine starts. Other lights indicate turn signal position, high beam, parking brake on, seat belt not fastened, and emergency flashers. Each vehicle manufacturer has its own test system. There has to be a system in place to

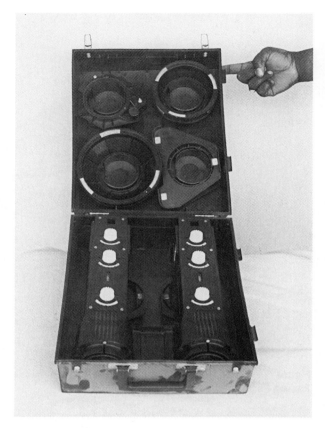

Figure 4.12 Headlight aimers. Headlight aimers installed on the lights are used to adjust the vertical and horizontal beam path. With this type aimer the lights are not on when set (courtesy of Training Enterprises Company).

check the warning light bulbs so they will come on to make the driver aware of a problem. Check the owner's manual for each vehicle setup and check out the warning system for the owner.

- Check the PCV valve. The positive crankcase ventilation (PCV) valve controls the amount of crankcase blowby gases allowed to be recirculated and burned in the combustion chamber (see Figure 4.13). This valve works in a dirty environment. If it is clogged, clean or replace it. Some can be cleaned, other replaced. Also inspect the PCV valve hose to see if it is clogged. Replace with hose materials that can withstand oil.
- Inspect the wiper blades and check the washer system. Inspect the edges of both wiper blades. Replace cut, torn, or hardened wiper blades. Check the spring tension of the arms by moving them out from the glass and gauging the tension. A weak pull on the wiper arms means the springs have stretched. Replace these wiper arms. Check the windshield washer system. Look

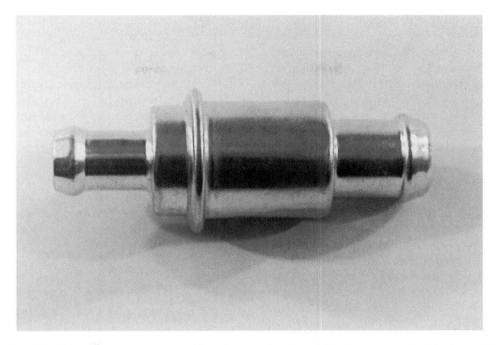

Figure 4.13 PCV valve. This valve is used to control the amount of crankcase blowby gases going into the engine intake (courtesy of Training Enterprises Company).

at the spray volume and the pattern by turning on the washer system and observing it work. This test was covered in Chapter 1.

LESSON 4–4 12,000 Mile/20,000 Km or Twelve-Month Maintenance Service

The three- and six-month maintenance checks should be made at this point. The service checks and inspections listed in this lesson are in addition to these regular checks.

Under-the-Vehicle Service

- Inspect front and rear suspension and tire balance. Alignments are performed by a specialist but the need for alignment is first detected by the service technician. Certain types of abnormal tire wear can be traced to improper alignment or balance (refer to Figure 16.73). Look for cupping, wear on the inside or outside of the tread, and feather edging. If the owner has been following the maintenance schedule suggested in this chapter, the tires have been rotated once. See if the original tire and the tire that was rotated the same position have identical wear patterns. The intent of tire rotation is to equalize the tire wear. Tire rotation will not help if the alignment is so bad that the tires are worn out in two rotations. Four rotations are normal.

- Make a tire rotation (second rotation). Go back to Lesson 4–2 and follow the directions for rotating tires. Be sure to adjust tire pressure and check for out-of-balance tires. Balance any tires that need it. Balancing is covered in Chapter 16.

Under-the-Hood Service

- Clean fuel injectors. Fuel injectors can stick closed or open and can produce an abnormal spray pattern. Black smoke out the exhaust, when caused by injectors, is the result of too much fuel entering the combustion chamber. If the injector is not firing, the cylinder will not receive fuel and the engine will skip or run rough. Some injector problems can be solved by cleaning. Follow the directions for injector cleaning in Chapter 11.

- Check the air conditioner compressor clutch. One periodic maintenance item related to air condition systems is adjusting the compressor clutch gap. Compressors cycle on and off when the engine is running. This places heavy wear on the compressor clutch friction materials. The gap between the clutch friction materials and the magnetic clutch widens. The gap has to be reset or the clutch will slip and burn out. Follow the directions in the air conditioning section of Chapter 19 to adjust the gap.

- Check the alternator charging rate. Alternators can have some internal damage and still produce a charge. Some common causes of alternator failure are shorted stators and diode failure in the rectifier section. Usually when a rectifier section is defective, the alternator changes sound and the charging rate drops below normal. This sound should not be confused with defective bearings. To determine if the alternator has an electrical or electronic problem, make a simple voltmeter test. Hook up a voltmeter in parallel across the battery terminals, connecting red to positive and black to negative (refer to Figure 3.19). Read the voltage with the engine running. The normal charging rate should be from 14.1 volts to 15.5 volts. For greater accuracy, look up the exact specifications for the vehicle you are testing. Most problems cause a drop in the charging voltage but there are several that cause higher than normal charging rates. Both low and high charging rates need to be corrected.
- Check starter amperage draw. One of the first indications of a starter problem is when the starter cranking speed gets slower than normal. The starter also makes a different sound. Technicians call this "dragging." This problem can be caused by worn bushings, brushes, and shorted field coils. There also is another cause, not related to a bad starter. Too much load can be placed on the starter by burned-out engine bearings or an accessory with bearing failure. Both these failures slow up the cranking speed and appear to be a starter problem. Use a voltmeter to check the amperage draw of the starter (refer to Figure 3.14). When the engine is cranked, the voltage should not drop below 9.6 volts. When battery voltage drops below this point on a fully charged battery, a very large amperage or load has been placed on the battery. If the excessive amperage load is caused by the starter, repair or replace it. To find out if an accessory is at fault, loosen each of the drive belts and repeat the test. A normal cranking voltage would eliminate the starter as a problem. For more details about starters, refer to Chapter 8.

LESSON 4–5 Two Years, Four Years, and As-Needed Vehicle Maintenance Service

Some maintenance and service are only performed after long periods of vehicle operation. We have placed these items in this section. Refer to this lesson when the time and mileage are right.

Two Years

- Replace accessory and timing belts. There are two types of belt systems used for accessories. One type has individual belts for one or two units. The other type has one belt for all the accessories (see Figure 4.14). This is called a

Figure 4.14 Serpentine belt. On most of the newer engines one belt (serpentine) is used to run most of the accessories. Correct belt tension is very important (courtesy of Training Enterprises Company).

"serpentine" system. This system has an automatic tensioner, which keeps the right force on the belt to prevent it from slipping. With the individual belt system, each belt must be tightened separately.

Belts must be replaced when they no longer drive the unit without slipping. They get glazed, cracked, and start to separate. Preventive maintenance plans require belt replacement every two years, and more often if the vehicle is driven more than the average yearly mileage. Outside belts have to be removed to replace inside belts. It is recommended that all belts be replaced at the same time, especially if an inside belt breaks and the outside belts have to be removed to make the repair. Always purchase dual belts in matched pairs so each belt has the same tension when installed and tightened.

The serpentine belt is more critical when it breaks. All units stop, including the power steering, alternator, air conditioner, air pump, and water pump. Do not run an engine without the water pump operating. The engine will overheat and internal damage could result. Belt tensioners on the serpentine belts should be adjusted so they keep the correct tension on the belt and prevent slipping.

Engine timing belts should be inspected once a year and replaced every two years. This belt is critical. It is not wise to run the engine until the belt breaks. This belt drives the engine camshaft or shafts (see Figure 4.15). When it breaks, the camshaft stops moving. Some valves will stop in the open position. The pistons can hit the open valves and bend or break the valves as well as damage the tops of the pistons. This is a very costly repair.

- Flush cooling system, and change thermostat and hoses. Every two years, drain the old coolant and run cleaner through the cooling system. This removes the rust and scale built up in the radiator and block.

A new thermostat should be installed at this time. This requires removal of the thermostat housing and installation of a new thermostat with the element placed toward the engine

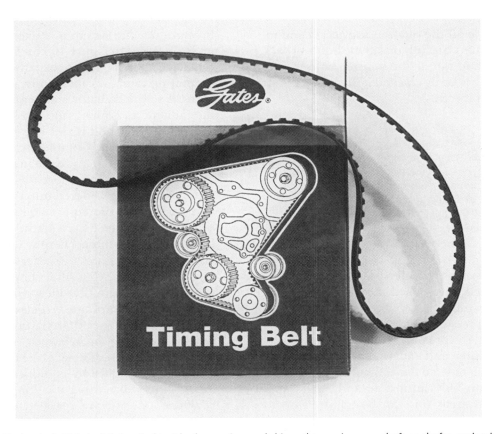

Figure 4.15   Timing belt. This belt is located inside the engine and drives the engine camshaft or shafts, maintaining the timing between the piston movement and the valves (courtesy of Training Enterprises Company).

Figure 4.16 Radiator core service. The radiator core can be replaced by soldering the old ends to the new core (courtesy of Training Enterprises Company).

block. Scrape off the old housing gasket and install a new one. Carefully install the housing back in position and torque the housing bolts evenly. The housing is easily cracked if the bolts are not tightened correctly.

> New types of coolant allow longer periods of time between flush and change intervals. Follow the manufacturer's recommendations for the correct flush and change intervals. As mentioned before, do not mix coolant types such as regular and extended life because it will reduce the change interval of the extended-life coolant.

Cooling system and heater hoses often fail during sustained high-speed driving conditions. This is the time the cooling system is at its maximum pressure. A dry or brittle hose will crack and let the pressurized coolant escape. Replace all heater and radiator hoses every four years. Install new coolant. The system should be filled with 50% antifreeze and 50% water. In very cold areas this can be adjusted up to 70% antifreeze for added protection. The new coolant contains additives that lubricate the water pump and prevent rust and scale buildup.

Pressure test the system to make sure there are no leaks (refer to Figure 10.16). Fix any leaks by replacing gaskets, hoses, expansion plugs, water pumps, radiator caps, and heater or radiator cores. A severe radiator leak requires removing the radiator and taking it to a radiator specialty shop. They will boil it out to restore the flow and repair the leak. Completely plugged radiator or heater cores require the insertion of a rod into each opening to remove the hard material. New cores can be soldered into the old radiator end parts when the core material deteriorates beyond repair (see Figure 4.16).

- Drain diesel fuel filter. There is a filter on diesel engines that separates the water out of the fuel (see Figure 4.17). This filter should be drained every six months, more often if the fuel/water separator light (on some vehicles) comes on.
- Replace gasoline fuel filter. Carburetor-type fuel systems can have an in-line or inlet-type filter (see Figure 4.18). Replace these filters every two years. Fuel injection–equipped vehicles have in-line filters that can go as long as 60,000 to 80,000 miles and are serviced only when required.
- Replace automatic transmission filter. When the transmission fluid smells burned or has been

Figure 4.17 Diesel fuel filter. This filter separates the water from the diesel fuel. Drain the water when the filter is saturated (courtesy of Training Enterprises Company).

30,000 miles or more, change the transmission filter and fluid. The transmission pan has to be removed, the old fluid drained out, and the filter changed (see Figure 4.19). The pan is cleaned and reinstalled with a new gasket. New fluid of the correct type is added until the dipstick reads full.

- Replace limited-slip differential fluid. Limited-slip differential fluid must be replaced more often than regular differential fluid. A limited-slip differential has friction discs that wear through regular use. This material contaminates the differential fluid and causes problems. To drain the fluid, remove either a drain plug or cover. Inspect the differential for wear, clean out the housing, and replace the cover. A new gasket should be used and the bolts should be tightened evenly. Skip around from side to side and top to bottom so the bolts will not be tightened all at one side first. Starting at one bolt and moving to the next in line can cause a "hinge" effect and distort the gasket. Be sure to use differential

Figure 4.18 Gasoline filters. An in-line fuel filter like this is installed to keep dirt and contaminants from entering the fuel injectors (courtesy of Training Enterprises Company).

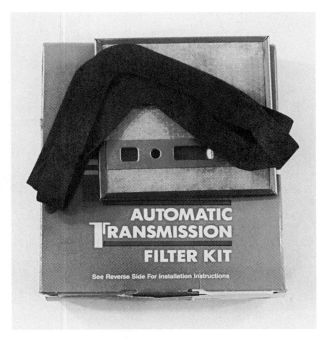

Figure 4.19 Automatic transmission filter. Remove the transmission pan and install a new transmission filter. The filter kit contains the new filter and pan gasket (courtesy of Training Enterprises Company).

fluid specifically recommended for limited-slip differentials when you refill the unit. Fill the unit to the bottom of the filler plug threads or to the "full" mark on the dipstick.

Four Years

- Replace fuel, PCV, and vacuum hoses. Four years is the recommended life of products such as hoses and lines because the material gets dry and brittle. Preventive maintenance plans suggest replacing all vacuum, heater, radiator, and fuel hoses every four years (see Figure 4.20). Cooling system hoses should be replaced at the same time the cooling system is flushed and new coolant installed.
- Replace standard transmission, power steering, and standard differential fluids. These units should have a fluid change when the old fluid becomes contaminated with dirt, water, or other fluids or materials. If the vehicle is moved to a different climate, fluids must be changed to a different viscosity. Power steering fluid can be removed by removing the return hose and letting the old fluid drain out. Be sure to use the correct fluid recommended for each vehicle.

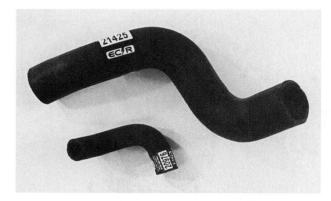

Figure 4.20 Types of hoses. Vacuum, heater, radiator, and fuel hoses such as these should be replaced every four years. The hoses get soft and brittle and fail under pressure or vibration (courtesy of Training Enterprises Company).

Standard transmissions and differentials usually have drain plugs. Both these units have filler plugs or dipsticks. Most of the time the same fluid is recommended for both units, but use caution as some units require special fluid. Always check the manufacturer's specifications and use only recommended fluid for both units. Fill both units to the bottom of the filler plug threads or to the "full" mark on the dipstick.

As-Needed Service

• Inspect brakes and repack wheel bearings. *Caution:* Brake systems contain asbestos. Use special equipment to vacuum asbestos dust away from brake systems before they are serviced. If you do not have this equipment, do not inspect brakes. To inspect brakes, the front wheels must be removed so you can look at the rotors and pads. Inspect rotors on both sides to see if they are grooved or scored. Evaluate the pad thickness to see how much additional mileage is left. Many vehicles still have drum and shoe systems in the rear. To inspect this system, the brake drum must be removed (see Figure 4.21). Check the inside of the drum for bell mouth, out-of-round, hard spots, and taper. If the drums are heavily scored, they have to be turned. This is a machine shop operation and is done when new brake shoes are installed. Check the brake shoe lining to see how much more use is in them before they have to be replaced. Look at the wheel cylinders to detect any brake fluid leaks. Worn-out wheel cylinder cups allow the brake fluid to pass around the cup and into the dust boot. Pull the dust boot back and check for dampness. Inspect return springs and hold-down springs. Lubricate the backing plate with high-temperature grease before reinstalling the drum brake drum.

Figure 4.21 Drum brake inspection. First remove the brake drum. Inspect the shoes, springs, parking brake, and wheel cylinder. Correct any problems (courtesy of Training Enterprises Company).

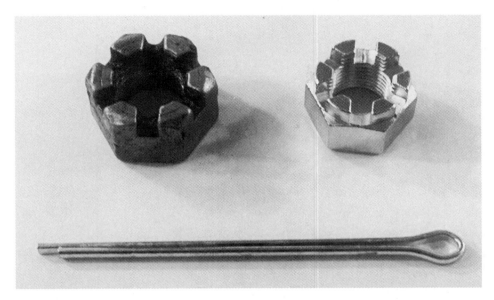

Figure 4.22 Axle nut and cotter key. To keep the axle nut from coming off, a cotter key is installed. This should never be left off (courtesy of Training Enterprises Company).

Wheel bearings are found in the front and rear of all vehicles. Some systems are sealed, and others require service. Wheel bearings should be repacked every 24,000 miles/40,000 km or twenty-four months. The bearings should be removed, cleaned, and inspected for damage, and repacked with grease. The hub assembly is reinstalled and the axle nut torqued. A cotter key is installed to keep the nut from turning (see Figure 4.22). Never leave this key out because the nut could loosen and fall out.

Pedal feel, noise, and stopping reaction are three good ways to evaluate brakes. Any abnormal pedal feel, noise, or stopping action should result in a complete brake inspection. Correct any problems and retest.

- Adjust manual clutch pedal travel. The manual clutch linkage must be adjusted when the clutch pedal is released and the clutch slips. As the clutch disc friction material wears, the system is designed so the pressure plate fingers move toward the throwout bearing (see Figure 4.23). This prevents the pressure plate from clamping down on the friction material on the clutch disc. The adjustment procedure moves the throwout bearing away from the pressure plate fingers. Mechanical linkage is adjustable. This should be

done every time the clutch pedal is released and the clutch slips.
- Rebuild hydraulic clutch. If either the hydraulic clutch master cylinder or the slave cylinder leak, they must be rebuilt or replaced (see Figure 4.24). Kits can be purchased to rebuild both parts but most technicians install new ones. This is a critical area and safety problems would occur if the hydraulic clutch were to fail while driving. When the parts are installed, you must "bleed" the system of air and adjust it so the clutch operates properly.

A refrigeration license is required to open and service an automotive air conditioning system. Refrigerant must be recovered rather than released into the air. Any technician can inspect the system and order further service from a licensed technician. Any technician in automotive servicing should work toward getting a license.

- Replace air conditioner filter and receiver dryer. When moisture and air enter an air conditioning system, both must be removed and a new receiver dryer installed (see Figure 4.25). There are line filters in most air conditioners. These must be replaced when they become blocked. Both problems can be detected by connecting service gauges to the system and reading them. You must obtain a license to open an air conditioning system for any type of repair. A

Figure 4.23 Clutch system. Friction material in the clutch wears. This requires periodic adjustments to keep the clutch from slipping and damaging internal parts (courtesy of Training Enterprises Company).

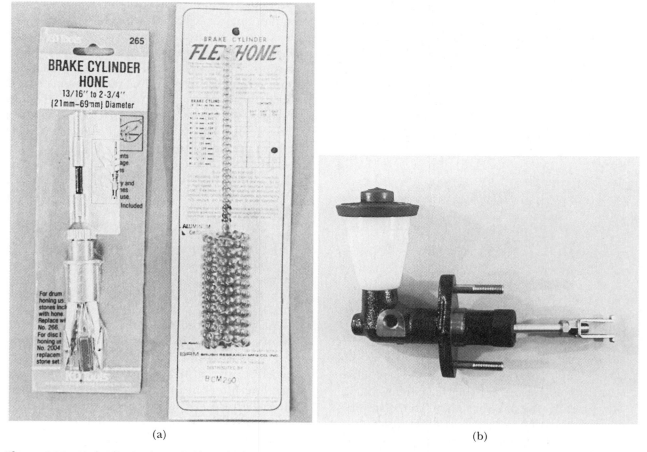

(a)   (b)

Figure 4.24 Hydraulic clutch repair. These hones (a) are used to rebuild hydraulic brake cylinders, clutch master cylinders (b), and both wheel and slave cylinders. The cylinders have to be honed and cleaned before new parts can be installed (courtesy of Training Enterprises Company).

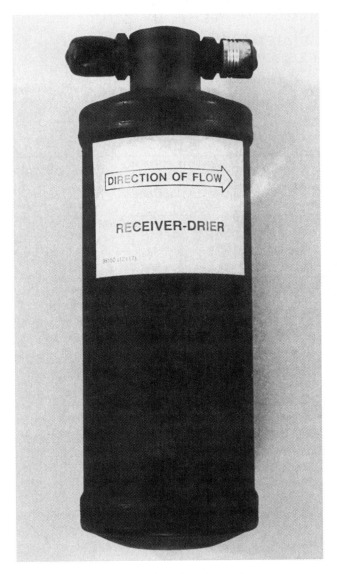

Figure 4.25 A/C filter and receiver dryer. These parts are replaced in an air conditioning system when moisture enters the system or when particles clog the lines (courtesy of Training Enterprises Company).

top nut can be removed, the shaft has to be held from turning. Before the new shock absorbers are installed, air must be removed from the internal fluid. The shock is slowly extended and retracted several times until the movement in both directions is smooth and steady. Shock absorbers should be replaced in pairs on the same axle. When one is worn out, the other will soon need replacement.

• Perform a state vehicle inspection (if required). This check should be made at least once during the year on the month the sticker expires (see Figure 4.26).

> Be sure to check out the inspection requirements for the state in which you will be working. Add to or revise the list provided in this chapter. Inspection requirements change from year to year. Emission requirements are some of the latest items added to inspections.

The headlights should all be burning and set properly. The high-beam indicator light should come on when the lights are switched to high beam.

Parking lights should all be burning. They should be amber in the front and red in the rear. All side marker lights should be burning and the correct color.

In the rear of the vehicle should be a license plate light. Tail lights should all be burning. When the brake pedal is applied, the brake lights should come on. All brake lights should be burning and the correct color.

Right and left directional signals should both work. They should flash and the indicator light on the dash should show which side is on.

The brake pedal should be firm or hard when pressed and not have excessive pedal movement at the start or as the pedal is held. The brake warning light should not be on or disconnected. This may be the same light used to indicate the parking brake is on. When the parking brake is off this light should be off unless there is a pressure failure in one side of the hydraulic brake system. The brakes should stop the vehicle in the normal amount of time based on speed and distance. No wheels should lock up. There should not be unusual sounds such as metal on metal in the brake system. There should not be any signs of leaks at the master cylinder or the wheel/calipers. No part of the brake system should be disconnected.

license is not required for making tests. Abnormal temperatures at the inside air conditioner ducts and gauges that read too high or low are two indications that the system needs to be repaired.

• Replace shock absorbers and suspension bushings. Shock absorbers are replaced when an inspection shows leaks and when the vehicle does not recover from road bumps properly. Cupping tires are another indication of bad shock absorbers. Shock absorbers are mounted in rubber bushings at the top and bottom (refer to Figure 4.3). Usually two bolts hold the shock at the bottom and one nut at the top. Before the

SI-15 (Rev. 6/92)

North Carolina Division of Motor Vehicles
RECEIPT AND STATEMENT
COVERING VEHICLE INSPECTION PROCEDURES

OWNER John Q. Motorist

ADDRESS Route 1

CITY Raleigh   **COUNTY** Wake

Inspection Fee $ _____

Certificate Fee $ _____

Repair Charge Made $ _____

LICENSE NUMBER	MAKE	YEAR	TYPE OF VEHICLE	VEHICLE IDENTIFICATION NO.	MILEAGE
ABC123	Chev	2000	☑ Auto ☐ Truck ☐ Trailer ☐ Station Wagon ☐ Bus ☐ Motorcycle	1A2BC34D5EF678912	10,123

COPY FROM PREVIOUS INSPECTION CERTIFICATE		ENGINE INFORMATION	

Mileage	Month of previous inspection
5,321	☐ Jan ☐ Feb ☐ Mar ☐ April ☐ May ☐ June ☐ July ☐ Aug ☐ Sept ☑ Oct ☐ Nov ☐ Dec

No. of Cylinders 6

Type Fuel: Gas ☑ **Diesel** ☐ **Other** ☐

SAFETY EQUIPMENT	APPROVED	DIS-APPROVED	CORRECTED	EXHAUST EMISSION CONTROLS TAMPERING CHECK	NOT APPLICABLE	CONNECTED	DIS-CONNECTED	CORRECTED
Headlights	✓			Catalytic Converter (CAT)		✓		
Beam Indicator Light/Switch	✓			Air Injection System (AIS)		✓		
Parking Lights	✓			PCV Valve		✓		
License Plate Light	✓			Unleaded Gas Restrictor		✓		
Tail Lights	✓			Exhaust Gas Recirculation Valve (EGR)		✓		
Stop Lights	✓			Thermostatic Air Control (TAC)		✓		
Clearance Lights (Buses, Trucks and Trailers)	✓			Oxygen (O2) Sensor		✓		
Reflectors	✓			Evaporative Emission System (EVP)		✓		
Directional Signals	✓				APPROVED	DIS-APPROVED	CORRECTED	
Foot Brake	✓							
Emergency Brake	✓			Exhaust System				
Steering Mechanism	✓							
Windshield Wiper	✓							
Horn	✓							
Tires	✓							
Rear View Mirrors	✓							
Window Tinting Installed Prior to 7-1-88								

John Q. Motorist

(Customer's Signature)

REPAIRS MADE BY: INSPECTION STATION ☐ OTHER ☐	MECHANIC'S SIGNATURE Bill Wrenchwielder

INSPECTION CERTIFICATE NUMBER 12345678

STATION NO. 1234	DATE OF INSPECTION 10/15/2000

REINSPECTION DATE	MECHANIC'S SIGNATURE

DISAPPROVED EQUIPMENT MAY BE REPAIRED BY THE OWNER OR AT A FIRM OF THE OWNER'S CHOICE AND BE REINSPECTED FREE OF CHARGE WITHIN 90 DAYS UPON PRESENTATION OF THIS RECEIPT TO THE SAME STATION CONDUCTING THE ORIGINAL INSPECTION; HOWEVER, THE INSPECTION DEADLINE IS NOT EXTENDED. OPERATION WITHOUT CURRENT "INSPECTION CERTIFICATE" OR DEFECTIVE EQUIPMENT SUBJECTS THE OPERATOR TO ARREST ACTIO

Figure 4.26   This form is typical of those used by state inspection stations when they perform a yearly safety inspection (courtesy of Training Enterprises Company).

The parking brake should have lever reserve when the brake is applied. Cables should be free to move and not be frayed. There should be no broken or missing cables. The brake lever should lock in position and the brake warning light should come on.

The horn should emit a sound that can be heard for at least 200 feet. It should not emit unusual sounds, such as tunes or music; the sound should be easily recognizable as a vehicle horn.

The steering mechanism should not have steering wheel play over 4 inches. If the vehicle is equipped with power steering, it must be operating. The front and rear suspension and tie rod ends must not be damaged or worn beyond safe limits.

The windshield wiper should be adequate to clean mud, snow, and rain from the windshield. If there were two wipers installed originally, both must work. They should have the proper tension and cannot have parts missing. They should have a control that the driver can operate.

Tires should not have a tread depth of less than 2/32 in. There should not be any exposed cords, broken belts, bulges, cut sidewalls, or exposed tread wear indicators. The tread wear indicators are bars across the face of the tire tread that show up as a line when the tread is worn down (see Figure 4.27).

Rear view mirrors must be placed so the vehicle operator can see the highway behind the vehicle. Most inspections require an outside mirror on the driver's side. These must be mounted so the driver can see traffic approaching on the left side of the vehicle. All approved mirrors cannot be obstructed by a blocked rear window or side window.

Exhaust systems must be operational, without holes or leaks. All vehicles are equipped with a muffler, that reduces excessive noise. The exhaust system includes the exhaust pipe, muffler, resonator, and tailpipe. Muffler cut-outs are prohibited in many states. A *cut-out* is a separate system, developed to bypass the muffler, that reduces back pressure on the engine. Without a muffler the engine is very loud.

All emission control devices originally installed on a vehicle should be operating. Air pump belts, catalytic converters, computer controls, and oxygen sensors are devices used to reduce pollutants. Most states require the vehicle to pass a three-gas emissions test. A vehicle could fail

Figure 4.27 Tire tread wear indicators. These bars in the tire tread warn the vehicle owner when the tire is worn to where it is unsafe. The bar looks like a straight line across the tire (courtesy of Training Enterprises Company).

these tests if a spark plug wire was defective or the engine needed a tuneup.

VOCABULARY

Use the listed words in the blanks beside the sentences to complete the definitions. Either write out the words or place the letters in the blanks.

A. Drain plug

B. Coolant

C. Combustion chamber

D. Abnormal tire wear

E. NLGI

F. Chassis grease

G. Compatible

H. Crankcase

I. Oil gauge

J. "Cold" mark

K. Belt tension

L. Glazed

M. Hydraulic clutch

N. DOT

O. Maintenance-free battery

P. Plastic "eye"

Q. Electrolyte level

R. Hydrometer

S. Coolant recovery reservoir

T. Lug nut pattern

U. Space saver tire

V. Transmission heat exchanger

W. Hydraulic lifters

X. Horizontal

Y. PCV

_____ 1. When the sides of a belt have been worn slick

_____ 2. Positive crankcase ventilation

_____ 3. A mixture of 50% water and 50% antifreeze

_____ 4. A lubricant suited for ball joints and suspensions

_____ 5. A built-in battery hydrometer

_____ 6. A sequence for installing lug nuts or bolts

_____ 7. A tire for emergency use only

_____ 8. The opposite of a verticle direction

_____ 9. When materials are made to work together without problems

_____ 10. Indicates oil system pressure

_____ 11. Where fluids can be drained from a standard transmission

_____ 12. Department of Transportation

_____ 13. Used to check coolant strength

_____ 14. Cools automatic transmission fluids

_____ 15. Saw-toothed tread pattern

_____ 16. Used to check power steering fluid level

_____ 17. A battery that does not need servicing

_____ 18. Where the coolant level is checked and maintained

_____ 19. Hydraulic part that used engine oil to operate

_____ 20. The fluid level in a battery

_____ 21. Amount of adjustment placed on a belt to prevent slipping

_____ 22. Where the fuel is burned in an engine

_____ 23. Clutch that used a master cylinder to operate a slave cylinder

_____ 24. Where the engine oil is stored

_____ 25. National Lubricating Grease Institute

REVIEW QUESTIONS

The following questions will help you determine if you have accomplished the tasks stated at the begining of this chapter. If you donot know many of the answers, go back and review the material before proceeding to the next chapter.

Lesson 4–1

1. What are two units that preventative maintenance is scheduled from?
2. What are two conditions that will increase the frequency of required maintenance?
3. List eight fluids that could be found leaking from a vehicle.
4. How is the fluid level checked on most standard transmissions?
5. What does a black sooty exhaust indicate?
6. Where are tire cold inflation pressures found?
7. What is the agency that rates grease?
8. What does it mean when parts move while being greased?
9. What would be a recommendation to correct uneven wear between tires?
10. After just installing engine oil, what is the correct engine starting procedure?
11. Is the engine running or stopped when checking automatic transmission fluid?
12. How is brake fluid quality rated?
13. What is the percentage of charge in a battery that has a dark or red dot in the "eye"?
14. What does the mark on a power steering dipstick just above the low mark mean?
15. What is the chemical makeup of coolant?
16. What lubricant can be used on hinges, latches, and doors?

Lesson 4–2

17. How often should tire rotation be performed?
18. Can all types of tires be rotated so they turn a different direction?
19. What tool when used reduces the chance of drum and rotor warpage?
20. Why should round air filters be rotated 1/4 turn after an inspection?
21. What are three things to look for when performing a cooling system inspection?
22. What is the name of the tool used to check cooling system protection levels?

23. How can automatic transmission fluid contaminate engine coolant?
24. How should the air conditioner sight glass look on a normal system?

Lesson 4–3
25. How are hydraulic lifters set?
26. What is the correct horizontal setting for headlights when using adjusters?
27. What are two items that should be checked on windshield wipers?
28. What are two things that should be checked on windshield washers?
29. What part must be removed before lifters can be adjusted?
30. What does the PCV valve do?

Lesson 4–4
31. Name three types of abnormal tire wear.
32. Who usually performs wheel alignment?
33. After tires have been rotated how should they be serviced?
34. What causes black exhaust smoke?
35. What two things can cause an alternator to change sound?
36. How is the need for most tire alignments detected?
37. What are three things that can happen to cause fuel injectors to fail?
38. What will happen if the air conditioner compressor clutch is never adjusted?
39. What is the normal alternator charging rate range?
40. How are starter problems detected?
41. What is the usual cause of starter dragging?

Lesson 4–5
42. What is a "serpentine" belt?
43. Name some common belt problems.
44. What can be the result in the engine if a timing belt breaks?
45. What is the normal life of heater and radiator hoses?
46. What type of gasoline filter is common on fuel injected vehicles?
47. How often should an automatic transmission filter be changed?
48. What types of fluid can be used in a limited-slip differential?
49. When should standard transmission, power steering, or standard differential fluid be changed?
50. How often should wheel bearings be repacked?
51. How can the driver tell if the brakes need attention?

52. Name four items that are checked during a state inspection.
53. What are the indications when a tire is no longer safe to run?

ASE QUESTIONS

Each question or incomplete statement in this test is followed by four suggested answers or completions. In each case select the *one* that best answers the question or completes the statement.

1. Technician A says the automobile should be level when checking engine oil. Technician B says the vehicle should be level when checking standard transmission fluid. Who is right?
   a. A only   b. B only
   c. Both A and B   d. Neither A nor B
2. Technician A says most rear wheel drive differentials are checked with a dipstick. Technician B says most rear wheel drive differentials are checked by removing a plug. Who is right?
   a. A only   b. B only
   c. Both A and B   d. Neither A nor B
3. Technician A says movement between parts being greased shows the grease is entering the part. Technician B says movement between parts being greased shows wear. Who is right?
   a. A only   b. B only
   c. Both A and B   d. Neither A nor B
4. Technician A says maximum tire inflation pressures can be found on the sidewall of the tire. Technician B says the maximum tire inflation pressures are located on a sticker either on the edge of the door or in the glove compartment. Who is right?
   a. A only   b. B only
   c. Both A and B   d. Neither A nor B
5. Technician A says shock absorbers should be checked by a visual inspection. Technician B says shock absorbers should be checked by a road test and checking tire wear. Who is right?
   a. A only   b. B only
   c. Both A and B   d. Neither A nor B
6. Technician A says wear of the center tread shows underinflation. Technician B says wear on both the outer and inner sides of the tire tread shows overinflation. Who is right?
   a. A only   b. B only
   c. Both A and B   d. Neither A nor B
7. Technician A says most power steering unit fluid level is checked by the plug method. Tech-

nician B says most power steering units fluid level is checked by the dipstick method. Who is right?

a. A only
b. B only
c. Both A and B
d. Neither A nor B

8. Technician A says it is normal for the brake fluid level to drop in the disc brake side of the master cylinder reservoir. Technician B says any drop in brake fluid level in the disc brake side of the master cylinder reservoir shows there is a leak in the system. Who is right?

a. A only
b. B only
c. Both A and B
d. Neither A nor B

9. Technician A says a clear eye at the built-in hydrometer in a maintenance-free battery indicates a need for a battery charge. Technician B says a dark eye shows a defective battery. Who is right?

a. A only
b. B only
c. Both A and B
d. Neither A nor B

10. Technician A says only a four-tire rotation plan can be used when the vehicle has a space saver tire. Technician B says a five-tire rotation plan can be used if the vehicle has a space saver tire. Who is right?

a. A only
b. B only
c. Both A and B
d. Neither A nor B

11. Technician A says a steady flow of refrigerant can be seen in the sight glass of a fully charged air conditioning system. Technician B says that no refrigerant flow can be seen in the sight glass of a fully charged air conditioning system. Who is right?

a. A only
b. B only
c. Both A and B
d. Neither A nor B

12. Technician A says there should be a gap between the valve stem and push rod on hydraulic lifter equipped engines. Technician B says there should be a gap between the valve stem and push rod on a solid lifter equipped engine. Who is right?

a. A only
b. B only
c. Both A and B
d. Neither A nor B

13. Technician A says that checking and setting headlights should be a part of every state inspection routine. Technician B says that a tire tread depth check should be a part of every state inspection. Who is right?

a. A only
b. B only
c. Both A and B
d. Neither A nor B

Engine Lubrication System Maintenance

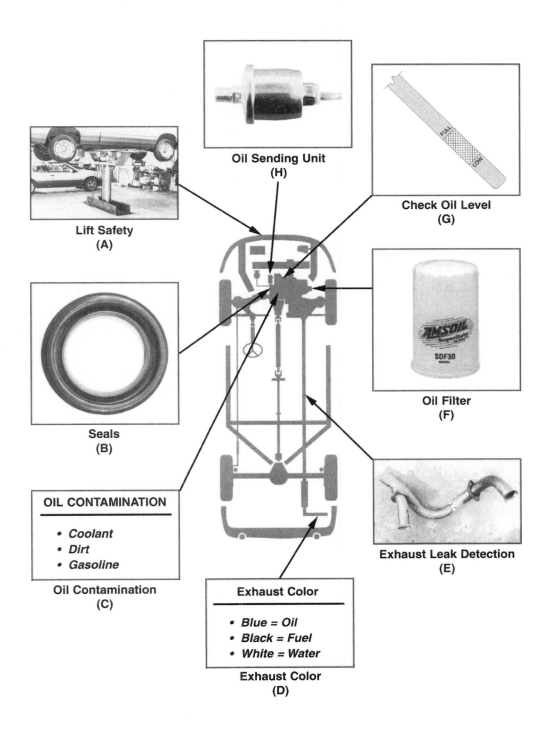

Oil Sending Unit
(H)

Check Oil Level
(G)

Lift Safety
(A)

Oil Filter
(F)

Seals
(B)

OIL CONTAMINATION

- *Coolant*
- *Dirt*
- *Gasoline*

Oil Contamination
(C)

Exhaust Leak Detection
(E)

Exhaust Color

- *Blue = Oil*
- *Black = Fuel*
- *White = Water*

Exhaust Color
(D)

Some of the most important automotive maintenance services include those simple checks and adjustments usually made when a vehicle is refueled. Most of us have probably performed some of these checks and adjustments without realizing their importance.

For an automotive engine to keep running it must have all its internal parts lubricated. Engine oil of the correct quality and viscosity is pumped under pressure through galleries or passageways to all the parts requiring lubrication. The oil is filtered and reused many times until it has reached the end of its product life. Engine lubrication service requires the selection of the right quality and viscosity of oil. It also requires changing the oil filter and the oil. Selecting the correct intervals between oil changes and the right oil viscosity is based on outside air temperature and engine running conditions. A lubrication specialist must know what oil products to use and when to replace them when they are no longer effective. The lubrication specialist must be able to select the right lubrication products to enable the engine to reach its maximum mileage and hours of service.

TASKS

The following are seven tasks to master before leaving this chapter:

Task 5-1. Study the engine lubrication system to learn how each part operates. Knowledge of how a system works makes service and troubleshooting easier.

Task 5-2. Learn how to check engine oil levels accurately and adjust the engine oil level when it is found to be either too high or too low.

Task 5-3. Learn how to select the correct engine oil for all types of engines, weather conditions, and driving conditions.

Task 5-4. Learn how to lift a vehicle correctly and safely for under-the-car service.

Task 5-5. Be able to perform an engine oil and filter change to factory standards.

Task 5-6. Be able to find the cause of excessive engine oil consumption, solve oil contamination problems, and repair oil leak problems.

Since the engine is the heart of any vehicle (see items in chapter opening illustration), to keep it running requires a heavy maintenance investment. The oil should be checked often (see part G). Oil filters (see part F) should be changed when dirty. Leaks may require new seal replacements (see part B). Oil can become contaminated (see chart C) and require engine repair as well as oil replacement. A technician must work hard to learn the skills necessary to maintain today's engines.

LESSON 5-1   Engine Lubrication System and Engine Oil

Every engine must have a lubrication system to provide a quantity of oil sufficient to lubricate the engine's moving parts. A typical lubrication system is shown in Figure 5.1. A study of these illustrations will help you understand how a lubrication system works. The *oil pan* at the bottom of the engine acts as a reservoir and holds the supply of oil.

Oil has to circulate to every moving part in the engine to prevent wear and friction. This is accomplished by a system of passageways called *oil galleries.* Figure 5.1 shows a typical General Motors four-cylinder engine. In this system, oil is stored in the oil pan, or *sump,* until the engine is started. When the engine starts, a rod from the distributor to the *oil pump* operates the pump. Oil is drawn in at the *pickup filter* and travels up the *oil pickup tube* into the pump. Gears in the pump cause the oil to be placed under pressure, and it is forced up through the *filter feed gallery* to the *oil filter.* There the oil filter removes dirt and particles from the oil. The filtered and cleaned oil leaves the filter and moves along the main oil gallery into the engine parts, which include the *camshaft, hydraulic lifters, main bearings, connecting rod bearings, valve train,* and *timing gears.* Oil is also sprayed into the cylinders and dripped on the timing gears. Splash oiling of the *cylinder walls* keeps the *pistons, piston pins,* and *piston rings* oiled. The piston rings control the oil on the cylinder walls by scraping the excess oil back into the oil pan. The *valves* are lubricated by oil running off the top of the *rocker arms.* In the case of *overhead cam* engines, pressurized oil is fed to the *cam bearings* and *lifters* (refer to Figure 5.1). Valve seals regulate the amount of oil that stays on the valve stems. Oil pressure is maintained by the condition of all the parts in the system and by a pressure relief valve at the oil pump. Excess pressure, above the oil pump relief valve pressure, is released allowing the oil to flow back to the oil sump. Thirty to sixty pounds per square inch (psi, as measured with a gauge) is the usual pressure found on most automobiles.

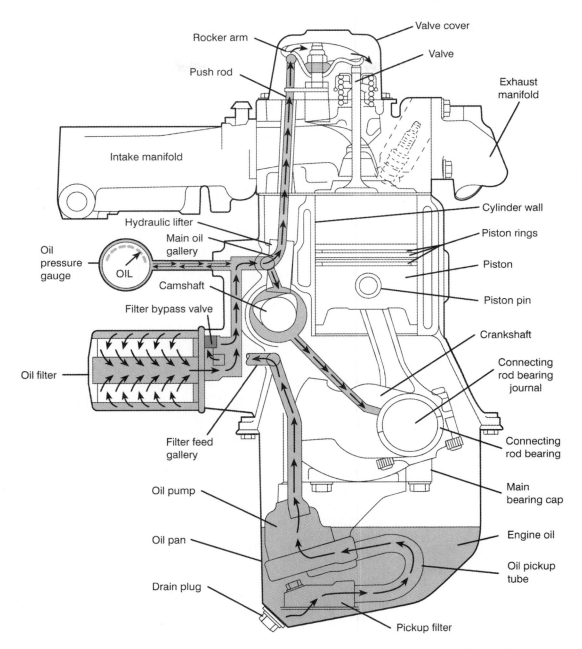

Figure 5.1 The lubrication system of a typical four-cylinder engine (courtesy of Chevrolet Motor Division, General Motors Corporation).

When the oil filter gets clogged, a *filter bypass valve* is forced open. This allows the oil to bypass the filter and go directly to the main oil gallery. This means that from this point until the filter is changed the oil is not properly filtered.

Oil pressure gauge readings are good indicators of engine wear. When the engine is at operating temperature and idle, oil pressure should not drop below twenty psi. Any engine with a lower than normal oil pressure has internal problems, such as a defective oil pump or worn engine parts. Engines equipped with oil pressure lights should have test gauges installed if the oil pressure light comes on at idle or anytime the engine is running (remember to check the oil level first!). The light will come on at about three to seven psi. This pressure would be too low to run at road speeds. Correct all oil pressure problems immediately—oil-starved parts have been known to fly through the sides of the engine when they fail. Any loud noise coupled with low oil pressure means that engine bearings and parts have failed and the engine must be repaired.

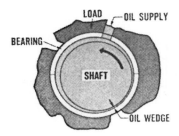

Figure 5.2 Cross-sectional view of oil film. Note that the oil film separates the bearing and the shaft, and thus minimizes friction and wear (courtesy of American Motors).

Oil

The oil that flows through the lubrication system performs many functions. The most important function is that of a *lubricant*. Any motion between parts in contact creates friction, and friction causes wear. To minimize wear, friction must be minimized. A lubricant reduces friction by flowing between parts in contact and providing a thin film that acts to separate the parts. The effect of a lubricating film is shown in Figure 5.2. Since this lubricating film can be wiped off or squeezed out by the motion of the parts, a constant supply of oil must be provided to maintain continuous lubrication.

Oil also helps to cool an engine. Because oil comes in contact with hot parts, the oil absorbs some of the heat and carries it back to the oil pan. Much of this heat is *dissipated,* or passed off, through the sides and bottom of the oil pan. The oil also tends to equalize the temperature of the engine parts by transmitting some of its heat to cooler parts.

Among the other functions oil performs is that of a *sealant.* The film of oil that forms between the cylinder walls and the piston rings helps in obtaining a seal between those parts.

The remaining functions of oil are for the most part handled by the *additives* in the oil. Additives are chemical compounds that are blended into the oil when it is refined and processed. Those additives include *detergents,* which are similar to the detergents used to wash clothes. Detergents in the oil act to dissolve dirt, sludge, and varnish deposits in the engine. If used continuously in new engines, oil containing detergents keep the insides of the engines from becoming dirty. Usually included with detergents are *dispersants,* which act to keep any dirt in suspension. If the dirt is kept in suspension, it cannot build up in the engine. Large dirt particles are trapped by the filter. The remaining dirt drains out with the old oil when it is changed.

Other additives include *viscosity index improvers* and *pour point depressants* that help to control the change in oil thickness with temperature change, and various *inhibitors* that decrease or prevent oxidation, rust, and corrosion. Additional agents reduce foaming and improve lubricating qualities.

Viscosity.   Oil is available in different thicknesses (see Figure 5.3). Oil can be as thin as water and flow very easily or it can be as thick as honey and flow very slowly. *Viscosity* is a measurement of how easily a liquid flows. Oil for use in automobile engines is graded in a viscosity index system developed by the Society of Automotive Engineers (SAE). In this system, oils are assigned numbers in relation to their thickness. Thin oils are given low numbers, and higher numbers are assigned to thicker oils.

Figure 5.3 Multiviscosity oil. Pictured here are four of the most popular multiviscosity oils used in today's engines. Outside temperature, engine condition, and driving conditions are some factors that determine viscosity selection (courtesy of Training Enterprises Company).

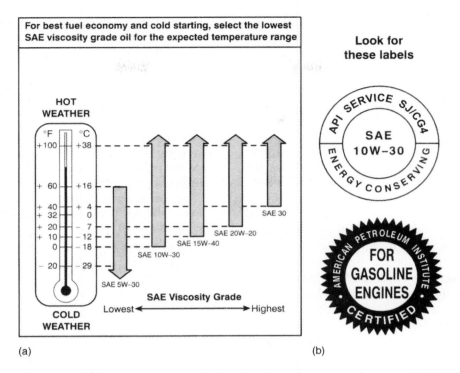

Figure 5.4 Viscosity chart. Typical oil viscosity recommendations based on temperature (courtesy of Chevrolet Motor Division, General Motors Corporation).

The most commonly specified oil viscosities for automobile engines range from SAE 5 or SAE 5W (Winter) for cold climate use to SAE 50 for use under high-temperature conditions. Figure 5.4 shows the oil viscosities recommended by one manufacturer for use within normal temperature ranges on the North American continent.

When oil is heated, it tends to thin out. An oil with a low viscosity flows easily between parts. This may provide excellent lubrication when a cold engine is first started. But when the engine reaches normal operating temperatures, the oil may be too thin and allow excessive wear. An oil with a higher viscosity may be ideal for high-temperature operation. However, it may not flow between the parts when the engine is cold, and thus allow wear when the engine is first started. To provide proper lubrication over a broad temperature range, *multigrade* or *multiviscosity* oils were developed.

In use, a multiviscosity oil performs as a low-viscosity oil when it is cold. When it is heated, it performs as a high-viscosity oil. As an example, an SAE 10W-30 oil flows as an SAE 10W oil when cold, but flows as an SAE 30 oil when hot. Multiviscosity oils are produced by the addition of viscosity index improvers as mentioned previously. These additives keep the oil from becoming too thin when heated.

Service Classification. This system was developed by the American Petroleum Institute (API). It provides a means of selecting an engine oil based on the service conditions under which a particular engine is operated. In this system, oils are divided into two categories: the "S" category (spark ignited) is mainly for oils to be used in gasoline-powered cars and trucks. The "C" category (combustion ignited) is mainly for oils designed for diesel engines.

These are the current classifications in the "S" category:

SA An obsolete oil. Oils with this classification do not contain any additives. They can be used only in engines that are operated under very mild conditions. This classification has no performance requirements.

SB Another obsolete oil. Oils with this classification can be used in engines in cars built before 1964. Oils in this classification have been in use since the 1930s and provide only antiscuff capability and resistance to oil oxidation and bearing corrosion. These oils should be used only under mild conditions where minimum protection is desired.

Another use for SB oils is to allow enough wear to reduce problems (break in) in an engine after it has been rebuilt. The new oils are so good that the rings do not wear to the contour of the cylinder walls. SB classification oil is nondetergent and allows enough wear in about 1000 miles to seat the rings and reduce oil consumption past the piston rings. After the break-in period, switch the engine oil to the recommended oil for the engine.

SC This classification was originally recommended for 1964 through 1967 cars and trucks. Oils designed for this service provide control of high- and low-temperature deposits, wear, rust, and corrosion in gasoline engines.

SD Oils with this classification can be used in gasoline engines in 1968 through 1970 models of cars and light trucks. Oils designed for this service provide more protection than oils classified SC against high- and low-temperature deposits, wear, rust, and corrosion.

SE These oils can be used in gasoline engines in cars and light trucks built from 1971 through 1979. They are suitable for severe service and offer more protection against deposits, rust, and corrosion. These oils meet the increased demands of the emission control devices used on these later engines.

SF Oil with this classification was recommended by many manufacturers beginning with 1980 cars and light trucks. These oils offer better antiwear performance and are specifically recommended for the new four-cylinder engines whose higher speeds place more demands on engine oil.

SG SG started in 1988 and was replaced in 1993 by SH. It replaces SF and all other previous classifications as the best oil available. This oil protects better than earlier oils and reduces wear problems in critical areas of the automobile, such as the camshaft and lifters.

SH This classification, was replaced in 1997. When compared to SG motor oil, this oil produces 19% less engine sludge, 20% less cam wear, 5% less engine varnish, 21% improved oxidation, 7% less piston varnish, 3% less engine rust, and 13% less bearing wear. As you can see, this is a superior product to anything used in the past and should prolong the life of any engine.

SJ This is the latest classification, and it meets the same minimum requirements in areas of deposit control, resistance to rust, and oxidation as the older classifications. It also allows the engine to run with less friction, which results in better fuel economy. This oil classification was introduced in 1997 and replaces all earlier API categories. The companies are working on the next classification, which will be labeled SK, but it is not ready at this date.

Energy Conserving. There are two other categories of motor oil, energy conserving and energy conserving II. These oils improve fuel economy by reducing internal friction in areas such as pistons, rings, and bearings. There should be a fuel economy increase of from 1.5% to 2% in the energy conserving category and greater than 2.7% in the energy conserving II category.

The API Service Classification System is "open ended" in that it allows the addition of new classifications as they become necessary. When engine design, operating conditions, or lubricant performance requires a new classification, SK will be added. With 20 letters of the alphabet remaining, this system should remain in use indefinitely.

Diesel Engines. For diesel engines, the "C" category contains these classifications:

CA These oils were in use in the 1940s and do not provide sufficient protection from deposits and wear in the engines built today (obsolete).

CB These oils are for engines in moderate-duty service. They contain additives that protect against bearing corrosion and high-temperature deposits (obsolete).

CC Oils with this classification can be used in engines used in moderate to severe duty and for lightly supercharged diesel engines. They are used in many farm tractors and construction equipment (obsolete).

CD These oils are for use in high-speed, heavy-duty, and supercharged engines. These oils are of higher quality than those classified CC, CB, and CA (obsolete).

CD-II This oil is used in two-stroke diesel engines. It reduces wear and deposits in the combustion chamber (obsolete).

CE The lowest combustion or commercial classification in use today. It can be used for diesels made after 1983. This oil gives increased protection to prevent high- and low-temperature deposits, reduce internal parts wear, and cut down on rust or corrosion.

CE-4 An oil suited for any high-speed, heavy-duty engine. Turbocharged engines with on-highway applications use this oil to control oil consumption and reduce piston deposits.

CF   An oil for off-road, indirect-injected, and other diesel engines. It's ideal for those engines that use diesel fuel with over 0.5% by weight of sulfur in the fuel. You can replace the CD oil classification with this classification.

CF-2   This is a replacement classification for the old CD-II category. It is made for two-stroke-cycle engines operated in severe conditions such as dirt, weather, and temperature.

CG-4   The current highest classification being used for four-stroke-cycle engines using less than 0.5% by weight of sulfur in the fuel. This is a replacement for CD, CE, and CF-4 oils.

All engine oil distributed by reputable refiners and manufacturers is labeled to identify its SAE viscosity and its API service classification. Typical container markings are shown in Figures 5.3 and 5.5.

Selecting Correct Oil

Weather and engine mileage are two factors that determine oil selection. As the engine begins to

Job 5A

IDENTIFY TERMS RELATING TO ENGINE OIL

SATISFACTORY PERFORMANCE
A satisfactory performance on this job requires that you do the following:

1. Identify terms and abbreviations relating to engine oil by placing the number of each term or abbreviation in front of the phrase that best describes it.
2. Correctly identify all the terms within 15 minutes.

PERFORMANCE SITUATION

1 SA	6 Detergent
2 Dispersant	7 Viscosity Index Improver
3 SH	8 Additives
4 SAE	9 Inhibitors
5 Viscosity	10 API

_____ Dissolves dirt and sludge in engines
_____ An oil classification that has no performance requirement
_____ American Petroleum Institute
_____ Super Activated
_____ Additives that decrease or prevent oxidation and rust
_____ Chemical compounds added to engine oil
_____ An oil classification meeting current requirements
_____ A measurement of the ability of a liquid to flow
_____ Severe Aeration Eliminator
_____ An Additive that controls viscosity change
_____ Society of Automotive Engineers
_____ An additive that holds dirt in suspension in the oil

Figure 5.5 API oil ring. To provide uniform identification of engine oils, the API has adopted this ring-shaped design (a) for the top of oil containers. The upper half of the ring contains the API classification. The center of the ring contains the SAE viscosity. The lower half of the ring is used for the words "energy conserving." The "starburst" symbol (b) identifies energy conserving II oils suitable for light-duty gasoline engine use (courtesy of Chrysler Corporation).

wear, the clearances increase between the bearings and the bearing journals. The low-viscosity oils no longer stay between these parts. A heavier viscosity oil has to be selected to be sure that the oil stays in place long enough to circulate through the entire engine. This change should be made when the oil pressure drops so low the engine can be damaged.

Weather extremes require viscosity changes, as any owner's manual will indicate. Very hot weather requires a switch from SAE 5W-30 motor oil to SAE 10W-30, 15W-40, or 20W-20. The lighter viscosity oil would not maintain the right oil pressure or lubricate the entire engine. Very cold temperatures require a switch from the hot weather oils to an SAE 5W-30. Engine starting in very cold weather is a critical time. The oil has to flow through the engine quickly. Thick or high-viscosity oils not flow properly and the engine bearings could be damaged from lack of oil before the engine gets warm enough for the oil to flow properly. Any of the multiviscosity oils are excellent choices for most weather temperatures in this climate. This oil flows like a low-viscosity oil when cold and thickens up like a high-viscosity oil when warm. Be careful not to use an oil that is too light in hot weather. Any 5W-20, -30, or -40 multiviscosity oil would not be recommended for high-speed driving in temperatures over 60°F (16°C).

CHECKING ENGINE OIL LEVEL

If there is insufficient oil in an engine, the engine parts may not receive proper lubrication and the oil may overheat. If there is too much oil in an engine, excessive oil consumption may result. An oil level that is too high may also result in the oil being *aerated*. That condition can occur when the rotating crankshaft and the ends of the connecting rods strike the surface of the oil in the oil pan. This action whips up the oil so that air bubbles are mixed with it. Air bubbles and foam in the system provide poor lubrication. An engine lubricating system functions properly only when the correct oil level is maintained.

The level of the oil is easily checked by means of a dipstick located on the engine. Most dipsticks have markings that indicate a safe oil level range, as shown in Figure 5.6. Check oil level only when the engine is not running and when the car is parked in a level position. Do not check oil level immediately after stopping an engine. Time must be allowed for all the oil to drain back into the oil pan. An accurate check can be made only when the engine has been off for at least 3 minutes and the vehicle is on level ground.

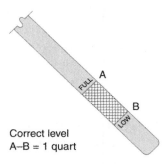

Correct level
A–B = 1 quart

Figure 5.6 Typical dipstick markings. On this dipstick, full and low levels are indicated, with the safe range between these two markings (courtesy of Training Enterprises Company).

The following steps outline a procedure for accurately checking engine oil level. Place the vehicle on level ground, raise the hood, use fender covers then;

1. Locate and remove the engine oil dipstick.
2. Using a clean rag or a paper towel, wipe all traces of oil from the dipstick.
3. Study the markings on the dipstick so that you can determine the location of the safe oil level range.
4. Insert the dipstick into its tube, pushing it down as far as it will go.
5. Remove the dipstick and hold it with the handle up (refer to Figure 5.7).

   Note: If you hold the dipstick so that the end is pointed upward, the oil will run down the dipstick and give you a false reading.

6. Read the oil level shown on the dipstick. Most vehicles require one full quart (0.95 liter) from the "add" mark to the "full" mark on the dipstick.
7. Observe the quality of the oil and look for traces of gasoline or coolant in the oil. Also evaluate the sludge content and overall condition of the oil.

   Note: Gasoline in the oil makes the oil thin and have a fuel smell. It will read above the full mark. Coolant turns the oil to a white milky sludge. Both conditions require further study, but fuel in the oil is an explosion and fire hazard. If you discover this condition, do not let the vehicle be started or driven until the problem is corrected.

8. Insert the dipstick into its tube.

Adjusting the Oil Level

If the oil level is in the safe range, no adjustment is necessary.

If the oil level is below the safe range, add 1 quart of oil to the engine. The oil filler cap is usually located in a valve cover at the top of an engine. Figure 5.8 shows the location of a typical oil filler cap. The use of a funnel minimizes the possibility of spilling oil on the engine. After adding oil, wait a few minutes for it

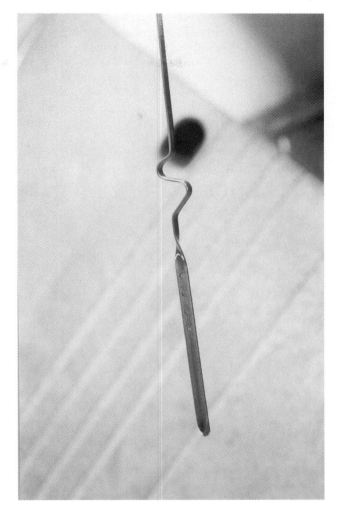

Figure 5.7 Holding engine oil dipstick. The dipstick should be held with the tip downward while checking the oil level (courtesy of Ford Motor Company, Dearborn, MI).

Figure 5.8 Typical engine oil filler caps. On an engine, they are usually located on the left or right side valve cover (courtesy of Training Enterprises Company).

to drain down into the pan. Recheck the oil level. If the level is still below the safe range, add another quart and repeat the oil level check. Never add oil so that the level goes above the safe range.

In most instances you will use a multiviscosity oil of SAE 10W-30 or SAE 10W-40 with an API Service Classification of SJ. Always consult the manufacturer's manual for the specifications for the oil to use in a particular engine.

Synthetic Oil Products and Improvers

Marvel Mystery Oil, STP Oil Treatment, Casite Engine Tune Up, and other similar products are oil additives. These are added to the regular motor oil to help reduce wear, clean the internal parts of the engine, and keep parts from sticking. Additives do not take the place of good motor oil. Oil has to be used with them. An additive can improve the qualities of the oil. Many of these additives stay on the parts and help during cold engine startup before the oil has a chance to circulate properly.

Some products can be added to the gasoline to clean carburetors and injectors. A top-quality motor oil, changed when it should be, is all the

protection you may ever need. Additives should be avoided if they affect the oxygen sensor and cause it to give a false reading to the computer.

Synthetic oils are products that have a different base stock. The oil is built just for use in an automotive engine and performs well in very cold and very hot temperatures. Synthetic oils can improve fuel economy because they reduce friction in the engine. The oil's ability to resist pressure is increased. This makes them ideal for camshaft and lifter protection. The oils have a special feature: they bond to the metal parts in the engine and keep lubricant on these parts even after the engine has stopped. The oil change frequency can be extended, but only to a point where there is not an excessive buildup of soot and water from the burning of fuel. At this point the soot and acids should be drained out with the oil.

Synthetic oils can be added to the regular oil between oil changes with no adverse effects. The major problem with synthetic oils is that they can cost up to five times per quart more than regular oil. Some high-performance vehicles recommend this oil. These oils may be worth the extra cost if internal engine wear is reduced and the vehicle engine life is extended.

Job 5B

CHECK AND ADJUST ENGINE OIL LEVEL

SATISFACTORY PERFORMANCE
A satisfactory performance on this job requires that you do the following:

1. Check the oil level in the engine assigned and adjust the oil level if required.
2. Following the steps in the "Performance Outline," complete the job within 10 minutes.
3. Fill in the blanks under "Information."

PERFORMANCE OUTLINE

1. Remove, clean, and insert the dipstick.
2. Remove the dipstick and determine the oil level.
3. Adjust the oil level if necessary.

INFORMATION

Vehicle identification _____
Reference used _____ Page(s) _____
Oil specified: SAE viscosity _____   API classification _____
Oil level was: Correct _____   Too low _____   Too high _____
Was oil added?   Yes _____   No _____
Oil added: SAE viscosity _____   API classification _____

LESSON 5–2 Proper Vehicle Lifting for Under-The-Vehicle Service

Raising and Supporting a Car

Many of the jobs you will perform require that you work under the car. Most of the time a car is raised by means of a hydraulic floor jack similar to the one shown in Figure 5.9. Whenever a car is raised with a jack, be careful where you place the jack. An improperly placed jack may let the car fall or may damage parts under the car.

The proper placement of a jack depends on whether the car is driven by the front or rear wheels and on the type of frame and suspension systems on the car. Because of the many different drive

Figure 5.9 A hydraulic floor jack similar to those used in most auto shops (courtesy of Hein-Werner Corporation).

systems, frames, and suspension systems in use, check the car maker's manual before you attempt to raise a car with a jack, Figures 5.10 and 5.11 are typical of the drawings found in service manuals. They show the areas where it is safe to place a jack. Some cars with front wheel drive require that a jack be used in special locations. Figures 5.12 through 5.17 show some of those locations.

> **!** **Safety Message:** Always use jack stands to hold up the vehicle after lifting it with a floor or bumper jack. A hydraulic jack can fail. The vehicle would immediately drop.

When using a jack always remember that it is made to raise cars, not to support them. Work-

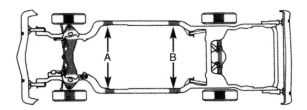

Figure 5.10 Safe frame jacking points. Drawing of a typical frame of a rear wheel drive car showing locations where it is safe to place a jack or car stands (courtesy of Chevrolet Motor Division, General Motors Corporation).

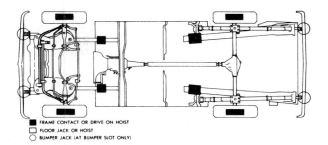

Figure 5.11 Unit body safe jacking points. Typical lifting and support locations on a rear wheel drive car of unit body design. Because a separate frame is not used, the jacks and car stands must by placed under reinforced areas of the floor pan or underbody (courtesy of Chrysler Corporation).

ing on a car that is held off the floor by a jack is very dangerous, because the car can easily slip off the jack. Any time you raise a car, even for a few minutes, always place *car stands,* or *jack stands,* under the car to support its weight. Typical car stands are shown in Figure 5.17. The drawings in the repair manual will also show where it is safe to place those stands (refer to Figures 5.10 and 5.11).

Although there are many different areas under a car where car stands may be positioned, there are only two ways a car can be supported. One is by the frame, or underbody, and the other is by the suspension systems. When a car is supported by the frame, or underbody, the wheels are free to drop down to the limits of their suspension systems. When a car is supported by its suspension systems, the wheels are held up in the approximate position they are in when the car is on the floor. The method used depends on the particular job to be done. The proper methods of raising and supporting a car are very important to your safety.

On many cars, the fuel tank is attached to the frame or underbody just ahead of the rear bumper. In that position, it may be damaged while using a jack to raise or lower the car. When both the front and the rear wheels of a car of that design must be raised from the floor, the rear of the car should be raised and supported first. The front of the car can then be raised. When the car is lowered to the floor, the front of the car should be lowered before the rear of the car is lowered. Those procedures minimize the possibility of fuel tank damage and the dangers of fuel leakage.

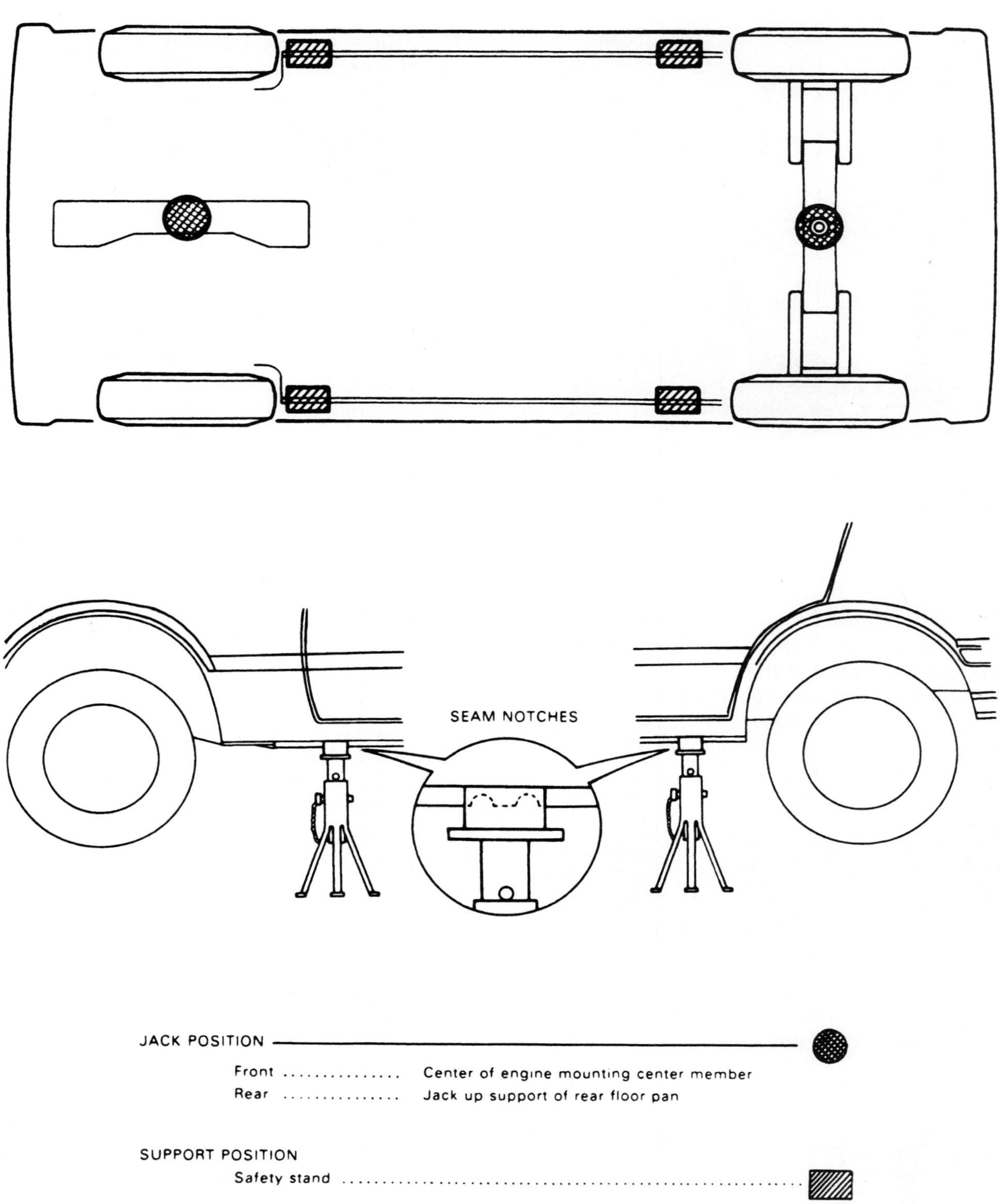

SEAM NOTCHES

JACK POSITION ─── ⬤

      Front ....   Center of engine mounting center member

      Rear ....   Jack up support of rear floor pan

SUPPORT POSITION

      Safety stand .... ▨

Figure 5.12 Jack and support positions specified for one particular front wheel drive car (courtesy of Chevrolet Motor Division, General Motors Corporation).

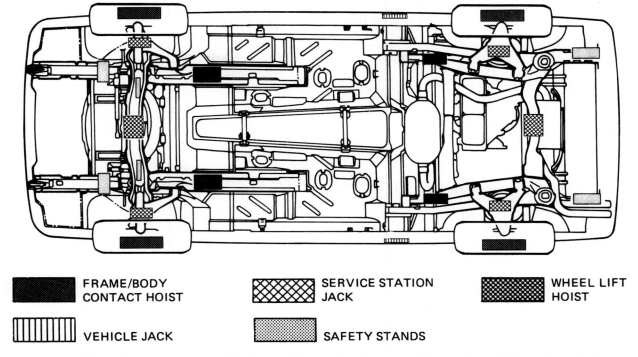

FRAME/BODY
CONTACT HOIST

SERVICE STATION
JACK

WHEEL LIFT
HOIST

VEHICLE JACK

SAFETY STANDS

Figure 5.13 Lifting and support points specified for a mid-engined car (courtesy of Pontiac Motor Division, General Motors Corporation).

Safety

There is always a risk involved when working under a raised vehicle. Never take a chance if you feel that a lift or jack is not placed correctly to allow work under the vehicle. Take time and reset the equipment. Always use safety glasses.

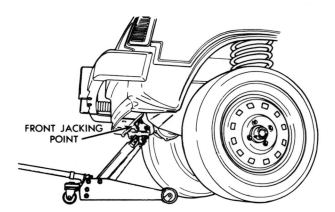

FRONT JACKING
POINT

Figure 5.14 Floor jack position. On some cars, the jack should be placed under a reinforced section of the underbody behind the front bumper (courtesy of Chrysler Corporation).

Raising a Car with a Lift

Many shops are equipped with hydraulic or electric lifts that raise and support cars. Most of those lifts are capable of raising a car high enough so that a technician can stand while working under the car. All of those lifts incorporate some type of safety system in their construction so that a car cannot drop suddenly in case of equipment failure. Some of those safety devices are automatic. Others must be manually set. Before you attempt to use a lift, be sure you understand the operation of its safety device.

Because there is such a variety of lifts in use, it is beyond the scope of this book to provide specific operating instructions for all of them. Lift manufacturers provide instruction manuals for the operation of each of the designs they make. Read the manual provided with the lift you have available. Lacking the manual, you should receive instructions from someone who is familiar with the operation of the lift you intend to use. Although the following steps (pp. 117–130) do not apply to the operation of some lifts, they outline procedures that are common to most lifts.

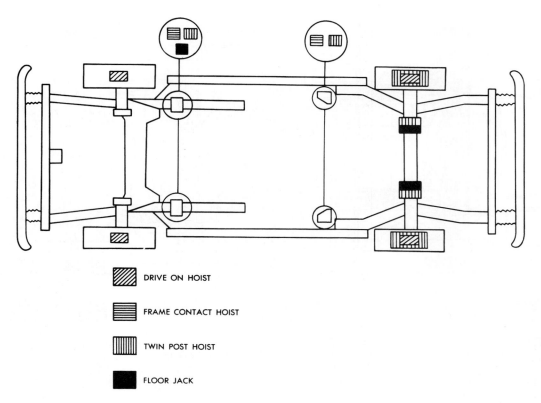

Figure 5.15   Lifting and jacking locations for one particular front wheel drive car (courtesy of Chrysler Corporation).

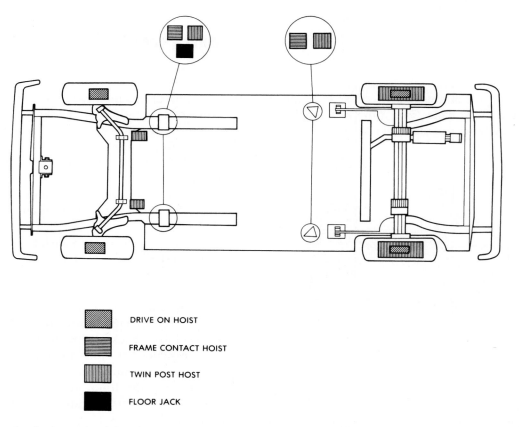

Figure 5.16   Chrysler front wheel drive lifting. On this front wheel drive car, a floor jack is not recommended for use at the rear (courtesy of Chrysler Corporation).

Figure 5.17   A pair of adjustable car stands. Always use car stands, often called jack stands and safety stands, to support a car after you raise it with a jack (courtesy of Hein-Werner Corporation).

<table>
<tr><td>

RAISING A REAR WHEEL DRIVE CAR AND SUPPORTING IT BY THE FRAME OR UNDERBODY

</td><td>

The steps that follow outline a typical procedure for raising a rear wheel drive car with a jack and supporting it with car stands placed under the frame or underbody. Check the manual for the car on which you are working for the correct lifting and support points.

</td></tr>
</table>

Rear
1. Roll a jack under the rear of the car. Raise the jack slightly and adjust its position so that it is centered under the rear axle housing (see Figure 5.18 and position A and C in Figures 5.19 and 5.20).
2. Operate the jack to raise the car until the wheels are clear of the floor by at least 10 in. (25 cm).
3. Place the car stands under the frame side rails or underbody reinforcements. (See positions B and D in Figures 5.19 and 5.20 and refer to Figure 5.13.) Raise the car stands as high as possible.
4. Lower the jack so that the car is supported by the stands.
5. Remove the jack.

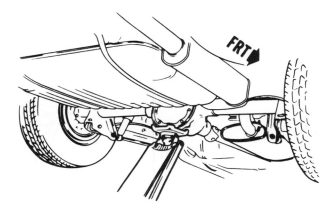

Figure 5.18   A floor jack positioned under the center of the rear axle or differential housing (courtesy of Chevrolet Motor Division, General Motors Corporation).

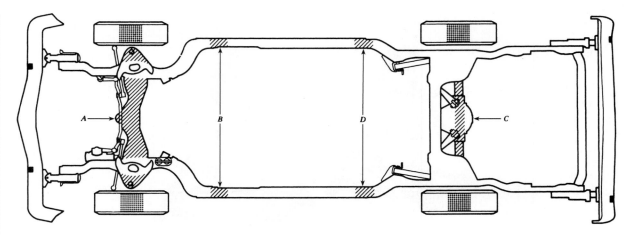

Figure 5.19 Drawing of a typical frame used on a rear wheel drive car. Note the locations for raising the car with a jack (A and C) and positions where car stands should be placed (B and D) for supporting the car by the frame (courtesy of Chevrolet Motor Division, General Motors Corporation).

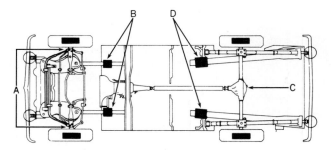

Figure 5.20 Drawing showing the reinforced areas on the underbody of a rear wheel drive car of unit body construction. Note the locations for raising the car with a jack (A and C) and the positions where car stands should be placed (B and D) for supporting the car by the underbody (courtesy of Chrysler Corporation).

Front 1. Roll a jack under the front of the car. Raise the jack slightly, and adjust its position so that it is centered under the front crossmember. (See Figure 5.21 and position A in Figure 5.22.)

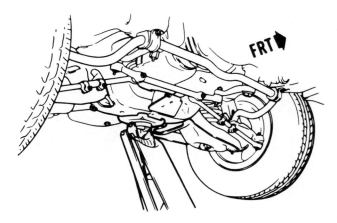

Figure 5.21 Raising the front of a rear wheel drive car by using a jack centered under the front crossmember (courtesy of Chevrolet Motor Division, General Motors Corporation).

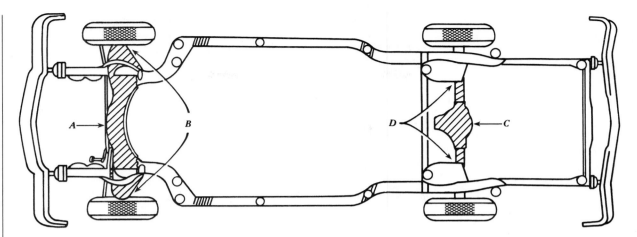

Figure 5.22   Position of car stands for a typical frame used on a rear wheel drive car. Shown are the locations for raising a car with a jack (A and C) and positions where car stands should be placed (B and D) for supporting the car by the suspension systems (courtesy of Chevrolet Motor Division, General Motors Corporation).

Note: On some cars, it is recommended that the front of the car be raised and supported one side at a time by positioning the jack under the outer ends of the lower controls arms. (See position A in Figure 5.20.)

2. Operate the jack to raise the car until the wheels are clear of the floor by about 6 in. (15 cm).

Note: If the car is raised one side at a time, each wheel should be raised about 8 in. (20 cm).

3. Place the car stands under the frame side rails or underbody reinforcements. (See position B in Figures 5.19 and 5.26 and refer to Figure 5.13.) Raise the car stands as high as possible.

4. Lower the jack so that the car is supported by the stands.

5. Remove the jack.

Job 5C

RAISE A REAR WHEEL DRIVE CAR AND SUPPORT IT BY THE FRAME OR UNDERBODY

SATISFACTORY PERFORMANCE

A satisfactory performance on this job requires that you do the following:

1. Using a floor jack, raise a rear wheel drive car from the floor and support it with car stands placed under the frame or underbody.
2. Following the steps in the "Performance Outline" and the recommendations of the car manufacturer regarding jack and car stand positioning, complete the job within 15 minutes.
3. Fill in the blanks under "Information."

PERFORMANCE OUTLINE

1. Raise the rear of the car.
2. Support the rear of the car with car stands.
3. Raise the front of the car.
4. Support the front of the car with car stands.
5. Lower the car to the floor.

INFORMATION

Vehicle identification_____
Reference used _____ Page(s) _____

Job 5D

RAISE A REAR WHEEL DRIVE CAR AND SUPPORT IT BY THE SUSPENSION SYSTEMS

SATISFACTORY PERFORMANCE

A satisfactory performance on this job requires that you do the following:

1. Using a floor jack, raise a rear wheel drive car from the floor and support it with car stands placed under the suspension systems.
2. Following the steps in the "Performance Outline" and the recommendations of the car manufacturer regarding jack and car stand placement, complete the job within 15 minutes.
3. Fill in the blanks under "Information."

PERFORMANCE OUTLINE

1. Raise the rear of the car.
2. Support the rear of the car with car stands.
3. Raise the front of the car.
4. Support the front of the car with car stands.
5. Lower the car to the floor.

INFORMATION

Vehicle identification_____

Reference used _____ Page(s) _____

RAISING A REAR WHEEL DRIVE CAR AND SUPPORTING IT BY THE SUSPENSION SYSTEM	The following steps outline a procedure for raising a rear wheel drive car with a jack and supporting it with car stands placed under the suspension systems. Be sure to consult an appropriate manual for the correct lifting and support points for the car on which you are working.

Rear
1. Roll a jack under the rear of the car. Raise the jack slightly, and adjust its position so that it is centered under the rear axle housing. (Refer to Figure 5.18 and see position C in Figures 5.22 and 5.23.)
2. Operate the jack to raise the car until the wheels are clear of the floor by at least 6 in. (15 cm).
3. Place car stands under the rear axle housing as close as possible to the wheels. (See Figure 5.24 and see positions D in Figures 5.22 and 5.23.) Raise the stands as close as possible to the axle housing.

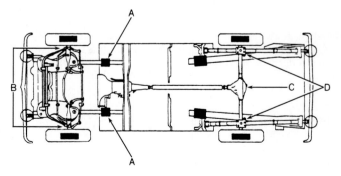

Figure 5.23 Car stand positions. Drawing of the underbody of a rear wheel drive car of unit body construction. Note the locations for raising the car with a jack (A and C) and the positions where car stands should be placed (B and D) for supporting the car by the suspension systems (courtesy of Chrysler Corporation).

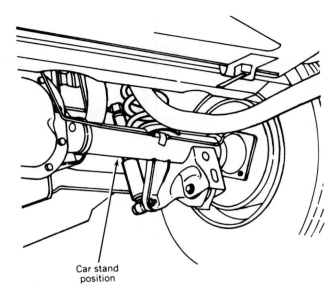

Car stand
position

Figure 5.24   Rear axle car stand positions. Car stands may be placed under the rear axle housing in the area shown (courtesy of Ford Motor Company, Dearborn, MI).

4. Lower the jack so that the car is supported by the stands.
5. Remove the jack.

Front 1. Roll a jack under the front of the car. Raise the jack slightly, and adjust its position so that it is centered under the front crossmember. (Refer to Figure 5.21 and see position A on Figure 5.22.)

   Note: On some cars, it is recommended that the front of the car be raised and supported one side at a time. At times, this can be done by placing the jack under the frame side rails or underbody reinforcements. (See positions B in Figure 5.23.)

2. Operate the jack to raise the car until the wheels are clear of the floor by about 6 in. (15 cm).
3. Place car stands under the lower control arms as close as possible to the wheels. (See Figure 5.25 and positions B in Figures 5.22 and 5.23.) Raise the car stands as close as possible to the lower control arms.
4. Lower the jack so that the car is supported by the stands.
5. Remove the jack.

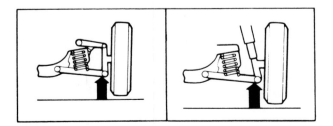

Figure 5.25   Rear wheel drive car stand positions. When positioning car stands under the lower control arms of rear wheel drive cars, place them as close as possible to the wheels (courtesy of Ford Motor Company, Dearborn, MI).

Job 5E

RAISE AND SUPPORT A FRONT WHEEL DRIVE CAR

SATISFACTORY PERFORMANCE
A satisfactory performance on this job requires that you do the following:

1. Using a floor jack, raise a front wheel drive car from the floor and support it with car stands.
2. Following the steps in the "Performance Outline" and the recommendations of the car manufacturer regarding jack and car stand positioning, complete the job within 15 minutes.
3. Fill in the blanks under "Information."

PERFORMANCE OUTLINE

1. Raise the rear of the car.
2. Support the rear of the car with car stands.
3. Raise the front of the car.
4. Support the front of the car with car stands.
5. Lower the car to the floor.

INFORMATION

Vehicle identification_____

Reference used _____ Page(s) _____

<table>
<tr><td rowspan="4" style="background:black;color:white;">**RAISING AND SUPPORTING A FRONT WHEEL DRIVE CAR**</td><td>Front wheel drive cars are found with many different underbody designs and are equipped with many different types of suspension and drive systems. Because of this, many different precautions and procedures are specified to raise and support these cars safely. The front and the rear of some front wheel drive cars can be raised by a jack placed under a central location on the underbody or under a bumper (refer to Figures 5.13 and 5.14). As shown in Figure 5.22, some cars must be raised one side at a time by a jack positioned under certain reinforced areas at the sides of the underbody. While most car makers caution against placing a jack under the suspension arms of front wheel drive cars, the reinforced brackets used to mount the suspension arms can often be used as jacking points (see Figure 5.26).</td></tr>
</table>

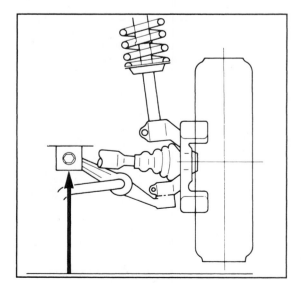

Figure 5.26   Control arm bracket position. While most manufacturers advise against using a jack under the control arms of front wheel drive cars, a control arm bracket often can be used as a lifting point (courtesy of Ford Motor Company, Dearborn, MI).

The steps that follow outline a typical procedure for raising a front wheel drive car with a jack and supporting it with car stands. You should consult an appropriate manual for the correct lifting and support points for the car on which you are working:

1. Position a jack under the lifting points specified by the car manufacturer. (Refer to Figures 5.13, 5.14, 5.15, 5.22, and 5.23.)
2. Operate the jack to raise the car until the wheels are clear of the floor by at least 6 in. (15 cm).
3. Place the car stand(s) under the specified support point(s). Raise the stand(s) as high as possible.
4. Lower the jack so that the car is supported by the stand(s).
5. Remove the jack.
6. Repeat steps 1 through 5 at other locations as required.

FRAME CONTACT LIFTS

A typical frame contact lift is shown in Figure 5.27. They are usually made with adjustable arms and contact pads. This allows the pads to be positioned to contact the correct lifting points on any car. As you learned when raising a car with a jack, the correct lifting points for any car can be found in the service manual for that car. Figure 5.28 shows

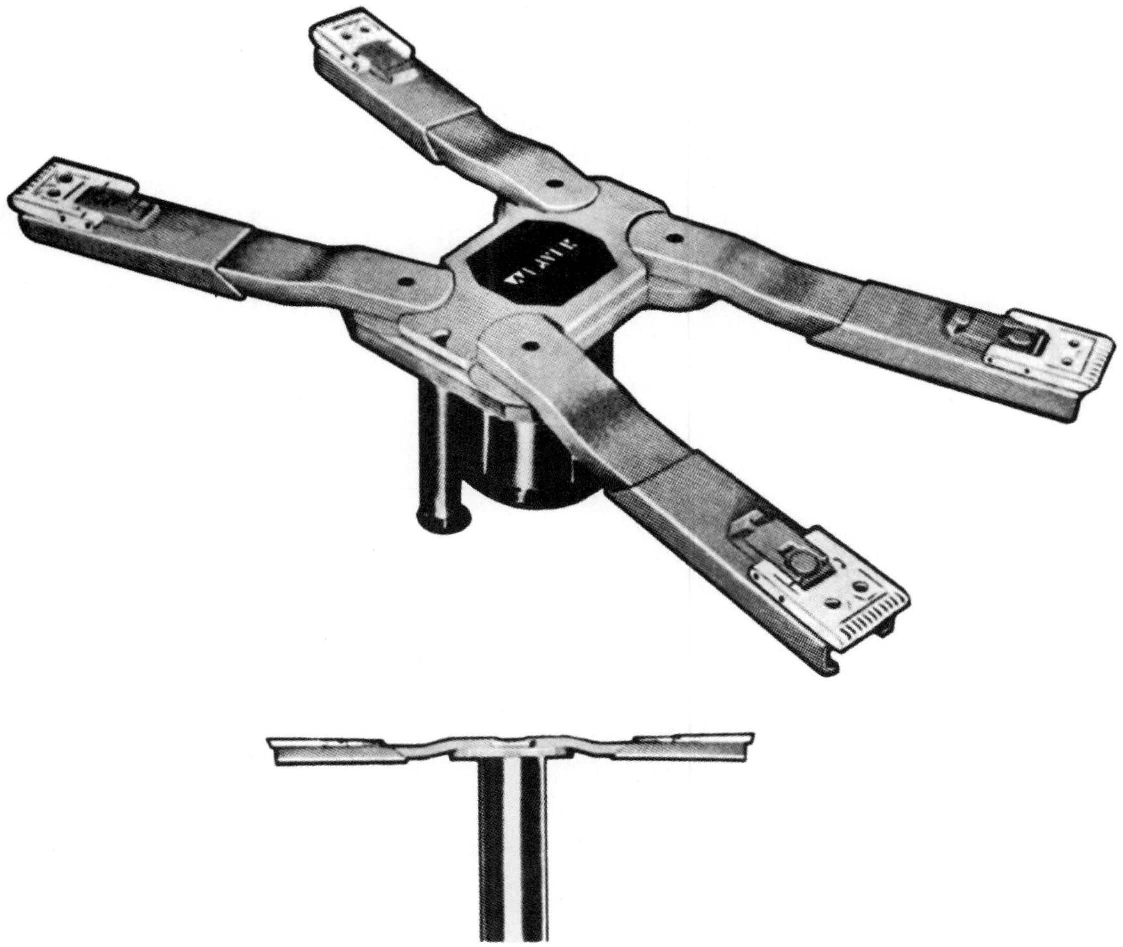

Figure 5.27 Frame contact lift. The arms are adjustable in both length and angle, and the pads or adapters at the ends of the arms are adjustable for different heights (courtesy of Weaver-Paris Div. Dura Corp.).

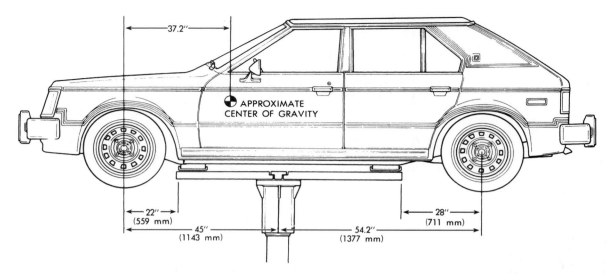

Figure 5.28 Lifting position points specified by one manufacturer. In addition to using the correct lifting points, it is very important to position the car so that its center of gravity is as close as possible to the center posts of the lift (courtesy of Chrysler Corporation).

the location of the lifting points specified by one manufacturer. The following steps outline a typical procedure for the operation of a frame contact lift:

Preparation

1. Check that the lift is all the way down and that the arms and pads will not come into contact with the underbody of a car driven over the lift. Lower the lift and move these parts if necessary.
2. Slowly drive the car over the lift so that the car is centered. Position the car so that the wheels are in place in the trough or against the stops on the floor. Turn off the engine, leave the parking brake off, and place the shift lever in the NEUTRAL position.
3. Check to see that the car is centered over (or between) the lift posts. Reposition the car if necessary.
4. Consult an appropriate manual to determine the correct lifting points.
5. Adjust the positions of the arms and pads so that they are directly under the lifting points (see Figures 5.29 and 5.30).

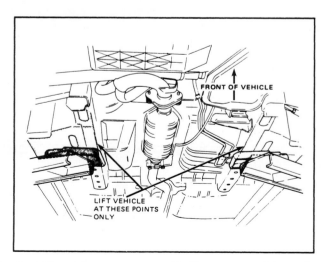

Figure 5.29 Front lift pad contact areas specified by one manufacturer (courtesy of Ford Motor Company, Dearborn, MI).

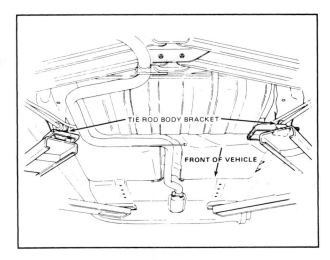

Figure 5.30 Rear lift pad positions. On this particular car, the manufacturer specified that the rear lift pads be placed beneath the rear tie rod brackets (courtesy of Ford Motor Company, Dearborn, MI).

Note: When positioning the pads and arms, try to keep the approximate center of gravity of the car over the post(s). (Refer to Figure 5.28.)

The center-of-gravity spot on a vehicle is the place where the vehicle weight is balanced between the front and the rear.

Lifting
1. Carefully operate the lift controls so that the lift rises from the floor. Stop the lift when the pads contact the underbody.
2. Check the position of each pad so you are sure that they are in firm contact with the correct lifting areas (see Figures 5.31 and 5.32).
   Note: The pads should extend beyond the sides of the frame or underbody supporting structure, as shown in Figure 5.33.
3. Raise the car until the tires are clear of the floor by about 1 in. (25 mm). By pushing on the bumpers and fenders, try to push the car off the lift.
   Note: It is better to have the car slip off the lift now, when there is little danger of damage or injury, than to have it slip off when raised several feet.
4. If the car is secure on the lift, continue to raise the car to the desired height.
5. Set and lock any manually operated safety devices that may be present.

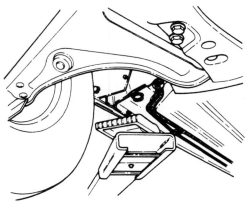

Figure 5.31 The pad of a frame contact lift positioned under the reinforced edge of a floor pan (courtesy of Chevrolet Motor Division, General Motors Corporation).

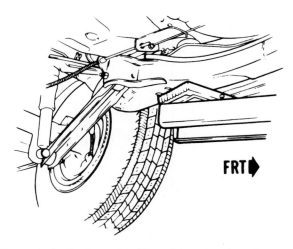

FRT ▶

Figure 5.32 The pad of a frame contact lift positioned under a frame siderail (courtesy of Chevrolet Motor Division, General Motors Corporation).

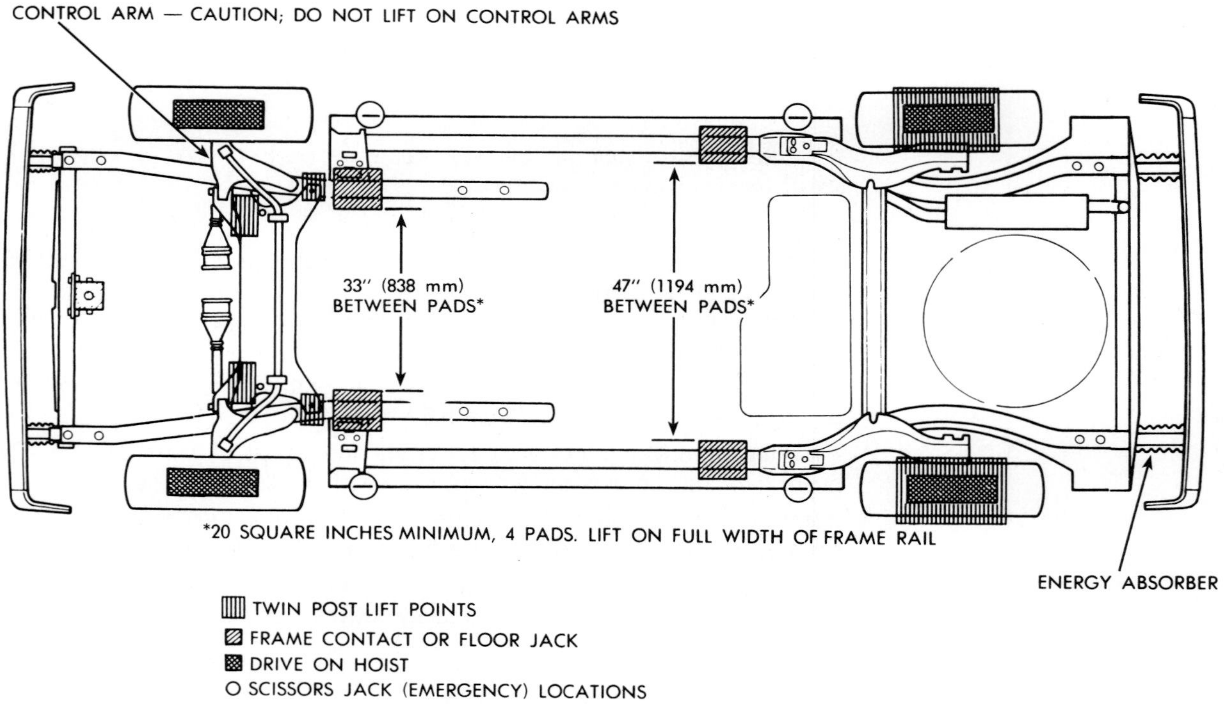

CONTROL ARM — CAUTION; DO NOT LIFT ON CONTROL ARMS

33" (838 mm) BETWEEN PADS*

47" (1194 mm) BETWEEN PADS*

*20 SQUARE INCHES MINIMUM, 4 PADS. LIFT ON FULL WIDTH OF FRAME RAIL

ENERGY ABSORBER

▦ TWIN POST LIFT POINTS
▨ FRAME CONTACT OR FLOOR JACK
▧ DRIVE ON HOIST
O SCISSORS JACK (EMERGENCY) LOCATIONS

Figure 5.33 Lift and support locations specified by one manufacturer. Note that the lift pads must be positioned so that they contact the full width of the frame rails or underbody reinforcement (courtesy of Chrysler Corporation).

Lowering

1. Clear the area under the car of any tools, equipment, wires, and hoses.
2. Release the safety devices.
3. Carefully operate the controls so that the car is lowered to the floor.
4. Adjust the position of the arms and pads under the car so that the car may be driven off the lift.

Suspension contact lifts have posts or heads that can be adjusted so that a car is lifted by the front lower control arms and the rear axle or axle housing. Figures 5.34 and 5.35 show these lifting points. Suspension contact lifts can be used to raise most rear wheel drive cars. Because of differences in drive and suspension systems, most car makers state that suspension contact lifts should not be used to raise cars with front wheel drive. The following steps outline a typical procedure for the operation of a suspension contact lift.

Preparation

1. Check that the lift is all the way down and that the heads will not come into contact with the suspension systems or the underbody of a car driven over the lift. Lower the lift and move those parts if necessary.

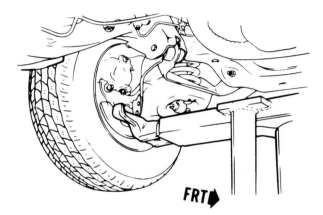

FRT

Figure 5.34 Suspension contact lift areas. A correctly positioned front lift head. Note that the head is in contact with the outer end of the lower control arm (courtesy of Chevrolet Motor Division, General Motors Corporation).

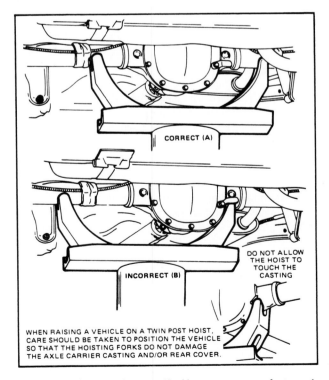

CORRECT (A)

INCORRECT (B)

DO NOT ALLOW THE HOIST TO TOUCH THE CASTING

WHEN RAISING A VEHICLE ON A TWIN POST HOIST, CARE SHOULD BE TAKEN TO POSITION THE VEHICLE SO THAT THE HOISTING FORKS DO NOT DAMAGE THE AXLE CARRIER CASTING AND/OR REAR COVER.

Figure 5.35 Rear lift head positioning specified by one car manufacturer (courtesy of Ford Motor Company, Dearborn, MI).

2. Slowly drive the car over the lift so that the car is centered. Position the car so that the wheels are in the troughs or against the stops on the floor. Turn off the engine, leave the parking brake off, and place the shift selector lever in the NEUTRAL position.
3. Check to see that the car is centered over the heads. Reposition the car if necessary.
4. Consult an appropriate manual to determine the correct lifting points.
5. Adjust the position of the heads so that they are directly under the lifting points.

Lifting

1. Carefully operate the lift controls so that the lift rises from the floor. Stop the lift when the heads contact the lower control arms and the rear axle housing.
2. Check the position of the heads to be sure that they are in firm contact and in the proper position. (Refer to Figures 5.34 and 5.35.)
3. Raise the car until the tires are clear of the floor by about 1 in. (25 mm). By pushing on the bumpers and fenders, try to push the car off the lift.

    Note: It is better to have the car slip off the lift now, when there is little danger of damage or injury, than to have it slip off when raised several feet.

4. If the car is secure on the lift, continue to raise the car to the desired height.
5. Set and lock any manually operated safety devices.

Lowering

1. Clear the area under the car of any tools, equipment, wires, and hoses.
2. Release the safety devices.
3. Carefully operate the controls to lower the car to the floor.
4. Adjust the position of the heads so that the car may be driven off the lift.

Job 5F

RAISE AND SUPPORT A CAR WITH A FRAME CONTACT LIFT

SATISFACTORY PERFORMANCE

A satisfactory performance on this job requires that you do the following:

1. Using a frame contact lift, raise and support the car assigned.
2. Following the steps in the "Performance Outline," the lift manufacturer's operating instructions, and the car maker's specifications regarding lifting points, complete the job within 15 minutes.
3. Fill in the blanks under "Information."

PERFORMANCE OUTLINE

1. Align the car on the lift and adjust the lift so that the pads will contact the lifting points and so that the car's approximate center of gravity is over the post(s).
2. Raise the car slightly and test the security of the points of contact.
3. Raise the car and engage the safety devices.
4. Lower the car to the floor and clear the lift so that the car can be removed.

INFORMATION

Vehicle identification_____
Lift identification and type _____
Reference used _____ Page(s) _____

Job 5G

RAISE AND SUPPORT A CAR WITH A SUSPENSION CONTACT LIFT

SATISFACTORY PERFORMANCE

A satisfactory performance on this job requires that you do the following:

1. Using a suspension contact lift, raise and support the car assigned.
2. Following the steps in the "Performance Outline," the lift manufacturer's operating instructions, and the car maker's specifications regarding lifting points, complete the job within 15 minutes.
3. Fill in the blanks under "Information."

PERFORMANCE OUTLINE

1. Align the car on the lift and adjust the leads so that they will contact the lifting points.
2. Raise the car slightly and test the security of the points of contact.
3. Raise the car and engage the safety devices.
4. Lower the car to the floor and clear the lift so that the car can be removed.

INFORMATION

Vehicle identification_____
Lift identification and type _____
Reference used _____ Page(s) _____

LESSON 5-3 Engine Oil and Engine Filter Changing
Changing Engine Oil

As with chassis lubrication, automobile manufacturers specify the intervals at which the engine oil in their cars should be changed. Oil change intervals are found in the appropriate service manuals and in the owner's manuals furnished with each car. Although changing engine oil is an easy task, it could result in extensive engine damage if it is improperly performed.

Safety. In order to change the oil and filter, the vehicle is raised on a lift or with a jack. Be sure to review the correct lifting techniques, presented in the previous lesson. Always wear safety glasses when working under a vehicle. If you are using a floor jack, place jack stands under the vehicle. Check to be sure the safety catches on the lift are working and lock into place. Exposure to used motor oil has been proven to cause skin cancer. Avoid any skin contact with used oil when removing the filter and engine oil. Dispose of the filter and oil properly by recycling both.

Oil Change Frequency. Most manufacturers prefer the shortest oil change interval the customer will accept. An oil and filter change every 3000 miles is a very good plan. Most of the life in the oil additives has been used up and the oil is starting to be saturated with corrosive chemicals from the burning of the fuel. Some vehicles have information centers built into the car that indicate by percentage how much oil life remains. These centers even flash a warning that an oil change should be considered within a certain number of miles. A final warning is given when this mileage has been reached. This leaves no doubt as to when manufacturers recommend an oil and filter change. They determine when the messages will be given to the driver.

Another method is to consult with the customer and decide on an oil change interval based on miles driven and driving conditions. At the time the oil is changed, the technician places a sticker with the oil change information where the driver can see it. When this mileage is reached, the driver comes in for the next oil and filter change. Here are some factors that determine the change interval:

1. The type of miles driven, such as long trip or city.

2. The season, which determines viscosity and weight of the oil.
3. Multiviscosity or single viscosity.
4. Oil quality and brand.
5. Whether to change the filter each time or every other time.
6. Conditions the vehicle will be working in, such as dust, off the road, or high humidity.

Oil Changing Procedures

Changing the engine oil requires removing the drain plug at the bottom of the oil pan. The location of a drain plug is shown in Figure 5.36. The oil pan drain plug is removed and installed many times during the life of an engine. Thus the plug, its gasket, and the threaded hole in the oil pan may be worn or damaged by improper service procedures. If the damage to those parts allows oil to leak from the oil pan, the engine can be ruined by lack of lubrication.

To avoid the possibility of causing damage and to avoid installing parts that may have been damaged in the past take the following precautions:

1. Remove the drain plug with a socket wrench or a box wrench of the proper size (see Figure 5.37). The use of these tools minimizes the possibility of "rounding-off" the corners of the hex-shaped top of the plug.

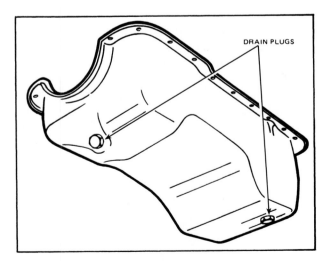

Figure 5.36 Oil pan drain plug locations. Most cars have but one drain plug in the engine oil pan, but some engines have a "dual sump," which requires that the oil be drained from two locations (courtesy of Ford Motor Company, Dearborn, MI).

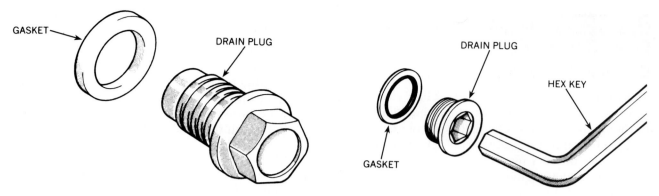

Figure 5.37   Pan plugs. While most oil pan drain plugs can be turned with a box wrench or a socket wrench, some plugs require the use of a hex key or Allen wrench (courtesy of Chrysler Corporation).

2. After the plug is removed, clean and examine the threads on the plug. If they appear worn, rounded, or contain metal slivers, replace the plug with a new one.

3. Clean and examine the gasket. If the gasket is crushed, cracked, or broken, replace it with a new one.

4. Examine the threads in the oil pan drain hole by carefully threading the plug approximately halfway into the hole. The plug should not feel loose in the hole and should resist any effort to pull it straight out. If the plug "wobbles" in the threads, or can be pulled out, repeat the test with a new plug. If the fit is improved with a new plug, discard the old plug. If the fit is not improved when tested with a new plug, an oversize replacement plug should be installed. An oversize replacement plug, shown in Figure 5.38, is made of hardened steel and will recut the worn threads in the drain hole as it is installed.

5. When installing the drain plug, start the plug by hand and thread it in place with your fingers to avoid cross-threading.

6. Tighten the plug carefully. A box wrench or a socket wrench should again be used. The plug should not be tightened with a great amount of force, but should be "snugged-up" just tight enough to compress the gasket slightly. One method you can use to avoid overtightening is to hold the wrench about 6 inches (15 cm) away from the plug. This will reduce the amount of leverage you can apply.

Changing the Oil Filter

All automobile engines in current production use a "full-flow" oil filtration system. As shown in Figure 5.39 all the oil that is pumped from the oil pan must flow through a filter before lubricating the internal parts of the engine. Because it is the job of the filter to trap dirt and other particles that contaminate the engine oil, the filter must be changed at regular intervals.

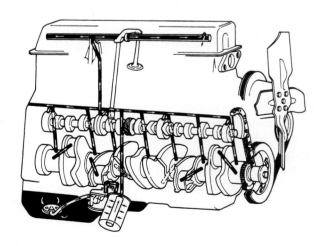

Figure 5.39   Typical engine lubrication system. Note that all the oil flows through the oil filter before it lubricates the engine parts (courtesy of American Motors).

Figure 5.38   Oversize drain plug. A plug of this type should be used when the threads in the oil pan drain hole are worn or stripped (courtesy of Dorman Products, Inc.).

OIL CHANGE PROCEDURE

Ideally, engine oil should be changed when it is hot. If the oil is cold, it is advisable to run the engine for about 5 minutes before draining the oil. You should consult an appropriate manual for the specifications and the amount of new oil to be installed. The following steps outline a typical procedure:

1. Be sure to use safety glasses and avoid skin contact with the used oil.
2. Locate the drain plug at the bottom of the pan.
3. Raise and support the vehicle. The location of the drain plug in the pan will determine how a vehicle will be raised when using floor jacks. The pan must be angled so that all the oil will drain out when the plug is removed.
4. Place a drain pan under the engine.
5. Locate the drain plug on the bottom of the oil pan.
6. Position a drain pan under the plug and remove the plug.

   Note: Hot engine oil can cause severe burns. When draining hot oil it is advisable to remove the plug with a socket on an extension, or to protect your hand with a folded wiper or rag.

7. Clean and examine the plug and the gasket. Replace any worn or damaged parts.
8. Examine the drain hole in the oil pain. Fit a new or oversize plug if required.
9. Carefully install the drain plug, making sure that the gasket is in place.

   Note: Thread the plug in by hand to avoid cross-threading.

> **!** ***Safety Message:*** **Used motor oil can cause skin cancer. Avoid daily contact, and use rubber gloves and clean up immediately when used oil is spilled on you.**

10. Use a six-point box wrench or a six-point socket wrench to place pressure on the drain plug. Finish by using a torque wrench to place the correct amount of pressure or torque on the plug. This will prevent getting the plug too tight or leaving it too loose.
11. Remove the drain pan from under the engine and pour the old oil into a waste oil receptacle or other suitable container for disposal. Clean the drain pan. Remember to recycle the used motor oil.
12. If the filter is not to be changed, continue on to step 13. If it is, go to "Changing the Oil Filter" for filter change directions.
13. Lower the car to the floor.
14. Fill the crankcase with the correct amount and type of oil specified by the car manufacturer.
15. Start the engine and allow it to run at idle speed. Check to see that the oil pressure warning light goes out or that the oil pressure gauge indicates that the engine has sufficient oil pressure.
16. Check the drain plug and the floor under the car for any evidence of leakage. Correct any leaks found.
17. Turn off the engine. After allowing a few minutes for the oil to drain back into the oil pan, check the oil level. Correct the oil level if necessary.

As with chassis lubrication and engine oil changes, the manufacturer of the vehicle specifies those intervals. In a few instances, it is recommended that the filter be replaced during every other oil change. About 1 pint (0.47 1) of old oil remains in the filter when the oil is changed. That old oil mixes with the new oil if the filter is not changed at the same time. Because of this mixing, most manufacturers recommend that the filter be changed with each oil change.

Job 5H

CHANGE ENGINE OIL
SATISFACTORY PERFORMANCE
A satisfactory performance on this job requires that you do the following:

1. Change the engine oil of the car assigned.
2. Following the steps in the "Performance Outline" and the specifications of the car manufacturer, complete the job within 30 minutes.
3. Fill in the blanks under "Information."

PERFORMANCE OUTLINE

1. Raise and support the car.
2. Drain the oil into a suitable container.
3. Examine the plug, the gasket, and the drain hole. Replace parts as required.
4. Install the plug.
5. Discard the waste oil and clean the drain pan.
6. Lower the car to the floor.
7. Fill the crankcase with the amount and type of oil specified by the car manufacturer.
8. Check for leaks and correct oil level.

INFORMATION

Vehicle identification_____
Reference used _____ Page(s) _____
Oil used: Amount _____ quarts
      SAE viscosity _____ API classification _____

| OIL FILTER REPLACEMENT | Most manufacturers use a disposable screw-on filter of the type shown in Figure 5.40. The filter mounts on the engine block as shown in Figures 5.41 and 5.42. You will need a special *oil filter wrench* similar to those shown in Figures 5.43 and 5.44 to loosen the filter. You should consult an appropriate manual for the specific instructions that may be necessary for the car on which you are working. The steps that follow (on pages 134–137) outline a typical procedure. |

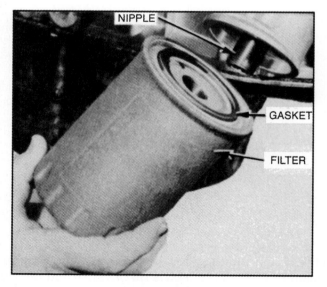

Figure 5.40 A disposable oil filter: Note that the filter fits on a threaded nipple on the engine block and that the gasket is cemented to the filter (courtesy of Buick Motor Division, General Motors Corporation).

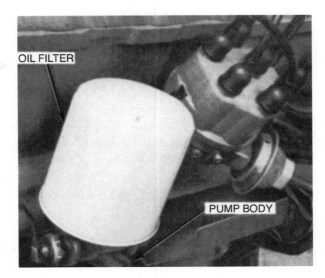

Figure 5.41 An oil filter mounted on the side of a six-cylinder engine (courtesy of Chrysler Corporation).

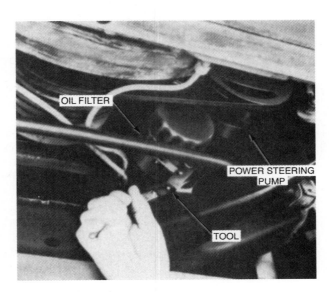

Figure 5.42 Filter wrench removing oil filter. An oil filter mounted under an eight-cylinder engine (courtesy of Chrysler Corporation).

Figure 5.43 Band and handle oil filter wrench. A universal oil filter wrench. The handle not only provides leverage, but tightens the band around the filter (courtesy of KD Tools, Lancaster, PA 17604).

Figure 5.44 3/8″ ratchet and filter wrench. A square drive filter wrench designed for hard-to-reach filters. This wrench can be turned with a 3/8″ ratchet and extension (courtesy of KD Tools, Lancaster, PA 17604).

1. Raise and support the car.

   Note: The vehicle may already be raised if the oil is being changed along with the filter.

2. Position an oil drain pan beneath the filter.

3. Using an oil filter wrench, turn the filter counterclockwise to loosen it (see Figure 5.45.

4. Remove the wrench and unscrew the filter by hand.

   Note: The filter will be filled with hot engine oil. Protect your hand with a folded wiper or rag. Hold the filter upright until it can be placed in a disposal container. Avoid letting the hot oil spill in your face or on your clothing.

5. Examine the old filter to determine if the old sealing gasket came off with the filter. If it did not, be sure to remove the old gasket from the mounting surface at the motor.

6. Compare the old filter with the new one to determine if you have the correct filter. Compare the size of the gasket and the diameter of the center mounting hole. Recycle the filter properly.

7. Use a marking pen to make a line on the end of the new filter. This line will be used to determine how much to tighten the filter.

8. Prime all filters that can be installed in the upright position. To prime the filter, fill it with new motor oil to about an inch from the top. This will prevent a prolonged no oil pressure period while the new filter is being filled. Bearings can be damaged during this period.

9. Lubricate the gasket on the new filter by using your finger to coat the gasket with clean engine oil.

   Note: Lubricating the gasket aids in installation and minimizes the possibility of gasket distortion when you tighten the filter.

10. Screw the new filter in place by hand and continue turning it until it makes contact with the engine block.

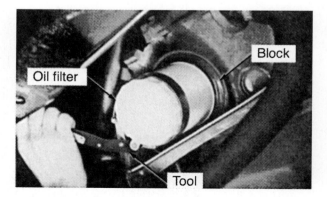

Figure 5.45 Using an oil filter wrench to loosen an oil filter (courtesy of Chrysler Corporation).

11. Tighten the filter by turning it 2/3 to 3/4 of a turn from the point where the filter gasket made initial contact with the block.

    Note: The tightening specification is usually indicated on the filter or on the filter box. Although it is usually recommended that the filter be tightened by hand, it is often necessary to use a filter wrench.

Preparation for Starting

12. Remove the drain pan from under the engine. Dispose of the old oil in a waste oil receptacle or other suitable container. Clean the drain pan.
13. Lower the car to the floor.
14. Check the engine oil level. Adjust the oil level if necessary.

> **!** **WARNING:** When changing both the engine oil and oil filter, be sure to add the required amount of new oil back into the crank case.

15. Start the engine and allow it to run at idle speed. Check to see that the oil pressure warning light goes out or that the oil pressure gauge indicates that the engine has sufficient oil pressure.

    Note: If oil pressure is not indicated within 10 seconds, turn off the engine and check for leaks.

16. If oil pressure is indicated, allow the engine to run for a few minutes.
17. Check the oil filter for leaks.
18. Turn off the engine. After allowing a few minutes for the oil to drain back to the oil pan, check the oil level. Adjust the oil level if necessary.

    Note: You should never have to add oil beyond the recommended number of quarts or liters. It may require an additional quart or liter when the filter is changed.

Job 5I

REPLACE AN ENGINE OIL FILTER

SATISFACTORY PERFORMANCE
A satisfactory performance on this job requires that you do the following:

1. Replace the engine oil filter on the car assigned.
2. Following the steps in the "Performance Outline" and the specifications of the car manufacturer, complete the job within 20 minutes.
3. Fill in the blanks under "Information."

PERFORMANCE OUTLINE

1. Raise and support the car.
2. Remove the oil filter.
3. Clean the filter mounting area.
4. Lubricate the filter gasket.
5. Install the replacement filter.
6. Lower the car to the floor.
7. Check for leaks.
8. Adjust the oil level if necessary.

INFORMATION

Vehicle identification_____

Reference used _____ Page(s) _____

Filter make _____ Part number _____

Tightening specification: _____ turns after contact

LESSON 5–4 Engine Oil Leak Inspection and Corrective Procedures

Many places in an engine can leak oil. Seals, gaskets, passageways, and PC, valves can let oil pass. The engine can be burning the oil in the combustion chamber. It does not take long for a quart of oil to leave an engine if there is a large leak. This can be dangerous on a long trip because the oil level may get so low the pump cannot pick up oil to work. This could result in engine damage.

> Oil leaks from the engine show as wet spots or puddles under the vehicle. When the vehicle moves these leaks drift toward the rear of the engine or vehicle. Clean the engine of all oil streaks and drive the vehicle. Keep looking for the oil leak. Once the leak is found, repair the problem.

Front Oil Seal

A seal, like the one in Figure 5.46, is located at the front of the engine. This seal keeps oil from

Figure 5.46 Engine front crankshaft seal. This seal prevents oil from leaving the front of the engine around the crankshaft. It is hard to seal around a moving shaft (courtesy of Training Enterprises Company).

leaking out of the engine around the crankshaft. Since the crankshaft is turning in the seal, any dirt or metal particles in the oil will wear the seal surface. After enough wear the seal can start leaking. The seal is usually placed in the timing cover, which surrounds the engine timing gear and chain. The cover is sealed between the engine block with a timing cover gasket. Leaks can occur between the cover and gasket as well as the seal. Check all the timing gear cover bolts and tighten any that are loose. Clean the oil from the area and check for any leaks. Remove the cover to replace a leaking seal.

Rear Oil Seal

The rear of the crankshaft has another oil seal. It too can leak after enough wear. Both the front and the rear seals can start leaking faster if the main engine bearings become worn. This allows the crankshaft to move. This movement can pound out the seals. A rear oil seal allows oil to leak out the flywheel cover (see Figure 5.47). This cover has a drain hole in the bottom to drain any oil that comes out the seal. This area is also a drain for leaking front transmission seals. Determine if the leaking oil is transmission fluid or motor oil. Repair or replace the necessary seals. The transmission has to be removed to replace many rear engine seals.

This is an excellent time to replace the transmission seals.

Oil Pan Leaks

Leaks at the oil pan can be from the pan gasket, drain plug, or a crack in the pan. Most engine oil leaks drip off the bottom of the pan. For this reason, be sure to locate the source of the leak before attempting to replace the pan gasket. Check the pan bolts and tighten any that are loose. Clean all oil from the bottom of the engine and see if the leak has been stopped. On a clean engine, the leaks show up close to the leak areas. Oil flows down the sides of the engine if the leak is higher than the oil pan. Correct all leaks.

> When replacing pan and valve cover gaskets be sure to use a thread lock on the hold-down bolts. This will prevent the bolt from backing out when the gasket compresses. Torque bolts like this again if the part being held gets loose enough to leak.

Oil Sending Unit

The oil sending unit has tapered pipe threads, like the one shown in Figure 5.48. When the sending unit is tightened to the right torque, the threads seal and prevent any oil leaks. *Caution:* To avoid any damage to the sending unit, be sure to use a sending unit socket. This puts pressure on the unit at the right spots to avoid damage to the unit. After tightening the unit, clean around it and start the engine to check for leaks and for correct sealing.

Valve Cover

The valve cover has RTV (tube sealer) or a gasket between the cover and the engine head. Overtime heat causes this gasket to harden and no longer seal. A valve cover leak shows up along the sides of the head. First, check all the valve cover bolts and tighten any that are loose. If this does not stop the leak, replace the gasket.

Positive Crankcase Ventilation (PCV) Valve

The PCV valve controls the movement of engine crankcase blowby gases (refer to Figure 1.15). When the engine is running and the gases

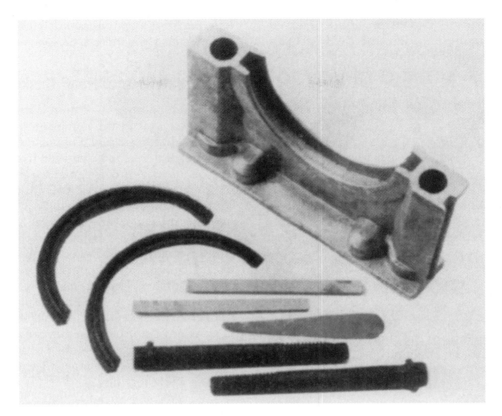

Figure 5.47   Rear engine oil seal. The crankshaft is sealed at the rear with an oil seal to prevent leaks. The seal can be damaged if the engine bearings are worn (courtesy of Training Enterprises Company).

accumulate, the valve opens and lets the gases flow to the intake system where they are drawn into the combustion chamber and burned. This prevents unburned hydrocarbons (blowby gases) from polluting the air. It also makes the engine more efficient because the recycled gases help fuel the engine. If the PCV valve or the passageways get stopped up, pressure is produced in the engine.

Figure 5.48   Oil sending unit. The oil sending unit is located in an oil galley where there is oil pressure. The unit has tapered pipe threads that seal when the unit is tightened to the correct torque (courtesy of Training Enterprises Company).

This pressure causes oil to be forced out of the engine everywhere there is a defective gasket or opening. If an engine looks as if every opening and gasket is leaking oil, check the condition of the PCV valve system. If it is clogged, clean it and install a new valve. Clean the oil from the engine with engine cleaner and see if the problem has been solved.

Oil Filler Cap

The cap should seal the opening used to put oil into the engine. Check to see if the cap is sealing properly and replace one that is cracked or that does not have a gasket (see Figure 5.49).

Air Cleaner

The air cleaner is used on many cars as a source of filtered air to replace the blowby gases that have been drawn into the engine from the oil pan. Excessive blowby from broken or worn rings creates too much pressure in the oil pan. This causes oil to be forced out the filter in the air cleaner. If you find that oil is pooled in the air cleaner and the filter for the crankcase is wet with oil, check the PCV valve system. If that does not correct the prob-

lem, perform a compression check of the engine cylinders to see if there are broken rings.

Rings, Valves, and Head Gasket

A problem in any one of these three areas can allow, oil to go into the combustion chamber and be burned with the fuel. Oil burned in the engine causes blue smoke to be emitted from the tailpipe. The piston rings are designed to scrape the excess oil from the cylinder walls. The valve guide-to-valve clearance and the condition of the valve seals keeps oil from entering at the valve area. Some passages are sealed between the head and the block by the condition of the head gasket. If you see blue smoke out the tailpipe, investigate all of these areas. Worn engine bearings journals can allow too much oil onto the cylinder walls. This results in the rings not being able to control the oil. The rings can be in excellent shape because they are receiving more than enough lubrication—the problem is the bearings. Low oil pressure at idle and when running are signs of worn bearings.

Under-the-Vehicle Inspection

External leaks show up as oil spots under a parked car. Train customers to check oil frequently and to look for signs of oil leaking down the sides of the engine and for puddles of oil where the car is parked. Leaks are always serious, but they are *dangerous* when more than a quart leaves the engine between oil changes. Always check the level of oil when a customer comes in for a regular oil change, and report any low readings. Look at all the areas mentioned in this lesson to discover where the leaks are and set up appointments to repair the problem. Problem leaks can be found if a dye is added to the engine oil and problem areas inspected under a black light. The dye will show up if the leak is from the engine.

Figure 5.49 Oil filler caps. Remove the cap and check the sealing surface or gasket. Some caps contain filters, while others are sealed (courtesy of Training Enterprises Company).

VOCABULARY

A. Sump

B. Oil pump

C. Oil filter

D. Hydraulic lifter

E. API

F. "S"

G. Filter by-pass valve

H. SAE

I. Multiviscosity

J. SJ

K. CG-4

L. API oil ring

M. Additive

N. Aerated

O. Dipstick

P. Safe oil range

Q. "Add" mark

R. Synthetic oil

S. Jack stand

T. Frame contact lift

U. Oversize plug

V. "Full flow"

W. Oil filter wrench

X. Oil seal

Y. Sending unit

_____ 1. Stands for service

_____ 2. The latest quality designation for automotive engine oil

_____ 3. Used to check fluid levels

_____ 4. Used with a jack for safety

_____ 5. Keeps oil inside an automotive unit

_____ 6. American Petroleum Institute

_____ 7. Where the engine oil is stored

_____ 8. Used to replace an oil stripped plug

_____ 9. The lower line on a dipstick

_____ 10. When all the oil is directed through the filter

_____ 11. Society of Automotive Engineers

_____ 12. Gets thicker when hot and thinner when cold

_____ 13. Uses oil to maintain a zero valve clearance

_____ 14. Has a manufactured base

_____ 15. Tool to remove an oil filter

_____ 16. Indicates the grade and quality of engine oil

_____ 17. Opens when the oil filter gets clogged

_____ 18. Maintains the pressure in an oil system

_____ 19. Designates the best quality commercial oil

_____ 20. When air mixes with the oil

_____ 21. Used to lift a vehicle when being serviced

_____ 22. Removes dirt and contamination from the oil

_____ 23. Added to the engine oil to improve it

_____ 24. Sends a signal to the oil light or gauge

_____ 25. Area on a dipstick between the add and full marks

REVIEW QUESTIONS

The following questions will help you determine if you have accomplished the tasks stated at the beginning of this chapter. If you do not know many of the answers, go back and review the material before proceeding to the next chapter.

Lesson 5–1

1. When does the filter bypass valve open?
2. Name three functions that are performed by engine oil.
3. Describe what a dispersant additive does in the oil.
4. How is viscosity measured?
5. In an SAE 5W can of oil, what does the "W" mean?
6. How does a multiviscosity oil perform when the temperature is cold?
7. What does the "S" stand for in the oil service classification?
8. What three facts about a can of motor oil can be found in the API circle?
9. Name two substances that can contaminate the oil.

Special Practice. Refer to Figure 5.1 and study each part italicized in the engine lubrication system lesson. Trace the oil flow and study how each part works and what job it has to do in the system.

Lesson 5–2

10. What should always be used to support the car after it is lifted?
11. On a vehicle with a fuel tank close to the rear bumper, should the front or rear be raised first?
12. What is the correct placement of jack stands when using lower control arms on rear wheel drive cars?
13. What should be the setting for the parking brake and transmission before lifting a vehicle with a suspension contact lift?
14. Before lowering a vehicle on a lift, what should be checked?
15. What is meant by the phrase *center of gravity*?

16. Before driving on a lift, what should be checked?
17. What is the purpose of lift safety catches?

Lesson 5–3

18. What should be used with a floor jack for added safety?
19. When the oil plug threads are stripped in the pan, what can be done to correct the problem?
20. What determines whether the vehicle should be jacked up from the front or rear to change the oil?
21. What part of the filter must be checked to see that it did not stick to the filter mounting surface?
22. What is the purpose of the mark placed on the end of the filter?
23. What is meant by priming the filter?
24. When putting the new oil into the engine, how do you know when you have put enough in the engine?

Lesson 5–4

25. In what part is the front engine seal usually found?
26. What engine parts cause seals to wear faster if they are worn?
27. What type of threads does the oil sending unit have?
28. When installing a sending unit, what tool prevents damage?
29. What are the signs of a clogged PCV valve?
30. What two problems can cause oil in the air cleaner?

ASE QUESTIONS

Each question or incomplete statement in this test is followed by four suggested answers or completions. In each case select the *one* that best answers the question or completes the statement.

1. Technician A says the engine cylinder walls are lubricated by spray. Technician B says the engine oil goes to the oil filter first before entering the engine oil galleries. Who is right?
   a. A only   b. B only
   c. Both A and B   d. Neither A nor B
2. Technician A says SAE 30 weight engine oil is suitable to use when the outside temperature is 0°F or hotter. Technician B says that SAE 10W- 30 weight engine oil is suitable for use at 0°F and above. Who is right?
   a. A only   b. B only
   c. Both A and B   d. Neither A nor B
3. Technician A says that SH is the latest and best classification for motor oil. Technician B says that SJ is the latest engine oil classification. Who is right?
   a. A only   b. B only
   c. Both A and B   d. Neither A nor B
4. What is the latest and best classification for commercial motor oil?
   a. CE-4   b. CF-3
   c. CG-4   d. CG-5
5. Technician A says that quality is an important consideration when selecting motor oil. Technician B says that viscosity is an important consideration when selecting motor oil. Who is right?
   a. A only   b. B only
   c. Both A and B   d. Neither A nor B
6. Technician A says that motor oil is brown in color and turns black with use. Technician B says that motor oil is black in color and turns brown with use. Who is right?
   a. A only   b. B only
   c. Both A and B   d. Neither A nor B
7. Technician A says that gasoline contamination of motor oil reduces the viscosity of the oil. Technician B says that coolant contamination of motor oil turns the motor oil white. Who is right?
   a. A only   b. B only
   c. Both A and B   d. Neither A nor B
8. Technician A says the center of gravity has to be balanced when a vehicle is placed on a lift. Technician B says a vehicle can be safely placed on a lift anywhere the pads are positioned to support the weight. Who is right?
   a. A only   b. B only
   c. Both A and B   d. Neither A nor B
9. Technician A says that hydraulic floor jacks are made to support a vehicle. Technician A says that floor jacks are made to lift the vehicle only. Who is right?
   a. A only   b. B only
   c. Both A and B   d. Neither A nor B
10. Technician A says anytime a vehicle is jacked up from the front it is ready for motor oil removal. Technician B says that a vehicle must be level before the motor oil is removed. Who is right?

a. A only b. B only
c. Both A and B d. Neither A nor B

11. Technician A says that used motor oil can cause skin cancer. Technician B says that used motor poses no threat and skin contact is allowed. Who is right?
a. A only b. B only
c. Both A and B d. Neither A nor B

12. Technician A says that the filter wrench is used to both remove and install an oil filter. Technician B says that the filter wrench is only used to remove an oil filter. Who is right?
a. A only b. B only
c. Both A and B d. Neither A nor B

13. Technician A says that it takes one pint of motor oil to go from the add mark to the full mark on the dipstick. Technician B says it takes one quart of motor oil to go from the add mark to the full mark. Who is right?
a. A only b. B only
c. Both A and B d. Neither A nor B

14. Technician A says that the oil sending unit does not require a gasket to seal the threads. Technician B says that the oil sending unit requires a copper gasket to prevent leaks. Who is right?
a. A only b. B only
c. Both A and B d. Neither A nor B

6

Battery System Maintenance

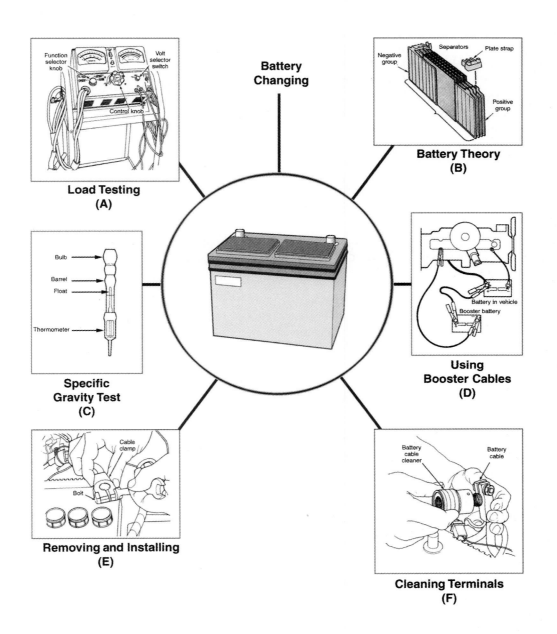

Load Testing
(A)

Battery
Changing

Battery Theory
(B)

Specific
Gravity Test
(C)

Using
Booster Cables
(D)

Removing and Installing
(E)

Cleaning Terminals
(F)

The battery is the heart of the electrical system. When the battery fails to do its job, the vehicle owner knows it immediately. The starter, which demands a high current draw from the battery, fails to crank the engine. This type of engine failure can be inconvenient or dangerous depending on when or where it happens.

A service technician must know how to test batteries for defects, select the right battery for each vehicle, clean and replace cables, and jump-start a vehicle battery or charge the battery (see Figure 6A–F). Some batteries require distilled water when the level drops to an unacceptable level. Others have a built-in hydrometer that must be read to determine the battery condition. Many batteries have been replaced that only needed a charge to be serviceable, and many defective batteries have led to the replacement of starters and alternators that were still in excellent condition and operating as they should. It is the job of the battery service technician to test for problems of this nature and service the good parts while replacing only those that are known to be defective.

TASKS

The following are six tasks to master before leaving this chapter:

Task 6-1. Study battery theory and parts. Knowledge of battery theory is important when performing testing, charging, and servicing operations.

Task 6-2. Learn battery safety procedures to avoid injury. There is a strong acid in batteries that turns to an explosive gas while being charged.

Task 6-3. Learn to select the right battery for all types of vehicle applications. There are many different size and strength batteries on the market. Not all batteries are suitable for every vehicle.

Task 6-4. Learn to service a battery and evaluate its condition. Service involves cleaning cables, charging, filling the cells, condition testing, replacing defective batteries, and activating new ones. These operations involve the use of both tools and test equipment.

Task 6-5. Learn how to charge a battery correctly, which involves the use of a battery charger and some test equipment.

Task 6-6. Learn to install jumper or booster cables correctly to start a vehicle with a "dead" battery. Incorrect installation of booster or jumper cables

can result in damage to many expensive electrical and electronic components in a vehicle. There is also the risk of an explosion if a spark is generated over a charging battery.

LESSON 6–1   Battery Operation and Terms
The Battery

The battery in an automobile serves four important functions:

1. It furnishes the electrical energy that cranks the engine for starting.
2. It supplies the current needed to operate the ignition system while starting.
3. It provides current to the electrical system when the engine is not running and when the demands of the system exceed the output of the charging system.
4. It acts as a stabilizer or cushion in the electrical system to minimize variations in system voltage.

Unless the battery performs each of these functions, the electrical system and its related components will not operate properly.

Battery Operation. Although a battery may sometimes be referred to as a "storage battery," a battery does not store electricity. A battery stores chemicals that react to produce electrical energy. Battery service includes certain chemical and electrical tests. But it is not enough to be able to perform the tests.

You must also be able to interpret the results of those tests. To do that, you must be knowledgeable about certain facts regarding battery operation and construction.

A battery operates through the application of a simple scientific principle. When two different metals are immersed in an acid solution, a difference in electrical pressure exists between them. Figure 6.1 shows how that pressure causes the flow of electricity.

Most batteries used in automobiles are of the *lead-acid type*. In a lead-acid battery, the different metals are *lead peroxide* and *sponge lead*. The lead peroxide forms the *positive* (+) plate. The sponge lead forms the *negative* (−) plate. The acid is *electrolyte*, a mixture of sulfuric acid and water.

Electrochemical Action. A lead-acid cell can be repeatedly discharged and charged. This is possible

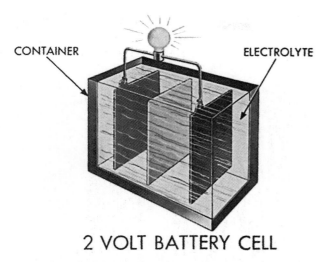

CONTAINER   ELECTROLYTE

2 VOLT BATTERY CELL

Figure 6.1 Two-volt battery cell. The difference in electrical pressure between the plates of a simple cell causes the flow of current. In this example, the current flows through the filament of a bulb (courtesy of Chevrolet Motor Division, General Motors Corporation).

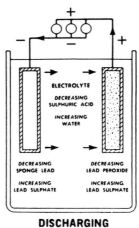

ELECTROLYTE

DECREASING
SULPHURIC ACID

INCREASING
WATER

DECREASING
SPONGE LEAD

DECREASING
LEAD PEROXIDE

INCREASING
LEAD SULPHATE

INCREASING
LEAD SULPHATE

DISCHARGING

Figure 6.3 The chemical condition of a battery that is discharging (courtesy of Exide Corporation).

because the chemical action in the cell can be reversed. If a higher external voltage is applied to the plates, the current flow can be reversed. Thus the energy used to start an engine can be restored by the charging system when the engine is running. If such were not the case, a battery would have to be discarded after a short period of use. Throughout its life, a battery is *cycled,* or partially discharged and recharged, thousands of times. At any time in its life, a battery will be in one of the following states.

Charged   Figure 6.2 shows the chemical condition of a fully charged battery. The positive plate consists of lead peroxide, the negative plate is sponge lead, and the electrolyte is at its full strength.

Discharging   When a load is placed across the plates, the battery discharges. The difference in electrical pressure between the plates causes current to flow. While that current is flowing, a chemical change takes place in the plates and in the electrolyte. As shown in Figure 6.3, the electrolyte becomes diluted and the plates become *sulfated.* Actually, the electrolyte (H_2SO_4) divides into hydrogen (H_2) and a sulfate radical (SO_4). The hydrogen (H_2) combines with some of the oxygen (O) formed at the positive plate and produces additional water (H_2O). The sulfate (SO_4) combines with the lead (Pb) in both plates and forms lead sulfate ($PbSO_4$).

Discharged   If a continuous load is placed on a battery, the chemical action continues until the battery is discharged. As shown in Figure 6.4, the electrolyte has been depleted and diluted until it is mostly water. The plates have both become lead sulfate, and they are no longer dissimilar.

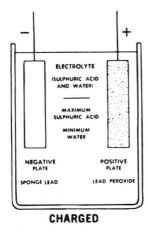

ELECTROLYTE
(SULPHURIC ACID
AND WATER)

MAXIMUM
SULPHURIC ACID

MINIMUM
WATER

NEGATIVE
PLATE

POSITIVE
PLATE

SPONGE LEAD

LEAD PEROXIDE

CHARGED

Figure 6.2 The chemical condition of a fully charged battery (courtesy of Exide Corporation).

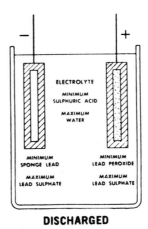

ELECTROLYTE

MINIMUM
SULPHURIC ACID

MAXIMUM
WATER

MINIMUM
SPONGE LEAD

MINIMUM
LEAD PEROXIDE

MAXIMUM
LEAD SULPHATE

MAXIMUM
LEAD SULPHATE

DISCHARGED

Figure 6.4 The chemical condition of a discharged battery (courtesy of Exide Corporation).

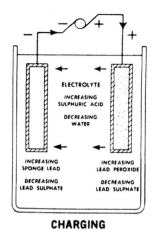

Figure 6.5 The chemical condition of a battery that is being charged (courtesy of Exide Corporation).

Charging   When a battery is being charged, the chemical action is reversed as shown in Figure 6.5, the lead sulfate ($PbSO_4$) is broken down, restoring the plates to their original composition (PbO_2 and Pb). The sulfate (SO_4) combines with the hydrogen (H_2) in the water (H_2O) to form sulfuric acid (H_2SO_4). The sulfuric acid increases the strength of the electrolyte.

> Battery cell voltage measures higher just after the battery has been charged or the engine turned off. To get an accurate voltage test reading, remove this "surface charge" by placing a load on the battery, such as turning on the lights, for ten seconds.

Cell Voltage.   Electrical pressure is measured in units called *volts*. A fully charged lead-acid cell produces a pressure of about 2.1 volts. Internal resistance reduces that pressure slightly, and a lead-acid cell is usually referred to as a 2-volt cell. Increasing the size of the plates, or increasing the number of plates in a cell, does not increase the voltage. To

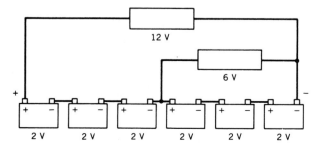

Figure 6.6 Cells in series. Cells are connected in series to form batteries. A 6-volt battery has three cells. A 12-volt battery has six cells.

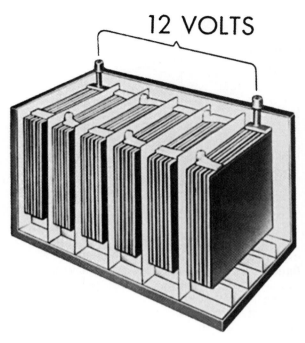

Figure 6.7 Typical arrangement of the cells in a 12-volt battery (courtesy of Chevrolet Motor Division, General Motors Corporation).

obtain higher voltage, cells must be connected in *series*, positive to negative, as shown in Figure 6.6. Figure 6.7 shows how the cells are arranged in the typical 12-volt battery used in most cars.

Battery Design.   Both "conventional" and "maintenance-free" batteries are in common use. There are many material and design differences between these two types. The most obvious difference is that a true maintenance-free battery is sealed and is not provided with removable vent plugs.

Conventional Battery Construction

The internal parts of a battery are not normally visible nor can they be serviced. Yet an understanding of those parts and how they are assembled is important if you are to interpret correctly the results of the various battery tests you will perform.

Grids.   The plates of a lead-acid battery are built on *grids*. A grid, shown in Figure 6.8, is a screen or mesh that forms the framework of a plate. A grid usually is made of an alloy of lead and antimony; pure lead is too soft and lacks the required strength.

Positive Plates.   A positive plate is built by filling all the openings in a grid with *active material*. The active material for a positive plate is a paste made

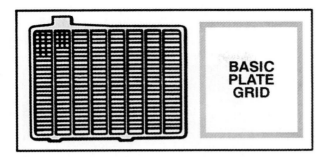

Figure 6.8 Basic plate grid. A basic plate grid is a screen or mesh made of lead alloyed with antimony (courtesy of General Motors Corporation).

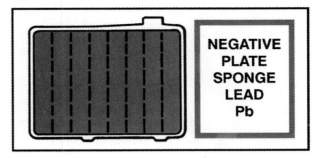

Figure 6.10 Negative plate. A negative plate is formed by coating a grid with sponge lead (courtesy of General Motors Corporation).

of lead oxide. The lead oxide is then converted to a hard, porous, dark brown lead peroxide (PbO_2) by giving the coated plate a "forming" charge (see Figure 6.9).

Negative Plates.   A negative plate is built by filling all the openings in the grid with a different active material. The active material used to build a negative plate consists of powdered lead (Pb) and an inert "expander" that keeps the lead porous or spongy (see Figure 6.10).

Separators.   Since the plates in a cell must not come into contact with each other, *separators* must be placed between them. In addition to being acid resistant, separators must be porous to allow electrolyte to pass through them. Various materials including rubber, plastic, and fiberglass are used for separators.

Plate Groups.   A plate group is a number of similar plates (positive or negative) joined together at their tops by a *plate strap* as shown in Figure 6.11. The plate strap contains a lug or post that allows it to be connected to another plate group in the next cell. The number of plates in a group determines

the *capacity* of the battery. Increasing the number of plates enables the battery to deliver more energy.

When positive and negative plate groups are built for a particular battery, the negative group is built with one more plate than the positive group. By increasing the total area of the negative plates, the efficiency of the battery is increased.

> The number and size of the battery plates determines how much amperage a battery can produce. All automotive batteries are kept at 12.6 volts by the number of battery cells. The battery amperage changes with the physical size of the battery such as length, height, and width.

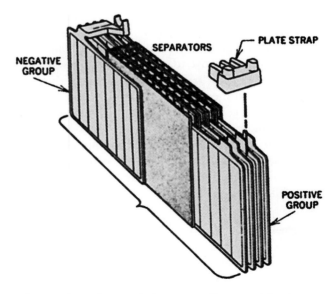

Figure 6.11 Plates and plate straps. Plates are joined together by plate straps. A number of similar plates joined together is referred to as a plate group (courtesy of General Motors Corporation).

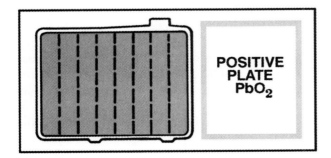

Figure 6.9 Positive plate. A positive plate is formed by coating a grid with lead peroxide (courtesy of General Motors Corporation).

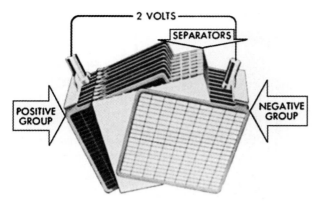

Figure 6.12 Forming an element. A group of positive plates and a group of negative plates are combined to form an element. Insulating separators are used to keep the plates from touching each other (courtesy of Chevrolet Motor Division, General Motors Corporation).

Elements. An *element* is composed of a positive plate group and a negative plate group placed together in an interlocking fashion as shown in Figure 6.12. Separators are placed between each of the plates so that they do not touch. Since the negative group has one more plate than the positive group, the assembled element has negative plates exposed on both sides.

The Battery Case. The battery case or *container* is molded of hard rubber or plastic. The case contains partitions that divide it into separate cells. The bottom of each cell has several *bridges* molded into place. Those bridges act as element rests that support the bottoms of the plates. When a battery is in service, electrochemical action and vibration combine to dislodge particles of active material from the plates. That active material eventually settles to the bottom of the battery container as sediment. Since this sediment is a conductor, it will cause a short in the cell if it contacts the bottom of the plates. The spaces between the bridges form *sediment chambers* that collect the active material shed from the plates. Sufficient space is provided to collect any sediment that may accumulate during the useful life of the battery.

Connectors. When all the elements are in place in each cell of the battery case, the plate straps of each element are joined by *connectors* so that the cells are connected in series. In some batteries, the cell connectors pass through holes in the case partitions as shown in Figure 6.13. In other designs, the connectors arch over the cell partitions.

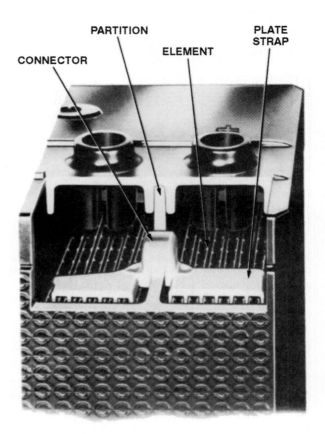

Figure 6.13 A cutaway view of a battery showing how the cell connectors pass through the partitions in the battery case (courtesy of Chevrolet Motor Division, General Motors Corporation).

Cell Covers. Most batteries have a one-piece cover that is cemented or bonded to the battery case. The cover provides a seal over each partition and contains a baffled opening for each cell as shown in Figure 6.14. The opening provides access to the cells for the addition of electrolyte, for testing the electrolyte, and for adding water when it is required. The baffled opening acts to deflect any electrolyte that may be splashed against the inside of the cover and, in most instances, is formed so that the correct electrolyte level can easily be determined.

Vent Plugs. The openings in the cell cover are fitted with *vent plugs*. These plugs or caps are vented to allow the escape of gases that are generated while the battery is working. As shown in Figure 6.15, they contain baffles to minimize the possibility of the escape of liquid electrolyte. On some batteries, the vent plugs are combined, usually in sets of three, and are friction-fitted so that they can be pulled off and pushed on. Single vent

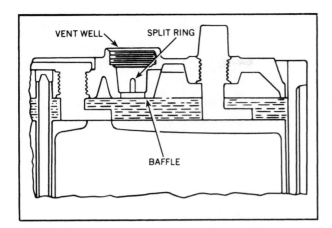

Figure 6.14 Vent hole and split ring. The vent hole in the cell cover is formed to act as a baffle. The split ring provides a means of checking the electrolyte level (courtesy of General Motors Corporation).

Figure 6.16 A typical post terminal battery (courtesy of Training Enterprises Company).

plugs may be friction-fitted or may be threaded to screw into the cell cover.

Battery Terminals. Two types of battery terminals are in common use. *Post terminals* extend through the top of the cell cover as shown in Figure 6.16. They consist of tapered posts to which a battery cable can be clamped. The positive (+) post is 11/16 in. (17.5 mm) in diameter at the top. The negative (−) post is 5/8 in. (15.9 mm) in diameter at the top. The positive (+) post is larger than the negative (−) post as an aid in determining polarity. Posts are also identified by color and letters. If color is used, the positive post is red and the negative post, black. The letters "Pos" and "Neg" may be written on some cases near the posts for identification. *Side terminals,* shown in Figure 6.17, are mounted on the side of the battery container and

consist of a reinforced threaded hole into which a special battery cable end can be threaded.

Maintenance-Free Battery Construction

Maintenance-free batteries differ from conventional batteries in that they do not require the addition of water during their normal service life. Although a true maintenance-free battery is sealed, it does have a small gas vent to prevent a rise in internal pressure. Both conventional and maintenance-free batteries operate through the same electrochemical action, but they are designed and constructed in a different manner.

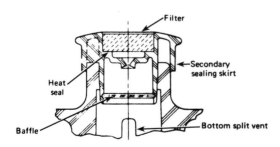

Figure 6.15 Flame arrester vent plug. The plug shown incorporates a filter that allows gases to escape but does not allow the entry of a hydrogen flame. A plug of this type prevents a flame or spark from entering the battery and causing an explosion (reprinted with permission from AC-Delco, General Motors Corporation).

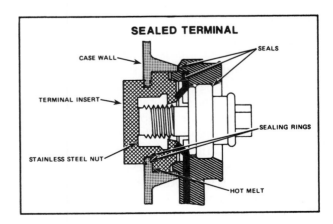

Figure 6.17 A cross-sectional view of a sealed terminal typical of those used in side terminal batteries (courtesy of General Motors Corporation).

Figure 6.18 A lead-calcium grid of modern design. The grid shown is cold worked, whereas traditional lead-antimony grids are cast (courtesy of General Motors Corporation).

Figure 6.19 Envelope separator. In some maintenance-free batteries, each plate is "bagged," or encapsulated in a porous plastic envelope to eliminate the need for separator (courtesy of General Motors Corporation).

Most water loss in a conventional battery is through the evaporation of water vapor. The water vapor is the result of *gassing* caused by the heat generated inside a battery. The heat is produced when a battery is working, especially when it is being charged by the charging system, and actually boils the water out of the electrolyte. It has been found that the antimony used to strengthen the grids is the main cause of gassing. The antimony requires a high charging current, which generates excessive heat. When the antimony in the grid alloy is replaced with calcium, less charging current is required, less heat is created, and less gassing occurs. The elimination of antimony in the alloy also increases the conductivity of the grids and thus improves the battery's capacity. Figure 6.18 shows a lead-calcium grid.

The shedding of active material from the plates of a conventional battery requires that sediment chambers be provided at the bottom of each cell. This causes the elements to be supported high in the case and close to the surface of the electrolyte. By replacing the traditional separators with microporous plastic envelopes, each plate can be separately "bagged" or encapsulated, as shown in Figure 6.19. The plastic envelopes also provide better cushioning for the plates to minimize the effects of vibration. The active material that is dislodged from the plates is trapped in the envelopes, held in contact with the plates, and not allowed to fall to the bottom of the cell. Since no sediment is formed, no sediment chambers are required, and the elements can be positioned lower in the battery case. This provides a larger volume of electrolyte above the tops of the plates.

Job 6A

IDENTIFY TERMS RELATING TO BATTERY OPERATION AND CONSTRUCTION

SATISFACTORY PERFORMANCE
A satisfactory performance on this job requires that you do the following:

1. Identify the terms relating to battery operation and construction by placing the number of each term in front of the phrase that best describes it.
2. Identify all the terms correctly within 15 minutes.

PERFORMANCE SITUATION

1. Electrolyte	6. Lead peroxide
2. Grid	7. Sponge lead
3. Separator	8. Lead sulfate
4. Calcium	9. Plate group
5. Element	10. Antimony

_____ The active material of a positive plate in a fully charged lead-acid cell

_____ The active material of a negative plate in a fully charged lead-acid cell

_____ The material used in the construction of separators

_____ A mixture of sulfuric acid and water

_____ An insulator used between plates

_____ The composition of the plates in a discharged cell

_____ The metal added to the lead used to make grids for a maintenance-free battery

_____ The metal added to the lead used to make grids for a conventional battery

_____ An assembly of a positive plate group and a negative plate group

_____ The meshlike framework of a plate

_____ An assembly of similar plates connected by a plate strap

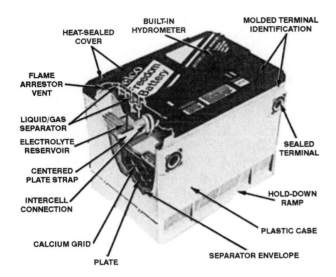

HEAT-SEALED COVER
BUILT-IN HYDROMETER
MOLDED TERMINAL IDENTIFICATION
FLAME ARRESTOR VENT
LIQUID/GAS SEPARATOR
ELECTROLYTE RESERVOIR
CENTERED PLATE STRAP
INTERCELL CONNECTION
CALCIUM GRID
PLATE
SEALED TERMINAL
HOLD-DOWN RAMP
PLASTIC CASE
SEPARATOR ENVELOPE

Figure 6.20 The component parts and features of a true maintenance-free battery (courtesy of General Motors Corporation).

Figure 6.20 shows a complete battery assembly. Study this illustration to become familiar with the component parts and their location.

LESSON 6–2 Battery Safety

Safety Precautions

Battery service exposes you to certain hazards. Because the electrolyte in batteries contains sulfuric acid, be extremely careful when working on or near a battery. Electrolyte can damage painted finishes. It can corrode metal. It can eat holes in your clothing. It can cause painful burns if spilled on your skin and blindness if splashed in your eyes.

For your personal protection, observe the following safety precautions:

1. Wear safety glasses any time you are working on or near a battery. These glasses should be equipped with side shields. A full face shield is a better choice for safety protection around a battery because it protects the entire face from acid and explosion damage.
2. Remove any jewelry such as rings and watches. Metal objects such as these could become shorted between the metal of the vehicle and the positive battery terminal. There have been cases where rings have been shorted between the wrench and the terminal. A person's ring finger could be burned by the extreme heat created on the ring by such a rapid battery discharge.

3. Use fender covers to protect the finish of the car. These covers should be the rubber-coated type that would prevent battery acid from soaking through to the vehicle finish. Battery acid will damage the vehicle paint.

Job 6B

IDENTIFY THE COMPONENT PARTS OF A BATTERY

SATISFACTORY PERFORMANCE
A satisfactory performance on this job requires that you do the following:

1. Identify the numbered parts or features on the drawing by placing the number of each part or feature in front of the correct part name or description.
2. Identify correctly 12 of the 14 parts or features within 15 minutes.

PERFORMANCE SITUATION
____ Calcium grid
____ Plastic case
____ Flame arrestor vent
____ Sealed terminal
____ Terminal identification
____ Liquid/gas separator
____ Hydrometer
____ Plate strap
____ Intercell connector
____ Reservoir
____ Sediment chamber
____ Cover
____ Plate
____ Cell partition
____ Hold-down ramp
____ Separator envelope

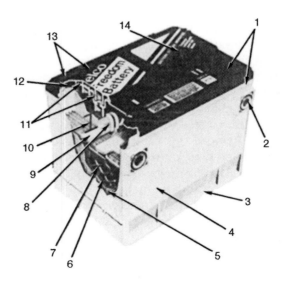

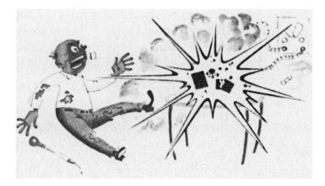

Figure 6.21 Battery safety poster. The explosive gases given off by a battery can be ignited by a spark or a flame (courtesy of Chevrolet Motor Division, General Motors Corporation).

> **!** **Warning:** Hydrogen and oxygen are produced by a battery during its normal operation. Those gases are vented from the battery and may explode if ignited by any open flame, spark, or lighted cigarette. The explosion usually bursts the battery and sprays electrolyte over a large area (see Figure 6.21).

4. When working with tools or other metallic objects on or near a battery, use care so that they do not short across the battery terminals or across the positive (+) terminal and ground. The resultant arc may ignite the vented gases. Any battery is capable of producing a very high amperage when a direct short is made. This high amperage is capable of melting wrenches and causing fires.

5. Use a nonmetallic filler or funnel when adding water to a battery.

6. Never disconnect a battery cable or a charger cable from a battery terminal if the circuit is live. The resultant arc may ignite the vented gases. Always turn the charger off first. Connect the negative lead to a good metal spot on the engine instead of the negative battery terminal. Remove this cable first after charging the battery. If an arc is produced it will not be where the explosive gases are located.

7. Always disconnect the negative battery terminal first. Connect it last to complete the battery installation. By removing this terminal first and connecting it last, it would not cause a short if your wrench were to contact the vehicle frame creating an accidental path to ground. The ground terminal is supposed to be connected to the frame. The positive terminal should never be shorted to ground or to the negative terminal.

8. There are many electronic items on today's vehicles. They will be damaged if the battery polarity is accidentally reversed. Always connect the positive vehicle cable (usually colored red) to the positive battery terminal (marked red, pos, or with a plus sign), and the negative vehicle cable (usually colored black) to the negative battery post (marked black, neg, or with a negative sign). This applies to the use of jumper cables to start a disabled vehicle. The misuse of jumper cables causes more electronic damage than any other single cause.

9. Always make sure the battery hold-down device (bracket) is in place and that it is in good shape. A battery can short out if it tips out of its holder into any metal parts completing an electrical path between the posts.

LESSON 6–3   Battery Selection

Battery selection should take into account vehicle carrier space, post location, power needed, and any special applications. At no time should you select a battery with less than the recommended cranking amperage or power output. This battery, even when fully charged, will not be strong enough to do the job it was intended for. It will not supply power enough to turn the starter fast enough and the starter could be damaged. As a vehicle gets older, the amount of battery power needed increases rather than decreases. Resistance in the circuits increases and more power is needed to overcome this.

Consider the following points when making replacement battery selections:

1. *Vehicle battery space.* Most vehicles limit the space size allotted for a battery. Vehicle designs with sloped hoods limit the battery height. When considering a battery with more amperage, measure the holder space to determine if the larger battery will fit.

2. *Cable length.* Since battery cables are limited in length, the new battery positive and negative terminals should be located in the same place as those on the old battery. The location of the positive terminal is the most critical. It must be located where it will not get into contact with the metal around the carrier or the hood. This would cause a direct short of the terminals and cause a fire or destroy the battery. Side mount cables require a side mount replacement battery so the cables will connect. These batteries

have the terminals located with the positive terminal on the right or the left as you face the battery, depending on the vehicle application.

3. *Amperage capacity.* The battery plate size determines how much amperage a battery is capable of producing. The more plates, or the larger the plate size, the more amperage can be produced by the battery. Most vehicles have enough room to install a larger battery. The size of the battery holder determines if a larger and more powerful battery can be purchased. A well-maintained vehicle should not require a battery replacement larger than the original.

4. *Cranking power.* The term *amp-hour* is used to determine how much amperage a battery produces in a given time. *Cranking amperage* or *cold cranking amperage* means the amount of amperage available to crank the starter for a given period of time. The plate materials and the size of the plates determine the cranking amperage and the amp-hour capacity of the battery. The correct replacement battery generates the same amperage output as the old battery. Higher capacity batteries can be used if the battery holder space permits.

5. *Special applications.* Lawn tractors, trucks, and boats are special applications, in part because they may be stored for long periods of time. Batteries stored for long periods of time without being used decrease in voltage or discharge. Batteries that stay idle for long periods of time at a reduced charge tend to sulfate. The plate materials harden and do not take a charge when the vehicle is needed. To prevent this from happening, place a *trickle* or very small charge on the battery when it is being stored for long periods of time. This keeps the battery charged and prevents sulfating. Batteries for vehicles that will be idle for long periods of time have a larger electrolyte area over the top of the plates.

LESSON 6–4 Battery and Cable Inspection
Visual Inspection

Begin battery service with a thorough visual inspection. A visual inspection of a battery and its mounting may reveal the need for other services. Figure 6.22 illustrates some of the more common faults that may be found.

A battery should be securely held in its *carrier* or *tray* by its *hold-down*. Some hold-downs grip the

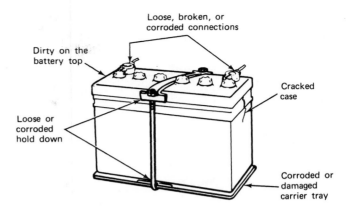

Figure 6.22 Battery visual inspection. Battery service should begin with a thorough visual inspection of the battery, its connections, and its mounting (courtesy of Ford Motor Company, Dearborn, MI).

battery by its base as shown in Figure 6.23. Other hold-downs grip the battery at the top and are secured by long bolts. Such an arrangement is shown in Figure 6.24. A loose or broken hold-down allows a battery to move. If a battery is not securely mounted, movement and vibration will damage the battery. Tighten a hold-down snugly so the battery cannot move, but not so tight that the battery case is distorted. If a hold-down is damaged so it cannot be tightened, replace it.

Some manufacturers provide heat shields to protect the battery from engine heat. Others provide air ducts that direct cool air around the battery.

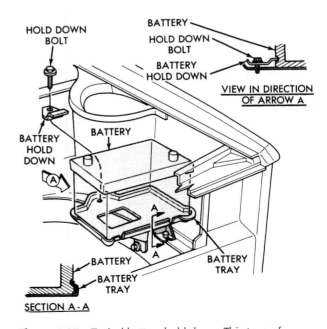

Figure 6.23 Typical battery hold-down. This type of hold-down secures the battery to the battery tray by means of grooves formed in the bottom edge of the battery case (courtesy of Chrysler Corporation).

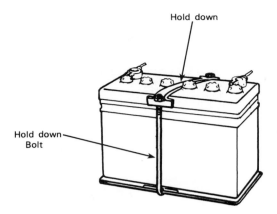

Figure 6.24 A hold-down that passes over the top of the battery (courtesy of Ford Motor Company, Dearborn, MI).

Figure 6.25 Corroded battery terminals. Badly corroded battery terminals and clamps often are the cause of electrical system problems (courtesy of General Motors Corporation).

An inspection of the hold-down should include an inspection of those devices.

A cracked case allows electrolyte to leak from the battery. Even if that leakage is slight, the electrolyte will corrode the battery tray and its surrounding parts. Replace a battery with a cracked case.

Corrosion caused by spilled electrolyte should be removed and neutralized. This can be done by cleaning the parts with a solution made by dissolving a teaspoonful of baking soda in a cup of water. (A disposable coffee container is handy for this job because it can be discarded after use.) After the parts have dried, protect them from further corrosion by a coating of oil or light grease.

Dirt on the top of a post terminal battery may hold spilled electrolyte. Because electrolyte conducts electricity, that coating may cause a battery to self-discharge. Always keep the top of a battery clean and dry.

Loose, broken, or corroded connections such as those shown in Figure 6.25 may restrict current flow. In an electrical circuit, a restriction to current flow is called *resistance*. The resistance of such connections often causes problems that may be incorrectly blamed on the battery or on the starter motor. Replace broken or damaged cables. Keep connections clean, tight, and in good condition.

LESSON 6–5 Cleaning Battery Terminals

Cleaning Battery Connections: Post Terminals

A visual inspection of the terminals on a battery with post terminals may reveal some of the faults shown in Figure 6.26. Although those faults require correction, a more serious fault may escape detec-

tion. Oxidation and corrosion between the post and the cable clamp as shown in Figure 6.27 are a common cause of high resistance. To eliminate that resistance, the cable clamps must be removed from the posts and all parts must be cleaned thoroughly. The following steps outline a suggested procedure:

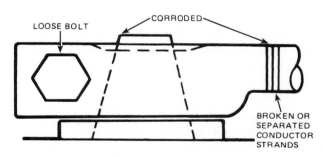

Figure 6.26 Cable clamp. A cable clamp should be clean, tight, and exhibit no broken or separated conductor strands (courtesy of Ford Motor Company, Dearborn, MI).

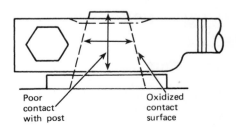

Figure 6.27 Clamp oxidation areas. Although a cable clamp may appear clean and tight, internal oxidation can create a bad connection (courtesy Ford Motor Company, Dearborn, MI).

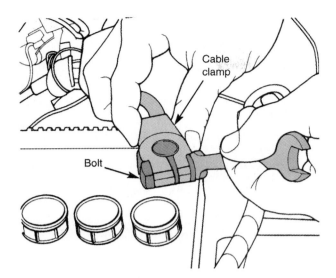

Figure 6.28 Loosening a battery cable clamp. Remove the ground cable first to minimize the dangers of arcing and a possible battery explosion (courtesy of Chrysler Corporation).

1. Make sure that all switches and controls are in the OFF position.
2. Loosen the clamp connecting the ground cable to the battery as shown in Figure 6.28. On most cars, the ground cable is connected to the negative (−) terminal.

   Note: If the nut on the clamp bolt is corroded or worn so that a wrench cannot be used, a pair of battery pliers similar to those shown in Figure 6.29 may prove helpful.
3. Remove the cable clamp from the battery post.

   Note: Never attempt to pry or twist a cable clamp from a battery post. To do so could damage the battery. If a clamp does not slide off easily, use a cable puller, similar to the one shown in Figure 6.30. Positioned over the clamp as shown in Figure 6.31, a puller will enable you to remove the clamp without damage to the battery.
4. Remove the remaining battery cable clamp.
5. Using a battery post and clamp cleaning tool similar to the one shown in Figure 6.32, clean the inside of the battery cable clamps. This operation is shown in Figure 6.33.

Figure 6.29 Battery pliers. This tool is designed for the removal of cable clamp nuts that are so corroded a wrench cannot be used (courtesy of KD Tools, Lancaster, PA 17604).

Figure 6.30 A typical battery cable clamp puller (courtesy of KD Tools, Lancaster, PA 17604).

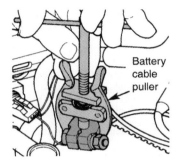

Figure 6.31 Using a puller to remove a battery cable clamp from a battery post (courtesy of Chrysler Corporation).

Figure 6.32 A typical battery post and clamp cleaning brush (courtesy of KD Tools, Lancaster, PA 17604).

6. Clean the battery posts as shown in Figure 6.34.
7. Clean the top of the battery. A solution of baking soda and water applied with a brush is ideal for cleaning because it neutralizes any spilled acid (see Figure 6.35).

   Note: Be careful that the solution does not enter the cells. The baking soda and water solution will weaken the electrolyte.
8. Install the cable that connects the battery to the starter motor or starter solenoid. On most cars, this cable connects to the positive (+) post of the battery.

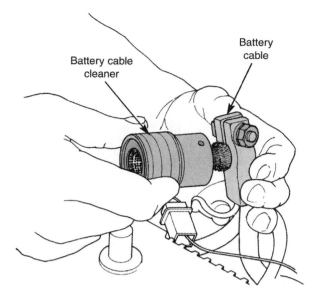

Figure 6.33 Cleaning the inside surfaces of a battery cable clamp (courtesy of Chrysler Corporation).

Note: Connect this cable first to minimize the dangers of shorting out the tools.

9. Install the ground cable. On most cars the ground cable is connected to the negative (−) post.

Note: Always install the ground cable last to minimize the dangers of arcing and possible battery explosion.

10. Coat the cable clamps with a thin coating of grease.

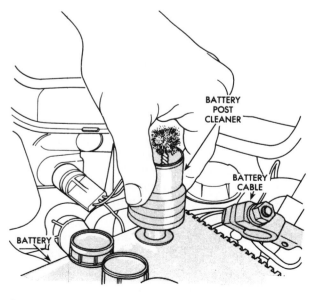

Figure 6.34 Cleaning a battery post (courtesy of Chrysler Corporation).

Job 6C

INSPECT A BATTERY, HOLD-DOWN, AND CARRIER TRAY

SATISFACTORY PERFORMANCE
A satisfactory performance on this job requires that you do the following:

1. Inspect the battery, hold-down, and carrier tray on the car assigned.
2. Following the steps in the "Performance Outline," complete the job within 10 minutes.
3. Fill in the blanks under "Information".

PERFORMANCE OUTLINE

1. Protect the fender of the car with a fender cover.
2. Inspect the terminals, clamps, and cables for damage, looseness, and corrosion.
3. Inspect the top of the battery for the presence of dirt and electrolyte.
4. Inspect the battery case for cracks and leakage.
5. Inspect the hold-down for looseness, damage, and corrosion.
6. Inspect the carrier tray for looseness, damage, and corrosion.
7. Inspect any heat shield or air duct that may be fitted for looseness, damage, and corrosion.

INFORMATION

Vehicle identification _____

Terminals, clamps, and cables:	____ Clean	____ Dirty
	____ Tight	____ Loose
Battery top:	____ Clean	____ Dirty
Battery case:	____ Intact	____ Cracked
Hold-down:	____ Clean	____ Dirty
	____ Tight	____ Loose
	____ OK	____ Damaged
Carrier tray:	____ Clean	____ Dirty
	____ Tight	____ Loose
Heat shield/air duct:	____ Tight	____ Loose
	____ OK	____ Damaged

Services required _____
_____
_____

Cleaning Battery Connections: Side Terminals

Side terminals are not as subject to corrosion as are post terminals, and the design of the cable ends makes it difficult to check for the presence of corrosion. Because of this, their maintenance is often neglected and a high-resistance condition is not detected. The procedure for cleaning the connections of a side terminal battery differs

Figure 6.35 Cleaning the top of a battery with a solution of baking soda and water (courtesy of Chrysler Corporation).

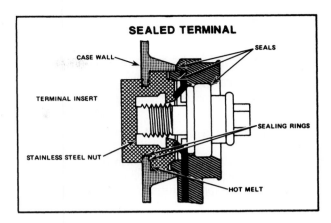

Figure 6.37 Sealed terminals. The sealed terminals of a side terminal battery are easily damaged by improper cable bolt alignment and torque (courtesy of General Motors Corporation).

slightly from the previous procedure and requires additional precautions. A suggested procedure follows:

1. Make sure that all switches and controls are in the OFF position.
2. Using a six-point socket of the correct size, loosen the bolt holding the ground cable to the battery terminal. On most cars, the ground cable is connected to the negative (−) terminal.

   Note: The head of the bolt is very small and easily damaged. Do not attempt to use an open-end wrench or a pair of pliers.

3. Remove the cable from the terminal.
4. Repeat steps 2 and 3 at the remaining terminal.
5. Using a cable and terminal cleaning tool of the type shown in Figure 6.36, clean the cable ends and the terminals on the battery.

6. Clean the top and side of the battery.
7. Install the cable that connects the battery to the starter motor or starter switch. On most cars, this cable connects to the positive (+) terminal and should be installed first to minimize the dangers of arcing and possible battery explosion.

   Note: Thread the cable bolt into place by hand to ensure that it is properly aligned. The bolt should be tightened to the torque specification (19 ft-lb—12 N.m). This should be done with a torque wrench. Excessive torque can damage the terminal in the case (see Figure 6.37).

8. Install the ground cable, tightening it to the torque specification as in step 7.

LESSON 6–6 Removing and Installing Batteries

Battery removal may be necessary for a thorough battery inspection and cleaning, for recharging, to gain access to the battery tray or other parts, or to install a replacement battery. The following steps outline a procedure that will enable you to remove and install a battery safely:

Removal

1. Wear safety glasses or a full face shield when working around a battery.
2. Make sure that all switches and controls are in the OFF position.

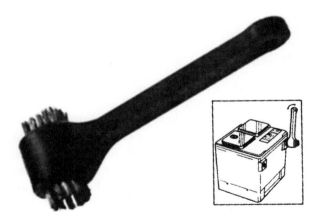

Figure 6.36 A wire brush tool for cleaning the cable end and the recessed terminals used on side terminal batteries (courtesy of KD Tools, Lancaster, PA 17604).

Figure 6.39 A battery carrier strap designed for use with side terminal batteries. Knurled headed screws provide a means of attaching the strap to the terminals (courtesy of KD Tools, Lancaster, PA 17604).

Job 6D

CLEAN BATTERY TERMINALS AND CABLE ENDS

SATISFACTORY PERFORMANCE
A satisfactory performance on this job requires that you do the following:

1. Clean the battery terminals and cable ends on the car assigned.
2. Following the steps in the "Performance Outline" and the recommendations and specifications of the car manufacturer, complete the job within 30 minutes.
3. Fill in the blanks under "Information."

PERFORMANCE OUTLINE

1. Disconnect the cables from the battery.
2. Clean the terminals and the cable ends.
3. Clean the battery top.
4. Install the cables.

INFORMATION

Vehicle identification _____
Battery type: _____ Post terminal
                                                 _____ Side terminal
Which cable was disconnected first?   _____ Positive
                                                 _____ Negative
If the battery was a side terminal battery:
    What was the wrench size of the cable bolt? _____
    What was the bolt torque specification? _____

3. Disconnect the ground cable from the battery terminal.

    Note: On most cars the ground cable is connected to the negative (−) battery terminal.

4. Disconnect the remaining cable.
5. Remove the battery holddown and any heat shield or air duct that may be present. Apply penetrating oil to the threads of the bolts to make this operation easier.

    Note: On some cars the battery hold-down is located at the bottom of the battery. (Refer to

Figure 6.23.) On other cars, the hold-down is positioned across the top of the battery. (Refer to Figure 6.24.)

6. Lift the battery from the battery tray and remove it from the car.

    Note: Take care in performing this step. Batteries are very heavy and contain acid. To avoid the possibility of dropping the battery, use a battery carrier. Figure 6.38 shows a battery carrier commonly used with post terminal batteries. Side terminal batteries can be safely lifted with a carrier similar to the one shown in Figure 6.39. That type of carrier is attached to the battery by bolts that screw into the battery terminals. Some shops use a clamp-type carrier. That type carrier can be used on both post terminal and side terminal batteries.

Some batteries have cases made of a soft, flexible plastic. Attempting to lift those batteries by hand by grasping them on their end walls may result in causing electrolyte to be forced through the vent plugs. If a battery carrier is not available, a battery should be lifted only by grasping it at diagonally opposite corners.

Installation

1. Clean the cable clamps or ends.
2. Inspect the battery tray. If any corrosion is present, clean the tray with a solution of baking soda and water. After drying the tray, coat it with light oil to retard future corrosion. Tighten or replace any loose or damaged bolts that secure the tray to the car. Check that no bolts or sharp edges protrude from the tray where they could contact the battery.
3. Using a battery carrier, carefully place the battery in the tray. Be sure that the terminals are in the correct position.

Figure 6.38 A typical battery carrier strap for use with post terminal batteries (courtesy of KD Tools, Lancaster, PA 17604).

Figure 6.40 Battery cable clamp spreading pliers. A tool of this type is useful for opening the clamp so that a cable can be installed on a new battery (courtesy of KD Tools, Lancaster, PA 17604).

Note: If the original battery is to be installed, clean the terminals and the battery before installing it in the tray.

4. Clean the hold-down assembly and any heat shield that was removed. Cleaning and oiling the threads on the attaching bolts and nuts will make their installation easier.

5. Install the hold-down assembly and any heat shield or air duct that was removed. Tighten the attaching bolts to the manufacturer's torque specifications.

6. Install the battery cables, connecting the ground cable last.

   Note: If the cable clamps will not fit over the terminals on a post terminal battery, they may be spread with the use of a tool similar to the one shown in Figure 6.40.

7. Tighten the clamp nuts or terminal bolts to the torque specifications of the manufacturer.

8. Coat the cable clamps with a thin coating of grease.

9. It may be necessary to reset any electronic accessories in the vehicle. The vehicle emission control computer will reset itself as the vehicle is used. Consult the owner's manual to reset clocks and other electronic items.

LESSON 6–7 Battery Specific Gravity Testing

Battery Testing

Routine maintenance requires testing a battery at regular intervals. The state of charge of some batteries can be determined by a *specific gravity test* that measures the "strength" of the electrolyte. Although it indicates the percentage of charge in a battery, a specific gravity test does not provide a total picture of the battery's condition. Other tests must be made to determine the battery's ability to deliver energy.

Job 6E

REMOVE AND INSTALL A BATTERY

SATISFACTORY PERFORMANCE
A satisfactory performance on this job requires that you do the following:

1. Remove and install the battery in the car assigned.
2. Following the steps in the "Performance Outline" and the specifications of the car manufacturer, complete the job within 30 minutes.
3. Fill in the blanks under "Information."

PERFORMANCE OUTLINE

1. Disconnect the battery cables.
2. Remove the hold-down and related parts.
3. Remove the battery.
4. Inspect and clean the cable ends and battery terminals.
5. Inspect and clean the battery tray.
6. Install the battery and secure it with the hold-down.
7. Install any heat shield or air duct that was removed.
8. Connect the battery cables.

INFORMATION

Vehicle identification _____
Reference used _____ Page(s) _____
Type of battery: _____ Post terminal
                                    _____ Side terminal
Type of hold-down: _____ Top mounted
                                    _____ Bottom mounted
Did the battery have a heat shield?_____ Yes
                                    _____ No
Did the battery have an air duct?   _____ Yes
                                    _____ No
Terminal bolt (nut) torque specification _____
Holddown bolt (nut) torque specification _____

A *high-rate discharge test* or *load test* provides a method of determining the service-ability of a battery while it is working under load. As its name implies, load testing consists of testing a battery while it is working under a load.

A *3-minute charge test* often is made on a battery when it is suspected to be sulfated. All battery tests must be performed in the correct sequence and, in some instances, must follow certain specifications if their results are to be accurate. In addition, all battery tests require the interpretation of test results.

Specific Gravity Testing. *Specific gravity* may be defined as "exact weight." For use as a standard, pure water has been given the arbitrary weight or specific gravity of 1.000. The weight of all other liquids, whether heavier or lighter than water,

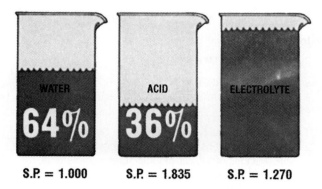

Figure 6.41 The composition, by weight, of a typical battery electrolyte (courtesy of American Motors).

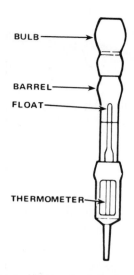

Figure 6.42 A typical battery hydrometer (courtesy of American Motors).

can be determined by comparing them to the weight of water. If a liquid is lighter than water, it will have a lower specific gravity. If a liquid is heavier than water, it will have a higher specific gravity.

Sulfuric acid is much heavier than water. It has a specific gravity of 1.835. Thus any mixture of water and sulfuric acid will have a specific gravity of more than 1.000 and less than 1.835. The specific gravity of any electrolyte is determined by the percentage of water and sulfuric acid that have been combined. One commonly used electrolyte consists of a mixture, by weight, of 64% water and 36% sulfuric acid. As shown in Figure 6.41, that electrolyte has a specific gravity of 1.270.

New batteries are usually filled with an electrolyte that has a specific gravity of 1.265. Most manufacturers consider a battery that has been in service to be fully charged if the electrolyte in the battery has a specific gravity of from 1.250 to 1.265.

The specific gravity of the electrolyte in a conventional battery with removable vent plugs is easily measured with a *hydrometer*. A hydrometer, shown in Figure 6.42, is a syringe-type device that enables you to withdraw a sample of electrolyte from a battery cell. As the electrolyte rises in the glass barrel of the hydrometer, it causes a calibrated float to rise. As shown in Figure 6.43, the float is marked for various specific gravities. If the electrolyte is heavy, as it is in a fully charged battery, the float will be high and will indicate a high specific gravity. If the electrolyte is light, as in a discharged battery, the float will be low and indicate a low specific gravity.

As you learned earlier, the electrolyte in a battery changes to water as the battery discharges. Thus the electrolyte becomes lighter as the battery dis-

charges. This change of weight, shown in Figures 6.44 through 6.47, provides a reliable indication of the battery's state of charge. The percentage of charge for various ranges of specific gravity is given in Figure 6.48.

The specific gravity of a liquid changes with its temperature. As a liquid is heated, it expands

Figure 6.43 A battery hydrometer float (courtesy of General Motors Corporation).

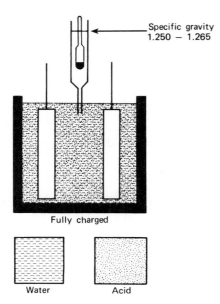

Figure 6.44 Specific gravity (fully charged). The electrolyte in a fully charged battery has a high concentration of acid and thus a high specific gravity.

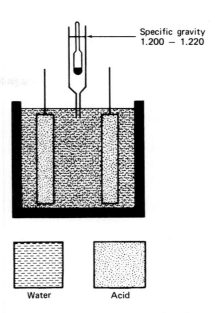

Figure 6.46 Specific gravity (discharged). A large amount of the acid in the electrolyte has combined with the plates. A battery in this condition may not have sufficient energy to start an engine.

and becomes less dense. Thus its specific gravity becomes lower. As a liquid is cooled, it contracts and becomes more dense. Thus its specific gravity becomes higher. Because of this, a partially discharged battery may appear to be fully charged if it is tested when it is cold. For the same rea-

son, a fully charged battery may appear to be partially discharged if it is tested when it is hot (see Figure 6.49).

The specific gravity readings and specifications for electrolyte are accurate only when the electrolyte temperature is 80°F (27°C). If the

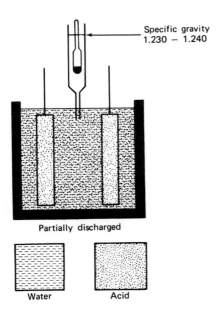

Figure 6.45 Specific gravity (almost discharged). As the battery discharges, the acid combines chemically with the plates, and the specific gravity drops.

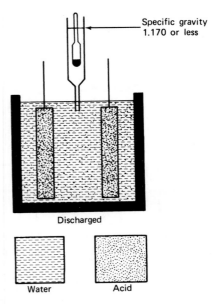

Figure 6.47 Specific gravity (fully discharged). Most of the acid in the electrolyte has combined with the plates. Since the electrolyte now consists mainly of water, it has a very low specific gravity.

PERCENT OF CHARGE	SPECIFIC GRAVITY RANGES
100	1.260–1.265
95	1.250–1.260
75	1.230–1.240
50	1.200–1.220
25	1.170–1.190

Batteries containing electrolyte with a lower specific gravity should be considered discharged.

Figure 6.48 Specific gravity and percent discharge. Approximate percentages of the state of charge for various ranges of battery electrolyte specific gravity.

electrolyte is at any other temperature, the hydrometer readings must be corrected. Most hydrometers contain a thermometer that enables you to determine the temperature of the electrolyte. Electrolyte temperature must always be considered when using a hydrometer to determine the state of charge of a battery.

The temperature correction chart in Figure 6.50 provides an easy method by which you can correct specific gravity readings within a wide range of temperatures. That chart reflects a 0.004 change in specific gravity for each 10°F (5.5°C) change in temperature. For every 10°F (5.5°C) over 80°F (27°C), 0.004 must be added to the hydrometer reading. For every 10°F (5.5°C) under 80°F (27°C), 0.004 must be subtracted from the hydrometer reading.

Interpreting Test Results. If the electrolyte temperature was approximately 80°F (27°C), the specific gravity readings may be considered accurate as recorded. Specific gravity readings of electrolyte at any other temperature must be corrected. Refer to Figure 6.50 to correct the specific gravity. Then refer to Figure 6.48 to determine the state of charge of the battery.

Batteries with electrolyte whose specific gravity is less than 1.240 may be charged to increase the specific gravity. Batteries with a specific gravity of less than 1.200 should be charged before any further testing is attempted.

The specific gravity of all the cells in a battery should not vary more than 0.050. If the readings vary more than 0.050, the battery may be sulfated and may require replacement.

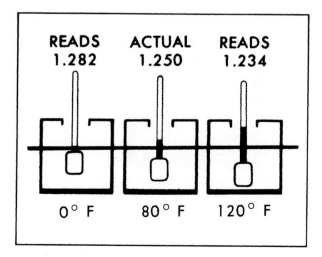

Figure 6.49 Temperature correcting readings. Specific gravity reading must be corrected for temperature. Conventional hydrometers are accurate only at 80°F (27°C) (courtesy of General Motors Corporation).

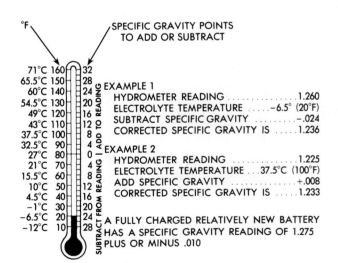

Figure 6.50 A hydrometer correction chart for correcting specific gravity readings for various electrolyte temperatures (courtesy of Chrysler Corporation).

The following steps outline a procedure for measuring the specific gravity of the electrolyte in a battery:

1. Place a fender cover over the fender nearest the battery.

   Note: Remember that electrolyte is an acid and is highly corrosive. Wear safety glasses and use care not to spill or splash any electrolyte during this procedure.

2. Remove the vent plugs or covers from the cells and place them on the battery as shown in Figure 6.51.

3. Squeeze the suction bulb of the hydrometer and insert the pickup tube into the cell closest to the positive (+) post.

   Note: Do not force the tube into the cell because you might damage the plates and the separators.

4. Slowly release the bulb and draw in sufficient electrolyte to halfway fill the barrel.

   Note: If there is insufficient electrolyte in the cell, an accurate test cannot be made. Water must be added to the cell and the battery must be charged so that the water will mix with the electrolyte.

5. Slowly squeeze the bulb to return the electrolyte to the cell.

   Note: This step adjusts the temperature of the hydrometer to that of the electrolyte and provides for a more accurate first reading.

6. Slowly release the bulb again and draw in sufficient electrolyte to cause the float to rise.

   Note: Hold the hydrometer in a vertical position so the float does not drag against the inside of the barrel.

7. Read the specific gravity indicated on the float. Be sure the float is floating free in the electrolyte and not in contact with the spacer at the top of the barrel.

   Note: An accurate reading requires that you bend down so the reading is taken at eye level, as shown in Figure 6.52. Do not remove the hydrometer from the battery because that will allow electrolyte leakage. Also note from Figure 6.53 that you should disregard the slight curvature of the electrolyte.

8. Note the temperature indicated by the thermometer.

9. Slowly squeeze the bulb and return all of the electrolyte to the cell.

10. Record the specific gravity and the electrolyte temperature.

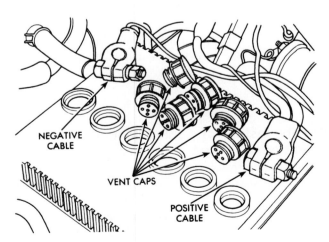

Figure 6.51 Vent cap removal. Remove all vent plugs or caps before testing specific gravity. Placing the caps on the battery minimizes the possibility of electrolyte damage to other surfaces (courtesy of Chrysler Corporation).

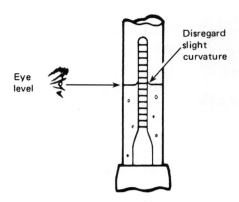

Figure 6.52 Reading a hydrometer. When reading a hydrometer, hold it vertically so the float does not touch the sides of the barrel. To obtain an accurate reading, the liquid should be at eye level (courtesy of American Motors).

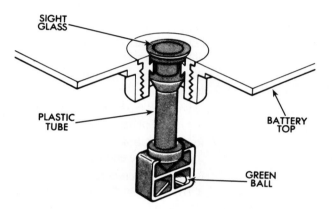

Figure 6.53 Built-in hydrometer. A built-in hydrometer of the type used in most sealed batteries. When the green ball floats in the electrolyte, it is visible in the sight glass. When the battery is discharged and the green ball sinks, the sight glass appears dark. When the electrolyte level drops below the hydrometer, the sight glass appears dear or light yellow (courtesy of Chrysler Corporation).

11. Repeat steps 3 through 10 for the remaining cells.
12. Install the vent plugs or covers.
13. Clean and dry the top of the battery.

Specific Gravity Testing of Sealed Maintenance-Free Batteries. A sealed, maintenance-free battery has no removable vent plugs. Therefore, a conventional hydrometer cannot be used to determine the state of charge. Most sealed batteries incorporate a built-in temperature-compensated hydrometer as shown in Figure 6.53. The sight glass is located in the battery top as shown in Figure 6.54. While the built-in hydrometer does not provide an accurate measurement of the specific gravity of the electrolyte in each cell, it does provide sufficient information for diagnosis.

As shown in Figure 6.55, the most commonly used type of built-in hydrometer provides three indications:

1. *Green dot visible.* Any green appearance should be considered a "green dot." This indicates that the state of charge is satisfactory and the battery is ready for further testing.
2. *Dark—green dot not visible.* A dark appearance without a green dot indicates that the battery is partially discharged. Further testing is required to determine if the battery can be charged or if it should be replaced.

Figure 6.54 A sealed battery with a built-in temperature-compensated hydrometer (courtesy of Pontiac Motor Division, General Motors Corporation).

3. *Clear or light yellow.* A clear or light yellow appearance indicates that the electrolyte level is

A maintenance-free battery can have a defective cell and still have a green dot visible in the hydrometer eye. The hydrometer only checks one cell. If a maintenance-free battery has less than 12.6 volts, charge the battery and check the voltage again. If the battery will not charge up to 12.6 volts and will not produce enough amperage to run the starter, the battery is defective and should be replaced.

so low that it is below the bottom of the built-in hydrometer. This usually means that the bat-

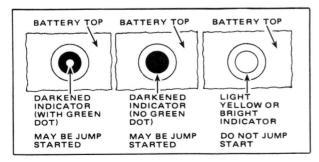

Figure 6.55 Reading provided by a built-in hydrometer (courtesy of Chevrolet Motor Division, General Motors Corporation).

tery is defective. If a clear or light yellow appearance is accompanied by a failure to crank the engine, the battery should be replaced. DO NOT ATTEMPT TO CHARGE, TEST, OR JUMP-START.

LESSON 6–8 Battery Load Testing
Load Testing

A hydrometer can be used to determine the state of charge of a battery, but it cannot measure the battery's ability to deliver energy. A *load test* provides a method of determining the service-ability of a battery. As its name implies, load testing consists of testing a battery while it is working under a load.

Many different instruments and procedures may be used to load test a battery. All of those instruments and procedures, however, require that battery voltage be measured while the battery is being discharged at a high rate. For this reason, a load test is often referred to as a *high-rate discharge test.*

A tester similar to the one shown in Figure 6.56 is most commonly used to load test a battery. In addition to various selector switches, the tester contains an adjustable resistance unit, an ammeter, and a voltmeter. The adjustable resistance unit is usually a *carbon pile.* A carbon pile is a stack of carbon discs that can be squeezed together to form a low-resistance unit capable of handling large amounts of current. The ammeter measures the amount of current flowing through the carbon pile. The voltmeter measures the battery voltage.

In use, the tester is connected across the terminals of a battery as shown in Figure 6.57. The carbon pile is adjusted by means of the control knob until a specified current is shown on the ammeter. That current will vary from 150 amperes to over 300 amperes depending on the battery being tested. The voltage indicated by the voltmeter is read after the load has been maintained for 15 seconds.

The following steps outline a typical procedure for load testing a battery. Consult an appropriate manual for the correct load to place on the battery you are testing.

1. Place a fender cover on the fender near the battery.
2. Test the specific gravity and temperature of the battery. If the specific gravity is less than 1.200, charge the battery before attempting a load test. If the temperature of the battery is less than 60°F (15.5°C), allow the temperature of the battery to rise before attempting a load test.

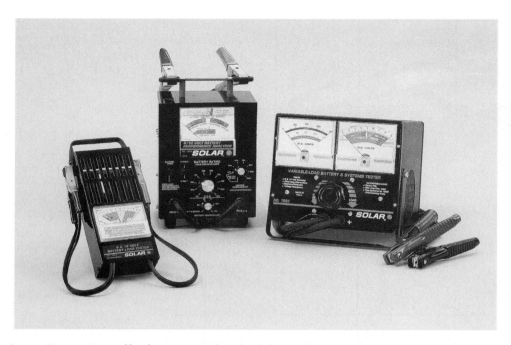

Figure 6.56 Battery Testers. Testers like these are used to check the condition of a battery or charging system. Some place a load on the battery to check the amperage output indirectly by measuring the voltage drop of the battery when loaded (courtesy of Century MFG. Co.).

3. Disconnect the battery cables from the terminals.

   Note: Disconnect the ground cable first. This will minimize the possibility of arcing and a resultant battery explosion.

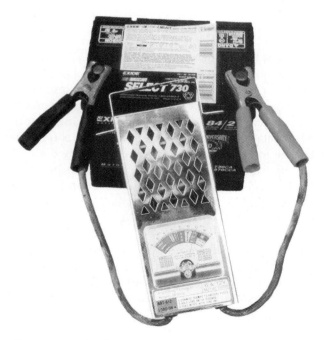

Figure 6.57 A volt-amp tester connected to perform a battery load test (courtesy of Training Enterprises Company).

4. Turn the control knob on the battery tester to the OFF position.
5. If the tester is fitted with a function control switch, turn the switch to the Battery Test position.
6. If the tester is fitted with a volt selector switch, turn the switch to select a voltage exceeding battery voltage.
7. Connect the heavy ammeter leads to the battery terminals. The positive (+) lead must be connected to the positive (+) terminal, the negative (−) lead to the negative (−) terminal.

   Note: When testing side terminal batteries, use post adapters or a post adapter tool similar to the one shown in Figure 6.58 so a good connection can be obtained.

8. Connect the voltmeter leads to the battery terminals. The positive (+) lead must be connected to the positive (+) terminal, the negative (−) lead to the negative (−) terminal.

   Note: The voltmeter leads should contact the battery posts or adapters. If the volt-meter leads are connected to the clamps on the ammeter leads, an inaccurate voltmeter reading may be obtained.

9. Refer to an appropriate manual for the correct load to place on the battery being tested.

Job 6F

TEST THE SPECIFIC GRAVITY OF BATTERY ELECTROLYTE AND INTERPRET THE TEST RESULTS

SATISFACTORY PERFORMANCE

A satisfactory performance on this job requires that you do the following:

1. Test the specific gravity of the electrolyte in the battery assigned.
2. Following the steps in the "Performance Outline," complete the job within 20 minutes.
3. Fill in the blanks under "Information."

PERFORMANCE OUTLINE

1. Remove the vent plugs.
2. Measure and record the specific gravity and the temperature of the electrolyte in each cell.
3. Install the vent plugs.
4. Clean and dry the battery top.
5. Correct the specific gravity readings if necessary and determine the state of charge of the battery.

INFORMATION

Vehicle identification _____
Battery identification _____

Test readings obtained:

Cell #	SPECIFIC GRAVITY	TEMPERATURE
1	_____	_____
2	_____	_____
3	_____	_____
4	_____	_____
5	_____	_____
6	_____	_____

Corrections and test interpretations:

CELL #	CORRECTED SPECIFIC GRAVITY	PERCENT OF CHARGE
1	_____	_____
2	_____	_____
3	_____	_____
4	_____	_____
5	_____	_____
6	_____	_____

Recommendations: _____

_____

_____

Note: Some manufacturers provide specific discharge rates for their batteries. An example of those specific loads is shown in Figure 6.59.

10. Turn the control knob clockwise as shown in Figure 6.60 until the desired discharge rate is indicated by the ammeter. Allow the control to remain in this position for 15 seconds and then turn the control to the OFF position.

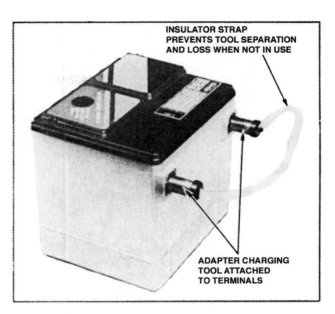

Figure 6.58 Side terminal adapters. Adapters can be attached to side terminal batteries to facilitate testing (courtesy of Pontiac Motor Division, General Motors Corporation).

Note: This initial load removes any "surface charge" from the battery and provides more accurate test results.

11. After waiting about 15 seconds, again turn the control knob clockwise until the desired discharge rate is indicated.

Conventional Batteries	
Battery Capacity (Ampere Hours)	Discharge Rate (Amperes)
36	155
41	145
45	190
53	175
54	225
68	220
77	228
Maintenance-Free Batteries	
Battery Capacity (Ampere Hours)	Discharge Rate (Amperes)
53	200
63	215
68	235

Figure 6.59 Discharge rates specified by one car manufacturer for batteries of different ampere-hour ratings.

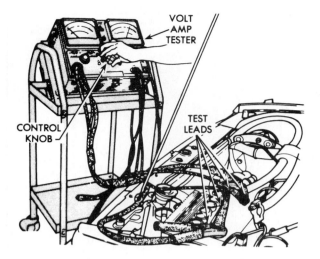

Figure 6.60 Applying a battery load. A load is applied to the battery by turning the control knob clockwise (courtesy of Chrysler Corporation).

12. Maintain the desired discharge rate for 15 seconds and note the voltage indicated by the voltmeter.
13. Immediately turn the control knob to the OFF position.

Note: It is not advisable to maintain the load for more than 15 seconds.

14. Disconnect the tester from the battery.
15. Connect the battery cables.

Note: Connect the cable that runs to the starter motor or starter switch first. Connect the ground cable last.

Interpreting Test Results

A 12-volt battery in good condition will maintain a voltage of at least 9.6 volts while the specific load is applied. Since battery temperature affects the indicated voltage, the chart in Figure 6.61 lists the

MINIMUM VOLTAGE UNDER SPECIFIED LOAD	BATTERY °F	TEMPERATURE °C
9.6	70	21
9.5	60	16
9.4	50	10
9.3	40	4
9.1	30	-1
8.9	20	-7
8.7	10	-12
8.5	0	-18

Figure 6.61 Minimum voltages during load testing.

Job 6G

LOAD TEST A BATTERY

SATISFACTORY PERFORMANCE
A satisfactory performance on this job requires that you do the following:

1. Perform a load test (high-rate discharge test) on the battery assigned.
2. Following the steps in the "Performance Outline" and the specifications of the manufacturer, complete the job within 20 minutes.
3. Fill in the blanks under "Information."

PERFORMANCE OUTLINE

1. Test the specific gravity of the battery electrolyte.
2. Disconnect the battery cables.
3. Connect the tester.
4. Apply the specified load.
5. Read the voltage while the battery is under load.
6. Remove the load.
7. Disconnect the tester.
8. Connect the battery cables.

INFORMATION

Vehicle identification _____
Battery identification _____
Reference used _____ Page(s) _____
Battery ampere-hour capacity _____
Hydrometer readings: 1 ____ 2 ____ 3 ____
　　　　　　　　　　 4 ____ 5 ____ 6 ____
Electrolyte temperature _____
Corrected hydrometer readings:
　　　　　　　　　 1 ____ 2 ____ 3 ____
　　　　　　　　　 4 ____ 5 ____ 6 ____
Specified discharge rate (test load)
Tester identification _____
Amount of time load was maintained _____
Voltage indicated while under load _____
Recommendations:
____ Battery should be returned to service.
____ Battery should be charged and returned to service.
____ Battery should be replaced.

minimum voltage allowable for temperatures lower than 70°F (21°C).

If the indicated voltage during a load test drops below those listed in Figure 6.61, the battery is defective and should be replaced.

LESSON 6–9　Battery Charging

A battery in good condition may occasionally fail. This usually is noticed by the car owner when the battery is unable to crank the engine fast enough so that it will start. The most common causes of a failure of this type are as follows:

1. The lights or other accessories were accidentally left on for an extended period of time.
2. Poor battery maintenance, including failure to maintain the electrolyte level, loose connections, dirty connections, or an improperly secured battery.
3. Problems in the charging system, including loose drive belts, a faulty alternator, a faulty regulator, or high resistance in connections and components.
4. Trips of short duration that do not allow sufficient time for the charging system to restore the energy used for starting.
5. Defects in the electrical system such as short circuits.
6. The application of electrical loads exceeding the capacity of the alternator. This is usually caused by the use of aftermarket equipment such as radio systems, air conditioners, and special lighting systems.
7. Battery self-discharge during a long period of inactivity.

A discharged battery in good condition can be charged and returned to service. To prevent a recurrence, the causes of the discharged condition should be determined and, if possible, corrected.

Many types of battery chargers are in use, but all chargers operate on the same principle. They apply an electrical pressure that forces current through the battery to reverse the electrochemical action in the cells (see Figure 6.62).

> **⚠ Warning:** When a battery is being charged, an explosive mixture of gases including hydrogen and oxygen is released from the electrolyte. Those gases are present in the cells and in the area surrounding the battery. To avoid the possibility of igniting those gases, observe the following precautions:

1. Never connect or disconnect live charger leads to a battery or otherwise break a live circuit at the battery. To do so may cause arcing and possibly ignite the gases. The charger should be turned OFF before the leads are disconnected, connected, or otherwise disturbed.
2. Keep all open flames away from a battery.

Figure 6.62 Battery Charger. When a battery needs to be recharged, a machine like this one is used. A high voltage (over 13 to 16 volts) and high amperage charge (up to 30 or 40 amps) is placed in the battery until the battery reaches its rated voltage (12.6 volts) (courtesy of Century MFG. Co.).

3. Do not smoke near a battery on charge or near a battery that has recently been charged.
4. If possible, charge batteries in a well-ventilated area.

Charging Rates. The amount of charge a battery receives is equal to the rate of charge, in amperes, multiplied by the amount of time, in hours, that the charge is applied. As an example, a battery charged at the rate of 5 amperes for a period of 5 hours would receive a 25 ampere-hour charge. To bring a battery to a fully charged condition, you must restore the ampere-hours that were removed from it. Since 100% efficiency cannot be obtained on recharging, approximately 20% must be added to your calculations to allow for losses in the charging process.

Slow Charging. If time allows, slow charging should be used to recharge a discharged battery. Slow charging consists of charging a battery at a

---

| **CHARGING A BATTERY** | The following steps outline a procedure for charging a battery. Consult the instructions provided with the charger you have available. The charging specifications should be obtained from an appropriate manual and used with consideration for the condition of the battery you will charge: |

1. Place a fender cover over the fender nearest the battery.
2. If the battery is not sealed, check the electrolyte level in all of the cells and adjust the level if necessary.

   Note: Do not attempt to charge a battery that appears to be frozen or if ice crystals are visible in the electrolyte. Allow the battery to thaw fully before charging is attempted.

3. If the battery is a sealed battery, check the built-in hydrometer. Do not attempt to charge the battery if the indicator appears clear or light yellow (refer to Figure 6.55).
4. Disconnect the battery cables. This prevents possible damage to electrical components in the car during charging.

   Note: Disconnect the ground cable first to minimize the possibility of arcing and a resultant battery explosion.

5. Clean the battery terminals and the battery top.
6. Consult an appropriate manual and determine the charging rate and time for the battery.
7. Turn the charger switch to the OFF position.
8. Connect the charger leads to the battery. The positive (+) lead must be connected to the positive (+) terminal, the negative (−) lead to the negative (−) terminal.

   Note: If you are charging a side terminal battery, install post adapters to ensure a good connection (refer to Figure 6.58).

9. Turn the charger switch to the ON position.

   Note: On some chargers, the timer must be set to turn on the charger.

10. Adjust the charging rate.
11. Adjust the timer.
12. Check the charging rate and the battery temperature after the battery has been charging for about 15 minutes. Adjust the charging rate if required.
13. Continue charging until the allotted time has elapsed or until the battery is fully charged.
14. Turn the charger switch to the OFF position.
15. Disconnect the charger leads from the battery.
16. Connect the battery cables.

    Note: Connect the ground cable last.

---

rate of about 5 amperes for a time sufficient to bring the specific gravity to its highest reading. Depending on the existing state of charge of the battery, slow charging may require 12 to 24 hours or more. During the charging period, the electrolyte temperature should not exceed 110°F (43°C). If the electrolyte temperature rises above this limit, the charging rate should be decreased.

> Slow charging is always preferred over fast charging. Fast charging produces more heat and can cause internal battery damage.

A battery on slow charge is considered fully charged when the electrolyte is *gassing*, or steaming freely, and when no further rise in specific

> Connect a voltmeter to a battery when using a battery charger to monitor the voltage charging rate. Do not let the voltage charging rate climb above 15.5 volts. This is the same voltage rate as the vehicle alternator charging rate and is safe for the battery.

gravity is noted during three successive hydrometer readings taken at intervals of 1 hour. A sealed battery should be slow charged until the green

Job 6H

CHARGE A BATTERY

SATISFACTORY PERFORMANCE

A satisfactory performance on this job requires that you do the following:

1. Recharge the battery assigned.
2. Following the steps in the "Performance Outline" and the charging recommendations of the manufacturer, complete the job within 30 minutes plus the charging time.
3. Fill in the blanks under "Information."

PERFORMANCE OUTLINE

1. Check the electrolyte level and adjust the level if required.
2. Disconnect the battery cables.
3. Clean the battery terminals and the battery top.
4. Determine the charging rate and time.
5. Connect the charger and adjust the charging rate and time.
6. Check the charging rate and the battery temperature.
7. Turn the charger OFF when completed.
8. Disconnect the charger.
9. Connect the battery cables.

INFORMATION

Vehicle identification _____
Battery identification _____
Reference used _____ Page(s) _____
Recommended charging rate: _____ amperes for _____ hours
Battery was charged at the rate of _____ amperes
Battery temperature during period of charge _____
Length of time battery was charged _____
Specific gravity of electrolyte at completion _____

dot appears. In some instances, a sealed battery must be tipped or shaken to allow the green dot to appear.

Fast Charging. If time is not available to slow charge a battery, fast charging at a high rate is permissible. Although fast charging does not fully recharge a battery, it restores the charge sufficiently to allow the battery to be used. If the charging system in the car is operating properly, the battery will continue charging in service.

Fast charging consists of charging a battery at a rate of from 10 to 50 amperes. The exact charging rate depends on the construction of the battery and the time available. The temperature of the electrolyte provides an indication of the correct charging rate. If the electrolyte temperature rises above 125°F (65°C), the charging rate is too high and should be reduced. Because a high charging rate and the resultant high temperatures can damage a battery, a battery should be charged at the lowest possible rate. Most car manufacturers specify the charging rates and charging times for their batteries. Figure 6.63 shows the specifications provided in the manual of one car maker.

LESSON 6–10 **Using Jumper Cables Jump Starting**

A booster battery is often used to jump-start the engine of a car that has a discharged battery. The

Watt Rating	5 Amperes	10 Amperes	20 Amperes	30 Amperes	40 Amperes	50 Amperes
Below 2450	10 Hours	5 Hours	2½ Hours	2 Hours		
2450–2950	12 Hours	6 Hours	3 Hours	2 Hours	1½ Hours	
Above 2950	15 Hours	7½ Hours	3¼ Hours	2 Hours	1¾ Hours	1½ Hours

*Initial rate for constant voltage taper rate charger.
To avoid damage, charging rate must be reduced or temporarily halted if:
    1. Electrolyte temperature exceeds 125° F.
    2. Violent gassing or spewing of electrolyte occurs.
Battery is fully charged when over a two hour period at a low charging rate in amperes all cells are gassing freely and no change in specific gravity occurs. For the most satisfactory charging, the lower charging rates in amperes are recommended.
Full charge specific gravity is 1.260–1.280 corrected for temperature with electrolyte level at split ring.

Figure 6.63 Typical charging rates. Typical charging rates and times for fully discharged batteries as recommended by one car manufacturer (courtesy of Buick Motor Division, General Motors Corporation).

Figure 6.64 A pair of jumper cables (courtesy of Perfect Parts, Inc., Carlstadt, NJ).

booster battery may be a separate battery brought to the disabled vehicle. It may also be the battery in another car. Jumper cables similar to those shown in Figure 6.64 are usually used to connect

the booster battery to the car with the discharged battery.

Properly connected, a booster battery enables you to provide an important emergency service. Improperly connected, a booster battery can cause serious damage to automotive electrical systems and may even cause a battery explosion.

Observe the following precautions when using a booster battery:

1. Wear safety glasses.
2. Do not allow electrolyte to contact your eyes, skin, clothing, or the finish of the vehicles.
3. Do not lean over a battery when connecting or disconnecting cables.
4. Do not allow the jumper cable clamps to touch each other when installed.
5. Keep open flame and sparks away from the batteries.
6. Do not connect a booster battery directly to a discharged battery (see Figure 6.65).

USING A BOOSTER BATTERY TO JUMP-START AN ENGINE

The following steps outline a typical procedure for using a booster battery to jump-start an engine. Some car manufacturers have established alternate procedures to protect certain electrical components used in their products. Consult an appropriate manual for the jump-starting procedures recommended by the manufacturer of the car you wish to start:

1. Check to see that all switches and other electrical controls in the car are in the OFF position.
2. If the discharged battery is a sealed, maintenance-free battery, check the charge indicator. If the charge indicator is light or yellow, as shown in Figure 6.55, *do not* attempt to jump-start the engine. Replace the battery.
3. If the discharged battery has removable vent plugs, remove them and check the electrolyte level.

   Note: During cold weather, the electrolyte in a discharged battery may freeze. If the electrolyte is not visible, or if it appears that the electrolyte is frozen, *do not* attempt to jump-start the engine. A frozen battery may rupture or explode if a booster battery is connected to it. Thaw a frozen battery by placing it in a warm area. After the battery has thawed, adjust the electrolyte level as necessary. Then test and charge the battery in the normal manner.

   > Always check the built-in hydrometer eye on batteries equipped with them before hooking up and starting the battery charger or attempting a jump start. A light yellow or bright indicator means DO NOT CHARGE OR JUMP-START.

4. If the electrolyte is not frozen, and if the level is above the tops of the plates, install CAPS.
5. Connect the jumper cables with the red marked ends between the positive (+) terminal of the discharged battery and the positive (+) terminal of the booster battery as shown in Figure 6.65.

   Note: Be sure the clamps on the jumper cables are firmly connected to the battery terminals.

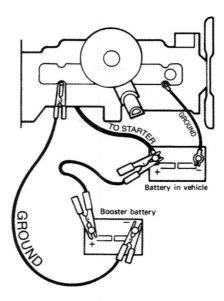

Figure 6.65 Correct jumper cable hookup. The correct placement of jumper cables when a booster battery is used to jump-start an engine. Note that the negative (−) jumper cable is connected to the engine (courtesy of American Motors).

6. Connect one end of the remaining black marked cable to the negative (−) terminal of the booster battery (see Figure 6.65).
7. Attach the remaining end of the black marked jumper cable to a good ground on the engine, away from the battery (see Figure 6.65).

   Note: Some manufacturers recommend that the negative (−) jumper cable be connected to the alternator bracket or to the air conditioner compressor bracket, as shown in Figure 6.66. Do not attach the cable to any part of the fuel system.

8. Making sure that the parking brake is applied and that the shift lever is in the PARK or NEUTRAL position, attempt to start the engine in the normal manner.
9. After the engine has started (or if the engine fails to start), the jumper cables should be disconnected in the reverse order by which they were connected.

   Note: Disconnect the negative (−) jumper cable from the ground on the engine FIRST.

10. Remove and discard the cloths that were used to cover the battery openings.
11. Install the vent plugs on the batteries.

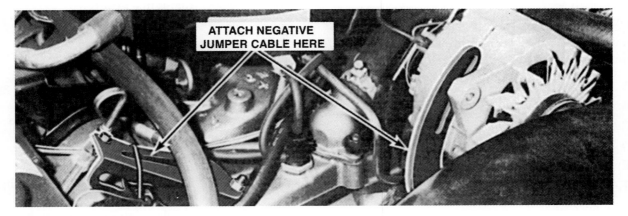

Figure 6.66 Where to attach negative cable. Some car manufacturers recommend a specific location, such as the alternator bracket or the air conditioner compressor bracket, for the attachment of a jumper cable (courtesy of Pontiac Motor Division, General Motors Corporation).

Job 6I

USE A BOOSTER BATTERY TO JUMP-START AN ENGINE

SATISFACTORY PERFORMANCE

A satisfactory performance on this job requires that you do the following:

1. Use a booster battery to start the engine of the car assigned.
2. Following the steps in the "Performance Outline" and the procedure and specifications of the car manufacturer, complete the job within 15 minutes.
3. Fill in the blanks under "Information."

PERFORMANCE OUTLINE

1. Determine that the discharged battery in the vehicle is in a condition that will allow safe starting.
2. Connect the booster battery to the car.
3. Start the engine.
4. Disconnect the booster battery.

INFORMATION

Vehicle identification _____

Vehicle battery condition:

Electrolyte level: ____ Above the tops of the plates
                   ____ Below the tops of the plates

Electrolyte temperature: ____ Above 40°F (4°C)
                         ____ Below 40°F (4°C)

The positive (+) booster cable was connected to:
____ The positive (+) terminal on the car's battery
____ A good ground on the engine

The negative (−) booster cable was connected to:
____ The negative (−) terminal on the car's battery
____ A good ground on the engine

Which cable was connected first?   ____ Positive
                                    ____ Negative

Which cable was disconnected first? ____ Positive
                                    ____ Negative

VOCABULARY

Use the listed words in the blanks beside the sentences to complete the definitions. Either write out the words or place the letters in the blanks.

A. Sponge lead

B. Electrolyte

C. Cycled

D. Charged

E. Cell voltage

F. Series

G. Plate strap

H. Capacity

I. Element

J. Battery case

K. Sediment chambers

L. Arc

M. Amp-hour

N. Cold cranking amperage

O. Trickle charge

P. Corrosion

Q. Resistance

R. Ground cable

S. Battery tray

T. Green dot

U. Dark dot

V. Light yellow dot

W. Carbon pile

X. Jump-start

Y. Fast charge

_____ 1. A positive and negative plate group complete with separators

_____ 2. A very small charge used to keep a battery at full strength

_____ 3. Indicates the battery is defective

_____ 4. 2.1 volts

_____ 5. Negative plate material used in a battery

_____ 6. When a battery is partially discharged and then recharged many times

_____ 7. Electrical spark that occurs when the battery charger leads are removed

_____ 8. A 64% water and 36% sulfuric acid solution

_____ 9. Determined by the number of plates in a group

_____ 10. Spaces between the bridges to collect active plate materials

_____ 11. The way the cells are connected in a battery

_____ 12. Shows when the battery has an adequate charge

_____ 13. When a battery is charged at a rate of 10 up to 50 amperes

_____ 14. Runs from the negative terminal to the engine

_____ 15. The amount of current being used each hour

_____ 16. Similar plates joined together by this part at the top

_____ 17. Used to place a load on a battery

_____ 18. The force opposing the flow of current in a wire

_____ 19. Amount of amperage to crank a battery for a period of time

_____ 20. Part used to place all the battery materials inside

_____ 21. When the specific gravity reaches its peak and the battery voltage equals 12.6 volts

_____ 22. When another system is used to crank an engine

_____ 23. Indicates when a battery is very badly discharged

_____ 24. Part the battery fits into in a vehicle

_____ 25. Oxidation and rust that prevents a good electrical connection

REVIEW QUESTIONS

The following questions will help you determine if you have accomplished the tasks stated at the beginning of the chapter. If you don't know many of the answers, go back and review the material before proceeding to the next chapter.

Lesson 6–1

1. What happens when two different metals are immersed in an acid solution?
2. What metals are used in automotive batteries?
3. What happens to the plates and electrolyte when a battery is discharging?
4. When do both battery plates turn to lead sulfate?
5. What should the voltage of a fully charged battery cell measure?
6. A true maintenance-free battery is _____ and is not provided with _____ vent plugs.
7. What are the plates of a lead-acid battery built on?
8. How is the lead oxide material on a positive grid changed to lead peroxide?
9. What two parts make up the element?
10. What kind of materials are used to make a battery case?
11. What part is also the battery vent on a serviceable battery?
12. What is meant by side terminals?
13. In a maintenance-free battery what replaces traditional separators?
14. How much voltage will a fully charged lead-acid battery cell produce?

Lesson 6–2

15. What can battery electrolyte do to paint and metal?
16. What piece of safety equipment is better for battery use than safety glasses?
17. What can happen to a ring if it shorts out a battery?
18. What gasses are being produced when a battery is being charged?
19. What should be done to a battery charger before removing the cables?
20. Which battery terminal should always be removed first and why?
21. What type of parts can be damaged in a battery if the polarity is reversed?

Lesson 6–3

22. When battery size is increased what is also increased?
23. Why is terminal location important in battery selection?
24. Which terminal should be kept from touching the vehicle metal when the cables are in place?
25. What does *amp-hour* mean?
26. What is the term used to indicate the amount of amperage available to crank the starter?
27. Name two special applications that require special batteries.
28. What can be done to prevent battery sulfating?
29. What is the difference in batteries made to run in vehicles idle for long periods of time?

Lesson 6–4

30. How should a battery be held in place?
31. What problem should be avoided when the hold-down is tightened?
32. How is heat from the engine prevented from damaging some batteries?
33. What mixture can be used to neutralize battery acid spills?
34. What can cause a battery to self-discharge?
35. Name three things to look for when making a battery inspection.
36. What is the result when the battery connections get corroded?

Lesson 6–5

37. What is a common cause of high resistance at the cable clamp?
38. What should be done to all switches and controls before the battery cables are removed?
39. Which battery cable should be removed first?
40. What is the name of the tool to be used if the cable clamp cannot be loosened?

41. What happens to a battery if baking soda and water enters the cells?
42. Which cable should always be installed first?
43. What is the torque tightening specification for a side terminal bolt?

Lesson 6–6

44. Name two common styles of hold-downs in use today.
45. What is the name of the tool used to lift a battery from the vehicle?
46. How should a battery with soft flexible plastic be removed by hand from a vehicle?
47. What should always be done before the original battery is installed back in the vehicle?
48. After the battery cables have been removed, what effect does this have on some electronic devices?
49. What happens to the electronic computer when a battery has been removed and reinstalled?

Lesson 6–7

50. What does a specific gravity test measure?
51. What is another name for a high-rate discharge test?
52. What is the definition of specific gravity?
53. What is the specific gravity of sulfuric acid?
54. What is the specific gravity of a mixture of 64% water and 36% sulfuric acid?
55. What will be the specific gravity range for batteries that have been in service?
56. What is the name of the tester used to test specific gravity?
57. What happens to the specific gravity readings of a battery that is being discharged?
58. At what temperature will the specific gravity readings not have to be temperature compensated?
59. At what specific gravity reading will a battery have to be charged before tests are made?
60. What does the green dot mean if showing in a built-in hydrometer?
61. If the "eye" is dark with the green dot not visible, what does this mean?
62. When there is a clear or light yellow "eye" showing, what does this mean?

Lesson 6–8

63. What does a hydrometer test not measure?
64. How long is the carbon pile load placed on the battery?
65. If the specific gravity of the battery is below 1.200, what should be done to the battery before it is load tested?

66. If the battery temperature is below____ , the battery should be warmed up before testing.
67. How is a surface charge removed from a battery?
68. What is the lowest voltage drop allowed for a battery at a temperature of 20°F?
69. What are the three major parts of a battery load tester?

Lesson 6–9

70. Give three reasons a good battery will fail.
71. The amount of charge a battery receives is equal to the rate of charge in _____ times the amount of time in _____.
72. How much time must be added to the charging time to allow for losses in the charging process?
73. How long, in hours, should a battery be slow charged?
74. When is a battery on slow charged considered finished?
75. How many ampere-hours would a battery receive that was charged for 3 hours at 14 amperes?
76. How long should a sealed battery be slow charged?
77. What is the fast charging ampere range?
78. What is used to make the determination on whether to charge a sealed battery?

Lesson 6–10

79. Can a vehicle with a frozen battery be jump-started?
80. Where on the disabled vehicle should the negative cable be attached?
81. On the vehicle used for the jump start, where should the negative cable be attached?
82. List three safety steps that should be followed when jump-starting a vehicle.

ASE QUESTIONS

Each question or incomplete statement in this test is followed by four suggested answers or completions. In each case select the *one* that best answers the question or completes the statement.

1. Technician A says the positive plate of a lead-acid battery cell is lead peroxide. Technician B says the negative plate is made up of sponge lead. Who is right?
   a. A only   b. B only
   c. Both A and B   d. Neither A nor B

2. Technician A says a battery surface charge must be removed before a voltage test will be accurate. Technician B says the surface charge will not affect a voltage test. Who is right?
   - a. A only
   - b. B only
   - c. Both A and B
   - d. Neither A nor B

3. Technician A says there are the same number of negative plates in a battery as there are positive plates. Technician B says there are more negative plates than positive plates. Who is right?
   - a. A only
   - b. B only
   - c. Both A and B
   - d. Neither A nor B

4. Technician A says a fully charged lead-acid battery cell will produce 2.1 volts. Technician B says that a fully charged lead-acid battery cell will produce 2 volts. Who is right?
   - a. A only
   - b. B only
   - c. Both A and B
   - d. Neither A nor B

5. Technician A says the positive battery post has a larger diameter than the negative post. Technician B says the battery posts are both the same diameter. Who is right?
   - a. A only
   - b. B only
   - c. Both A and B
   - d. Neither A nor B

6. Technician A says the size of a battery does not affect the amperage output of the battery. Technician B says the larger batteries will supply more voltage. Who is right?
   - a. A only
   - b. B only
   - c. Both A and B
   - d. Neither A nor B

7. Technician A says the sealed battery terminals can not be cleaned. Technician B says all terminals can be cleaned. Who is right?
   - a. A only
   - b. B only
   - c. Both A and B
   - d. Neither A nor B

8. Technician A says the negative battery terminal should be installed first. Technician B says the positive battery terminal should be removed first. Who is right?
   - a. A only
   - b. B only
   - c. Both A and B
   - d. Neither A nor B

9. Technician A says that a battery hydrometer measures the cell voltage. Technician B says a battery hydrometer measures specific gravity. Who is right?
   - a. A only
   - b. B only
   - c. Both A and B
   - d. Neither A nor B

10. Technician A says a specific gravity reading of 1.200 to 1.220 indicates a 50% state of charge. Technician B says a battery with a 100% charge will have a specific gravity of 1.360 to 1365. Who is right?
    - a. A only
    - b. B only
    - c. Both A and B
    - d. Neither A nor B

11. Technician A says when a green dot is showing on a maintenance-free battery it is fully charged. Technician B says that a dark eye means the battery is defective and should be replaced. Who is right?
    - a. A only
    - b. B only
    - c. Both A and B
    - d. Neither A nor B

12. What voltage should a battery in good condition and fully charged maintain during the specified test load at $70°F$ ($20°C$)?
    - a. 10.6 volts
    - b. 9.6 volts
    - c. 8.6 volts
    - d. 7.6 volts

13. What is the correct slow charging amperage rate?
    - a. 3 amps
    - b. 4 amps
    - c. 5 amps
    - d. 6 amps

14. When fast charging a battery, the amperage rate should be kept between what values?
    - a. 5 to 30 amps
    - b. 10 to 25 amps
    - c. 10 to 50 amps
    - d. 10 to 75 amps

15. Technician A says when using jumper cables the negative terminal of the boost battery should be connected to a metal part on the disabled vehicle's motor. Technician B says the negative terminal should be connected to the negative terminal of the disabled vehicle's battery. Who is right?
    - a. A only
    - b. B only
    - c. Both A and B
    - d. Neither A nor B

7

Charging System Maintenance

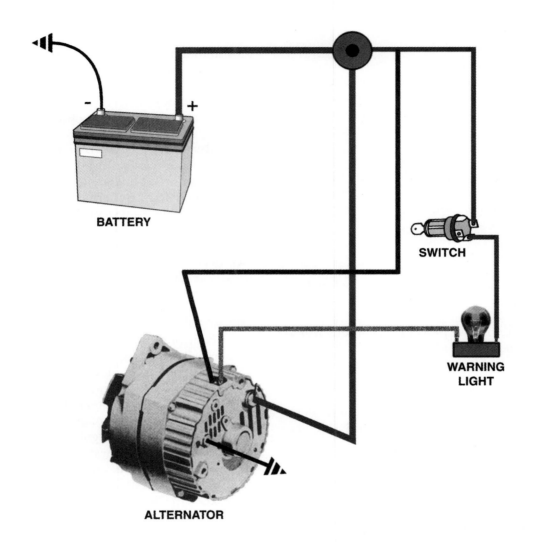

BATTERY

SWITCH

**WARNING
LIGHT**

ALTERNATOR

Automotive charging systems use alternators to convert mechanical energy to electrical energy. (see Figure 7) This electrical energy is needed to operate electrical systems in the vehicle and to maintain the state of charge of the battery. If the charging system fails, the battery will soon discharge to the point where the starter will not work and the engine will not run. The charging system alternator produces a direct current voltage higher than the battery voltage. This voltage is kept in a range from 14.5 volts to 15.5 volts. Most alternators produce at least sixty amperes of current. When the battery will hold a charge, the alternator produces more than enough voltage and amperage to keep the battery charged and provide extra power during times of heavy battery load. The most recent trend is to replace a defective alternator rather than rebuild it. Even with this trend there still are service operations to be performed, and testing becomes more important.

TASKS

The following are three tasks to master before leaving this chapter:

Task 7-1. Know the parts of a charging system and the theory of operation of each part, which involves electrical, mechanical, and electronic theory.

Task 7-2. Know how to evaluate and test charging system components using electrical and electronic test equipment.

Task 7-3. Learn how to service, repair, and replace charging system components.

LESSON 7–1 Charging System Parts, Terms, and Operation

In this lesson you will learn how charging systems operate. You will learn about the components used and how they function. And you will diagnose the cause of problems, isolate those causes, and perform the needed repairs. Your specific objectives are to perform the following jobs.

The Charging System

The charging system is responsible for maintaining the state of charge of the battery and supplying electrical power to the vehicle when the engine is running. If the charging system fails, the battery can provide energy for only a limited time. Repairs to the charging system should be based on diagnosis. And that diagnosis is based on a knowledge of the system, its components, and their function.

Charging System Components

Most automotive charging systems include four major components: (1) the alternator, (2) the regulator, (3) the battery, and (4) the indicating device. Figure 7.1 shows the location of those components in a typical charging system (also see Figure 7).

The Alternator.   An alternator, shown in Figure 7.2, is a generator that produces alternating current. For this reason it is sometimes referred to as an *AC generator*. The alternator is driven by a belt from the engine crankshaft, as shown in Figure 7.3 Through magnetism, the alternator converts mechanical energy to electrical energy. Some of this electrical energy is used by the various other electrical systems. And some of this energy is converted to chemical energy and stored in the battery.

The Regulator.   The regulator acts as an automatic control in the charging system. The regulator keeps the charging voltage from 14.5 volts up to 15.5 volts. Sometimes at idle the voltage will drop below 14.5 volts if the amperage load is heavy on the battery and charging system. The voltage should increase to the normal range when the engine is speeded up. Without a regulator, an alternator always operates at its highest possible output. It will do this even when the energy it produces is not needed. Uncontrolled, alternator output voltage will exceed the limits of the other electrical systems in a car. Bulbs and other electrical components

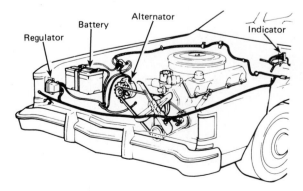

Figure 7.1   The location of the components in a typical charging system (courtesy of Ford Motor Company, Dearborn, MI).

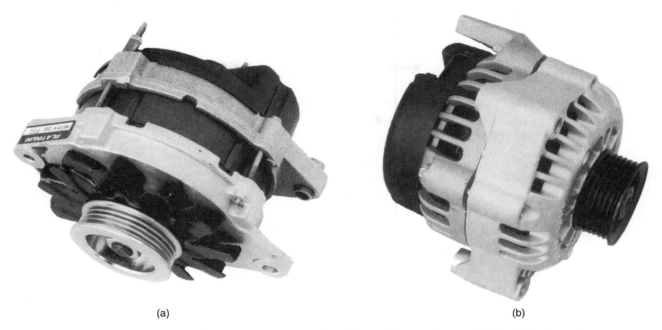

(a)   (b)

Figure 7.2 Alternator. Alternators of this type have an integral regulator and are used on vehicles built by General Motors Corporation (courtesy of Pontiac Motor Division, General Motors Corporation).

will burn out. The battery will be damaged by over-charging. And, within a very short time, the alternator will burn itself out.

The Battery. Although the battery converts and stores energy, it also acts as a "cushion" or "shock absorber" in the system. The battery does this by balancing out slight differences in the energy supplied by the alternator and the energy demanded by the other systems.

The Indicating Device. The indicating device provides the driver with a way to monitor the charging system. On most cars the indicating device con-

sists of a warning light on the instrument panel. If that light remains on while the engine is running, it indicates that the alternator is not charging the battery.

Some cars have an ammeter as an indicating device. These meters usually are not as accurate as those you use for testing. However, they do inform the driver of the approximate amount of current that is flowing in the electrical system. Ammeters used on instrument panels show current flow in two directions. Current flowing into the battery moves the meter needle to the CHARGE side of the dial. When the needle moves to the DISCHARGE side, it means that current is flowing out of the battery. Figure 7.4 shows a typical automotive ammeter.

On other cars, a voltmeter is provided as the indicating device. The voltmeter indicates system voltage, or between 14.5 volts up to 15.5 volts. Figure 7.5 illustrates such a meter.

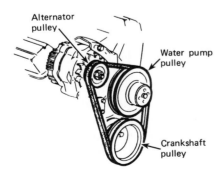

Figure 7.3 Alternator belt. On most cars, the alternator is driven by a belt from the crankshaft (courtesy of Pontiac Motor Division, General Motors Corporation).

Figure 7.4 Ammeter. Some cars have an ammeter that indicates approximate charge or discharge rates (courtesy of Stewart-Warner Corporation).

Job 7A

IDENTIFY THE PARTS IN A CHARGING SYSTEM

SATISFACTORY PERFORMANCE
A satisfactory performance on this job requires that you do the following:

1. Identify the numbered parts in the drawing by placing the number of each part in front of the correct part name.
2. Complete the job by correctly identifying all the parts within five minutes.

PERFORMANCE SITUATION

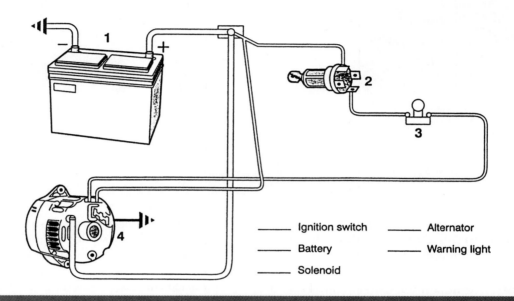

_____	Ignition switch	_____	Alternator
_____	Battery	_____	Warning light
_____	Solenoid		

> One way to check the accuracy of an analog-type voltmeter is to compare the reading with one taken on a digital voltmeter. Use the same battery for both readings.

Charging System Circuits

Many different circuits are used to connect the components in the charging system. Those circuits vary even among cars built by the same manufac-

Figure 7.5 Voltmeter. Some instrument panels incorporate a voltmeter to monitor system voltage (courtesy of Stewart-Warner Corporation).

turer. Figure 7.6 shows a typical circuit. When a diagram for the charging circuit in a particular car is needed, it is best found in the car manufacturer's manual. Different circuits require different testing procedures. These procedures are covered later in this chapter.

Charging System Component Operation

Many different types of alternators and regulators are used in automotive charging systems. Because of the different service procedures required, a knowledge of how these components operate is very important.

Alternators. As we learned earlier in our discussion of ignition coils, when a magnetic field is moved across a conductor, a current is induced in that conductor. In an alternator, an electromagnet called a *rotor* turns inside a set of stationary wire coils, or windings, called a *stator*. Those parts are shown in Figure 7.7. As the rotor turns, its magnetic lines of force move across all the windings in

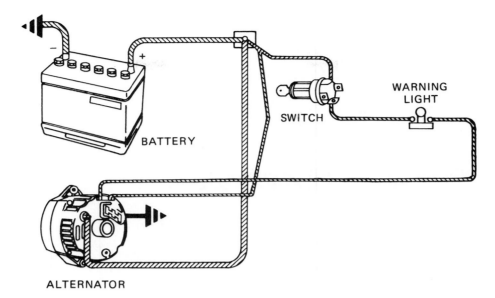

Figure 7.6 Internal regulator system. A charging system circuit used when the regulator is housed within the alternator (courtesy of Pontiac Motor Division, General Motors Corporation).

the stator. This action induces current in all the stator windings.

As the rotor turns, the poles of its magnetic field at the stator continuously alternate from north to south. Therefore, the current induced in the stator windings is *alternating current.* The polarity of alternating current continuously changes back and forth from positive (+) to negative (−). The battery and the electrical systems of the car require *direct current.* Direct current does not change polarity.

To be of use in an automotive electrical system, alternating current must be *rectified,* or converted

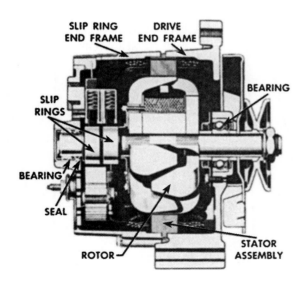

Figure 7.7 A cutaway view of a typical alternator (courtesy of Pontiac Motor Division, General Motors Corporation).

to direct current. A rectifier is used for this task. Figure 7.8 shows a rectifier and its location in an alternator. A rectifier usually consists of a group of *diodes.* A diode is an electrical check valve that conducts current in only one direction (see Figure 7.9) Both positive (+) and negative (−) diodes are used in pairs to "split" the alternating current. Most rectifiers contain six diodes. Half the diodes conduct positive (+) current and half the diodes conduct negative (−) current. Thus the alternating current is converted to direct current before it leaves the alternator.

The voltage produced by an alternator depends largely on the strength of the rotor's magnetic field. This magnetic field is created by a coil of wire inside the rotor. Figure 7.10 shows this *field coil.* Battery voltage is conducted to the field coil by a pair of brushes that contact a pair of slip rings on the rotor shaft (refer to Figure 7.7). By controlling the amount of current that flows through the field coil, the output voltage of the alternator is controlled. Current flow through the field coil is controlled automatically by a regulator.

Regulators. As mentioned, regulators control alternator output by controlling the amount of current that flows in the field coil winding. This keeps the system at the normal regulated charging range of 14.5 up to 15.5 volts.

Transistorized Regulators. Most late model cars have transistorized regulators. Often called

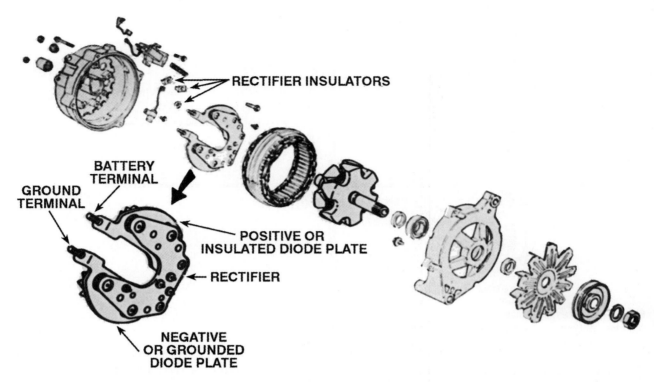

Figure 7.8 Ford alternator exploded view. A typical rectifier assembly and its location in an alternator (courtesy of Ford Motor Company, Dearborn, MI).

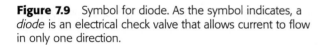

Figure 7.9 Symbol for diode. As the symbol indicates, a *diode* is an electrical check valve that allows current to flow in only one direction.

electronic regulators, they have no moving parts but use transistorized circuits to replace the mechanical switches. Many types of transistorized regulators are in use. Some are mounted separate from the alternator. A regulator of this type is shown in Figure 7.11.

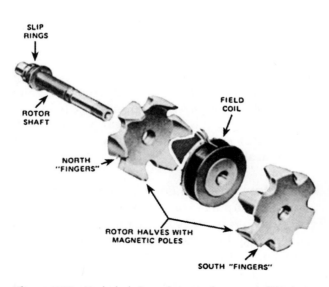

Figure 7.10 Exploded view of a rotor (courtesy of Ford Motor Company, Dearborn, MI).

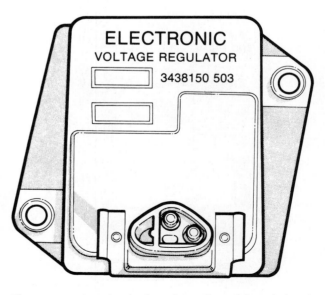

Figure 7.11 Transistorized regulator. The unit is sealed and has no moving parts (courtesy of Chrysler Corporation).

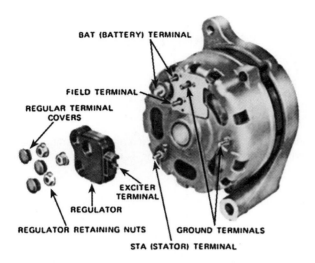

Figure 7.12 A transistorized regulator that is mounted on the rear of an alternator (courtesy of Ford Motor Company, Dearborn, MI).

Others are mounted externally on the rear of the alternator, as shown in Figure 7.12. Still others are mounted inside the alternator as an integral part of that assembly (see Figure 7.13). And on some cars, the functions of the regulator are handled by circuitry within the computer.

Warning Lights. Most cars have an alternator warning light on the instrument panel to warn

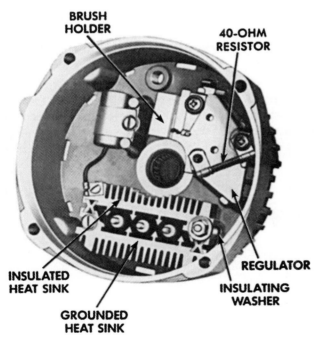

Figure 7.13 A transistorized regulator mounted inside the rear housing of an alternator (courtesy of Chevrolet Motor Division, General Motors Corporation).

Job 7B

IDENTIFY THE FUNCTION OF THE PARTS IN A CHARGING SYSTEM

SATISFACTORY PERFORMANCE
A satisfactory performance on this job requires that you do the following:

1. Identify the function of the listed charging system parts by placing the number of each part in front of the phrase that best describes its function.
2. Complete the job by correctly identifying all the parts within 10 minutes.

PERFORMANCE SITUATION

1. Alternator
2. Stator
3. Rotor
4. Diode
5. Rectifier
6. Battery
7. Electro-mechanical regulator
8. Transistorized regulator
9. Field winding
10. Brushes and slip rings

____ Converts and stores energy
____ Uses magnetically operated switches to control voltage
____ Conducts current to the field winding
____ Converts alternating current to direct current
____ Conducts current to the stator
____ Converts mechanical energy to electrical energy
____ Acts as an electrical check valve
____ Creates a magnetic field in the rotor
____ Uses transistorized circuits to control voltage
____ Moves a magnetic field across the stator windings
____ Receives current through induction

the driver of a charging system failure. Figure 7.14 shows the three phases of warning light operation.

LESSON 7–2 Charging System Service

Routine maintenance of the charging system consists of (1) keeping the alternator drive belt in

SWITCH	ENGINE	LAMP
Off	Stopped	Off
On	Stopped	On
On	Running	Off

Figure 7.14 Warning light phases. The charging system warning light operates in three phases.

PRELIMINARY ELECTRICAL CHECKS

If the battery is discharged, an accurate test of the charging system cannot be made.

Test the Battery

Check the specific gravity of the battery electrolyte and charge the battery if necessary. If the battery is defective the alternator will be unable to keep it charged. Load test the battery and replace it if it is defective.

Check the Battery Posts, Terminals, and Cable Clamps

Loose, dirty, and corroded connections prevent the alternator from maintaining the state of charge of a battery. Clean and tighten the connections as necessary.

Test the Voltage Drop in the Cables and Their Connections

Even though the battery cable connections may appear to be clean and tight, they may have excessive resistance. The steps that follow outline a procedure similar to the one you used when you tested for voltage drop in the starting system:

In performing the following tests, crank the engine with the starter motor. When working on a car with a catalytic converter, crank the engine for as short a time as possible. Extended cranking can deposit an excessive amount of fuel in the converter, causing it to overheat and pose a possible fire hazard.

1. Disable the ignition by removing the center wire from the distributor cap and grounding it.

   Note: An alternate disabling procedure may be used.

2. Apply the parking brake.
3. If the car has an automatic transmission, place the transmission selector lever in the PARK position. If the car has a manual transmission, place the shift lever in the NEUTRAL position.
4. Connect a remote starter switch to the starter relay.
5. Adjust a voltmeter to the low scale.
6. Connect the positive (+) voltmeter lead to the positive (+) battery post as shown in Figure 7.15.

   Note: The voltmeter lead must contact the battery post, not the cable clamp.

7. Connect the negative (−) voltmeter lead to the terminal bolt on the battery side of the starter relay (refer to Figure 7.15).

   Note: The voltmeter lead must contact the terminal bolt, not the battery cable terminal.

8. Crank the engine and observe the voltmeter reading.

   Note: The voltage reading should not exceed 0.2 volt. A reading of more than 0.2 volt indicates excessive resistance in the cable or its connections. Clean and tighten the connections. Replace the cable if necessary.

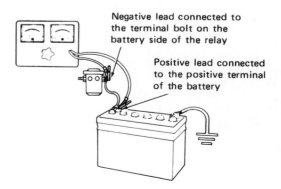

Figure 7.15 Connections for checking voltage drop in the battery cable and its connections (courtesy of Ford Motor Company, Dearborn, MI).

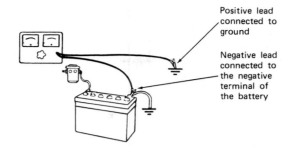

Positive lead connected to ground

Negative lead connected to the negative terminal of the battery

Figure 7.16 Connections for checking voltage drop in the battery ground cable and its connections (courtesy of Ford Motor Company, Dearborn, MI).

9. Disconnect the voltmeter.

10. Connect the positive (+) voltmeter lead to a good ground on the engine, as shown in Figure 7.16.

11. Connect the negative (−) voltmeter lead to the negative (−) battery post (refer to Figure 7.16).

    Note: The voltmeter lead must contact the battery post, not the cable clamp.

12. Crank the engine and observe the voltmeter reading.

    Note: The voltage reading should not exceed 0.2 volt. A reading of more than 0.2 volt indicates excessive resistance in the battery ground cable or its connections. Clean and tighten the connections. Replace the cable, if necessary.

13. Remove the voltmeter.

14. Restore the ignition system to operating condition.

Check the Alternator Drive Belt
A loose belt will slip and the alternator will not be driven at the proper speed. Use a belt tension gauge as shown in Figure 7.17. Adjust the belt if the tension is not within specifications. Replace the belt if it is glazed or damaged.

Check the Wiring
An open circuit or a short circuit in the wiring is a common cause of charging system problems. Check for loose connections and damaged wires.

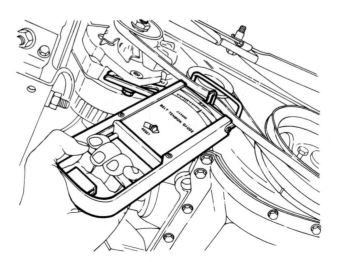

Figure 7.17 Using a gauge to check the tension of an alternator belt (courtesy of American Motors).

adjustment, and (2) keeping all the electrical connections in the system clean and tight.

Other services may be required when problems arise in the system. These services should include the replacement of parts after they have been determined to be defective. Alternators are not rebuilt at the shop like they used to be. Instead they are exchanged for factory rebuilt or new units.

Alternator rebuilding requires replacing bearings, brushes, and rectifier sections and checking the rotor, stator, and front and rear housings. If any alternator needed this much repair it would be cheaper to get the factory rebuilt part.

The best way to test an alternator for electrical or electronic problems is with the oscilloscope. These problems cannot escape the oscilloscope and always show up as an abnormal pattern. After you make repairs or if you are quality checking any shop or factory unit, use the oscilloscope. Sometimes a factory rebuilt unit may not pass the normal pattern test.

Learn each of the parts in the charging system and how they function. Based on this knowledge, most charging system problems can be solved by following a logical test procedure (see Preliminary Electrical Checks on page 188).

Fusible Links

Some cars have *fusible links,* sometimes called *fuse links,* in the charging circuit to protect the alter-

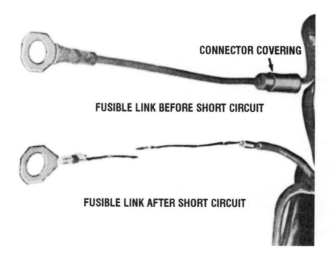

Figure 7.18   Charging circuit fusible links. On some cars, fusible links are used in the charging circuit to protect the parts from damage caused by excessive current flow (courtesy of Oldsmobile Motor Division, General Motors Corporation).

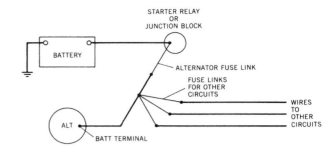

Figure 7.19   Fuse link schematic (series). On some cars, the fuse link that protects the alternator is wired in series with other fuse links that protect other circuits. If the alternator fuse link burns out, it will stop the flow of current to the other circuits.

nator. A fuse link is a short length of special wire built into the wiring harness. The fuse link is several gauges smaller than the wire used in the circuit it protects. Thus, when excessive current flows in that circuit, the fuse link wire acts as a fuse and burns out (see Figure 7.18). To prevent the possibility of a fire, fuse links are covered with a special insulation that does not burn. The insulation on some fuse links "bakes" to an ash; others have insulation that blisters and discolors. Fuse links in the charging circuit are often burned out when a booster battery or a battery charger is incorrectly connected.

The locations of fuse links and the circuits that they protect vary with different cars and are best found by reference to an appropriate manual. On some cars, the fuse link that protects the alternator is wired as shown in Figure 7.19. If that fuse link burns out, current cannot flow to other electrical equipment. Some cars are wired as shown in Figure 7.20. When wired in that manner, a burned-out fuse link in the charging circuit has no effect on the other circuits.

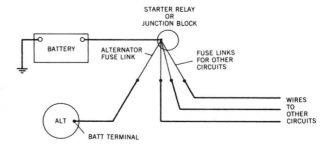

Figure 7.20   Fuse link schematic (parallel). On some cars, the alternator fuse link is wired in parallel with the fuse links that protect other circuits. If the alternator fuse burns out, the other circuits will still function.

Job 7C

PERFORM BASIC CHARGING SYSTEM CHECKS

SATISFACTORY PERFORMANCE
A satisfactory performance on this job requires that you do the following:

1. Perform basic charging system checks on the car assigned.
2. Following the steps in the "Performance Outline" and the procedures and specifications of the vehicle manufacturer, complete the job within 45 minutes.
3. Fill in the blanks under "Information."

PERFORMANCE OUTLINE

1. Inspect the drive belt(s) and check the belt tension.
2. Test the specific gravity of the battery electrolyte.
3. Load test the battery.
4. Check the battery terminals and cable clamps.
5. Clean and tighten the connections if necessary.
6. Test the voltage drop in the cables and connections.
7. Check the system wiring for loose connections and damaged wires.
8. Clean and tighten connections as required.
9. Check the condition of the fuse link(s) (if present).

INFORMATION

Vehicle identification _____
Reference used _____ Page(s) _____
Alternator drive belt(s):
    Belt condition: _____ Good _____ Glazed _____ Damaged
    Belt tension specification _____
    Belt tension measurement _____
    Was belt adjusted? _____ Yes _____ No
Specific gravity of battery electrolyte:
    Cell 1 _____ Cell 2 _____ Cell 3 _____
    Cell 4 _____ Cell 5 _____ Cell 6 _____
Does the battery require charging? _____ Yes _____ No
Battery load test:
    Battery ampere-hour capacity _____
    Amount of time load was maintained _____
    Voltage indicated while under load _____
    Approximate battery temperature _____
    Recommendations: _____ Battery is serviceable
                          _____ Battery should be replaced
Battery terminals and connections:
                 _____ Were found clean and tight
                 _____ Were cleaned and tightened
Voltage drop test results:
    Battery positive (+) cable: _____ volts
    Battery negative (−) cable: _____ volts
Were cable services required? _____ Yes _____ No
Wiring condition: _____ OK _____ NG
    Defect(s) found _____

Fuse link condition: _____ OK _____ Burnt

LESSON 7-3 Three-Stage Charging Test

In performing the previous jobs, some problems may have been found and corrected in the charging system. Now perform a three-stage charging test. This test will tell you if the charging system is operating correctly. This test can verify your repairs and check for other problems that may be present.

PERFORMING A THREE-STAGE CHARGING TEST

The following steps outline a procedure for performing a three-stage charging test:

Stage 1 This part of the test provides you with a base voltage reading to which you can compare the readings you obtain in stages 2 and 3.

1. Adjust a voltmeter to a scale exceeding battery voltage.
2. Connect the voltmeter to the battery terminals as shown in Figure 7.21.
3. Read the voltmeter and record the reading as the base voltage (see Figure 7.22).

   Note: The engine should not be running and all accessories should be turned off.

4. If the voltage is higher than normal, the battery has a surface charge. This will make the test inaccurate. Remove the surface charge by placing a load on the battery for 15 seconds. One way to do this is to turn on the headlights.

Stage 2 This part of the test provides you with a no-load voltage reading with the engine running.

1. Apply the parking brake.
2. If the car has an automatic transmission, place the transmission selector lever in the PARK position. If the car has a manual transmission, place the shift lever in the NEUTRAL position.

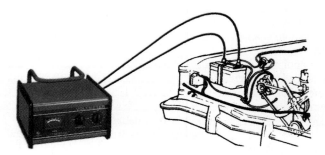

Figure 7.21 Voltmeter connected to battery. All the readings taken during a three-stage charging test are taken with a voltmeter connected to the battery (courtesy of Ford Motor Company, Dearborn, MI).

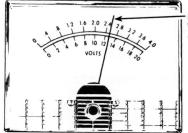

Figure 7.22 Base voltage reading. The base voltage reading is a measurement of battery voltage. It is taken with the engine and all electrical loads off (courtesy of Ford Motor Company, Dearborn, MI).

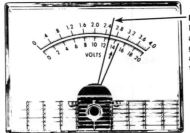

BASE VOLTAGE
Not more than 2.0 volts above base voltage with engine running @2000 RPM and all electrical loads turned off.

Figure 7.23 No-load voltage reading. The no-load voltage reading is a measurement of the charging circuit voltage taken while the engine is running approximately 2000 rpm with all electrical loads off (courtesy of Ford Motor Company, Dearborn, MI).

3. Start the engine and let it run at approximately 2000 rpm.

   Note: Be sure that all accessories are turned off.

4. Read the voltmeter and record the reading as the no-load voltage.

   Note: You may have to let the engine run for a short time if the voltmeter reading keeps rising. Read the voltmeter when the needle stops rising.

5. Compare the no-load voltage with the base voltage (see Figure 7.23).

   Note: The no-load voltage should exceed the base voltage, but by no more than 2.0 volts. A no-load voltage of more than 2.0 volts over the base voltage may indicate an overcharging condition. The reading obtained in Stage 3 will verify this.

Stage 3 This part of the test will provide a load voltage reading while the engine is running and with a heavy load on the charging system.

1. Turn the headlights on in the high beam position.
2. Turn the heater blower motor switch to the HIGH position.
3. Run the engine at approximately 2000 rpm.
4. Read the voltmeter and record the reading as the load voltage.
5. Turn off the engine, the headlights, and the heater blower.
6. Disconnect the voltmeter.
7. Compare the load voltage with the base voltage (see Figure 7.24).

   Note: The load voltage should exceed the base voltage by at least 0.5 volt, but not more than 2.0 volts. If the load voltage is within this range, the charging system is operating correctly. If the difference is less than 0.5 volt, the system is undercharging. If the difference is more than 2.0 volts, the system is overcharging. Additional tests are required in both instances.

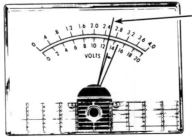

BASE VOLTAGE
At least 0.5 volt above base voltage with engine running @2000 RPM and headlights and blower turned on.

Figure 7.24 Load voltage reading. The load voltage reading is a measurement of the charging circuit voltage taken while the engine is running approximately 2000 rpm with a heavy load on the circuit (courtesy of Ford Motor Company, Dearborn, MI).

Job 7D

PERFORM A THREE-STAGE CHARGING CIRCUIT TEST

SATISFACTORY PERFORMANCE

A satisfactory performance on this job requires that you do the following:

1. Perform a three-stage test on the charging circuit of the car assigned.
2. Following the steps in the "Performance Outline," complete the job within 45 minutes exclusive of any charging time required.
3. Fill in the blanks under "Information."

PERFORMANCE OUTLINE

1. Perform the preliminary circuit checks.
2. Perform any repairs required.
3. Measure the base voltage.
4. Measure the no-load voltage.
5. Measure the load voltage.
6. Compare the readings.

INFORMATION

Vehicle identification _____

Reference used _____ Page(s) _____

Specific gravity of electrolyte:

   Cell 1 _____   Cell 2 _____   Cell 3 _____

   Cell 4 _____   Cell 5 _____   Cell 6 _____

Did battery require charging? _____ Yes _____ No

Was battery charged?   _____ Yes _____ No

Load Test:

   Battery ampere-hour capacity _____

   Discharge rate (test load) _____

   Amount of time load was maintained _____

   Voltage indicated while under load _____

   Approximate battery temperature _____

   Recommendations: _____ Battery is serviceable

                      _____ Battery should be replaced

Battery terminals and connections:

   _____ Were found clean and tight

   _____ Were cleaned and tightened

Voltage drop test results:

   Battery positive (+) cable _____

   Battery ground cable _____

   Were cable services required? _____ Yes _____ No

Alternator drive belt:

   Belt tension specification _____

   Belt tension measurement _____

   Was belt adjusted? _____ Yes _____ No

   Belt condition _____ Good _____ Glazed _____ Damaged

Three-stage charging test:

   Base voltage _____

   No-load voltage _____

   Load voltage _____

   Interpretation of test results _____

The test procedures that follow are typical of those recommended by the various vehicle manufacturers. There are many different types of charging systems in use. And these systems use a variety of components. For these reasons, you consult an appropriate service manual for the specific test procedures recommended for the system on which you are working. In all instances, do not attempt these test procedures until the preliminary checks and the three-stage charging test have been performed:

Systems Using Alternators with Internal Regulators (Delcotron)

Alternators of the type shown in Figure 7.25 have a *test hole* in the slip ring end frame. This hole allows you to bypass the internal regulator. The following procedure should be used:

1. Locate the test hole in the rear of the alternator.

   Note: On some cars, access to the test hole is blocked. On those cars, the alternator must be removed for bench testing.

2. Insert a small screwdriver into the test hole as shown in Figure 7.26. Check to see that it will touch both the side of the hole and the *test tab* inside the alternator.

   Note: The test tab is about 3/4 inch (19 mm) inside the hole. Do not insert the screwdriver into the hole for a distance of more than 1 in. (25 mm). To do so may damage internal parts. If you cannot touch the test tab, the alternator must be removed for bench testing.

3. Adjust a voltmeter to a scale exceeding battery voltage.
4. Connect the voltmeter to the battery terminals (refer to Figure 7.21).
5. Apply the parking brake.
6. If the car has an automatic transmission, place the transmission selector lever in the PARK position. If the car has a manual transmission, place the shift lever in the NEUTRAL position.
7. Start the engine and allow it to idle.

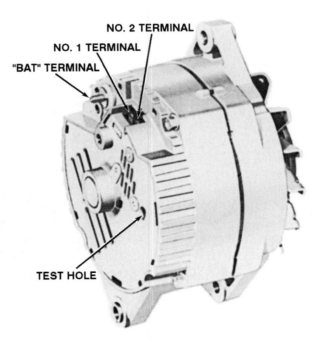

Figure 7.25   Internal regulator Delcotron. A Delcotron alternator with an integral regulator. A test hole is provided so that the regulator can be bypassed for testing (courtesy of Pontiac Motor Division, General Motors Corporation).

Figure 7.26   Bypassing internal regulator. This operation is often referred to as "full fielding" an alternator (courtesy of Pontiac Motor Division, General Motors Corporation).

8. Insert the small screwdriver into the test hole so that it contacts both the side of the hole and the test tab (refer to Figure 7.26).
9. Gradually accelerate the engine and observe the voltmeter while holding the screwdriver in place. The reading should rise to at least 2.0 volts above the battery voltage.
10. Remove the screwdriver and turn off the engine.

Interpretation of Test Results   If the voltage rises considerably, the regulator in the alternator is defective. If the voltage does not rise, and the wiring is known to be in good condition, the alternator is defective. In both instances the alternator must be repaired or replaced.

Alternators of the type shown in Figures 7.27 and 7.28 are controlled by regulators mounted separately. The following procedure explains how these regulators can be bypassed with jumper wires:

Figure 7.27   Ford alternator. Alternators of this type are used on some vehicles built by Ford Motor Company (courtesy of Training Enterprises Company).

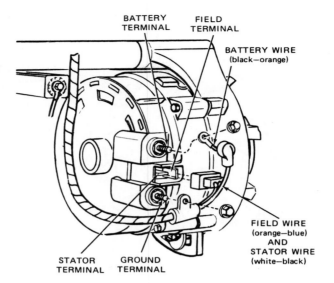

Figure 7.28 An externally regulated alternator with side mounted terminals. Alternators of this type are used on some vehicles built by Ford Motor Company (courtesy of Ford Motor Company, Dearborn, MI).

1. Determine the location of the battery (BAT) terminal and the field (FLD) terminal on the alternator. (Refer to Figures 7.27 and 7.28.)
2. Disconnect the regulator from the circuit.

   Note: Most wiring harnesses have a plug that connects to the regulator. This plug can be unlocked by using a screwdriver as shown in Figure 7.29.
3. Adjust a voltmeter to a scale exceeding battery voltage.
4. Connect the voltmeter to the battery terminals (refer to Figure 7.21).
5. Apply the parking brake.
6. If the car has an automatic transmission, place the transmission selector lever in the PARK position. If the car has a manual transmission, place the shift lever in the NEUTRAL position.
7. Start the engine and allow it to idle.
8. Connect a jumper wire to the battery (BAT) terminal and the field (FLD) terminals as shown in Figure 7.30.
9. Gradually accelerate the engine and observe the voltmeter reading. The reading should rise at least 2.0 volts above the battery voltage.
10. Remove the jumper wire and turn off the engine.

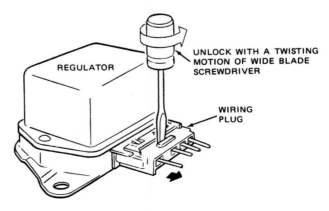

Figure 7.29 Disconnecting regulator plug. Jumper wire connections for checking alternator output (courtesy of Ford Motor Company, Dearborn, MI).

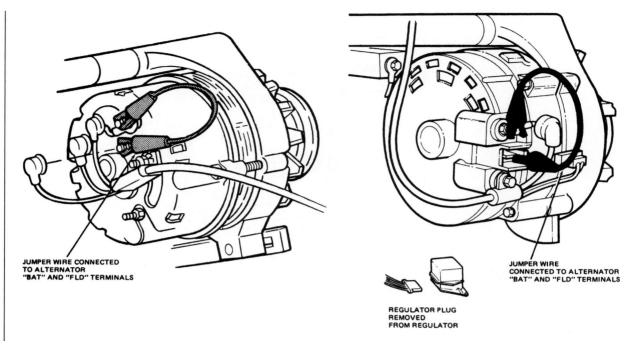

Figure 7.30 Checking Ford alternator output. Jumper wire connections for checking alternator output (courtesy of Ford Motor Company, Dearborn, MI).

Interpretation of Test Results   If the voltage does not rise, the alternator is defective and must be repaired or replaced. If the voltage rises considerably, the alternator is functioning properly. The cause of the undercharging lies either in the regulator or in the wires connecting the regulator to the alternator. To isolate the problem, continue with step 11.

11. Connect a jumper wire between the "A" and "F" contacts in the plug that you disconnected from the regulator (see Figure 7.31).
12. Restart the engine.
13. Gradually accelerate the engine and observe the voltmeter reading.
14. Turn off the engine and remove the jumper wire.

Interpretation of Test Results   If the voltage rises considerably, the regulator is defective and should be replaced. If the voltage does not rise, the problem is caused by a break in the "A" wire or in the "F" wire. To isolate the problem, continue with step 15.

15. Connect a jumper wire to the "F" contact in the plug and to the positive (+) battery terminal as shown in Figure 7.32.
16. Restart the engine.
17. Gradually accelerate the engine and observe the voltmeter reading.
18. Turn off the engine and remove the jumper wire.

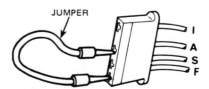

Figure 7.31 Jumper wire connections for bypassing the regulator at the wiring harness plug (courtesy of Ford Motor Company, Dearborn, MI).

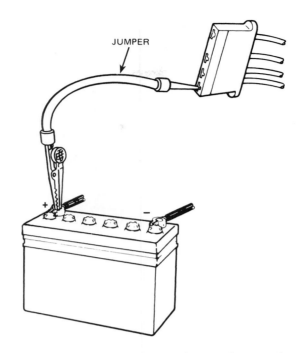

JUMPER

Figure 7.32 Jumper wire connections for testing the wires between the regulator and the alternator (courtesy of Ford Motor Company, Dearborn, MI).

Interpretation of Test Results

If the voltage does not rise, the problem is caused by a break in the "F" wire. If the voltage rises, the problem is caused by a break in the "A" wire. Perform the needed repair. Verify the repair by performing a three-stage charging test.

Systems Using Alternators with Separate Regulators (Chrysler)

Alternators of the type shown in Figure 7.33 are controlled by regulators that are mounted separately. These regulators control the alternator field through the ground circuit as shown in Figure 7.34. The following procedure explains how the regulators can be bypassed with a jumper wire:

1. Determine the location of the field (FLD) terminal on the rear of the alternator (refer to Figure 7.33).
2. Disconnect (unplug) the wire from the field (FLD) terminal.
3. Adjust a voltmeter to a scale exceeding battery voltage.
4. Connect the voltmeter to the battery terminals (refer to Figure 7.21).
5. Apply the parking brake.
6. If the car has an automatic transmission, place the transmission selector lever in the PARK position. If the car has a manual transmission, place the shift lever in the NEUTRAL position.
7. Start the engine and allow it to idle.
8. Connect a jumper wire to the field (FLD) terminal on the alternator and to a good ground.
9. Gradually accelerate the engine and observe the voltmeter. The reading should rise to at least 2.0 volts above the battery voltage.
10. Remove the jumper wire and turn off the engine.

Interpretation of Test Results

If the voltage does not rise, the alternator is defective and must be repaired or replaced. If the voltage rises considerably, the alternator is functioning properly. The cause of the undercharging lies either in the regulator ground, in the regulator, or in the wire that connects the field terminal to the regulator. To isolate the problem, continue with step 11.

Figure 7.33   Chrysler alternator. Alternators of this type are used by Chrysler vehicles (courtesy of Training Enterprises Company).

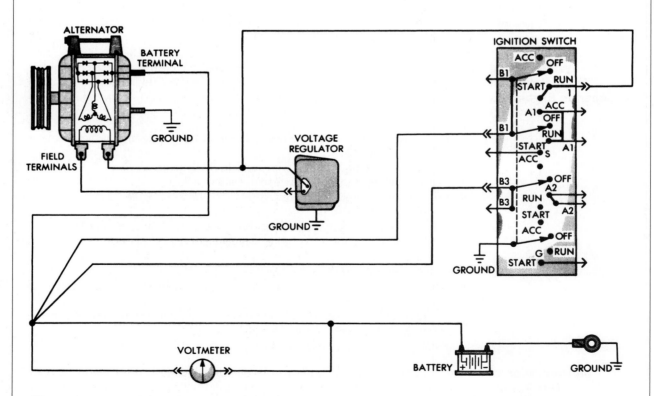

Figure 7.34   A typical wiring diagram for a Chrysler alternator used in a vehicle equipped with a voltmeter (courtesy of Chrysler Corporation).

11. Connect the field wire to the field (FLD) terminal on the back of the alternator.
12. Connect a jumper wire between the base of the regulator and a good ground.
13. Start the engine.
14. Gradually accelerate the engine and observe the voltmeter. The reading should rise to at least 2.0 volts above battery voltage.
15. Turn off the engine and remove the jumper wire.

Interpretation of Test Results

If the voltage rises considerably, the regulator has a poor ground. Remove the regulator and clean the regulator base to obtain a good connection with the body. The use of lock washers on the attaching screws is recommended. Verify the repair by performing a three-stage charging test. If the voltage does not rise, the cause of the undercharging lies in the regulator or in the wire connecting the regulator to the field (FLD) terminal. To isolate the cause of the problem, continue with step 16.

16. Disconnect the field wire from the regulator.

    Note: On vehicles with an electromechanical regulator, remove the green wire from the terminal. On vehicles with an electronic regulator, disconnect the wiring plug by releasing the locking tab (see Figure 7.35).

17. Turn the ignition switch to the ON position, but do not start the engine.
18. Remove the positive (+) voltmeter lead from the battery and touch it to the disconnected green wire.
19. Observe the voltmeter reading. The meter should indicate battery voltage.
20. Turn the ignition switch to the OFF position.

Interpretation of Test Results

If battery voltage is indicated, the regulator is defective and should be replaced. If no voltage is indicated, the wire connecting the regulator to the field (FLD) terminal is broken and should be repaired. Verify the repair made by performing a three-stage charging test.

Figure 7.35 A typical electronic regulator. Notice the locking tab, which must be released to remove the plug (courtesy of Chrysler Corporation).

Job 7E

DETERMINE THE CAUSE OF UNDERCHARGING

SATISFACTORY PERFORMANCE
A satisfactory performance on this job requires that you do the following:

1. Determine the cause of undercharging indicated by a three-stage charging test.
2. Following the steps in the "Performance Outline" and the procedure and specifications of the manufacturer, complete the tests required within 30 minutes.
3. Fill in the blanks under "Information."

PERFORMANCE OUTLINE

1. Bypass the regulator.
2. Check the system with the regulator bypassed.

INFORMATION

Vehicle identification _____
Reference used _____ Page(s) _____
Test results: Alternator _____ OK _____ NG
                  Regulator _____ OK _____ NG
                  Wiring   _____ OK _____ NG
Recommendations _____

TESTING FOR THE CAUSE OF OVERCHARGING	

The following test procedures are typical of those recommended by the various vehicle manufacturers. Consult an appropriate manual for the specific procedures recommended for the system on which you are working. In all instances, attempt these procedures only after the preliminary checks and the three-stage charging test have been performed.

Systems Using Alternators with Internal Regulators (Delcotron)

Overcharging in a system using alternators of this type (refer to Figure 7.25) is usually caused by an internal failure in the alternator. The alternator should be repaired or replaced.

Systems Using Alternators with Separate Regulators (Ford or Motorcraft)

The following steps outline a procedure for determining the cause of overcharging in systems using alternators of this type (refer to Figure 7.27 and 7.28):

1. Adjust a voltmeter to a scale exceeding battery voltage.
2. Connect the voltmeter to the battery terminals (refer to Figure 7.21).
3. Read the voltmeter and record the reading as the base voltage.
4. Connect a jumper wire to the base of the regulator and to a good ground (see Figure 7.36).
5. Apply the parking brake.
6. If the car has an automatic transmission, place the transmission selector lever in the PARK position. If the car has a manual transmission, place the shift lever in the NEUTRAL position.
7. Start the engine and run it at approximately 2000 rpm.
8. Read the voltmeter. The indicated voltage should not exceed 2.0 volts above the base voltage.
9. Turn off the engine and remove the jumper wire.

Interpretation of Test Results

If the voltage does not exceed 2.0 volts over the base voltage, the regulator has a bad ground. Remove the regulator and clean the regulator base to obtain a good connection with the body. The use of lock washers on the attaching screws is recommended. Verify your repair by repeating steps 7 and 8. If the voltage exceeds 2.0 volts above the base voltage, continue with step 10.

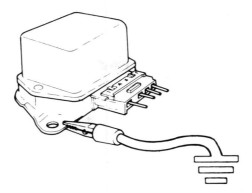

Figure 7.36 Checking regulator ground. A poor regulator ground can be detected by grounding the regulator with a jumper wire (courtesy of Ford Motor Company, Dearborn, MI).

10. Disconnect the wiring plug from the regulator (refer to Figure 7.29)
11. Start the engine and run it at approximately 2000 rpm.
12. Read the voltmeter. The voltage should not rise above the base voltage.
13. Turn off the engine.

Interpretation of Test Results

If the voltage rises above the base voltage, there is a short circuit in the wiring between the regulator and the alternator. Most likely, the "A" and the "F" wires are in contact with each other. Check the wiring and perform the needed repairs. Verify your repair by repeating steps 11 through 13. If the voltage does not rise, the regulator is defective and should be replaced. Verify your repair by performing a three-stage charging test.

Systems Using Alternators with Separate Regulators (Chrysler)

The following steps outline a procedure for determining the cause of overcharging in systems using alternators of this type (refer to Figure 7.33):

1. Adjust a voltmeter to a scale exceeding battery voltage.
2. Connect the voltmeter to the battery terminals (refer to Figure 7.21).
3. Read the voltmeter and record the reading as the base voltage.
4. Disconnect the wire from the field (FLD) terminal on the alternator (refer to Figure 7.33).
5. Apply the parking brake.
6. If the car has an automatic transmission, place the transmission selector lever in the PARK position. If the car has a manual transmission, place the shift lever in the NEUTRAL position.
7. Start the engine and allow it to idle.
8. Gradually accelerate the engine and observe the voltmeter. The reading should remain at the base voltage.
9. Turn off the engine.

Interpretation of Test Results

If the voltage rises above the base voltage, the alternator is defective and should be repaired or replaced. Verify your repair by performing a three-stage charging test. If the voltage does not rise above the base voltage, continue with step 10.

10. Disconnect the field wire from the regulator.

    Note: On vehicles with an electro-mechanical regulator, remove the green wire from the terminal. On vehicles with an electronic regulator, disconnect the wiring plug (refer to Figure 7.35).

11. Disconnect the negative (−) voltmeter lead from the battery and connect it to the field wire.
12. Read the voltmeter. The voltmeter should indicate no voltage.
13. Disconnect the voltmeter lead.

Interpretation of Test Results	If voltage is indicated by the voltmeter, the field wire between the regulator and the alternator is grounded. Repair the wire. Verify your repair by repeating steps 11 through 13. If the voltmeter indicates no voltage, the regulator is defective and should be replaced. Connect the field wire to the field (FLD) terminal on the alternator and verify your repairs by performing a three-stage charging test.

Job 7F

DETERMINE THE CAUSE OF OVERCHARGING

SATISFACTORY PERFORMANCE
A satisfactory performance on this job requires that you do the following:

1. Determine the cause of overcharging indicated by a three-stage charging test.
2. Following the steps in the "Performance Outline" and the procedure and specifications of the manufacturer, complete the tests required within 30 minutes.
3. Fill in the blanks under "Information."

PERFORMANCE OUTLINE

1. Bypass the regulator as required.
2. Check the system to isolate the defect.

INFORMATION

Vehicle identification _____
Reference used _____ Page(s) _____
Test results: Alternator _____ OK _____ NG
                  Regulator _____ OK _____ NG
                  Wiring   _____ OK _____ NG
                  Grounds   _____ OK _____ NG
Repairs required _____
_____

LESSON 7–4   Alternator Removal and Replacement

ALTERNATOR REPLACEMENT	On most cars, the alternator is mounted so that it is accessible from under the hood. On some cars, it must be removed from under the car. Figure 7.37 to 7.39 show typical alternator installations and the attaching hardware and brackets. Cars equipped with power steering and air conditioning may have the alternator mounted in a location different from similar cars without those options.
    The following steps outline a general procedure for replacing an alternator. There are many variations in alternator mountings and many different replacement procedures. Therefore, consult an appropriate manual for the procedure required for the car on which you are working.
Removal	1. Disconnect the battery ground cable. 2. If the alternator must be removed from under the car, raise the car and support it with jack stands. 3. Loosen the alternator adjustment bolts and remove the belt from the alternator pulley. 4. Disconnect the wires from the alternator. 5. Remove any brackets, braces, or shields as necessary. 6. Remove the alternator.

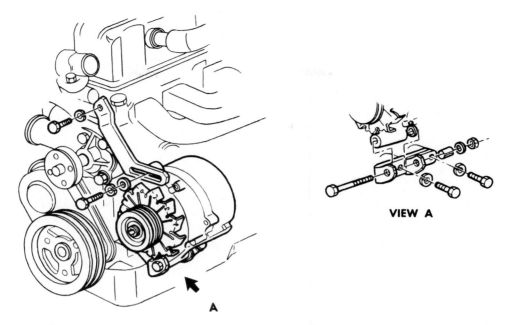

Figure 7.37   A typical alternator mounting on an inline engine (courtesy of Chevrolet Motor Division, General Motors Corporation).

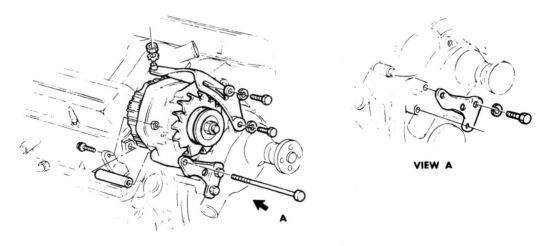

Figure 7.38   A typical alternator mounting on a V-type engine (courtesy of Chevrolet Motor Division, General Motors Corporation).

Preparation for Installation

Many replacement alternators are supplied without a pulley. The pulley must be removed from the old alternator and installed on the replacement alternator.

On most alternators, the pulley is held on the rotor shaft by a nut as shown in Figure 7.40. The rotor shaft usually has a hex-shaped hole in its end. That hole enables you to hold the shaft with an *Allen*, or hex, wrench. As shown in Figure 7.41, the nut can then be removed with a box wrench. When the pulley is installed on the replacement alternator, it should be tightened to the manufacturer's torque specification. Figure 7.42 shows how a torque wrench can be used on an *Allen* socket.

Some alternators do not use a nut to retain the pulley. The hole in the pulley is slightly smaller than the diameter of the rotor shaft. The pulley is forced on the shaft to obtain a very tight *interference fit*. Special pullers usually are required to remove

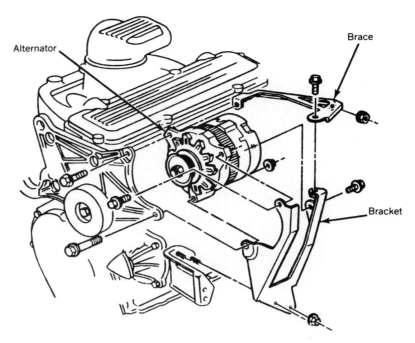

Figure 7.39 An alternator mounting with reinforcing braces (courtesy of Chevrolet Motor Division, General Motors Corporation).

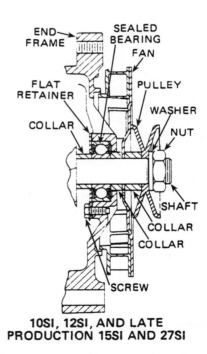

10SI, 12SI, AND LATE PRODUCTION 15SI AND 27SI

Figure 7.40 Typical pulley nut. On most alternators, the pulley is held to the shaft by a nut and a lock washer (courtesy of Chevrolet Motor Division, General Motors Corporation).

interference fit pulleys. Some pulleys have a small groove machined on the end. Figure 7.43 shows how a special puller fits on a pulley of that type. As shown in Figure 7.44, other pulleys require a special puller that fits inside the pulley. Pulleys of this type are removed as shown in Figure 7.45.

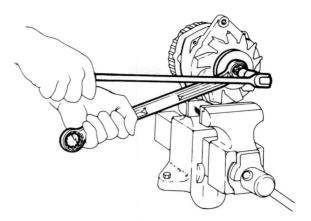

Figure 7.41 Removing an alternator pulley nut. Notice that the nut is turning with a box wrench while the rotor is held by an Allen wrench (courtesy of American Motors).

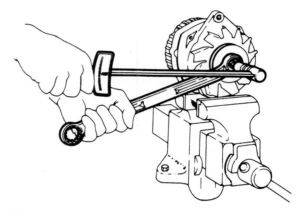

Figure 7.42 Tightening an alternator pulley nut. A torque wrench can be used on the Allen wrench socket (courtesy of American Motors).

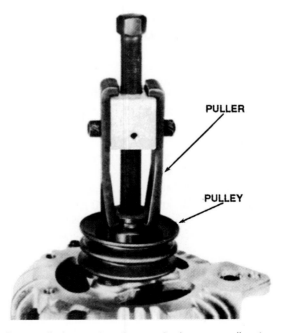

Figure 7.43 A puller installed on an interference fit alternator pulley (courtesy of Chrysler Corporation).

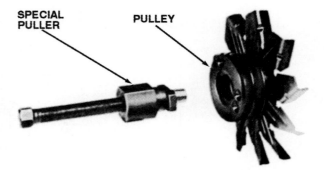

Figure 7.44 Chrysler special puller. Some pulleys require a special puller that fits inside the pulley (courtesy of Chrysler Corporation).

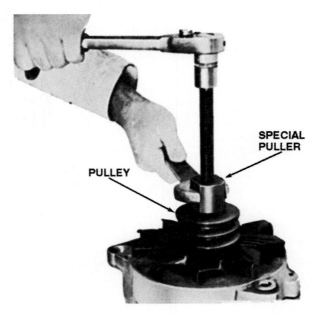

Figure 7.45 Removing an interference fit pulley with a special puller (courtesy of Chrysler Corporation).

The installation of interference fit pulleys usually requires the use of a press as shown in Figure 7.46. In most instances, the alternator must be disassembled so that the rear of the rotor shaft can be properly supported.

Installation
1. Hold the alternator in position and install the mounting bolts by hand.

   Note: Do not attempt to tighten any of the bolts until all the bolts have been installed.

2. Alternately tighten the bolts until they are all snug.
3. Install the belt(s) on the pulley.
4. Adjust the belt tension.
5. Tighten all the bolts to the manufacturer's torque specification.
6. Connect the wires to the alternator.
7. Connect the battery ground cable.

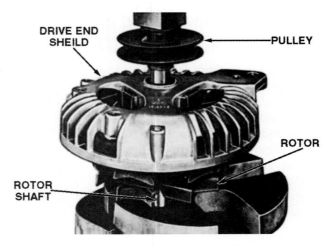

DRIVE END
SHEILD

PULLEY

ROTOR

ROTOR
SHAFT

Figure 7.46 Using a press to install an interference fit pulley. Note that the alternator has been disassembled so that the rotor shaft can be supported on the press table (courtesy of Chrysler Corporation).

8. Check the operation of the alternator.
9. If the car is supported by jack stands, lower the car to the floor.

> Most factory rebuilt alternators now come ready to install with the pulley and fan in place. It is difficult to change pulleys without some special tools. There is no advantage to getting a rebuilt or new unit without the pulley already in place.

Job 7G

REPLACE AN ALTERNATOR

SATISFACTORY PERFORMANCE
A satisfactory performance on this job requires that you do the following:

1. Replace the alternator on the car assigned.
2. Following the steps in the "Performance Outline" and the procedure and specifications of the manufacturer, complete the job within 200 percent of the manufacturer's suggested time.
3. Fill in the blanks under "Information."

PERFORMANCE OUTLINE

1. Disconnect the battery ground cable.
2. Raise and support the car if necessary.
3. Remove the alternator.
4. Install the replacement alternator.
5. Connect the battery ground cable.
6. Check the operation of the alternator.
7. Lower the car to the floor.

INFORMATION

Vehicle identification _____
Reference used _____ Page(s) _____
Was the pulley exchanged? _____ Yes _____ No
Does the replacement alternator operate correctly? _____ Yes _____ No

LESSON 7-5 Oscilloscope Testing a Charging System

Although the voltmeter is the simplest method to check charging output, it will not tell you exactly what is wrong internally. The oscilloscope is another matter. If the operator knows how to read the patterns, it will indicate what parts are defective. The only requirement is that the alternator be producing some voltage. This voltage causes a pattern to be displayed on the screen. The defective pattern determines what parts need repair. This test is accurate and fast. Connect tester leads to the battery or at the alternator terminals. Start the engine. The pattern is either normal or defective. The technician who can read abnormal patterns will know immediately what has to be repaired. In this lesson we study oscilloscope testing.

An *oscilloscope* is a tester that resembles a television set. A pattern is produced on the oscilloscope indicating voltage strength in relation to elapsed time. Voltage is indicated in the vertical direction and time in the horizontal direction. Figure 7.47 shows the relationship between voltage strength and time on an oscilloscope tube.

> The oscilloscope is the most accurate way to check for alternator problems. All electrical or electronic problems will show up as an abnormal pattern. The oscilloscope does not check for mechanical problems, which requires either hearing a noise or disassembly and individual parts inspection.

For easier communication, you need to know the following terms and definitions:

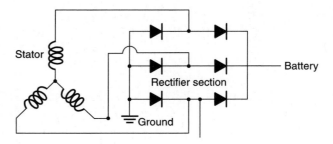

Figure 7.48 Alternator schematic. This shows the three positive and three negative diodes inside the alternator. The alternator has three phases. One positive and one negative diode is connected to the end of each phase (courtesy of Training Enterprises Company).

1. *Diode.* A diode is an electrical device that allows current to flow in only one direction. It blocks the current flow in the opposite direction. An automotive alternator uses six diodes. Three of these are positive polarity and three are negative polarity. They rectify the alternating current produced by the alternator to direct current needed to charge the battery. There may be other diodes used to protect the electronic parts in the alternator from voltage surges, which could damage these parts (see Figure 7.48)

2. *Open circuit.* This type circuit exists when broken wires, cut wires, open switches, and loose or corroded connections prevent the flow of current. For current to flow there has to be a complete circuit away from one battery post, to the circuit components, and back to the other battery post (see Figure 7.49)

3. *Short circuit.* A short circuit forms when the current takes a path that was not its original one. When a coil of wire has a short circuit, the wire

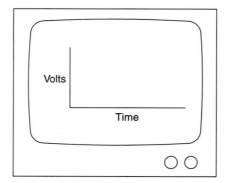

Figure 7.47 Voltage vs. time on scope. Voltage is measured on the vertical line. The horizontal line represents time (courtesy of Training Enterprises Company).

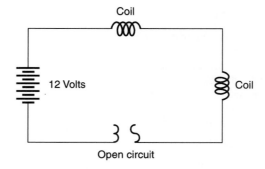

Figure 7.49 Open circuit. The circuit in this figure has an "open." This prevents any current flow in that circuit until the "open" wire is repaired (courtesy of Training Enterprises Company).

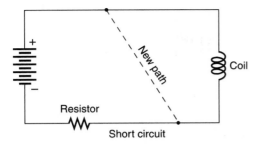

Figure 7.50 Short circuit. The circuit in this figure has a short. The current can still flow but it takes a path that is not planned (courtesy of Training Enterprises Company).

insulation breaks down and allows the current to take a shorter path rather than going the entire length of the wire. When diodes short circuit, they no longer block current flow and instead allow current to flow in both directions (see Figure 7.50).

4. *Polarity*. Polarity is determined by the battery. One battery post is "positive" and the other is "negative." A cable clamped to the negative battery post is considered a negative polarity wire.

5. *Phase*. In the stator section of the alternator are three coils of wire. Each of these coils is called a *phase*. The three coils of wire are placed in the stator in an overlapped position. This allows the alternator to produce more amperage between engine idle speed and maximum speed. One positive and one negative diode are attached to the end of each coil. The coil of wire and the diodes make up one phase (see Figure 7.51).

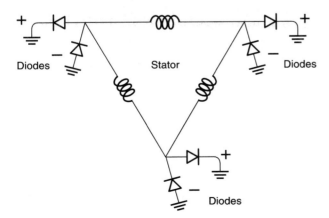

Figure 7.51 Phases and diodes. The stator contains three coils of wire. Each coil is a phase. The diodes are used to convert the alternating current to direct current. It takes direct current to charge a battery (courtesy of Training Enterprises Company).

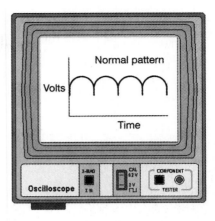

Figure 7.52 Normal pattern. This represents how a normal alternator pattern would look on a scope. Any deviation from this pattern means there is a problem in the electronic or electrical part of the alternator (courtesy of Training Enterprises Company).

6. *Pattern*. A pattern is the picture produced on the oscilloscope tube by the part being tested. Any defect in the part shows up as an abnormal pattern. To use an oscilloscope, the technician must recognize normal patterns and be able to identify the problem if the pattern is abnormal.

The normal alternator pattern looks like the one in Figure 7.52. When this pattern appears on the oscilloscope screen, no further testing is necessary. Any other pattern shape indicates a problem.

1. *Open diode, any phase*. One of the six diodes attached to the ends of the stator wires is open (no longer makes a complete path). The abnormal pattern in Figure 7.53 is what an

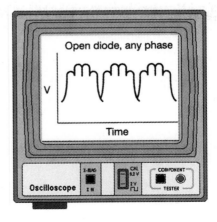

Figure 7.53 Open diode, any phase. One of the six diodes used in the rectifier section of the alternator has an "open." The diode can either be positive or negative polarity (courtesy of Training Enterprises Company).

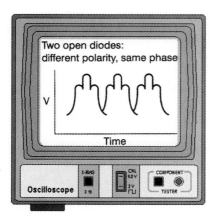

Figure 7.54 Two open diodes, different polarity, same phase. One negative and one positive diode have opened. These diodes are attached to the same stator coil (courtesy of Training Enterprises Company).

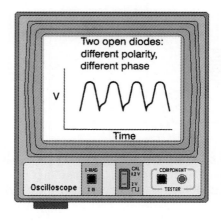

Figure 7.56 Two open diodes, different polarity, different phase. One negative and one positive diode have opened. They will be attached to two different stator coils (courtesy of Training Enterprises Company).

open diode would look like on the oscilloscope screen.

2. *Two open diodes, different polarity, same phase.* Figure 7.54 indicates how this pattern would look on the oscilloscope. Both the diodes attached to one phase or stator wire have opened. One was positive polarity and the other was negative.

3. *Two open diodes, same polarity, different phase.* Figure 7.55 shows how this pattern would look. Either two negative or two positive diodes have open circuits. These would have to be on different phases because no phase has two same-polarity diodes attached to it.

4. *Two open diodes, different polarity, different phase.* Figure 7.56 indicates what this situation would

look like. Notice that all pulses of the alternator would be affected and the output of the alternator is reduced.

5. *One shorted diode, either polarity, any phase.* Notice that shorted diodes reduce the alternator output more than open diodes (see Figure 7.57).

6. *Two diodes shorted, same polarity, different phase.* As you can see by Figure 7.58, only one phase is in operation while the output of the other phases is zero.

There are many other alternator problems that can reduce the output. No problem can escape the oscilloscope. The pattern will be normal or distorted. By comparing the pattern produced with those we have detailed in this lesson, you will have

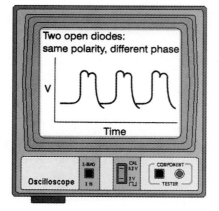

Figure 7.55 Two open diodes, same polarity, different phase. Either two positive or two negative diodes have opened. They will be attached to two different stator coils (courtesy of Training Enterprises Company).

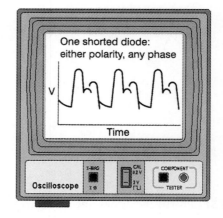

Figure 7.57 One shorted diode, either polarity, any phase. One of the six diodes has a short circuit (courtesy of Training Enterprises Company).

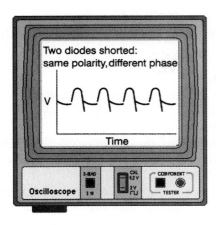

Figure 7.58 Two shorted diodes, same polarity, different phase. Either two positive or two negative diodes have shorted. They will be attached to different stator coils (courtesy of Training Enterprises Company).

a better idea what is wrong. The oscilloscope is a superior method for testing an alternator. It is more accurate and gives more detailed information than the conventional voltage and amperage output tests. This test method shows you what is happening inside the alternator without having to remove it and test individual parts.

Some electronics problems in an alternator cause the alternator to sound like it has a mechanical failure such as a bearing. If a disassembly and inspection indicates the bearings and mechanical parts are not damaged, concentrate on clearing up all the electrical and electronics problems. There should no longer be any noises in the rebuilt alternator.

VOCABULARY

Use the listed words in the blanks beside the sentences to complete the definitions. Either write out the words or place the letters in the blanks.

A. Alternator
B. Regulator
C. Indication device
D. Ammeter
E. Charge
F. Discharge
G. Voltmeter
H. Rotor
I. Stator

J. Alternating current
K. Direct current
L. Rectified
M. Diodes
N. Field coil
O. Voltage drop
P. Fusible link
Q. Overcharging
R. Open circuit
S. Short circuit
T. Interference fit
U. Oscilloscope
V. Pattern
W. Phase
X. Torquing
Y. Puller

_____ 1. A measure of the voltage decrease along a wire
_____ 2. When battery voltage is below 12.6 and the vehicle is running
_____ 3. Keeps the alternator charging rate between 13.5 and 15.6 volts
_____ 4. Part that contains three coils of wire
_____ 5. A revolving electromagnet
_____ 6. When the charging rate goes above 15.5 volts
_____ 7. A broken wire
_____ 8. Used to remove pulleys
_____ 9. Voltage supplied to the rotor
_____ 10. A one-way electrical valve
_____ 11. When the pulley opening is smaller than the pulley shaft
_____ 12. Informs the driver how well the charging system is working
_____ 13. Used to bring the battery voltage back to normal
_____ 14. When AC current is changed to DC current
_____ 15. Current that can only move in one direction
_____ 16. Used to measure current flow in a circuit
_____ 17. When the current flow takes a different path than intended
_____ 18. Device that shows a picture of the current flow in a circuit
_____ 19. Unit used by the vehicle to keep the battery charged while moving

_____ 20. When current moves in two directions in a wave pattern

_____ 21. Used to protect circuits from overload

_____ 22. Name for a coil of wire in the stator

_____ 23. An oscilloscope picture

_____ 24. Device to measure voltage in a circuit

_____ 25. When a bolt is tightened a measured amount

REVIEW QUESTIONS

The following questions will help you determine if you have accomplished the tasks stated at the beginning of the chapter. If you don't know many of the answers, go back and review the material before proceeding to the next chapter.

Lesson 7–1

1. What are the names of three devices used to tell the driver the condition of the charging system?
2. What current is being controlled by the regulator in an alternator system?
3. Are there moving parts in the transistorized regulator?
4. How many diodes are there in the rectifier section of an automotive alternator?
5. What is the name of the alternator part that revolves inside the stator?
6. What type of current is required to charge a battery?
7. What are the four major components that make up the charging system?
8. The alternator converts ___ energy to ___ energy.
9. How will a alternator react if not regulated?
10. What does a red charging system light mean?
11. Where is the best place to find a specific charging system diagram?
12. What are the stationary wire coils called inside an alternator?
13. What type of current does an alternator produce before rectification?
14. How does a diode work?
15. In an automotive alternator half the diodes will be ___ and half will be ___ polarity.
16. What determines the amount of voltage produced by an alternator?
17. The voltage of an alternator is controlled between what range?

18. At what two times during the operation of a vehicle should the charging system warning light be off?

Lesson 7–2

19. Can an accurate test of a charging system be made if the battery is dead?
20. How does a fusible link work?
21. Should polarity be followed when checking cable voltage drop?
22. Long periods of time without starting the engine can harm what emission control device?
23. Why is ordinary wire not a good replacement for fuse link wire?

Lesson 7–3

24. What is the normal standing voltage of a 12-volt battery after the surface charge has been removed?
25. The stage 2 no-load voltage should exceed the base voltage by how much?
26. The stage 3 load voltage should exceed the base voltage by how much?
27. How fast should the engine be run for the load voltage test?
28. What is the type of test instrument used to make a three-stage charging test?

Lesson 7–4

29. Can all alternators be removed from under the hood?
30. Why should the battery ground cable be disconnected before alternator removal?
31. What tool is used to remove and replace interference fit pulleys?
32. What tool is used to get the correct pulley nut tightness on alternators with pulley nuts?

Lesson 7–5

33. How many diodes have positive polarity in an automotive alternator?
34. What is an open circuit?
35. What is a short circuit?
36. What is meant by the term *observing polarity*?
37. What is a phase?
38. What is a pattern?
39. How many separate coils of wire does the stator have?
40. What does the horizontal line on an oscilloscope pattern represent?

ASE QUESTIONS

Each question or incomplete statement in this test is followed by four suggested answers or completions. In each case select the *one* that best answers the question or completes the statement.

1. Technician A says that when the alternator fails, the engine ignition system will not operate. Technician B says the ignition system will operate but fail when the battery gets low. Who is right?
   a. A only
   b. B only
   c. Both A and B
   d. Neither A nor B

2. Technician A says the alternator produces alternating (AC) current. Technician B says the alternator produces direct (DC) current. Who is right?
   a. A only
   b. B only
   c. Both A and B
   d. Neither A nor B

3. What is the charging system voltage range?
   a. 12.5 to 14.5 volts
   b. 13.5 to 14.5 volts
   c. 14.5 to 15.5 volts
   d. 15.5 to 16.5 volts

4. Technician A says there are two wires going from the alternator to the battery. Technician B says there is only one wire and the other path is the frame of the vehicle. Who is right?
   a. A only
   b. B only
   c. Both A and B
   d. Neither A nor B

5. Technician A says in an alternator the rotor turns and the stator becomes an electromagnet. Technician B says the rotor turns and becomes an electromagnet. Who is right?
   a. A only
   b. B only
   c. Both A and B
   d. Neither A nor B

6. Technician A says only direct (DC) current can be used to charge a battery. Technician B says the alternator produces alternating (AC) current and it is used to charge the battery. Who is right?
   a. A only
   b. B only
   c. Both A and B
   d. Neither A nor B

7. Technician A says an accurate test of the charging system can be made even if the battery is discharged. Technician B says the battery must be charged before checking the charging system. Who is right?
   a. A only
   b. B only
   c. Both A and B
   d. Neither A nor B

8. Technician A says the regulator can be the cause of overcharging and undercharging of the battery. Technician B says that a defective regulator will only cause overcharging. Who is right?
   a. A only
   b. B only
   c. Both A and B
   d. Neither A nor B

9. Technician A says an alternator has four phases. Technician B says an alternator has only two phases. Who is right?
   a. A only
   b. B only
   c. Both A and B
   d. Neither A nor B

10. Technician A says diodes can be either negative or positive in polarity. Technician B says diodes have only positive polarity. Who is right?
    a. A only
    b. B only
    c. Both A and B
    d. Neither A nor B

11. Technician A says an open diode will not show up on an oscilloscope test. Technician B says any electrical problem will be detected by an oscilloscope. Who is right?
    a. A only
    b. B only
    c. Both A and B
    d. Neither A nor B

12. Technician A says that an alternator can have open or shorted diodes and still charge a battery. Technician B says open or shorted diodes will cause an alternator to not charge at all. Who is right?
    a. A only
    b. B only
    c. Both A and B
    d. Neither A nor B

13. Technician A says that current can flow in both directions through a diode. Technician B says that current will only flow in one direction through a diode. Who is right?
    a. A only
    b. B only
    c. Both A and B
    d. Neither A nor B

14. Technician A says the purpose of the alternator field current is to magnetize the rotor. Technician B says the purpose of the field current is the magnetize the stator. Who is right?
    a. A only
    b. B only
    c. Both A and B
    d. Neither A nor B

15. Technician A says an oscilloscope checks amperage. Technician B says an oscilloscope checks voltage. Who is right?
    a. A only
    b. B only
    c. Both A and B
    d. Neither A nor B

8

Starting System Maintenance

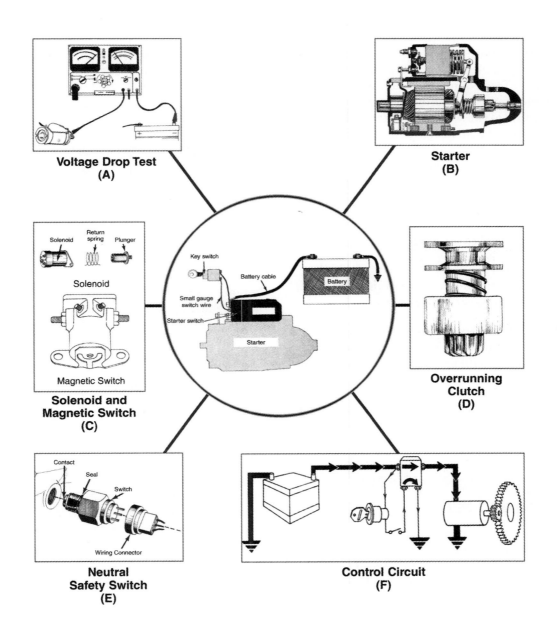

Voltage Drop Test
(A)

Starter
(B)

Solenoid and Magnetic Switch
(C)

Solenoid   Return spring   Plunger

Solenoid

Magnetic Switch

Overrunning Clutch
(D)

Key switch

Battery cable

Battery

Small gauge switch wire

Starter switch

Starter

Neutral Safety Switch
(E)

Contact

Seal

Switch

Wiring Connector

Control Circuit
(F)

The starter cranks the engine, which moves the parts necessary to bring fuel into the engine and compress it. The starter is a high-torque electric motor that requires large amounts of battery current to operate. Thus the battery should always be in good shape before starter problems can be solved. The starter solenoid, cables, and control circuit all need to be serviced along with the starter. Starter service requires a knowledge of mechanical systems, electricity, and parts removal or replacement. Test equipment such as voltmeters and ammeters are used to diagnose starter problems. Listening to the sounds a starter makes when in operation can be an accurate way to determine some types of solenoid and starter problems. The service technician should be able to test all kinds of starters and make any necessary repairs.

TASKS

The following are three tasks to master before leaving this chapter:

Task 8-1. Study the starting system component parts and learn how each part operates.

Task 8-2. Be able to test and evaluate each part of a starting system, which requires using electrical testing equipment and listening for normal starter operation.

Task 8-3. Be able to service a starting system, which may require replacing component parts in the starting system.

LESSON 8–1   Starting System Operation and Parts

The starting system converts electrical energy to mechanical energy and uses that energy to crank the engine (see Figure 8). The engine must be cranked to start the four-stroke cycle. Once the fuel and air mixture in the cylinders burns and exerts sufficient pressure on the pistons, the starting system is no longer needed.

If the starting system cannot crank the engine fast enough, or for a sufficient length of time, the engine will not start. Proper maintenance of the starting system will minimize system failure. A correct diagnostic procedure will enable the technician to locate the cause of any problems that may occur.

The starting system consists of two circuits. One circuit operates the starter motor through a gear system to crank the engine. The other circuit is a control circuit. It enables the driver to turn the motor circuit on and off by means of a small switch. This switch is usually incorporated in the ignition switch. Figure 8.1 shows the two circuits in a typical starting system.

Starter system problems may show up as follows:

1. No starter action when the key is turned.
2. Slow starter action when the key is turned.
3. Starter action but no engine cranking.
4. A loud clicking from the solenoid with no starter action or intermittent action.
5. Starter action and cranking with intermittent no engine cranking.
6. Starting action after the key is released.

It is up to the technician to listen for these problems and determine the cause.

Two circuits are needed because the starter motor requires a large amount of current to crank the engine. A simple switch could be used as a control in the starting system. But the switch would have to be quite large to handle the large amounts of current without being damaged. In addition, long, heavy cables would have to be used to conduct the current to and from the switch. Figure 8.2 shows the location of both circuits in a typical automobile.

The Motor Circuit

The motor circuit consists of the battery, the relay, and the starter motor. These parts are connected by heavy cables that can handle large amounts of current (refer to Figure 8.1).

The Battery. The battery is the power source in the circuit. It supplies the electrical energy needed by the starter motor. A battery converts chemical energy to electrical energy. In the starting system, the starter motor converts electrical energy to mechanical energy.

A fully charged battery can deliver large amounts of energy in the form of electrical current. But this current can be delivered for only a short amount of time. If the battery is partially discharged, it may not deliver sufficient current to crank the engine fast enough to start, or may not be able to deliver the current for a long enough period of time. Because the battery provides the

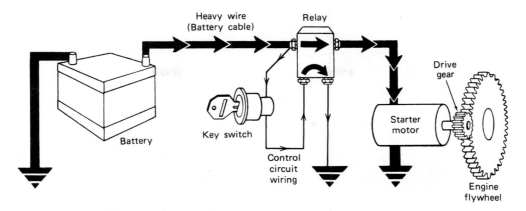

Figure 8.1 Typical starting system. Notice that the system contains two circuits. The motor circuit has its parts connected by heavy cables. The control circuit uses small-gauge wires (courtesy of Chevrolet Motor Division, General Motors Corporation).

energy that cranks the engine, its state of charge is very important.

The Relay. The relay is a magnetically operated heavy-duty switch. Many types of relays are used, but they all serve the same function. They allow a small amount of current in the control circuit to control a large amount of current in the motor circuit. When the driver turns the ignition switch to the START position, a small amount of current energizes the magnet in the relay. The magnet closes a switch with large contacts and current flows to the starter motor.

The Starter Motor. The starter motor is a heavy duty electric motor. Figure 8.3 shows one type of

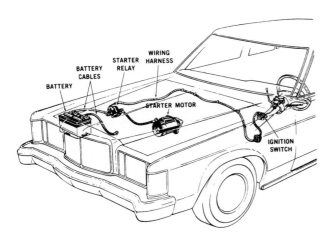

Figure 8.2 Location of starter components in a typical automobile. Notice that the parts in the motor circuit are close together in the engine compartment. The parts of the control circuit are widely separated and are connected by wires in a wiring harness (courtesy of Ford Motor Company, Dearborn, MI).

starter motor. The starter motor turns a small gear, called the *drive pinion*, Which turns the engine fly-wheel. (Refer to Figure 8.1.) The drive pinion is part of a drive system that shifts the pinion in and out of mesh with the flywheel *ring gear*. As shown in Figure 8.4, the ring gear is a toothed ring that en-circles the flywheel. When the motor circuit is en-ergized, the drive pinion is moved into mesh with the ring gear. When the starter switch is released, the drive pinion is moved back out of mesh by a spring.

The Cables. All the parts in the motor circuit must be connected by conductors capable of han-dling large amounts of current. Small gauge wire offers too much resistance to the flow of the cur-rent required. If small gauge wires were used, the starter motor would not be able to crank the en-gine, and the wires would overheat and possibly melt.

The Control Circuit

The control circuit consists of the battery, the relay, and the starter switch. On many cars, a *neutral safety switch* is also used. This switch is placed in series in the circuit. Because the control circuit requires very little current, the components are connected by small gauge wires. (Refer to Figure 8.1.)

A good battery has a standing voltage (no load) of 12.6 volts and produces enough power to operate a normal starter without dropping below 9.6 volts. At very cold temperatures the voltage may be allowed to drop lower.

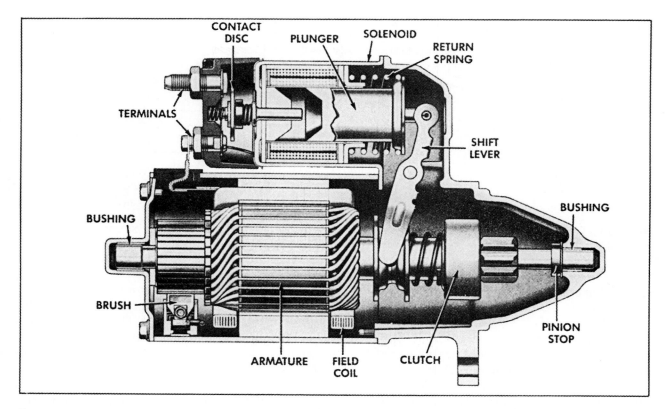

Figure 8.3   Cross-sectional view of a typical starter motor (courtesy of Pontiac Motor Division, General Motors Corporation).

The Battery.   The battery is shared by both circuits. In the control circuit, it provides the energy to operate the relay.

The Relay.   The relay is also shared by both circuits. The control circuit delivers the current that operates the relay. Most relays used in starting

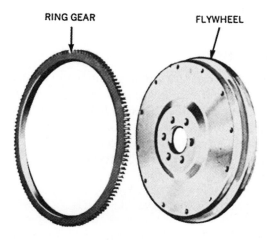

Figure 8.4   Ring gear and flywheel. The ring gear is mounted on the flywheel and turned by the drive pinion (courtesy of Ford Motor Company, Dearborn, MI).

systems are of the solenoid type. Some are mounted on an inner fender panel between the battery and the starter motor (refer to Figure 8.2). A relay of that type acts only as a switch to close the motor circuit. Others are mounted on the starter motor (refer to Figure 8.3). In addition to acting as a switch, they serve a mechanical function. The plunger of the solenoid moves a shift lever, which engages the drive pinion with the flywheel ring gear.

The Starter Switch.   The starter switch opens and closes the control circuit. In most cars, it is a set of contacts built into the ignition switch, as shown in Figure 8.5. When the driver turns the key to the START position, the starter switch contacts are brought together. A spring returns the switch to the IGNITION or ON position and opens the starter control circuit when the key is released.

The Neutral Safety Switch.   To prevent the accidental starting of an engine when the shift selector lever is in any position except NEUTRAL or PARK, most control circuits incorporate a neutral safety switch. The switch is placed in series with the starter switch. Some cars with manual or standard transmissions have a neutral safety switch operated

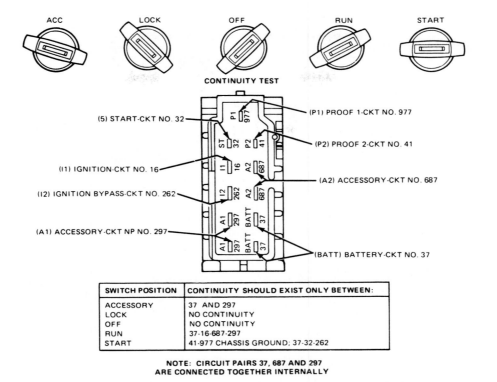

SWITCH POSITION	CONTINUITY SHOULD EXIST ONLY BETWEEN:
ACCESSORY	37 AND 297
LOCK	NO CONTINUITY
OFF	NO CONTINUITY
RUN	37-16-687-297
START	41-977 CHASSIS GROUND; 37-32-262

NOTE: CIRCUIT PAIRS 37, 687 AND 297
ARE CONNECTED TOGETHER INTERNALLY

Figure 8.5 Switch positions. In most cars, the starter switch contacts are built into the ignition switch. Shown are typical switch positions and test points (courtesy of Ford Motor Company, Dearborn, MI).

by the clutch linkage. When a switch of that type is used, it is closed only when the clutch pedal is depressed.

> Never disable or bypass the neutral safety switch. It is a very important safety device and prevents the engine from being started in drive or reverse.

On some cars, a neutral safety switch is placed between the starter switch and the relay, as shown in Figure 8.6. On other cars, a switch is used

between the relay and the ground, as shown in Figure 8.7.

LESSON 8-2 Starting System Components

All starting systems in late model cars have two circuits and operate in the same manner. But the systems used by various manufacturers are different and use different components. To service these

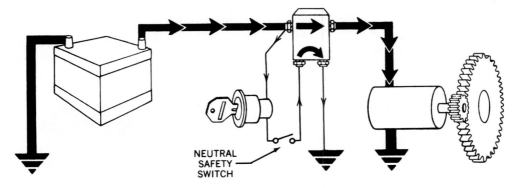

Figure 8.6 Starter control circuit. The control circuit in some starting systems incorporates a neutral safety switch between the starter switch and the relay (courtesy of Chevrolet Motor Division, General Motors Corporation).

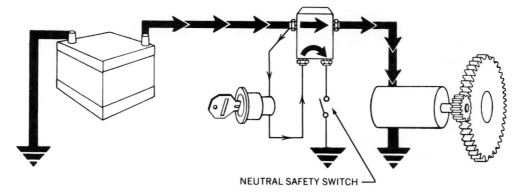

NEUTRAL SAFETY SWITCH

Figure 8.7   Location of neutral safety switch. On some cars, a neutral safety switch is wired between the relay and ground (courtesy of Chevrolet Motor Division, General Motors Corporation).

systems properly, you must be aware of these differences.

Relays

Relays are magnetic switches. They use magnetism to close switch contacts. These contacts can handle large amounts of current. Two types of relays are commonly used. One type, shown in Figure 8.8, uses an electromagnet to move an armature and cause two switch contacts to come together. A relay of that type is used in the control circuit of some cars built by the Chrysler Corporation and is shown in Figure 8.9.

The other type of relay is commonly called a *solenoid*. A solenoid is an electromagnet with a movable core. Figure 8.10 shows a relay of that type. A large metal disc is attached to the core. When magnetism pulls the core, the disc contacts two large terminals. A solenoid is used as a relay on many cars built by Ford Motor Company. It is usually mounted on the inner fender panel near the battery, as shown in Figure 8.11.

A solenoid can exert a very strong pull. On many cars, a large solenoid is mounted on the starter motor (refer to Figure 8.3). The solenoid is used to shift the drive pinion into mesh with the flywheel ring gear. In some applications, the solenoid on the starter motor performs an additional task. It also acts as a relay, eliminating the need for a separate relay. Many cars now use the solenoid to perform both functions.

Starter Motors

Many different types of starter motors are used (see Figure 8.12). Some car manufacturers design and build the starter motors for their cars. Others purchase starter motors from independent makers of electrical equipment or from other car makers. Because of these practices, you will find different starter motors used on apparently similar cars built by the same car maker. Regardless of the make of the starter, most starter motors in use can be classified into three different types.

Starter Motors with the Drive Pinion Shifted by a Solenoid.
Figure 8.13 shows a typical starter motor of this type. An externally mounted solenoid operates a shift fork to slide the drive pinion out, as shown in Figure 8.14. Starter motors of this type

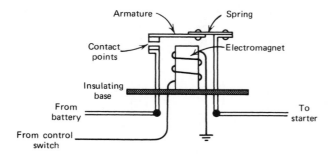

Figure 8.8   Typical relay construction. When current flows from the control switch, the electromagnet pulls the armature down, closing the contact points. Current then flows from the battery to the starter motor.

Figure 8.9   Typical starter relay. A typical starter relay of the type used on certain cars built by Chrysler Corporation.

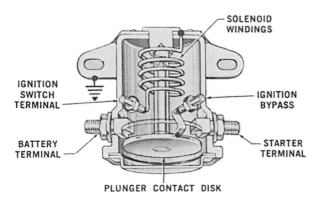

Figure 8.10 Solenoid switch starter relay. A solenoid switch used as a starter relay. When current passes through the solenoid winding, the plunger and the large disc are pulled upward. The disc then contacts the two large terminals (courtesy of Ford Motor Company, Dearborn, MI).

are very common and found on various cars built by almost all manufacturers.

Gear Reduction Starter Motors with the Drive Pinion Shifted by a Solenoid.

As shown in Figure 8.15, starter motors of this type incorporate a gear reduction system to increase torque. Gear reduction starter motors of various designs are used on some cars built by Chrysler Corporation and by General Motors, and on a few imported cars.

> A damaged or defective starter drive clutch often fails to crank the engine and many times lets the starter motor run but not engage the flywheel. This makes a whirring noise in place of the normal cranking sounds. If the vehicle does start it should be driven immediately in for repair to save a tow charge.

Starter Motors with the Drive Pinion Shifted by a Movable Field Pole Shoe.

Starter motors of this type, shown in Figure 8.16, do not use a sep-

Figure 8.11 Solenoid mounting. The starter motor solenoid is usually mounted on an inner fender panel or on the firewall (courtesy of American Motors).

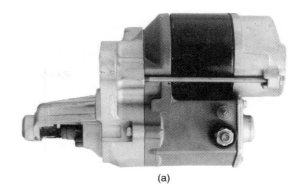

(a)

(b)

(c)

Figure 8.12 Starter motors. Starter motors like A, B, and C are used to crank the engine to start the vehicle (courtesy of Training Enterprises Company).

arate solenoid to move the drive pinion. One of the field windings in the starter motor acts as a solenoid winding. A movable pole shoe takes the place of a solenoid plunger. This type of starter motor is used on some cars built by Ford Motor Company and on some cars built by American Motors Corporation.

Starter Drive Clutches

If the starter motor is to crank the engine, the drive pinion must be held in mesh with the flywheel ring gear. On most cars, the solenoid serves that function as long as the ignition switch is held in the START position. That means that when the engine

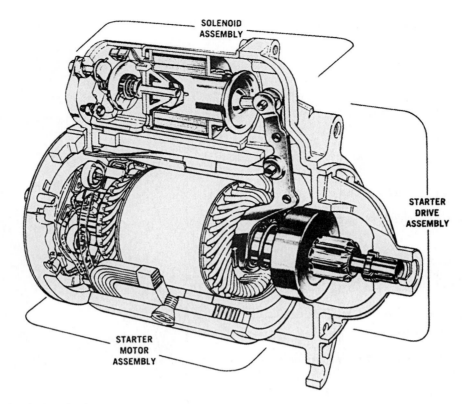

Figure 8.13 Sectional of Ford solenoid. A starter motor that uses an externally mounted solenoid to shift the drive pinion (courtesy of Ford Motor Company, Dearborn, MI).

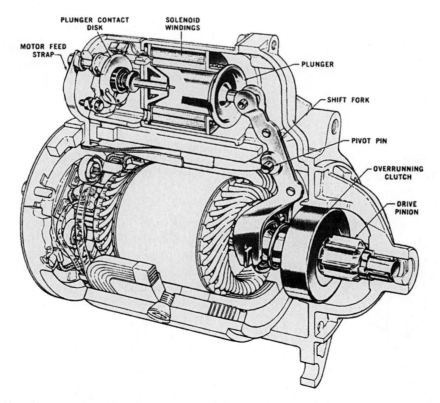

Figure 8.14 Ford solenoid engaged position. A starter motor that uses an externally mounted solenoid to shift the drive pinion. Notice that in this view the shift fork has moved the drive pinion outward (courtesy of Ford Motor Company, Dearborn, MI).

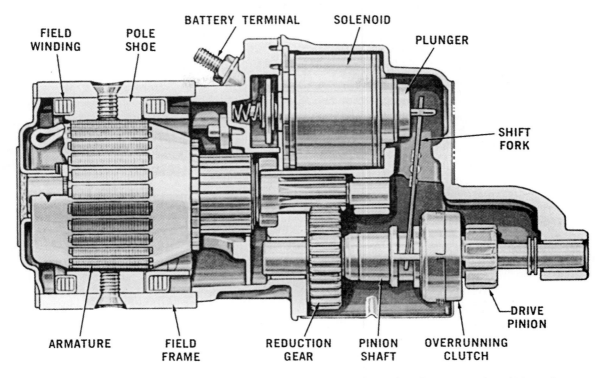

Figure 8.15 A typical gear reduction starter motor. Notice that the solenoid is enclosed (courtesy of Ford Motor Company, Dearborn, MI).

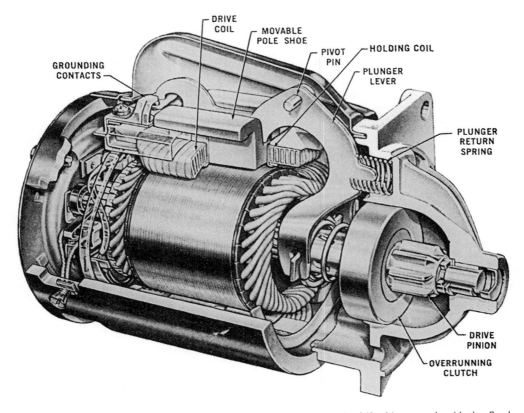

Figure 8.16 Movable pole shoe starter. A starter motor where the drive pinion is shifted into mesh with the flywheel ring gear by means of a movable pole shoe. The field coil winding performs the function of a solenoid (courtesy of Ford Motor Company, Dearborn, MI).

starts, the flywheel turns the drive pinion until the driver releases the switch.

To enable a small starter motor to crank a large engine, the gear ratio between the starter motor and the engine must allow the starter motor to spin fast enough to develop sufficient torque. The average drive pinion has about 10 teeth. Depending on the diameter of the flywheel, the number of teeth on a ring gear varies from about 150 to 200. This provides a gear ratio of from 15:1 to 20:1. When the engine starts, the speed of the flywheel increases above its cranking speed and the flywheel now turns the drive pinion. If the engine runs at 1000 rpm, the drive pinion is turned from 15,000 to 20,000 rpm. If the starter motor armature is rotated at these speeds, centrifugal force will cause the armature windings to be torn loose, destroying the starter motor. Therefore, the armature must be instantly disconnected from the drive pinion when the engine starts. That function is performed by an *overrunning clutch.*

An overrunning clutch, shown in Figure 8.17 is a device that allows torque to be transmitted in only one direction. The clutch locks to allow the starter armature to turn the drive pinion. However, it releases when the pinion tries to turn the armature. Since it transmits torque in only one direction, an overrunning clutch is sometimes referred to as a *one-way clutch.*

As shown in Figure 8.17, an overrunning clutch consists of a set of rollers housed in a ring whose inner surface is formed in the shape of ramps. Those ramps form wedge-shaped pockets for the rollers. Small springs push the rollers up the ramps and wedge them between the outer housing

and an extension of the drive pinion. When the armature turns, the ramped housing turns and increases the wedging action. This locks the drive pinion to the housing and allows the armature to turn the drive pinion.

When the engine starts, the flywheel ring gear turns the drive pinion at a speed faster than the armature. This causes the extension of the drive pinion to move faster, or *overrun,* the housing turned by the armature. The rollers are rolled down the ramps, releasing their grip on the housing and the drive pinion extension. This allows the drive pinion to rotate freely without turning the armature.

LESSON 8–3 Starting System Service

The starting system requires very little maintenance. That maintenance usually consists of (1) keeping the battery in a high state of charge and

> An experienced technician can tell when certain parts of the starting system fail by how the starter sounds when being used. A whirring noise and no engine cranking sound is a defective starter drive clutch. A click and no motor startup is a defective solenoid. A dragging sound with a good battery is excessive resistance. This can be either too much motor resistance or internal starter problems.

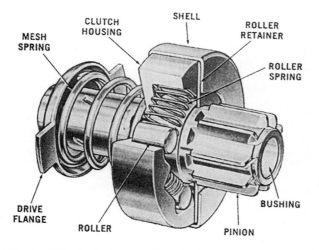

Figure 8.17 Typical overrunning clutch used in a starter drive system (courtesy of Ford Motor Company, Dearborn, MI).

MESH SPRING · CLUTCH HOUSING · SHELL · ROLLER RETAINER · ROLLER SPRING · DRIVE FLANGE · ROLLER · PINION · BUSHING

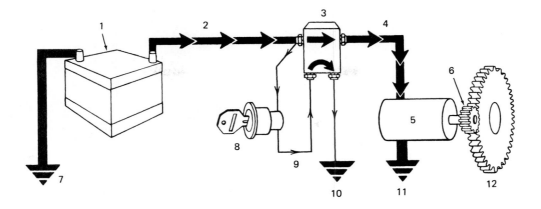

Job 8B

IDENTIFY THE FUNCTION OF THE PARTS IN A STARTING SYSTEM

SATISFACTORY PERFORMANCE
A satisfactory performance on this job requires that you do the following:

1. Identify the functions of the listed starting system parts by placing the number of each part in front of the phrase that best describes its function.
2. Complete the job by correctly identifying all the parts within 10 minutes.

PERFORMANCE SITUATION

1. Battery	7. Starter motor ground
2. Control circuit ground	8. starter cable
3. Control circuit wiring	9. Flywheel
4. Battery cable	10. Battery ground
5. Starter switch	11. Relay
6. Drive pinion	12. Starter motor

____ Provides a path for the return of current to the battery
____ Conducts current to the relay
____ Provides a path for the return of control circuit current
____ Turns the flywheel
____ Provides a bypass for excess starter current
____ Conducts current to the starter motor
____ Provides the control in the control circuit
____ Conducts current in the control circuit
____ Provides a path for the return of motor circuit current
____ Turns the crankshaft
____ Provides the energy for the system
____ Provides the control in the motor circuit
____ Converts electrical energy to mechanical energy.

(2) keeping all the electrical connections in the system clean and tight. When problems arise in the system, other services may be required. Those services include the replacement of parts. But before attempting to replace any part, first determine if the part is defective.

Basic Starting System Tests

The diagnosis of starting system problems is easy if you understand how the system operates and follow a logical test procedure. Many starting problems are caused by dirty or loose battery terminals or by a partially discharged battery. Cables that are badly corroded or otherwise damaged should be replaced. Remember to disconnect the negative (−) cable from the battery first before you attempt to remove any cable.

> **!** **Warning** The starter was never intended to be used for long periods of time and this includes during tests. If an engine cranks but does not start quickly, find the engine starting problem and correct it before the starter is damaged. If the starter is used for making tests on engine components, let it cool after periods of extended use.

In most instances, the control circuit can easily be checked simply by attempting to start the engine. If the circuit is functioning, you usually can hear the relay or solenoid operate. If the relay or solenoid does not appear to be functioning, connect a test light between the S terminal and a good ground, as shown in Figures 8.18 to 8.20. The light will tell you if current is reaching the relay when the key is turned to the START position.

If current is available and the relay or solenoid does not operate, the relay or solenoid is probably at fault. If current is not available, there is an open in the control circuit. The ignition switch or the neutral safety switch may require adjustment or replacement, or there may be a bad connection or a break in the circuit wiring. The test light may be used to check for current at the switches, or the switches may be bridged with a jumper wire for testing.

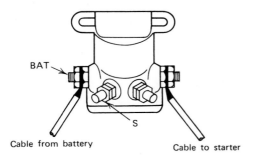

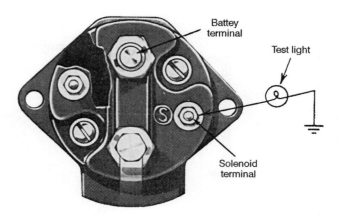

Figure 8.18 Solenoid test. When connected between the S terminal and ground, a test lamp can be used to check the operation of the starter control circuit. If the lamp lights when the key is turned to the START position, the starter switch and the neutral safety switch are functioning.

Figure 8.20 Delco solenoid testing. Connected as shown to a solenoid mounted on a starter motor, the test lamp should light when the ignition switch is turned to the START position (courtesy of Chevrolet Motor Division, General Motors Corporation).

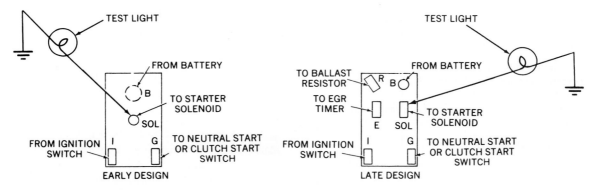

Figure 8.19 Starter relay testing. Connected as shown to the starter relay used on some cars built by Chrysler Corporation, a test lamp should light when the ignition switch is turned to the START position (courtesy of Chrysler Corporation).

TESTING STARTER CURRENT DRAW

A starter current draw test provides a quick check of the entire starting system. This test is performed with a battery starter tester of the type shown in Figure 8.21. You use a tester of this type when you load tested batteries.

The following steps outline a procedure for performing a starter current draw test. Consult the manual furnished with the tester that you have available for any special procedure that may be necessary with that instrument. The specification for starter current draw varies with different cars and must be obtained from an appropriate manual.

1. Always wear safety glasses when working under a vehicle. Dirt, fluids, rust, or other items may fall in your eyes.
2. Place a fender cover on the fender near the battery.
3. Test the specific gravity of the battery electrolyte. If the specific gravity is less than 1.200, charge the battery before attempting a starter current draw test.
4. Check the battery terminals and cable clamps. Clean the terminals and clamps if necessary.

   Note: The battery connections must be clean and tight to obtain accurate test results.

5. Turn the carbon pile control knob on the tester to the OFF position.

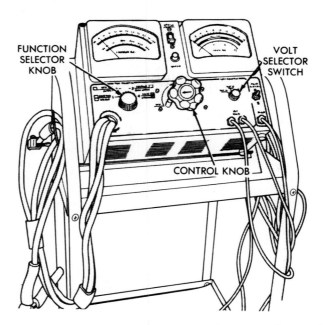

Figure 8.21 Typical battery and starter tester. A typical tester used to test batteries and starting systems (courtesy of Chrysler Corporation).

6. If the tester is fitted with a function control switch, turn the switch to the STARTER TEST position.
7. If the tester is fitted with a volt selector switch, turn the switch so that a voltage exceeding battery voltage is selected.
8. Connect the heavy ammeter leads to the battery terminals. The positive (+) lead must be connected to the positive (+) terminal, the negative (−) lead to the negative (−) terminal.
9. Connect the voltmeter leads to the battery terminals. The positive (+) lead must be connected to the positive (+) terminal, the negative (−) lead to the negative (−) terminal.

   Note: The voltmeter leads should contact the battery terminals as shown in Figure 8.22. If the voltmeter leads are connected to the clamps on the ammeter leads, an inaccurate voltage reading may be obtained.

Figure 8.22 Voltage/current testing. Connections for performing a starter current draw test. Notice that the voltmeter leads are not attached to the ammeter leads, but are in contact with the battery posts (courtesy of American Motors).

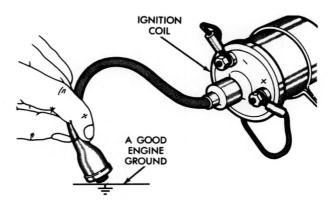

Figure 8.23 Grounding coil wire. On most cars, the ignition system can be disabled by removing the coil wire from the center terminal of the distributor cap and grounding it (courtesy of Chrysler Corporation).

10. Disable the ignition system by removing the center wire from the distributor cap and grounding it, as shown in Figure 8.23.

    Note: In some ignition systems, the coil is located within the distributor cap and no center wire is used. Systems of this type may be disabled by disconnecting a connector at the distributor cap, as shown in Figure 8.24.

11. Apply the parking brake.

12. If the car has an automatic transmission, place the transmission, selector in the PARK position. If the car has a standard or manual transmission, place the shift lever in the NEUTRAL position.

13. Crank the engine for about 3 seconds while observing the voltmeter. Record the voltage indicated.

    Note: You may use a remote starter switch similar to the one shown in Figure 8.25. Figures 8.26 to 8.28 show how to connect a remote starter switch.

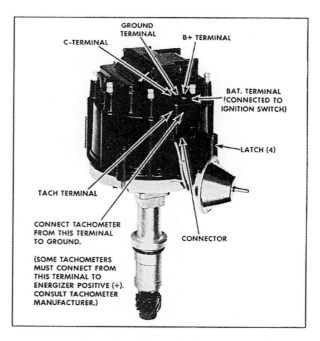

Figure 8.24 Electronic distributor disabling. In an electronic distributor of this type, the coil is housed inside the distributor cap. Unplugging the connector disables the system (courtesy of Pontiac Motor Division, General Motors Corporation).

Figure 8.25 Remote starter switch. A remote starter switch enables you to crank an engine while working under the hood (courtesy of Snap-on Tools Corporation).

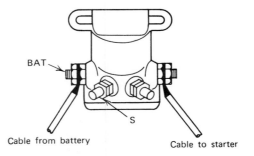

BAT

S

Cable from battery   Cable to starter

Figure 8.26 Starter remote connections. A starter solenoid of the type often used by Ford Motor Company and by American Motors Corporation. Remote starter switch connections should be made at the BAT and S terminals.

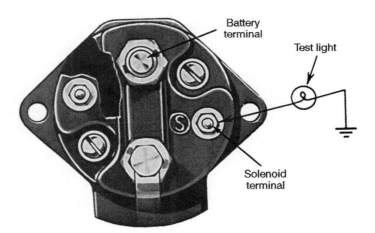

Battery terminal

Test light

S

Solenoid terminal

Figure 8.27 GM remote terminal connections. A front view of a starter solenoid often used on cars built by General Motors Corporation. When using a remote starter switch, it should be connected to the battery terminal and the solenoid (S) terminal (courtesy of Chevrolet Motor Division, General Motors Corporation).

> Disable the ignition system cautiously. Refer to the manufacturer's recommendations in each case. Avoid long periods of starter use with the ignition disabled. Large amounts of gasoline down into the catalytic converter can damage the converter. Long periods of starter use can damage the starter.

14 Turn the carbon pile control knob clockwise until the voltmeter indicates the voltage that you recorded in step 12. Read the current indicated by the ammeter and immediately turn the control knob counterclockwise to the OFF position.

15. Record the current indicated by the ammeter.

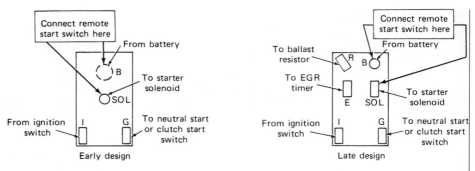

Figure 8.28 Chrysler remote terminal connections. Relays of the type shown are found on some cars built by Chrysler Corporation. Remote starter switch connections should be made at the battery and solenoid (S) terminals (courtesy of Chrysler Corporation).

16. Compare the meter reading with the car manufacturer's specification for starter current draw or with Figure 8.29.
17. Disconnect and remove the tester.
18. Restore the ignition system to operating condition.

AVERAGE STARTER CURRENT DRAW 12 Volt Systems	
CYLINDERS	**AMPERES**
4	120–160
6	150–180
8	160–210

Figure 8.29 Average starter current draw. Average starter current draw specifications. Current draw varies with the temperature, oil viscosity, and the condition of the engine.

Interpretation of Test Results

The specifications for starter current draw vary with different engines produced by different manufacturers. Figure 8.29 shows the specification range for cars with 12-volt systems. Because of the wide range of specifications, the results of the test can be interpreted only when you know the specification for the particular car on which you are working.

Three test results are possible. The indicated starter current draw may be within specifications, above specifications, or below specifications.

Within Specifications. If the ammeter reading falls within the manufacturer's specified range, the starting system is in good condition and should require no repairs.

Above Specifications. If the indicated current draw exceeds the manufacturer's specifications, several problems may be indicated. In most instances, the starter motor is at fault and will require repair or replacement. High current draw also may be caused by the use of high-viscosity oil, high engine temperature, internal engine damage, or very cold temperatures.

Below Specifications. If the starter current draw falls below the specifications of the manufacturer, it usually is an indication of high resistance in the motor circuit. All the connections, including the ground connections, should be checked, cleaned, and tightened.

Interpretation of Test Results

Test 1. The indicated voltage should not exceed 0.5 volt . A reading of 0.5 volt or less indicates that the resistance in the "hot" side of the motor circuit is acceptable. The reading of tests 2 and 3 can be disregarded. Move to test 4.

A reading of more than 0.5 volt indicates excessive resistance in the "hot" side of the motor circuit. Move to test 2.

Test 2. The indicated voltage should not exceed 0.3 volt. A reading of 0.3 volt or less indicates that excessive resistance is present between the relay and the starter motor. The starter cable connections should be cleaned and tightened. The cable should be replaced if necessary.

TESTING VOLTAGE DROP

All conductors have resistance, but their resistance is usually very low. When conductors are corroded, those connections offer more resistance. If the connections are clean and tight, the additional resistance will also be slight. However, if the connections are dirty, loose, or corroded, the resistance may increase so that current flow is restricted.

The starter motor requires large amounts of current. If there is high resistance in the motor circuit, the starter motor will be unable to receive the current it requires. Any resistance in a circuit will cause a drop in voltage. Therefore, a voltage drop test can be used to detect resistance.

The steps that follow outline the procedure for a series of four voltage drop tests in a starting system. These tests, performed in the sequence given, will enable you to find the exact location of any high resistance. Since the voltmeter readings taken will be in tenths of 1 volt, a voltmeter with a low scale is required for accuracy.

In performing the following tests, you will energize the starter motor to crank the engine. When working on a car with a catalytic converter, crank the engine for as short a time as possible. Extended cranking can deposit an excessive amount of fuel in the converter, causing it to overheat and pose a possible fire hazard.

Preparation
1. Place a fender cover on the fender near the battery.
2. Test the specific gravity of the electrolyte in the battery. If the specific gravity is less than 1.200, the battery should be charged.
3. Disable the ignition system by removing the center wire from the distributor cap and grounding it (refer to Figure 8.23).

   Note: In some ignition systems, the coil is located within the distributor cap and no center wire is used. Systems of this type can be disabled by disconnecting a connector at the distributor cap (refer to Figure 8.24).

4. Apply the parking brake.
5. If the car has an automatic transmission, place the selector lever in the PARK position. If the car has a standard or manual transmission, place the shift lever in the NEUTRAL position.
6. Connect a remote starter switch to the relay or solenoid (refer to Figures 8.26 to 8.28).
7. Adjust a voltmeter to the low scale.

Test 1 This test measures the voltage drop in the "hot" side of the motor circuit.

1. Connect the positive (+) voltmeter lead to the positive (+) battery post as shown in Figure 8.30.

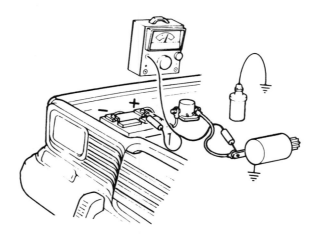

Figure 8.30 "Hot" side voltage drop test. Meter connections for performing a voltage drop test of the "hot" side of the starting system motor circuit (courtesy of American Motors).

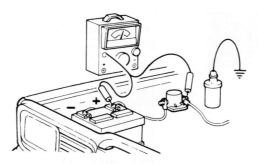

Figure 8.31 Battery-to-starter voltage drop test. Meter connections for performing a voltage dorp test on the "hot" side of the motor circuit between the battery and the starter side of the relay (courtesy of American Motors).

Note: The voltmeter lead should contact the battery post, not the battery cable clamp.

2. Connect the negative (−) voltmeter lead to the terminal bolt on the starter motor. (refer to Figure 8.30).

Note: The voltmeter lead should contact the starter terminal bolt and not the terminal on the end of the cable.

3. Crank the engine and observe the voltmeter reading. Record the voltage indicated.
4. Disconnect the negative (−) voltmeter lead.

Test 2   This test measures the voltage drop between the battery and the starter side of the relay.

1. Connect the negative (−) voltmeter lead to the terminal bolt on the starter side of the relay, as shown in Figure 8.31.
2. Crank the engine and observe the voltmeter reading. Record the voltage indicated.
3. Disconnect the negative (−) voltmeter lead.

Test 3   This test measures the voltage drop between the battery and the battery side of the relay.

1. Connect the negative (−) voltmeter lead to the terminal bolt on the battery side of the relay as shown in Figure 8.32.
2. Crank the engine and observe the voltmeter reading. Record the voltage indicated.
3. Disconnect both voltmeter leads.

Test 4   This test measures the voltage drop in the ground side of the motor circuit.

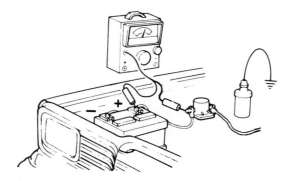

Figure 8.32 Battery-to-solenoid voltage drop test. Meter connections for performing a voltage drop test of the "hot" side of the motor circuit between the battery and the battery side of the relay (courtesy of American Motors).

1. Connect the positive (+) voltmeter lead to the starter motor housing as shown in Figure 8.33.
2. Connect the negative (−) voltmeter lead to the negative (−) battery post (refer to Figure 8.33).

   Note: The voltmeter lead must contact the battery post, not the cable clamp.

3. Crank the engine and observe the voltmeter reading. Record the voltage indicated.
4. Disconnect both voltmeter leads.
5. Restore the ignition system to operating condition.

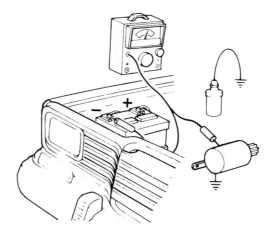

Figure 8.33 Ground side voltage drop test. Meter connections for performing a voltage drop test of the ground side of the motor circuit (courtesy of American Motors).

Job 8C

TEST STARTER CURRENT DRAW

SATISFACTORY PERFORMANCE
A satisfactory performance on this job requires that you do the following:

1. Perform a starter current draw test on the car assigned.
2. Following the steps in the "Performance Outline" and the specifications of the manufacturer, complete the job within 15 minutes.
3. Fill in the blanks under "Information."

PERFORMANCE OUTLINE

1. Test the specific gravity of the battery electrolyte.
2. Check the battery connections and clean them if necessary.
3. Connect the tester.
4. Disable the ignition system.
5. Read the voltage while the starter motor is cranking the engine.
6. Read the amperage while using the carbon pile to duplicate the voltage reading.
7. Compare the reading with the manufacturer's specifications.
8. Interpret the test results.

INFORMATION

Vehicle identification _____
Engine identification _____
Specification for starter current draw _____ amperes
Starter current draw indicated by test _____ amperes
Test interpretation and recommendations _____

A reading of more that 0.3 volt indicates excessive resistance between the battery and the starter terminal on the relay. Move to test 3.

Test 3.   The indicated voltage should not exceed 0.2 volt. A reading of 0.2 volt or less indicates that excessive resistance is present in the relay or in the relay connections. The connections should be cleaned and tightened. The relay should be replaced if necessary.

A reading of more than 0.2 volt indicates excessive resistance is present between the battery and the relay. The battery cable connections should be cleaned and tightened. The battery cable should be replaced if necessary. Move to test 4.

Test 4.   The indicated voltage should not exceed 0.3 volt. A reading of 0.3 volt or less indicates that the resistance in the ground side of the motor circuit is acceptable.

Job 8D

TEST THE VOLTAGE DROP IN A STARTING SYSTEM

SATISFACTORY PERFORMANCE
A satisfactory performance on this job requires that you do the following:

1. Test the voltage drop in the motor circuit of the starting system of the car assigned.
2. Following the steps in the "Performance Outline" and the specifications of the manufacturer, complete the job within 20 minutes.
3. Fill in the blanks under "information."

PERFORMANCE OUTLINE

1. Prepare the vehicle and the meter for the test.
2. Measure the voltage drop in the entire "hot" side of the motor circuit.
3. Measure the voltage drop between the battery and the starter side of the relay.
4. Measure the voltage drop between the battery and the battery side of the relay.
5. Measure the voltage drop in the ground side of the motor circuit.
6. Restore the vehicle to operating condition.
7. Compare your readings with the specifications of the manufacturer.

INFORMATION

Vehicle identification _____
Reference used _____ Page(s) _____
Meter identification _____
Meter scale used _____

TEST PERFORMED	*TEST RESULTS*	*SPECIFICATION*
Voltage drop in the entire "hot" side of the circuit	_____ volts	_____ volts
Voltage drop between the battery and the starter side of the relay	_____ volts	_____ volts
Voltage drop between the battery and the battery side of the relay	_____ volts	_____ volts
Voltage drop in the ground side of the circuit	_____ volts	_____ volts

INTERPRETATION OF TEST RESULTS

_____ Resistance of the entire motor circuit is within specifications.
Excessive resistance may be present in the:
_____ Positive battery terminal and the cable clamp connection
_____ Battery cable
_____ Battery cable connection at the relay
_____ Relay
_____ Starter cable connection at the relay
_____ Starter cable
_____ Starter cable connection at the starter motor
_____ Negative battery terminal and the cable clamp connection
_____ Ground cable
_____ Ground cable connection at the engine
_____ Starter motor mounting

A reading of more than 0.3 volt indicates excessive resistance in the ground connections. The battery ground cable should be cleaned and tightened. The starter mounting bolts should be checked and tightened.

Verification of Repair

The appropriate voltage drop test should be repeated after any repair has been made.

LESSON 8–4 Replacing a Starter Motor and Relay

Starters are not rebuilt as often as they were in the past. Instead they are exchanged for a factory rebuilt or new one. This has the added advantage of a warranty.

If the starter is to be repaired the most common items replaced during a repair are the brushes, brush springs, field coils armature, front and rear bushings, one-way clutch, and any damaged housings. See Figure 8.3 for a picture of these parts. If all this is needed to be replaced it would cost more than the cost of an exchange unit.

One common method is to disassemble the starter and examine the parts. If the damage is

---

Job 8E

REPLACE A STARTER RELAY

SATISFACTORY PERFORMANCE
A satisfactory performance on this job requires that you do the following:

1. Replace the starter relay on the assigned car.
2. Following the steps in the "Performance Outline," complete the job within 20 minutes.
3. Fill in the blanks under "information."

PERFORMANCE OUTLINE

1. Disconnect the battery ground cable.
2. Remove the relay.
3. Install the replacement relay.
4. Connect the battery ground cable.
5. Test the operation of the relay.

INFORMATION

Vehicle identification _____
Reference used _____ Page(s) _____

---

minor, replace the parts. If not, reassemble the starter and exchange it for a rebuilt or new one without doing any repair. Labor is expensive so there is not too much profit margin to work with.

REPLACING A STARTER RELAY	The steps that follow outline a typical procedure for replacing starter relays and solenoids that are mounted separate from the starter motor. Consult an appropriate manual for any specific procedures that may be necessary for the car on which you are working.

1. Protect the fender of the vehicle with a fender cover.
2. Disconnect the ground cable from the battery terminal.
3. Disconnect the wires and cables from the relay.

   Note: Arrange the wires so they will be installed in the same position.

4. Remove the relay.
5. Install the replacement relay.
6. Install the cables and wires.
7. Connect the battery ground cable.

REPLACING A STARTER MOTOR	Removing a starter motor from an engine and installing a replacement is a relatively simple job. However, when the engine is located in a crowded engine compartment, the job becomes a bit more difficult. The starter motor on some cars can be removed by working under the hood. On others, you must raise the car, support it, and work underneath.

Two methods of mounting a starter motor on a engine are in common use. One method uses two or three short bolts to hold the starter motor to the flywheel housing as shown in Figures 8.34 and 8.35. The other method uses two long bolts to hold the starter motor to the bottom of the flywheel housing as shown in Figures 8.36 and 8.37.

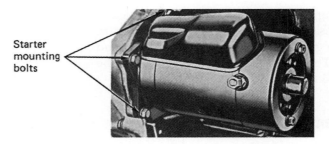

Figure 8.34 Ford starter installation. In this installation, the starter motor is held to the front of the flywheel housing by three bolts (courtesy of Ford Motor Company, Dearborn MI).

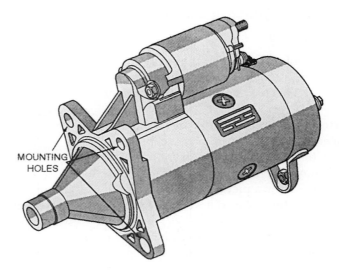

Figure 8.35 Starter mounting flange. Some starter motors have a mounting flange or "ears" by which the starter is bolted to the flywheel housing (courtesy of Chrysler Corporation).

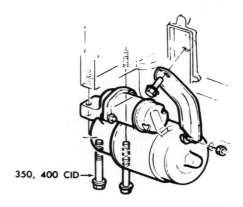

Figure 8.36 Bolt and bracket starter mounting. In this installation, the starter motor is held to the bottom of the flywheel housing by two bolts. A bracket reinforces the mounting (courtesy of Chevrolet Motor Division, General Motors Corporation).

On some cars, the steering linkage blocks the removal of the starter motor. Turning the steering wheel to the extreme left or to the extreme right may provide sufficient clearance. In some instances, the steering linkage must be disconnected and moved.

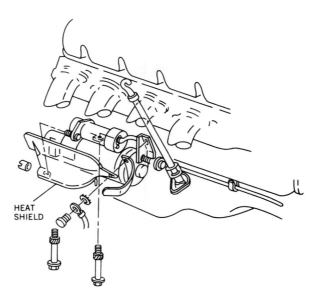

Figure 8.37 Starter heat shield. On some cars, the starter motor is protected from the heat of the exhaust manifold by a heat shield (courtesy of Chevrolet Motor Division, General Motors Corporation).

There are many variables in engine and chassis design, even among cars built by the same manufacturer. Many of those variables require different starter motor removal procedures. The steps that follow outline a general procedure. Consult an appropriate manual for the specific procedure required for the car on which you are working.

Removal

1. Disconnect the battery ground cable.
2. If the starter must be removed from under the car, raise the car and support it with car stands.

   Note: On some cars, supporting the car under the frame provides more clearance at the steering linkage and allows easier starter removal.

3. Remove any reinforcing brackets, braces, or heat shields that may be present. (Refer to Figure 8.37.)
4. Disconnect the wires and cables connected to the starter motor.

   Note: Be sure to observe or tag the location of each wire so you can install them in the correct location on the replacement starter motor.

   Note: On some cars, it is difficult to gain access to the terminals on the starter motor or on the solenoid. On those cars, it is easier to remove the starter mounting bolts first. Then the starter motor can be positioned for better access to the terminals.

5. Remove the bolts holding the starter motor to the flywheel housing.

   Note: On some engines, shims are used between the starter motor and the flywheel housing, as shown in Figure 8.38. Be sure to save any shims present so you can install them with the replacement starter motor.

6. Remove the starter motor.

   Note: Starter removal may be blocked by other engine and chassis components. Consult an appropriate manual for the manufacturer's recommended removal procedure.

Installation

1. Clean the starter motor mounting surface on the flywheel housing.
2. Position the replacement starter motor against the flywheel housing and start the mounting bolts, inserting any shims that may have been removed.
3. Turn all the bolts into place gradually, holding the starter motor in position.

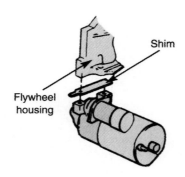

Shim

Flywheel
housing

Figure 8.38 Starter shim positions. On some engines, shims are used between the starter motor and the flywheel housing to provide a means for adjusting gear mesh (courtesy of Pontiac Motor Division, General Motors Corporation).

4. Tighten the bolts to the manufacturer's torque specification.
5. Install the wires and cables if not previously installed.
6. Install any brackets, braces, and heat shields that were removed. Tighten the attaching bolts.
7. Install any engine or chassis components that were removed to allow starter motor removal.
8. Connect the battery ground cable.
9. Check the operation of the starter motor.
10. Lower the car to the floor.

Job 8F

REPLACE A STARTER MOTOR

SATISFACTORY PERFORMANCE
A satisfactory performance on this job requires that you do the following:

1. Replace the starter motor on the car assigned.
2. Following the steps in the "Performance Outline" and the procedure and specifications of the manufacturer, complete the job within 200 percent of the manufacturer's suggested time.
3. Fill in the blanks under "Information."

PERFORMANCE OUTLINE

1. Disconnect the battery ground cable.
2. Raise and support the car if necessary.
3. Remove all parts necessary to gain access to the starter motor.
4. Remove the starter motor.
5. Install the replacement starter motor.
6. Install all parts removed to gain access.
7. Connect the battery ground cable.
8. Check the operation of the starter motor.
9. Lower the car to the floor.

INFORMATION

Vehicle identification _____
Reference used _____ Page(s) _____

VOCABULARY

Use the listed words in the blanks beside the sentences to complete the definitions. Either write out the words or place the letters in the blanks.

A. Crank

B. Start position

C. Relay

D. Drive pinion

E. Ring gear

F. Neutral safety switch

G. Ignition position

H. Neutral

I. Magnetic switch

J. Solenoid

K. Field coil

L. Polo shoe

M. Shift fork

N. Armature

O. Holding coil

P. Plunger

Q. Roller

R. Current draw

S. Battery starter tester

T. Voltage drop

U. Starter shim

V. Starter bracket

W. Heat shield

X. Above specifications

Y. Contact disc

_____ 1. A part located on the edge of flywheel that meshes with the starter pinion

_____ 2. A part that causes the pole shoes to become electromagnets when energized

_____ 3. When the engine turns over prior to starting

_____ 4. Provides power when energized to various vehicle parts

_____ 5. One of the transmission selector positions for cranking the engine

_____ 6. Part that moves into position to lock the drive pinion so the starter will crank the engine

_____ 7. The measure of voltage strength from one wire terminal to another

_____ 8. Keeps heat from going into the starter and overheating the starter parts

_____ 9. Connects the end of the starter cable to the battery cable

_____ 10. Moves the shift fork into position when the solenoid is energized

_____ 11. Moves the pinion into mesh with the ring gear

_____ 12. Becomes a magnet when the field coil has current

_____ 13. Remote part that both connects the battery to the starter and shifts the drive pinion

_____ 14. The key position used to crank the engine

_____ 15. Keeps the starter from being energized if the selector position is not in park or neutral

_____ 16. Part that rotates to make the starter become a motor

_____ 17. Helps locate the starter in the correct position in relation to the ring gear

_____ 18. The amount of amperage needed to operate the starter

_____ 19. Holds the end of the starter in place to reduce vibration

_____ 20. Connects starter wire to the battery

_____ 21. When the starter draw is above normal for the vehicle engine being tested

_____ 22. Keeps the solenoid on or energized during the starting operation

_____ 23. A check of battery voltage during starting

_____ 24. The part located between the armature and the ring gear

_____ 25. Key position after the vehicle has started

REVIEW QUESTIONS

The following questions will help you determine if you have accomplished the tasks stated at the beginning of the chapter. If you don't know many of the answers, go back and review the material before proceeding to the next chapter.

Lesson 8–1

1. The starting system converts _____ energy to _____ energy.
2. What two circuits make up the starting system?
3. The battery, relay, and the starter motor make up what circuit?
4. What is the purpose of the starter relay in the starting system?
5. The starter is a heavy-duty _____ ?
6. What is the purpose of the drive pinion?
7. What is the purpose of the ring gear?
8. What three parts make up the control circuit?
9. Most starter switches are part of ___ ?
10. When does the neutral safety switch prevent the starter from operation?
11. How is the neutral safety switch placed in relation to the starter switch?
12. Why is the battery state-of-charge important to the starter testing?

Lesson 8–2

13. What is another name for relay?
14. How should a test light react if place between the "S" terminal and ground on a Ford relay?
15. What is a solenoid?
16. On many vehicles what does the solenoid do besides provide current to the starter?
17. What is the purpose of a starter armature?
18. What is the purpose of the field winding?

19. What part meshes with the flywheel ring gear?
20. What part is defective when the starter motor runs but the engine does not crank?
21. How many teeth does the average drive pinion have?
22. What is the purpose of the overrunning clutch?

Lesson 8–3

23. Starter maintenance consists of doing what two things?
24. What battery and cable problems can affect starter operation?
25. When the key is turned to the "start" position and current is reaching the relay, what is at fault if the starter does not turn over?
26. If current is not reaching the relay, what part may be defective?
27. Where is the voltmeter connected to make the starter current draw test?
28. What should be done to make sure the vehicle does not run when making a starter current draw test?
29. How many amps of current will a typical six-cylinder, 12-volt starter draw if the system is normal?
30. What are the problems when the starter current draw test is above specifications?
31. What are the problems when the starter current draw test is below specifications?
32. What does observing polarity mean when making voltage tests?
33. What is considered a good voltage reading for the hot side voltage drop test?

Lesson 8–4

34. Can all starters be removed from under the hood?
35. What is the purpose of starter bracket?
36. Why should the battery be disconnected when working on a starter?
37. What is the purpose of starter shim?
38. What is sometimes placed around a starter to protect it?

ASE QUESTIONS

Each question or incomplete statement in this test is followed by four suggested answers or completions. In each case select the *one* that best answers the question or completes the statement.

1. Technician A says the relay is part of the starter motor circuit. Technician B says the relay is part of the control circuit. Who is right?
   a. A only   b. B only
   c. Both A and B d. Neither A nor B

2. Technician A says the starter meshes with a gear on the crankshaft. Technician B says the starter meshes with the flywheel ring gear. Who is right?
   a. A only   b. B only
   c. Both A and B d. Neither A nor B

3. Technician A says the neutral safety switch allows the engine to be started in PARK. Technician B says the neutral safety switch allows the engine to be started in NEUTRAL. Who is right?
   a. A only   b. B only
   c. Both A and B d. Neither A nor B

4. Technician A says the relay used an electromagnet to close the switch. Technician B says the switch is closed by a mechanical link from the ignition switch. Who is right?
   a. A only   b. B only
   c. Both A and B d. Neither A nor B

5. Technician A says both the starter relay and solenoid use contact points. Technician B says only the starter relay uses points. Who is right?
   a. A only   b. B only
   c. Both A and B d. Neither A nor B

6. Technician A says the starter is an electric motor. Technician B says the starter is an electric generator. Who is right?
   a. A only   b. B only
   c. Both A and B d. Neither A nor B

7. Technician A says that all starters use the field coils as a solenoid. Technician B says that some Ford starters use the field coils as a solenoid. Who is right?
   a. A only   b. B only
   c. Both A and B d. Neither A nor B

8. Technician A says the starter overrunning clutch allows torque to be applied in only one direction. Technician B says the overrunning clutch allows torque to be applied in both directions. Who is right?
   a. A only   b. B only
   c. Both A and B d. Neither A nor B

9. The average starter current draw for an eight-cylinder engine is between what amperage range?
   a. 120 to 160 amps   b. 150 to 180 amps
   c. 160 to 210 amps   d. 190 to 250 amps

10. Technician A says a starter that tests with a higher than normal current draw will have internal starter damage. Technician B says a

starter that tests with a higher than normal current draw could have a motor with too high a viscosity engine oil. Who is right?

a. A only
b. B only
c. Both A and B
d. Neither A nor B

11. Technician A says a starter with the current draw testing below normal will have high resistance in the motor circuit. Technician B says a starter testing with the below normal current draw will have low motor circuit resistance. Who is right?

a. A only
b. B only
c. Both A and B
d. Neither A nor B

12. Technician A says adjustment bolts are used to correct starter to flywheel positioning. Technician B says shims are used to adjust starter to flywheel positioning. Who is right?

a. A only
b. B only
c. Both A and B
d. Neither A nor B

13. Technician A says most starters are exchanged for either a rebuilt or new one. Technician B says most starters are rebuild by the technicians in the shop. Who is right?

a. A only
b. B only
c. Both A and B
d. Neither A nor B

14. Technician A says that normal battery to starter cable will have resistance of 1 volt. Technician B says that normal battery to starter cable resistance will be .5 volts or lower. Who is right?

a. A only
b. B only
c. Both A and B
d. Neither A nor B

15. Technician A says a clicking noise without hearing the starter motor is usually solenoid failure. Technician B says a clicking noise without hearing the starter motor is usually the ignition starter switch. Who is right?

a. A only
b. B only
c. Both A and B
d. Neither A nor B

Ignition System Maintenance

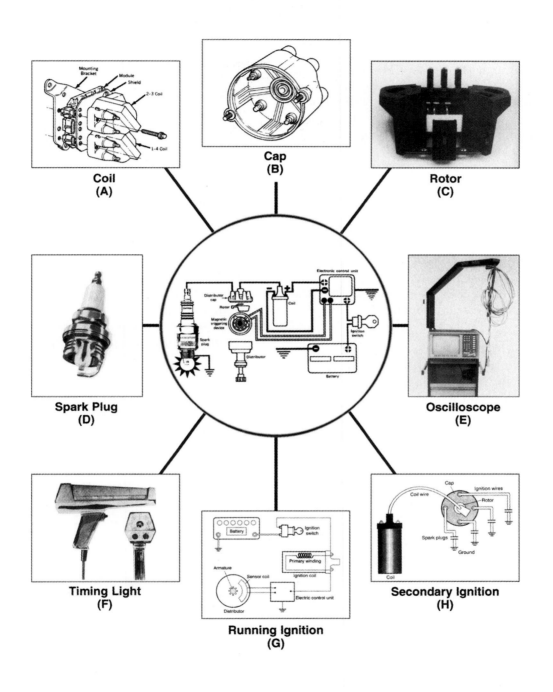

Coil
(A)

Cap
(B)

Rotor
(C)

Spark Plug
(D)

Oscilloscope
(E)

Timing Light
(F)

Running Ignition
(G)

Secondary Ignition
(H)

The ignition system (see Figure 9) supplies the spark that ignites the fuel and air mixture in the engine's cylinders. Ignition systems have two main circuits. The primary circuit voltage is the low-voltage side of the ignition system and by the coil increases the voltage high enough to jump the spark plug gap (see Figure 9G). This normally is between 7000 and 15,000 volts depending on how wide the spark gap is set and the gap condition due to wear. The system also controls the ignition timing so the spark ignites the fuel and air mixture when maximum power is delivered from the burning fuel. The secondary circuit provides the high-voltage path to the spark plugs. This path is from the coil to the distributor (if the vehicle has one) along the spark plug wires and to the spark plug (see Figure 9H).

The service technician has to deal with both the mechanical side of the ignition system and the electrical or electronic side. Knowledge of electrical test equipment (see Figure 9E) is needed to find and solve ignition system problems. Electricity cannot be seen unless a tester such as an oscilloscope is used. With this piece of test equipment electrical problems become easy to spot and solve.

TASKS

The ignition system on most vehicles today is loaded with electronics. These systems are usually dependable, but when something fails it takes real skill to find and correct the problem. Ignition system maintenance is an important area to concentrate your study. Ignition problems are brought to the technician to solve because the average vehicle owner cannot do ignition repair without the equipment and the knowledge.

The following are six tasks to master before leaving this chapter:

Task 9-1.   Study the parts of an ignition system and know how they operate.

Task 9-2.   Be proficient in the removal, selection, and replacement of spark plugs. Be able to "read" the conditions that caused premature spark plug failure.

Task 9-3.   Be able to test, remove, and replace ignition wires, distributor or sensor parts, and ignition coils.

Task 9-4.   Study the function of a primary circuit.

Task 9-5.   Be able to set ignition timing and on older systems set and adjust dwell.

Task 9-6.   Be able to use test equipment to evaluate the ignition parts accurately in both the primary and secondary systems.

LESSON 9–1   Ignition System Parts and Operation

A spark plug, shown in Figure 9.1, contains a pair of electrodes that are spaced, or *gapped,* so that the high voltage will push current across the gap, causing a spark. Most ignition systems contain two circuits. A *primary circuit* handles battery voltage. A *secondary circuit* handles the high voltage produced to jump the gap at the spark plugs.

The Primary Circuit

The primary circuit actually is the control circuit of the ignition system. Two basic types of primary circuits are used in automotive ignition systems. Most older cars have a primary circuit that uses a set of mechanically operated *breaker points.* Cars in current production do not use breaker points. Electronic components eliminate the need for those mechanically operated parts.

Figure 9.1   Typical spark plug. A spark occurs when high voltage jumps the gap between the two electrodes (courtesy of Chevrolet Motor Division, General Motors Corporation).

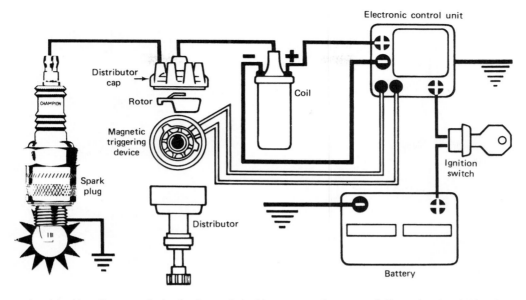

Figure 9.2 A pictorial wiring diagram of a basic electronic ignition system (courtesy of Champion Spark Plug Company).

A primary circuit using breaker points consists of the battery, the ignition switch, the *ignition coil,* a set of breaker points, and a condenser.

A primary circuit using electronic components consists of the battery, the ignition switch, the ignition coil (or coils), an *electronic control unit,* and/or *module,* and some type of *magnetic triggering device.* Figure 9.2 shows a basic system, but many different systems are in use.

Primary Circuit Components

The Battery. The battery supplies the energy to operate the system during cranking and during those times when the charging system is not producing sufficient current.

The Ignition Switch. The ignition switch enables the driver to control the system, and thus the engine, on and off.

The Ignition Coil. The ignition coil boosts the battery voltage to the high voltage needed to push current across the gap of the spark plugs. Since the coil handles both low and high voltage, it is actually a part of both the primary and secondary circuits.

A typical coil, shown in Figure 9.3, consists of two separate windings of insulated wire. Those windings are wrapped around a laminated iron core. The *primary winding* is part of the primary circuit and consists of about 100 turns of heavy wire. The *secondary winding* is part of the secondary circuit and consists of several thousand turns of very fine

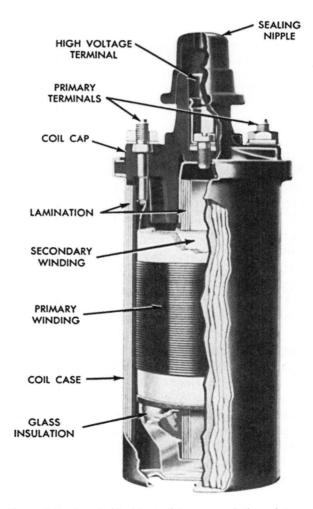

Figure 9.3 A typical ignition coil (courtesy of Chevrolet Motor Division, General Motors Corporation).

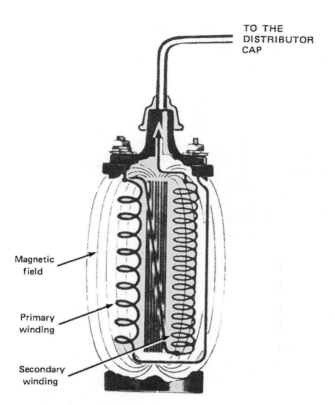

TO THE
DISTRIBUTOR
CAP

Magnetic field

Primary winding

Secondary winding

Figure 9.4 Coil operation. When battery current flows in the primary winding of a coil, a magnetic field is created. When the current is cut off, the magnetic field collapses, inducing high voltage in the secondary winding (courtesy of Chevrolet Motor Division, General Motors Corporation).

Figure 9.5 Distributor electronic control module. A small electronic control unit in common use. Units of this type are usually called *modules* and are mounted inside the distributor (courtesy of Training Enterprises Company).

wire. When current from the battery flows through the primary winding, a strong magnetic field is produced. The magnetic field is aligned and reinforced by the iron core and the iron case surrounding the coil (see Figure 9.4). When the flow of current through the primary winding is interrupted, the magnetic field collapses. When the magnetic field collapses, a surge of voltage is *induced,* or generated, in the secondary winding. Due to the difference in the number of turns in the two windings, the induced voltage is very high.

Electronic Circuitry. In a breakerless system, electronic circuitry takes the place of the points and the cam that operates them. A transistorized circuit controls the flow of current in the primary winding of the coil. Since the circuitry has no moving parts, it does not require adjustment or replacement because of wear. Figures 9.5 to 9.7 show some of the units in common use. Most electronic units are operated by a *magnetic triggering device.*

These systems use a crankshaft position sensor (see Figures 9.8 and 9.10) to signal an electronic

control module when it is time to fire the spark plug. The control module regulates the flow of current to the primary winding of the coil. The module also controls the spark advance so the engine develops maximum power and speed. All this is accomplished electronically and replaces the old systems that used centrifugal advance and vacuum advance units. The new distributors do not have to be rotated to set base timing. The distributor is locked in place and only touched if the distributor has to be removed from the engine. There are many items that have to be serviced in the new systems.

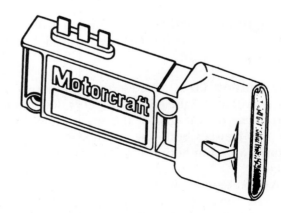

Figure 9.6 Ford electronic module. Some electronic ignition systems use a small module of this type attached to the outside of the distributor (courtesy of Ford Motor Company, Dearborn, MI).

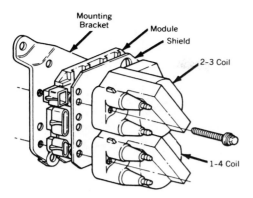

Figure 9.7 Direct ignition system. In this distributorless ignition system, called a Direct Ignition System (DIS), the module is mounted under the coils (courtesy of Chevrolet Motor Division, General Motors Corporation).

Figure 9.8 Crankshaft sensor. This part sends a signal to a computer that is used to trigger the ignition coil into producing high voltage to jump the spark plug gap (courtesy of Training Enterprises Company).

Figure 9.9 Trigger wheel and sensor. The sensor detects changes in the magnetic field when the trigger wheel rotates inside. The magnetic field changes are detected by a computer and used to time the response of the coil as it produces the spark plug high voltage (courtesy of Training Enterprises Company).

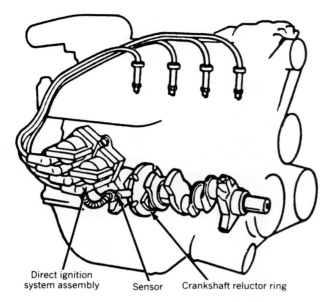

Figure 9.10 caption labels: Direct ignition system assembly, Sensor, Crankshaft reluctor ring

Figure 9.10 Distributorless ignition system. In this distributorless system, a notched reluctor ring on the crankshaft takes the place of a trigger wheel. The sensor is positioned in the engine block near the ring (courtesy of Chevrolet Motor Division, General Motors Corporation).

Coils have to be checked for shorts, excessive resistance, and open wires. Caps and rotors have to be checked for cracks, corrosion, and carbon paths. Spark plug and coil wires have to be checked for open circuits and excessive resistance. The crankshaft sensor has to be checked to see if it is sending the right signal at the right time. All these parts are replaceable and may cause trouble.

Spark Plug Coil. On some General Motors applications there are separate wires for the brand of coil being used. The Melco coil uses a wire that is 145 mm (5.70 in.) in length, and the Delphi coil uses a wire that is 110 mm (4.30 in.) in length. On both wires the total ohms resistance should not exceed 3000 ohms.

The Importance of the Scan Tool. To accurately check out the entire range of sensors and electronic switches used on an engine, a place is made in the wiring harness especially to hook up a scan tool. By following a program built into the machine the technician can easily check out the working condition of all the computer sensors. Learn to use this tool accurately because it is the heart of computer service. One sensor malfunction and the vehicle can run very poorly. Service technicians can no longer guess and change parts. They have to test and replace those that are bad. Without a scan tool it would be almost impossible to produce fast and accurate repair work.

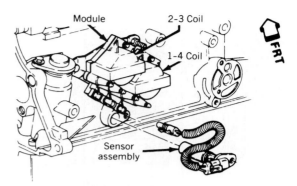

Figure 9.11 labels: Module, 2-3 Coil, 1-4 Coil, FRT, Sensor assembly

Figure 9.11 Sensor mounting for DIS system. The location and mounting of the sensor and the coils of a distributorless system (courtesy of Chevrolet Motor Division, General Motors Corporation).

The Magnetic Triggering Device. This usually consists of some type of *pickup assembly,* or *sensor,* and an *armature,* or *trigger wheel.* In some systems, the sensor and trigger wheel are mounted in the distributor as were breaker points and the cam (See Figures 9.8 and 9.9). The sensor detects changes in a magnetic field caused by the motion of the trigger wheel. The trigger wheel is rotated by the distributor shaft as is the cam in a breaker point system (see Figure 9.9).

In other systems, the distributor has been eliminated. The function of the trigger wheel is handled by a *reluctor ring* mounted on the crankshaft. The sensor is mounted in the engine block so that it can detect changes in a magnetic field caused by notches on the reluctor ring. In those systems, multiple coils are used (see Figures 9.10 to 9.12).

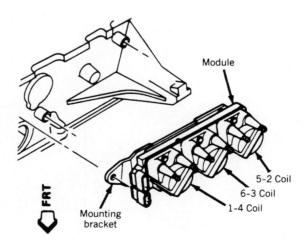

Figure 9.12 labels: Module, 5-2 Coil, 6-3 Coil, 1-4 Coil, FRT, Mounting bracket

Figure 9.12 Six-cylinder DIS mounting. A Direct Ignition System (DIS) for a six-cylinder engine. Note the use of three coils (courtesy of Chevrolet Motor Division, General Motors Corporation).

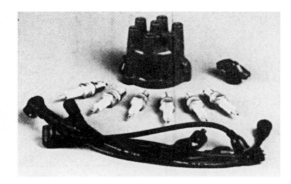

Figure 9.13 Secondary circuit components. The secondary circuit components of a six-cylinder engine. Shown is the distributor cap, rotor, spark plugs, and high-tension wires (courtesy of American Motors).

The Secondary Circuit

The secondary circuit in both breaker point systems and electronic systems is basically the same. The function of the secondary circuit is to distribute the high voltage surges to each cylinder, where it can jump the spark plug gap. The secondary circuit consists of the ignition coil(s), the spark plugs, the secondary wires, the *distributor cap,* and the *rotor.* Figure 9.13 shows those components.

On systems that do not use a distributor, the distributor cap and rotor are not required.

Secondary Circuit Components

The Ignition Coil.   As mentioned previously, the coil is shared by both the primary and secondary circuits. The high voltage induced in the secondary winding flows out through the tower at the top of the coil (refer to Figures 9.3 and 9.4). The high-voltage surges are carried to the center tower of the distributor cap or, in distributorless systems, directly to the spark plugs by a secondary, or *high-tension,* wire.

The Distributor Cap.   This part is made of plastic or other insulating material. In addition to the center tower, the distributor cap has other towers or terminals spaced around its circumference. One tower is provided for each of the engine's cylinders. Inside the cap, at the base of each of those towers, is a metal post as shown in Figure 9.14. Those posts, one at a time, receive a surge of high voltage from the center tower by means of a rotating contact called a *rotor.*

Figure 9.14 Distributor cap. This is an eight-cylinder electronic distributor cap. The spark plug wires are connected to the eight extended parts. A carbon button is in the center of the cap to make contact with the rotor button (courtesy of Training Enterprises Company).

Figure 9.15 Electronic distributor rotor button. The rotor button directs the high voltage from the coil to the terminals of each spark plug wire. A metal conductor rests on a carbon button in the center of the cap. High voltage comes from the coil through the metal conductor and out the tip of the rotor. It then jumps over to the spark plug wire terminal (courtesy of Training Enterprises Company).

The Rotor. The rotor, usually made of plastic, is mounted on the distributor shaft and turns with it. A typical rotor is shown in Figure 9.15. A metal strip or spring on the rotor contacts a *button* or *brush* at the base of the center tower (refer to Figure 9.14). As the shaft rotates, the tip of the rotor passes from one outer terminal to the next. This allows the high-voltage surge to flow to each terminal in turn. Thus, in one turn of the distributor shaft, high voltage is distributed to all the outer terminals.

The Spark Plugs. There are many types of spark plugs, but they all serve the same purpose. A spark plug provides the gap, or air space, across which the high voltage can jump. A spark occurs when the high voltage jumps the gap. Spark plugs are threaded so they can be screwed into the cylinder head(s) of an engine. This places the gap inside the combustion chamber as shown in Figure 9.16.

The Secondary Wires. Since the secondary circuit may handle in excess of 100,000 volts, special wires must be used. Those wires, commonly

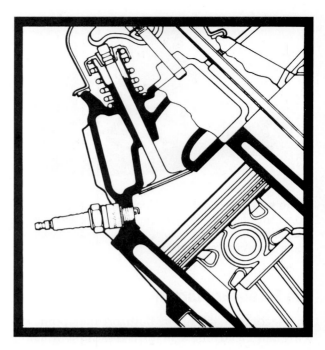

Figure 9.16 The position of the spark plug inside a typical combustion chamber (courtesy of Champion Spark Plug Company).

called *spark plug wires,* must have extra insulation to prevent any leakage of that high voltage (see Figure 9.17). Factory-installed wires have a nonmetallic conductor.

The construction of those two types of spark plug wires is shown in Figure 9.18. To provide good connections at the distributor cap and at the spark plugs, special terminals are used at the ends of the wires. Some of those terminals are shown in Figure 9.19.

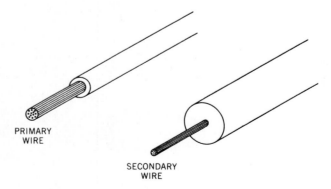

Figure 9.17 Primary and secondary wire. Primary wire is insulated to prevent the leakage of low voltage. Secondary wire or high-tension wire has much heavier insulation, as it may be subjected to electrical pressures of over 30,000 volts.

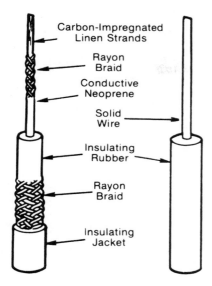

Figure 9.18 High-tension wire construction. The construction of the two types of high-tension wire used in the secondary circuit. Notice that the conductor has a very small cross section compared to the cross section of the insulation (reprinted with permission from AC-Delco, General Motors Corporation).

Job 9A

IDENTIFY THE PARTS IN A BASIC IGNITION SYSTEM

SATISFACTORY PERFORMANCE

A satisfactory performance on this job requires that you do the following:

1. Identify the numbered parts on the drawing by placing the number of each part in front of the correct part name listed below.
2. Correctly identify all the parts within 10 minutes.

PERFORMANCE SITUATION

____ Rotor
____ Spark plug
____ Electronic control unit
____ Magnetic triggering device
____ Distributor
____ Ignition coil
____ Coil wire
____ Distributor cap
____ Battery
____ Ignition switch

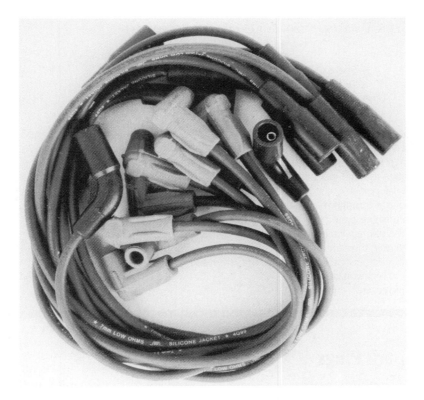

Figure 9.19 Spark plug wires. Special insulated spark plug wires are used on electronic ignition systems. These wires have heavier insulation than the old-style conventional ignition systems. These wires are factory made with both the spark plug and distributor cap ends installed. Wires such as these can be bought in sets or individually as needed (courtesy of Training Enterprises Company).

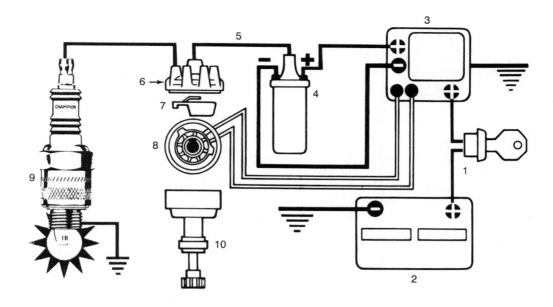

Job 9B

IDENTIFY THE FUNCTION OF IGNITION SYSTEM PARTS

SATISFACTORY PERFORMANCE
A satisfactory performance on this job requires that you do the following:

1. Identify the function of the ignition system parts listed below by placing the part number in the space provided in front of the correct part function.
2. Correctly identify the function of all the parts within 15 minutes.

PERFORMANCE SITUATION

1. Ignition coil	6. Spark plugs
2. Electronic control unit	7. Primary wires
3. Breaker points	8. Armature and sensor
4. High-tension wires	9. Ignition switch
5. Condenser	10. Battery

_____ Provides current for the ignition system while the engine is cranking
_____ Conducts high voltage from the distributor cap to the spark plugs
_____ Generates high voltage through induction
_____ Minimizes arcing at the points
_____ Conducts battery voltage through the system
_____ Allows the driver to turn the system on and off
_____ Makes and breaks the primary circuit in a breakerless ignition system
_____ Generates high voltage in the primary circuit
_____ Makes and breaks the primary circuit in an ignition system using breaker points
_____ Provides a gap for the high voltage to jump
_____ Triggers the electronic control unit

LESSON 9-2   Spark Plugs

Of all the parts in an ignition system, the spark plugs usually require the most service and the most frequent replacement. This is understandable when you consider the conditions under which they operate.

When the average car has traveled 10,000 miles (16,000 km), each spark plug in the engine has fired about 15 to 20 million times. Each time a plug fires, the spark is pushed across the gap by a voltage surge that can exceed 30,000 volts. During the combustion of the fuel and air mixture, the plug is exposed to temperatures of over 5000°F (2760°C)

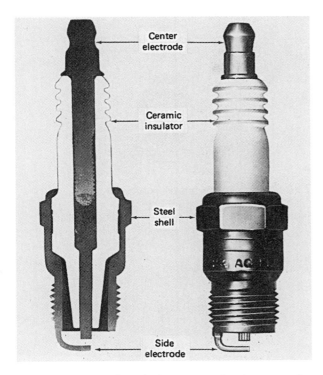

Figure 9.20 Typical spark plug construction (courtesy of Chevrolet Motor Division, General Motors Corporation).

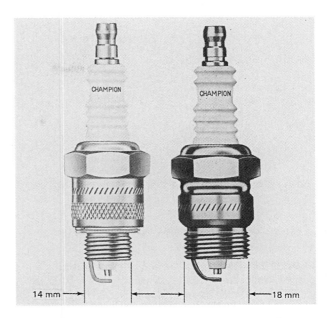

Figure 9.21 Two types of spark plug thread sizes. The two most commonly used spark plug thread sizes are 14 mm and 18 mm (courtesy of Champion Spark Plug Company).

and subjected to pressures that can exceed 700 psi (4226 kPa).

The skills required for spark plug service are easily developed, but the application of those skills must be based on an understanding of spark plug construction and operation.

Spark Plug Construction

As shown in Figure 9.20, a spark plug consists of a *center electrode* enclosed in a ceramic *insulator* held by a steel *shell*. The center electrode provides one side of the gap that the spark must jump. The remaining side of the gap is formed by a *side electrode*, or ground electrode, that is welded to the shell.

The lower part of the shell is threaded to fit a threaded hole in the cylinder head. The upper part of the shell is hexagonal, allowing you to use a socket to remove and install the plug.

Spark Plug Design Differences

Although most spark plugs appear similar, they have many design differences. Some of those differences are not apparent. Although a certain spark plug may appear to fit a particular engine, its use

may cause poor engine performance and even serious engine damage.

Thread Size. Thread size, or thread diameter, is the most obvious design difference. Most car manufacturers have adopted two sizes as standard. As shown in Figure 9.21, those sizes are 14 and 18 mm. Spark plugs with other thread sizes are available, but they rarely are used in automobile engines.

Seat Types. When a spark plug is installed in an engine, it must provide a perfect seal against the pressures of compression and combustion. This seal must also allow heat to flow from the plug to the cylinder head. A tight, heat-conducting seal is provided between the spark plug seat and a matching seat that is machined in the cylinder head. In some engines, gaskets made of soft metal are used between the seats. In other engines, no gaskets are used.

Two commonly used seat designs are shown in Figure 9.22. On plugs that use gaskets, the seat is flat. The gasket is compressed between the seat on the plugs and a matching flat seat in the cylinder head. On plugs that do not use gaskets, the seat is tapered. A tapered seat spark plug is designed to wedge into a similar taper formed in the cylinder head. Since the seats in all cylinder heads are not the same, the selection of plugs with the wrong seat

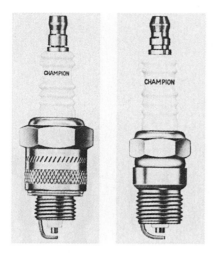

Figure 9.22   Examples of flat and tapered spark plug seat designs. Notice that the plug with the flat seat is fitted with a gasket (courtesy of Champion Spark Plug Company).

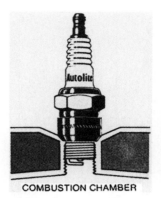

Figure 9.24   Example of wrong reach plug installed. A spark plug with a short reach installed in a cylinder head designed for a plug with a long reach (courtesy of Allied Automotive).

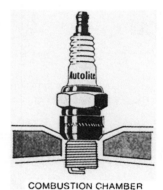

Figure 9.25   Example of too long a reach. A spark plug with a long reach installed in a cylinder head designed for a plug with a short reach (courtesy of Allied Automotive).

will allow leakage around the spark plug thread and will restrict heat flow.

Reach.   Reach, or thread length, is the distance between the seat and the end of the thread. Figure 9.23 shows some of the thread lengths in common use. If the reach of a plug is too short for a particular engine, the electrodes will not be properly positioned in the combustion chamber. This condition is shown in Figure 9.24. Moreover, the exposed threads in the cylinder head will become filled with carbon and other deposits of combustion. Those deposits will make it difficult for you to install the correct plug at a later date.

If the reach of a spark plug is too long, as shown in Figure 9.25, the plug will extend too far into

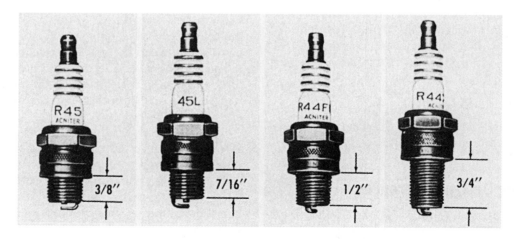

Figure 9.23   Examples of spark plug reach. Different engines require plugs with different thread length or reach (reprinted with permission from AC-Delco, General Motors Corporation).

the combustion chamber. This can cause trouble in several ways:

1. The threads of the plug will become filled with combustion deposits. This will make it difficult to remove the plug.
2. The exposed threads may glow when heated causing the fuel and air mixture to ignite before the spark jumps the gap. This early firing, called *pre-ignition*, can cause damage to the spark plug and to the engine.
3. The end of the plug may contact the valves or the piston when the engine is running. That contact can cause serious engine damage.

Heat Range. Spark plug heat range is the range of temperature within which a spark plug normally operates. Heat range is determined by the plug's ability to dissipate heat. To provide good performance, the spark plugs in a particular engine must operate within a certain temperature range. If a plug's operating temperature is too low, the plug will become *fouled*. As shown in Figure 9.26, fouling is a buildup of oil, carbon, and other combustion deposits on the insulator tip and in the shell. Those deposits conduct electricity and allow secondary voltage to leak to ground. Since the spark does not jump the gap, the plug misfires and combustion does not occur.

If the operating temperature of a spark plug is too high, the electrodes wear rapidly. Under extreme conditions, pre-ignition, spark plug failure, and engine damage will result. Figure 9.27 shows a spark plug whose heat range was too hot for the engine in which it was installed.

The heat range of a plug is usually determined by the length of its lower insulator (Figure 9.28). As shown in Figure 9.29, the short insulator tip in the "cold" plug provides a short path for heat to flow from the insulator tip to the cylinder head, where it is dissipated in the coolant. Since the plug can

Figure 9.27 Example of pre-ignition damage. Pre-ignition damage caused by the installation of a plug whose heat range was too high (courtesy of Ford Motor Company, Dearborn, MI).

pass off its heat rather rapidly, its operating temperature remains low. The "hot" plug has a long insulator that requires heat to travel a greater distance before it is dissipated. Thus its operating temperature remains high.

Extended Tips. On some spark plugs, the electrodes and the tip of the insulator are extended so that they project farther beyond the end of the shell. A spark plug of that design is shown in Figure 9.29. In some engines, that design extends the heat range of the plug. When the engine is running at low speed, the extended tip retains more heat and acts as a hotter plug. This prevents fouling, which is common when an engine is operated at low speeds. At higher speeds, when a colder plug is desirable, the extended tip is cooled by the flow of the incoming fuel and air mixture. Due to

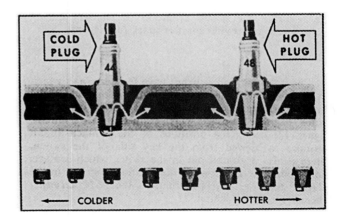

Figure 9.28 Heat ranges of spark plugs. Examples of spark plugs with different heat ranges. The ability of a plug to dissipate heat is determined by the length of its insulator tip (courtesy of Chevrolet Motor Division, General Motors Corporation).

Figure 9.26 Fouled spark plug (courtesy of Ford Motor Company, Dearborn, MI).

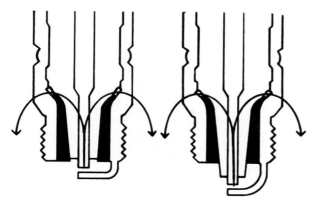

Figure 9.29 Examples of tip design. Conventional and extended-tip design spark plugs. Notice the heat flow paths (courtesy of Allied Automotive).

engine design differences, extended-tip spark plugs cannot be used in all engines.

> Replacement spark plugs must have the correct seat type, reach, heat range, gap, and resistor value if they are to work right in the engine. After any of these problems are introduced into an engine they are hard to find and correct. The engine may have to be hot before the incorrect heat range will cause skipping, or one plug gapped incorrectly may not cause a problem until the engine is under load.

Resistor Types.   Most spark plugs have a built-in resistor. The resistor forms a part of the center electrode, as shown in Figure 9.30. The resistor serves two purposes: (1) It reduces radio and television interference caused by the ignition

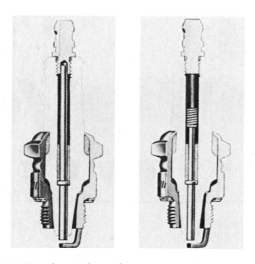

Figure 9.30   Comparison of a conventional plug and a resistor plug. The resistor forms a part of the center electrode (courtesy of Champion Spark Plug Company).

system, and (2) it reduces electrode wear and thus extends spark plug life.

Spark Plug Selection

The correct spark plugs for a particular engine are determined by the engine manufacturer. Spark plugs are identified by code numbers and letters. The identifying code is a specification and can be found in owner's manuals, shop manuals, and the catalogs of spark plug manufacturers.

Spark Plug Catalogs.   The catalogs distributed by the manufacturers of spark plugs are as important as the shop manuals that you use. Different plug makers use different code systems and explain their system in their catalogs. As an example, one of those code systems is explained in Figure 9.31.

At times, the replacement plugs that you have available may be of a different brand than those specified by the engine manufacturer. In those instances, you must be able to convert from one code system to another. The catalogs contain conversion charts so you can easily locate the correct identification code for the replacement plugs.

"Reading" Spark Plugs

You will occasionally find that an engine requires spark plugs different from those specified by the manufacturer. The problem usually is one of incorrect heat range. The condition of the electrodes and of the insulators of the plugs that you remove from an engine provide a fairly accurate means of determining (1) the condition of the engine and (2) the type of service to which the engine is subjected. With a little practice, you can learn to "read" a spark plug and select the correct replacement.

Normal Appearance.   The spark plug shown in Figure 9.32 was removed from an engine that is in good condition and is in average service. The insulator tip has a light tan or gray color and the electrodes are not excessively burned. No heavy deposits are present. The heat range of this plug obviously is correct for the engine from which it was removed. The replacement plug should be of the same heat range.

Oil-Fouled Plugs.   Worn piston rings, cylinder walls, bearings, and valve guides may allow excessive amounts of oil to enter the combustion chambers of an engine. The oil is not completely burned during combustion, and oily carbon deposits build up on the spark plug tip. In a short time, the plug

AC Spark Plug Identification Table

Prefix	Suffix	

B — Series Gap
C — Commercial
CS — Chain Saw
F — Fine Line 14 mm (⅝") Hex
G — Gas Engine
H — High altitude (aircraft) or
     weather proof (shield
     connector ¾-20 thread)
M — Marine
MC— Motorcycle types (are now S)
LM — Lawn mower type
R — Resistor
S — Shielded (⅝-24 thread)
S — Sport Vehicle
SR — Shielded Resistor
SN — Snow Types (are now S)
TC — Tractor-Commercial
     (now C types)
V — Surface Gap
W — Water proof (shield connector,
     ⅝-24 thread)
WR— Waterproof – Shielded Resistor
	A — Clip Gap
	C — Copper Core Center
	     Electrode
	C — Colder Version of M44 Plug
	E — Special Design Electrode,
	     Extended Tip
	F — ½" (12.7 mm) reach
	FF— ½" (12.7 mm) reach, fully
	     threaded
	G — Pin Gap (Cold Running)
	I — Iridium Center Electrode
	K — Special Design, Marine
	L — $7/16$" (11.1 mm) reach
	LT — Long reach, .715" (18.16
	     mm), Tapered Seat
	M — Special Design Electrode
	N — ¾" (19 mm) reach, ⅜" (9.5
	     mm) threaded
	O — Threaded Terminal (no
	     screw-on nut)
		P — Platinum electrodes
		R — Resistor (Sport
		     Vehicle Plugs)
		S — Extended tip
		S — ⅞" (22.3 mm) Moderate
		     Long reach $23/32$"
		     (18.25 mm)
		T — Tapered Seat Shell Design
		TS— Tapered seat with
		     extended tip
		W — Recessed termination
		X — Wide Gap (H.E.I.)
		XL— Extra Long reach, ¾"
		     (19 mm) fully threaded
		Y — 3 prong cloverleaf electrode
		Z — Special gap (usually
		     denotes wide gap)
		Z — European applications
		6 — .060" (1.5 mm) gap
		8 — .080" (2 mm) gap

Prefixes are sometimes combined, e.g. VB, CR.	**Suffixes are combined to form such AC suffix designation as: FG, XLS, TS, FFM, TSX, SZ, etc.**	

Numbering

1st number denotes THREAD SIZE	2nd number denotes HEAT RANGE
4 = 14 mm 2 = ½-inch taper 8 = 18 mm 5 = ½-inch 10 = 10 mm 6 = ¾-inch 12 = 12 mm 7 = ⅞-inch	0–1–2–3–4–5–6–7–8–9 COLD ———————— HOT The higher the second digit, the "hotter" the plug; the lower the last digit, the "cooler" the plug (except Z types). (The numbering of Z type plugs is opposite to that for other types and the heat rating is indicated by the last two digits: the higher the number, the cooler the plug.)

Figure 9.31 AC spark plug codes. (reprinted with permission from AC-Delco, General Motors Corporation).

Figure 9.32 Normal spark plug. A spark plug with normal deposits. The insulator tip is light tan or gray in color (courtesy of Ford Motor Company, Dearborn, MI).

becomes oil fouled and it misfires. A typical oil-fouled plug is shown in Figure 9.33. An oil-fouled plug usually indicates the need for major engine repairs. When it is not practical for those repairs to be made, the use of a hotter plug may help to burn off the oil-fouling deposits before the plug misfires.

Carbon-Fouled Plugs. As shown in Figure 9.34, a carbon-fouled plug has dry, fluffy carbon deposits on the insulator, shell, and electrodes. Such a condition may be caused by excessive idling or low-speed operation. If that is the case, a hotter spark plug may be appropriate. Since the dry, fluffy carbon is caused by unburned fuel, also check for a plugged air filter and other faults that may cause the fuel and air mixture to be too rich.

Figure 9.33 Oil-fouled spark plug. Wet, oily carbon deposits cover the firing tip (courtesy of Ford Motor Company, Dearborn, MI).

Figure 9.34 Carbon-fouled spark plug. The firing tip is coated with dry, fluffy carbon (courtesy of Ford Motor Company, Dearborn, MI).

Overheating. A plug operating at too high a temperature exhibits a white insulator tip containing random colored specks. The electrodes may appear burned. A plug that has been overheated is shown in Figure 9.35. An overheated plug usually indicates excessive combustion chamber temperatures and may indicate that the plug is too hot. Replace a plug that shows overheating with a colder plug, but check the engine and its accessories for other causes of high-combustion temperatures.

Figure 9.36 provides additional illustrations of spark plugs that have been removed from various

Figure 9.35 Overheated spark plug. The insulator is white or light gray with random colored specks (courtesy of Ford Motor Company, Dearborn, MI).

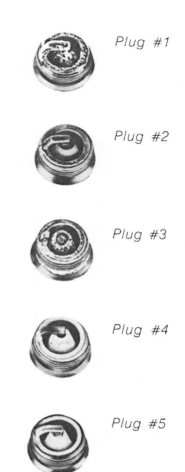

Plug #1

Plug #2

Plug #3

Plug #4

Plug #5

Job 9C

IDENTIFY SPARK PLUG OPERATING CONDITIONS

SATISFACTORY PERFORMANCE

A satisfactory performance on this job requires that you do the following:

1. Identify the operating conditions of the spark plugs shown below by placing the number of each plug in front of the description of the condition.
2. Identify correctly four of the five conditions indicated within 5 minutes.

PERFORMANCE SITUATION

Plug # 1   Wet, black deposits on the insulator, shell interior, and electrodes
Plug # 2   Black, dry, fluffy deposits on the insulator, shell interior, and electrodes
Plug # 3   Melted electrodes, blistered insulator
Plug # 4   White or light gray insulator, with small black or gray-brown spots
Plug # 5   Light tan or gray deposits on the insulator tip

____ Overheating   ____ Pre-ignition
____ Ceramic fusing   ____ Normal appearance
____ Carbon fouled   ____ Oil fouled

CARBON FOULED	**GAP BRIDGED**	**OIL FOULED**

IDENTIFIED BY BLACK, DRY FLUFFY CARBON DEPOSITS ON INSULATOR TIPS, EXPOSED SHELL SURFACES AND ELECTRODES. CAUSED BY TOO COLD A PLUG, WEAK IGNITION, DIRTY AIR CLEANER, DEFECTIVE FUEL PUMP, TOO RICH A FUEL MIXTURE, IMPROPERLY OPERATING HEAT RISER OR EXCESS IDLING. CAN BE CLEANED.	IDENTIFIED BY DEPOSIT BUILD-UP CLOSING GAP BETWEEN ELECTRODES. CAUSED BY OIL, OR CARBON FOULING. IF DEPOSITS ARE NOT EXCESSIVE, THE PLUG CAN BE CLEANED.	IDENTIFIED BY WET BLACK DEPOSITS ON THE INSULATOR SHELL BORE ELECTRODES. CAUSED BY EXCESSIVE OIL ENTERING COMBUSTION CHAMBER THROUGH WORN RINGS AND PISTONS, EXCESSIVE CLEARANCE BETWEEN VALVE GUIDES AND STEMS, OR WORN OR LOOSE BEARINGS, CAN BE CLEANED. IF ENGINE IS NOT REPAIRED, USE A HOTTER PLUG.
LEAD FOULED	**NORMAL**	**WORN**

IDENTIFIED BY DARK GRAY, BLACK, YELLOW OR TAN DEPOSITS OR A FUSED GLAZE COATING ON THE INSULATOR TIP. CAUSED BY HIGHLY LEADED GASOLINE, CAN BE CLEANED.	IDENTIFIED BY LIGHT TAN OR GRAY DEPOSITS ON THE FIRING TIP. CAN BE CLEANED.	IDENTIFIED BY SEVERELY ERODED OR WORN ELECTRODES. CAUSED BY NORMAL WEAR. SHOULD BE REPLACED.
FUSED SPOT DEPOSIT	**OVERHEATING**	**PRE-IGNITION**

IDENTIFIED BY MELTED OR SPOTTY DEPOSITS RESEMBLING BUBBLES OR BLISTERS. CAUSED BY SUDDEN ACCELERATION. CAN BE CLEANED.	IDENTIFIED BY A WHITE OR LIGHT GRAY INSULATOR WITH SMALL BLACK OR GRAY BROWN SPOTS AND WITH BLUISH-BURNT APPEARANCE OF ELECTRODES, CAUSED BY ENGINE OVERHEATING, WRONG TYPE OF FUEL, LOOSE SPARK PLUGS, TOO HOT A PLUG, LOW FUEL PUMP PRESSURE OR INCORRECT IGNITION TIMING. REPLACE THE PLUG.	IDENTIFIED BY MELTED ELECTRODES AND POSSIBLY BLISTERED INSULATOR. METALLIC DEPOSITS ON INSULATOR INDICATE ENGINE DAMAGE. CAUSED BY WRONG TYPE OF FUEL, INCORRECT IGNITION TIMING OR ADVANCE, TOO HOT A PLUG, BURNT VALVES OR ENGINE OVERHEATING. REPLACE THE PLUG.

Figure 9.36 Spark plug diagnostic chart. A diagnostic chart for "reading" spark plugs (courtesy of Ford Motor Company, Dearborn, MI).

engines. Each illustration depicts a different engine operating condition. By studying the illustrations you can become skilled at reading spark plugs.

> Always take out the old plugs and identify the cylinder where they were installed. If the plug is not burning normally this can help determine if there is any engine damage.
>
> When new plugs are installed they should be "broken in" (driven carefully for the first 500 miles).
>
> The new plugs can be fouled by deposits in the cylinder. The new plug is more efficient and burns hotter. This leads to fouling if the cylinder is not allowed to clear itself of old deposits. Heavy acceleration should be avoided during the break-in period.

LESSON 9-3   Spark Plug Service

As an automotive technician, you will be required to perform spark plug services. Those services are (1) the adjustment of spark plug gap, (2) the installation of new spark plugs, and (3) the reconditioning of used spark plugs.

Adjusting Spark Plug Gap

The distance between the spark plug electrodes must be adjusted to a specification. Although the gap on all new spark plugs is preset by the plug manufacturer, the gap may not be correct for the engine on which you are working. The plugs also may have been dropped during handling and shipping, and the gap may have been changed. Different gap measurements are required for different engines. The correct measurement may range from 0.025 inch (0.635 mm) to 0.080 inch (2.03 mm). Refer to an appropriate shop manual or a spark plug catalog for the gap measurement specified for the engine on which you are working. To ensure the quality of your work, always check the gap of a new plug and adjust it if adjustment is required.

> Always check or reset the gap of every new plug before installation. Never assume the gap is correct or set at the factory. The same plug may be used in several vehicles and the gap may be different in each. You might get the wrong setting for the job.

Spark plug gap is easily measured by using a wire *feeler gauge* or a *spark plug gap gauge* of the type shown in Figure 9.37. A wire of the correct gap

measurement is passed between the electrodes. If the wire passes through with a slight drag, as shown in Figure 9.38, the gap is correct.

If, as shown in Figure 9.39, the wire passes through loosely, without touching both electrodes,

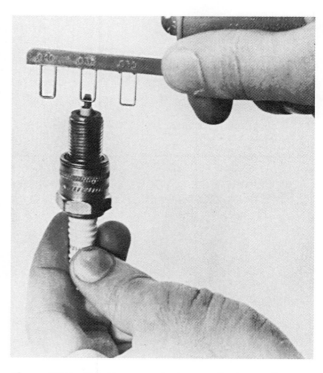

Figure 9.37   Checking a spark plug gap (courtesy of American Motors).

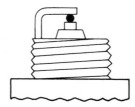

Figure 9.38   Correctly adjusted spark plug gap. The gauge wire slides between the electrodes and touches both of them.

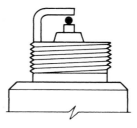

Figure 9.39   Too wide a spark plug gap. The gauge wire does not contact both electrodes.

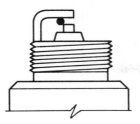

Figure 9.40 Too narrow a spark plug gap. The gauge wire does not fit between the electrodes.

the gap is too large. If the wire will not pass between the electrodes, as shown in Figure 9.40, the gap is too small.

The gap of a spark plug is adjusted by bending the side electrode. This is easily done with the bending tool attached to the gauge. The use of that tool is shown in Figure 9.41.

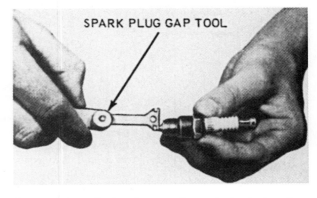

Figure 9.41 Adjusting the gap of a spark plug by bending the side electrode (courtesy of Ford Motor Company, Dearborn, MI).

| REPLACING SPARK PLUGS | Spark plugs are the most frequently replaced parts in an engine. The accessibility of the spark plugs varies from car to car, but the procedure you follow is the same. The following steps outline the procedure, but refer to an appropriate manual for the specifications required for the car on which you are working. |

Removal

1. Grasp the rubber boot at the end of the spark plug wire and twist it as shown in Figure 9.42. This will loosen the boot on the plug. Continue twisting the boot and pull it off the spark plug.

   Note: Special pliers such as those shown in Figure 9.43 can be used for this step. If you attempt to remove the boot from the plug by pulling on the wire, you may pull the wire from the boot or cause the wire to break within the insulation.

2. Label the wire with a piece of masking tape numbered to the cylinder number, or position the wire so you can reinstall it on the correct plug.

3. Remove and label or position the remaining wires in the same manner.

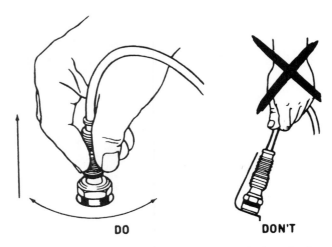

DO   DON'T

Figure 9.42 Correct way to remove a wire. Remove a spark plug wire from a spark plug by twisting and pulling on the boot. Never attempt to remove a wire by pulling on the wire (courtesy of Delco-Remy Division of General Motors Corporation).

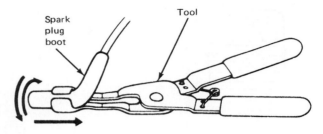

Figure 9.43 Using a boot removal tool. A spark plug boot can be removed from a spark plug without damage to the wire by using special pliers (courtesy of Ford Motor Company, Dearborn, MI).

4. Using a spark plug socket, loosen all the spark plugs about one full turn.
5. Using a compressed air blowgun, blow away all dirt from around the base of the plugs. This will minimize the possibility of dirt entering the engine when the plugs are removed.

   Note: Be sure to wear your safety glasses during this step.

6. Using a spark plug socket, remove all the plugs and arrange them in the order of their position in the engine. The use of a rack similar to the one shown in Figure 9.44 is suggested.

   Note: By arranging the plugs in order, you can determine which cylinder(s) may be causing problems if one or more of the plugs have an abnormal reading.

7. Read the spark plugs to determine if they are of the correct heat range and if engine defects are indicated.

Installation The replacement spark plugs should be of the type specified by the engine manufacturer. If, by reading the old plugs, you have determined that hotter or colder plugs are required, consult an appropriate spark plug catalog to find the identification code of the correct plug. Change heat range by only one or two steps or numbers. Too great a change may cause poor performance or possible engine damage.

> Never Seize compound can be used on spark plug threads before installation. This will make plug replacement easier the next time.

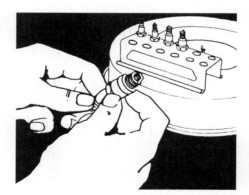

Figure 9.44 Spark plug inspection and tray. When removing spark plugs from an engine, you should place them in a tray or rack so that you can identify any cylinders that may have trouble (reprinted with permission from AC-Delco, General Motors Corporation).

1. Check to be sure the gap of all the replacement plugs meets the engine manufacturer's specifications. Adjust the gaps as necessary (refer to Figure 9.41).
2. Thread all the spark plugs into place using finger pressure only.

   Note: Do not use a wrench for this step. If access to the spark plug holes is difficult use a boot from a discarded spark plug wire as an installation tool. The use of a wrench or ratchet handle to install spark plugs may result in your stripping the threads on the plugs and in the spark plug holes.
3. After all the plugs have been threaded into their holes, tighten the plugs to the torque specification of the engine manufacturer.

   Note: When the use of a torque wrench proves difficult, you can apply the proper torque by an alternate method shown in Figure 9.45.
4. Install the wires on the plugs, making sure they are installed in their original locations.

   Note: Spark plug wires must be installed to conform to the *firing order* of the engine. The firing order specifies the sequence in which the plugs fire. This specification can be found in an appropriate manual. Typical firing orders and wire locations are shown in Figures 9.46 to 9.48. On some engines with electronic ignition systems, the inside of the boots should be coated with a silicone dielectric compound prior to installation. The engine manufacturer's manual will advise you as to the need for this operation and the specifications of the compound that may be required.

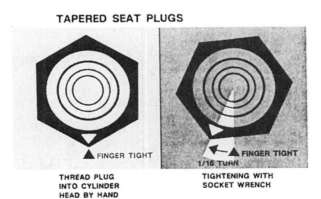

Figure 9.45 Plug tightening without torque wrench. Suggested methods of tightening spark plugs when a torque wrench cannot be used (courtesy of Champion Spark Plug Company).

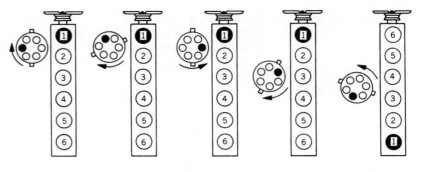

FIRING ORDER
1-5-3-6-2-4

Figure 9.46 Cylinder identification. Although all these inline six-cylinder engines have the same firing order, the location of the no. 1 wire, the direction of distributor rotation, and even the numbering of the cylinders are different.

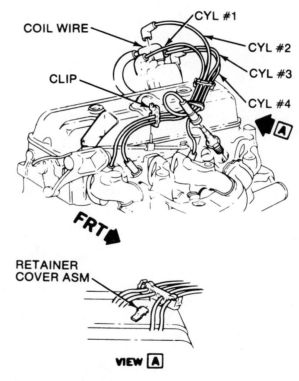

Figure 9.47 Spark plug routing. Spark plug wire routing on a typical four-cylinder engine (courtesy of Chevrolet Motor Division, General Motors Corporation).

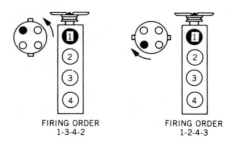

FIRING ORDER
1-3-4-2

FIRING ORDER
1-2-4-3

Figure 9.48 Distributor rotation and firing order. Although these two four-cylinder engines may appear similar, the firing order, the direction of distributor rotation, and the location of no. 1 wire are different.

Job 9D

REPLACE SPARK PLUGS

SATISFACTORY PERFORMANCE

A satisfactory performance on this job requires that you do the following:

1. Replace the spark plugs in the assigned engine.
2. Following the steps in the "Performance Outline" and the procedure and specifications of the manufacturer, complete the job within 200 percent of the manufacturer's suggested time.
3. Fill in the blanks under "Information."

PERFORMANCE OUTLINE

1. Disconnect the wires from the plugs.
2. Loosen the plugs and blow away the dirt from around the base of the plugs.
3. Remove the plugs.
4. Read the plugs.
5. Select the correct replacement plugs.
6. Check the gap on the replacement plugs and adjust to specifications if necessary.
7. Install the plugs.
8. Tighten the plugs to the manufacturer's torque specifications.
9. Install the wires.

INFORMATION

Vehicle identification _____
Engine identification _____
Reference used _____ Page(s) _____
Spark plug brand and identification code specified _____
_____
Spark plug gap specification _____
Spark plug torque specification _____
Brand and identification of plugs removed _____
_____
Spark plugs removed were:
_____ Normal _____ Too hot _____ Too cold
Brand and identification code of plugs installed _____
_____

LESSON 9–4 Spark Plug Wires, Distributor Cap, and Rotor

The spark plug wires, the distributor cap, and the rotor are responsible for delivering the high voltage to the spark plugs. Excessive resistance in those parts may prevent a spark from jumping the plug gap. Defects in the insulation of those parts may allow voltage to leak to ground before it reaches the plug. Problems in the secondary circuit may require that you inspect and test those parts and replace those found defective.

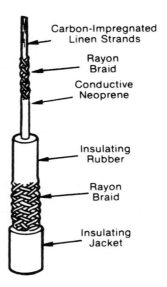

Figure 9.49 Construction of a resistance wire. Wires of this type are usually marked TVRS to indicate television-radio suppression (reprinted with permission from AC-Delco, General Motors Corporation).

Spark Plug Wires

Most spark plug wires used as original equipment have a nonmetallic conductor. As shown in Figure 9.49, the core of those wires is usually made of carbon-impregnated strands of linen or other similar material. The carbon conducts electricity, but has a relatively high resistance. Those *resistance wires* (1) *suppress,* or reduce, radio and television interference caused by the ignition system and (2) reduce spark plug electrode wear. The core of a spark plug wire is easily broken and can be pulled loose from its terminal. Therefore, handle spark plug wires carefully and remove them from spark plugs only by twisting and pulling on the boots. (Refer to Figures 7.42 and 7.43.)

Spark plug wires must be able to handle up to 80,000 volts while being subjected to almost continuous vibration. The wires also are exposed to extremes in temperature and are many times wet with fuel, oil, and water. Because of those severe service conditions, spark plug wires deteriorate and occasionally require replacement. A spark plug wire may fail in many ways.

1. *The insulation may fail.* Heat may cause the insulation and the boots and nipples to dry and crack. Contact with an exhaust manifold can melt the insulation. Oil and fuel may cause the insulation to become porous. Any failure of the insulation can allow voltage to leak to ground and cause the plug to misfire.

2. *The resistance of the wire may increase.* Vibration and stress may cause the carbon particles in the core to separate slightly. The separation increases the voltage required to fire the plug. When the required voltage exceeds the voltage available from the coil, the plug will misfire.

3. *The continuity of the wire may be lost.* The conductive core may have an internal break or may have been pulled loose from one of its terminals. Current must then jump the gap in the wire as well as the gap of the plug. The break in the wire will burn increasingly larger until the available voltage can no longer jump both gaps. The plug will then misfire.

The condition of the insulation can be checked visually. The resistance and continuity should be checked with an *ohmmeter.* An ohmmeter, shown in Figure 9.50, is an instrument that measures resistance. The scale of an ohmmeter is calibrated in ohms (Ω) from zero (0) to infinity (∞). An ohmmeter is self-powered. It contains a small battery to push current through the part being tested. If the part has no resistance to the flow of that current, the meter will indicate zero (0). If the part does not allow the flow of any current, the meter will indicate infinity (∞). If the part has resistance that allows a partial flow of current, that resistance will be indicated in ohms (Ω).

Figure 9.50   Multimeter tester. A tester such as this can check voltage and resistance. Resistance tests are needed to check the condition of spark plug wires for excessive resistance or open circuits (courtesy of Training Enterprises Company).

INSPECTING AND TESTING SPARK PLUG WIRES

The following steps outline a procedure for inspecting and testing the spark plug wires used on most cars. The specifications for wire resistance should be obtained from an appropriate manual, but usually fall into the ranges shown in Figure 9.51. When two or more wires on an engine fail to pass the inspection or tests, it is advisable to replace the entire set. The remaining wires have been subjected to equal service, and they most likely will fail within a short time.

1. Carefully remove one wire from a spark plug.
2. Remove the remaining end of the wire from its distributor cap or coil tower.

WIRE LENGTH	RESISTANCE (Ω)
6 to 15 in. (15 to 38 cm)	3000 to 10000
15 to 25 in. (38 to 63 cm)	4000 to 15000
25 to 35 in. (63 to 88 cm)	6000 to 20000
Over 35 in. (Over 88 cm)	8000 to 25000

Figure 9.51   Typical spark plug wire resistance specifications.

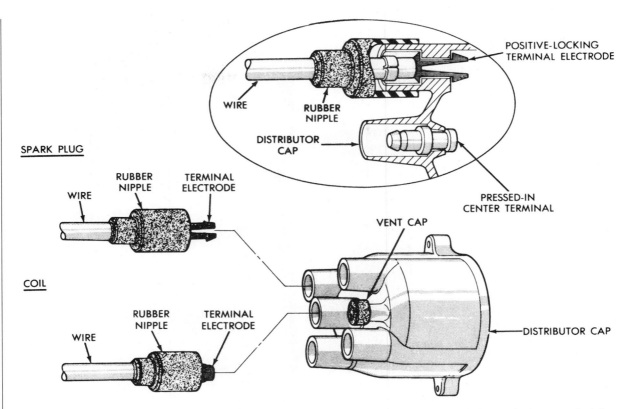

Figure 9.52 Locking wires and cap. In some electronic ignition systems, the terminals on the spark plug wires lock into the cap and take the place of the terminals at the base of the towers (courtesy of Chrysler Corporation).

Note: The manufacturers of some cars do not recommend removing the wires from the cap for testing. On those cars, the distributor cap can be removed to gain access to the inner tower terminals (see Figures 9.52 and 9.53). Be sure to check an appropriate manual for the procedure recommended for the car on which you are working.

3. If the wire is dirty or oil soaked, clean the insulation with a rag or a wiper wet with cleaning solvent and dry the wire.

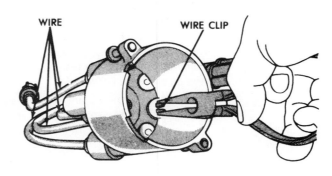

DISTRIBUTOR CAP

Figure 9.53 Removing locking-type wires. Spark plug wires that lock into the distributor cap can be released by squeezing the ends of the terminal electrodes with a pair of needle-nose pliers (courtesy of Chrysler Corporation).

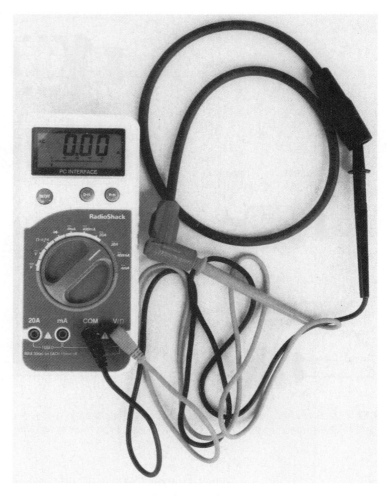

Figure 9.54 Using an ohmmeter to check the resistance of a spark plug wire (courtesy of Training Enterprises Company).

4. Examine the wire insulation, the boot, and the nipple for cracks, burned areas, abrasions, porosity, and other damage. Check the metal terminals at the ends of the wire. They should be clean and bright and show no corrosion.
5. Turn the selector switch on the ohmmeter to the "×1000" scale.
6. Clip the ends of the ohmmeter test leads together and turn the "Zero Adjustment" knob so that the meter indicates zero (0).
7. Connect the ohmmeter test leads to the terminals on the ends of the spark plug wire as shown in Figure 9.54.

   Note: It may be necessary to insert an adapter or a short piece of wire into the spark plug boot to contact the terminal at that end.
8. Read and record the resistance indicated by the meter.

   Note: Be sure to multiply the meter reading by 1000 because the meter is set on the "×1000" scale. A reading of zero (0) indicates that the wire is not a resistance wire, but contains a metallic conductor. A reading of infinity (∞) indicates that the wire lacks continuity—that is, there is a break in the wire.
9. Compare the resistance of the wire to the manufacturer's specifications (refer to Figure 9.51).

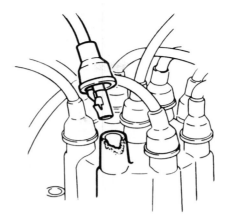

Figure 9.55 Eroded distributor cap wire tower. A distributor cap with an eroded or cracked tower should be replaced (courtesy of Delco-Remy Division of General Motors Corporation).

Note: Manufacturers' specifications will vary, but as a general rule, the resistance should not exceed 8000 ohms per 12 inches (30 cm).

10. If the wire was removed from the distributor cap, inspect the cap tower. The tower should not be cracked or eroded, as shown in Figure 9.55. The metal insert in the tower should be clean and have no corrosion.

   Note: The use of a mirror and a droplight or flashlight will enable you to inspect the inside of a distributor cap tower when it is otherwise impossible to do so.

11. Slide the nipple up on the wire.
12. Insert the wire into the cap tower, pushing it firmly down in place until you feel the terminal bottom in the tower.
13. Slide the nipple down over the tower, squeezing it to expel any air that may be trapped inside.

   Note: Some manufacturers recommend coating the inside of the nipple with a silicone dielectric compound prior to installation. Be sure to check the manual for this recommendation and the specification of the compound that may be required.

14. Install the remaining end of the wire on the spark plug, pushing the boot firmly over the insulator.

   Note: Some manufacturers recommend coating the inside of the boot with a silicone dielectric compound.

15. Position the wire so that it will not contact the exhaust manifold, and secure it in any guides or wire holders that may be present.
16. Repeat the previous steps on the remaining wires.

   Note: It is advisable to remove, test, and install each wire one at a time. By following that procedure, you will maintain the correct firing order and wire positions.

Job 9E

INSPECT AND TEST SPARK PLUG WIRES

SATISFACTORY PERFORMANCE
A satisfactory performance on this job requires that you do the following:

1. Inspect and test the spark plug wires on the car assigned.
2. Following the steps in the "Performance Outline" and the procedure and specifications of the manufacturer, complete the job within 60 minutes.
3. Fill in the blanks under "Information."

PERFORMANCE OUTLINE

1. Disconnect one wire.
2. Clean and inspect the wire.
3. Test the wire for continuity and resistance.
4. Connect the wire.
5. Repeat the above steps on the remaining wires.

INFORMATION

Vehicle identification _____
Reference used _____ Page(s) _____
Wire resistance specifications _____
Test results:

WIRE #	INSULATION		LENGTH	CONTINUITY		RESISTANCE
1	_____ OK	_____ NG	_____	_____ Yes	_____ No	_____
2	_____ OK	_____ NG	_____	_____ Yes	_____ No	_____
3	_____ OK	_____ NG	_____	_____ Yes	_____ No	_____
4	_____ OK	_____ NG	_____	_____ Yes	_____ No	_____
5	_____ OK	_____ NG	_____	_____ Yes	_____ No	_____
6	_____ OK	_____ NG	_____	_____ Yes	_____ No	_____
7	_____ OK	_____ NG	_____	_____ Yes	_____ No	_____
8	_____ OK	_____ NG	_____	_____ Yes	_____ No	_____

Is the resistance of all the wires within specifications? _____ Yes _____ No
Which wires, if any, should be replaced? _____

Distributor Caps and Rotors

Distributor caps and rotors should be inspected for cracks, erosion, corrosion, and damage. Cracks and erosion on these parts provide a path for voltage to leak to ground. Corrosion increases the resistance to current flow. These defects can usually be located by a visual inspection.

Inspecting Distributor Caps

A distributor cap may be cracked and eroded internally without any external sign of those defects. Therefore, remove the distributor cap from the distributor for a thorough inspection. The following three methods are commonly used to hold a distributor cap on a distributor.

Spring Clips. The most commonly used method of retaining a distributor cap is by spring clips, as shown in Figure 9.56. Hinged at the distributor, spring clips hook into projections on the side of the cap. They are easily removed by prying them loose with a screwdriver. When you wish to install the cap, the spring clips can be snapped back into position.

Spring-Loaded Hooks. As shown in Figure 9.57, some caps are fitted with spring-loaded hooks. Those hooks engage in notches on the bottom of the distributor. Caps retained in that manner are removed by turning the slotted head of the hooks 180° with a screwdriver. When installing these caps, the hooks are pushed down with a screwdriver and turned so that they fit into their notches under the distributor.

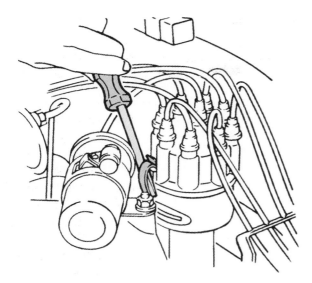

Figure 9.56 Removing spring-type cap. A distributor cap retained by spring clips. The clips can be released by prying with a screwdriver as shown (courtesy of Delco-Remy Division of General Motors Corporation).

Screws. Some distributor caps are held to the distributor by screws. In most instances, screws are built into the cap so that they cannot be dropped and lost. A cap of that type is shown in Figure 9.58.

All distributor caps are made with a tab or key that aligns with a notch in the distributor. When

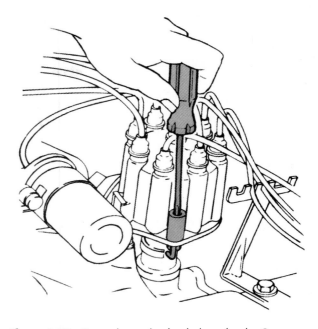

Figure 9.57 Removing spring-loaded cap hooks. Some distributor caps are retained by spring-loaded hooks. They are released by using a screwdriver (courtesy of Delco-Remy Division of General Motors Corporation).

installing a distributor cap, check the position of the cap before attempting to secure it. A properly positioned cap cannot be rotated on the distributor.

Figure 9.58 A distributor cap that is retained by screws (courtesy of Training Enterprises Company).

DISTRIBUTOR CAP INSPECTION

The following steps outline a procedure for inspecting a distributor cap that has been removed from a distributor. A cap that exhibits cracks, erosion, carbon paths, corrosion, or damage should be replaced.

1. Clean the outside surface of the cap, carefully examining it for cracks and erosion.

   Note: Cracks and erosion are usually indicated by the presence of a carbon path, as shown in Figure 9.59. A carbon path is formed when high voltage leaks along a crack or flaw in the cap and erodes the cap surface.

2. Clean the inside of the cap with a wiper or with a compressed air blowgun, as shown in Figure 9.60. Check for cracks, carbon paths, and erosion of the terminals.

   Note: Be sure to wear your safety glasses when cleaning parts with compressed air.

3. Check the carbon ball or brush under the center tower.

   Note: Where a carbon brush is used, it is backed by a small spring that holds the brush out in contact with the rotor. In caps of that type, the brush should be checked for freedom of movement (see Figure 9.61).

Figure 9.59   Checking cap for carbon paths outside. The outside surfaces of a distributor cap should be cleaned and checked for cracks and carbon paths (courtesy of Chevrolet Motor Division, General Motors Corporation).

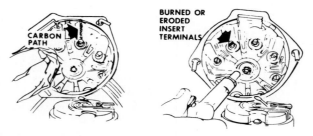

Figure 9.60   Checking inside of cap for problems. The inside of a distributor cap should be thoroughly cleaned and checked for cracks, carbon paths, and burned or eroded terminals (courtesy of Chevrolet Motor Division, General Motors Corporation).

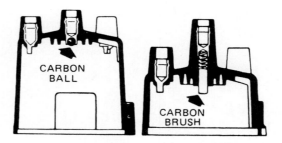

Figure 9.61   Checking carbon ball or brush. A distributor cap inspection should include a check of the carbon ball or brush under the center tower (courtesy of Delco-Remy Division of General Motors Corporation).

Figure 9.62 Example of a rotor button. This type of distributor rotor slides over the distributor shaft. It is positioned by a flat or a keyway on the shaft (courtesy of Training Enterprises Company).

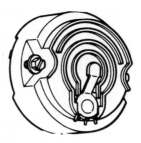

Figure 9.64 Screw-held rotor button. Some rotors are held to the distributor shaft by screws (courtesy of Ford Motor Company, Dearborn, MI).

Inspecting Rotors

While the distributor cap is off, remove and inspect the rotor. Many different types of rotors are used. The rotors shown in Figure 9.62 is pushed on over the distributor shaft. It is positioned by a projection or key that fits into a matching flat or keyway on the shaft. Rotors of this type are removed by pulling them off the shaft as shown in Figure 9.63.

Rotors of the type shown in Figure 9.64 are held by two screws. Correct positioning of most rotors of this type is obtained by two protrusions on the bottom of the rotor. One protrusion is round; the other is square. The two protrusions fit into matching holes in a plate on the distributor shaft. After the screws are removed, the rotor can be lifted from the distributor (see Figure 9.65).

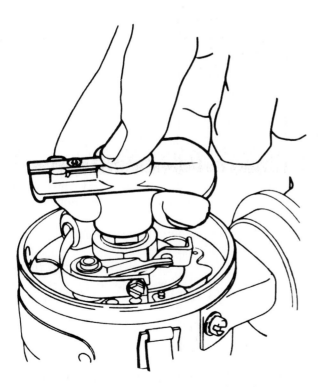

Figure 9.63 Removing a distributor rotor button (courtesy of Delco-Remy Division of General Motors Corporation).

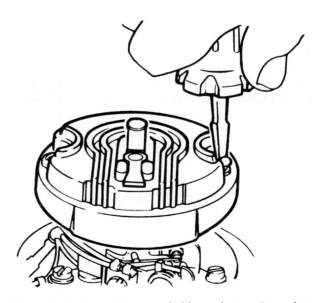

Figure 9.65 Removing screw-held rotor button. Removing the screws holding a rotor to a distributor shaft (courtesy of Delco-Remy Division of General Motors Corporation).

Job 9F

REPLACE A DISTRIBUTOR CAP

SATISFACTORY PERFORMANCE
A satisfactory performance on this job requires that you do the following:

1. Replace the distributor cap on the car assigned.
2. Following the steps in the "Performance Outline" and the procedure and specifications of the manufacturer, complete the job within 200 percent of the manufacturer's suggested time.
3. Fill in the blanks under "Information."

PERFORMANCE OUTLINE

1. Remove and inspect the distributor cap.
2. Remove and inspect the rotor.
3. Install the rotor.
4. Install the distributor cap.
5. Check the firing order and the wire locations.

INFORMATION

Vehicle identification _____
Reference used _____ Page(s) _____
Results of distributor cap inspection:
_____ Defective _____ Suitable for reuse
Defect found _____
Cap was secured by:
_____ Spring clips
_____ Spring-loaded hooks
_____ Screws

Clean and inspect the rotor for cracks, corrosion, and insufficient spring tension, as shown in Figure 9.66. The rotors used in electronic systems should be checked carefully for carbon tracks and carbon smudges on their underside. This indicates that current has been leaking through the rotor to the distributor shaft. Replace rotors that exhibit these faults.

When installing a rotor, be sure it is correctly positioned and securely in place. Failure to do so may result in damage to the rotor and to the cap.

Replacing Distributor Caps

Replacing a distributor cap is an easy job, but each wire must be installed in its correct tower. To avoid mixing the wires, remove each wire from the old cap and immediately install in the replacement cap. The old cap and the replacement cap should be aligned and held side by side. If space permits, install the new cap on the distributor. Then transfer the wires one at a time.

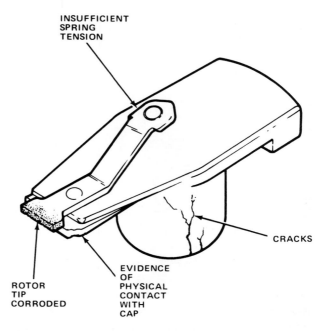

Figure 9.66 Possible rotor defects (courtesy of American Motors).

LESSON 9-5 Electronic Primary Ignition Circuit

Although the parts used in most secondary circuits are common, electronic ignition systems use many different primary circuits containing many different parts. These differences are found even among vehicles built by the same manufacturer. Because of these differences, diagnostic and repair procedures in those circuits are beyond the scope of this text.

The primary circuit is actually the control circuit of the ignition system. As such, it performs the following functions:

1. It provides current to the primary winding of the coil so that a strong magnetic field is created.
2. It interrupts the flow of that current so the magnetic field collapses.
3. It times the occurrence of the first two functions so a high-voltage surge is produced in the secondary circuit at the exact instant it is required.

To appreciate the performance of the primary circuit, consider the speed at which it operates. At cruising speed in a car with an eight-cylinder engine, the primary circuit must perform its functions about 200 times per second.

Primary Circuit Components and Their Functions

The primary circuits of the various electronic ignition systems are designed to require practically no maintenance. Each of the systems was designed to meet the requirements of the car manufacturer for a particular application. Thus the components and circuitry differ greatly, even in cars built by the same maker. When service is required in those systems, a detailed procedure established by the manufacturer must be followed. Those procedures are listed in appropriate factory manuals and are not within the scope of this book.

Systems using breaker points require the frequent inspection and adjustment of certain components. All those systems use similar components and circuitry. Therefore, common procedures are followed in the maintenance of most of those systems. If you are to follow the procedures correctly, a knowledge of the components used in the primary circuit of breaker point systems is necessary.

Primary Circuit Inspection

Primary circuit inspection includes those checks and tests that enable you to determine if the circuit is operating within specifications. Based on the results of that inspection, you can make the necessary adjustments and replace the required parts.

Other Electronic Ignition Parts

What used to be mechanical is now accomplished by electronics. The distributor, distributor cap, and rotor button are still being used on some new engines. These parts are checked and serviced just like similar parts we have had through the years (refer to Figure 9.4). One design change is to replace the distributor with a crankshaft sensor (see Figure 9.10). In this type of system a reluctor ring takes the place of a trigger wheel. On a typical four-cylinder engine with this type of system, the number 2 and 3 cylinders share one coil and the number 1 and 4 cylinders share another coil. It is possible to have a weak or burned-out coil and the engine still run on the other two cylinders. It would, of course, run very poorly depending on how much high voltage the defective coil is producing and how often it would fire those two spark plugs.

Service on the distributorless systems requires checking and replacement of crankshaft sensors, reluctor rings, coils, distributor wires, and spark plugs. Each coil should be checked for primary and secondary coil resistance. On the General Motors Delphi coils the resistance of the secondary winding of each coil should be between 3K up to 7K ohms at room temperature. The continuity between the shield and the electrical connector ground pin should be from no resistance up to 10K ohms resistance. All ignition coils have a primary and secondary winding. These can both be checked for resistance, and if the values are not within specifications, the coil should be replaced.

The oscilloscope is a very accurate and useful tool to find coil problems. Any defective coil causes a distorted pattern on the scope for both the cylinders the coil serves. Replace any coil that does not produce a normal pattern. After replacing the coil, use the oscilloscope to see if the patterns are back to normal and the repair was successful.

LESSON 9-6 Dwell and Ignition Timing

Dwell can be defined as the amount of time, measured in degrees of distributor shaft rotation or reluctor rotation, that current flows in the primary winding of the coil. In electronic ignition systems, the correct dwell is maintained by the electronic control unit, and no adjustment is necessary. In systems using breaker points, dwell is adjusted by changing the point gap. Closing the gap increases the amount of time that the points remain closed, increasing the dwell. Opening the point gap decreases the amount of time the points remain closed, decreasing the dwell.

Dwell is measured electrically with a dwell meter. Point gap is set manually with a feeler gauge inserted between the points gap. The use of a dwell meter on a breaker point system can, in most instances, eliminate the mechanical and human error that can affect the measurement of the point gap with a feeler gauge. The dwell meter provides another advantage. It can be used while an engine is running or while an engine is being cranked by the starter motor.

If the dwell on an electronic system is changing, there is a problem with the reluctor ring and the pickup sensor. The bearings in the distributor can also be worn, causing the reluctor-to-sensor gap to change. Normally there should not be any change in dwell at any speed, and the only setting on the distributor-type systems is the gap between the reluctor ring and the pickup sensor. The distributorless systems have reluctor rings and pickup sensors, but there is not an adjustment provided to change the dwell.

With timing changed from a mechanical operation to an electronic one, it is no longer necessary to change timing and set base timing in the newer systems. The crankshaft sensor and the reluctor now provide information to a computer, and based on this information the ignition timing is advanced or retarded to fire the spark plugs at the right time. This produces maximum power by burning the fuel so it can create maximum power in the engine. A timing light can still be used on the electronic systems to observe the amount of advance, but this is only useful if the electronic system is not advancing the timing or not advancing the timing as much as it should for the vehicle engine speed.

CHECKING SPARK TIMING	All engines are provided with a means by which spark timing can be checked. Most engines have timing marks on the crankshaft pulley and on the front of the engine. On some engines, the pulley is marked in degrees of crankshaft rotation. Those degree markings usually extend both before TDC (BTDC) and after TDC (ATDC). The desired degree marking can be aligned with a pointer attached to the front of the engine. Timing marks of that type are shown in Figure 9.67. Other engines have a single mark or notch on the pulley as shown in Figure 9.68. That mark can be aligned with the desired marking on a degree scale attached to the engine.

Still other engines have the timing marks on the flywheel or torque converter and on the bell housing. On some engines the degree markings are on the flywheel and

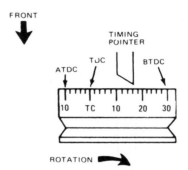

Figure 9.67   Crankshaft pulley timing marks. Typical timing marks as found on a crankshaft pulley. These marks can be aligned with a pointer attached to the engine. Notice that in this drawing the crankshaft is at 16° before top dead center (BTDC) (courtesy of Ford Motor Company, Dearborn, MI).

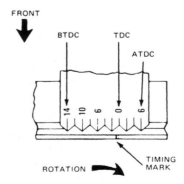

Figure 9.68   Typical Ford timing marks. Typical timing marks as found on the front of an engine. The mark or notch on the crankshaft pulley can be aligned with those marks. Notice that in this drawing the crankshaft is at 1° before top dead center (BTDC) (courtesy of Ford Motor Company, Dearborn, MI).

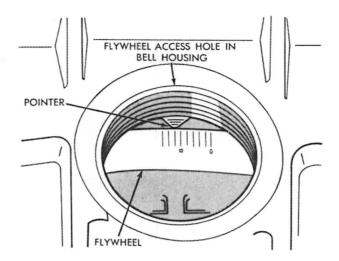

Figure 9.69   Flywheel timing marks. On some engines, the degree markings are on the flywheel. These marks can be aligned with a pointer by looking through an access hole in the bell housing (courtesy of Chrysler Corporation).

can be aligned with a pointer on the bell housing as shown in Figure 9.69. You also will find engines with degree markings on the bell housing. On those engines, the flywheel or torque converter is notched or marked (see Figure 9.70).

Timing marks are used to check the *initial spark timing*, which is the starting point for all spark timing. It indicates when the spark occurs while an engine is idling and before any of the spark advance systems begin to function. The specifications for initial spark timing vary with different engines and with different engine applications. The specifications for a particular car should be obtained from the tuneup decal or from an appropriate manual.

Initial spark timing can be checked and adjusted while an engine is not running. This method is known as *static timing.* Static timing may be necessary after a distributor has been replaced, but it is rarely used during routine service.

Most mechanics check spark timing *dynamically,* or while the engine is running. Since the marks cannot be aligned while the crankshaft is turning, a *timing light,* or *strobe light,* is used to "stop" the pulley or flywheel. A typical timing light is shown in Figure 9.71. A timing light provides brilliant flashes of light. When that light is directed at moving parts, those parts appear to be at rest.

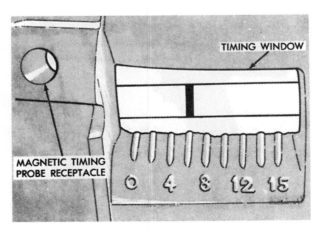

Figure 9.70   Bell housing timing marks. On some engines, the degree markings are found on the bell housing. A timing mark or notch on the flywheel or torque converter can be aligned with those markings by observing the mark through a window or opening in the bell housing (courtesy of Chrysler Corporation).

Figure 9.71 Timing light. A typical portable power timing light. The two small wires are attached to the car battery. The remaining wire is connected to the spark plug wire for the No. 1 cylinder (courtesy of Kal-Equip Company).

Most portable timing lights are connected to the car battery and to the spark plug wire that leads to the No. 1 cylinder. When the high voltage surge flows to the No. 1 plug, it triggers the light. Thus the light flashes at exactly the same time that the plug fires. When the light flashes, the timing marks can easily be seen. The alignment of the marks indicate when the plug fires in relation to the position of the crankshaft. If the spark occurs when the piston is at TDC, the timing marks are illuminated at the instant the pointer is aligned with the TDC mark. Figure 9.72 shows a timing light in use.

A timing light also can be used to check the operation of the advance systems. As the engine is accelerated, the change in spark timing causes the timing marks to move. This movement can be observed and, with some timing lights, measured. Figure 9.73 shows a timing light combined with an advance meter.

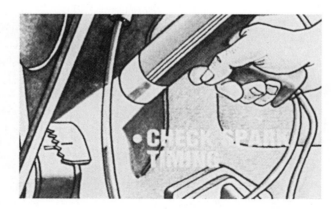

Figure 9.72 Using a timing light. A timing light "stops" the motion of the crankshaft pulley or flywheel so that the timing marks can be observed while the engine is running (courtesy of American Motors).

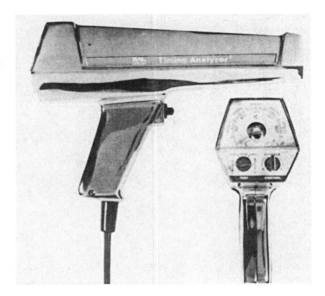

Figure 9.73 Spark advance meter timing light. A timing light that incorporates a spark advance meter. This instrument will check initial spark timing and measure spark advance (courtesy of Kal-Equip Company).

The following steps outline a procedure for checking spark timing with a timing light. Timing specifications and the location and type of timing marks vary with different engines. Such information should be obtained from an appropriate manual.

1. Connect a tach-dwell meter to the engine and check the dwell. Any change in dwell will cause the timing to change. Before the timing can be accurately checked, the dwell must be checked and, if necessary, be adjusted to specifications.

   Note: Leave the dwell meter connected after this step as it will be used later in this procedure.

2. Locate the initial timing specification and the information giving the type of timing marks and their location. (Refer to Figures 9.67 through 9.70.)

3. Using a droplight or a flashlight, locate the timing marks on the engine and on the pulley or flywheel.

   Note: On some cars, it is easier to locate pulley markings from under the car.

4. Thoroughly clean the markings on the engine and on the pulley or flywheel.

   Note: It is suggested that you accent the pointer and the degree mark specified. A sharp piece of chalk or a stiff piece of wire dipped in light-colored paint can be used. The accented marks are easier to see when the engine is running.

5. Connect the timing light battery leads to the battery terminals.

6. Connect the remaining timing light lead to the wire that runs to the spark plug in the No. 1 cylinder.

   Note: If the timing light is equipped with an induction pickup, merely clamp the pickup over the wire (refer to Figure 9.67). If the timing light does not have an induction pickup, disconnect the spark plug wire from the plug or from the distributor cap. An adapter can then be used as shown in Figure 9.74. Never pierce a spark plug wire or attempt to insert a probe between the boot and the wire. To do so will damage the wire.

7. Position the timing light so it cannot fall when the engine is started. Make sure that the wires are clear of the fan and the drive belts.

8. Disconnect and plug the vacuum hose(s) that may be connected to the distributor diaphragm.

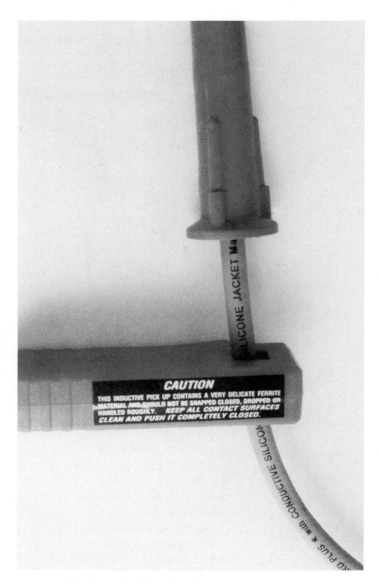

Figure 9.74 Attaching timing light lead to plug. When you connect test equipment to a spark plug wire, use an adapter between the wire and the plug or between the wire and the distributor cap tower. Never pierce a wire or insert a probe between the wire and a boot or nipple (courtesy of Delco-Remy Division of General Motors Corporation).

Note: Failure to disconnect and plug the hose(s) may result in a false timing indication.

9. Set the function switch on the tach-dwell meter to TACH and the cylinder selector switch to the number of cylinders in the engine.
10. Apply the parking brake.
11. If the car has an automatic transmission, place the transmission selector lever in the PARK position. If the car has a manual transmission, place the shift lever in the NEUTRAL position.
12. Start the engine and allow it to idle.
13. Check the idle speed and, if necessary, adjust it to specifications.

Note: If the idle speed is too high, the spark timing may advance, causing a false reading when you check the initial timing.

14. Aim the timing light at the timing marks and observe their position. The pointer and the specified degree mark should be aligned.

    Note: If the marks are not aligned, the initial spark timing must be adjusted. The procedure for that adjustment follows the completion of the procedure for checking timing.

15. Check the operation of the spark advance mechanisms.

    a. *Electronic spark advance.* If the system being checked advances the timing electronically, the advance specifications and measurement procedures for that particular system should be obtained from an appropriate service manual.

    b. *Centrifugal spark advance.* If the distributor incorporates a centrifugal advance mechanism, slowly accelerate the engine while watching the timing marks. The marks should move in the BTDC direction and may even move beyond the range of the markings. When the engine is returned to idle, the marks should return to their original position.

    c. *Vacuum spark advance.* If the distributor is fitted with a vacuum diaphragm, operate the engine at about 2000 rpm and observe the location of the timing marks. Unplug and connect the hose(s) you previously disconnected. Again accelerate the engine to about 2000 rpm. The marks should move farther ahead in the BTDC direction than they did when the hose(s) was (were) disconnected. Allow the engine to return to idle. The marks should return to their original position.

16. Turn the ignition switch to the OFF position.

17. If the initial spark timing is correct, disconnect and remove the timing light and the tach-dwell meter. If the initial spark timing requires adjustment, continue with the following procedure.

Adjusting Spark Timing

Initial spark timing is adjusted on most engines by rotating the distributor. The distributor is held in position by a clamp as shown in Figure 9.75. After the bolt holding the clamp is loosened, the distributor can be rotated in either direction. On some engines, access to that bolt is extremely limited. A special distributor wrench similar to one of those shown in Figure 9.76 may be required. On some engines, the distributor is secured with a special bolt as shown in Figure 9.77. Those bolts require the use of a special wrench.

The following steps outline a procedure for adjusting spark timing. Because these steps are a continuation of the previously listed steps for checking initial spark timing, they are numbered in the same sequence:

18. Disconnect and plug any vacuum hose(s) that may be connected to any distributor diaphragm.

    Note: Failure to disconnect and plug the hose(s) may result in an incorrect adjustment.

19. Loosen the bolt or nut that secures the distributor clamp (refer to Figure 9.75).

20. Start the engine and allow it to idle.

    Note: Check the tachometer to be sure the engine is idling at the specified idle speed.

21. While watching the timing marks, carefully rotate the distributor until the specified degree marking and the pointer are aligned.

    Note: To advance timing, the distributor should be rotated in the direction opposite that of shaft rotation. Rotating the distributor in the same direction as shaft rotation will retard the timing.

22. Tighten the bolt or nut that holds the distributor clamp.

23. Recheck the alignment of the timing marks.

24. Recheck the idle speed and, if necessary, adjust it to specifications.

25. Turn the ignition switch to the OFF position.

26. Connect the vacuum hose(s) to the distributor diaphragm.

27. Disconnect and remove the timing light and the tach-dwell meter.

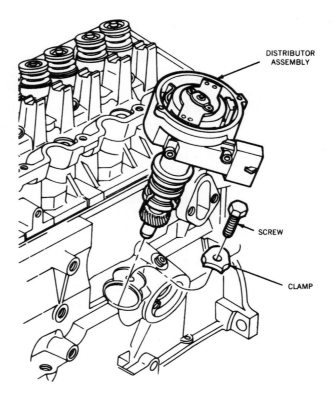

DISTRIBUTOR
ASSEMBLY

SCREW

CLAMP

Figure 9.75   Preparing distributor to set timing. Most distributors are held in place in the engine by a clamp. After loosening the clamp bolt or nut, the distributor can be rotated to adjust the initial timing (courtesy of Ford Motor Company, Dearborn, MI).

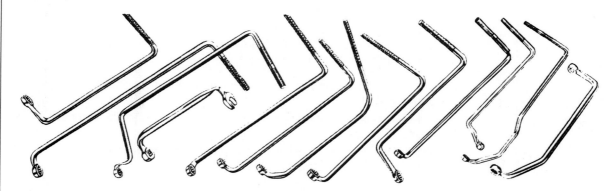

Figure 9.76   Assortment of distributor wrenches. Special distributor wrenches are needed on some engines. These are but a few of the many types and sizes available (courtesy of Snap-on Tools Corporation).

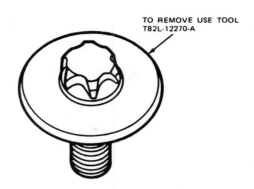

Figure 9.77 Security-type hold-down bolt. On some engines, the distributor is locked by a special "security-type" hold-down bolt. This prevents tampering with the timing adjustments by those who may not be qualified to make the proper adjustment (courtesy of Ford Motor Company, Dearborn, MI).

Job 9G

CHECK AND ADJUST SPARK TIMING

SATISFACTORY PERFORMANCE
A satisfactory performance on this job requires that you do the following:

1. Check and, if necessary, adjust the timing on the car assigned.
2. Following the steps in the "Performance Outline" and the procedures and specifications of the manufacturer, complete the job within 30 minutes.
3. Fill in the blanks under "information."

PERFORMANCE OUTLINE

1. Check and, if necessary, adjust the dwell and the engine idle speed.
2. Check the initial spark timing and compare it to the specifications.
3. Check the operation of the advance systems.
4. Adjust the initial spark timing if necessary.

INFORMATION

Vehicle identification _____
Engine identification _____
Reference used _____ Page(s) _____
Specifications: Dwell _____
                  Initial timing _____
                  Idle speed _____
Measurements taken: Dwell _____
                      Initial timing _____
                      Idle speed _____
Adjustments made: Dwell _____
                    Initial timing _____
                    Idle speed _____
Operation of advance systems:
Electronic   ____ OK   ____ NG
Centrifugal   ____ OK   ____ NG
Vacuum   ____ OK   ____ NG

LESSON 9–7 Oscilloscope Testing an Ignition System

An ignition system has many parts. Electrical problems are not easy to spot because they remain hidden and invisible. When using an oscilloscope to test electrical circuits the problems are easy to spot. Some mechanical problems also show up on the scope patterns. The ignition system is divided into two parts, the primary side (see Figure 9.78) and the secondary side (see Figure 9.79). The primary side is the 12-volt or low-voltage side and the secondary side is the 80,000-volt or the high-voltage side.

Primary ignition parts are as follows:

1. Pickup coil and module in electronic ignition systems

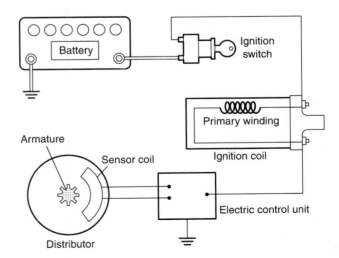

Figure 9.78 Primary ignition side. This side of the ignition system is the low-voltage or the 12-volt side (courtesy of Training Enterprises Company).

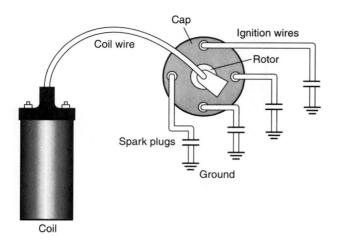

Figure 9.79 Secondary ignition side. This side of the ignition system is the high-voltage or 30,000-volt side (courtesy of Training Enterprises Company).

2. Battery or power source
3. Ignition switch and wires
4. Ballast resistor or coil resistor
5. Resistor bypass circuit or starting circuit
6. Distributor ground circuit
7. Low-voltage side of the coil

Secondary ignition parts are the following:

1. Spark plug
2. Distributor cap
3. Rotor button
4. High-voltage side of the coil
5. Spark plug wires
6. Coil wire (if used)

The oscilloscope (see Figure 9.80) presents a picture of how well these parts are working in the vehicle. The primary and secondary patterns are different. Each pattern is displayed separately. In this lesson we discuss the normal primary and secondary pattern, and some of the problems that cause an abnormal pattern. Consult the materials that came with the oscilloscope for a more in-depth look at abnormal patterns. If the pattern is not normal, keep looking for the problem until a normal pattern is displayed. If you can read the abnormal patterns, your search for the problem will be shortened.

Primary Ignition Patterns (Conventional and Electronic)

Figure 9.81 is a normal primary pattern and what all primary patterns should look like. Any pattern

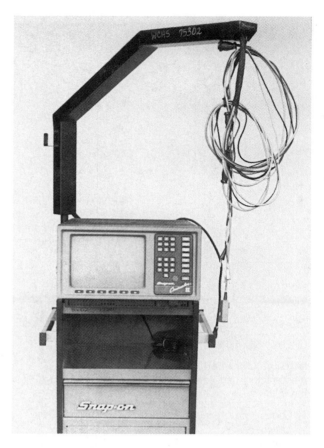

Figure 9.80 Oscilloscope tester. This is an electronic machine used to check the low- and high-voltage side of the ignition system. A picture is presented on a screen. If anything is wrong with the system, the pattern on the screen will be abnormal (courtesy of Training Enterprises Company).

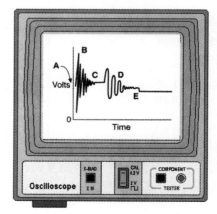

Figure 9.81 Normal primary pattern. This is what the low-voltage pattern of a normal primary ignition system looks like on an oscilloscope (courtesy of Training Enterprises Company).

that does not look like this is indicating the failure of an ignition part. Dirt, corrosion, shorts, opens, loose wires, and damaged mechanical parts all can distort this pattern from normal.

1. Point A is the transistor off or points open signal. This is where the battery current is turned off going to the ignition coil.
2. Point B is the primary peak voltage. After the battery current is turned off there will be a slight surge of voltage. This is what that surge looks like on the scope.
3. Point C is primary coil oscillations pattern. This is where we see the steady decline of the voltage used to energize the coil. The collapse of the magnetic lines of force in the coil is producing the voltage necessary to fire the spark plugs. As long as the spark plug fires, the oscillations show up on the scope pattern.
4. Point D is the coil condenser oscillations pattern. This represents the energy bouncing between the coil and the condenser and resembles a spring. This bouncing action gradually weakens until it is used up.
5. Point E is the points close or transistor on signal. This is how the scope pictures the place where the battery current is turned on to the coil. The amount of time elapsed between the points close signal and the points open signal is called the *dwell*. This should be the same for all cylinders.

Important points to remember are that defects in the primary circuit directly affect the secondary circuit, and most problems in the primary circuit will be common to all cylinders.

Secondary Ignition Patterns (Conventional and Electronic)

Figure 9.82 is a normal secondary pattern. Use this pattern as a model when making comparisons of secondary test patterns.

1. Point A indicates spark plug firing voltage. This line represents the amount of voltage it takes to jump across the spark plug gap. The size of the spark plug gap directly affects the height of this line. The larger the gap, the longer the line display.
2. Point B represents the amount of voltage it takes to keep the spark plug firing. It does not take as much voltage to maintain the spark plug fire as it does to start firing the plug. The hor-

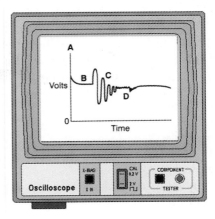

Figure 9.82 Normal secondary pattern. This is what the high-voltage pattern of a normal secondary ignition system will look like on an oscilloscope (courtesy of Training Enterprises Company).

izontal length of this line represents the spark plug firing duration or time.
3. Point C represents the coil/condenser oscillations pattern, the dissipation of the unused energy left over from firing the spark plug. The oscillations represent the voltage "moving" back and forth between the condenser and the coil. This action resembles a spring and tapers down to a straight line.
4. Point D is the points close or transistor on signal. There should be a slight oscillation action as the current is turned on in the coil circuit. The amount of time the points are closed or transistor stays on is the *dwell*. The battery voltage to the coil has been turned on during this time and the coil is being saturated with magnetic lines of force. When the voltage is turned off and these lines of force collapse, the high voltage is created in the secondary side of the coil and increases high enough to jump the gap in the spark plug.

Corrosion in distributor cap wire towers, burned points, corroded spark plug wires, open spark plug wires, lean fuel, rich fuel, and fouled plugs are just a few problems that will show up clearly on the scope patterns. Each of the parts listed at the beginning of this lesson can become damaged or worn out. What the scope operator has to do is study patterns so when they appear in the signals, the defective parts can be identified. Sometimes multiple problems have to be solved by correcting a problem and checking with the scope to see if the problem has been corrected. If not, other areas have to be checked until a normal pattern is obtained.

Other Scope Patterns

The oscilloscope can be used to check many sensors and current producing devices on the vehicle. Following are some of the items that can be tested:

1. Ignition modules
2. Triggers
   a. Inductive
   b. Hall effect switches
   c. Optical triggers
3. Fuel injector driver circuits
4. Potentiometer
5. "Knock" sensors
6. Mass air flow sensors
7. MAP/BARO sensors
8. Antilock brake testing
9. Coolant sensor testing
10. Speed sensors

These sensors have patterns that fall into several categories.

Square Wave Pattern.   A pattern like the one in Figure 9.83 is the result of the power being turned on for one period of time and turned off for another. The voltage stays steady at some set value and then drops to zero when the power is shut off. The duration of the off and on times determines how long the horizontal scope lines will be. Remember, the horizontal lines represent time and the vertical lines represent voltage.

Pulse Pattern.   Some units produce a pulse pattern like Figure 9.84. This pattern is the result of voltage being produced at set intervals. A

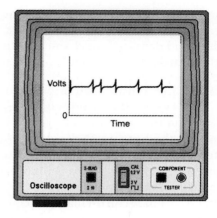

Figure 9.84   Pulse pattern. A pattern like this would be produced by a crankshaft sensor (courtesy of Training Enterprises Company).

crankshaft sensor is one unit that would produce such a pattern.

Steady Voltage Pattern.   Some sensors produce a steady voltage such as the signal in Figure 9.85. A steady voltage produces a straight line on the scope at the point on the vertical scale that represents the strength of the voltage. The scope is set to a certain voltage scale and the marks on the tube represent that voltage. A unit producing 7 volts would produce a straight-line pattern at the 7-volts mark. This would continue all across the scope because the horizontal direction represents time.

There are all kinds of patterns. The signal being produced is a direct result of voltage received

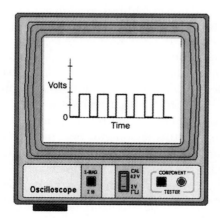

Figure 9.83   Square wave pattern. On-and-off current produces a pattern like this on an oscilloscope (courtesy of Training Enterprises Company).

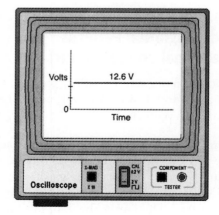

Figure 9.85   Steady voltage pattern. A steady voltage that does not vary in strength would produce a pattern like this one. The standing voltage of a battery when the engine is off would produce a voltage of 12.6 on the scope (courtesy of Training Enterprises Company).

by the scope at any given time. Consult the manufacturers' training materials to study the different normal and abnormal patterns produced by each automobile. With most sensors there is no way to make repairs. They either perform as they should or they are replaced. A study of normal patterns should come first. Later it may be to your advantage to know exactly what was wrong with the part even though you could do nothing to correct the problem except replace it.

VOCABULARY

Use the listed words in the blanks beside the sentences to complete the definitions. Either write out the words or place the letters in the blanks.

A. Spark plug

B. Breaker points

C. Ignition coil

D. Secondary winding

E. Induced voltage

F. Pickup assembly

G. Armature

H. Reluctor ring

I. Distributor cap

J. High-tension wire

K. DIS

L. Electrode

M. Reach

N. Pre-ignition

O. Heat range

P. Misfire

Q. Colder plug

R. Adjusting plug gap

S. Wire resistance

T. Ignition timing

U. BTDC

V. Timing marks

W. Firing order

X. Square wave pattern

Y. Pulse pattern

_____ 1. Part that the wires are fastened into on a distributor

_____ 2. Ignites the fuel in a engine combustion chamber

_____ 3. How the wires are positioned in a distributor cap

_____ 4. The amount of ohms it takes to move current in a wire

_____ 5. When a plug does not fire

_____ 6. High-voltage side of a coil

_____ 7. Part that produces the voltage necessary to jump the spark plug gap

_____ 8. Adjusting the firing of the spark plugs with the movement of the pistons and valves

_____ 9. Bending the outside electrode to obtain a certain measurement between electrodes

_____ 10. Before top dead center

_____ 11. Determines how hot or cold a plug will run in an engine

_____ 12. Opens and closes to control the voltage to a coil

_____ 13. Used for spark plug wires

_____ 14. Place where the spark jumps on the tip of a spark plug

_____ 15. Takes the place of a trigger wheel on a crank shaft

_____ 16. A sensor that reacts to changes in a magnetic field

_____ 17. A magnetic device in an electronic distributor

_____ 18. Creates a magnetic field when current to coil is shut off

_____ 19. An ignition system that does not use a distributor

_____ 20. The term used for spark plug thread length

_____ 21. Made with a shorter insulator tip

_____ 22. Electronic picture of voltage staying on for a short period of time and then going off

_____ 23. When the fuel in the combustion chamber is burned before the engine is ready

_____ 24. An electronic picture of voltage being produced at set intervals

_____ 25. Marks on either the crankshaft pulley or flywheel cut in degrees of rotation

REVIEW QUESTIONS

The following questions will help you determine if you have accomplished the tasks stated at the beginning of this chapter. If you do not know many of the answers go back and review the material before proceeding to the next chapter.

Lesson 9–1

1. What two circuits does an ignition system contain?
2. What has replaced breaker points in a modern primary circuit?
3. What unit is part of both the primary and secondary circuit?
4. What is the function of a trigger wheel and sensor?
5. How long is the wire used with a Melco coil?
6. In systems without a distributor what takes the place of the trigger wheel?
7. How much voltage is a secondary circuit able to produce?
8. Which wire requires the heavier insulation, primary or secondary?

Lesson 9–2

9. When the average vehicle has traveled 10,000 miles, how many times has each spark plug fired?
10. Name the parts that provide the gap on a spark plug.
11. Which spark plug seat type does not require a gasket?
12. What is spark plug reach?
13. What is the definition of heat range?
14. What will be the result of too low a spark plug heat range?
15. What are two purposes of a resistor plug?
16. What does the end of an overheated plug look like?

Lesson 9–3

17. What is the spark plug gap range for most plugs?
18. How is a plug gap set?
19. What number do all firing orders start with?

Lesson 9–4

20. What are three ways a spark plug wire fails?
21. What tool is used to check a spark plug wire?
22. How much resistance should be expected in a wire 10 inches long?
23. Can a rotor be placed on a distributor shaft in one or two positions?

Lesson 9–5

24. What are three jobs of a primary circuit?
25. In an eight cylinder engine, how many time per second must the primary circuit perform?
26. On a crankshaft sensor system of a four cylinder engine, what cylinders share each coil?
27. What is the ohms reading of the secondary winding in a Delphi coil?

Lesson 9–6

28. How is dwell measured?
29. What does ATDC mean?
30. What are timing marks?
31. How is timing set?

Lesson 9–7

32. Is the ballast resistor found on the primary or secondary ignition side?
33. What causes a square wave pattern?
34. What will produce a pulse pattern?
35. What type of pattern will a battery produce?

ASE QUESTIONS

Each question or incomplete statement in this test is followed by four suggested answers or completions. In each case select the *one* that best answers the question or completes the statement.

1. Technician A says the primary circuit of the ignition system is the high-voltage side. Technician B says there is high voltage on both the primary and secondary side of the ignition system. Who is right?
   a. A only   b. B only
   c. Both A and B   d. Neither A nor B

2. Technician A says the high voltage in the coil is produced when the current to the coil is shut off. Technician B says the high voltage is produced when the current is turned on. Who is right?
   a. A only   b. B only
   c. Both A and B   d. Neither A nor B

3. Which part is not needed in an electronic ignition system that uses a distributor?
   a. Coil   b. Points
   c. Trigger wheel   d. Sensor

4. Technician A says the wires are placed in a distributor cap according to the engine firing order. Technician B says the wires are placed in the cap according to distributor rotation. Who is right?
   a. A only   b. B only
   c. Both A and B   d. Neither A nor B

5. Technician A says a rotor can be placed on a distributor shaft in two positions. Technician B says that rotors can only be installed in one position. Who is right?
   a. A only   b. B only
   c. Both A and B   d. Neither A nor B

6. What is the maximum temperature in degrees Fahrenheit that a spark plug or combustion chamber can reach?
   a. 1000   b. 2000
   c. 3000   d. 5000

7. Technician A says if the thread size and plug reach are right, the heat range will be right. Technician B says that the heat range to use is determined by the engine combustion chamber temperatures. Who is right?
   a. A only   b. B only
   c. Both A and B   d. Neither A nor B

8. Technician A says that when oil, carbon, and other deposits are on the insulator tip of a spark plug it is fouled. Technician B says a plug will foul when the operating temperature in the combustion chamber gets too hot. Who is right?
   a. A only   b. B only
   c. Both A and B   d. Neither A nor B

9. Technician A says pre-ignition can be caused by installing a plug with too low a heat range. Technician B says pre-ignition can be caused by installing a plug with too high a heat range. Who is right?
   a. A only   b. B only
   c. Both A and B   d. Neither A nor B

10. Technician A says resistor-type plugs reduce radio noise. Technician B says resistor-type plugs reduce electrode wear. Who is right?
    a. A only   b. B only
    c. Both A and B   d. Neither A nor B

11. Technician A says the spark plug gap is set by moving the center electrode. Technician B says the spark plug gap is set by moving the outside electrode. Who is right?
    a. A only   b. B only
    c. Both A and B   d. Neither A nor B

12. Technician A says Never Seize compound can be used on spark plug threads to make future replacement easier. Technician B says that nothing should be used on spark plug threads because of the extreme heat. Who is right?
    a. A only   b. B only
    c. Both A and B   d. Neither A nor B

13. Technician A says the number one spark plug wire is used to time an engine. Technician B says a timing light can be used on any spark plug wire to time an engine. Who is right?
    a. A only   b. B only
    c. Both A and B   d. Neither A nor B

14. Technician A says dwell is measured in degrees of distributor shaft rotation. Technician B says dwell is measured in degrees of crankshaft rotation. Who is right?
    a. A only   b. B only
    c. Both A and B   d. Neither A nor B

10

Engine Cooling System Maintenance

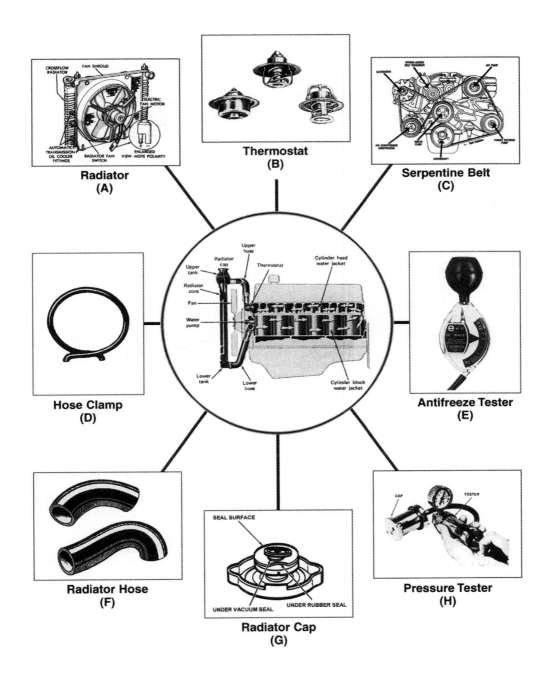

Radiator
(A)

Thermostat
(B)

Serpentine Belt
(C)

Hose Clamp
(D)

Antifreeze Tester
(E)

Radiator Hose
(F)

Radiator Cap
(G)

Pressure Tester
(H)

One of the hardest working systems in an automobile is the cooling system (see Figure 10). A very large quantity of heat is developed as the fuel is burned in the engine. This heat has to be carried away from the inside of the engine or the internal temperature will cause the engine parts to melt. We have all seen vehicles along the highway with the hood up and steam coming out of the engine compartment. This means the cooling system has failed.

The life of hoses and belts is about four years. These products start out as soft rubber and as engine heat reacts on them they begin to harden. As the engine moves and vibrates, the hardened parts crack and rupture. Normal short distance driving does not get the cooling system up to maximum heat and pressure. When starting on a long trip and getting up to highway speeds the system is under maximum stress. If anything is going to fail, it will be at this time. A dirty, clogged system and stop-and-go driving in heavy traffic for long periods of time is another high-pressure situation.

The cooling system should be maintained on a seasonal basis. The system should be cleaned and flushed when needed. The hoses and belts should be changed at least every four years. This means plenty of maintenance work for a technician.

TASKS

The following are eight tasks to master before leaving this chapter:

Task 10-1. Know how an engine cooling system operates and what each part does in the system.

Task 10-2. Be able to test a cooling system for leaks and coolant strength.

Task 10-3. Know how to clean and flush a cooling system correctly.

Task 10-4. Know how to inspect and replace defective cooling system parts.

Task 10-5. Be able to inspect, adjust, and replace defective drive belts.

Task 10-6. Be able to test and replace defective temperature-sensitive switches accurately.

Task 10-7. Be able to test and replace defective fans.

Task 10-8. Be able to identify the source and solve contamination or leak problems.

LESSON 10–1 Cooling System Operation and Parts

The cooling system must remove about 35% of the heat of combustion and dissipate it into the air. Without a cooling system, a car could be driven only a few miles before its engine would be ruined. But the cooling system must not remove too much heat. For efficient operation, an engine must run within a certain temperature range. The cooling system must remove enough heat to maintain the correct engine temperature range.

The combustion of the fuel and air mixture in an engine can raise internal temperatures to near $5000°F$ ($2760°C$). If this heat is not quickly dissipated, considerable engine damage will result. To carry off most of the heat, a typical liquid-cooled engine requires the circulation of thousands of gallons of coolant per hour. Obviously, a large amount of coolant is not required because the coolant in the system is continuously cooled and recirculated.

If a cooling system is to operate efficiently, it must receive regular routine maintenance. Most of the tests, adjustments, and repairs you will perform are relatively simple. But you will find that a knowledge of how a cooling system operates is essential for diagnosing problems.

Cooling System Operation

Figure 10.1 shows coolant circulation in a cooling system. A *water pump*, driven by a belt from the crankshaft, circulates the coolant. The pump pulls coolant from the discharge side of the radiator through the lower hose. It then pushes the coolant through *water jackets* in the cylinder block. Water jackets consist of passages that surround the cylinders and combustion chambers. As the coolant passes through the block water jackets, it absorbs heat from the cylinder walls.

From the block, the coolant is directed upward into the cylinder head water jackets through holes in the head gasket. As the coolant passes through the head, it absorbs more heat from the combustion chambers and the valve seats. The hot coolant leaves the cylinder head through the upper hose and enters the intake side of the radiator. The coolant then flows down through the radiator core,

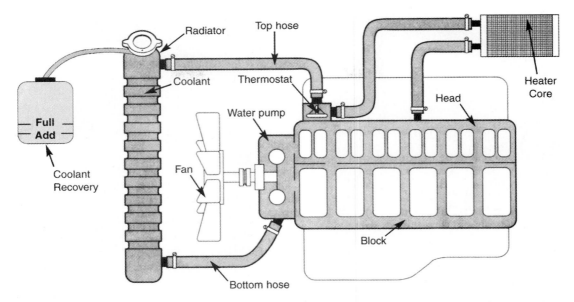

Figure 10.1 A sectioned view of a simple cooling system showing coolant circulation (courtesy of Ford Motor Company, Dearborn, MI).

a section of which is shown in Figure 10.2. As the coolant flows through the tubes of the core, it passes off heat to the air flowing through the fins. When the coolant reaches the lower tank, it has cooled sufficiently to be recirculated.

To provide for the flow of air through the radiator, even when the car is not in motion, a fan is used. On most rear wheel drive cars, the fan is usually attached to the water pump and rotates with it (refer to Figure 10.1). On most front wheel drive cars, the fan is driven by an electric motor as shown in Figure 10.4. Electric coolant fans usually operate only when the coolant temperature exceeds a certain limit.

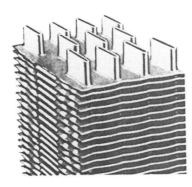

Figure 10.2 A section of a typical "tube and fin" radiator core. Coolant flowing through the tubes passes off heat to the tubes and fins. This heat, in turn, is passed off to the air that flows between the fins and the tubes (courtesy of Ford Motor Company, Dearborn, MI).

Coolant can be found inside the engine, heater system, and radiator (see Figure 10.1). The new generation of coolants are nitrite, phosphate, and silicate free (see Figure 10.3b). Coolants of this type meet the Japanese and European automotive manufacturers' standards where these chemicals are not to be used. The shelf life of coolants has increased from eighteen months to about eight years.

One type of coolant has a propylene glycol base, and the other still uses the conventional ethylene glycol (see Figure 10.3a). Both coolants provide superior protection for aluminum, brass, cast iron, steel, solder, and copper. This means the life of the coolant is extended and water pump life is improved because the pump seals last longer. Heat transfer between the engine and coolant is improved which reduces summer boil-over. These products both provide superior winter freeze protection. They are 100% biodegradable if never used, but the percentage falls slightly when used in a vehicle. This means they should not be poured out on the ground but disposed of properly.

If the older conventional ethylene glycol coolant (see Figure 10.3a) is added during service to this new extended-life coolant, a dilution of over 10% will decrease the extended-life protection. When adding coolant, use the same product. Use extended-life ethylene glycol (see Figure 10.3b) if that is in the cooling system and extended-life propylene glycol where that is found. The best maintenance plan is to always add the same base

(a)   (b)

Figure 10.3   Radiator coolant. The old coolant (see 10.2a) is what we have been using. In the latest vehicles the extended-life coolant is currently the new replacement (see 10.2b) (courtesy of Training Enterprises Company).

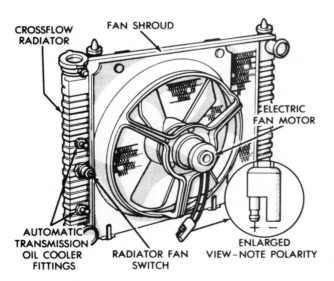

Figure 10.4   Electric fan. Many cars have an electric fan mounted behind the radiator. The fan motor is operated by a heat-sensitive switch. Note that in this installation, the fan switch is mounted in the radiator tank (courtesy of Chrysler Corporation).

extended-life coolant to the radiator system during service and change the coolant at the maximum recommended vehicle mileage and years. This can be as long as five years and 150,000 miles, which is longer than a great many owners drive their automobiles before trading.

A chemical coolant system flush is not recommended as a service procedure unless there are visible deposits inside the radiator and the tubes are restricted. If you do use the flush, be sure to neutralize the cleaner by running at least two clear water flushes before adding the nitrite-free extended-life coolant. Be sure the cleaner is out of the heater system as well. Use at least two water flushes when changing from conventional coolants to the extended-life coolants to reduce the possibility of contamination.

In extreme cold weather temperatures the ratio of extended-life coolant to water can be changed up to 60% coolant and 40% water. Do not go over 67% or under 40% for maximum benefits and protection.

Temperature Control

The average liquid-cooled engine operates most efficiently when its temperature is in the 195 to 240°F (90 to 115°C) range. In the simple cooling system just described, the engine temperature changes with the outside air temperature and with the loads placed on the engine. To maintain engine temperature within the most efficient range, a *thermostat* is used. A thermostat, shown in Figure 10.5, is a heat-operated valve that regulates the amount of coolant that flows through the cooling system. A thermostat is placed in the system at the base of the upper radiator hose (refer to Figure 10.1).

When an engine is cold, the thermostat is closed. When a cold engine is started, the coolant cannot flow from the engine to the radiator. A small amount of coolant is circulated through the block and head by means of a bypass port. While the engine is warming up, this is the only coolant circulation in the system. A typical bypass port is shown in Figure 10.6.

When the coolant in the engine reaches a temperature of about 195°F (90°C), the thermostat starts to open. This allows some coolant to flow through the radiator. As the engine temperature increases, the thermostat continues to open and the coolant flow increases. When the coolant reaches a temperature of from 215° to 220°F (101° to 104°C), the thermostat is completely open and full circulation is allowed.

If the outside air temperature is very low, the thermostat opens slowly, and may never open completely. This restricts coolant circulation and allows engine temperature to remain as close as possible to the ideal range. If the outside air temperature is very high, the thermostat opens quickly and completely. This allows full circulation while maintaining the engine temperature within its most efficient range.

During average driving in moderate temperatures, the thermostat automatically regulates the

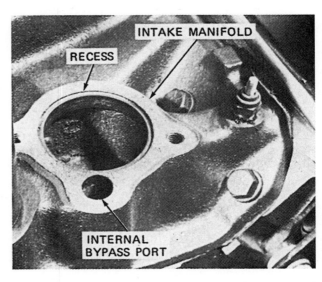

Figure 10.6 The coolant outlet port and the bypass port of a V-8 engine. The thermostat fits into the recess of the coolant outlet port. The bypass port allows coolant circulation through the head and block when the thermostat is closed (courtesy of American Motors).

flow of coolant through the system. It closes slightly to restrict the flow when the engine temperature drops. And it opens to increase the flow when engine temperature rises.

Pressure Control

As you learned in a previous chapter, modern cooling systems are pressurized. A pressurized cooling system is more efficient because it allows the coolant to absorb more heat without boiling. It also allows the coolant to dissipate more heat through the radiator.

The average pressure cap maintains a pressure of about 15 psi (103 kPa) in the system. Because a

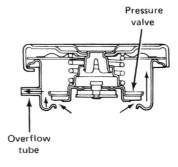

Figure 10.7 Radiator cap (pressure). Pressure valve operation in a radiator pressure cap. The pressure valve is pushed off its seat and coolant escapes through the overflow tube (courtesy of American Motors).

Figure 10.5 Various types of thermostats (courtesy of Chrysler Corporation).

Job 10A

IDENTIFY COOLING SYSTEM PARTS AND THEIR FUNCTION

SATISFACTORY PERFORMANCE

A satisfactory performance on this job requires that you do the following:

1. Identify the numbered parts on the drawing by placing the number of each part in front of the correct part name.
2. Identify the function of the numbered parts by placing the number of each part in front of the phrase that best describes its function.
3. Correctly identify all the parts and their functions within 15 minutes.

____ Radiator cap   ____ Fan
____ Water pump   ____ Thermostat
____ Upper hose   ____ Recovery tank
____ Radiator   ____ Lower hose
____ Cylinder head water jacket
____ Cylinder block water jacket
____ Controls the circulation of coolant
____ Circulates coolant through the system
____ Transfers heat from the coolant to the air
____ Allows coolant to contact the outer surfaces of the cylinder walls
____ Carries the coolant from the engine to the radiator
____ Forces the coolant from the head to the block
____ Allows coolant to contact the outer surfaces of the combustion chambers and valve seats
____ Pulls air through the radiator core
____ Carries the coolant from the radiator to the engine
____ Maintains pressure in the system

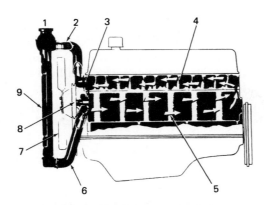

pressure of 1 psi (6.9 kPa) raises the boiling point of a liquid about 3°F (1.6°C), coolant in the system can be heated to over 250°F(121°C) without boiling.

If the pressure in a system exceeds the rating of the cap, a pressure valve in the cap opens, as shown in Figure 10.7. This allows pressurized coolant to escape through the overflow tube to the coolant recovery bottle.

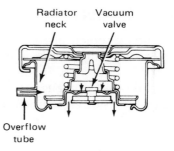

Figure 10.8 Radiator cap (vaccum). Vacuum valve operation in a radiator cap. The vacuum valve is lifted off its seat and coolant returns through the overflow tube (courtesy of American Motors).

As engine temperature drops, the coolant pressure drops. As the coolant contracts, it can form a partial vacuum in the system. As shown in Figure 10.8, the vacuum valve in the cap opens and allows coolant in the recovery bottle to return to the radiator.

LESSON 10–2   Coolant Testing

As you learned in a previous chapter, coolant is a mixture of 50 percent water and 50 percent antifreeze. A new generation of coolants has been introduced for electric, gas, and diesel vehicles. One has the ethylene glycol base with new organic acid corrosion inhibitors, and the other is a new propylene glycol base with these new inhibitors. Both types are nitrate, nitrite, borate, phosphate, silicate, and amine free. This new technology protects the six basic metal alloys found in the engine systems: aluminum, brass, cast iron, steel, solder, and copper.

Very often you will find that the coolant in a cooling system has been diluted with water. There are two common causes of this dilution:

1. Coolant loss through a leak in the system was replaced by the addition of water.
2. The level of coolant in a system without a recovery bottle was repeatedly raised by the addition of water when the system was cold. When the coolant was heated, it expanded, and the excess coolant was forced out the overflow tube and was lost.

Diluted coolant may freeze in cold weather and may cause overheating in warm weather. To protect the cooling system and maintain its efficiency, the 50/50 ratio of the coolant mixture should be maintained. As with battery electrolyte, the specific

Figure 10.9 A coolant hydrometer, or antifreeze tester. With this type, the number on the float is aligned with the top of the thermometer column to provide temperature-corrected freezing and boiling points (courtesy of E. Edelmann & Co., Skokie, IL 60076).

gravity of coolant can be measured. This measurement can be used to determine if sufficient ethylene glycol is present in the coolant.

The specific gravity of coolant is measured with a special hydrometer. Various types of coolant hydrometers, usually called *antifreeze testers*, are available. Some of these testers are shown in Figures 10.9 and 10.10. When you measure the specific gravity of electrolyte, some hydrometers require a compensation for the temperature of the coolant. Other hydrometers automatically compensate for different temperatures.

> The hydrometer is the correct tester to use when testing ethylene glycol. A new tester called a refractometer has been introduced to give accurate readings for the new coolants. It uses light reflection rather than specific gravity to test the amount of coolant protection. Since accuracy is important the new tester should be used.

An antifreeze tester is easy to use. A sample of the coolant is drawn into the tester from the upper

radiator tank. The tester then indicates the freezing point of the coolant. Because you know that the freezing point of a 50/50 coolant mixture is about −34°F (−37°C), you can determine if the coolant contains sufficient ethylene glycol.

In addition to testing the "strength" of the coolant, an antifreeze tester provides a simple way to check the condition of the coolant. Because the body of the tester is usually made of clear glass or plastic, the coolant can be examined for contamination by dirt or rust. Some antifreeze testers contain a series of plastic balls of different weight. The number of balls that float in the coolant indicates its relative "strength." An antifreeze tester of this type is shown in Figure 10.11.

Most antifreeze contains a dye that gives it a yellow-green color. This color should be quite obvious in the coolant. If the coolant contains dirt or rust particles, or if it appears dark or dirty, it should be drained and discarded. Flush the cooling system to remove loose dirt and rust, and install new coolant.

When testing ethylene glycol, the current testers are already accurate for the 1.080 specific gravity.

Figure 10.10 Dial indicating antifreeze tester. This type provides a temperature-compensated direct reading (courtesy of E. Edelmann & Co., Skokie, IL 60076).

| **TESTING COOLANT MIXTURE AND STRENGTH** | The following steps outline a procedure for testing coolant. Consult the instructions furnished with the antifreeze tester you have available for the correct use of that instrument: |

> **!** **WARNING:** Never remove the radiator cap when the engine coolant is hot. Failure to follow this advice could cause serious burns and possible damage to the cooling system. Because scalding hot coolant or steam may erupt from the radiator filler neck, use extreme care when removing a radiator filler cap. It is best to wait until the engine has cooled.

1. Wrap a heavy rag or wiper around the radiator cap.
2. Turn the radiator cap counterclockwise until you feel it stop at its first "stop" or detent. This position releases the pressure in the system.

   Note: If pressure is released, stand away from the radiator until you are sure that all pressure is released. Do not attempt to remove the cap in one motion. The pressure in the system could force hot coolant or steam to erupt from the filler neck.

3. Wiggle the cap to be sure it is loose and has released all the pressure in the system.
4. Push down on the cap and slowly turn it counterclockwise to its second "stop" and lift the cap from the filler neck.
5. Insert the tester into the radiator and draw up sufficient coolant to operate the tester.

   Note: Some testers are accurate only when the coolant is at or near its normal operating temperature. Be sure to check the instructions furnished with the tester.

6. Read the tester to determine the freezing point of the coolant.
7. Hold the tester up to a light source and check the condition of the coolant.
8. Return the coolant sample to the radiator tank.
9. Repeat steps 5 through 8 to verify your findings.
10. Install the radiator cap.

Figure 10.11 Pocket-type coolant tester. A pocket-type coolant tester that is in common use. The degree of protection is measured by the number of floating balls (courtesy of Thexton Mfg. Co. Inc.).

Since there is a slight difference in the specific gravity of propylene glycol (1.038), there will be a slight difference in the reading if the ethylene glycol tester is used, but not enough to cause serious errors. For all practical purposes the same tester scales can be used. The error induced with the testing of propylene glycol tends to indicate the need for more coolant to be added to reach the target temperature. Always temperature compensate any specific gravity tester readings.

Adjust the coolant protection level as needed, but never let the percentage of coolant ratio get over 60% or under 40% of coolant to water. The ideal solution is the 50% coolant to 50% water that has been the norm for many years (see Figure 10.12). Change both the old conventional coolant and the extended-life coolant as recommended by the automotive manufacturers and the coolant manufacturers. Five years or 150,000 miles

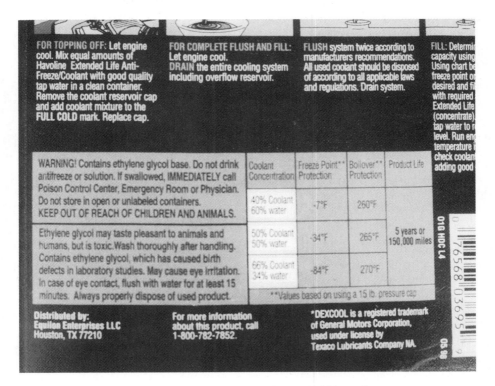

Figure 10.12 A coolant mixture chart showing the freezing points of extended-life coolants.

is the recommendation for the new extended-life coolant.

Determining the Amount of Coolant Required

Use the chart shown in Figure 10.13 to determine the amount of coolant in a cooling system. The capacity of the system and the approximate freezing point of the coolant are all you need to know. The cooling system capacity can be found in the owner's manual or in a shop manual. The antifreeze tester provides the approximate freezing point.

To use the chart simply read across the line provided for the capacity and find the approximate freezing point. The number of quarts of ethylene glycol in the coolant is noted above that column.

Once you know how much antifreeze is in the coolant, determine how much, if any, additional antifreeze should be added to obtain a 50/50 mixture. The following is an example of how this chart can be used.

A test made of the coolant in a system containing 14 quarts indicates that it will provide protection against freezing down to a temperature of about −18°F(−27°C). As shown in Figure 10.13, in

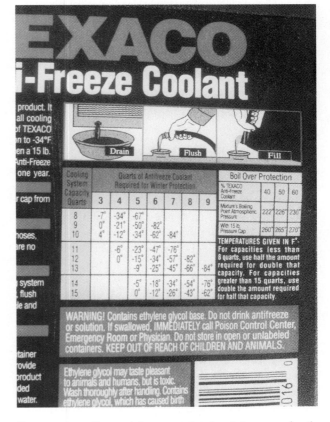

Figure 10.13 Determining protection level. An example of how the coolant mixture chart can be used to determine the amount of ethylene glycol in a cooling system.

Job 10B

TEST COOLANT MIXTURE AND CONDITION

SATISFACTORY PERFORMANCE
A satisfactory performance on this job requires that you do the following:

1. Test the mixture and condition of the coolant in the car assigned.
2. Following the steps in the "Performance Outline" and the instructions supplied with the tester used, complete the job within 15 minutes.
3. Fill in the blanks under "Information."

PERFORMANCE OUTLINE

1. Remove the radiator cap.
2. Determine the freezing point of the coolant.
3. Check the condition of the coolant.
4. Install the radiator cap.

INFORMATION

Vehicle identification _____
Reference used _____ Page(s) _____
Cooling system capacity _____
Tester used _____
Indicated freezing point of coolant _____
Temperature of coolant: _____ Hot _____ Cold
Is additional antifreeze required? _____ Yes _____ No
How much antifreeze should be added to bring the freezing point of the coolant to approximately −34°(−37°C)? _____
_____
Is the coolant dirty? _____ Yes _____ No
Should the coolant be changed? _____ Yes _____ No

Figure 10.14 Radiator chemical cleaners. Materials like these are used to clean and flush radiators (courtesy of Training Enterprises Company).

reading across the line for a system with a 14-quart capacity, you will find a box for −18°F. This column indicates that the system contains approximately 6 quarts of ethylene glycol. Add one additional quart of ethylene glycol to restore the coolant to its correct 50/50 proportions.

LESSON 10–3 Cooling System Cleaning

Most car makers recommend that cooling systems be drained, flushed, and refilled with fresh coolant at intervals of about 2 years or 30,000 miles (48,000 km). Machines are made that drain and fill cooling systems (see Figure 10.17). They are very fast and efficient. They are also environmentally safe. The antifreeze and antiboil prop-

erties of the coolant may still be effective after that period of usage. But the rust and corrosion inhibitors in the mixture are usually depleted. In addition, a considerable amount of rust and dirt particles may be in the coolant. As those particles are circulated through the system, they may build up in certain passages and restrict coolant flow.

A properly maintained cooling system can usually be cleaned by use of a chemical cleaner (see Figure 10.14). Chemical cleaners loosen and dissolve deposits of dirt, rust, and corrosion and hold them in suspension. When the cleaner is drained, the dissolved deposits are removed. Most chemical cleaners contain acids, and they should be respected for the injury and damage that acids can inflict. Depending on the acid content, some cleaners require that the system be treated with a *neutralizer* following the cleaning process. The neutralizer stops the action of any acid that may remain in the system.

If the cooling system is to be changed over to the new extended-life coolant and there is a minimum of deposits in the system, use just water as a flush. Flush both the cooling system and the heater system at least twice. If chemical flushes are used, be sure all chemicals are flushed out of the system before adding the extended-life coolant. Again, perform at least two clear water flushes and more if needed.

<table>
<tr><td>

**CLEANING A
COOLING SYSTEM**

</td><td>

The following steps outline a procedure for cleaning a cooling system by using a chemical cleaner. Because the procedures for use vary with different chemical cleaners, carefully read and follow the instructions furnished with the particular cleaner you have available.

</td></tr>
</table>

1. Drain the coolant from the system.

    Note: Most cooling systems can be drained through a *petcock,* or valve, located in a radiator tank. Such a valve is shown in Figures 10.15 and 10.16. Although the petcock is located in the lowest part of the system, a considerable amount of

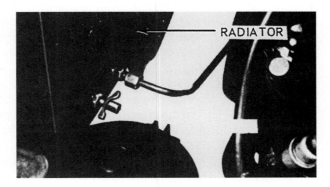

Figure 10.15 Petcock location. Most cooling systems can be drained by means of a petcock located in the lower radiator tank (courtesy of Ford Motor company, Dearborn, MI).

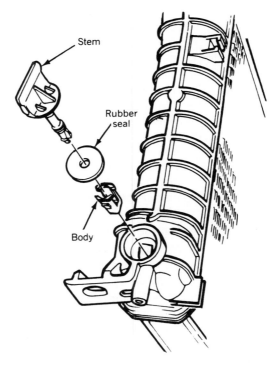

Figure 10.16 Plastic drain cock. Many radiators constructed of aluminum and plastic are equipped with a plastic drain cock of this type (courtesy of Chevrolet Motor Division, General Motors Corporation).

coolant will remain in the block water jackets. On some engines, this coolant can be drained by removing threaded plugs from the water jackets. Because the plugs may be difficult to remove, many technicians leave them in place. They raise the rear of the car with a jack and support it with car stands. This procedure allows more coolant to drain from the radiator petcock.

2. After the coolant has drained, close the petcock and fill the system with clean water to a level of about 2 in. (5 cm) below the base of the filler neck.

3. Apply the parking brake.

4. Place the transmission selector level in the PARK or NEUTRAL position and start the engine.

5. Adjust the heater temperature control to its highest position. This allows circulation of the cleaner through the heating system.

6. Allow the engine to run until it reaches its normal operating temperature.

   Note: Check the water level frequently during this period of operation. When the thermostat opens, the water level may drop. Adjust the water level as necessary.

7. Add the chemical cleaner.

8. Allow the engine to run at its normal operating temperature for the period of time specified by the instructions furnished with the cleaner.

9. Turn the engine off and drain the cleaning mixture.

10. After the cleaning mixture has been drained, close the petcock (see Figure 10.16) and fill the system with clean water.

    Note: Some cleaners require that a neutralizer be added to the water at this step.

11. Run the engine for the specified amount of time to dilute and neutralize the cleaner remaining in the system.

    Note: Be sure to check the water level frequently.

12. Drain the water from the system.

    Note: It is advisable to again raise the rear of the car so that sufficient water will drain from the system to allow for the addition of the ethylene glycol.

13. Check an appropriate manual to determine the capacity of the cooling system.

14. Determine the amount of ethylene glycol required. (Most manufacturers recommend 50% of the system capacity.)

15. After the water has drained, close the petcock and add the required amount of ethylene glycol to the system.

16. Add water to the system to a level of about 2 in. (5 cm) below the base of the filler neck.

    Note: The design of some cooling systems causes them to trap air in parts of the system. This air must be purged or "bled" from the system. Consult a repair manual for specific "bleeding" procedures that may be required for the car on which you are working.

17. Start the engine and allow it to run until it reaches its normal operating temperature.

    Note: Check the coolant level frequently during this period of operation. When the thermostat opens, the water level may drop. Adjust the coolant level with water if necessary.

18. Allow the engine to run and check the operation of the heater to be sure that hot coolant is circulating through the heater core.

19. Install the radiator cap.

20. Turn the engine off.

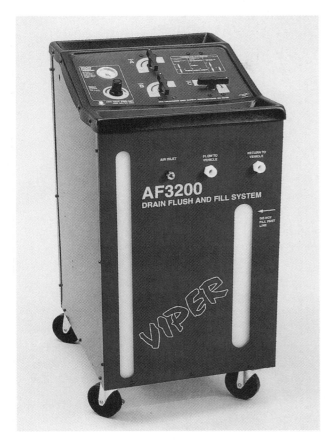

Figure 10.17 Coolant drain, fill, and flush machine. Machines like this take the place of the old methods of servicing cooling systems (Courtesy of Century MFG. Co.).

Job 10C

DRAIN, FLUSH, AND REFILL A COOLING SYSTEM

SATISFACTORY PERFORMANCE
A satisfactory performance on this job requires that you do the following:

1. Drain, flush, and refill the cooling system of the car assigned.
2. Following the steps in the "Performance Outline" and the instructions furnished with the chemical cleaner available, complete the job within 60 minutes plus the time required for the circulation of the cleaner.
3. Fill in the blanks under "Information."

PERFORMANCE OUTLINE

1. Drain the coolant.
2. Fill the system with fresh water and flush the system in accordance with the instructions furnished with the cleaner.
3. Add the required amount of ethylene glycol.
4. Adjust the coolant level with water.
5. Check the circulation of the coolant and readjust the coolant level if necessary.

INFORMATION

Vehicle identification _____
Reference used _____ Page(s) _____
Chemical cleaner used _____
Was a neutralizer required? ____ Yes ____ No
Cooling system capacity _____
Amount of ethylene glycol added _____

LESSON 10-4 Cooling System Leakage

Any leakage in a cooling system can cause a loss of coolant, a loss of pressure, and overheating. Test a cooling system for leaks as part of routine maintenance. Many times, a system will not leak until it is hot and is operating near its maximum pressure. Those conditions can be duplicated in the shop by using a *pressure tester* similar to the one shown in Figure 10.18.

A pressure tester consists of a hand pump that can be attached to the radiator filler neck. A gauge on the tester enables you to pressurize the system to the maximum pressure the system will be subjected to in use. Figure 10.19 shows a pressure tester connected to a radiator. The tester can be used to test radiator pressure caps by means of an adapter. This test is shown in Figure 10.20.

Figure 10.18 A typical cooling system pressure tester and adapter (courtesy of American Motors).

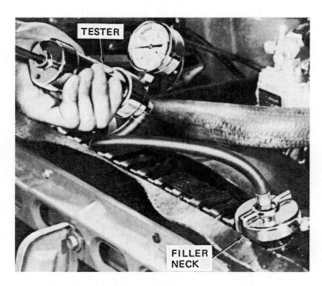

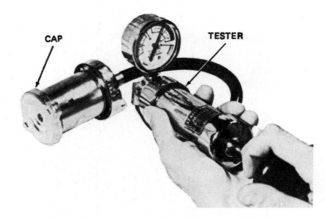

Figure 10.20   Testing a radiator pressure cap (courtesy of American Motors).

Figure 10.19   Pressure testing a cooling system (courtesy of American Motors).

PRESSURE TESTING A COOLING SYSTEM

The following steps outline a typical procedure for pressure testing a cooling system. Consult the instruction manual furnished with the tester you have available for any specific procedure that may be necessary for that instrument.

1. Carefully remove the radiator cap.

   Note: Do not attempt to remove the cap in one motion. Remember that if there is pressure in the system it could force hot coolant to erupt from the radiator and cause you painful burns.

2. Carefully wipe out the inside of the filler neck and examine the seat, or sealing surface, in the neck for dirt or damage that could cause a faulty seal between the seat and the pressure cap (see Figure 10.21).

3. Adjust the coolant level if necessary.

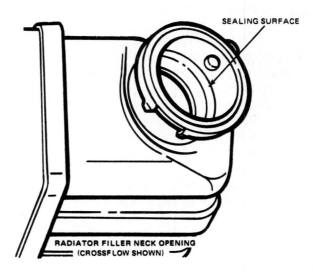

Figure 10.21   Radiator sealing surface. The seat inside the radiator filler neck provides the sealing surface for the pressure cap (courtesy of Ford Motor Company, Dearborn, MI).

4. Apply the parking brake, place the transmission selector lever in the PARK position, and start the engine.
5. Allow the engine to run until it reaches its normal operating temperature.
6. Turn off the engine.
7. Locate the manufacturer's specification for cooling system pressure in an appropriate manual.

    Note: The pressure cap is usually marked to indicate its opening pressure. Because the cap may be a replacement with an incorrect pressure rating, do not rely on the cap markings to indicate the system operating pressure.

8. Attach a pressure tester to the filler neck as you would install a radiator cap.
9. Operate the tester pump until the gauge indicates that the system is pressurized to the specification (refer to Figure 10.20).
10. Observe the gauge:
    a. If the gauge needle holds steady and the pressure is maintained for at least two minutes, the system has no serious leaks.
    b. If the gauge needle drops slowly, seepage or small leaks are indicated. Use a drop light or a flashlight and examine all hoses, connections, and gaskets for leaks.
    c. If the gauge needle drops quickly, serious leaks are indicated.
11. Slowly release the pressure in the system.

    Note: This can be safely done on some testers by tipping the metal "stem" that connects the hose to the tester cap.

12. Remove the tester from the radiator.

PRESSURE TESTING A RADIATOR PRESSURE CAP

The following steps outline a procedure for testing a radiator pressure cap. Consult the instruction manual furnished with the tester you have available for any specific procedure that may be necessary for that instrument:

1. Clean both sides of the rubber seal and under the vacuum valve inside the cap. Check for any dirt or damage that could cause it to leak (see Figure 10.22).
2. Wet the rubber seal with water and install the cap on the adapter as you would install the cap on the radiator.
3. Attach the adapter to the pressure tester.

    Note: Some testers require an adjustment before the tester can be fitted to the adapter. Other testers require the use of a special rubber spacer washer. The correct

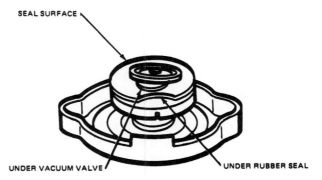

SEAL SURFACE

UNDER VACUUM VALVE   UNDER RUBBER SEAL

Figure 10.22 The parts of a pressure cap that require cleaning and inspecting (courtesy of Ford Motor Company, Dearborn, MI).

method for fitting the adapter is described in the instruction manual furnished with the tester.

4. Operate the tester pump until the gauge indicates its highest reading. (Refer to Figure 10.20.) This reading indicates the cap release pressure and should agree with the manufacturer's specifications.
5. Observe the gauge:
   a. If the gauge needle holds steady and some pressure is maintained for at least 30 seconds, the cap is in good condition. (A slight pressure drop is acceptable.)
   b. If the gauge needle drops rapidly, the cap is defective.
6. Remove the cap from the tester.

Job 10D

PRESSURE TEST A COOLING SYSTEM AND RADIATOR CAP

SATISFACTORY PERFORMANCE
A satisfactory performance on this job requires that you do the following:

1. Pressure test the cooling system and the radiator cap of the car assigned.
2. Following the steps in the "Performance Outline" and the instructions furnished with the tester used, complete the job within 15 minutes.
3. Fill in the blanks under "Information."

PERFORMANCE OUTLINE

1. Bring the engine up to its normal operating temperature.
2. Install the pressure tester.
3. Pressurize the system to the manufacturer's specification.
4. Observe the pressure gauge and locate any leaks.
5. Remove the pressure tester.
6. Pressure test the cap.
7. Remove the cap from the tester and install the cap on the radiator.

INFORMATION

Vehicle identification _____

Reference used _____ Page(s) _____

Cooling system operating pressure specification _____

Test results _____

_____

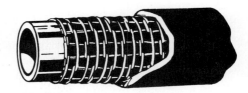

Figure 10.23 Radiator hose construction. Most quality radiator hoses use a lockstitch knit reinforcement pattern that keeps the hose from expanding and losing its shape under pressure (courtesy of NAPA Belts/Hose, Denver, CO).

facturer as original equipment are usually *molded*, or curved. A pair of molded hoses installed on a radiator is shown in Figure 10.24. Molded hoses are formed to a particular shape so that they will clear the fan and other parts at the front of the engine. Although molded hoses are available as replacement parts, in many instances flexible hoses of the type shown in Figure 10.25 are used. These hoses are reinforced with steel wire and can be bent to duplicate the curves of many molded hoses.

As shown in Figure 10.26, hoses also connect the engine to the heater. These hoses, usually called *heater hoses*, allow hot coolant to circulate through a small radiator called a *heater core* (see Figure 10.27). Air passing through the heater core is heated and used to warm the passenger compartment. Some heater hoses are cut from straight lengths of flexible hose; others are of molded construction (see Figure 10.28). Formable heater hose, as shown in Figure 10.29, is also available for use where sharp bends are required.

The hoses in the cooling system are repeatedly subjected to movement, vibration, and extremes in temperature and pressure. Thus they have a limited service life. Routine maintenance requires that the hoses in a cooling system be inspected at regular intervals. Most car makers suggest that all hoses and their connections be checked at least once each year or every 15,000 miles (24,000 km).

LESSON 10-5 Hoses

The radiator and the engine are connected by flexible rubber hoses. These hoses allow the engine to vibrate and move slightly in its mounts without damaging the radiator. To withstand cooling system pressures, the hoses are reinforced internally, usually by lockstiched nylon cord as shown in Figure 10.23. The radiator hoses installed by the car manu-

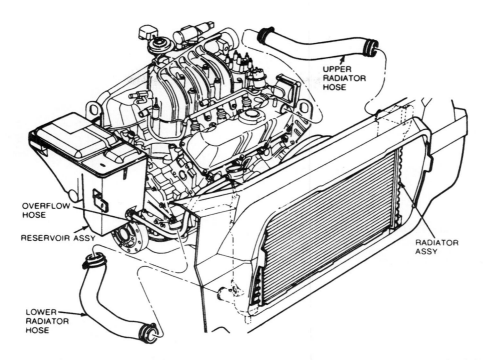

Figure 10.24 Radiator hose location. A pair of molded radiator hoses used on a V-6 engine in a front wheel drive car (courtesy of Ford Motor Company, Dearborn, MI).

Inspecting Hoses

A careful check of the hoses in a cooling system may reveal leaks or damage and deterioration that could cause a hose to fail in service. Replace any hose that fails to pass the following inspections.

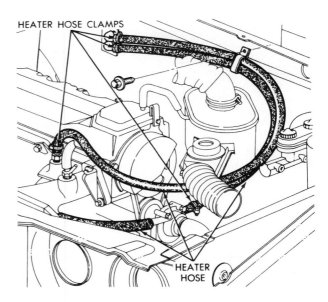

Figure 10.25 A flexible or bendable radiator hose. Hoses of this type can often be used to replace many of the molded types (courtesy of The Gates Rubber Company, Denver, CO).

Figure 10.26 Typical heater hose routing between the engine and the heater core (courtesy of Chrysler Corporation).

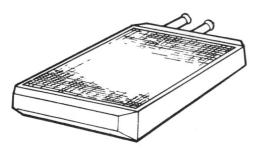

Figure 10.27   A typical heater core (courtesy of Ford Motor Company, Dearborn, MI).

Figure 10.28   Molded radiator hose. Some cooling systems use a short length of molded bypass hose to reroute coolant back to the water pump (courtesy of NAPA Belts/Hose, Denver, CO).

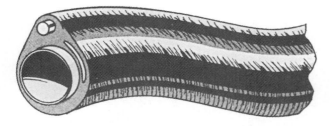

Figure 10.29   Formable radiator hose. In some installations, molded heater hose can be replaced with formable hose. Note that the hose has a special wire spline that can be bent to various shapes without kinking the hose (courtesy of NAPA Belts/Hose, Denver, CO).

Visual Inspection.   Using a drop light or a flashlight, check the outer surfaces of the hoses. Look for coolant stains and other signs of leakage. Check for cracks, exposed cords, and damage by abrasion (see Figures 10.30 through 10.32). The hoses should appear smooth, with no signs of swelling,

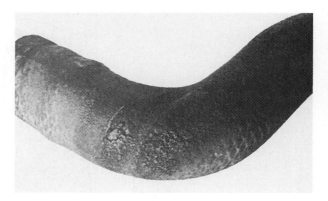

Figure 10.30   A hose damaged by heat, usually from a nearby hot engine part such as an exhaust manifold (courtesy of NAPA Belts/Hose, Denver, CO).

Figure 10.31   Oil-damaged radiator hose. Oil damages hose by causing it to soften, swell, and separate, layer by layer. The oil may be dripping on the hose from an external leak, or the oil could be leaking into the cooling system from a defective transmission cooler or other damaged components (courtesy of NAPA Belts/Hose, Denver, CO).

Figure 10.32   Dry and cracked hose. Aging, plus flexing of the hose and fittings, causes cracks to appear at the hose end. Retightening the clamp may reduce the chance of leakage, but the hose should be replaced (courtesy of NAPA Belts/Hose, Denver, CO).

blisters, or bubbles. Connect a pressure tester to the system and check for leakage, swelling, and blisters while the system is pressurized.

Manual Inspection.   Remove the pressure tester and squeeze the hoses. They should be firm but not hard. A hose that feels hard is usually brittle and may crack if it is bent. A hose that is rotted internally usually feels soft or spongy. A hose that feels slippery or oily may have been softened by oil or fuel spills.

Hose Clamps

A hose that is in good condition often leaks at its connection to the engine, radiator, or heater core. The clamp holding the hose to its fitting may be loose or defective. Tightening or replacing the clamp may eliminate the leak. Several types of clamps are in common use.

Radial-Type Hose Clamps.   Clamps of this type, also referred to as *screw-tower clamps,* are used by some manufacturers as original equipment. Shown in Figure 10.33, a clamp of this type can sometimes be tightened with a screwdriver. Quite often you will find that a clamp of this type is so rusted or corroded that an adjustment cannot be made. In those instances the clamp must be replaced. The use of a tool similar to the one shown in Figure 10.34 will enable you to cut off the defective clamp without damage to the hose.

"Perma-Quik" Hose Clamps.   At times you will find heater hoses and bypass hoses that are secured with clamps of this type. Shown in Figure 10.35, these clamps are designed for onetime use. They are *crimped,* or squeezed, on the hose and are not adjustable. Clamps of this type are easily removed by cutting them off with a tool similar to the one shown in Figure 10.36.

Figure 10.33   Radial-type hose clamp. Clamps of this type are often used as original equipment (courtesy of NAPA Belts/Hose, Denver, CO).

Figure 10.34   Radial-type hose clamp cutter. A special cutter for removing radial-type hose clamps without damaging the hose. The insert shows how the tool is used (courtesy of KD Tools, Lancaster, PA).

Figure 10.35   Perma-Quik hose clamp. This type of clamp is crimped in place and is not reusable (courtesy of KD Tools, Lancaster, PA).

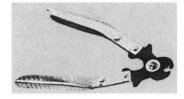

Figure 10.36   Perma-Quik hose clamp cutter. A special cutter for removing Perma-Quik hose clamps (courtesy of KD Tools, Lancaster, PA).

Figure 10.37   A screw-drive or "Wittek" hose clamp (courtesy of The Gates Rubber Company, Denver, CO).

Screw-Drive Hose Clamps.   Clamps of this type, shown in Figure 10.37, are commonly used to replace clamps used as original equipment. Sometimes called *Wittek clamps* or *worm-drive clamps,* they provide a positive grip over a wide range of adjustment. In addition, clamps of this

Figure 10.38 Corbin hose clamp. Clamps of this type are self-tightening (courtesy of KD Tools, Lancaster, PA).

type can be opened, allowing you to install them without removing the hose.

Corbin Hose Clamps. Made of heavy spring steel wire as shown in Figure 10.38, a Corbin clamp is another type of clamp in common use. A Corbin clamp is self-tightening and self-adjusting. A special pair of *hose clamp pliers,* similar to those shown in Figure 10.39, should be used to remove and install a clamp of this type.

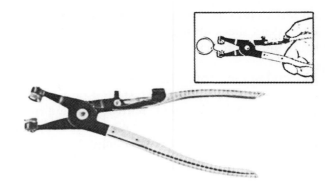

Figure 10.39 Hose clamp pliers. Hose clamp pliers used to remove and install Corbin clamps. The insert shows how the pliers are used to grip and expand a clamp (courtesy of KD Tools, Lancaster, PA).

| REPLACING RADIATOR HOSES | The following steps outline a procedure for replacing radiator hoses in a typical cooling system. |

Removal
1. Drain the coolant into a suitable clean container.
2. Loosen or remove the clamps at the ends of the hose to be replaced.
3. Twist the hose to break its bond with its connections and slide it off the fittings.

   Note: Do not force a hose off its fittings, because you may cause damage. If a hose is tight on its fittings, use a knife as shown in Figure 10.40 to carefully split the hose.

Installation
1. Compare the replacement hose with the hose you removed and determine its position.
2. Clean all traces of dirt and old sealer from the hose fittings (see Figure 10.41).
3. Place the clamps on the hose.

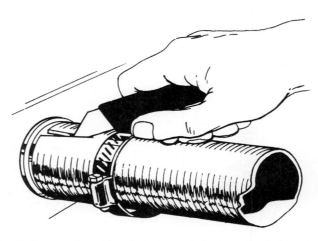

Figure 10.40 Knife removing old radiator hose. If the hose is stuck to the fitting, don't force or pry it off. This could damage the fitting. Use a sharp knife to cut and peel the hose away (courtesy of NAPA Belts/Hose, Denver, CO).

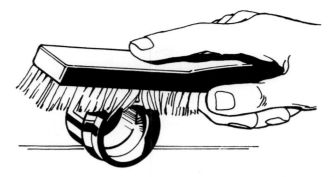

Figure 10.41 Cleaning radiator hose fittings. To minimize the possibility of leakage, gently clean the fittings with a wire brush or emery cloth (courtesy of NAPA Belts/Hose, Denver, CO).

Note: Most technicians prefer to use new clamps when replacing a hose. The old clamps may not provide leakproof connections.

4. Install the hose on its fittings, aligning it so that it clears the fan, the belts, and other parts.

Note: Some manufacturers advise coating the fittings with a water-resistant sealer before installing a hose.

5. Slide the clamps so they are positioned approximately 1/4 in. (about 6 mm) from the ends of the hose, as shown in Figure 10.42.

6. Tighten the clamps.

Note: Be sure that the *bead,* or ridge, on the fitting is not under the clamp. The clamp should be between the bead and the end of the hose, as shown in Figure 10.43.

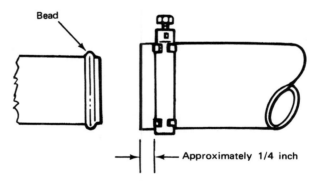

Figure 10.42 Hose clamp position on hose. A hose clamp should be positioned so that it is about 1/4 in. (6 mm) from the end of the hose (courtesy of Ford Motor Company, Dearborn, MI).

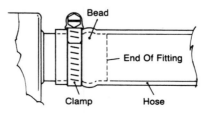

Figure 10.43 Installing hose clamp position. A hose clamp should be positioned so that it is between the end of the hose and the bead on the radiator or engine outlet (courtesy of NAPA Belts/Hose, Denver, CO).

7. Fill the system with the drained coolant.
8. Apply the parking brake, place the shift selector lever in PARK or NEUTRAL, and start the engine.
9. Allow the engine to run until it reaches normal operating temperature.

   Note: Be sure to check the coolant level repeatedly during warmup. The level may drop when the thermostat opens.

10. Turn the engine off.
11. Pressure test the system for leaks.

REPLACING HEATER HOSES

The following steps outline a procedure for replacing heater hoses.

Removal

1. Drain the coolant into a suitable clean container.
2. Loosen or remove the clamps at the ends of the hose to be replaced.
3. Twist the hose to break its bond with the fittings, and remove the hose.

   Note: Do not attempt to remove a heater hose by force. The fittings at the heater core are easily damaged. If a hose is tight on its fittings, use a sharp knife to carefully split the hose (refer to Figure 10.40)

4. Free the hose from any brackets or straps that position the hose. (Refer to Figure 10.26.)

Installation

1. Determine the diameter of the replacement hose required.

   Note: Hose size is determined by its inside diameter as shown in Figure 10.44. The most commonly used sizes are 5/8 in. and 3/4 in.

2. Cut a length of replacement hose to match the length of the hose you removed.

   Note: Some technicians prefer to cut the new hose a few inches longer than the old hose. If the hose proves to be too long, it can be trimmed on installation.

3. Clean all traces of dirt and old sealer from the hose fittings.
4. Place the clamps on the hose.

   Note: Most technicians prefer to use new clamps as insurance against leakage.

5. Position the hose in its retaining brackets or straps.
6. Install the hose on its connections, aligning it so that it is clear of the exhaust manifold and any other parts that may cause wear or damage.

   Note: Some manufacturers advise coating the fittings with a water-resistant sealer before installing a hose.

7. Slide the clamps so that they are positioned approximately 1/4 in. (about 6 mm) from the ends of the hose (refer to Figure 10.42).
8. Tighten the clamps.

   Note: Be sure that the bead, or ridge, on the fitting is not under the clamp. The clamp should be between the bead and the end of the hose (refer to Figure 10.43).

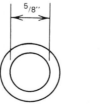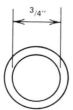

Figure 10.44   Determining heater hose size. Hose size is determined by the inside diameter. The two most commonly used heater hose sizes are 5/8 in. and 3/4 in.

9. Fill the system with the drained coolant.
10. Apply the parking brake and place the shift selector lever in PARK or NEUTRAL. Start the engine.
11. Allow the engine to run until it reaches normal operating temperature.

    Note: Be sure to check the coolant level repeatedly during warmup. The level may drop when the thermostat opens.

12. Position the heater controls in the HEAT position and check the operation of the heater.
13. Turn the engine off.
14. Pressure test the system for leaks.

Job 10E

REPLACE COOLING SYSTEM HOSES

SATISFACTORY PERFORMANCE
A satisfactory performance on this job requires that you do the following:

1. Replace the designated hoses on the car assigned.
2. Following the steps in the "Performance Outline" and the procedure and specifications of the manufacturer, complete the job within 200% of the time suggested by the manufacturer.
3. Fill in the blanks under "Information."

PERFORMANCE OUTLINE

1. Drain the coolant.
2. Remove the designated hose(s).
3. Install the replacement hoses(s).
4. Check the operation of the system.
5. Pressure test the system.

INFORMATION

Vehicle identification _____
Reference used _____ Page(s) _____
Hose(s) replaced:
_____ Upper radiator   _____ Lower radiator
_____ Heater supply   _____ Heater return
_____ Water pump bypass
Heater hose size: _____ 5/8 in.   _____ 3/4 in.
Cooling system pressure specification _____
Cooling system was pressure tested to _____ psi

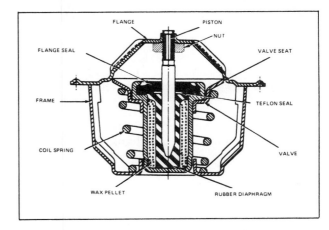

Figure 10.45 A sectional view of a typical thermostat (courtesy of Pontiac Motor Division, General Motors Corporation).

cools, the temperature-sensitive material contracts and allows a spring to close the valve.

When the engine, and thus the coolant, is cold, the valve remains closed. This prevents the coolant from circulating through the radiator. By means of a bypass, coolant circulates through the water jackets, as shown in Figure 10.46. This allows the engine to warm up quickly and evenly. As the coolant temperature rises, the valve opens slightly and allows coolant to flow through the radiator. Depending on the temperature of the coolant, the valve opens and closes, permitting the flow of sufficient coolant to keep the engine operating temperature within a specified range.

LESSON 10–6 Thermostats

A *thermostat* is an automatic valve that controls the flow of coolant in a cooling system. The parts of a typical thermostat are shown in Figure 10.45. The valve is actuated by the expansion of a temperature-sensitive material sealed within a cup and piston assembly. When the assembly is heated, the material expands and opens the valve. When the assembly

Diagnosing Thermostat Problems

If the valve in a thermostat remains open or partially open, the following problems may occur.

1. Extended engine warmup time
2. Engine operating temperature below specifications

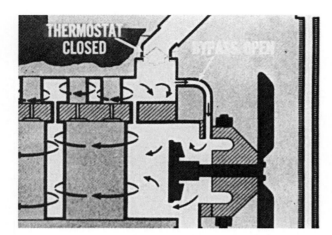

Figure 10.46 Thermostat closed position. When the coolant is cold, the thermostat is closed. The coolant does not flow through the radiator, but is pumped through the water jackets (courtesy of Chrysler Corporation).

3. Insufficient heat from the heater
4. Unacceptable levels of exhaust emissions

If the valve of a thermostat remains closed or does not open sufficiently, the following problems may occur:

1. Overheating
2. Coolant loss
3. Internal engine damage

Occasionally the thermostat may be missing from the cooling system of some cars. The thermostat may have been removed by someone in an attempt to "cure" a problem of overheating. All thermostats, even when wide open, provide a restriction in the cooling system. This restriction is designed

Figure 10.47 A typical coolant thermometer (courtesy of KD Tools, Lancaster, PA).

to slow down the flow of coolant and ensure complete circulation through the water jackets.

If the thermostat is removed, coolant flow to the rear of the water jackets is usually decreased. This results in uneven engine temperatures. The front cylinders may be overcooled, whereas the cylinders at the rear of the engine may not be cooled enough. Uneven engine temperatures result in engine wear and damage caused by improper lubrication and improper combustion.

An engine should not be operated without a thermostat in the cooling system. If an engine overheats continuously when the proper thermostat is installed, the thermostat is usually not the cause of the problem. Overheating can be caused by many things including plugged radiator core tubes, improper fan operation, and clogged water jackets. These and many other causes are listed in appropriate service manuals together with the required repairs.

A coolant thermometer similar to the one shown in Figure 10.47 will help determine if a thermostat is operating correctly. When inserted in the filler neck of the radiator, it provides you with a fairly accurate measurement of coolant temperature.

REPLACING THERMOSTATS

The following steps outline a typical procedure for replacing a thermostat. Because of the many variations in thermostat mounting and placement, consult an appropriate manual for the specific procedure and specifications required for the car on which you are working.

Removal
1. Drain the coolant into a suitable clean container.
2. Disconnect the upper radiator hose from the coolant outlet connection (see Figure 10.48)
3. Using a socket wrench, remove the bolts that hold the outlet connection to the engine (see Figure 10.49).
4. Remove the coolant outlet and the thermostat.

Instead of a gasket between the thermostat housing and the block, some applications now use a gasket on the thermostat and do not have a gasket over the entire surface of the thermostat housing.

Figure 10.48 Removing thermostat. The radiator hose should be disconnected from the coolant outlet before attempting to remove the thermostat (courtesy of Chevrolet Motor Division, General Motors Corporation).

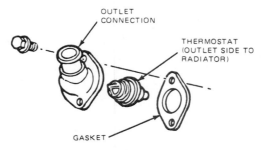

Figure 10.49 Thermostat installation. Disassembled view of the coolant outlet, thermostat, and gasket (courtesy of Ford Motor Company, Dearborn, MI).

Installation

1. Clean all traces of sealer and old gasket material from the outlet connection and its mating surface on the engine.
2. Check the replacement thermostat to be sure that it is the correct type and that it has the correct opening temperature.

   Note: Most thermostats are marked with their opening temperature.

3. Install the thermostat so the actuating pellet is toward the engine. Most thermostats are marked to indicate the correct position.

   Note: The outer edge of a thermostat fits into a recess. On some cars the recess is in the engine, as shown in Figure 10.50. On other cars the recess is in the outlet connection, as shown in Figure 10.51. If the thermostat is not seated in this recess, the outlet connection may crack when the bolts are tightened. Some technicians place a few small daubs of assembly cement on the rim of the thermostat to ensure that it will stay in place during assembly. Some car manufacturers provide a means of locking the thermostat in the recess. The thermostat is inserted in the outlet connection and turned clockwise to lock it in place (refer to Figure 10.51).

4. Coat a new gasket with water-resistant sealer and position the gasket over the thermostat.

   Note: Some car makers do not use a gasket at the water outlet. They specify the use of an RTV (room temperature vulcanizing) sealant.

5. Position the outlet connection over the engine and install the attaching bolts.

   Note: Be careful not to dislodge the thermostat from its position in the recess.

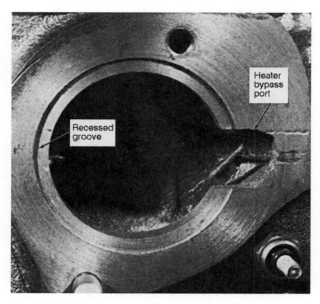

Figure 10.50   A typical thermostat recess in an engine (courtesy of American Motors).

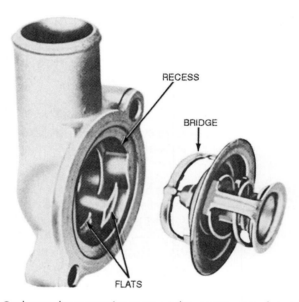

Figure 10.51   Coolant outlet connection recess. A thermostat recess formed in the coolant outlet connection. This outlet also has flats into which the thermostat can be locked to ensure proper installation (courtesy of Ford Motor Company, Dearborn, MI).

6. Tighten the bolts to the torque specification of the car maker.
7. Connect the upper hose.
8. Fill the system with the drained coolant.
9. Pressure test the system for leaks.
10. Apply the parking brake and place the shift lever in PARK or NEUTRAL. Start the engine and allow it to run until its normal operating temperature is reached.

    Note: Be sure to check the coolant level repeatedly during warmup. The level may drop when the thermostat opens.
11. Check the temperature of the coolant.

Job 10F

REPLACE A THERMOSTAT

SATISFACTORY PERFORMANCE
A satisfactory performance on this job requires that you do the following:

1. Replace the thermostat in the cooling system of the car assigned.
2. Following the steps in the "Performance Outline" and the procedure and specifications of the car manufacturer, complete the job within 200% of the manufacturer's suggested time.
3. Fill in the blanks under "Information."

PERFORMANCE OUTLINE

1. Drain the coolant.
2. Disconnect the upper hose.
3. Remove the thermostat.
4. Install the replacement thermostat.
5. Connect the upper hose.
6. Install the coolant.
7. Pressure test the system.
8. Check the operation of the system.

INFORMATION

Vehicle identification _____
Reference used _____ Page(s) _____
Manufacturer's specifications for:
Thermostat opening temperature _____
Coolant outlet connection bolt torque _____
System operating pressure _____
Opening temperature of thermostat installed _____
Location of thermostat recess: _____ Coolant outlet
                               _____ Engine
System was pressure tested to _____
Coolant temperature at completion of test _____

LESSON 10–7 Drive Belts

Many engine accessories, including the fan and the water pump, are driven by V belts. These belts are turned by a pulley on the engine crank-shaft. On some cars, the fan is attached to the water pump shaft. Then the fan and the water pump are driven by the same belt. In addition to driving the fan and the water pump, many *fan belts* also drive the alternator. On many cars, a failure of the fan belt results in the failure of both the cooling and the charging systems. Include an inspection and adjustment of the fan belt as a part of routine maintenance.

Several types of V belts are in common use (see Figure 10.52). The type of belt is chosen by the car maker to meet the performance requirements of the particular application. Conventional V belts are most commonly used. As shown in Figure 10.53, they will be found in both single and multiple arrangements. A cogged belt, a variation of the conventional belt, is often used where the belt must bend around a pulley of small diameter.

Where space considerations are a factor, V-rib belts are often used. As shown in Figure 10.54, one V-rib belt can be used to replace several

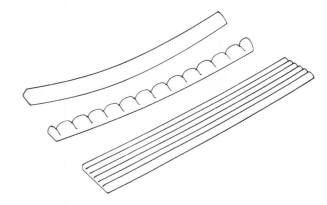

Figure 10.52 Commonly used drive belts (courtesy of Ford Motor Company, Dearborn, MI).

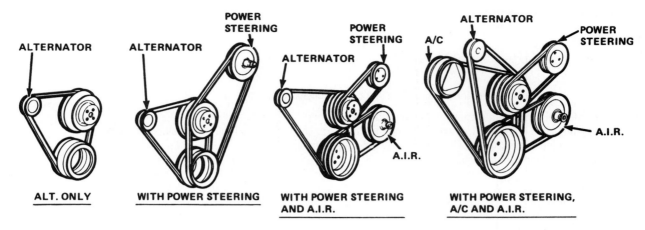

Figure 10.53 Typical drive belt arrangements (courtesy of Pontiac Motor Division, General Motors Corporation).

conventional belts. The thin profile of a V-rib belt (see Figure 10.55) gives the belt greater flexibility. This allows it to be bent backward over a pulley so that it can transmit power through the flat top section of the belt. As shown in Figure 10.56, a V-rib belt usually weaves in and out around the pulleys on an engine. Because of its snakelike arrangement,

a V-rib belt is often referred to as a *serpentine belt.* Figure 10.56 shows the system used to keep tension on a V-rib belt.

Inspecting Drive Belts

Before any attempt is made to adjust a belt, inspect the belt. The underside of the belt should have no cracks (see Figure 10.57). If cracks are found, replace the belt. The tapered sides of a belt should be smooth. As shown in Figures 10.58 through 10.62, a belt showing separation, tensile breaks, or a worn cover should be replaced. A loose belt slips, and some slipping belts develop glazing. A belt is glazed when its sides have a shiny, glasslike surface (see Figure 10.60). A glazed belt will continue to slip, even after it has been properly adjusted. For this reason, a glazed belt should be replaced. In most cases, an oil-soaked belt (see Figure 10.60) indicates that the seal at the end of the crankshaft is leaking. An oil-soaked belt must also be replaced, and the location of

Three Standard Belts   V-Rib Belt Drive

Figure 10.54 Single and multiple belts. To avoid the necessity for multiple belts, some car makers use a single V-rib belt like the one on the right to drive the accessories (courtesy of NAPA Belts/Hose, Denver, CO).

Figure 10.55 Cross section of V-rib belt. Cross section of a V-rib belt used on serpentine and multipulley engine drives. The belt can transmit power from both the flat and ribbed sides (courtesy of NAPA Belts/Hose, Denver, CO).

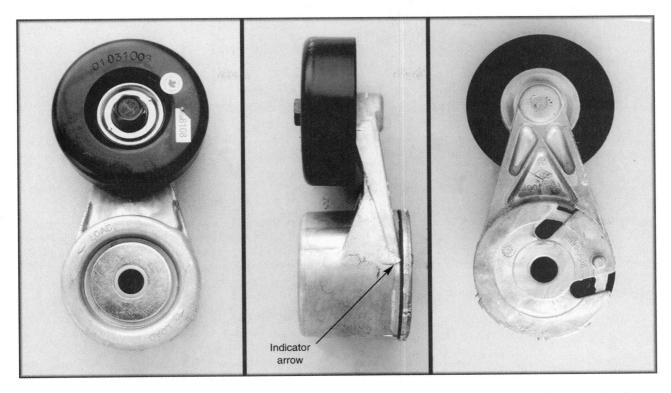

Figure 10.56 Serpentine belt system pulley and tensioner parts. Serpentine belt systems save space and weight under the hood by allowing one longitudinally ribbed belt to replace two, three, and sometimes four different V-belts to drive the engine accessories (courtesy of Training Enterprises Company).

the leak must be found and the required repair performed.

A loose belt cannot drive the fan, water pump, and alternator at the proper speed. In addition, a loose, slipping belt will eventually destroy itself through overheating and, by heat transfer through the pulleys, can "bake" the lubricants in the bear-ings of the accessories. A loose belt that passes the above inspections should be adjusted to increase its tension.

Most fan belts are adjusted by moving the alter-nator in or out on its mountings. This operation

Figure 10.57 Deep belt cracks. Deep cracks on a belt indicate that it is turning over a pulley that is too small. Or, if the failed belt is a replacement, it should have been a cogged, or notched, belt designed for small pulleys (courtesy of NAPA Belts/Hose, Denver, CO).

Figure 10.58 Belt layer separation. Layer separation is the most common indication of impending belt failure. As the lower sidewalls of the belt become excessively worn, the belt layers separate. Normally, the belt will then turn over, break, or flip off the drive pulleys (courtesy of NAPA Belts/Hose, Denver, CO).

Figure 10.59 Tensile cord breakage. Tensile cord breakage is usually caused by forcing the belt over a pulley during installation, by a high shock load from the drive, or by a foreign object wedged between the belt and a pulley. When installing a belt, an accessory should be moved so that the belt can be slipped onto the pulley (courtesy of NAPA Belts/Hose, Denver, CO).

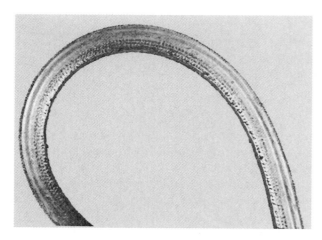

Figure 10.60 Glazed belt. Glazed belt sidewalls are the result of slippage caused by low belt tension or worn pulley grooves. Grease or oil on the belt can also cause this condition (courtesy of NAPA Belts/Hose, Denver, CO).

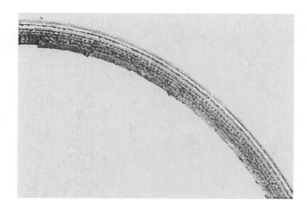

Figure 10.61 Burned and pitted belt. Burned and pitted belt sidewalls indicate that the belt has been slipping for an extended period of time. This extreme case was caused by low belt tension (courtesy of NAPA Belts/Hose, Denver, CO).

Figure 10.62 Pulled-apart belt. A belt pulled apart usually means that a pebble or piece of gravel has shot up into the drive and become lodged between the belt and a pulley groove (courtesy of NAPA Belts/Hose, Denver, CO).

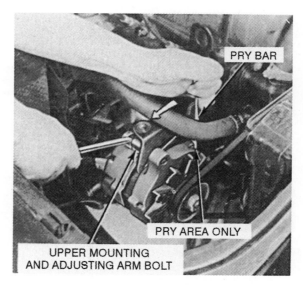

Figure 10.63 Belt adjustment. On most cars, the fan belt tension is adjusted by prying the alternator outward in its mountings (courtesy of Ford Motor Company, Dearborn, MI).

is shown in Figure 10.63. Most car makers specify the tension to which the belts on their cars should be adjusted (see Figure 10.64). After a belt is inspected, its tension should be measured. Belt tension is easily measured by the use of a *belt tension gauge*. A typical belt tension gauge is shown in Figure 10.65. The gauge is positioned on the belt as shown in Figure 10.66. Compare the tension indicated on the gauge to the manufacturer's specifications. If the tension is within the specified range, no adjustment is necessary. If the tension is too low or too high, an adjustment is required.

ENGINE	TENSIONING	GENERATOR	POWER STEERING	AIR CONDITIONING
L–4	NEW	650 N (146 LB)	650 N (146 LB)	750 N (168 LB)
	USED	222–350 N (50–80 LB)	222–350 N (50–80 LB)	289–422 N (65–95 LB)

Figure 10.64 Belt tension specifications. Belt tension specifications specified by one manufacturer for one particular engine. Note that the specifications for a "used" belt are approximately half those for a "new" belt. A belt that has been in service for more than 15 minutes can be considered "used" (courtesy of Chevrolet Motor Division, General Motors Corporation).

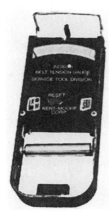

Figure 10.65 A typical belt tension gauge (courtesy of American Motors).

Figure 10.66 Installing a belt tension gauge on the fan belt. The gauge is placed between the alternator and the water pump (courtesy of Chevrolet Motor Division, General Motors Corporation).

ADJUSTING A FAN BELT

The following steps outline a typical procedure for adjusting a fan belt. Consult an appropriate manual for the particular procedure and for the tension specifications required for the car on which you are working.

1. Position a belt tension gauge on the belt as shown in Figure 10.67.
2. Loosen the adjustment nuts or bolts on the alternator slightly so that the alternator can be moved on its mountings (see Figure 10.68).
3. Carefully pry the alternator in the appropriate direction until the correct tension is indicated on the gauge (refer to Figure 10.63).

   Note: Some manufacturers specify the pry points for each application and may even specify the use of a special tool (see Figures 10.69 and 10.70).

4. While maintaining the correct belt tension, tighten the adjustment bolts or nuts to the manufacturer's torque specifications (see Figure 10.71).
5. Remove the belt tension gauge.

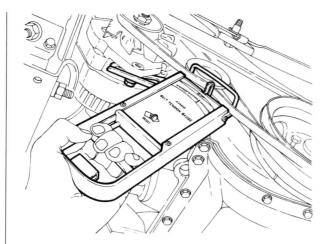

Figure 10.67 Checking alternator belt tension with a belt tension gauge. As shown, in some instances it is easier to check the belt tension from under the car (courtesy of American Motors).

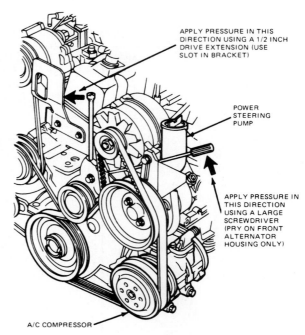

Figure 10.69 Pry points and adjustment. On some applications, more than one belt will require adjustment. Note that pry points for both the alternator and the idler pulley are specified (courtesy of Ford Motor Company, Dearborn, MI).

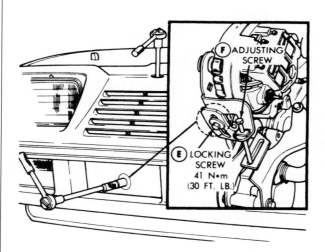

Figure 10.68 Belt adjustment access hole. On some cars, access holes are provided for alternator belt adjustment. Note that this mounting has a separate locking screw to secure the adjustment (courtesy of Chrysler Corporation).

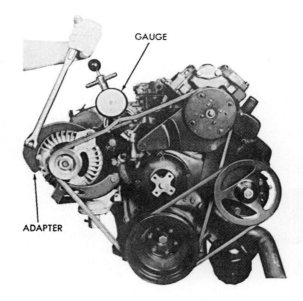

Figure 10.70 Using belt adjustment tools. Adjusting the tension of a belt using a special tool to grasp the alternator (courtesy of Chrysler Corporation).

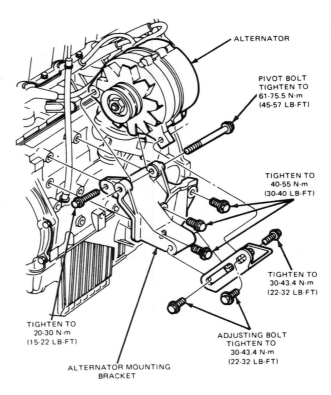

ALTERNATOR

**PIVOT BOLT
TIGHTEN TO
61-75.5 N·m
(45-57 LB·FT)**

**TIGHTEN TO
40-55 N·m
(30-40 LB·FT)**

**TIGHTEN TO
30-43.4 N·m
(22-32 LB·FT)**

**TIGHTEN TO
20-30 N·m
(15-22 LB·FT)**

**ADJUSTING BOLT
TIGHTEN TO
30-43.4 N·m
(22-32 LB·FT)**

**ALTERNATOR MOUNTING
BRACKET**

Figure 10.71 Alternator adjustment and torque. Typical alternator mounting and adjusting locations and torque specifications (courtesy of Ford Motor Company, Dearborn, MI).

Job 10G

ADJUST A FAN BELT

SATISFACTORY PERFORMANCE
A satisfactory performance on this job requires that you do the following:

1. Adjust the fan belt tension on the car assigned.
2. Following the steps in the "Performance Outline" and the manufacturer's procedure and specifications, complete the job within 200% of the manufacturer's suggested time.
3. Fill in the blanks under "Information."

PERFORMANCE OUTLINE

1. Measure the belt tension.
2. Compare the tension with the specifications.
3. Loosen the adjustment nuts or bolts.
4. Adjust the belt tension to the specifications.
5. Tighten the nuts or bolts to the torque specification.

INFORMATION

Vehicle identification _____

Reference used _____ Page(s) _____

Belt tension specification _____

Belt tension at the start of the job _____

Belt tension at the completion of the job _____

<table>
<tr><td>

REPLACING A FAN BELT

</td><td>

The following steps outline a procedure for replacing a fan belt. On many cars, other belts must be removed to gain access to the fan belt (refer to Figure 10.53). Therefore, consult an appropriate manual for the particular procedures and specifications that may be necessary for the car on which you are working.

1. Determine if other belts must be removed to gain access to the fan belt.
2. Loosen the adjustment and mounting bolts or nuts necessary to relieve the tension on the belt(s).
3. Remove the belt(s).
4. Install the replacement belt(s).
5. Position a belt tension gauge on the fan belt (refer to Figures 10.66 and 10.67).
6. Carefully pry the alternator in the appropriate direction until the correct tension is indicated on the gauge (refer to Figures 10.69 and 10.70).
7. Tighten the adjustment and mounting bolts and nuts to the manufacturer's torque specifications while maintaining the correct belt tension (refer to Figure 10.71).
8. Repeat steps 5 to 7 on any remaining belts.

</td></tr>
</table>

Job 10H

REPLACE A FAN BELT

SATISFACTORY PERFORMANCE

A satisfactory performance on this job requires that you do the following:

1. Replace the fan belt on the vehicle assigned.
2. Following the steps in the "Performance Outline" and the manufacturer's procedure and specifications, complete the job within 200% of the manufacturer's suggested time.
3. Fill in the blanks under "Information."

PERFORMANCE OUTLINE

1. Loosen the necessary adjustment and mounting bolts or nuts.
2. Remove the belt(s).
3. Install the replacement belt(s).
4. Adjust the tension of the belt(s) to specifications.
5. Tighten the adjustment and mounting bolts and nuts to the torque specifications.

INFORMATION

Vehicle identification _____
Reference used _____ Page(s) _____
Part number of replacement belt _____
Belt type:
____ Conventional ____ Cogged ____ V-rib
Fan belt tension specification _____
Accessory belt tension specifications _____

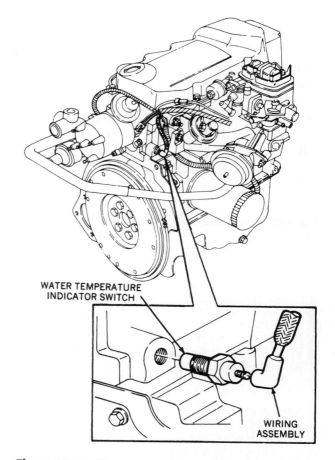

Figure 10.72 Water temperature sending unit location. The water temperature warning light sending unit is usually fitted in a threaded hole in the cylinder head (courtesy of Ford Motor Company, Dearborn, MI).

LESSON 10–8 Temperature-Sensitive Sending Units

Most warning light circuits that indicate excessive engine temperature are triggered by a temperature-sensitive sending unit mounted in the cylinder head of the engine, as shown in Figure 10.72. Temperature-sensitive sending units, sometimes called *thermal sending units*, open and close a circuit with changes in temperature. The

Figure 10.73 Typical temperature-sensitive sending units used to operate warning lights.

sending unit is positioned so its sensing bulb or element is immersed in the coolant. When the temperature of the coolant exceeds a certain specification, the contacts of the sending unit close, completing the circuit for the light.

Most thermal sending units used in warning light circuits are built to close when the coolant reaches a temperature of approximately 5 to 10°F below the boiling point of the coolant mixture. If plain water without ethylene glycol is used in the system, the warning light usually will not operate, even though the water may be boiling. Proper operation of the system and the warning light requires that a mixture of approximately 50% water and 50% ethylene glycol be used in the system.

Most sending units used to control the temperature warning light complete the circuit to ground and have but one terminal, as shown in Figure 10.73. In some cars, however, the sending unit

Job 101

REPLACE A TEMPERATURE-SENSITIVE SENDING UNIT

SATISFACTORY PERFORMANCE
A satisfactory performance on this job requires that you do the following:

1. Replace the designated temperature-sensitive sending unit in the car assigned.
2. Following the steps in the "Performance Outline" and the procedure and specifications of the manufacturer, complete the job within 200% of the manufacturer's suggested time.
3. Fill in the blanks under "Information."

PERFORMANCE OUTLINE

1. Drain the coolant.
2. Remove the switch.
3. Install the replacement switch.
4. Install the coolant.
5. Check for leaks.
6. Check the operation of the switch.

INFORMATION

Vehicle identification _____
Reference used _____ Page(s) _____
Switch replaced _____

performs additional duties. Those sending units are usually found with two or more terminals (see Figure 10.74). They are often used to control the operation of electric fans, and to signal

REPLACING TEMPERATURE SENSITIVE SENDING UNITS	Temperature-sensitive sending units are easily changed. Since most are provided with a hex head, they can be removed from the engine with a socket or a box wrench. Since the switch enters the engine water jacket and is in contact with the coolant, the system must be drained to prevent leakage and loss of coolant. The following steps outline a procedure to perform the job safely:

1. Drain the coolant into a suitable clean container.

   Note: The entire system need not be drained, but the coolant level must be lowered to below the location of the sending unit.

2. Disconnect the wire from the sending unit.
3. Using an appropriate socket or box wrench; remove the sending unit.
4. Install and tighten the replacement sending unit.

   Note: Some car makers recommend coating the sending unit threads with a sealing compound or Teflon tape.

5. Connect the wire to the sending unit.
6. Close and tighten the petcock.
7. Install the drained coolant.
8. Pressure test the system for leaks.
9. Add coolant if necessary.

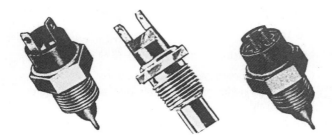

Figure 10.74 Two-prong warning light sending units. Temperature-sensitive sending units with two or more terminals are often used in other circuits as well as in warning light circuits.

computer-controlled engine systems of changes in engine temperature.

LESSON 10–9 Electric Cooling Fans

As shown in Figure 10.75, many vehicles are equipped with a radiator fan driven by an elec-

tric motor. The motor is usually controlled by a temperature-sensitive switch located in the radiator tank or in the cylinder head of the engine (see Figure 10.76). When the coolant in contact with the switch exceeds a predetermined temperature, the switch contacts close, energizing the motor. When the coolant temperature drops below the operating range of the switch, the contacts open, breaking the circuit.

On some cars, the switch merely completes the ground side of the fan motor circuit as shown in Figure 10.77. On others, it operates a relay that sends current to the fan motor (see Figure 10.78).

On air conditioned cars that have the air conditioning condenser mounted in front of the radiator, additional air flow through the condenser and the radiator is often required when the air conditioner is operating. On some cars, the fan motor is energized at all times when the air conditioner is turned on. On others, the fan is energized by both a temperature-sensitive switch in the cooling system and by a pressure-sensitive switch in the air

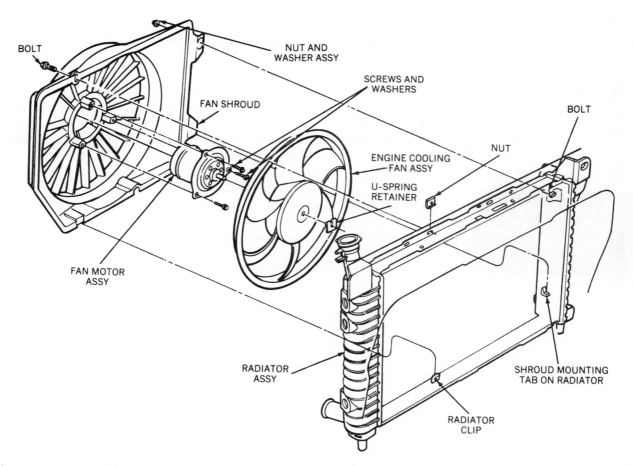

Figure 10.75 Typical electric fan assembly. The fan motor is mounted in a shroud that is attached to the radiator (courtesy of Ford Motor Company, Dearborn, MI).

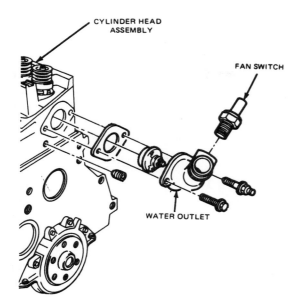

Figure 10.76 Fan switch location. In this application, the fan switch is installed in the coolant outlet connection of the cylinder head (courtesy of Ford Motor Company, Dearborn, MI).

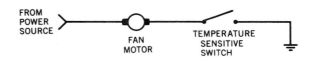

Figure 10.77 Temperature switch schematic. On some cars, the temperature-sensitive switch is placed in the ground side of the motor circuit.

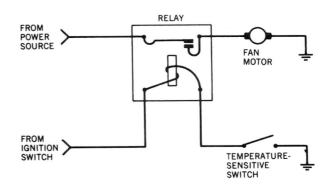

Figure 10.78 Motor circuit with relay. Some fan motor circuits incorporate a relay to actuate the fan motor.

conditioning system. Some cars have a two-speed fan motor to provide the correct air flow for different operating conditions.

> ⚠ **Safety Message 1:** Keep hands out of an electric cooling fan when a hot engine has just been shut off. The fan is operated by a temperature-sensitive thermostat and can start up even when the key and engine are shut off.

On some cars, the fan operates at any time that the contacts in the temperature-sensitive switch are closed, even if the ignition switch is turned off.

> ⚠ **Safety Message 2:** To avoid the possibility of injury from the fan blades, disconnect the fan wire connector when working near the fan (refer to Figure 10.75).

TESTING ELECTRIC COOLING FANS	Several different fan operating systems are in common use, each requiring a slightly different test procedure. The following steps outline a typical procedure, but reference to an appropriate manual is suggested:

1. Check the coolant level in the radiator.

   Note: Never remove the radiator cap when the engine is running. Failure to follow this advice could result in severe burns. It is best to wait until the engine has cooled.

2. Adjust the coolant level if necessary.

   Note: The coolant should consist of a mixture of approximately 50% water and 50% ethylene glycol. The addition of water will dilute the coolant and will adversely affect the operation of the cooling system.

3. Start the engine and allow it to run for several minutes until the coolant temperature rises to above the specified operating temperature of the temperature-sensitive switch. (The specified temperature may range from 195°F [91°C] to 225°F [107°C]).

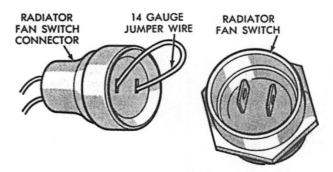

Figure 10.79 Jumper used to check fan switch. A jumper wire can be used to bridge the terminals in the fan switch connector (courtesy of Chrysler Corporation).

    a. If the fan operates, the circuit can be considered to be working correctly.
    b. If the fan does not operate, turn off the engine and continue with step 4.

4. Disconnect the wire connector from the temperature-sensitive switch in the radiator tank or in the cylinder head.

5. If the connector has a single wire, ground the wire with a jumper. If the connector has two wires, use a jumper as shown in Figure 10.79 to bridge the two wires. Turn on the ignition switch.

    a. If the fan operates, the temperature-sensitive switch should be replaced.
    b. If the fan does not operate, continue with step 6.

6. Turn off the ignition switch.

7. Connect the wire connector to the temperature-sensitive switch.

8. Unplug the wire(s) at the fan (refer to Figure 10.75).

9. Using jumper wires from the battery, energize the fan motor at its connector. (refer to Figure 10.75).

    a. If the fan does not operate, the fan motor should be replaced.
    b. If the fan operates, refer to an appropriate manual or wiring diagram and check the wires and any fuses and relays that may be used in the circuit.

FAN AND MOTOR REPLACEMENT

On most cars, the fan motor is mounted on a *shroud* or frame that is bolted to the radiator (refer to Figure 10.75). As shown in Figures 10.80 and 10.81, the entire assembly must be removed from the radiator for service. The replacement procedure may vary slightly with different systems. The following steps outline a typical replacement procedure:

1. Unplug the wire connector at the fan and free the wires from any clips or brackets that may be present.

2. Remove the bolts or nuts holding the shroud or fan frame to the radiator.

3. Remove the assembly from the vehicle.

4. Remove the nut or clip that holds the fan to the motor shaft (see Figure 10.82).

5. Remove the fan from the motor shaft.

   Note: If the fan is cracked, bent, or damaged in any way, it should be replaced. Never attempt to straighten, weld, or otherwise repair a damaged fan.

6. Remove the nuts holding the fan motor to the shroud or frame and remove the fan motor.

   Note: On some cars, the fan motor is not considered a separate part, and the entire assembly must be replaced.

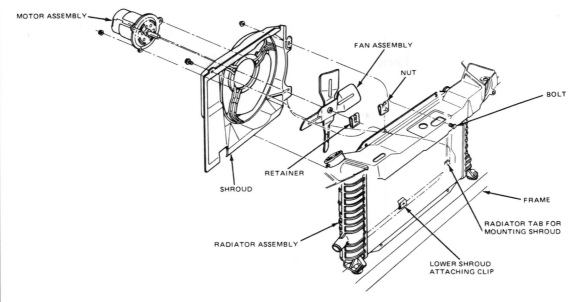

Figure 11.80 Typical fan assembly. An exploded view of a typical fan assembly. In this application, the fan motor is mounted in a shroud (courtesy of Ford Motor Company, Dearborn, MI).

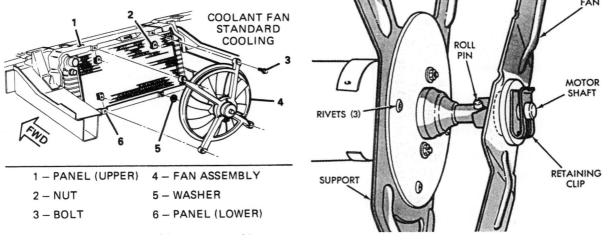

1 – PANEL (UPPER)	4 – FAN ASSEMBLY
2 – NUT	5 – WASHER
3 – BOLT	6 – PANEL (LOWER)

Figure 10.81 Frame mounted fan system. In this application, the fan motor is mounted in a simple frame and a shroud is not used (courtesy of Pontiac Motor Division, General Motors Corporation).

Figure 10.82 Clip mounted fan. On some cars, the fan is held to the motor shaft by a retaining clip (courtesy of Chrysler Corporation).

7. Install the replacement motor in the shroud or frame.
8. Install the fan and the retaining nut or clip.
9. Position the assembly on the radiator and install the mounting nuts or bolts.
10. Connect the fan wires.
11. Check the operation of the fan.

Job 10J

TEST AND REPLACE COOLING FAN CIRCUIT PARTS

SATISFACTORY PERFORMANCE
A satisfactory performance on this job requires that you do the following:

1. Test the parts and wires in a radiator fan circuit and repair or replace the parts required.
2. Following the steps in the "Performance Outline" and the procedure and specifications of the car manufacturer, complete the job within 200% of the manufacturer's suggested time.
3. Fill in the blanks under "Information."

PERFORMANCE OUTLINE

1. Check the coolant level.
2. Check the fan operation.
3. Check the switch.
4. Check the motor.
5. Check to remaining circuit parts.
6. Perform the required repairs.

INFORMATION

Vehicle identification _____
Reference used _____ Page(s) _____
Defect(s) found _____
Repairs performed _____
Parts replaced _____

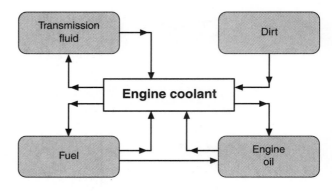

Figure 10.83 Fluid contamination. Coolant can become contaminated by fuel, engine oil, dirt, and transmission fluid. Coolant can contaminate engine oil and transmission fluid. Fuel contamination can be found in the engine oil (courtesy of Training Enterprises Company).

LESSON 10–10 Coolant Contamination, Leaks, and Troubleshooting

Coolant contamination is a serious problem. Coolant and other fluids contaminating the coolant start out being separated in their own closed and separate systems. See Figure 10.83. If they are mixing it means there is a hole somewhere between the systems holding the two fluids apart. This could be a simple repair, or may mean an engine block replacement.

Coolant Contamination

Coolant in the Oil.   This is usually found during a routine engine oil check. When coolant enters the oil, the oil becomes a white sludge-looking fluid. Look for cracks in the engine or a blown head gasket. There is a problem between the engine water jackets and the oil passages (refer to Figure 10.1).

Oil in the Coolant.   This shows up when making a check of the radiator coolant level. Again the result is a white sludge. Look for a crack between the engine water jackets and the oil passages. A blown head gasket can also give this result.

Coolant and Automatic Transmission Fluid. Any time sludge is in the automatic transmission or in the radiator, the automatic transmission fluid and coolant are mixing. When this happens there is a leak in the transmission cooler (see Figure 10.84). This is a heat exchanger inside the radiator. The transmission fluid is circulated through the cooler by lines to and from the transmission. The automatic transmission fluid is under pressure and could be forced into the radiator coolant. The radiator is pressurized when hot and could force coolant into the transmission cooler. The radiator has to be removed and the transmission cooler replaced or the leak patched. Both the radiator and the transmission should be flushed and new fluids installed.

Coolant Leaks

Leaks can occur under pressure or with no pressure. Hoses have a life of about four years. After this, they can crack, balloon, and soften depending on their exposure to heat and chemicals. Look for leaks around the hose clamps and check the hoses for hardness. (Refer to Figures 10.30, 10.31, and 10.32.) Coolant running down the sides of the engine can come from cracks in the metal or from the expansion plugs along the sides. A leak can occur if the head gasket is blown or if the head bolts

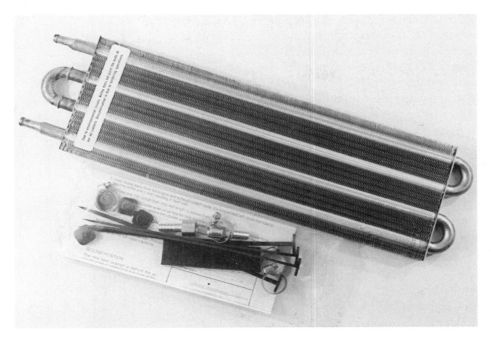

Figure 10.84 Transmission cooler. There are two types of transmission coolers. One is separate from the radiator and the other (Figure 10.83) is part of the radiator (courtesy of Training Enterprises Company).

are loose. The water pump can leak if the seals and bearings wear out. Figure 10.85 indicates some of the common leak points along the coolant system. Coolant running down the sides of the radiator can be the result of holes in the radiator.

If leaks cannot be found by a visual inspection, they are either internal leaks or pressure leaks. You can find these leaks by placing the cooling system under pressure and seeing if the pressure remains steady. A drop in pressure indicates a leak. To see

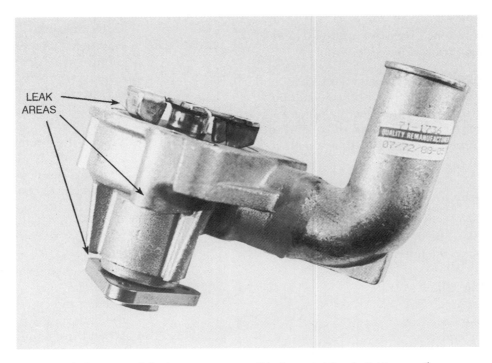

Figure 10.85 Water pump leak areas. A defective water pump will leak around the shaft. Here are the common cooling system leak points (courtesy of Training Enterprises Company).

if it is an internal leak, remove the spark plugs and pressurize the system. If coolant runs out any of the cylinders, there is either a crack or failed head gasket. Fix *all* leaks because the system must be able to hold pressure. Many vehicle operators avoid fixing leaks and just replace the coolant with water. Coolant has lubricants to protect the water pump seals and bearings. It is very harmful to an engine to add water to a cooling system when it is hot. This can cause cracks in the head and cylinders.

Troubleshooting

Overheating is the most common cooling system problem. Check the following items when overheating is the problem:

1. Coolant loss
2. Loose or broken pump belt
3. Mechanical fan clutch not engaging
4. Electrical fan not operating
5. Clogged or restricted radiator
6. Thermostat not operating
7. Restricted air flow over radiator
8. Radiator cap not holding pressure
9. Radiator hoses collapsing

If the cooling system is not reaching the correct temperature, check the following:

1. The thermostat—it could be stuck open or missing.
2. The water pump. Listen for unusual sounds that could indicate an impeller failure.

Check the coolant protection level on a seasonal basis. Coolant should be 50% antifreeze and 50% water. Look at the protection level by using a hydrometer (refer to Figures 10.9 and 10.10) and add additional antifreeze if the protection level is too low.

VOCABULARY

Use the listed words in the blanks beside the sentences to complete the definitions. Either write out the words or place the letters in the blanks.

A. Fahrenheit
B. Hose
C. Coolant recovery
D. Fin
E. Ethylene glycol
F. Thermostat
G. Coolant
H. Pressurized
I. Diluted
J. Antifreeze
K. Hydrometer
L. Freezing point
M. Neutralize
N. Pressure tester
O. Radiator cap
P. Water pump
Q. Heater core
R. Hose clamp
S. RTV
T. Serpentine belt
U. V-rib belt
V. Glazed
W. Thermal switch
X. Ground side
Y. Contamination

_____ 1. Keeps a hose from leaking
_____ 2. Circulates coolant in a cooling system
_____ 3. A 50% water and 50% antifreeze solution
_____ 4. When the sides of a belt are worn shiny and slick
_____ 5. A term for temperature measurement
_____ 6. One type of belt used to drive all accessories
_____ 7. Removable seal at the top of a radiator
_____ 8. When the water temperature reaches −32°F
_____ 9. Chemical used to prevent freezing in vehicle cooling systems
_____ 10. The radiator part air passes around to take heat from the coolant
_____ 11. The base antifreeze is made from
_____ 12. Heat exchanger used to provide passenger heat
_____ 13. Voltage and current path back to the battery
_____ 14. When the chemical cleaning in a cooling system is stopped
_____ 15. Rubber tube used to make paths for coolant

_____ 16. A reduction in coolant strength and protection

_____ 17. Used to capture coolant and re-cycle it

_____ 18. When dirt and oil get mixed with the coolant

_____ 19. Temperature-sensitive valve used to control the flow of coolant in the system

_____ 20. Used to control a warning light when the engine is overheating

_____ 21. Allows the system to absorb more heat

_____ 22. Type of belt used in small radius areas

_____ 23. Tests specific gravity of the coolant

_____ 24. Used to coat the threads of thermal switches to avoid leaks

_____ 25. Places the system under pressure to test for leaks

REVIEW QUESTIONS

The following questions will help you determine if you have accomplished the tasks stated at the beginning of this chapter. If you do not know many of the answers, go back and review the material before proceeding to the next chapter.

LESSON 10–1
1. How hot can an engine get internally?
2. How many gallons per hour does a cooling system circulate?
3. What is the best operating range for the engine coolant temperature?
4. Why is a pressurized cooling system more efficient?
5. What would happen to the engine if the cooling system failed?
6. What is the maximum temperature the combustion system reaches?
7. What causes air to move through the radiator when the vehicle is not moving?
8. What is the normal temperature range for a cooling system?

LESSON 10–2
9. What is the percentage of both liquids in a coolant?
10. What are two causes of a diluted coolant?
11. What tool is used to measure coolant strength?

12. When more balls float in an antifreeze tester, what does this indicate about the protection level?
13. What percentage of coolant is added to water to fix a normal coolant mixture?
14. What does a coolant hydrometer measure?
15. Describe how a cap should be removed from a hot radiator.
16. A 50% antifreeze and 50% water solution protects down to what temperature?

LESSON 10–3
17. What type of material is used to clean a cooling system?
18. How is trapped air removed from a cooling system after cleaning and refilling?
19. What additives are depleted from coolant after long use?
20. What is the recommended change interval for the extended-life coolants?
21. Describe the radiator system flush procedures for the extended-life coolants.
22. What is the purpose of a neutralizer?

LESSON 10–4
23. What could be a problem when the cap markings are used to pressure test a cap?
24. What does it indicate when the pressure tester gauge needle drops quickly while testing a cooling system?
25. Name three parts of a pressure cap that should be cleaned and inspected.
26. Name two types of cooling system leaks.
27. What piece of equipment is used to find cooling system leaks?
28. How much pressure should be used to test a radiator cap?

LESSON 10–5
29. Name two types of radiator hoses.
30. What are some hose problems that can be found with a manual inspection?
31. Can a Perma-Quik hose clamp be reused?
32. What is a molded radiator hose?
33. Describe what happens to hoses with age and heat.
34. What is different about a Corbin hose clamp?
35. Why can't a Perma-Quik hose clamp be reused?
36. Between what two areas should a hose clamp be installed?

LESSON 10–6
37. What is a thermostat?
38. Can coolant circulate through the radiator when the engine is cold?

39. Should an engine be operated without a thermostat?
40. Which way does the operating pellet go in relation to the engine?
41. What is the problem with the thermostat if engine warmup time is extended?
42. Describe what the thermostat does in the cooling system.
43. What happens internally to the rear of the engine block if the thermostat is removed?
44. How is a thermometer used to detect thermostat problems?

LESSON 10–7

45. What two parts are driven by the same belt on most cars?
46. What does the thin profile of a V-rib belt allow it to do?
47. What is belt separation?
48. What is the name of the tool used to check belt tension?
49. What is the normal cause of deep belt cracks?
50. How can oil soak into a belt?
51. Can a glazed belt be adjusted so it will not slip?
52. What is the usual cause of a pulled apart belt?

LESSON 10–8

53. At what temperature does the thermal switch close?
54. What are both terminals used for on a two-terminal temperature switch?
55. If a temperature switch lead becomes grounded what happens?
56. What is another name for a temperature-sensitive switch?
57. What are one-terminal temperature switches used for?

LESSON 10–9

58. Are there vehicles that operate the electric fan anytime the air conditioner is on?
59. Would lack of proper coolant strength affect fan operation?
60. Will grounding the fan switch wire cause all types of fans to operate if the motor is not defective?
61. A switch that completes the ground circuit in a cooling system usually controls what part?
62. Explain why it is not safe to touch an electric fan just after a hot engine has just been shut off.
63. Explain how a jumper wire is used to test an electric fan.

LESSON 10–10

64. What does oil in the coolant look like?
65. How can transmission fluid enter the radiator?
66. How can pressure leaks be found?
67. What tool is used to check coolant protection levels?
68. Describe how coolant changes and what it looks like from oil contamination.
69. Explain how automatic transmission fluid can mix with coolant.
70. Describe what a cooling system pressure leak is and when it occurs.
71. Name some ways coolant can leak into the engine cylinders.

ASE QUESTIONS

Each question or incomplete statement in this test is followed by four suggested answers or completions. In each case select the *one* that best answers the question or completes the statement.

1. Technician A says the life of cooling system belts and hoses is about six years. Technician B says the belts and hoses should be replaced every four years. Who is right?
   a. A only   b. B only
   c. Both A and B   d. Neither A nor B

2. Technician A says thousands of gallons of coolant circulate through a typical cooling system each hour. Technician B says hundreds of gallons of coolant circulate through a typical cooling system each hour. Who is right?
   a. A only   b. B only
   c. Both A and B   d. Neither A nor B

3. Technician A says coolant flows from the top of a radiator to the bottom. Technician B says coolant flows from the bottom up to the top of the radiator. Who is right?
   a. A only   b. B only
   c. Both A and B   d. Neither A nor B

4. Technician A says the fan is used to flow air through the radiator fins. Technician B says air flows through the radiator fins when the vehicle is moving. Who is right?
   a. A only   b. B only
   c. Both A and B   d. Neither A nor B

5. Technician A says the new types of coolants are nitrate and nitrite free. Technician B says the new coolants contain borate and phosphate. Who is right?
   a. A only   b. B only
   c. Both A and B   d. Neither A nor B

6. Technician A says the thermostat is used to heat up the engine. Technician B says the thermostat is used to cool down the engine. Who is right?
   a. A only
   b. B only
   c. Both A and B
   d. Neither A nor B

7. Technician A says a pressurized cooling system allows the coolant to absorb more heat. Technician B says a pressurized cooling system is used to circulate the coolant faster. Who is right?
   a. A only
   b. B only
   c. Both A and B
   d. Neither A nor B

8. Technician A says that normal coolant has 20% antifreeze to 80% water. Technician B says that normal coolant is 50% water and 50% antifreeze. Who is right?
   a. A only
   b. B only
   c. Both A and B
   d. Neither A nor B

9. Technician A says a radiator runs under pressure when hot. Technician B says a radiator forms a vacuum when cooling. Who is right?
   a. A only
   b. B only
   c. Both A and B
   d. Neither A nor B

10. Technician A says the strength of a coolant can be determined by the color. Technician B says a hydrometer is used to determine the coolant strength. Who is right?
    a. A only
    b. B only
    c. Both A and B
    d. Neither A nor B

11. A 16-quart radiator requires how much antifreeze to make a normal coolant?
    a. 5 quarts
    b. 6 quarts
    c. 7 quarts
    d. 8 quarts

12. Technician A says a coolant system leak can be determined by moisture and puddles on the ground. Technician B says a cooling system leak must be found by using a pressure tester. Who is right?
    a. A only
    b. B only
    c. Both A and B
    d. Neither A nor B

13. Technician A says a Corbion-type hose clamp never has to be tightened. Technician B says all types of hose clamps have to be tightened. Who is right?
    a. A only
    b. B only
    c. Both A and B
    d. Neither A nor B

14. Technician A says the best way to remove old hoses is to twist and pull them. Technician B says the best way to remove old hoses is to cut them off. Who is right?
    a. A only
    b. B only
    c. Both A and B
    d. Neither A nor B

15. Technician A says heater hose size is determined by the inside diameter. Technician B says heater hose size is determined by outside diameter. Who is right?
    a. A only
    b. B only
    c. Both A and B
    d. Neither A nor B

16. Technician A says a serpentine belt is tightened by moving a unit such as the alternator or power steering pump. Technician B says a serpentine belt is kept tight by a tensioner. Who is right?
    a. A only
    b. B only
    c. Both A and B
    d. Neither A nor B

17. Technician A says there is no way automatic transmission fluid can enter the cooling system. Technician B says there is no way engine oil can enter the cooling system. Who is right?
    a. A only
    b. B only
    c. Both A and B
    d. Neither A nor B

11 Fuel, Fuel Injection, and Emission Control Systems Maintenance

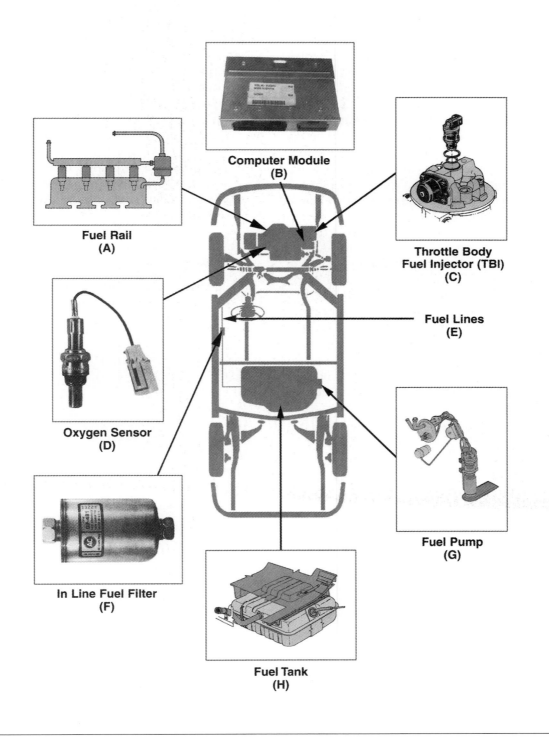

Fuel Rail
(A)

Computer Module
(B)

Throttle Body
Fuel Injector (TBI)
(C)

Oxygen Sensor
(D)

Fuel Lines
(E)

In Line Fuel Filter
(F)

Fuel Pump
(G)

Fuel Tank
(H)

Power in an internal combustion engine is developed by burning fuel in a combustion chamber. Fuel injectors are used to bring fuel directly into the combustion chamber where it is mixed with air and ignited. Vehicle fuel efficiency is measured by the distance in miles or kilometers the vehicle will travel on a gallon or liter of fuel. If the fuel efficiency drops, it is a signal to the driver or technician that something is wrong. The fuel delivery system has many parts (see Figure 11), and all of them must be inspected, tested, and repaired in order to get the maximum efficiency designed in the system. A problem could be as simple as replacing a clogged air filter or as complicated as replacing a defective oxygen sensor.

Air pollution is becoming a problem as it relates to the vehicles moving on our highways. The engine emission control system is designed to reduce the amount of harmful gases the vehicle is emitting into the air from the exhaust. Today's systems use a computer to control the amount of fuel allowed to enter the combustion chamber. The air-to-fuel ratio is maintained as close to the needs of the engine as the technology will allow. This means that the computer needs information fed to it so it can make changes in the fuel delivery. A fuel system with its complicated electronics, mechanical systems, electrical systems, air delivery systems, and fuel delivery systems makes troubleshooting and repair very complicated. A complex system such as the fuel system presents a great opportunity for the service technician. Keeping the system operating properly goes beyond simple maintenance. Solving fuel system problems can be a "bread and butter" item for any service technician.

TASKS

The following are five tasks to master before leaving this chapter:

Task 11–1. Study the internal combustion engine and how it is designed.

Task 11–2. Study motor fuel and how it is used.

Task 11–3. Know the parts in a fuel system and how they work.

Task 11–4. Learn how to service a fuel system.

Task 11–5. Learn to troubleshoot a fuel system.

LESSON 11–1   Engine Operation

An engine develops sufficient power only when it receives the correct fuel mixture. The four-stroke cycle engine used in most automobiles burns a fuel mixture of gasoline and air. This chapter covers the basic operating principles of this engine and its fuel system.

The fuel system stores and delivers gasoline and mixes it with air in the correct proportions. In addition, the fuel system must limit the emissions of both burned and unburned gases that pollute the atmosphere.

Most automobiles are powered by an *internal combustion* engine fueled by gasoline. An internal combustion engine is one that burns fuel internally, converting heat energy to the energy of motion. The most popular type of engine operates on the *four-stroke cycle* principle. Before you attempt to work on a fuel system or any other engine system, you should have an understanding of the four-stroke cycle.

The Four-Stroke Cycle

A four-stroke cycle engine utilizes a piston that moves up and down in a cylinder. By means of

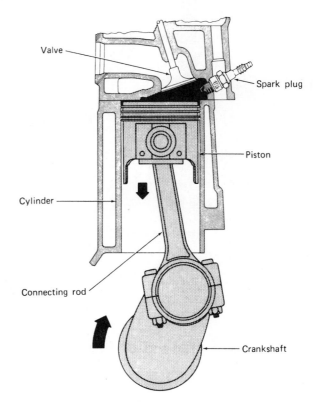

Figure 11.1   The major parts of a four-stroke cycle engine (courtesy of Ford Motor Company, Dearborn, MI).

a connecting rod, the piston is connected to a crankshaft. Through this arrangement, the *reciprocating*, or up and down, motion of the piston is converted to rotary motion. Figure 11.1 shows a four-stroke cycle engine and identifies the major parts. Study this illustration so you will be familiar with these parts.

During each stroke of the piston, the crankshaft rotates one-half turn (180°). Therefore, a complete four-stroke cycle requires that the crankshaft rotate two full turns (720°). Fuel is burned and power is delivered to the crankshaft only during one stroke. The remaining three strokes are required to fill the cylinder with a fuel and air mixture, to compress the mixture, and to exhaust the burned gases.

The Intake Stroke.

The intake stroke starts with the piston at the extreme top of the cylinder. This position is called *top dead center*, or *TDC*. As the crankshaft turns, the piston is pulled down in the cylinder as shown in Figure 11.2. The intake valve opens, allowing atmospheric pressure to push a mixture of gasoline vapor and air into the cylinder. The intake stroke is completed when the piston reaches the limit of its travel at the bottom of the cylinder. This position is called *bottom dead center*, or *BDC.*

All four strokes overlap each other. The intake stroke starts before the exhaust stroke has finished. This is the same with the power stroke. The exhaust stroke starts before the power stroke has finished. The shape of the camshaft lobes determines when the valves open, how long they stay open, and when they close.

The Compression Stroke.

The fuel and air mixture in the cylinder must be squeezed, or *compressed*, for efficient burning. The intake valve closes and the rotating crankshaft forces the piston back up in the cylinder as shown in Figure 11.3. Because the fuel and air mixture cannot escape, it is compressed into a small space between the cylinder head and the top of the piston. This space is called the *combustion chamber* (refer to Figure 11.1). The

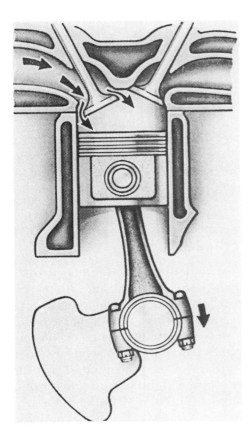

Figure 11.2 Intake stroke. The intake valve opens and the piston is pulled down in the cylinder, creating a partial vacuum. Atmospheric pressure forces the fuel and air mixture into the cylinder through the intake port (courtesy of Chevrolet Motor Division, General Motors Corporation).

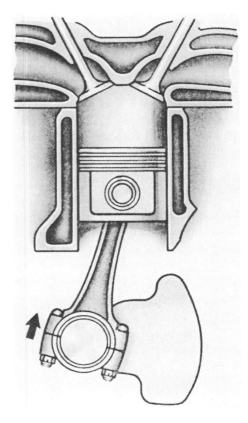

Figure 11.3 Compression stroke. The piston is pushed up in the cylinder while both valves remain closed. The fuel and air mixture is compressed into the combustion chamber (courtesy of Chevrolet Motor Division, General Motors Corporation).

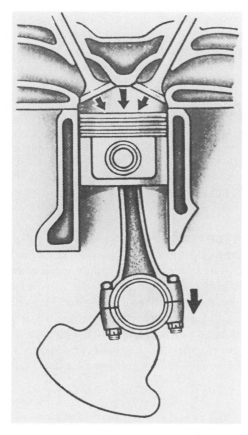

Figure 11.4 Power stroke. The fuel and air mixture is ignited and the pressure created by the burning mixture pushes the piston down in the cylinder (courtesy of Chevrolet Motor Division, General Motors Corporation).

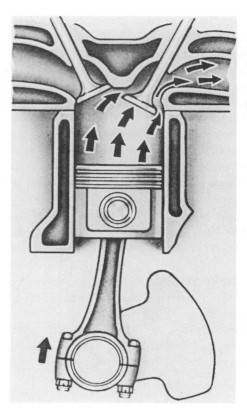

Figure 11.5 Exhaust stroke. The exhaust valve opens and the piston is pushed up in the cylinder. The burned gases are forced out of the cylinder through the exhaust port (courtesy of Chevrolet Motor Division, General Motors Corporation).

compression stroke is completed when the piston reaches TDC.

The Power Stroke. A spark produced at the spark plug located in the combustion chamber ignites the compressed mixture. Both valves remain closed and the expansion of the burning mixture forces the piston down as shown in Figure 11.4. The fuel mixture is completely burned and the power stroke is completed when the piston reaches BDC.

> Some automotive manufacturers produce a two-cycle engine. On these engines the intake and exhaust strokes are combined, and the compression and power strokes are together. Engines like these are widely used in lawn mowers and marine applications.

The Exhaust Stroke. The cylinder is now filled with burned gases, which must be expelled. As shown in Figure 11.5, the exhaust valve opens. The rotating crankshaft pushes the piston back up

into the cylinder, forcing the burned gasses out through the exhaust port. When the piston reaches TDC, the exhaust stroke is completed and the cycle is repeated.

Multicylinder Engines

A single-cylinder engine delivers power to the crankshaft only once during two revolutions. Therefore, these engines run roughly, especially at low speed. The use of multiple cylinders provides a smoother running engine. Most automobile engines have four, six, or eight cylinders. The power strokes of all the cylinders are timed so that they occur within the same two revolutions of the crankshaft. In a four-cylinder engine, a power stroke occurs during each 180° of crankshaft rotation. In most six-cylinder engines, a power stroke occurs every 120°. In eight-cylinder engines, power is delivered to the crankshaft during each 90° of crankshaft rotation.

Job 11A

IDENTIFY THE FOUR STROKES OF THE FOUR-STROKE CYCLE AND RELATED ENGINE PARTS

SATISFACTORY PERFORMANCE
A satisfactory performance on this job requires that you do the following:

1. Identify the four strokes of the four-stroke cycle shown by placing the letter of each stroke in front of the correct stroke name.
2. Identify the numbered engine parts shown by placing the number of each part in front of the correct part name.
3. Correctly identify all the strokes and parts within 10 minutes.

PERFORMANCE SITUATION

STROKES

____ Intake   ____ Compression
____ Power   ____ Exhaust

PARTS

____ Piston   ____ Cylinder
____ Intake port   ____ Exhaust valve
____ Exhaust port   ____ Intake valve
____ Connecting rod   ____ Spark plug
____ Cam shaft   ____ Crankshaft

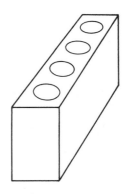

Figure 11.6 Cylinder arrangements of in-line engines.

Cylinder Arrangement

Although many different cylinder arrangements have been used, the most popular are the *in-line* and the *V*. These cylinder arrangements are shown in Figures 11.6 and 11.7. Most four-cylinder engines are in-line. To avoid excessive length, most eight-cylinder engines are of the V type. Six-cylinder engines are built in both in-line and V designs. In-line and V-type engines are shown in Figures 11.8 and 11.9.

LESSON 11–2   Gasoline

Gasoline is a mixture of *hydrocarbons*. Hydrocarbons are chemical compounds made up of hydrogen and carbon. Although gasoline is purchased in liquid form, liquid gasoline will not burn in an engine. Before the energy in gasoline can be harnessed, the gasoline must be *vaporized*, or changed from a liquid to a vapor. When gasoline is vaporized and mixed with air, it is referred to as a *fuel and air mixture*. If the proportions of fuel and air are within a certain range, the mixture burns rapidly and releases a great amount of heat energy.

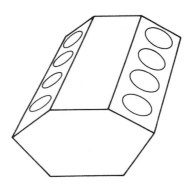

Figure 11.7 Cylinder arrangements of V-type engines.

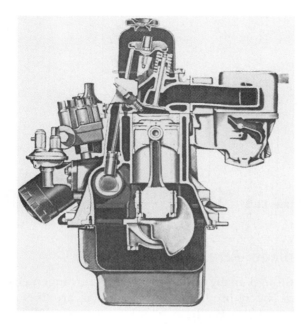

Figure 11.8 A sectional view of a typical in-line engine as seen from the front (courtesy of American Motors).

Fuel-to-Air Ratios

Fuel-to-air ratios are determined by weight. As shown in Figure 11.10, about 9000 gallons of air are required to burn 1 gallon of gasoline. By converting these amounts from volume to weight, the

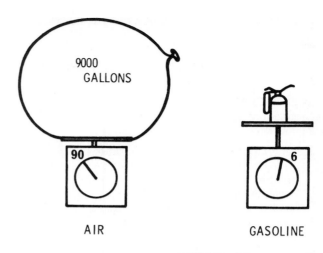

Figure 11.10 Air-to-fuel ratio. Approximately 9000 gallons of air are required to burn 1 gallon of gasoline in an engine (courtesy of Chevrolet Motor Division, General Motors Corporation).

numbers are easier to work with. A mixture of 15 pounds of air and 1 pound of gasoline has a ratio of 15 to 1 and can be considered an average mixture. A mixture that contains less air (or more gasoline) is called a *rich mixture*. A mixture that contains more air (or less gasoline) is called a *lean mixture*. As shown in Figure 11.11, a mixture richer than 8 to 1 usually will not burn in an engine. At the other extreme, a mixture leaner than 18.5 to 1 will also fail to burn.

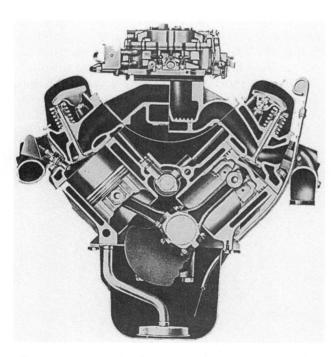

Figure 11.9 A sectional view of a typical V-type engine as seen from the front (courtesy of American Motors).

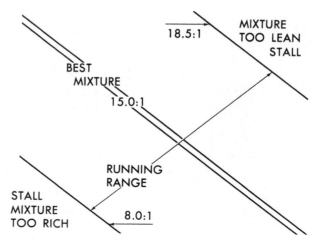

Figure 11.11 Fuel-to-air ratio running range (courtesy of Chevrolet Motor Division, General Motors Corporation).

Rich Mixtures. A rich mixture may be needed at times when maximum power is required. However, the gasoline in a rich mixture is not completely burned during combustion. In addition to providing poor fuel economy, mixtures that are too rich cause (1) the spark plugs to become carbon fouled, (2) carbon deposits to build up in the engine, and (3) the engine to emit polluting unburned hydrocarbons.

Lean Mixtures. A lean mixture is desirable for reasons of economy and because it burns more completely. By burning more completely, a lean mixture emits fewer unburned hydrocarbons, resulting in less pollution. The use of a mixture that is too lean for a particular engine can result in engine damage. A lean mixture usually creates combustion chamber temperatures that are higher than normal. This excess heat can (1) damage spark plugs, (2) cause valves to burn, and (3) cause piston damage.

Detonation

Ideally, the fuel and air mixture should burn at a controlled rate. In this manner, the released energy acts to push the piston down in the cylinder rather than to drive it down. Detonation occurs when the smooth, progressive burning of the fuel and air mixture is interrupted by an explosion. Figure 11.12 shows how *detonation occurs.* When the mixture *detonates,* or explodes, its energy is released too rapidly. This sudden release of energy imparts a hammerlike blow to the piston and can cause extensive engine damage. Figure 11.13 shows a piston damaged by detonation.

> Detonation is detected by the antiknock sensor. When detonation occurs a signal is sent to the computer. The computer makes changes in engine timing and fuel injection timing until the knocking stops. Sometimes the condition can be helped by using a higher octane fuel.

Because detonation is an explosion, it can often be heard. Detonation is usually heard when an engine is under load, such as when a car is accelerating or when it is climbing a hill. Audible detonation is often referred to as *pinging* or *spark knock.*

Detonation results when a fuel and air mixture is exposed to a combination of temperature and pressure too great for it to withstand. Engine design, operating conditions, and even weather

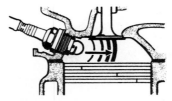

When the spark plug ignites the fuel-air mixture, a flame front moves across the combustion chamber. The burning is controlled and the energy released exerts a push against the piston.

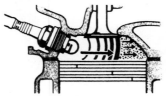

The flame front continues across the combustion chamber and the pressure and temperature of the unburned mixture ahead of the flame front increases.

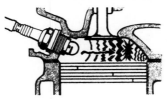

The temperature of the unburned mixture rises so high that the mixture starts to burn at another location. When the opposing flame fronts collide, an explosion occurs.

Figure 11.12 Detonation of a fuel and air mixture (courtesy of Ford Motor Company, Dearborn, MI).

conditions are factors that affect detonation. In many instances, detonation can be minimized by using a fuel that burns slower. Slower burning fuels are usually identified by a high octane rating.

Octane Ratings

The octane rating of a fuel provides an indication of the fuel's ability to resist detonation. The octane rating of a fuel can be adjusted during the refining process by blending different hydrocarbons and by using additives.

The octane number assigned to a fuel is based on the results of comparative testing. A sample of fuel is burned in a special laboratory engine. The antiknock quality of the fuel is then matched to that of a control fuel composed of *isooctane* and *heptane.* These two hydrocarbons have widely differing antiknock qualities. Isooctane is rated at 100, whereas heptane is rated at 0. If the fuel tested has the same antiknock quality as a mixture of 80% isooctane and 20% heptane, the fuel is rated at 80 octane.

Figure 11.13 Detonation piston damage. Piston damage caused by the explosive force of detonation (courtesy of Champion Spark Plug Company).

The octane rating of the different fuel selections is posted on the pump at the station. Higher octane fuels have additives that reduce the fuel's burn qualities and ability to cause knocking. Most fuels range from the middle 80s up to the high 90s in octane value. It is not always true that the higher octane fuels produce more energy. They just react differently in the combustion chamber of the engine.

Gasoline Safety

When gasoline is burned in an engine, the heat energy released is harnessed and put to work. If gasoline is ignited outside an engine, the energy released can rarely be controlled. Gasoline fires have caused staggering property losses, extremely painful and disfiguring injuries, and much loss of life. When working on an automobile or in an auto shop, always remember that gasoline and gasoline vapors are usually present. Observe the following safety rules to help you avoid a serious accident:

1. Never use gasoline to wash parts or equipment.

Job 11B

IDENTIFY THE DEFINITIONS OF TERMS RELATING TO GASOLINE

SATISFACTORY PERFORMANCE
A satisfactory performance on this job requires that you do the following:

1. Identify terms relating to gasoline by placing the number of each term in front of the phrase that best identifies it.
2. Correctly define all the terms within 15 minutes.

PERFORMANCE SITUATION

1.	Hydrocarbon	6.	Detonation
2.	Octane rating	7.	Rich mixture
3.	Lean mixture	8.	Vaporization
4.	Isooctane	9.	Heptane
5.	Spark knock	10.	Gasoline

_____ An explosion that occurs when a fuel is subjected to excessive pressure and temperature
_____ A hydrocarbon that has a very high resistance to detonation
_____ A fuel composed of a mixture of hydrocarbons
_____ A chemical compound made up of hydrogen and carbon
_____ A fuel additive that increases the amount of energy released during combustion
_____ An indication of a fuel's ability to resist detonation
_____ A hydrocarbon that has very little resistance to detonation
_____ An audible indication of detonation
_____ A fuel and air mixture that has an excess of fuel
_____ The changing of a vapor to a liquid
_____ A fuel and air mixture that has an excess of air
_____ The changing of a liquid to a vapor

2. Never smoke while in the vicinity of gasoline or where gasoline vapors may be present.
3. Use care when working on parts of a fuel system. Fuel is usually spilled when lines are disconnected and parts removed.
4. Never attempt to start an engine if gasoline has been spilled on the engine. Dry up all spills with rags and dispose of the rags outdoors where the fuel can evaporate.
5. Do not attempt to weld or braze on or near fuel system parts.
6. When gasoline must be stored in other than underground tanks, it should be stored only in small quantities in special gasoline safety cans.
7. Never refuel a vehicle indoors. A buildup of gasoline vapors will occur. Outdoor refueling allows fuel vapors to dissipate.

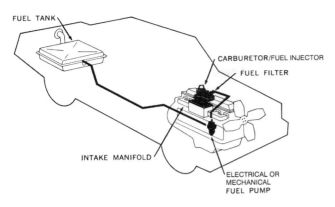

Figure 11.14 A basic automotive fuel system (courtesy of Ford Motor Company, Dearborn, MI).

LESSON 11-3   The Fuel System

An automotive fuel system must (1) store fuel, (2) deliver the fuel to the engine, and (3) vaporize the fuel and mix it with the correct amount of air. In addition, the system should contain devices that filter the fuel, filter the air, and prevent the escape of polluting fuel vapors. Figure 11.14 shows the major parts of a typical fuel system. Study this illustration

so you become familiar with these parts and their location.

The Fuel Tank

Although some plastic fuel tanks exist, most fuel tanks are made of sheet steel. The tank is usually attached to the frame or underbody of the car as shown in Figure 11.15. Most fuel tanks have a filler pipe, an outlet tube, and one or more vent tubes. Some fuel tanks incorporate a fuel return tube. An electrical device using a movable float operates the fuel gauge on the instrument panel, as shown in Figure 11.16.

Fuel tanks on cars that require unleaded gasoline have a restricted filler pipe. The small opening prevents refueling from pumps that dispense leaded gasoline. As shown in Figure 11.17, some filler pipes incorporate a spring-loaded valve. This valve cannot be opened by the nozzle of a leaded gasoline pump.

The fuel tank outlet tube is connected to the fuel line that runs to the fuel pump. The vent tube(s) allow air to enter the tank as the fuel is used. The vent tube(s) also prevent pressure changes in the

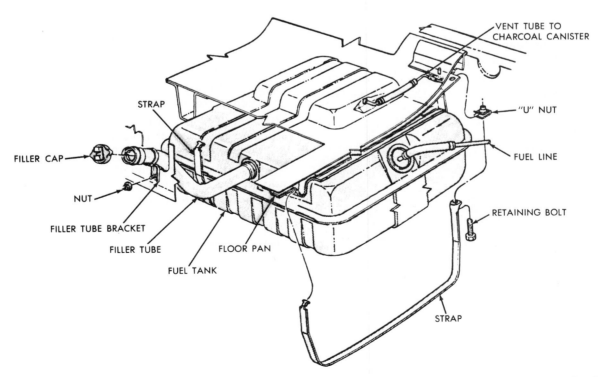

Figure 11.15 Typical fuel tank assembly. Note that the tank is secured to the car's floor pan by straps (courtesy of Chrysler Corporation).

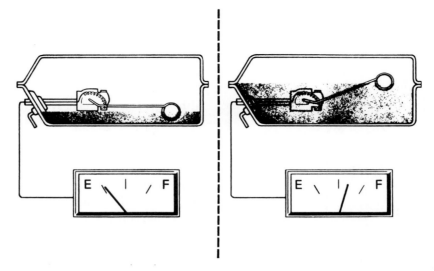

Figure 11.16 The operation of an electric fuel gauge. The movable float operates a variable resistance, which in turn operates the gauge (courtesy of Ford Motor Company, Dearborn, MI).

tank when the fuel expands or contracts with temperature changes.

Maintenance on fuel tanks requires checking and repairing leaks. The vent tube and fuel line have fuel hoses that should be replaced when cracked or hard (see Figure 11.15). When a filler cap loses its seal, replace it to keep the tank under pressure. There is a filter in the tank, and on fuel-injected systems the fuel pump is located in the tank. If the fuel gauge becomes inaccurate the float may have become porous and allowed fuel inside, causing it to not float. The float drops to the bottom of the tank and stays there. Inspect the

straps that hold up the tank on a regular basis for rust and damage. A full tank of fuel is heavy, and rusted straps have been known to fail.

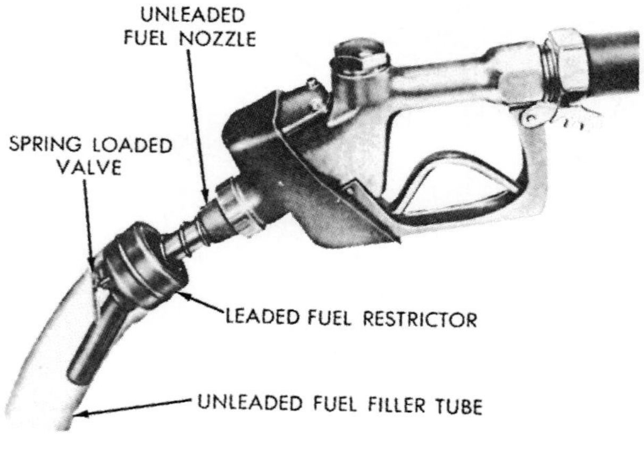

The Fuel Pump

The mechanical fuel pump must perform two jobs. It must pull gasoline from the fuel tank, and it must push gasoline to the carburetor or injection system. Some cars use a mechanically operated diaphragm pump mounted on the engine. As shown in Figure 11.18, a pump of this type is operated by an eccentric on the cam shaft. Most fuel injected cars have electric fuel pumps. Electric fuel pumps are sometimes installed in the fuel line between the tank and the carburetor or injection system. On most cars, electric fuel pumps are mounted inside the fuel tanks, as shown in Figure 11.19. They push gasoline into the injector rails.

The Carburetor

A *carburetor* is a device that mixes gasoline and air in the correct amounts so that the mixture can be burned in the engine. As shown in Figure 11.20, the carburetor must perform three functions. It must (1) *meter,* or measure out, the correct amount of fuel; (2) *atomize,* or break up, the liquid gasoline into a fine mist; and (3) *mix* the atomized fuel with the air flowing into the engine. Carburetors are no longer used and have been replaced with fuel injection on the new model engines.

UNLEADED
FUEL NOZZLE

SPRING LOADED
VALVE

LEADED FUEL RESTRICTOR

UNLEADED FUEL FILLER TUBE

Figure 11.17 Unleaded filler pipe. A filler pipe used on cars that require unleaded gasoline. Note that the restrictor has a spring-loaded valve that must be pushed open by the fuel nozzle (courtesy of Chrysler Corporation).

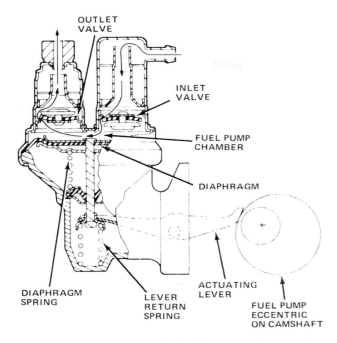

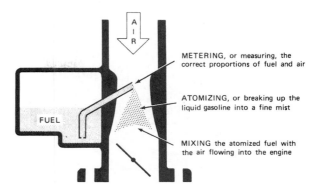

Figure 11.20 The three basic functions of a carburetor (courtesy of Chevrolet Motor Division, General Motors Corporation).

Figure 11.18 A typical mechanical fuel pump. An eccentric on the camshaft moves an actuating lever. As the diaphragm moves downward, fuel is pulled from the tank. When the diaphragm is returned by the spring, fuel is pushed to the carburetor (courtesy of American Motors).

The Fuel Injection System

Most cars are equipped with a fuel injection system in place of a carburetor. Fuel injection, especially when controlled by a computer, offers many advantages over carburetion. These advantages include greater engine efficiency, improved performance, and reduced exhaust pollution.

In a fuel injection system, fuel is introduced into the engine by means of an *injector*, or nozzle-type valve (see Figures 11.21 and 11.24). That valve is operated by magnetism and is opened by an electrical signal from a computerized control module. The amount of fuel injected is determined by the length of time the valve is held open. Two types of fuel injection systems are in common use. They are

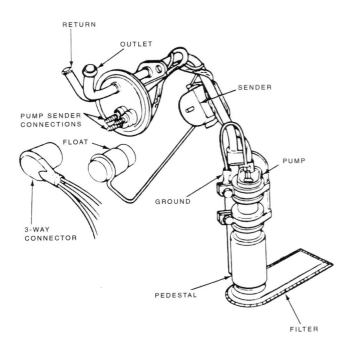

Figure 11.19 Typical in-tank fuel pump. Note that the pump is combined with the fuel gauge sender unit (courtesy of Ford Motor Company, Dearborn, MI).

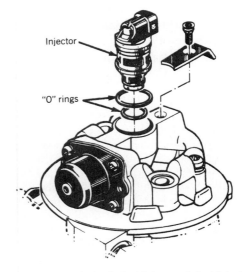

Figure 11.21 Throttle body fuel injector. A fuel injector as installed in a throttle body injection (TBI) unit (courtesy of Chevrolet Motor Division, General Motors Corporation).

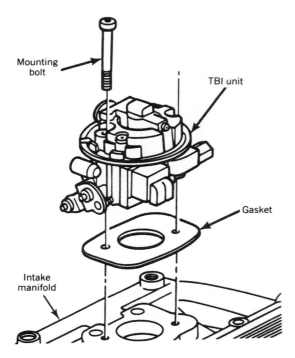

Figure 11.22 TBI mounting. A throttle body injection (TBI) unit is mounted on the intake manifold (courtesy of Chevrolet Motor Division, General Motors Corporation).

usually referred to as *throttle body fuel injection* and *port type,* or *multipoint fuel injection.*

Throttle Body Fuel Injection.

Throttle body fuel injection utilizes an assembly that is mounted on the intake manifold in the same location as a carburetor (see Figure 11.22). Depending on the size of the engine and its design, the assembly contains one or two injectors mounted over one or two throttle plates. The throttle plates are similar to those used in carburetors. They are opened and closed by the accelerator pedal and control the amount of air that enters the engine.

In fuel-injected engines, the fuel is sprayed into the air stream as it enters the intake or at each cylinder just before the air enters the combustion chamber. This mixture of air and fuel is kept in the correct ratio by the length of time the injectors are fired. Information is fed by the oxygen sensor to the computer on how much oxygen is mixed with the fuel. Based on this and other sensor information, the computer either increases or decreases the injector firing time to keep the correct ratio of air to fuel.

Port Type, or Multipoint Injection.

In a system of this type, shown in Figure 11.23, an injector

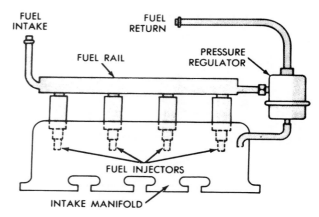

Figure 11.23 Multipoint fuel injection parts. The fuel supply system of a multipoint fuel injection system. Notice that an injector is provided for each cylinder (courtesy of Chrysler Corporation).

is placed in each of the intake ports. Figure 11.24 shows the injector type usually used. As with throttle body injection systems, air flow is controlled by a throttle plate operated by the accelerator pedal.

Fuel Injection System Components

Regardless of the type of fuel injection system, they all contain various mechanical and electronic subsystems. Some of these subsystems raise and regulate fuel pressure, and handle fuel and air delivery. Others sense engine operating conditions, and determine the correct ratio of the fuel-to-air mixture.

Filters

All automobile fuel systems contain filters. These filters remove dirt and other foreign matter from

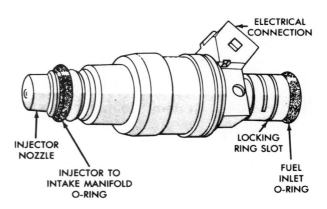

Figure 11.24 A fuel injector of the type used in a multipoint fuel injection system (courtesy of Chrysler Corporation).

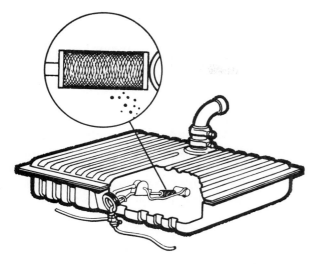

Figure 11.25 Fuel tank mesh filter. Most manufacturers install a mesh filter on the pickup end of the outlet tube in the fuel tank (courtesy of Ford Motor Company, Dearborn, MI).

Figure 11.26 In-line fuel filter. An in-line filter installed in the fuel line between the fuel pump and the carburetor (courtesy of Chrysler Corporation).

both the fuel and the air that is mixed with the fuel. Dirt in the fuel can plug small passages in the carburetor and in a fuel injection system. Dirt in the air can cause abrasive wear in the engine and shorten its life.

Fuel Filters. Most automobiles have at least two filters in the fuel system. A primary filter is usually used in the fuel tank. As shown in Figure 11.25, this filter is attached to the end of the outlet pipe. The primary filter prevents much of the dirt that accumulates in the tank from entering the fuel line. A secondary filter is usually installed between the fuel pump and the carburetor or fuel injection system. This filter removes any dirt that passes through the primary filter. In some systems, a third filter is used to further clean the fuel.

> Air and gasoline filters should be replaced on a regular basis depending on driving conditions. If the vehicle is used off-road in dirt, the filters should be inspected often and replaced as needed.

The most commonly used secondary filters are the *in-line filter* and the *fuel inlet filter*. An in-line filter, as its name implies, is installed in the fuel line between the fuel pump and the carburetor or fuel injection system. Figure 11.26 shows such an installation. A fuel inlet filter, shown in Figure 11.27,

is housed in the carburetor where the fuel line is connected.

Air Filters. Most car makers use an air filter made of porous paper. The paper is pleated, or accordion folded, so that a large filtering area is provided. As shown in Figures 11.28 and 11.29, the filter is contained in a housing mounted on or near the carburetor or air induction part of the fuel injection system.

Pollution Control Devices

It is estimated that about 50% of the pollutants that poison our atmosphere is emitted by automobiles. Most of those pollutants are emitted from the

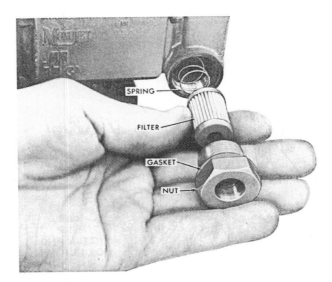

Figure 11.27 In-carburetor fuel filter. A typical fuel inlet filter as it is removed from a carburetor (courtesy of Chevrolet Motor Division, General Motors Corporation).

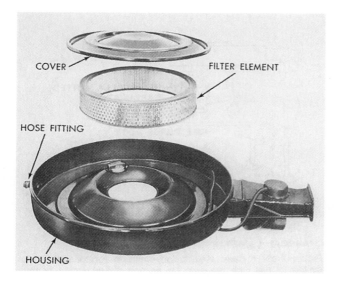

Figure 11.28 An air cleaner assembly used on an engine equipped with a carburetor (courtesy of Chrysler Corporation).

engine and from the fuel system. Automobile emissions can be traced to three sources: (1) engine exhaust, (2) fuel evaporation, and (3) crankcase vapors.

Engine Exhaust Emissions. Engine exhaust is responsible for about 60% of automotive pollution. The exhaust from a gasoline engine contains three products that are polluting:

1. *Unburned Hydrocarbons (HC).* Because it is almost impossible to burn all the fuel in a fuel and air mixture, some, unburned fuel is present in the exhaust. Under certain conditions, unburned hydrocarbons combine with sunlight to form a compound called *photochemical smog.* Photochemical smog is an eye and lung irritant.

2. *Nitrogen Oxides (NOx).* Nitrogen oxides are various compounds of nitric acid and nitrogen dioxide. They are formed when the nitrogen and oxygen in the air are exposed to high temperatures. Oxides of nitrogen aid the formation of smog under certain conditions.

3. *Carbon Monoxide (CO).* Carbon monoxide is a normal by-product of combustion, but it is produced in quantities larger than normal when the fuel and air mixture is rich. Carbon monoxide is an invisible, odorless, poisonous gas.

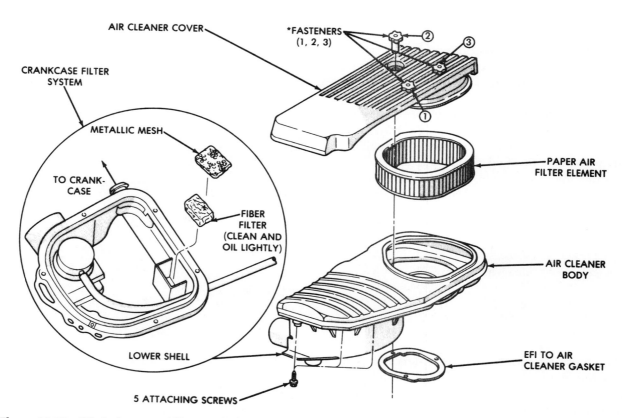

Figure 11.29 EFI air cleaner and filter. An air cleaner and crankcase filter system used on an engine equipped with electronic fuel injection (courtesy of Chrysler Corporation).

Exhaust emissions are controlled by many means. The devices and methods used vary with each engine design. The maintenance of exhaust emission control devices is a specialized area and is not within the scope of this text.

> Engine exhaust emissions are tested by machines that sample and analyze the exhaust gases. All vehicles are expected to meet standards set by the Environmental Protection Agency (EPA). A vehicle that doesn't meet the standards that vehicles of the same year and type are supposed to meet is given a rejection slip and reinspected when repairs are made. If it is found that the vehicle has been tampered with, the owner or technician could face a stiff penalty.

Fuel Evaporation Emissions. Gasoline vapors from the fuel tank and from the carburetor amount to about 20% of automotive emissions. On most cars, the fuel tank and the carburetor bowl are vented into a cannister containing activated charcoal. The charcoal absorbs the gasoline vapors, which are then drawn into the engine and burned. A typical evaporation emission control system is shown in Figure 11.30.

Crankcase Vapor Emissions. During the power stroke, a small amount of unburned gases leak past the piston and enter the crankcase. This leakage is called *blowby* and amounts to about 20% of automotive emissions. On most cars, the unburned fuel and the burned gases are removed

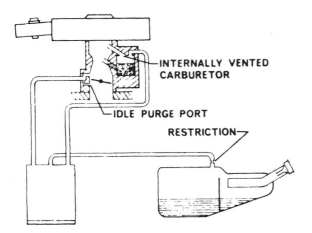

Figure 11.30 A basic evaporation emission control system. A system of this type prevents the escape of fuel vapors to the atmosphere (courtesy of Pontiac Motor Division, General Motors Corporation).

INTERNALLY VENTED CARBURETOR

IDLE PURGE PORT

RESTRICTION

Job 11C

IDENTIFY THE FUNCTION OF FUEL SYSTEM PARTS

SATISFACTORY PERFORMANCE

A satisfactory performance on this job requires that you do the following:

1. Identify the function of the listed fuel system parts by placing the part number in front of the phrase that best describes its function.
2. Correctly identify nine parts within 15 minutes.

PERFORMANCE SITUATION

1. Fuel injector
2. Fuel tank vent
3. PCV system
4. In-line fuel filter
5. Fuel pump
6. Restricted filler pipe
7. Fuel tank
8. Fuel inlet filter
9. Fuel evaporation canister
10. Air filter

____ Stores fuel vapors so they can be burned in the engine

____ Pulls fuel from the fuel tank and pushes it to the carburetor

____ Sprays fuel into air stream

____ Vaporizes fuel before it reaches the fuel pump

____ Cleans the air that enters the engine

____ Stores fuel in liquid form

____ Removes dirt from the fuel as it passes through the line between the fuel pump and the carburetor or fuel injection system

____ Draws clean air into the crankcase and removes the harmful vapors so that they can be burned

____ Prevents refueling from the nozzle of a leaded gasoline pump

____ Mixes air with the gasoline as it flows through the fuel line

____ Minimizes pressure differences in the fuel tank as the fuel expands and contracts with temperature changes

____ Removes dirt and other foreign matter from the fuel as it enters the carburetor

---

by a *positive crankcase ventilation (PCV)* system. This system draws fresh air through the crankcase and directs the harmful gases to the engine, where they are burned.

LESSON 11-4 Fuel System Service

The services necessary to maintain a fuel system are specified by the vehicle manufacturer. Mileage intervals are given for the inspection, cleaning, and replacement of parts. Routine maintenance of the fuel system requires certain knowledge and skills. You now know the major parts of the system and are aware of their functions. The skills required are easily developed.

CLEANING AN AIR FILTER

Within mileage limitations, a pleated paper air filter can be cleaned and reused. The following steps outline a typical procedure. Consult an appropriate manual for the correct service interval.

1. Remove the air cleaner cover. Some covers are held in place with a wing nut as shown in Figure 11.31. Others, as shown in Figure 11.32, are secured with clips or bails.
2. Lift the cover and remove the air filter as shown in Figure 11.33.
3. Using a compressed air blowgun, blow through the filter from the inside as shown in Figure 11.34. By blowing in the reverse direction of normal air flow, most of the dust and dirt will be dislodged from the filter.

   Note: Always wear safety glasses during this operation. Avoid placing the blowgun too close to the filter because the concentrated air blast can puncture the paper.

4. Using a rag or wiper dampened in cleaning fluid, wipe out the inside of the air filter housing.
5. Install the filter in the housing.
6. Install the cover and secure it.

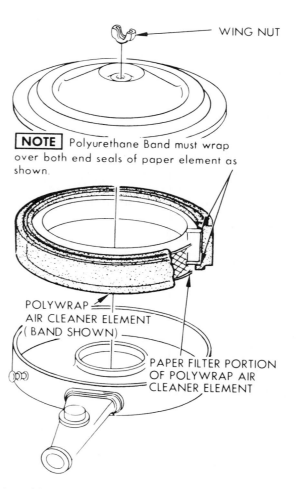

Figure 11.31   Dissembled view of a typical air cleaner. Note that this filter is wrapped with a polyurethane band (courtesy of Chevrolet Motor Division, General Motors Corporation).

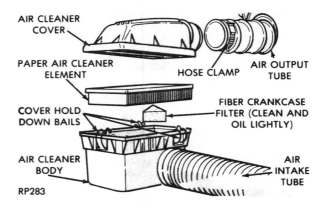

Figure 11.32 Rectangular air cleaner. In this assembly, the air cleaner cover is held in place by clips or bails (courtesy of Chrysler Corporation).

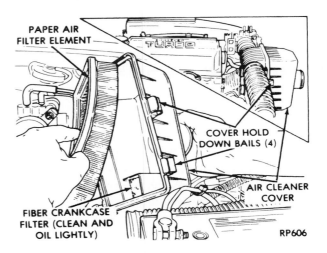

Figure 11.33 Removing air filter. On most cars, the filter housing need not be removed to gain access to the filter (courtesy of Chrysler Corporation).

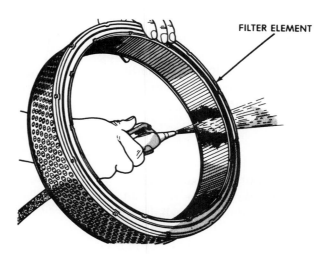

Figure 11.34 Cleaning air filter. The air blast should be directed in the reverse direction of normal air flow (courtesy of Chrysler Corporation).

Job 11D

SERVICE AN AIR FILTER

SATISFACTORY PERFORMANCE
A satisfactory performance on this job requires that you do the following:

1. Service the air filter on the car assigned.
2. Following the steps in the "Performance Outline" and the specifications of the manufacturer, complete the job within 15 minutes.
3. Fill in the blanks under "Information."

PERFORMANCE OUTLINE

1. Remove the filter from its housing.
2. Clean the filter.
3. Install the filter.

INFORMATION

Vehicle identification _____

Reference used _____ Page(s) _____

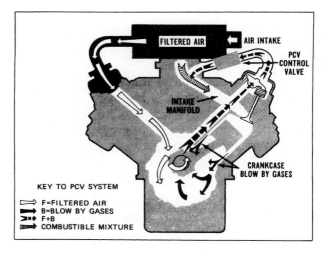

Figure 11.35   The operation of a typical PCV system (courtesy of Chevrolet Motor Division, General Motors Corporation).

Air Filter Service

Air filters require periodic service if they are to function properly. An air filter that is plugged with dirt restricts the flow of air to the engine. In some instances, the reduced air flow causes the fuel and air mixture to be too rich. This results in poor fuel economy and increased pollution. The filter may be damaged or installed so that all the dirt is not removed from the air. If dirt and dust are allowed to enter the engine, they can cause rapid wear of the moving parts.

Air filters should be serviced at intervals of from 5000 to 30,000 miles. The correct interval is specified in the owner's manual or in the manufacturer's manual for the vehicle on which you are working. If the vehicle is operated under dusty conditions, check the air filter at intervals more frequently than specified.

PCV System Service

A positive crankcase ventilation system pulls fumes from the crankcase by using intake manifold vacuum. The flow of air and fumes through the system must be controlled so that the fuel and air mixture is not affected. A *PCV valve,* shown in Figure 11.35, provides this control. The PCV valve is located between the intake manifold and the crankcase. Figure 11.37 shows a typical location.

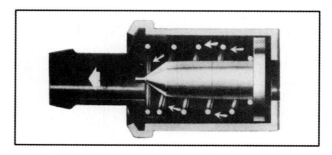

Figure 11.36   A sectioned view of a typical PCV valve (courtesy of Chevrolet Motor Division, General Motors Corporation).

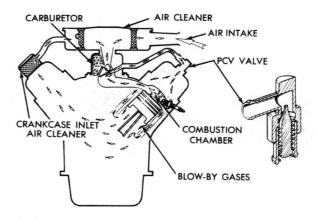

Figure 11.37   The location of the parts in a typical PCV system used on a V-8 engine (courtesy of Chrysler Corporation).

A PCV valve functions in three positions. These positions, described next, are determined by intake manifold vacuum, which must move the valve against spring pressure.

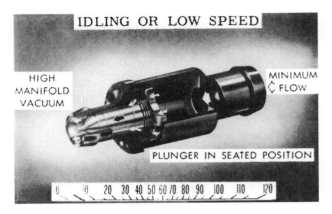

Figure 11.38 PCV valve at idle. When manifold vacuum is high, the valve plunger is pulled off its seat. The nose of the plunger restricts the air flow to a minimum (courtesy of Chevrolet Motor Division, General Motors Corporation).

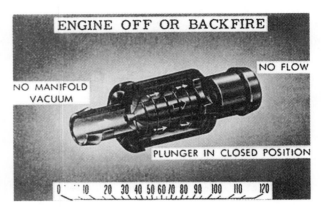

Figure 11.40 PCV valve at engine off/backfire. When the engine is not running, spring pressure closes the valve. The valve also closes when the engine backfires (courtesy of Chevrolet Motor Division, General Motors Corporation).

Partially Open. When the engine is idling or when the car is decelerating, intake manifold vacuum is very high. As shown in Figure 11.38, this high vacuum pulls the valve plunger, or shuttle, off its rear seat. As the valve is pulled to the limit of its travel, the nose of the plunger partially restricts the flow of air. This results in a minimum flow of gasses through the valve.

Fully Open. When the engine is running at higher speeds, manifold vacuum decreases. As shown in Figure 11.39, the spring pushes the plunger back slightly. This changes the position of the tapered nose on the plunger and allows the maximum flow of gasses through the valve.

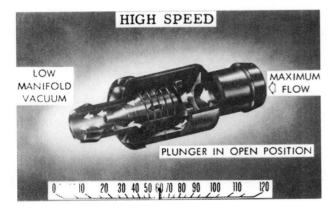

Figure 11.39 PCV valve at high speed. At high speeds, the valve plunger is held in a middle position, allowing the maximum flow of air (courtesy of Chevrolet Motor Division, General Motors Corporation).

Closed. When the engine is turned off, manifold vacuum drops to zero. The spring then closes the valve, as shown in Figure 11.40. The valve also closes during periods of heavy acceleration and high road

Job 11E

SERVICE A PCV SYSTEM

SATISFACTORY PERFORMANCE
A satisfactory performance on this job requires that you do the following:

1. Service the PCV system on the vehicle assigned.
2. Following the steps in the "Performance Outline" and the procedure established by the vehicle manufacturer, complete the job within 15 minutes.
3. Fill in the blanks under "Information."

PERFORMANCE OUTLINE

1. Test the PCV valve for freedom of movement.
2. Test the PCV valve for the passage of air.
3. Test for the presence of a vacuum in the crankcase.
4. Check the condition of the PCV system air filter.
5. Clean or replace parts as necessary.

INFORMATION

Vehicle identification _____
Reference used _____ Page(s) _____
Location of PCV valve _____
Did the valve click or rattle when shaken? ___ Yes ___ No
Did air flow through the valve? ___ Yes ___ No
Did you detect a vacuum in the
   crankcase? ___ Yes ___ No
Did the PCV valve require replacement? ___ Yes ___ No
Was the PCV system air filter dirty? ___ Yes ___ No
Was the PCV system air filter serviced? ___ Yes ___ No

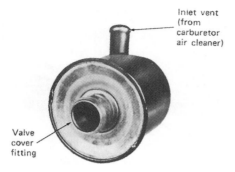

Figure 11.41 Crankcase air filter. An air cleaner used to filter the air that enters the crankcase (courtesy of Chrysler Corporation).

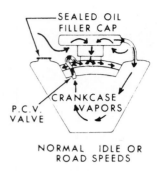

Figure 11.43 The normal flow of crankcase vapors when the PCV valve is open (courtesy of Pontiac Motor Division, General Motors Corporation).

speeds. If the engine backfires, the PCV valve acts as a check valve and closes. If flame from a backfire enters the crankcase, the vapors present could ignite and explode.

As fumes are removed from the crankcase, fresh, filtered air must be allowed to enter. Some systems use a small air cleaner that mounts on a valve cover. An air cleaner of this type is shown in Figure 11.41. Other systems use a small filter fitted inside the air filter housing, as shown in Figure 11.42. In most instances, the air enters through a hose connected to the air filter housing.

All PCV systems now in use are *closed systems*. This means that both the inlet and outlet hoses are connected so that all crankcase fumes are burned by the engine. Figure 11.43 shows the normal air flow when the PCV valve is open. During the short periods of time when the PCV valve is closed, crankcase pressure increases which forces fumes out through the inlet hose. Figure 11.44 shows the air flow during these periods.

Fuel Filter Service

Fuel filters are designed to trap and hold dirt and other foreign matter that may be present in the fuel. Therefore, if a fuel filter is working properly, it will eventually become clogged or restricted. Fuel filters should not be cleaned, but replaced instead. Car makers suggest that fuel filters be replaced at regular service intervals. These intervals are specified in the service manuals, and vary from 12,000 miles (19,200 km) to 30,000 miles (48,000 km).

Replacing a Fuel Filter

In most instances, the fuel filter is located between the fuel pump and the carburetor or fuel injection system. In this location, the fuel is under slight pressure, even when the engine is not running. This pressure causes a certain amount of fuel to leak when the filter is disconnected. Because of the possibility of fire, never attempt to change a fuel filter while the engine is hot. Place a rag or a cloth wiper under the filter to catch leaking fuel before you

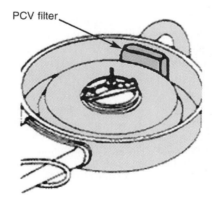

Figure 11.42 Air cleaner PCV filter. On some cars, the filter for the PCV system is located inside the air filter housing (courtesy of Chevrolet Motor Division, General Motors Corporation).

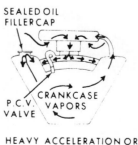

Figure 11.44 The flow of crankcase vapors when the PCV valve is closed (courtesy of Pontiac Motor Division, General Motors Corporation).

**CHECKING THE
OPERATION OF A
PCV SYSTEM**

Three simple tests should be made to determine if a PCV system is functioning properly. The procedures for making these checks follow:

1. Locate the PCV valve and disconnect it from the engine.

    Note: The PCV valve is usually located at the end of a hose that leads to the intake manifold. On most engines, the PCV valve plugs into a rubber *grommet,* or ring, on a valve cover.

2. Holding the hose, shake the PCV valve as shown in Figure 11.45. You should hear a clicking or rattling noise, which indicates that the valve plunger, or shuttle, is free to move.

3. Apply the parking brake.

4. If the car has an automatic transmission, place the selector lever in the PARK position. If the car has a standard transmission, place the shift lever in the NEUTRAL position.

5. Start the engine and allow it to operate at idle speed.

6. Listen to the PCV valve. You should hear a hissing noise as air passes through the valve.

7. Place one of your fingers over the valve opening as shown in Figure 11.46. You should feel a strong vacuum.

8. Push the PCV valve back into its grommet.

9. Locate and remove the inlet air cleaner or hose.

    Note: The cap or hose is usually located in a valve cover.

10. Position a piece of stiff paper, such as a parts tag, over the inlet opening, as shown in Figure 11.47. As the pressure drops in the crankcase, the paper should be pulled against the opening with a noticeable force.

11. Install the inlet cap or hose.

12. Turn the engine off.

If the PCV system fails to pass any of the tests previously described, replace the PCV valve. The tests should then be repeated. If a new PCV valve does not improve the operation of the system, additional diagnosis is required.

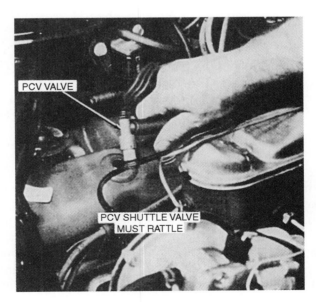

Figure 11.45 Checking PCV valve rattle. When shaken, a PCV valve should rattle. This usually indicates that the valve is not sticking (courtesy of Chrysler Corporation).

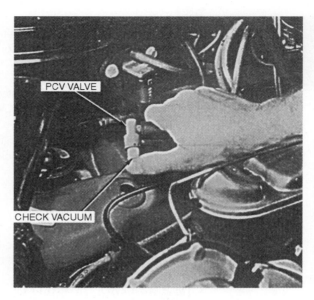

Figure 11.46   Checking PCV valve vacuum. A strong vacuum should be felt at the PCV valve when the engine is running (courtesy of Chrysler Corporation).

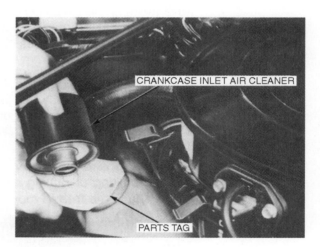

Figure 11.47   Checking crankcase vacuum. Vacuum in the crankcase can be checked by holding a stiff piece of paper over the opening in the valve cover (courtesy of Chrysler Corporation).

loosen any connections. When the fuel has stopped leaking, dispose of the rag properly where the fuel vapors can dissipate.

In-Line Filters.   The typical in-line filter is connected in the fuel line by two short hoses (refer to Figure 11.26). The filter is easily removed by loosening or removing the hose clamps. Many replacement filters are furnished with new hoses and clamps. The replacement of all these parts is recommended for a leak-proof installation.

Most fuel filters are *directional*. This means that the fuel should flow through in a certain direction. To aid in proper installation, in-line filters are usually marked with an arrow to indicate the correct direction of fuel flow. Install the filter so the arrow points toward the carburetor. Some in-line filters incorporate a vapor return fitting, as shown in Figure 11.48. Install filters of this type so the vapor return fitting is positioned at the top.

In-Line Filters at the Carburetor.   As shown in Figure 11.49, some in-line filters have a threaded

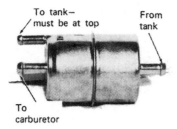

Figure 11.48 An in-line filter that contains a vapor vent (courtesy of American Motors).

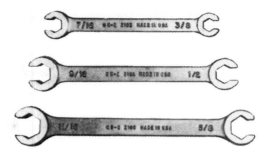

Figure 11.50 Flare nut wrenches. Flare nut wrenches should always be used when loosening and tightening fuel line fittings (courtesy of KD Tools, Lancaster, PA).

outlet that screws into the carburetor. When removing these filters, disconnect the hose before attempting to turn the filter. Carburetor castings are made of very soft metal. Therefore, thread the replacement filter into place by hand to avoid stripping the threads in the carburetor. Use a wrench only for the final tightening. Here, too, it is suggested that a new hose and new clamps be used to complete the installation.

Fuel Inlet Filters. Fuel inlet filters are housed inside the carburetor body (refer to Figure 11.27). The fuel inlet fitting, or nut, must be removed to gain access to the filter. Before the nut can be removed, the fuel line must be disconnected. When loosening or tightening a fuel line fitting, always use a *flare nut wrench*. Flare nut wrenches, shown in Figure 11.50, are designed so that they will not damage fuel line fittings. When disconnecting the fuel line, hold the nut with a large open-end wrench while turning the fitting with a flare nut wrench.

Fuel inlet filters are directional. They must be installed so the open end of the filter faces outward. To function properly, the filter must be held against

the nut by a spring. Figure 11.51 shows the order in which the filter and its related parts must be installed.

Other examples of fuel filters are shown in Figures 11.27, 11.48, and 11.59. Some filters require tubing nut wrenches to remove and replace. Others require hose clamp pliers. Replace fuel filters on a regular schedule. A clogged fuel filter can cause the engine to stall. Other conditions can be a loss of power or a rough-running engine. As the filter pores close up these conditions will continue to get worse.

The threads on the nut and in the carburetor are very soft. Thus the threads in the soft carburetor body are easily stripped. When installing a fuel inlet filter, be sure the gasket is in place on the nut. Then, carefully screw the nut all the way in with finger

Figure 11.49 An in-line filter that is threaded into the carburetor inlet (courtesy of Ford Motor Company, Dearborn, MI).

Figure 11.51 GM inlet filter. A fuel inlet filter and its related parts must be installed in this order (courtesy of Pontiac Motor Division, General Motors Corporation).

Job 11F

REPLACE A FUEL FILTER

SATISFACTORY PERFORMANCE
A satisfactory performance on this job requires that you do
the following:

1. Replace the designated fuel filter on the car assigned.
2. Following the steps in the "Performance Outline" and the
   procedure and specifications of the manufacturer,
   complete the job within 200% of the manufacturer's
   suggested time.
3. Fill in the blanks under "Information."

PERFORMANCE OUTLINE

1. Position a rag to catch any spilled gasoline.
2. Remove the filter and its related parts.
3. Install the replacement filter.
4. Start the engine and check for leakage.

INFORMATION

Vehicle identification _____
Reference used _____ Page(s) _____
Type of filter replaced:
_____ In-line _____ In-line at carburetor _____ Fuel inlet
Part number of replacement filter _____

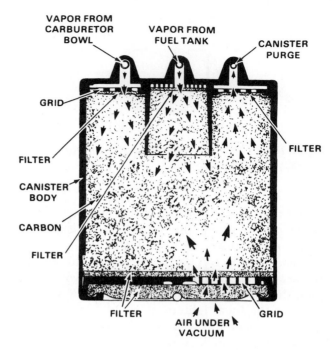

Figure 11.52 Vapor storage canister. The flow of air and
fuel vapors in a vapor storage canister (courtesy of Pontiac
Motor Division, General Motors Corporation).

pressure only. Use a flare nut wrench only for the
final tightening.

Evaporation Emission Control Service

Evaporation emission control systems are relatively simple. Their sole function is to prevent
the escape of fuel vapors to the atmosphere. Vapors from the fuel tank and the carburetor float
bowl are conducted to a vapor storage canister
by hoses. While the engine is running, the vapors
are pulled into the engine and burned. Vapors
that form while the engine is not running are absorbed by and stored in a bed of activated charcoal. When the engine is started, the canister is
purged, or cleaned (see Figures 11.52 and 11.53).
The amount of fuel vapors that are burned at any
time is very small. The burning of these vapors
has no effect on engine performance or on fuel
economy.

Evaporation emission control systems require
little maintenance. An inspection of the hoses
and their connections and, on some cars, a replacement of a filter is all that is needed. Disconnected or damaged hoses could allow fuel vapors to

Job 11G

SERVICE AN EVAPORATION EMISSION CONTROL SYSTEM

SATISFACTORY PERFORMANCE
A satisfactory performance on this job requires that you do
the following:

1. Service the evaporation emission control system on the car
   assigned.
2. Following the steps in the "Performance Outline" and the
   procedure and specifications of the manufacturer,
   complete the job within 200% of the manufacturer's
   suggested time.
3. Fill in the blanks under "Information."

PERFORMANCE OUTLINE

1. Check the condition of the hoses and their connections.
2. Repair or replace hoses as required.
3. Check the condition of the canister filter.
4. Replace the filter if required.

INFORMATION

Vehicle identification _____
Reference used _____ Page(s) _____
Condition of hoses and connections _____ OK _____ NG
Were hoses repaired or replaced? _____ Yes _____ No
Condition of filter _____ OK _____ NG
Was filter replaced? _____ Yes _____ No
Manufacturer's recommended service interval is _____ miles.

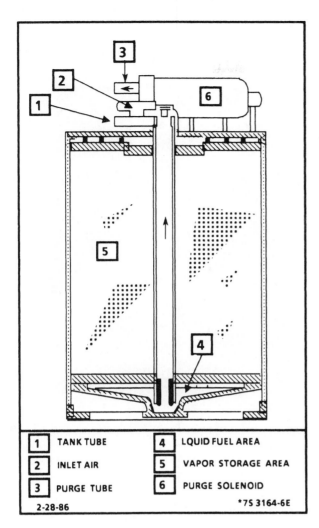

1	TANK TUBE	4	LQUID FUEL AREA
2	INLET AIR	5	VAPOR STORAGE AREA
3	PURGE TUBE	6	PURGE SOLENOID

2-28-86   *7S 3164-6E

Figure 11.53 Vapor canister without filter. Some canisters do not incorporate an air filter (courtesy of Chevrolet Motor Division, General Motors Corporation).

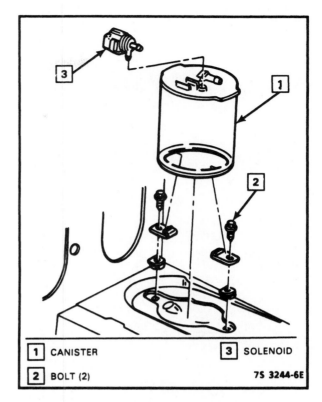

| 1 | CANISTER | 3 | SOLENOID |
| 2 | BOLT (2) | | 7S 3244-6E |

Figure 11.54 A typical vapor storage canister mounting (courtesy of Chevrolet Motor Division, General Motors Corporation).

LESSON 11-5 Fuel Injection System Parts

One of the major changes that has occurred in the automobile has been the way fuel is placed in the engine cylinders. For many years the carburetor

escape. A quick check of the hoses will disclose these faults. A hose with a split end can often be cut back and reinstalled. If a hose is damaged and must be replaced, use only hoses suitable for fuel systems.

Canisters are found in many different shapes and in different locations. Some are made of metal, and others are of molded plastic (see Figure 11.54). Some canisters are fitted with a filter (refer to Figure 11.52). Replace this filter at the mileage interval specified by the car manufacturer. Because the filter is usually located at the bottom of the canister, you may have to remove the canister to replace the filter. Before you disconnect the canister hoses, mark them so you can reconnect them in their proper location. As shown in Figure 11.55, the filter is easily replaced with your fingers.

Figure 11.55 Replacing canister filter. In most instances, a canister must be removed and inverted to replace the filter (courtesy of Chrysler Corporation).

Figure 11.56 Throttle body fuel injector. One or two injectors like this are used to spray fuel directly into the air intake at the throttle body (courtesy of Training Enterprises Company).

Figure 11.57 In-tank fuel pump. An electric fuel pump is used to move the fuel from the fuel tank to the injector rails. The pump also maintains fuel pressure to the rail (courtesy of Training Enterprises Company).

system was the only method used. It got the job done but wasted fuel in the process. With environmental concerns and the desire to reduce unburned hydrocarbons in fuel leaving the tailpipe, the manufacturers had to produce more fuel-efficient engines. To have better control over the air-to-fuel ratios, fuel injection was introduced. By using a computer to control the injectors, fuel economy has improved and exhaust emission problems have been reduced.

Two commonly used methods of fuel injection are throttle body fuel injection and port, or multipoint, fuel injection (refer to Figures 11.21 through 11.24). With the throttle body method, one or several injectors are used to spray fuel into the air intake manifold (see Figure 11.56). Port fuel injection requires the use of individual injectors at each cylinder. Fuel is sprayed behind the intake valve into the incoming air flow.

Fuel Injection Parts

Space does not permit the listing of all the parts for all the systems used. We cover some of the major parts here.

1. *Fuel pump.* This part moves the fuel from the fuel tank to the injector (see Figure 11.57). The pump also keeps the fuel under pressure so when the injector opens the fuel will spray into the air stream. Fuel pressures are critical for fuel injected vehicles and range from 5 to 45 psi at idle. General Motors' throttle body injected (TBI) fuel pressures range from 5.5 to 13 psi. Their multiple fuel injected (MFI) vehicles have pressures from 24 to 47 psi. When checking for fuel pump pressure, look up the exact range for the fuel system being serviced. Sufficient fuel pump pressure is needed to fire the injectors. Most fuel injection systems have pressure regulators that keep the pressure within the correct range.

Figure 11.58 Fuel pressure regulator. Fuel pressure is kept at the right value by a pressure regulator. This pressure is critical and should never fall too low or get too high (courtesy of Training Enterprises Company).

2. *Fuel pressure regulator.* This part controls the fuel pressure in relation to the needs of the engine (see Figure 11.58). Vacuum and a spring act together to increase or decrease the amount of pump pressure. Vacuum lowers when the throttle is opened. Fuel pressure is increased during this time. When the vacuum increases, the engine will be running slower or at idle speed. Fuel pressure is decreased at this time.

> **Safety Message 1:** When a fuel injector rail has to be removed, the fuel inside can be under pressure. Use caution because sprayed fuel is always a fire and safety hazard, especially around a hot engine.

3. *In-line filter.* A 10 to 20 micron (size of the filter holes) filter is used to keep fine particles from getting into the injector nozzles. The filter is connected directly into the fuel supply line and requires tubing nut wrenches to

Figure 11.59 In-line fuel filter. Fuel is filtered between the tank and the injector rail by an in-line filter. This prevents dirt and trash from getting into the injectors and causing failure (courtesy of Training Enterprises Company).

remove. This filter should be changed every 30,000 miles/48,000 km (see Figure 11.59).

4. *In-tank filter.* A woven plastic filter is used to keep dirt and water from entering the fuel pickup tube. This filter requires no maintenance unless the water and dirt in the tank are so severe that the filter is completely covered. To correct this problem, remove and clean the tank and filter.

5. *Fuel lines.* Two lines carry fuel. One supplies the fuel to the injectors. The other is the return line for the pressure regulator. Service requires replacement of any worn or damaged flex hoses and making sure all the fittings are tight.

6. *Fuel injector.* Fuel is sprayed into the air stream of the engine to mix with the air to be burned for power. Injectors are used for this purpose (see Figure 11.60). The injectors are electrically controlled so they can be open for varying lengths of time. This makes it possible for a computer to control the amount of fuel injected.

7. *Electronic control module.* This computer is designed to control the injectors (see Figure 11.61). Several sensors transmit information to the computer. The computer takes this information and controls the injector timing.

   a. *Coolant temperature sensor.* This part (see Figure 11.62), is located in the coolant system of the vehicle and tells the computer whether the engine is cold or warm.

   b. *Manifold pressure sensor.* This sensor provides information to the computer about engine load. Vacuum and air flow in the engine decrease as load increases (see Figure 11.63).

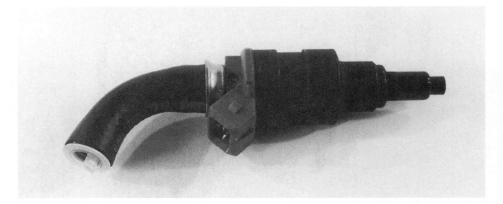

Figure 11.60   Fuel injector. These parts spray the right amount of fuel to be mixed with the incoming air. This mixture is burned in the engine and creates the power to operate the engine. Injector patterns are timed and result in better fuel control and economy (courtesy of Training Enterprises Company).

c. *Throttle position sensor.* This sensor tells the computer where the throttle is set, from idle to wide open (see Figure 11.64). This information is critical to the computer so it can determine how much fuel to inject into the cylinders.

d. *Engine rpm.* The distributor pulses are timed in some engines to determine engine speed or revolutions per minute (rpm). As the speed increases, the time between pulses decreases.

e. *Oxygen sensor.* The amount of oxygen in the exhaust gases is measured by this sensor (see Figure 11.65). This information is fed to the computer and used to determine the length of time gasoline should be injected into the engine. If the air and fuel mixture does not contain enough fuel (lean), the fuel is increased. Fuel is reduced if the gases are too rich.

f. *Distributor hall effect switch.* This unit tells the computer if the engine is running or

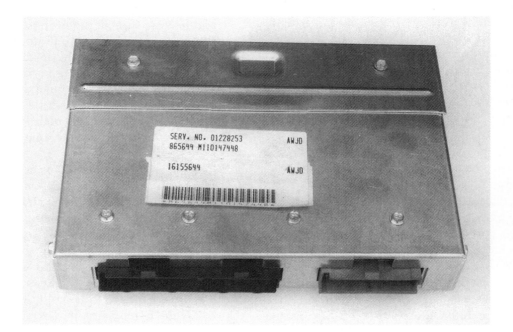

Figure 11.61   Electronic control module. This is the heart of the new fuel systems. Sensors tell the control what is happening in the engine. This information is used to control the amount of fuel injected into the engine (courtesy of Training Enterprises Company).

Figure 11.62 Coolant temperature sensor. Used to tell the computer whether the engine is warm or cold (courtesy of Training Enterprises Company).

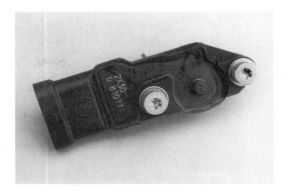

Figure 11.64 Throttle position sensor. This sends a signal back to the computer when the throttle is moved by the operator. The computer uses this information to increase or decrease the fuel injector timing (courtesy of Training Enterprises Company).

stopped (see Figure 11.66). This is an electronic device that emits a voltage signal that is sent to the computer.

When the computer receives the signals from the sensors, the information is used to control parts and units on the vehicle. These can be in the transmission, brakes, engine, and air conditioning systems, and at other locations. A test computer is installed on the vehicle to tell if all the sensors are working properly.

LESSON 11–6　Fuel Injection System Service

The fuel system needs periodic service. Injectors can get clogged or damaged, filters need changing, and rubber parts deteriorate. Some service items require only hand tools, and others require expensive pieces of equipment. If you do not have the

Figure 11.63 Manifold pressure sensor. This sensor is located so it can send information back to the computer about the manifold pressure and air movement (courtesy of Training Enterprises Company).

Figure 11.65 Oxygen sensor. This sensor is located in the exhaust system and measures the amount of fuel in the exhaust. Too little fuel is considered lean and too much fuel is rich. When a lean condition is detected the fuel is added, and when too rich it is reduced (courtesy of Training Enterprises Company).

right equipment, you cannot perform the checks and tests. Make every effort to take training on the tools needed to do the more complicated jobs.

Injectors can stick open, leak, or fail to open. Service involves finding the lifters that are not working or are defective and either cleaning them or replacing them. The scan can help determine fuel system problems (see Figure 11.67).

Trouble Codes

The electronic fuel injection system has a built-in diagnostic testing procedure to help keep it working properly. If a sensor fails, a two-number trouble code will be set in the computer memory. Use a scan tool to discover what codes are set and test how well the sensors are doing their job (see Figure 11.67). Without the scan tool, it would be very difficult and time consuming to determine what information is being sent to the computer and how the computer is reacting.

Figure 11.66 Distributor hall effect switch. The computer must be given information about engine speed. It must also know if the engine is running. This switch supplies this information (courtesy of Training Enterprises Company).

Figure 11.67 ECM scan tool. This computer is used to check out the sensors in a vehicle to see if they are working as they were intended (courtesy of Training Enterprises Company).

Fuel Filter Replacement

The fuel filter between the fuel tank and the injectors should be changed every 12,000 miles. This filter can be found near the fuel tank on some models and near the engine on others. Replace the filter as follows:

Step 1 Locate the filter. It could be in the front near the engine or in the rear next to the gasoline tank.

Step 2 Match the new filter with the old one to determine if the part is correct.

Step 3 Relieve the fuel line pressure at the service port on the fuel rails.

Step 4 Use tubing nut wrenches or clamp pliers to remove the old filter.

Step 5 Put the new filter in place with the flow arrow in the correct direction.

Step 6 Install the new filter and put clamps in position or tighten the fittings.

Step 7 Turn the ignition switch on and check for leaks. The electric fuel pump will start and the lines will be pressurized. Correct all leaks.

Air Filter

Millions of gallons of air enter the engine between oil changes. Small particles and dirt in the air can cause premature wear in the engine if they enter the cylinders. The air filter is designed to prevent this. This filter should be checked every oil change and replaced if dirty or restricted. A restricted filter will prevent air from entering the engine and the fuel-air mixture will be too rich (too much fuel and not enough air). Engine performance will be reduced and fuel economy (miles per gallon) will be low.

Round filters should be rotated 1/4 turn at each oil change. This places a new part of the filter at the air entrance. Inspect the filter with a light (see Figure 11.68), to see how much dirt has been trapped in the element. Replace the filter when the light will not shine through. Anytime a filter is inspected, be sure to clean the air filter housing and not let dirt fall into the air system.

Hoses and Wiring Inspection

At each oil change interval, check the sensor hoses and wiring. Hoses get hard from engine heat and can either crack or break. Wiring connectors get corroded. Rubber hoses should be replaced every four years. Carefully inspect all hoses and connectors. Clean connectors with chemical sprays or by using a wire brush on the terminals.

Exhaust Gas Testing

Testers are made that sample the exhaust gases for unburned hydrocarbons, carbon monoxide, and nitrogen oxides. All the many emission control devices were designed to reduce these pollutants. Any vehicle that emits any of these above the levels determined to be safe by the Environmental Protection Agency (EPA) should be checked to determine what parts need to be replaced or adjusted.

Injector Cleaning and Testing

Injectors are tested by measuring the amount of fuel pressure drop between injectors as they are hand fired. They are cleaned by running a cleaning solution into the fuel rail and through the injector (see Figure 11.69) Injectors should be cleaned and tested when cylinders are not receiving the right amounts of fuel—when they are either too lean or too rich. Injectors should be cleaned first and then

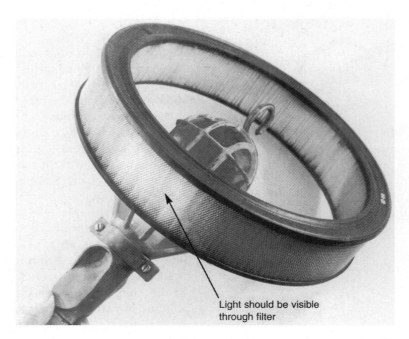

Light should be visible
through filter

Figure 11.68   Light inspection of an air filter. The condition of an air filter can be checked by using a light inside the filter and looking to see how much light is going through the element. A dirty filter will completely block the light (courtesy of Training Enterprises Company).

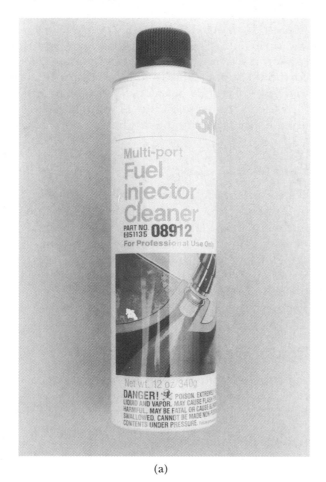

(a)

(b)

Figure 11.69   Fuel system cleaners. Some cleaners are fed into the fuel (see Figure 11.69a), and others are poured into the fuel tank (see Figure 11.69b) (courtesy of Training Enterprises Company).

tested. If they still do not inject the correct volume of fuel, replace them. Consult the manufacturer's specifications for the right injection volume. Follow these steps to clean injectors:

Step 1 Mix up a solution of injector cleaner. Follow the mixture recommendation of the product. Some manufacturers recommend a 95:5 mixture (95% gasoline to 5% cleaner).

Step 2 Disable the fuel pump by removing the fuse or disconnecting the pump electrical wires.

Step 3 Attach the cleaner hose to the vehicle fuel rail at the service port (a covered part that looks like a tire valve on the fuel rail).

Step 4 Turn off the cleaner hose valve and pressurize the cleaner tank to about 25 psi.

Step 5 Open the cleaner tank valve about 1/4 turn.

Step 6 Start and run the engine to about 2000 rpm. Run the engine for about 10 minutes, and for an additional 5 to 10 minutes if needed. If the injectors do not clean up in this length of running time, replace them.

Step 7 Turn off the vehicle engine and close the cleaner hose valve. Remove the cleaner hose from the service port.

Step 8 Close the service port by installing the cap and reconnect the fuel pump electrical wires.

Step 9 Start and run the engine about 5 minutes to purge the cleaner fluid from the injectors and lines.

Once the injectors are clean they will perform as they should or will be either too rich or lean. An injector test will determine which injectors are defective. Run the injector test as follows:

Step 1 Install the pressure tester at the fuel service rail.

Step 2 Release all air in the gauge lines.

Step 3 Turn the key on so the fuel pump puts pressure on the fuel rail.

Step 4 Disconnect the control wires to the injectors.

Step 5 Connect the tester to one of the injectors.

Step 6 Fire the injector and record the gauge pressure drop.

Step 7 Repeat the firing of all injectors. If the pressure drop is not the same for all injectors, repeat the test.

Step 8 Too large a pressure drop means the injector is injecting too much fuel and that cylinder will be too rich. Too small a drop means the injector is too lean and may be plugged. Replace all injectors that did not respond to the cleaning and that will not inject the right amount of fuel.

VOCABULARY

Use the listed words in the blanks beside the sentences to complete the definitions. Either write out the words or place the letters in the blanks.

A. Internal combustion

B. Piston

C. Crankshaft

D. Compression stroke

E. Air-to-fuel ratio

F. Exhaust stroke

G. Hydrocarbons

H. PCV

I. Lean mixture

J. Isooctane

K. Heptane

L. Carburetor

M. Meter

N. Atomize

O. Port fuel injection

P. Air filter

Q. Pressure regulator

R. Charcoal canister

S. Blowby

T. Electronic control module

U. Fuel line

V. Throttle position sensor

W. Oxygen sensor

X. Hall effect switch

Y. ECM scan tool

_____ 1. Point where engine gets rid of burned gasses

_____ 2. More air and less fuel in the fuel-to-air ratio

_____ 3. When combustion gases escape around the piston rings

_____ 4. Moves in the cylinder to compress the fuel and air mixture

_____ 5. Path for the fuel to move between the fuel tank and the engine

_____ 6. Stores the fuel vapors that evaporate from the fuel system

_____ 7. Used to check out the sensors and controls in a fuel system

_____ 8. Part that moves the pistons and rods up and down

_____ 9. The percentage of air to fuel

_____ 10. Measures the amount of oxygen in the exhaust gases

_____ 11. Positive crankcase ventilation

_____ 12. When the fuel is changed into a vapor from the liquid form

_____ 13. Sensor that tells the computer how the throttle is set

_____ 14. Produced by unburned fuel

_____ 15. Unit that controls and mixes fuel with air to be burned in the engine

_____ 16. A fuel system that has injectors for each cylinder

_____ 17. Prevents dirt and dust from entering the engine

_____ 18. Computer system that controls the injectors

_____ 19. When the fuel and air is compressed prior to ignition

_____ 20. A material rated at 100 octane and used to adjust the fuel antiknock qualities

_____ 21. Controls the fuel pressure in the fuel rails

_____ 22. To measure out the correct amount of fuel

_____ 23. Relays the engine speed to the computer

_____ 24. Used to control antiknock problems in fuel

_____ 25. Burning fuel in a combustion chamber

REVIEW QUESTIONS

The following questions will help you determine if you have accomplished the tasks stated at the beginning of this chapter. If you do not know many of the answers, go back and review the material before proceeding to the next chapter.

Lesson 11–1

1. What type of cycle is used in most automotive engines?
2. What type of combustion process is used in most automotive engines?
3. What is another name for the up-and-down motion of the piston?
4. How many degrees does the crankshaft rotate during one stroke of the piston?
5. What are the three strokes other than the power stroke used for?
6. When the piston is at the top of the cylinder, what is this position called?
7. What is the position called when the piston reaches the limit of its travel at the bottom of the cylinder?
8. What is the name of the stroke where the fuel and air mixture is compressed?
9. What are the positions of the exhaust and intake valves during the exhaust stroke?
10. After how many degrees of crankshaft rotation does a power stroke occur?
11. What are two popular cylinder arrangements?

Lesson 11–2

12. Gasoline is a mixture of what chemical compounds?
13. What must happen to the gasoline before the energy can be harnessed?
14. How many gallons of air does it take to burn 1 gallon of gasoline?
15. What is the ideal or best mixture of gasoline to air for maximum efficiency?
16. Below what value will the gasoline-to-air mixture fail to burn?
17. What are three problems that occur when the gasoline-to-air mixture is too lean?
18. What is the ratio of gasoline to air of a too rich mixture?
19. What is detonation?
20. What are the two compounds used to determine the octane rating of a fuel?
21. Why is using gasoline to wash parts a bad practice?

Lesson 11–3

22. What three things should an automotive fuel system do?
23. What is the material used to make most fuel tanks?
24. What two things do the fuel tank vent tubes do?
25. What are the three jobs that a carburetor performs?

26. What are the two most common types of fuel injection systems in use?
27. In a fuel injection system what determines the amount of fuel injected?
28. What controls the air flow in a fuel injection system?
29. What is the name of the part that prevents dirt from entering the injectors?
30. What are two commonly used secondary fuel filters?
31. What material is used to make an air filter element?
32. Automobiles cause what estimated percentage of air pollution?
33. What are the three sources of automotive emissions?
34. What are the three products from gasoline engine exhausts that are considered pollutants?
35. Where is the fuel tank and carburetor bowl vented?
36. When gases leak by the piston and enter the crankcase, what are they called?

Lesson 11–4

37. What happens to the fuel-to-air mixture when the air filter is plugged?
38. What is used to clean dust and dirt from an air filter?
39. Between what parts is the PCV valve located?
40. What is the PCV valve operation when the engine is at idle?
41. When the engine is at high speed what is the PCV valve operation?
42. What is meant by the term *closed PCV system?*
43. Should fuel filters be cleaned or replaced?
44. Between what parts are fuel filters located?
45. When is it a safety risk to try and replace a fuel filter?
46. For correct installation what should be done to a fuel filter?
47. How should a fuel filter with a vapor return fitting be installed?
48. What caution should be followed before removing or replacing an in-line threaded filter?
49. What is the name of the tool used to remove or install a fuel line fitting?
50. What is the purpose of an evaporation emission control system?
51. What two areas supply vapors to the vapor storage canister?
52. Where is the filter located on the vapor storage canister?

Lesson 11–5

53. What are two commonly used methods of fuel injection?
54. What is the name of the part that places the fuel under pressure in an injection system?
55. Where is the fuel pump located in fuel injected systems?
56. When vacuum is high, what happens to the injector pressure?
57. What controls the fuel pressure?
58. What are the size of the filter holes on an in-line fuel injection system filter?
59. What keeps dirt from entering the fuel pump?
60. What are the purposes of the two lines that carry fuel between the injector system and the fuel tank?
61. What does the oxygen sensor do?
62. What does the hall effect switch do?
63. What is the purpose of the scan tool?
64. How often should a fuel filter be replaced?
65. Why should round air filters be rotated after being checked?
66. How often should rubber fuel hoses be changed?
67. On an injector test, what does too little a pressure drop mean?

Lesson 11–6

68. How can an electronic fuel system tell if a sensor has failed?
69. How should a new filter be installed?
70. What are three exhaust gases that can be detected by machine?
71. What test is made to see if injectors are working correctly?
72. What has to be done to the fuel pump if using a pressure injector cleaner?

ASE Questions

Each question or incomplete statement in this exercise is followed by four suggested answers or completions. In each case select the *one* that best answers the question or completes the statement.

1. Technician A says the automotive engine uses external combustion to operate. Technician B says the automotive engine uses internal combustion to operate. Who is right?
   a. A only   b. B only
   c. Both A and B   d. Neither A nor B

2. Technician A says the intake stroke starts at TDC (top dead center). Technician B says the intake stroke starts at BDC (bottom dead center). Who is right?
   a. A only
   b. B only
   c. Both A and B
   d. Neither A nor B

3. Technician A says that during two strokes, both valves are closed. Technician B says that there are two strokes when a valve is open. Who is right?
   a. A only
   b. B only
   c. Both A and B
   d. Neither A nor B

4. Technician A says a single cylinder delivers power to the crankshaft every revolution. Technician B says a single cylinder engine delivers power only once every two crankshaft revolutions. Who is right?
   a. A only
   b. B only
   c. Both A and B
   d. Neither A nor B

5. Technician A says that most fuel injection systems have the fuel pump inside the fuel tank. Technician B says that most fuel injection systems have the fuel pump operated by the engine camshaft and it is bolted to the side of the engine. Who is right?
   a. A only
   b. B only
   c. Both A and B
   d. Neither A nor B

6. Technician A says most in-line fuel filters have filter material with holes measured from 5 to 8 microns. Technician B says most in-line filters have filter material with holes from 15 to 30 microns. Who is right?
   a. A only
   b. B only
   c. Both A and B
   d. Neither A nor B

7. Technician A says that no vacuum should be felt on the end of a PCV valve while the engine is at idle. Technician B says that a strong vacuum pull should be felt on the end of a PCV valve while the engine is at idle. Who is right?
   a. A only
   b. B only
   c. Both A and B
   d. Neither A nor B

8. Technician A says that an in-line filter is directional. Technician B says that fuel filters are made so they can be installed in either direction. Who is right?
   a. A only
   b. B only
   c. Both A and B
   d. Neither A nor B

9. Technician A says that most blowby comes from compression leaks around the valves and guides. Technician B says that most blowby comes from compression leaks around the piston and rings. Who is right?
   a. A only
   b. B only
   c. Both A and B
   d. Neither A nor B

10. Technician A says air filters are made of paper. Technician B says air filters are made of charcoal. Who is right?
    a. A only
    b. B only
    c. Both A and B
    d. Neither A nor B

11. Technician A says automotive pollution comes from unburned hydrocarbons. Technician B says automotive pollution comes from nitrogen oxides. Who is right?
    a. A only
    b. B only
    c. Both A and B
    d. Neither A nor B

12. Technician A says the restrictor in the gasoline filler pipe prevents dirt and dust from entering the tank during refueling. Technician B says the restrictor prevents the adding of unleaded gasoline to the tank. Who is right?
    a. A only
    b. B only
    c. Both A and B
    d. Neither A nor B

13. Technician A says that a gasoline float with a hole in it makes the fuel gauge read empty even if the tank is full. Technician B says a float with a hole in it makes the gauge read full when the tank is empty. Who is right?
    a. A only
    b. B only
    c. Both A and B
    d. Neither A nor B

14. Technician A says it takes about 900 gallons of air to burn 1 gallon of gasoline. Technician B says it takes about 9000 gallons of air to burn 1 gallon of gasoline. Who is right?
    a. A only
    b. B only
    c. Both A and B
    d. Neither A nor B

15. Technician A says that weather conditions can cause detonation in an engine. Technician B says that detonation is caused by operating conditions. Who is right?
    a. A only
    b. B only
    c. Both A and B
    d. Neither A nor B

16. Technician A says a mixture of 8% air to 1% gasoline will explode rather than burn. Technician B says a mixture leaner than 18.5% air to 1% gasoline will damage the engine. Who is right?
    a. A only
    b. B only
    c. Both A and B
    d. Neither A nor B

12 Exhaust System Maintenance

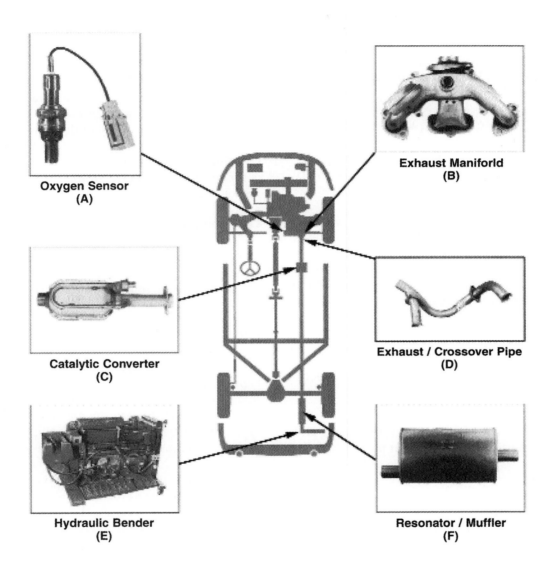

Oxygen Sensor
(A)

Exhaust Maniforld
(B)

Catalytic Converter
(C)

Exhaust / Crossover Pipe
(D)

Hydraulic Bender
(E)

Resonator / Muffler
(F)

The exhaust system (see Figure 12) performs many functions. It carries burned exhaust gases away from the engine and out the rear of the vehicle. Mufflers placed in the system reduce the engine noise. The catalytic converter cuts down on harmful pollutants that damage the environment. An oxygen sensor located in the exhaust manifold helps the computer gather information about the oxygen content of the exhaust flow. This information is used to regulate the timing of the fuel injectors. Most states require an exhaust system inspection to find rusted-out parts and converter damage. Parts of the exhaust system, such as the converter, should be in place and working to help reduce exhaust gas emissions.

If holes develop in the exhaust system that allow exhaust gases into the passenger compartment, all who are in the car are at risk from carbon monoxide.

One of the joys of today is to listen to great stereo and tape players as you roll along the highway. A rusted-out muffler would make it difficult to hear over the loud background noise. In fact, there are ordinances against too much vehicle noise and the vehicle owner could receive a ticket for a defective exhaust system.

TASKS

The following are seven tasks to master before leaving this chapter:

Task 12-1. Know what an exhaust system is and be able to identify the component parts.

Task 12-2. Learn exhaust system safety practices.

Task 12-3. Learn how to service a catalytic converter.

Task 12-4. Learn how to test and replace an oxygen sensor.

Task 12-5. Learn how to service an exhaust system.

Task 12-6. Learn how to test and replace exhaust system parts.

Task 12-7. Learn what the different exhaust smoke colors mean.

LESSON 12–1   The Exhaust System

The exhaust system carries the burned gases from the engine out the rear of the vehicle. The muffler keeps noise down and prevents the engine sounds from disturbing the passengers. The last job for the exhaust system is to reduce exhaust emissions. We describe the complete exhaust system here.

Exhaust System Parts

Exhaust Manifold. As the engine burns the fuel, exhaust leaves the engine, going directly into a manifold, which funnels all the individual cylinder exhausts down to one pipe (see Figure 12.1). One emission control part located in the manifold is the oxygen sensor. We go into detail about the sensor later.

Crossover Pipe. On a V-6 or a V-8 engine, a *crossover* pipe is needed to bring the exhaust gases from each side of the engine into one pipe. When vehicles are modified to have dual exhausts, the crossover pipe is removed and separate exhaust systems installed for each side (see Figure 12.2).

Catalytic Converter. To remove some of the harmful gases given off by the engine, a catalytic converter is installed in the system (see Figure 12.3). A catalyst is placed inside a muffler-shaped container and the exhaust gases have to go over the catalyst. The poison gases are changed to harmless materials. Vehicles so equipped do not pollute the air as much as did earlier ones.

Muffler. The internal combustion engine is very noisy. To reduce the noise, a muffler is placed in the system (see Figure 12.4). As the sound moves into the muffler, it moves into a series of baffles. This reduces the noise and makes the vehicle more pleasant for those inside and around the vehicle. The passengers can carry on a conversation or listen to music without having engine sounds interfere.

Resonator. As the engine speed increases and decreases, there are points where the sound *resonates,* or echoes. This can be very annoying to the driver and passengers, so a mufflerlike device called a *resonator* is installed in the exhaust system, which prevents the echo (see Figure 12.5).

Tailpipe and Hangers. The tailpipe carrier the sound and exhaust to the rear of the vehicle. This is a large-diameter steel pipe bent to go around

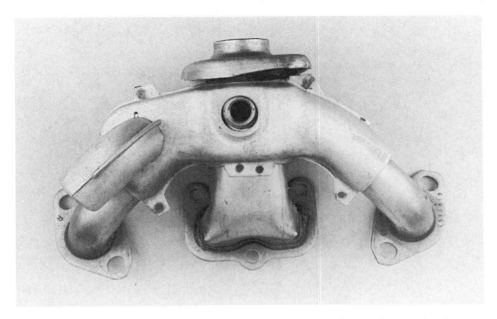

Figure 12.1 Exhaust manifold. This part is bolted to the engine with a gasket seal. V6 and V8 engines have a manifold on each bank (courtesy of Training Enterprises Company).

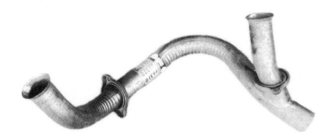

Figure 12.2 Crossover pipe. This part attaches to the manifolds of a V-6 or V-8 engine and funnels the exhaust into one pipe leading to the rear (courtesy of Training Enterprises Company).

obstacles under the vehicle (see Figure 12.6). The tailpipe is kept in place by hangers. These are rubber-mounted parts that suspend the pipe under the vehicle and don't allow it to touch the body parts. The motor moves as torque is applied. This causes the exhaust system to move. The hangers prevent the tailpipe from making noise against anything along the exhaust path.

Oxygen Sensor.   The computer has to know how rich or lean the gasoline mixture is in the exhaust flow. A special sensor called an oxygen sensor (see

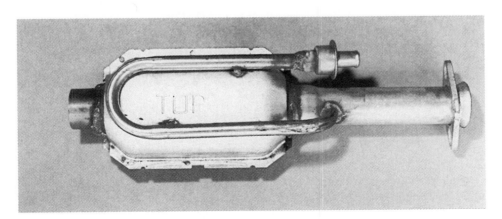

Figure 12.3   Catalytic converter. The converter is designed to change harmful exhaust gases into harmless gases. It does this by forcing the gases through a catalyst (courtesy of Training Enterprises Company).

Figure 12.4   Muffler. Welded or clamped in the exhaust system is a muffler. This part is designed to reduce the noise made when the fuel mixture is exploded in the engine combustion chamber (courtesy of Training Enterprises Company).

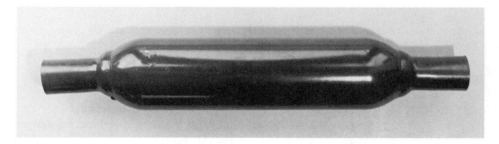

Figure 12.5   Resonator. This part is made to reduce resonate noise made when the engine exhaust noise reaches certain levels. Resonating sound can be very annoying (courtesy of Training Enterprises Company).

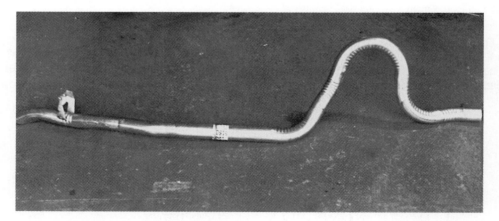

Figure 12.6   Tailpipe. This pipe carries the exhaust and sound out the rear of the engine. The pipe is kept in place by hangers (courtesy of Training Enterprises Company).

Figure 12.7) is installed in the exhaust flow at the exhaust manifold. As the mixture becomes lean or rich, a voltage signal is sent to the computer. The computer uses this information to control the amount of fuel injected into the cylinders. We discuss the oxygen sensor in detail in Lesson 12–4.

LESSON 12–2   Exhaust System Safety

Carbon Monoxide

This gas, a component of automobile exhaust, cannot be seen or smelled. A person breathing it

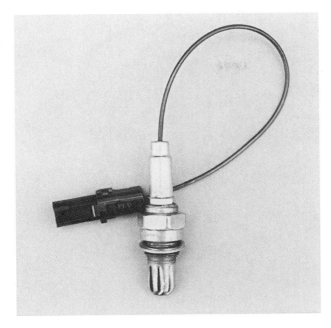

Figure 12.7 Oxygen sensor. This sensor is placed in the exhaust flow to detect the amount of oxygen in the gases. This information is sent to the computer and used to control the fuel injectors (courtesy of Training Enterprises Company).

will soon lose consciousness and die from lack of oxygen. The danger from this gas makes exhaust leaks very serious. Carbon monoxide allowed to enter the passenger compartment could cause all who are there to lose their lives. There have been cases where drivers have been overcome just enough to be involved in an accident. When vehicles are operated in closed areas, carbon monoxide fills the room and displaces the oxygen. As a result, all people that stay in the room either get very sick or soon die.

Heat and Fire

The exhaust system and the converter get very hot. If the vehicle is parked over a pile of leaves or some paper, there could be enough heat to ignite these materials. The manifold, crossover pipe, oxygen sensor, and converter get hotter than the rest of the system, as they are located closer to the engine where the heat is produced. Let a vehicle cool before starting to work around exhaust system parts. Many technicians have received very serious burns when they got careless and touched hot exhaust areas.

Other Gases

Most of the recent changes in the engine area have been to reduce the amounts of harmful gases produced by the automobile engine. Nitrogen oxides, hydrocarbons, and carbon monoxide are three gases that are being reduced. The gases are changed as follows:

1. Nitrogen oxides are changed to nitrogen and water.
2. Carbon monoxide is changed to carbon dioxide.
3. Hydrocarbons are changed to oxygen and water.

LESSON 12-3 Catalytic Converter Service

The catalytic converter is welded into the exhaust system so it is only serviced when it has a major problem (refer to Figure 12.3). Converters experience three major problems. The catalyst gets damaged, the converter gets stopped up, and both the inside and outside rust out.

Major catalyst damage can occur when the wrong fuel is burned in the engine. It is very important that only unleaded fuel be used in the engine. Leaded fuel coats the pellets in the converter. The catalyst can no longer react and remove the pollutants from the exhaust. The result is a converter that has to be repaired or replaced.

Over time the catalyst becomes used up and is no longer effective. In some cases the catalyst melts together and clogs the passages that allow the exhaust to flow through the converter. This problem has to be repaired immediately because the engine cannot develop power or the vehicle cannot reach road speeds.

Rusted-out internal and external converter parts require replacement of the converter. There is only one type of converter that can be serviced. In the pellet-type converter, there is a way that the pellets can be replaced when needed. A converter that has been in service a long period of time usually has internal rust, and replacement of the catalyst would only be a temporary solution to the problem. It may not be economical to replace the catalyst in an old unit.

LESSON 12-4 Oxygen Sensor

A very important emission control part is located in the exhaust manifold. This is the oxygen sensor (refer to Figure 12.7). It helps the computer to regulate the amount of fuel being injected into the engine cylinders, by telling the computer how much fuel and oxygen is present in the exhaust.

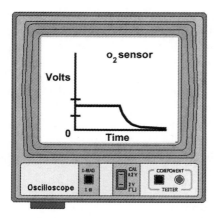

Figure 12.8 Oxygen sensor signal in relation to time. This shows how a typical oxygen sensor would vary the signal voltage to the computer in relation to time (courtesy of Training Enterprise Company).

Figure 12.9 A typical scan tool. Tools like this are needed to check the sensor operation in a vehicle (courtesy of Training Enterprises Company).

The oxygen sensor reacts to changes in the fuel mixture, especially the changes in the amount of oxygen in the exhaust flow. The oxygen sensor has to first get up to a temperature of about 315°C (600°F) to begin working. If the exhaust gas is lean (more oxygen to fuel) a very low voltage signal is sent to the computer. This voltage can be as low as 0.10 volt and as high as 0.45 volt.

A rich exhaust gas mixture causes a high voltage signal (from 0.45 volt up to 1 volt) to be sent to the computer. As the computer changes the injection time, the oxygen content in the exhaust flow changes, the signal voltage constantly changes, and the computer reacts. Figure 12.8 shows how a typical oxygen signal would change in relation to time.

Trouble codes

We are going to look at the General Motors method of telling the technician when a problem exists. When the oxygen sensor does not respond as it should, the computer detects this and a *trouble code* is set in the computer memory. If the exhaust flow stays too lean for at least 60 seconds, a code 44 is set. If the oxygen sensor voltage stays between 0.3 and 0.6 volt too long, a code 13 is set. Voltage that stays above 0.7 volt at least 30 seconds, in closed loop, sets a code 45. There are other conditions that have to be present along with the voltage problems to cause the codes to be set. Other systems have their own methods for self-testing. The result is the same. Trained technicians can get help from the internal diagnostic systems if they know how to check the system.

One of the best methods to find out about computer systems on any vehicle is to use a scan tool (see Figure 12.9). Part of your training should include the correct use of this equipment. The oxygen sensor is just one of many sensors that have to be checked to solve other problems in the computer area.

Always repair the condition causing any oxygen sensor failure before running a new sensor. If unleaded gasoline was at fault, drain it and add new fuel. The new sensor can become damaged just like the old one if you do not pay attention to failure causes and their correction.

Replacing an Oxygen Sensor

The oxygen sensor can become contaminated. When RTV silicone gasket materials are used where they can get into the fuel, they can damage the sensor. Using leaded fuel instead of unleaded fuel can be a major problem for both the oxygen sensor and the catalytic converter. The lead in the fuel glazes the sensor and reduce its ability to react to the oxygen flow. Some of the methanol fuels can dissolve the protective coating in the gas tank, exposing the lead tank walls to gasoline and adding some of the lead to the fuel. A vehicle that burns large amounts of oil or allows antifreeze to leak into the combustion chamber can result in oxygen sensor damage.

When the sensor needs to be replaced, follow these steps:

1. Warm the engine by letting it run several minutes. A cold sensor is hard to remove. Do not let the exhaust get so hot it becomes a hazard to work around.
2. Disconnect the sensor lead (refer to Figure 12.7).
3. Install the special sensor socket and turn the socket counterclockwise to remove the unit.
4. New sensors have a special compound of glass beads and liquid graphite placed on the threads at the factory. This material makes it possible to remove the sensor when it becomes defective.
5. Torque the new sensor to 30 foot-pounds, or 41 Newton-meters, of torque. The special torque wrench is needed for this step (see Figure 12.10).
6. Connect the sensor lead.
7. Start the engine and check the operation of the new unit.
8. Examine the old sensor and determine if any of the following problems are present.
   a. Silicone contamination
   b. Lead contamination
   c. Oil contamination

The new sensor will fail if you do not correct these problems. Multiple sensor failure requires that the cause be corrected and then the sensor changed.

LESSON 12-5 Exhaust System Service
Leaks

Leaks are both noisy and dangerous. If the sound is allowed to bypass the muffler, the engine noise increases. The larger the leak, the more noise will be produced. There is a possibility that the poison gases can enter the passenger compartment from a leak in the front of the exhaust system. The intake for the heater air or air conditioner air, which is located in the front, will draw the gases into the passenger compartment. Leaks are repaired by replacing parts or tightening clamps.

Visual and Audio Exhaust System Inspection

All inspections of the exhaust system start at the engine exhaust manifold and continue out the end of the exhaust pipe. An audio (listening) inspection starts with jacking up the vehicle, starting the engine, and listening for areas in the system that have

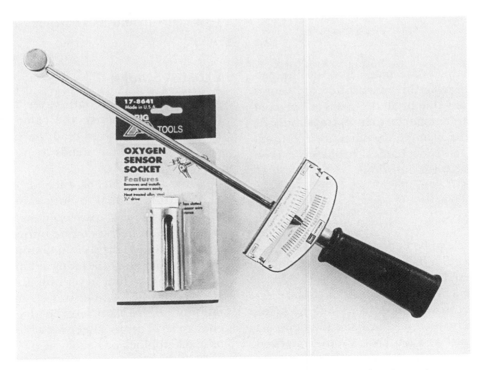

Figure 12.10 Torque wrench and sensor installation tool. To install a new sensor a special socket and a torque wrench are used. The torque wrench will help get the sensor as tight as it should be without damage (courtesy of Training Enterprises Company).

become louder than normal. This also may mean holding your hand near these parts and feeling for escaping exhaust gases (be careful because these gases can be very hot).

Continue the inspection by looking for bent, rusted-out, collapsed, and missing parts. Any problems found of this type will require the repair of the damaged sections. Parts can be purchased or made to replace each damaged pipe section, resonator, or muffler. Be sure all hangers and clamps are in place with no missing parts. Mufflers and resonators can be rusted out inside and not look rusted on the outside. Replace any of these parts that have increased in noise level.

After the new parts are installed, give the system a sound test and look for leaks around all areas where parts were replaced. Be sure there are no leaks before you release the vehicle.

Damage

Each time the vehicle is raised for an oil change, the entire exhaust system should be checked. Look for dents, rusted-out areas, broken hangers, and loose or missing clamps. If the system seems to be getting louder, try to determine where the problem is by starting the engine and looking for puffs of exhaust along the system. Sometimes it helps to lightly run your hand around an area that is suspect. Be careful, the system can be very hot.

Testing

Exhaust gas analyzers are made that tell the percentage of each gas in the exhaust flow as it leaves the tailpipe. If any one or all the gases are present in too high a percentage, further testing should be made, and perhaps engine repairs are required. Electrical, fuel, and mechanical problems can all cause high exhaust gas emissions.

Replacement

Welded parts have to be cut out of the exhaust system to be replaced. A hacksaw, chain cutter, or cutting torch are used (see Figure 12.11).

There are machines that bend and shape exhaust pipes, crossover pipes, and tailpipe (see Figure 12.12). The technician shapes the new part using the old part as a pattern. Another method is to buy the parts already shaped for each of the areas where they are needed. These parts are assembled and then welded or clamped to prevent exhaust leaks around the joints.

There are gaskets between the exhaust manifolds and the engine block (see Figure 12.13). A gasket placed in this extreme heat has to be made of special heat-resistant materials. In some cases, along with a gasket replacement, the matching parts have to be machined smooth. There are machine shops that specialize in this type of work.

Manifold bolts should be of the right quality and torqued to the correct specifications. Manifold leaks should never be left for long periods of time because the hot exhaust gases will channel grooves in the matching surfaces. It can be very costly to have these surfaces refinished. Sometimes the engine has to removed and partially disassembled.

A round (donut-shaped) gasket is commonly found between the end of the manifold and the crossover or exhaust pipe (see Figure 12.14). To seal the exhaust in this area there will be two or three studs in the manifold and a plate to put pressure on the gasket. The nuts will often be made of brass. These will loosen easily when the gasket needs to be replaced. When the studs deteriorate, they are hard to remove. One common method is to use a torch, heating the studs. Getting a bolt or stud hot will release the rust on the threads and make removal without breaking possible.

Hangers are clamped and bolted into place. Some hangers are special parts, and others can be replaced with universal hangers (see Figure 12.15).

Exhaust Smoke

When certain materials enter the combustion chamber, they change the color of the exhaust smoke. If you learn to read the smoke color, you can determine what needs to be adjusted or repaired.

White smoke means water or coolant is being burned. It is normal to notice some white smoke when the engine is first started on a cold day. Water condensation in the engine burns and will create a white smoke. This should disappear after the vehicle has reached operating temperature. Clouds of white smoke that never quit indicate that water is entering the combustion chamber. Constantly monitor the coolant level in the radiator. If the coolant level drops, check for a blown head gasket, or cracked block or head.

Black smoke means excessive fuel is getting into the combustion chamber. Some areas to investigate

Figure 12.11 Cutting torch. This equipment is used to remove welded exhaust system parts when new ones need to be installed (courtesy of Training Enterprises Company).

are leaking injectors, stuck choke, leaking carburetor float needle, and fuel-saturated float. The oxygen sensor can be defective and give a signal to the computer that the exhaust is lean. This will cause the computer to lengthen the injector times and place more fuel in the engine.

Blue smoke means engine or transmission oil is getting into the engine. Check for damaged piston rings, worn valve guides, head gasket problems, or a ruptured transmission vacuum modulator. Monitor the transmission fluid level and the engine oil level to see which one is dropping. Excessive oil in the exhaust flow will cause damage to the oxygen sensor. The oil problem has to be solved before the sensors will do the job they are designed for.

Figure 12.12 Hydraulic pipe bender. This machine bends tailpipe stock to match the original. This reduces the need to keep a large assortment of tailpipes in stock. The machine allows the technician to make custom exhaust systems (courtesy of Training Enterprises Company).

Figure 12.14 Round gasket. The round "donut-shaped" gasket is commonly used between the end of the crossover pipe and the exhaust pipe (courtesy of Training Enterprises Company).

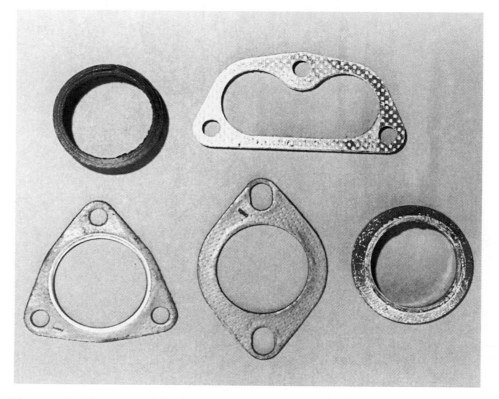

Figure 12.13 Exhaust gasket. These are typical exhaust gaskets that are installed between the exhaust manifold and the engine block. Some gaskets contain asbestos, which has to be handled with care (courtesy to Training Enterprises Company).

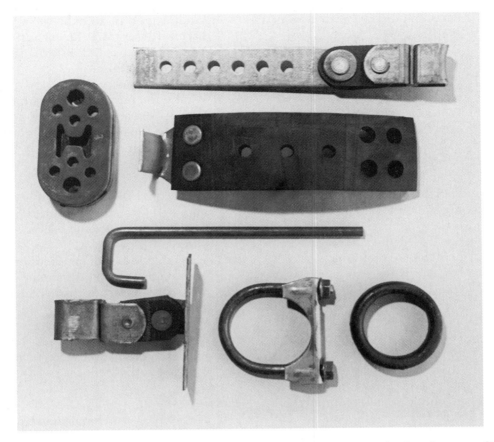

Figure 12.15 Hangers. Shown are some of the hangers used to hold the exhaust system in place (courtesy of Training Enterprises Company).

VOCABULARY

Use the listed words in the blanks beside the sentences to complete the definitions. Either write out the words or place the letters in the blanks.

A. Manifold

B. Oxygen sensor

C. Muffler

D. Baffles

E. Resonator

F. Tailpipe

G. Torque

H. Rich mixture

I. Nitrogen oxides

J. Hydrocarbons

K. Unleaded fuel

L. Engine cylinders

M. Low-voltage signal

N. Scan tool

O. RTV silicone

P. Glaze

Q. Methanol

R. Glass beads

S. Silicone contamination

T. Clamp

U. Chain cutter

V. Cutting torch

W. Gasket

X. Stud

Y. Black smoke

_____ 1. A part that reduces noise and echo

_____ 2. Part on the engine connected to the exhaust pipe

_____ 3. Result of too much fuel being burned in the combustion chamber

_____ 4. When the percentage of air to fuel is reduced

_____ 5. Parts that direct the air flow in a muffler

_____ 6. Detects the oxygen level in the exhaust flow

_____ 7. 0.1 to 1.0 volts produced by the oxygen sensor

_____ 8. When a hard film is produced over the catalyst

_____ 9. Part of the catalyst in a converter

_____ 10. A tool with cutting wheels used to cut tailpipe

_____ 11. Fuel that has all the lead removed

_____ 12. An exhaust part that reduces noise

_____ 13. A seal used on exhaust parts at the point where they join

_____ 14. Part of the exhaust system at the end

_____ 15. Uses acetylene to heat and cut metal

_____ 16. To turn an object to a specified amount of foot-pounds

_____ 17. Changed to nitrogen and water

_____ 18. Small handheld computer used to check vehicle computer systems

_____ 19. Changed to oxygen and water

_____ 20. Part of an engine where the pistons move

_____ 21. Part where exhaust nuts are installed

_____ 22. Liquid gasket material

_____ 23. Used with gasoline as a motor fuel

_____ 24. When the gasket sealer harms the catalyst

_____ 25. Part that tightens around the exhaust pipe to prevent leaks and hold in place

REVIEW QUESTIONS

The following questions will help you determine if you have accomplished the tasks stated at the beginning of this chapter. If you do not know many of the answers, go back and review the material before proceeding to the next chapter.

Lesson 12–1

1. What exhaust part funnels all the exhaust gases into one pipe?
2. Name two emission control parts located in the exhaust system.
3. What is the name of the part on a V-8 or V-6 engine that brings the exhaust gases into one pipe?
4. What is used in an exhaust system to remove harmful gases from the exhaust stream?
5. What part is used in an exhaust system to reduce engine noise?
6. What is a resonator?
7. What is the purpose of the tailpipe?
8. How are exhaust system parts held in place?
9. How can the computer tell if the exhaust flow is rich or lean?

Lesson 12–2

10. What could be the result if a work area gets saturated with carbon monoxide?
11. Explain how a catalytic converter can be a fire hazard.
12. What should be the preparation done before working on an exhaust system?
13. What does the converter change to nitrogen and water?
14. What kind of gasoline damages a catalytic converter?
15. What are the hydrocarbons changed into by the catalytic converter?

Lesson 12–3

16. What types of materials harm a catalytic converter?
17. Explain how a catalytic converter can get clogged.
18. What determines whether it is economical to replace the catalyst in a converter?
19. What are some of the major problems that require a converter replacement?

Lesson 12–4

20. The oxygen sensor does not react below what temperature?
21. If the exhaust gases are lean, what is the voltage signal range sent to the computer?
22. What are the conditions that cause a code 13 to be set in the computer?
23. What kind of tester is made to troubleshoot a fuel system?
24. What problems do methanol fuel cause in the fuel system?
25. What are two substances that cause oxygen sensor failure?
26. What must be done before a new oxygen sensor is installed to prevent multiple sensor failure?
27. How is a torque wrench used to install an oxygen sensor?

Lesson 12–5

28. What can cause an exhaust leak to become a danger to the driver and passengers?

29. What is the usual method for finding exhaust leaks?
30. What information can be learned from an exhaust gas analyzer?
31. What are three tools used to remove old exhaust system parts?
32. Explain what a bender is and how it is used.
33. What keeps exhaust parts from leaking at the joints?
34. If the gasket between the manifold and engine will not seal, what can be done?
35. What is a common method used to prevent bolt breakage during removal on manifolds?
36. What is a common material used for exhaust system nuts and bolts?
37. What damage can be done if exhaust manifold leaks are not repaired quickly?
38. What can cause large amounts of white smoke to come out the tailpipe?
39. What are some causes of black smoke coming out the tailpipe?
40. What are some causes of blue smoke coming out the tailpipe?
41. What type of material is used to make exhaust gaskets?

ASE QUESTIONS

Each question or incomplete statement in this test is followed by four suggested answers or completions. In each case select the *one* that best answers the question or completes the statement.

1. A code 13 was set in the vehicle computer system. Technician A says the exhaust flow was too lean. Technician B says the exhaust flow was too rich. Who is right?
   a. A only   b. B only
   c. Both A and B   d. Neither A nor B

2. An engine noise increases in decibels. Technician A says a manifold gasket has blown. Technician B says the muffler or other parts have a hole in them. Who is right?
   a. A only   b. B only
   c. Both A and B   d. Neither A nor B

3. An exhaust noise gets louder only at certain speeds. Technician A says the resonator should be replaced. Technician B says the converter should be replaced. Who is right?
   a. A only   b. B only
   c. Both A and B   d. Neither A nor B

4. Carbon monoxide is produced by the engine during combustion. Technician A says it is eas-

ily detected by smell and taste. Technician B says it it cannot be tasted or smelled. Who is right?
   a. A only   b. B only
   c. Both A and B   d. Neither A nor B

5. Hydrocarbons are produced by the engine combustion process. Technician A says the catalytic converter changes these to carbon dioxide. Technician B says the converter changes these to oxygen and water. Who is right?
   a. A only   b. B only
   c. Both A and B   d. Neither A nor B

6. When a converter is inspected the pellets are coated and damaged. Technician A says leaded fuel was burned in the engine. Technician B says oil entered the combustion chamber and was burned. Who is right?
   a. A only   b. B only
   c. Both A and B   d. Neither A nor B

7. When a manifold is removed and inspected there were grooves cut into the gasket surface. Technician A says this is the result of improper manifold bolt torque. Technician B says this is the result of a defective gasket that was left too long before repair. Who is right?
   a. A only   b. B only
   c. Both A and B   d. Neither A nor B

8. A manifold bolt is rusted in place. Technician A says a torch can be used to help remove the bolt without damage. Technician B says the bolt can be removed successfully with a torque wrench. Who is right?
   a. A only   b. B only
   c. Both A and B   d. Neither A nor B

9. Blue smoke is coming out the end of the exhaust pipe when the engine is running. Technician A says this is the result of too much fuel being burned in the engine. Technician B says this is the result of either oil or transmission fluid entering and being burned in the engine. Who is right?
   a. A only   b. B only
   c. Both A and B   d. Neither A nor B

10. The exhaust flow of an engine stays too lean for over one minute. Technician A says the computer will show a code 45 has been set. Technician B says a code 46 will be set. Who is right?
    a. A only   b. B only
    c. Both A and B   d. Neither A nor B

11. An oxygen sensor is inspected and found to be glazed. Technician A says the cause is the use

of a methanol fuel in the engine. Technician B says a leaded fuel was used in the engine. Who is right?

a. A only
b. B only
c. Both A and B
d. Neither A nor B

12. An engine without any fuel, electrical, or mechanical problems in the engine or drive train will not reach maximum speed or develop normal power. Technician A says the catalyst in the converter is melted and has restricted the exhaust system. Technician B says there is a bend or crimp in the exhaust pipe of the exhaust system that has reduced the exhaust flow. Who is right?

a. A only
b. B only
c. Both A and B
d. Neither A nor B

13

Manual Transmission, Clutch, and Automatic Transmission System Maintenance

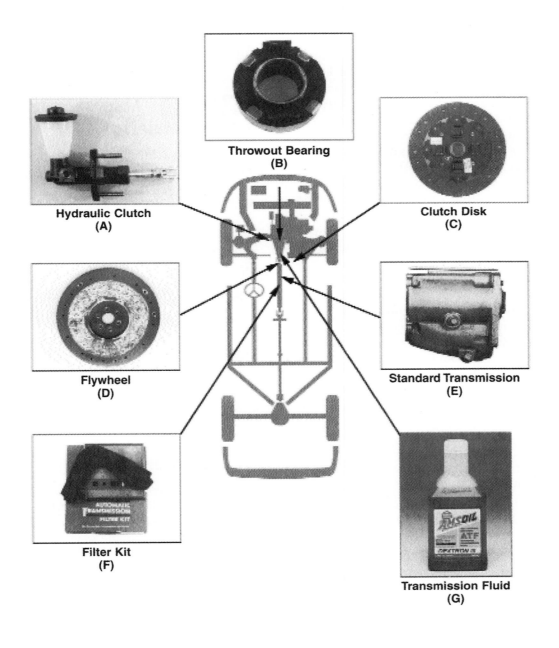

Throwout Bearing
(B)

Hydraulic Clutch
(A)

Clutch Disk
(C)

Flywheel
(D)

Standard Transmission
(E)

Filter Kit
(F)

Transmission Fluid
(G)

Both manual and automatic transmissions are used throughout the automotive industry. Smaller vehicles and trucks tend to have manual transmissions and larger passenger cars, automatic transmissions. The popular all-wheel-drive vehicles increase the amount of service and maintenance required, especially if used off-road (through the mud, water, and dust). All transmissions should have the fluid level checked, maintained, and changed on a regular basis. Leaks should be repaired, when found, because they can lead to internal unit damage if the fluid gets too low. Failure to change the fluid is a major cause of transmission failure.

It is almost as expensive to rebuild a manual transmission as it is an automatic. All-wheel-drive transmissions and those with overdrive are the most costly to replace or rebuild. Fluids with different viscosities should be used in cases of severe cold or hot weather in manual transmissions. If a vehicle with an automatic transmission is used to tow boats or trailers, special tow packages should be installed to keep the transmission fluids from overheating. Automatic transmissions can stand only a limited amount of extreme fluid heat before they fail.

The service technician needs to learn how to check, repair, adjust, and replace the fluids and parts in all the many different types of transmissions on the market (see Figure 13). Just keeping track of the different types of fluids in use is a fairly complicated job and requires constant research. Since the transmission is a major component in the automobile, customers require a high level of service skill and training from their technician. Transmissions last a very long time in terms of vehicle mileage when correctly maintained but fail rapidly when abused and allowed to run low on fluid.

TASKS

The following are nine tasks to master before leaving this chapter:

Task 13-1. Study the parts of a manual transmission.

Task 13-2. Learn how to service a manual transmission.

Task 13-3. Learn how to troubleshoot a manual transmission for problems.

Task 13-4. Study the parts of a clutch system.

Task 13-5. Learn how to service a clutch system.

Task 13-6. Learn how to troubleshoot a clutch system for problems.

Task 13-7. Study the parts of an automatic transmission.

Task 13-8. Learn how to service an automatic transmission.

Task 13-9. Learn how to troubleshoot an automatic transmission for problems.

LESSON 13-1   Manual Transmission Parts and Materials

The manual transmission has more parts and uses more types of materials than most people realize. We describe some of these parts in the following paragraphs.

Manual Transmission GL Classifications

GL-1 for spiral-bevel and worm gear axles and some manual transmissions under mild service

GL-2 for worn gear axles that require more than a GL-1 lubricant protection

GL-3 for manual transmissions and spiral bevel axles under moderately severe service

GL-4 for hypoid gears in normal severe service but not for those with severe shock loading

GL-5 for hypoid gears in severe service that may be shock loaded

Transmission Lubricant

Manual transmissions on rear wheel drive vehicles use a gear lubricant that varies from 60 to 90 weight. A multiviscosity weight is used in cold winter climates, and a heavier single weight is used for hot weather and high temperature. Gear lubricant prevents gear and bearing damage in the transmission from friction. Chapter 1 has additional information on gear lubricants. An American Petroleum Institute (API) rating of GL-5 is the best quality gear lubricant produced at the present time. A Society of American Engineers (SAE) 75W-90 gear lubricant would be a good selection for both cold and hot weather.

Figure 13.1 Gear set. A typical three-speed transmission has three forward gears: high, second, and low. There is also a reverse gear (courtesy of Training Enterprises Company).

The number one problem with manual or standard transmissions is the lack of regular lubrication changes. The old lubricant gets contaminated with dirt and metal chips, which soon causes major bearing and shaft wear. This results in a complete overhaul that can be very expensive. Change the fluid on a regular schedule according to the vehicle manufacturer's recommendations.

Transmission Parts

Gears. Each speed uses a different set of gears (see Figure 13.1). A three-speed transmission has a low, second, and high gear set. Separate gears are used for reverse. Three-speed, four-speed, and five-speed are the most common types of standard transmissions used in passenger vehicles and light trucks.

Needle Bearings and Shafts. The gears roll on hardened steel shafts, and needle-shaped bearings are used to reduce friction (see Figure 13.2). On heavy-duty transmissions there are two sets of needle bearings on each end of the shafts.

Drain and Filler Plugs. On the bottom of the transmission at the lowest point you will find a pipe-threaded plug (see Figure 13.3). Pipe threads are used because they are tapered and prevent fluid loss by sealing as the plug is tightened. This bottom plug is removed to drain the lubricant from the transmission when it needs to be changed. On the side of the transmission another plug is placed so the bottom edge of the plug hole is exactly where the fluid level in the transmission should be kept.

This plug is removed to check the fluid level or to replace fluid.

Shift Forks. Gears in the transmission have to be moved into and out of mesh as different speeds are selected. The shift forks are attached to the gears and slide the gears into the mesh or neutral position.

Case. The housing of the transmission that holds all the parts is called the *case*. It also is a container to hold the gear lubricant (see Figure 13.4).

Side or Top Cover. The cover provides a place to inspect the internal parts of the transmission without removing it from the vehicle. On some models the cover contains the shift forks and levers. The cover is bolted to the case and uses a gasket to prevent lubricant leaks (see Figure 13.5).

Tail Shaft. The rear section of the transmission is called the *tail shaft*. It covers a splined output shaft that the drive shaft fits over. A grease seal at the end of the tail shaft prevents lubricant from leaking out the rear of the transmission. On some transmissions the tail shaft holds the speedometer gear parts (see Figure 13.6).

Seals and Gaskets. Where two parts come together a gasket is used to prevent leaks. Seals are placed where shafts turn to prevent the loss of lubricant. Following are some places where seals and gaskets are found:

1. Shift fork levers
2. Front bearing flange
3. Side or top cover

Figure 13.2   Needle bearings and shaft. Needle or roller bearings are used to reduce friction on the gears that turn on the shafts. Heavy-duty transmissions have two sets of bearings at each end (courtesy of Training Enterprises Company).

Figure 13.3   Drain and filler plug. The pipe-threaded plug at the bottom of the transmission is to drain the fluid out. The plug in the side is for adding and checking the fluid level (courtesy of Training Enterprises Company).

Figure 13.4 Transmission case. The *case* is the outer shell of the transmission where the internal parts are installed. Most cases are made out of aluminum or cast iron (courtesy of Training Enterprises Company).

4. Tail shaft to case gasket and a seal in the end of the tail shaft housing
5. Speedometer gear
6. Plug seals at the ends of the gear shafts
7. Side and bottom filler and drain plugs

Synchronizers. Synchronizers are used when it is necessary to shift gears to either a higher or lower speed (see Figure 13.7). These parts help during gear changes by forcing both gears to rotate at the same speed so the meshing of the gears will

Figure 13.5 Side or top cover. A plate is bolted to either the side or the top of the transmission. This plate is sealed with a gasket and sometimes has a vent hole. Gears can be inspected by removing the cover (courtesy of Training Enterprises Company).

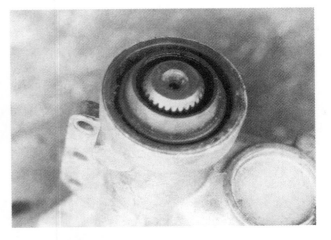

Figure 13.6 Tail shaft. Bolted to the rear of the transmission is the tail shaft. This encloses the rear drive shaft of the transmission. A grease seal is installed in the tail shaft to prevent loss of lubricant out the rear. There is a gasket between the tail shaft and the case (courtesy of Training Enterprises Company).

Figure 13.7   Synchronizers. This part is designed to force the gears to rotate at the same speed, which allows easier shifting. Gear changes would be difficult and damage hard to avoid without such devices (courtesy of Training Enterprises Company).

Figure 13.8   Thrust washer. Thrust washers control the amount of movement from front to rear of the internal parts of the transmission. They also reduce wear inside the case (courtesy of Training Enterprises Company).

occur without damage. It is very hard on gears when a different gear speed is selected. Two very fast moving parts are brought together. Synchronizers wear rapidly through regular use and should be replaced when it becomes difficult to shift gears without clashing.

Thrust Washers.   On the end of the gears next to the case are washers that act as bearings to prevent the sides of the gears from wearing the case (see Figure 13.8). Dirt in the lubricant and normal wear cause these washers to wear thinner. When this happens, the end play in the transmission increases. This can result in gear damage. The transmission has to be removed and disassembled to repair thrust washer wear.

LESSON 13-2   Manual Transmission Service

With all the moving parts in a manual transmission, service is important if vehicle owners are to avoid a major expense. We discuss service in this lesson.

> Always remember when checking and changing manual transmission lubricant to keep the vehicle level both front to rear and side to side. If this cannot be done, only refill the transmission with the correct amount of lubricant recommended by the manufacturer.

Lubrication

Most vehicle manufacturers recommend changing the transmission gear lube every 30,000 miles. Dirt and metal chips in the old fluid can damage gears and wear out bearings. Old fluid is drained by removing the drain plug at the bottom of the transmission case and letting the old fluid drain out (refer to Figure 13.3). New fluid of the correct viscosity is installed through a plug opening on the side of the transmission. The vehicle should be level and the fluid added until it reaches the bottom of the plug hole threads. This hole is designed to be at the top level of the correct amount of fluid needed to keep the transmission lubricated. Never overfill the transmission, and always check the fluid level during a regular engine oil change and suspension grease job. To check the fluid level, remove the side plug and use a finger to touch

the fluid inside. If you cannot touch the fluid, add lubricant until it reaches the bottom of the hole.

Linkage Inspection and Adjustment

The linkage should be adjusted so that each gear, when selected, will be placed in complete mesh. The levers should take each gear completely out of mesh. Each shift rod can be adjusted by making it shorter or longer. Start by placing the transmission in neutral (no gears in mesh). Adjust the levers until the shift selector arm in the vehicle is in the neutral position. Tighten the adjustments. Have someone move the shifter arm around while you look to see if it will shift each gear to the full mesh position.

No adjustment is necessary on many floor-mounted gear selectors, because the shift arm is attached directly to the top of the transmission and does not use linkage.

> Liquid gasket material can replace a leaking gasket or stop leaks around bolts. It is better to use a gasket made for the job, but if this is not possible, the liquid gasket material can take the place of the original gasket.

Leak Inspection

Gaskets and seals are potential leak points. A seal at the rear of the transmission prevents lubricant loss from the rotating drive shaft (refer to Figure 13.6). Lubricant loss at the front of the transmission can damage the clutch facing by causing it to slip and grab. Tighten bolts and replace seals if leaks are found. Never let the transmission run without sufficient lubrication.

Backup Light and Interlock

When the transmission is shifted into reverse, a switch is turned on that lights the backup lights (see Figure 13.9). The light should go out when the selector is taken out of reverse. On linkage-type systems this switch has to be adjusted.

Recent vehicles have a switch that prevents the vehicle engine from starting when the transmission is in gear. Either the clutch has to be disengaged or the shift level has to be in neutral. This is a safety system and must be repaired if defective.

Figure 13.9 Backup light switch. When the transmission is shifted into reverse, a switch is turned on to light the backup lights. The lights should come on when the transmission is in reverse and go off when shifted out of this gear (courtesy of Training Enterprises Company).

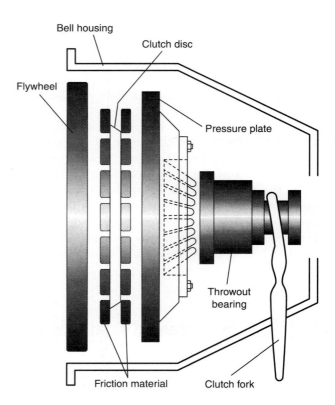

Figure 13.10 Shown is a diagram of the complete clutch system. The clutch is designed to disconnect the engine from the transmission so the transmission can be shifted into a different gear (courtesy of Training Enterprises Company).

LESSON 13–3 Clutch System

The clutch system is the other half of a manual transmission system. It is the system that disengages the engine from the transmission while the different gear speeds are selected (see Figure 13.10).

Clutch System Parts

Flywheel. The flywheel is bolted directly to the crankshaft of the engine. The side of the flywheel is used as a surface for the clutch disc friction materials to grip against when the clutch is engaged (see Figure 13.11).

Pressure Plate. The other part used for the clutch disc to grip against is the pressure plate. This plate closes against the flywheel surface and applies pressure on the clutch disc (see Figure 13.12). This connects the engine to the transmission because the clutch disc is splined directly to the input shaft of the transmission. When the driver depresses the clutch pedal, the pressure

plate releases its force on the clutch disc lining and the engine is no longer connected to the transmission.

Clutch Disc. A part with friction material on both sides is placed between the flywheel and the pressure plate (see Figure 13.13). When the pressure plate puts pressure on the clutch disc, the friction materials lock the flywheel to the clutch disc. This transmits power to the transmission because the clutch disc is splined to the transmission output shaft. When the pressure plate is disengaged, the flywheel and the pressure plate rotate freely without driving the clutch disc, and no power is transmitted to the transmission from the engine. The clutch disc is in a very wear-intensive area and usually is the first item to suspect if the clutch pedal is released and slipping occurs.

Throwout Bearing. The part that contacts the fingers of the pressure plate when the clutch pedal is pushed is called the *throwout bearing* (see Figure 13.14). This bearing is a sealed roller bearing. The face of the bearing rotates with the fingers of the

Figure 13.11 Flywheel. One part of the clutch system uses the flywheel surface. The clutch disc is forced against the flywheel (courtesy of Training Enterprises Company).

Figure 13.12 Pressure plate. This plate supplies the pressure that forces the clutch disc against the flywheel. The pressure plate also releases the pressure on the clutch disc when the operator pushes in the clutch pedal (courtesy of Training Enterprises Company).

Figure 13.13 Clutch disc. There is friction material on both sides of this disc. When the clutch disc is clamped between the pressure plate and the flywheel, the power of the engine is transferred to the transmission (courtesy of Training Enterprises Company).

Figure 13.14 Throwout bearing. This bearing is forced against the fingers of the pressure plate when the operator wants to disengage the clutch (courtesy of Training Enterprises Company).

pressure plate. A loud noise when the clutch pedal is pushed in usually means the throwout bearing has lost its lubricant. When the throwout bearing needs to be replaced, the transmission must be taken out of the vehicle. Usually the pressure plate is resurfaced, the flywheel resurfaced, and the clutch disc replaced at the same time because most of these parts have to be removed to replace the throwout bearing.

Bell Housing, Clutch Fork, and Throwout Bearing.

The vehicle operator controls the clutch by pushing the clutch pedal. Linkage from the pedal goes to the clutch fork. The throwout bearing is on the end of the clutch fork (see Figure 13.15). Pressure is placed on the throwout bearing and it pushes against the pressure plate fingers. This releases the pressure plate force on the clutch disc. As the clutch disc friction materials wear, the pressure plate moves closer to the flywheel. This reduces the amount of clutch pedal travel before the clutch begins to release. The pedal travel is a

Figure 13.15 Bell housing, clutch fork, and throwout bearing. The clutch pedal is foot operated and by linkage moves the clutch fork. The clutch fork moves the throwout bearing against a pressure plate. This releases and engages the clutch (courtesy of Training Enterprises Company).

maintenance item. The clutch linkage can be adjusted so that the pedal travel can be kept at about 1 in. before clutch release. The driver of the vehicle can tell when this adjustment is needed by watching the pedal movement before release.

Hydraulic Clutches

Instead of linkage, many vehicles now use a hydraulic system to connect the clutch pedal to the end of the clutch fork (see Figure 13.16a and b). A master cylinder is used at the end of the clutch pedal. Hydraulic lines transmit the hydraulic pressure to a slave cylinder at the shift fork. The shift fork is moved by the hydraulic pressure from the slave cylinder. This system is similar to the brake system used on vehicles. Brake fluid is used in the master cylinder and the fluid level should be checked as a routine maintenance item. Keep the fluid level about 1/4 in. from the top of the master cylinder reservoir. The slave cylinder rod has an adjustment on some vehicles. Adjust the rod so there is some movement in the clutch fork. Check for leaks at the master cylinder and the slave cylinder.

If a master cylinder or slave cylinder fails, the operator will not have any way to disengage the clutch. This can be extremely dangerous if failure occurs while waiting for a traffic light. When the system fails, if the car is in gear, the vehicle will move forward. This means that the only ways to stop the vehicle are to stall the engine with the brake, pull the transmission out of gear, or shut the engine off. This could result in an accident if

it happens without warning. Routine maintenance of the hydraulic clutch is very important.

LESSON 13-4   Clutch Service

The service procedures on clutch systems should be followed each time the car is given an engine oil change and suspension grease job. Following are the service details.

> A clutch system continues to wear down the friction material until it slips. A slipping system that cannot be adjusted will cause damage to the flywheel and pressure plate surfaces. If the clutch disc is replaced before this damage occurs, the cost of the repair will be reduced. It is very expensive to replace the pressure plate and have the flywheel resurfaced.

Throwout Bearing Adjustment

Adjust the clutch pedal when it moves less than 1 in. before releasing the clutch disc. If the clutch pedal is released and the clutch does not lock the engine and transmission together, there is either an adjustment problem or a worn-out clutch. Several methods are used to connect the clutch pedal to the end of the shift fork; one uses linkage rods, and another uses cables. Both methods require adjustment when the "free" clutch pedal travel is less than the specified distance. This is usually about 1 in.

There are adjustment nuts on the rod type clutch linkage. Turning the adjustment either

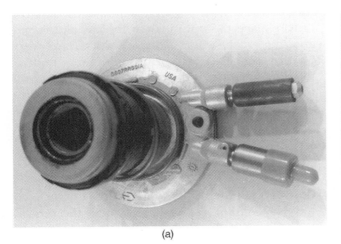

(a)

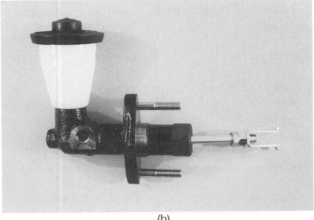

(b)

Figure 13.16 Hydraulic clutch. Many clutches are operated by hydraulic pressure. They have master cylinders (a) and slave cylinders (b). These systems use regular brake fluid (courtesy of Training Enterprises Company).

lengthens or shortens the linkage. There should always be a little movement between the end of the shift fork and the linkage. The throwout bearing should be allowed to completely back away from the fingers of the clutch disc. A constantly moving throwout bearing would rapidly wear out if it is locked against the fingers. Be sure to consult individual repair manuals to adjust all the different types of systems.

Linkage Lubrication

There are grease fittings on most mechanical clutch linkage at the points where it moves. Look for these grease fittings, and use the same grease used to lubricate the suspension system.

Contaminated Lining

There is an inspection cover that can be removed to inspect the clutch system. This is located over the flywheel and under the bell housing. If fluid is dripping out the hole in this cover, remove it and look for the leak. Three fluids can leak into this pan: engine oil, transmission fluid, and engine coolant. If any one of these fluids gets on the clutch disc lining, it will cause the clutch to slip or grab. All leaks should be repaired. The presence of coolant may mean that you must replace an expansion plug. It could also mean a cracked block. Transmission fluid can leak from a failed front bearing flange gasket or loose bolts. An overfilled transmission can result in fluid leaving the end of the bearing flange. Engine oil can leak from a damaged rear main bearing seal.

When the inspection cover is removed at the bottom of the bell housing, look for the following problems:

1. Worn and damaged clutch disc friction material
2. Bent or damaged clutch plate fingers
3. Broken springs in the clutch disc and clutch plate
4. Throwout bearing damage
5. Shift fork damage
6. Flywheel or pressure plate friction face damage

A noisy throwout bearing can be detected by leaving the transmission in neutral and starting the engine while depressing the clutch. When the clutch is depressed the bearing will rotate and if defective should make a sound.

Hydraulic Clutch Repair

The master cylinder is the heart of the hydraulic clutch. If you must constantly maintain the fluid level, the hydraulic system must have a leak. Look for leaks at the master cylinder, fluid lines, and the slave cylinder. Both the master cylinder and the slave cylinder can be repaired by removing the internal parts and replacing them with new parts from a rebuild kit. Both units should be cleaned and honed out before installing kits. If air gets into the system or parts are replaced, the system will have to be bled. A bleeder screw is located on the master cylinder and the slave cylinder (refer to Figure 13.16). Pressure is placed on the system by holding down the clutch pedal. The bleeder screw is opened and fluid removed until all air bubbles are removed. This process may have to be repeated several times until the clutch pedal feels solid to the foot. Air makes the pedal feel spongy, and it will not operate the clutch fork as it should.

The rod on the end of the slave cylinder that moves the clutch fork may have to be adjusted as the clutch disc wears. Adjust the rod so there is some movement of the clutch fork without pressure on the clutch pedal.

Replace any hydraulic fluid in the clutch master cylinder with DOT 3 brake fluid. This is the same fluid used in the brake master cylinder.

LESSON 13–5   Automatic Transmission Parts and Materials

The automatic transmission is a complicated unit that contains many finely machined parts. Most drivers place the transmission in gear and forget about it except when it doesn't work right. Very few drivers check the transmission fluid or replace the fluid and filter on a regular basis. To make you more familiar with the parts of an automatic transmission, we discuss the major components in this lesson.

Transmission Components

Converter. There are three parts to the converter system: an input device called the *turbine*, a one-way clutch called the *stator*, and the pump. Hydraulic fluid (transmission fluid) is *pumped* through the stator and into the turbine. The force of the fluid hitting the turbine blades drives the transmission and the vehicle. The one-way clutch prevents the fluid from driving the turbine in reverse as the speeds vary between the turbine and the pump.

Transmission. Simply put, an automatic transmission works by a complex planetary gear system, which uses clutches and bands to hold certain components and to let others turn to change gears. A governor in the transmission detects the speed of the engine and directs hydraulic fluid where it is needed to apply the clutches and bands for gear changes.

Transmission Fluid. Dextron III/Mercon is the new automatic transmission fluid, introduced in 1994. Some vehicles still use some of the earlier fluids. Check the manufacturer's recommendations before using any new fluids. Transmission fluid must be able to withstand extreme heat and still maintain the correct viscosity. The fluid is used to lubricate all gears and bearings. It also helps keep the parts clean and cool. Some of the valves in the hydraulic control section of the transmission have very close working clearances. The fluid has to prevent these parts from sticking (see Figure 13.17).

Cooler. Transmission fluid gets very hot when it goes through the converter and works in the transmission. To remove some of this heat, the fluid is pumped to a heat exchanger located in the bottom of the engine radiator (see Figure 13.18). Heat from the transmission fluid is removed and absorbed into the engine coolant. The ram air going through the radiator passes the coolant heat off into the outside air. If the vehicle is to be used when towing a camping trailer or a boat, a towing package may be installed. This is a separate heat exchanger that is just like a miniature radiator. This is more efficient than the other system and keeps the fluid cooler (see Figure 13.19).

Linkage. Cable linkage goes between the transmission levers and the driver shift selector arm. There is an adjustment on the linkage to make it shorter or longer. The transmission should shift into the park, drive, and reverse positions.

Case, Pan, and Tail Shaft. The case houses all the internal parts of the transmission. The pan holds the transmission reserve fluid until it can be picked up by the pump and circulated through the transmission. The tail shaft covers the output shaft of the transmission and is like the tail shaft

TRANSMISSION FLUID		
Type	**Description**	**Application**
Type A	Early General Motors fluid	Early General Motors products.
Type F	Early Ford products	Where Ford specification M2C33–F is required.
Mercon®	Wide range of transmissions that require a friction modified fluid	Use in all automatic transmissions made in North America starting with 1988. Can be used where Dextron, Dextron II, and Type H are recommended. *NOT* for type F applications.
FA	Replacement for type F fluids	Where Ford specification M2C33–F is recommended.
Dextron® II–e/Mercon®	Replacement for earlier Dextron fluids	Use for all transmissions except those that require a Ford M2C33F or M2C116–H fluid.
Dextron®III/Mercon®	A 1994 product that replaces the earlier Dextron® II–e/Mercon® product.	Use where a friction modifying fluid is required. Do not use in Ford products that

Figure 13.17 Transmission fluid. This is a special fluid used in automatic transmissions. The fluid supplies lubrication to the parts and hydraulic pressure to operate the transmission (courtesy of Training Enterprises Company).

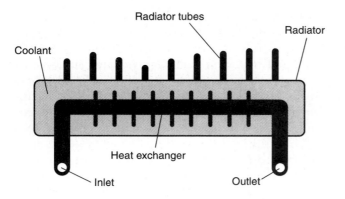

Figure 13.18 Transmission cooler. Transmission fluid would get so hot it would thin out or burn. To prevent this, the transmission fluid is cooled by a heat exchanger built into the bottom of the radiator (courtesy of Training Enterprises Company).

of the manual transmission. A seal prevents transmission fluid from leaking out the rear (refer to Figure 13.6).

LESSON 13–6 Automatic Transmission Service

The automatic transmission is expensive to repair, and therefore should be serviced and checked on a regular basis. Following are the service details.

Servicing Transmission Fluids

Fluid Checking. The engine has to be running to check the transmission fluid level. This means that the fluid is being pumped through all the passages and parts in the converter and transmission while the level is being checked. The vehicle should be level and the fluid should be warm. To check the fluid, warm the transmission by letting it come up to temperature and remove the dipstick. Wipe it clean and replace it, making sure it is fully installed. Remove it a second time and read the fluid level on the end of the stick (see Figure 13.20).

Fluid and Filter Changing. The transmission fluid is filtered to prevent small particles of metal or dirt from entering the valves and hydraulic parts of the transmission. The tolerances of the working parts are very close. The filter is located in the end of the pump fluid pickup tube, which is in the bottom of the pan. To change the filter, the pan has to be removed to uncover the filter. The filters are usually attached with screws or a clip. The new filter has a gasket or a seal (see Figure 13.21) that prevents leaks where the filter attaches to the pickup tube. A new gasket is installed on the pan, and it is bolted to the transmission case. Enough transmission fluid has to be replaced to

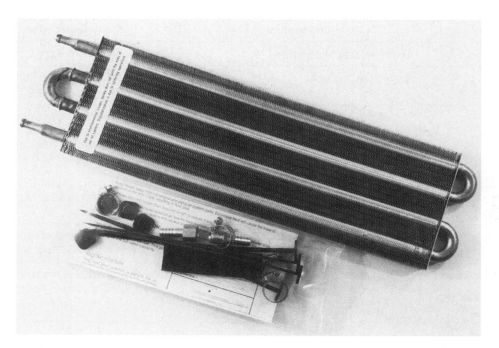

Figure 13.19 Outside cooler. Heavy-duty operations such as towing a trailer may require the installation of an outside transmission cooler to prevent damage due to overheating the fluid (courtesy of Training Enterprises Company).

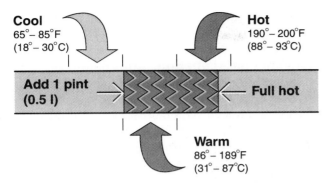

Figure 13.20 Reading an automatic transmission dipstick. The dipstick should be read when the fluid is "hot," with the transmission in "park," and the engine at "idle." It is normal for the fluid to check below the "add" mark when "cool" and "low" when "warm" (courtesy of Training Enterprises Company).

make sure the correct level reads on the dipstick. For a complete fluid change, the converter must also be drained and refilled. This is accomplished on some by removing a plug on the converter, draining it, and adding enough fluid to refill it. The engine has to be started to pump the fluid into the converter.

Transmission Fluid Exchange. At filling stations and express lubrication stations a new

method is being used to change automatic transmission fluid (see Figure 13.22). The transmission fluid change machine removes the old fluid and flushes the system without removal of the transmission pan or old filter. The flushing action also cleans the filter. All fluid is removed, even that in the converter, so when the new fluid is added none of the old fluid is left to contaminate the new. If you suspect that the old filter is beginning to clog and reduce oil flow, replace it. This requires removing the pan.

Change the automatic transmission fluid and filter every 30,000 miles. Adjust this mileage interval for driving conditions. Dirty, dusty conditions reduce the mileage interval, and long trip road miles extend the change mileage. Monitor the fluid condition at each dipstick check for either dirty or burnt-smelling fluid. When you detect this, change the fluid and make this the new change interval.

Some places change automatic transmission fluid by vacuuming the fluid out the filler pipe. This removes all the fluid, even that trapped in the converter. This method cannot be used every time because the filter will not be changed. Filters get clogged and need replacement along with the fluid. A clogged filter can result in expensive transmission internal parts damage.

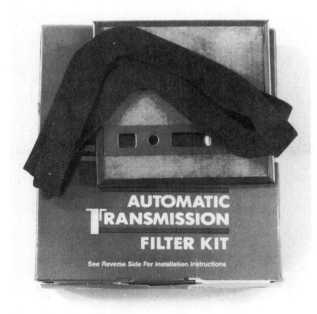

Figure 13.21 Filter and gasket kit. Part of the routine maintenance of an automatic transmission is filter replacement. The transmission pan is removed and a new filter installed (courtesy of Training Enterprises Company).

Figure 13.22 Transmission Fluid Change Machine. Machines like this remove the old fluid, flush the system, and clean the filter (courtesy of Century MFG. Co.).

Leak Detection. Transmission fluid is red. When it leaks, it usually flows from the front to the pan and along the pan to the ground. The underside of the transmission is usually wet with transmission fluid. A rear seal leak does not show up as a wet pan, but makes a wet area at the rear of the transmission. There are front and rear seals, pump gasket, pan gasket, tail shaft gasket, and linkage seals that can become possible leak points (see Figure 13.23) Dry the area around the suspected leak and run the engine. When the leak starts up again, the defective gasket or seal can usually be spotted. Fix all leaks, because they can result in the transmission being run while low on lubrication.

Coolant Contamination.   Most automatic transmissions use a heat exchanger in the bottom of the engine radiator to take the heat out of the transmission fluid (refer to Figure 13.18). A hole in the exchanger can result in transmission fluid entering the radiator coolant or radiator coolant entering the transmission. When the engine is cold, inspect the radiator coolant to check for any problems. Look for rust and the presence of oil. Anytime the

---

TRANSMISSION LEAK POINTS

1. Front
   A.   Converter
   B.   Front pump gasket and bolts
   C.   Front seal
   D.   Cracked case

2. Sides
   A.   Lever seals
   B.   Servo cover seals
   C.   Transmission cooler lines
   D.   Speedometer gear seal
   E.   Filler pipe tube seal
   F.   Cracked case
   G.   Pressure gauge plugs
   H.   Governor seal
   I.   Modulator loose or internal damage

3. Bottom
   A.   Pan bolts loose
   B.   Pan gasket
   C.   Damaged pan or cracked case

4. Rear
   A.   Rear housing seal
   B.   Governor
   C.   Modulator
   D.   Speedometer
   E.   Tail housing gasket or bolts loose (some models)

5. Oil out vent pipe
   A.   Transmission overfilled
   B.   Water in transmission fluid
   C.   Pump gasket and cover problems

6. Coolant in transmission or transmission oil in coolant
   A.   Heat exchanger in radiator has a hole

7. Blue smoke out exhaust pipe
   A.   Modulator letting fluid go into vacuum hose and engine intake

---

Figure 13.23   Transmission leak points. Shown are the areas to check when transmission fluid is leaking out of an automatic transmission (courtesy of Training Enterprises Company).

transmission dipstick indicates a white-looking substance mixed with the fluid, coolant is entering the transmission. The best way to fix this problem is to add an outside transmission cooler and plug the radiator fittings (refer to Figure 13.19). The radiator and the transmission have to be flushed and clean fluid installed.

Road Testing

A road test can be valuable when trying to determine the condition of a transmission. Look for the following problems:

1. No drive in any shift range
2. Slipping
3. Rough, early, or late shifting
4. Engine speed-up during any shift
5. Unusual noises in any range

Some of these problems can be corrected by adjusting linkage, replacing modulators, or cleaning the valve body. About 80% of all transmission problems can be corrected without taking the transmission from the car.

Pressure Testing

On most transmissions there will be a place to install a hydraulic fluid pressure tester. Too high or too low a pressure at these points means some repair is needed. This makes the repair easier, because you can go directly to the areas in the transmission that are causing the problems. Figure 13.24 is a pressure point checklist.

Other Services

Linkage Adjustment. The throttle in a wide-open position should make the transmission downshift. There is a cable or linkage connecting the transmission to the throttle. This is an adjustment point, and should be adjusted if the transmission is not downshifting when it should.

PRESSURE POINTS	
#1 Main Pressure	#2 Reverse
#3 Fourth Clutch	#4 Servos
RESULTS	
Pressure normal	Pressure too low
Pressure too high	Pressure changes
No pressure	Pressure changes with rpm
ABNORMAL PRESSURE CAUSES	
Transmission filter clogged	Pump defective
Worn internal seals	Sticking valves
Modulator defective	Pressure regulator defective
Low fluid level	Dirt in control body
Dirt in passages	Contaminated fluid

Note: We have not covered all the possible causes of abnormal line pressures. Consult the individual repair manual for the transmission you are testing for additional causes. Any abnormal pressure is a cause for concern and must be corrected. The pressure gauge can be a very useful tool to help solve a transmission problem.

Figure 13.24 Pressure points. A pressure gauge can be installed in several parts of the transmission hydraulic system. Abnormal pressure can mean the transmission must be serviced or repaired (courtesy of Training Enterprises Company).

More electronic parts are being placed in automatic transmissions to replace mechanical operating ones. These electronic parts can be checked with bench or handheld computer analyzers.

Backup Light. When the transmission is shifted into reverse, the backup light should come on. This should occur at all times, day or night. This lets those behind you know that you are ready to back up. When the backup switch needs adjustment, the light will either stay on all the time or not come on at all (refer to Figure 13.9). If the light does not come on at all, check the bulbs first and the adjustment next.

Neutral Safety Switch. The ignition should not start the engine if the transmission is in any gear selection position. When in park or neutral, the ignition should work. If the engine will start in drive or reverse, adjust the neutral safety switch (see Figure 13.25). If the ignition does not start in park or neutral, check the neutral safety switch for possible problems such as improper adjustment or electrical failure.

LESSON 13–7 Troubleshooting Manual Transmissions

Problems with these units fall into five categories:

1. Shifting
2. Moving or "jumping" out of gear
3. Unusual noise
4. Failure to drive in gear
5. Lubrication and leaks

Shifting problems can be caused by improper linkage adjustment, synchronizer damage, no lubrication, thick and dirty lubrication, bent shift forks, worn shafts, worn gear bushings, and case detente damage.

Moving out of gear can be caused by improper shift linkage adjustment, damaged gear teeth, broken shift fork, and many of the same problems that would cause shifting problems as outlined in the previous paragraph (see Figure 13.26).

If you hear any unusual noises from a standard transmission, immediately check the lubrication level. If this level is all right, look for worn bearings, bushings, and shafts. Noise can also be generated by damaged or broken gear teeth. Low or no lubrication noises should increase rapidly as the damage increases. Lubrication fluid that is thick or dirty can cause rapid gear, bushing, and bearing damage. Look for leaks if the lubrication level constantly drops in between checks. Immediately change any dirty or contaminated lubricant (see Figure 13.27).

Failure to drive in gear can be the result of broken gear teeth, but first make sure the linkage is adjusted properly and that the lever is actually shifting the gears into mesh. Broken teeth usually make loud grinding noises. To prevent more damage, repair the transmission immediately (see Figure 13.28).

Never drive a manual transmission with damaged gear teeth. The teeth are hardened steel, and if they get caught in any of the other teeth they will cause the transmission to be destroyed beyond rebuilding. It is better and more economical to stop and get damage like this repaired rather than driving the vehicle trying to never shift into the damaged gear.

Clutches

Problems with these units fall into four categories:

1. Slipping or chatter
2. Failure to disengage
3. Failure to engage
4. Noise

When it is determined that the clutch is slipping, look first at the linkage adjustment. As a clutch wears and the clutch disc gets thinner, the clutch adjustment changes. Eventually the clutch is

Figure 13.25 Neutral safety switch. Both standard and automatic transmissions have switches that prevent starting the engine unless the shifter is in NEUTRAL or PARK (courtesy of Training Enterprises Company).

MOVING OUT OF GEAR		
Gear	**Problem**	**Solution**
First or Reverse	Shift linkage adjustment Worn reverse idler gear bearings Worn reverse idler shaft Worn reverse gear teeth Worn low speed gear teeth Worn first and reverse shift fork Worn shift lever shafts First speed synchronizer worn	Adjust linkage. Replace worn parts.
Second speed and High	Worn second/high gears Worn or damaged synchronizers Worn countershaft needle bearings Worn thrust washers Worn high/second shift fork Worn shift lever Damaged cover detente system Missing or worn pilot bearing Worn third/direct gear thrust washer	Repair or replace all damaged, worn, and missing parts.

Figure 13.26 Moving out of gear. Refer to this chart if a manual transmission does not stay in the selected gear (courtesy of Training Enterprises Company).

prevented from engaging. Adjust the linkage so there will be some pedal movement at the start before any clutch disengagement. Worn-out clutch disc friction material, pressure plate problems, and contamination of the lining by grease or oil are some areas to check after linkage adjustment has been attempted.

Chatter is caused by rough spots on the flywheel or pressure disc, cracked or rough clutch lining,

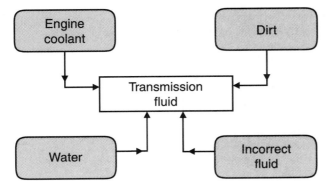

Figure 13.27 Transmission fluid contamination. Dirt, water, and engine coolant are three common contaminants found in automatic transmission fluid. Using the wrong fluid is another common problem (courtesy of Training Enterprises Company).

clutch disc damage, and pressure plate damage. Contaminated lining can also cause chatter (see Figure 13.29).

Failure to disengage can be the result of a linkage problem, sticking clutch disc facings, bent clutch disc, damaged pressure plate fingers and levers, or a swollen clutch lining.

Failure to engage can be the result of pressure plate damage, worn clutch facings, and linkage adjustment (refer to Figure 13.28).

The most often-heard noise is that of throwout bearing failure. This bearing is sealed and through use becomes dry of lubricant. Every time the clutch is engaged, a damaged throwout bearing makes a loud noise. This noise will continue as long as the clutch is kept engaged and will increase or decrease as the engine speed varies.

When the clutch disc facing wears down to the metal parts and rivets, this will result in slipping and noise. Warped clutch discs can make noise, as can worn-out pilot bearings. Loose flywheels and pressure plate bolts cause noise. Anytime there is a noise in the clutch area, remove the flywheel cover and make a visual inspection (refer to Figure 13.29). Check flywheel bolts and pressure plate bolts for correct torque. Tighten up all bolts and replace any that are missing.

FAILURE TO DRIVE IN GEAR OR TO ENGAGE	
Problem	**Solution**
Damaged detente	Inspect detente.
Linkage adjustment	Adjust linkage.
Damaged or broken shift fork	Replace shift fork.
Damaged synchronizer	Replace synchronizer.
Stripped gear teeth	Replace damaged gear.
Linkage out of shift arm	Place linkage back and key.
Worn shaft bearings	Replace bearings.
Damaged clutch gear sleeve	Replace gear sleeve.
Transmission shifted into two gears	Remove cover and repair.
Clutch plate worn out	Replace clutch plate.
Damaged pressure plate	Replace pressure plate.

Figure 13.28   Failure to drive in gear or to engage. Use this chart to determine problems if the transmission will not drive in any gear or engage into a gear (courtesy of Training Enterprises Company).

Automatic Transmissions

Problems with these units fall into four categories:

1. Upshift problems
   a. No upshift
   b. Delayed upshifts
2. No reverse or forward drive
3. Slipping or engine flareups
4. No downshift

We do not go into all the causes of these problems, because their repair is beyond the scope of a lubrication text. There are some basic things that should be done for any problem with an automatic transmission.

Basic maintenance starts with an investigation of the fluid quality and level. If the level is low it should be adjusted to the full mark. If the transmission is overfull, fluid must be removed until the

> It is reported that over 80% of all automatic transmission problems can be repaired without taking the transmission out of the vehicle. This is why it is important to make tests and pinpoint the problem before suggesting a complete overhaul.

CHATTER OR NOISE	
Problem	**Solution**
Low transmission fluid	Check and fill to correct level.
Worn bearings (needle/roller)	Replace bearings.
Excessive end play	Replace thrust washers.
Worn synchronizer	Replace synchronizers.
Worn gears or shafts	Replace gears and shafts.
Worn gear teeth	Replace gear.
Worn shift fork	Replace shift fork.
Missing or worn pilot bearing	Replace pilot bearing.
Linkage grommets missing	Replace grommets.
Bent shafts	Replace damaged shafts.
Loose pressure plate bolts	Tighten bolts.
Damaged pressure plate	Replace pressure plate.
Damaged clutch plate	Replace clutch plate.

Figure 13.29   Chatter or noise. Use this chart to determine the source of a problem of chatter or noise. Most of the time the transmission has to be removed to correct the problem (courtesy of Training Enterprises Company).

DIRTY FILTER PROBLEMS

Problem	Cause
No drive condition	Pump cannot develop pressure by picking up fluid from pan.
Slipping in all ranges	Pump pressure reduced by dirty filter.
Slow engagement	Servos and bands are not being applied with enough pressure.
Engine flareup	Pump pressure is not being maintained when the filter restricts flow.
Burned smell on the dipstick	The pressure is not strong enough to keep the bands and clutches from slipping.
Intermittent slipping and nonengagement	Low pressure at times will cause slipping and nonengagement.

Figure 13.30   Dirty filter problems. Use this chart to determine if the transmission has a clogged or dirty filter. Follow the manufacturer's maintenance plan to change the automatic transmission filter to prevent transmission damage (courtesy of Training Enterprises Company).

correct level is reached. An overfull transmission causes air to enter the fluid from contact with moving gears. Air in hydraulic fluid causes bands and clutches to slip from not being applied correctly. Transmission fluid should be changed on a regular schedule. In most cases the pan is removed and a new filter installed and a new pan gasket installed. If the converter is not drained, only a part of the fluid is changed during this operation. A complete change involves draining the converter and the pan. Regular filter and fluid changes prevent many of the problems associated with clogged filters and dirty fluid (see Figure 11.30). When the filter gets clogged, the pump pressure is reduced and clutches and bands are allowed to slip and burn. Repairing this damage involves a complete transmission overhaul.

Adjust cable and mechanical linkage when it gets out of adjustment. Replace ruptured or swollen vacuum modulator hoses when found. If there is blue smoke at the exhaust and the transmission fluid level drops, look for a ruptured vacuum modulator

LEAK PROBLEMS

Problem	Solution
Liquid foams	Level too high or wrong fluid.
Cracked case	Repair/replace damaged case.
Loose tail shaft bolts	Tighten bolts.
Damaged gaskets	Replace gaskets.
Damaged front or rear seals	Replace seals.
Damaged lever seals	Replace seals.
Loose retainer bolts	Tighten bolts.
Speedometer housing seal bad	Replace "O" ring seal.
Clogged breather tube	Open tube.

Figure 13.31   Leak problems. Use this chart to determine how leak problems can be solved (courtesy of Training Enterprises Company).

diaphragm. Remove the vacuum line to the modulator and if there is fluid present, replace the modulator. Repair any fluid leaks when found. Most common leak points are front or rear seals, pan gasket, around shift linkage, and around the filler tube (see Figure 13.31).

> The two most common problems with automatic transmissions is not changing the fluid and filter on time and running the transmission with the fluid too low. Both these problems can result in internal damage to the transmission. A leaking transmission can result in the fluid being low—the best reason to repair leaks immediately.

VOCABULARY

Use the words listed below to complete the definitions. Either write out the words or place the letters in the blanks.

A. Gear lubricant

B. GL-5

C. SAE

D. Gear

E. Side cover

F. Tail shaft

G. Seal

H. Filler plug

I. Thrust washer

J. Linkage

K. Interlock

L. Backup light switch

M. Clutch disc

N. Slave cylinder

O. Stator

P. Add mark

Q. Contamination

R. Slipping

S. Chatter

T. Automatic transmission filter

U. Master cylinder

V. Synchronizer

W. Pressure plate

X. Pedal travel

Y. Resurface

_____ 1. Society of American Engineers

_____ 2. Caused by worn friction lining

_____ 3. Toothed part that is driven or drives another

_____ 4. Operates the shift fork in a hydraulic clutch

_____ 5. Prevents wear on the end of a shaft

_____ 6. Prevents grease loss around a shaft

_____ 7. Best quality of gear oil

_____ 8. Distance the clutch pedal travels before the clutch disengages

_____ 9. Dextron III

_____ 10. 75W-90

_____ 11. Rear section of a transmission

_____ 12. Part that matches gear speeds for smooth shifting

_____ 13. Closes the opening where gear oil is added or checked

_____ 14. Part that has friction material on each side

_____ 15. One part of an automatic transmission converter

_____ 16. Operates the vehicle backup lights when transmission is in reverse

_____ 17. A machining operation used on flywheels and pressure plates to get them smooth

_____ 18. Vibrational and intermittent defect in a clutch disc operation

_____ 19. When dirt enters a lubricant

_____ 20. Hydraulic part that supplies the force to operate the slave cylinder

_____ 21. Line on a dipstick indicating where fluid should be added

_____ 22. Prevents the transmission from starting in gear

_____ 23. Supplies force to the clutch disc to lock the parts together and operate the transmission

_____ 24. Covers an opening in a transmission used for inspection of the gears

_____ 25. Parts that go from the transmission shift arms to the shift levers

REVIEW QUESTIONS

The following questions will help you determine if you have accomplished the tasks stated at the beginning of this chapter. If you do not know many of the answers, go back and review the material before proceeding to the next chapter.

Lesson 13–1

1. What is the weight range for manual transmission gear lubricant?
2. What is the best API rating placed on gear lubricant?
3. What would be a good multiviscosity gear lubricant for both cold and hot weather?
4. What are the most common transmission speeds for automotive vehicles?
5. How many sets of needle bearings are found per shaft in heavy-duty transmissions?
6. What type of threads are found on a transmission drain plug?
7. Where is the filler plug located in a manual transmission?
8. What are two purposes for the filler plug opening?
9. What do the shift forks do in a manual transmission?
10. What is the primary purpose for having a side cover?
11. What is placed at the end of the tail shaft to prevent fluid loss?
12. What kind of gaskets and seals are found in a standard transmission?
13. What is the purpose of a synchronizer?
14. Where are the thrust washers placed in a standard transmission?

Lesson 13–2

15. How often should the manual transmission gear lubricant be changed?
16. Why should a vehicle be level when checking gear lubricant?
17. What type of gear level checking system is most common on a standard transmission?
18. How does a technician know when the gear linkage is adjusted right?
19. How is an adjustment made on a shift rod?
20. In what gear position should the shift adjustment procedure start?
21. What two transmission areas are potential leak points?
22. What can happen to the vehicle operation if transmission fluid leaks out the front?
23. When is the backup light turned on?
24. What is the purpose of an interlock?

Lesson 13–3

25. Why is it necessary to have a clutch system?
26. What is the rear face of the flywheel used for?

27. What two parts does the clutch disc grip against?
28. How is a clutch disc constructed?
29. When the pressure plate is released, what two parts rotate freely?
30. What does a loud noise usually mean when the clutch pedal is pushed?
31. What parts should be replaced when a clutch system needs repair?
32. What parts are usually resurfaced when a clutch system is rebuilt?
33. What is the name of the part contacting the fingers of the pressure plate?
34. What has happened when the clutch pedal travel starts getting smaller?
35. How much clutch pedal travel is right?
36. What are the names of the two hydraulic parts in a hydraulic clutch?
37. What type and quality fluid is used in a hydraulic clutch?
38. Why is it very important from a safety standpoint to make sure the hydraulic clutch is inspected and repaired before it fails completely?

Lesson 13–4

39. What are the adjustment nuts on the rod-style clutch linkage for?
40. Explain how to adjust the throwout bearing.
41. What is the problem if the throwout bearing does not rotate freely from the fingers of the pressure plate?
42. What prevents clutch linkage from wear?
43. What are the problems if a clutch pedal is released and the clutch system slips?
44. What three fluids can drip out the bottom of the inspection plate cover?
45. What happens if fluid leaks on a clutch system?
46. What tools are used to prepare the slave and master cylinder for the rebuild kits?
47. What is the process called that removes air from the hydraulic system?
48. What is the problem if there is a spongy-feeling pedal on a hydraulic clutch system?

Lesson 13–5

49. What are the three parts of the torque converter called?
50. What prevents the converter fluid from driving the transmission in reverse?
51. What type of gear system runs an automatic transmission?

52. What do the clutches and bands do in an automatic transmission?
53. What is the name of the part in the transmission that reacts to engine speed?
54. What is the latest transmission fluid for GM and Ford?
55. What was the first Ford automatic transmission fluid called?
56. What unit in the transmission gets hot and heats up the fluid?
57. What is the purpose of the heat exchanger?
58. Where is the heat exchanger located?
59. What changes must be made to prevent heat damage if heavy towing is involved?
60. What is the job of the transmission pan?

Lesson 13–6

61. What three conditions should be met before the fluid can be checked accurately?
62. What is the most common method used to check automatic transmission fluid?
63. What happens to transmission fluid before it enters the pump?
64. How is the torque converter drained of lubricant?
65. What color is automatic transmission fluid?
66. What transmission temperature range is considered cool? Warm? Hot?
67. How much fluid does it take to go from the add mark to the full mark on the dipstick?
68. How can coolant mix with the transmission fluid?
69. How does transmission fluid look after it is contaminated by coolant?
70. What are five things to look for on a transmission road test?
71. What is the purpose of a hydraulic fluid pressure test?
72. What is the purpose of a neutral safety switch?

Lesson 13–7

73. What are five problem areas to look for when troubleshooting a manual transmission?
74. What causes chatter in a manual transmission system?
75. What are three problems that can cause failure to engage in a manual transmission?
76. What is the most probable cause of a noise each time the clutch is engaged?
77. Can most throwout bearings be lubricated?
78. What is the usual cause of a slipping clutch?
79. What is the first step to take if noise is heard inside a standard transmission?

80. What are four causes of automatic transmission fluid contamination?
81. Where are three common leak points for an automatic transmission?

ASE QUESTIONS

Each question or incomplete statement in this test is followed by four suggested answers or completions. In each case select the *one* that best answers the question or completes the statement.

1. A manual transmission requires lubricant. Technician A says the best lubricant is marked GL-4. Technician B says the best lubricant is marked GL-3. Who is right?
   a. A only   b. B only
   c. Both A and B   d. Neither A nor B

2. When a transmission is disassembled there were two sets of needle bearings on the shafts. Technician A says this is normal for all manual transmissions. Technician B says this is found only on heavy-duty transmissions. Who is right?
   a. A only   b. B only
   c. Both A and B   d. Neither A nor B

3. A manual transmission is to be filled with lubricant. Technician A says the level should be up to the bottom threads of the filler hole. Technician B says the amount of lubricant should be added until it reaches halfway up to the filler hole. Who is right?
   a. A only   b. B only
   c. Both A and B   d. Neither A nor B

4. A standard transmission is leaking. Technician A says the leak can be coming from the seals. Technician B says it can be coming from the gaskets. Who is right?
   a. A only   b. B only
   c. Both A and B   d. Neither A nor B

5. A standard transmission does not go into mesh without gear noise. Technician A says the synchronizers could be damaged. Technician B says the thrust washers could be worn out. Who is right?
   a. A only   b. B only
   c. Both A and B   d. Neither A nor B

6. A standard transmission is shifted into reverse and the motor shut off. The engine will not start. Technician A says the backup light switch could be defective. Technician B says an interlock could be defective. Who is right?

a. A only   b. B only
c. Both A and B   d. Neither A nor B

7. A clutch disc is being inspected and friction material is found on only one side. Technician A says this is a defective clutch disc because friction material should be on both sides. Technician B says this is normal because the disc is splined to the output shaft of the transmission and doesn't require friction material on both sides. Who is right?
a. A only   b. B only
c. Both A and B   d. Neither A nor B

8. There is 1/4 in. of pedal travel before a clutch disengages. Technician A says this is too little and it should be adjusted to 1 in. Technician B says this amount of travel is correct and it will get larger as the clutch disc wears. Who is right?
a. A only   b. B only
c. Both A and B   d. Neither A nor B

9. A throwout bearing adjustment is being checked. The bearing just touches the fingers of the pressure plate. Technician A says this adjustment is correct as long as the pedal travel is right. Technician B says the bearing should not touch the fingers. Who is right?
a. A only   b. B only
c. Both A and B   d. Neither A nor B

10. Fluid is dripping out the bottom hole of the inspection cover. Technician A says engine oil and transmission can leak into this area. Technician B says that engine coolant can leak into this area. Who is right?
a. A only   b. B only
c. Both A and B   d. Neither A nor B

11. A hydraulic clutch pedal is spongy feeling when the clutch is applied. Technician A says the slave cylinder needs to be adjusted. Technician B says the hydraulic system should be bled. Who is right?
a. A only   b. B only
c. Both A and B   d. Neither A nor B

12. A torque converter operates in both directions. Technician A says it should be prevented from working in reverse by a one-way clutch. Technician B says this is normal and needed to operate the vehicle in reverse. Who is right?
a. A only   b. B only
c. Both A and B   d. Neither A nor B

13. Some transmission fluid needs to be added to a new General Motors vehicle. Technician A says the best fluid to use is Dextron II. Technician B says the best fluid to use is Dextron IV. Who is right?
a. A only   b. B only
c. Both A and B   d. Neither A nor B

14. At what temperature range Fahrenheit is an automatic transmission fluid considered warm?
a. 72–85°   b. 145–195°
c. 86–189°   d. 190–200°

15. The engine of an automatic transmission equipped vehicle speeds up during any shift. Technician A says this problem can be corrected by a linkage adjustment. Technician B says it can be solved by repairing the governor. Who it right?
a. A only   b. B only
c. Both A and B   d. Neither A nor B

16. A manual transmission has shifting problems and does not go into gear normally. Technician A says the linkage should be adjusted. Technician B says the synchronizers should be checked. Who is right?
a. A only   b. B only
c. Both A and B   d. Neither A nor B

17. A clutch system chatters. Technician A says the noise can be caused by rough spots on the flywheel. Technician B says it can be caused by a contaminated clutch lining. Who is right?
a. A only   b. B only
c. Both A and B   d. Neither A nor B

18. An automatic transmission needs a new filter and lubrication change. Technician A says the converter needs to be drained also. Technician B says that when the pan is removed, all the fluid is drained. Who is right?
a. A only   b. B only
c. Both A and B   d. Neither A nor B

14

Drive Shaft, Universal Joint, and Differential System Maintenance

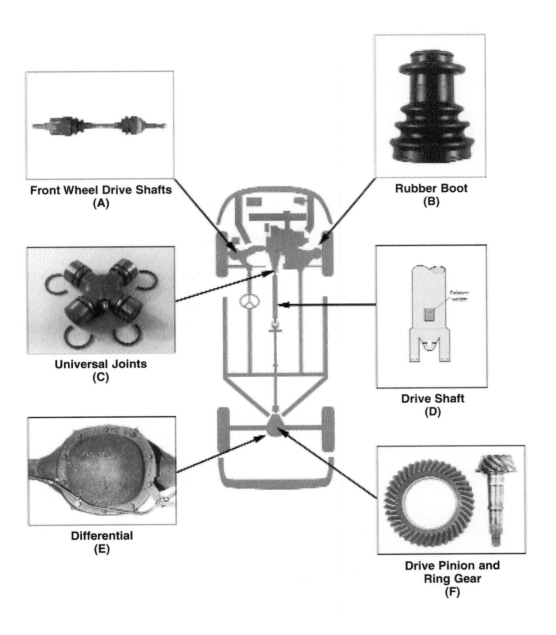

Front Wheel Drive Shafts
(A)

Rubber Boot
(B)

Universal Joints
(C)

Drive Shaft
(D)

Differential
(E)

Drive Pinion and
Ring Gear
(F)

On front wheel drive vehicles, a short drive shaft extends from a differential built into the transmission (transaxle) to each front wheel. Rear wheel drive vehicles have one large drive shaft extending from the rear of the transmission to a differential. The purpose of a drive shaft is to transmit the engine power from the transmission to the differential, which turns the wheels. Universal joints allow the shaft right, left, or up-and-down movement and still keep engine power flowing to the differential. In front wheel drive vehicles, power flows from the transmission through a transaxle and then to the drive shaft. On rear wheel drive vehicles power flows from the transmission to the drive shaft and then to a differential. A differential allows the outside wheels to move faster than the inside wheels when a vehicle is in a curve. Without a differential or transaxle, the vehicle would not go into a curve without sliding the rear or front wheels.

Much important lubrication information is needed to service these parts and the technician must use many types of lubrication materials and equipment.

As we see in this chapter, drive shafts, universal joints, differentials, and transaxles (see Figure 14) use a large assortment of lubrication products and require routine testing and checking. These parts work in severe conditions such as ice, mud, dust, and water. It is very important for the service technician to check seals and dust retainers along with fluid levels to keep these parts free from damage and wear.

TASKS

The following are six tasks to master before leaving this chapter:

Task 14-1.   Learn the parts of a drive shaft and universal joint.

Task 14-2.   Study how to service a drive shaft.

Task 14-3.   Learn how to troubleshoot a drive shaft.

Task 14-4.   Learn the parts of a differential and transaxle.

Task 14-5.   Study how to service a differential and transaxle.

Task 14-6.   Learn how to troubleshoot a differential and transaxle.

LESSON 14–1   Drive Shaft (Propeller Shaft) and Universal Joints

The drive shaft connects the transmission to the differential on rear wheel drive vehicles, and the transaxle directly to the wheels on front wheel drive vehicles. Because the rear differential or front wheels move up and down, there has to be method for the parts to move independently of each other. Universal joints allow this. The distance between the parts changes. A sliding yoke allows for these distance changes (see Figure 14.1). We describe

Figure 14.1   Drive shaft yoke and seal. The sliding yoke moves in and out of the tail shaft of the transmission where the rear seal is located. The outside of the yoke is the seal surface (courtesy of Training Enterprises Company).

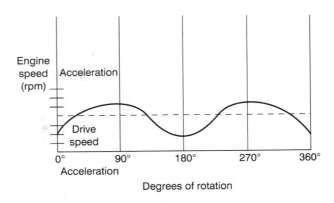

Figure 14.2 Transmission seal. The seal at the rear of the transmission shaft prevents lubricant from leaving the transmission (courtesy of Training Enterprises Company).

Figure 14.3 Drive shaft power. This illustrates how the drive shaft moves faster and slower as it turns one rotation. The shaft transmits full power to the differential even when the speed changes (courtesy of Training Enterprises Company).

the parts of this system in the following paragraphs.

Drive Shaft and Universal Joint Parts

Sliding Yoke. This part is attached to the front of the drive shaft by the front universal joint. Spines inside the yoke fit over the rear shaft of the transmission. The outside surface of the yoke is used to seat against the seal found in the end of the transmission tail shaft (see Figure 14.2).

Universal Joint. Universal joints allow side-to-side and up-and-down motion between parts. They are necessary as the differential moves up and down as the rear wheels follow the road. Full power is transmitted to the differential as the drive shaft speeds up and slows down (see Figure 14.3).

Drive Shaft (Propeller Shaft). The *drive shaft* is a hollow metal tube welded to parts holding the universal joints. Metal weights are placed on the side of the propeller shaft to keep the shaft in balance (see Figure 14.4).

Constant Velocity System. On some vehicles, instead of a long drive shaft, there is a constant velocity universal joint between the front and rear universal joints (see Figure 14.5). The speed of a drive shaft varies even when the motor speed remains constant. This speed changing makes the transfer of power from the transmission to the differential very rough. The constant velocity

universal joint helps smooth out the power transfer and cuts down on vehicle vibration.

Center Bearing Support. In many vehicles, such as trucks, the distance between the end of the transmission and the differential is great. In these applications, the drive shaft is separated in two parts (see Figure 14.6). There is a universal joint at the rear of the transmission with one section of drive shaft going to a center support bearing. This is a bearing mounted in rubber that holds the end of the shaft. The last section of drive shaft is splined into the first section at the support bearing. These parts are free to move just like a regular drive shaft, and this section is built just like a regular drive shaft only much shorter.

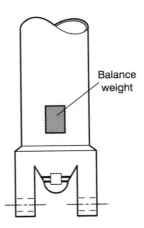

Figure 14.4 Drive shaft weights. These weights are used to balance the drive shaft and prevent vibration (courtesy of Training Enterprises Company).

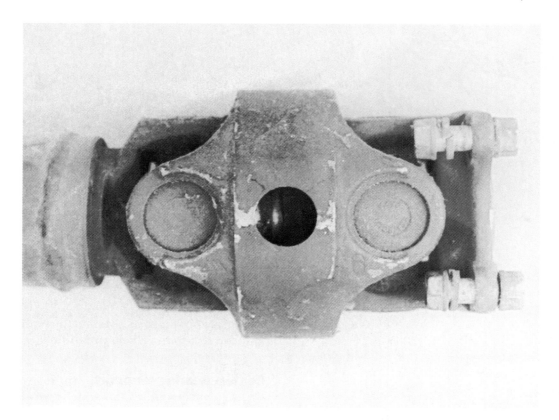

Figure 14.5   Constant velocity universal joint. This type of drive shaft is used to reduce the amount of variation between the engine speed and the drive shaft speed (courtesy of Training Enterprises Company).

Figure 14.6   Center bearing support. A center support is used on longer drive shafts, such as those under pickup trucks. A two-part drive shaft is used and most of the up-and-down movement is restricted to the rear section (courtesy of Training Enterprises Company).

Front Wheel Drive Systems

On front wheel drive vehicles a drive shaft extends out from each side of the transmission, which is placed where the drive shafts can be attached directly to the front wheels (see Figure 14.7). This location places a strain on the drive shafts. Each wheel is moving up and down to follow the road as the driver is moving the wheels from side to side to steer the vehicle. On these systems there is an inner and outer constant velocity joint. These joints are packed with special grease and sealed from dirt by large rubber boots (see Figure 14.8).

LESSON 14–2   Drive Shaft (Propeller Shaft) and Universal Joint Service
Inspection and Testing

While the vehicle is raised to change the oil is also an excellent time to inspect the drive shaft. Look for unusual movement when the shaft is turned by hand. Factory-installed universal joints seldom have grease fittings. Through use they eventually get dry of lubricant, which results in needle bearing

Figure 14.7 Front wheel drive shafts. These shafts have to move up and down and allow the front wheels to turn (courtesy of Training Enterprises Company).

damage. At this point there will be a noticeable movement of the cross shaft in the cups when the parts are inspected and moved by hand. The driver will notice a vibration at low speeds and again at higher speeds.

While under the vehicle to change the oil and lubricate the suspension, check the drive shaft. Hold one part of the drive shaft and try to twist the other. Any movement between the parts indicates wear and needle bearing damage.

Jack up the wheels and rotate the drive shaft by hand. Any binding should be checked further by removing the drive shaft and rotating the parts. As the needle bearings get dry, they start to cut into the end of the cross shaft. This is the major cause of binding. With the vehicle on jack stands, the engine can be started and the wheels turned. Watch the drive shaft and look for a jerky motion or a bent shaft. Look for vibration and listen for noise. With the wheels on the ground, make a reverse and forward test. Put your foot on the brake and place the transmission in drive and then reverse. Worn universal joints make a loud "clunk" when going from forward to reverse.

> It is not good lubrication policy to use different types of chassis lubricant in a universal joint unless you are sure they are compatible. Some lubricants do not mix well and the result causes the original lubricant to thin out and lack the correct viscosity. This causes the lubricant to flow away from the part and results in friction damage.

Inspect front wheel drive vehicles for inner and outer boot damage. The wheels can be jacked up and each wheel rotated by hand. On road tests, a "clicking" noise, especially on turns, means the lubricant has become dry and the steel balls are making a noise. When a boot is torn, you have very little time left to save the universal joints. Dirt and water will rapidly destroy the internal parts. Inspect the joint for worn parts. If there is no damage, it can be cleaned and repacked. After a new

Figure 14.8 Rubber boots. These protect the universal joints, keeping out dirt and water. If the boots become damaged the life of the universal joints is very short (courtesy of Training Enterprises Company).

Figure 14.9   Front wheel drive seal inspection. There is a seal where the drive shaft enters the transaxle. Leaking seals should be replaced (courtesy of Training Enterprises Company).

boot is installed, the joint can be placed back into service. Don't forget to look at each area for seal damage where the front wheel drive shaft enters the transaxle housings. If the drive shaft has to be removed, the seal should be replaced. This is inexpensive insurance to prevent a future leak (see Figure 14.9).

Lubrication

Those universal joints that have grease fittings should be lubricated at the same time the oil is changed. Use regular chassis lubricant. The area where the yoke slides on the splined transmission shaft should be kept free by grease. There may be grease fittings in these parts. If not, they may be lubricated by grease from the inside. Those shafts with center support bearings should be checked carefully. They have to be kept lubricated or the support bearing will be damaged if the yoke will not slide.

Universal Joint Replacement

Many times the problems with universal joints cannot be checked without taking the drive shaft out of the vehicle. Moving and shifting the yoke will determine if there is any binding. When the universal joints need replacement, follow these steps:

Removal

1. Remove the drive shaft from the vehicle. Mark the parts so they can be reassembled in the same relationship to each other (see Figure 14.10). This prevents causing an out-of-balance problem, especially if the parts were balanced at the factory. One method is to use a prick

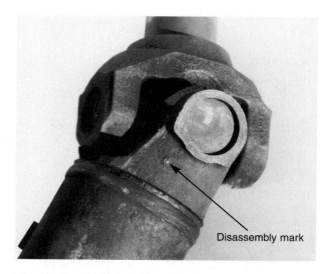

Figure 14.10   Disassembly marks. Use a punch and mark the sections of drive shaft so when reassembled the marks can be put together. This reduces the chance of causing out-of-balance problems (courtesy of Training Enterprises Company).

Figure 14.11 Lock removal. The universal joint cups are held in place by locks. Remove them for disassembly (courtesy of Training Enterprises Company).

Figure 14.12 Lock installation. Reinstall the locks to keep the drive shaft from flying apart. The lock has to be down into a groove and fully expanded (courtesy of Training Enterprises Company).

punch and place one dot on the first parts and two dots on the second parts, and so on.

2. Remove any internal or external clips that hold the universal joint cups in place at the yoke and drive shaft (see Figure 14.11).

3. Lay the cross shaft of the universal joint on the open jaws of a vise. With a brass hammer, tap on the yoke just back of the cup. The cup should start moving out of the yoke. Turn the drive shaft over in the vise to remove the cup at the other end. To remove the other two cups, repeat the process.

Installation

4. To install the new universal joint, first install the yoke end and then the drive shaft end. (Take great care to not let the needle bearings drop down inside the cups.)

5. Put one cup in place in the yoke. Use the vise to carefully force it into the yoke. Put the cross shaft into the open end and fit it back into the

installed cup. Place the other cup over the end of the cross shaft and into the yoke. Keep the cross shaft in place on both cups as you use the vise to force the cups together. Use a socket to seat the cups enough to get the locks into place. If the cups do not move together enough to get the locks in place, the needle bearings have dropped into the cup. The cup will have to be removed and the bearings placed back into the correct position. Install both locks to keep the cups from falling out (see Figure 14.12).

6. Put your identification marks in the right place and install the drive shaft to the yoke. Repeat step 5 to install both cups. Install the locks.

7. Install the grease fitting. Some are press fit and others screw into place (see Figure 14.13). Lubricate the universal joint. It uses the same grease that is used on the suspension system.

8. Install the drive shaft. Put all parts together using the alignment marks you made in the first step. Torque all bolts and make sure the

Figure 14.13 Universal joint grease fitting. Install the grease fitting and add lubrication with a grease gun. Be sure to add this fitting to the list when performing routine service (courtesy of Training Enterprises Company).

cups are down into place on the strap type systems.

9. Road test the vehicle. Drive shaft balance problems are usually felt at 30 to 45 miles per hour and again at 55 to 60 miles per hour. Drive shafts can become bent or out of balance.

When the universal joints have been replaced and there is still a vibration, it may be that the drive shaft parts were installed in the wrong position during a previous repair. The drive shaft parts should be changed to new assembly positions to see if the vibration stops. A drive shaft that cannot be used because of vibration or is bent will have to be replaced.

LESSON 14-3   Differential

The differential is needed to transmit the engine power from the drive shaft to the wheels. As a vehicle goes around a turn, the outside wheel will move faster than the inside wheel. The differential construction allows this to happen and still keeps the engine power going to the wheels.

Differential Parts

Case.   In rear wheel drive vehicles, the differential case is located in the middle with the right and left axle shafts extending out each side (see Figure 14.14). The case is a cast iron part that supports all the other parts. There is a cover on most models bolted to the back and sealed with a gasket. In the bottom is a drain plug and on the side, even with

Figure 14.14   The location of a typical rear wheel drive differential (courtesy of Training Enterprises Company).

DIFFERENTIAL DRAINING	
Plug method	Look for a plug at the front or rear of the unit and remove it to drain out the fluid.
Cover method	Remove the cover and bolts to drain. Install a new cover gasket.
FILLING	
Dipstick method	Add fluid through the dipstick tube. Constantly check to see when the level is correct.
Plug method	Look for a plug in the front or rear of the differential housing at the "full" level. Use only man-ufacturer's recommended fluid and fill to the bottom of the filler plug hole. If too much is added, let it drain out before installing the plug. The plug has pipe threads and should be torqued to specifications.
CHECKING	
Level differential	Be sure to place the vehicle so the differential is level.
Plug method	Remove the fill plug. Use your little finger to check the fluid level inside the filler plug open-ing. The correct level should be up to the bottom of the filler plug hole when the differential is level.
Dipstick method	Pull out the dipstick and wipe it clean. Install and remove the dipstick. "Read" the fluid level on the dipstick.

Figure 14.15 Draining, filling, and checking differentials. This chart describes the most common methods for draining, filling, and checking differentials. Be sure to check the fluid for contamination and dirt (courtesy of Training Enterprises Company).

the correct fluid level, is a filler plug (see Figure 14.15).

Drive Pinion. The drive shaft is attached to the end of the drive pinion. On the other end of the pinion is a gear that drives the ring gear. The pinion rotates on roller bearings and has a grease seal to prevent grease from leaving around the pinion shaft (see Figure 14.16).

Ring Gear. The ring gear is driven by the drive pinion. The ring gear and the pinion make it possible for the engine power to take a 90° turn and place power on the rear wheels through axles (refer to Figure 14.16).

Pinion Gears, Side Gears, and Gear Shafts. When a vehicle makes a turn, the inside wheel slows while the outside wheel accelerates. The pinion gears, side gears, and gear shafts make it possible for each wheel to rotate at different speeds and still receive power from the engine.

Axles, Wheel Bearings, and Axle Housings. An axle extends to each rear wheel and is splined into the side gears. The axle housing covers the axle and contains wheel bearings on the outside near the wheels. These bearings support the weight of

the vehicle and allow the axle to rotate to drive the wheel. A grease seal at the end of the axle housing prevents lubricant loss into the brake system (see Figure 14.17).

LESSON 14–4 **Differential Service**

It takes some effort to inspect and service a differential or transaxle. To make a lubricant check the vehicle must be level and a plug removed from either the rear or front, in the case of a differential, or the side for a transaxle. For the lubricant level to be normal it must be up to the bottom threads of the inspection plug opening. Refer to the Figure 14.18 chart to find the correct lubricant, if any, that has to be added.

The technician will find that not too many vehicle owners service a differential. In many cases it will be run until it gives trouble. They are very complicated parts and require special lubricant.

Leak Inspection

There are three seals on a rear wheel drive differential. One is located at the front, and one is on each side at the ends of the axles. If the grease seals leak

Figure 14.16 Drive pinion and ring gear. The drive pinion operates on bearings and has a seal preventing fluid loss. The pinion turns the ring gear, which is connected to the axles in a rear wheel drive vehicle (courtesy of Training Enterprises Company).

at the axle ends, there should be grease streaks on the inside of the tires. This will also affect the brake system, as the fluid will go inside the drum and on the brake lining. Grease streaks from the front to the rear of the differential housing could mean the drive pinion seal is defective. Defective seals often mean the bearings are also defective. Worn bearings cause the parts to move and the seals get damaged from this movement. If the seals need to be replaced, it is a good time to replace the bearings, because they will be exposed when you replace the seals.

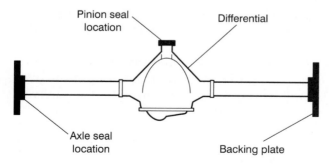

Figure 14.17 Differential grease seals. Three grease seals hold the grease in the differential, one pinion seal and two axle seals. They are located as in this illustration (courtesy of Training Enterprises Company).

Both the filler plug and the drain plug are possible leak points. They are tapered pipe threads that usually seal when the plug is torqued to specifications (see Figure 14.19).

The differential cover (on differentials that have them) is sealed with a gasket and by proper torque on the cover bolts. If there is a leak, try torquing the bolts first before trying to replace the gasket. A new gasket can be made by using the new RTV soft gasket materials.

Fluid Change

Differential fluid should be changed every two years or 30,000 miles. The quality of the fluid should be monitored at each oil change when the level is checked. Excessive dirt and metal particles in the fluid will cause damage to the bearings, seals, gears, and shafts. Eight types of gear oil, or fluid, are used in differentials. Regular fluid is used in all differentials other than positive traction. The positive traction differentials require a special lubricant (see Figure 14.18). *Never* put regular lubricant in a positive traction differential. This will damage the friction plates that lock up the differential when one wheel tries to spin. This would require a complete disassembly and some parts replacement.

DIFFERENTIAL GEAR OIL	
API service classifications	GL–1 to GI–5 are manufactured. The most common classifications used today are GL–4 and GL–5. GL–4 has two types. One has regular "extreme pressure" additives and the other has special nonreactive additives that avoid internal damage.
Viscosity grades	Some common grades are 75W, 80W, 80, 90, and 140. Common multigrades are 75W–90, and 80W–90. Multigrades and low common grade numbers are used where cold temperatures have an effect.
Limited slip	Either mix an additive with the gear oil or a special GL–5 rated gear oil for limited-slip differentials.
HP	Hypoid gear oil used with some Dana and Ford axles.
HP (limited slip)	Made to be used with limited-slip and positive traction differentials.
EP gear oil	An extreme pressure gear oil recommended by some manufacturers where there is high pressure placed on the gears.
GL special gear oil	Recommended for many limited-slip differentials. This oil is rated at GL–5 but only recommended for limited-slip applications.
Others	Some manufacturers only recommend a gear oil made specially for their gear systems. This oil has to be ordered through the manufacturer. These products have been supplied to solve special problems and it is not recommended that anything else be used.

NOTE: Always consult the manufacturer's recommendations before adding any product to a differential. Use the correct quality, classification, and viscosity. Use caution when newer products are marketed—they might not be suitable for older vehicles. Be sure the manufacturer has approved them as a substitute.

Figure 14.18 Differential gear oil. This chart covers most of the common differential fluids in use. Always consult the manufacturer's recommendations for rating, viscosity, additives, cold weather, and newer products (courtesy of Training Enterprises Company).

Axle Bearings

When the axle bearings become noisy or a vibration is felt, the axle bearings should be checked. The most common way to do this on standard differentials is to jack up one rear wheel at a time and use the engine to run the wheel that is off the ground. Listen for noise and check for any vibration. Replace any axle bearings that make a noise. Two types of axle bearings are on rear wheels. Type one is where the bearing and race are built together and the bearing is pressed on the axle shaft. It is held in place with a metal retainer ring. Type two is where the surface of the axle serves as a bearing race. When this bearing fails, it usually damages the axle making an axle replacement necessary along with the bearing. The axle in this system is held from moving by a horseshoe-shaped lock placed in the differential.

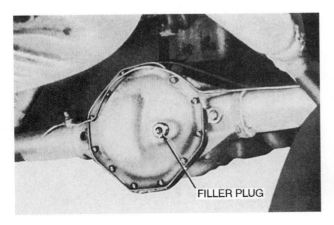
FILLER PLUG

Figure 14.19 A filler plug located in the differential cover of a rear wheel drive car (courtesy of Chrysler Corporation).

Rear axle seals are usually damaged when the axle bearing fails. Never replace the seal without checking the bearing for damage or wear. Always replace the seals when new bearings are installed.

Seals

Grease seals on the ends of the axles prevent the differential lubricant from leaving the end of the axle housing and going into the brake system. There is a third seal around the pinion shaft (see Figure 14.17). Seals fail rapidly if the lubricant is not changed on a regular schedule. Contaminated lubricant causes the bearings to wear prematurely. A loose bearing lets the axle move in the seal and damages the seal surface. The seal will no longer keep the lubricant in the differential.

Ring and Pinion Adjustment

When the *backlash*, or the movement between the pinion and the ring gear, becomes excessive, it should be adjusted. The differential cover has to be removed and the ring gear set closer to the pinion gear.

Backlash is checked with a dial indicator. There should be enough backlash between the gears to allow for heat expansion. If there is at least 0.008 in. backlash, this should allow enough expansion room for most applications and still not allow any gear noise. To be certain, always check the manufacturer's specifications for the vehicle. Since the gears are wedge shaped, as the ring gear is adjusted closer to the pinion, the backlash gets smaller. Consult with each manufacturer's repair manuals to get the proper settings and adjustment procedures.

LESSON 14–5   Troubleshooting Drive Shaft (Propeller Shaft)

Drive shafts can become bent or out of balance, and can have yoke damage. To determine if the drive shaft is bent, jack the vehicle up and install jack stands under the frame. Start the engine and place the transmission in drive. While the wheels are turning, look under the vehicle at the rotating drive shaft. A bent drive shaft is easy to spot. Out-of-balance drive shafts can also be detected when the vehicle is jacked up and being driven. The vehicle should vibrate at low speed and later as the speed is increased. Vibration can also be produced if the universal joints are worn or damaged. When vibration is traced to the drive shaft, remove the shaft and check the universal joints by moving them. Replace a binding or worn universal joint.

CHECKING DIFFERENTIAL LUBRICANT LEVEL

Checking the level of lubricant in a differential also requires that you go under the car. Differentials have filler holes too, but they can be in different locations. Figure 14.19 shows a filler plug located in the rear cover of the differential of a rear wheel drive car. Some similar differentials have the filler plug in the side of the housing in front of the axle. Such a location is shown in Figure 14.20, Figure 14.21 shows the location of the differential filler plug on a front wheel drive car. As with manual transmissions, the plug is positioned so that the correct level of lubricant is present when the surface of the lubricant is near the bottom edge of the hole. The location and size of the filler hole in

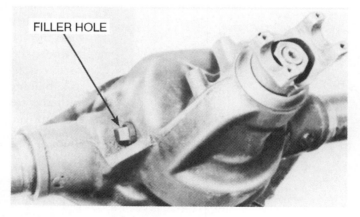

FILLER HOLE

Figure 14.20   A filler plug located in the side of a differential housing (courtesy of Chrysler Corporation).

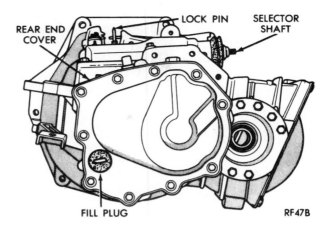

REAR END COVER — LOCK PIN — SELECTOR SHAFT

FILL PLUG   RF47B

Figure 14.21 The fill plug is on the side of this transaxle used on a front wheel drive car (courtesy of Chrysler Corporation).

The transaxle lubricant level is checked just like a rear differential if the side plug method is used. Level the vehicle and check the fluid height at the filler plug hole. It should be up to the bottom threads of the hole. Select the right lubricant from the chart in Figure 14.18 if fluid needs to be added.

some differentials makes it difficult, if not impossible, to use your finger as a gauge. In those units, you can bend a piece of welding rod or coat hanger wire to form a dipstick. If excess lubricant is found, it should be allowed to drain out.

The following steps outline a typical procedure for checking the level of lubricant in a differential. Consult an appropriate manual or lubrication chart for the specific lubricants and procedures that may be necessary for the car on which you are working.

1. Raise and support the car so that it is level.
2. Remove the filler plug on the differential (refer to Figures 14.19 through 14.21).

   Note: Some differentials are fitted with a "press-in" type filler plug of the type shown in Figure 14.22. Plugs of this type must be pried out carefully to avoid damage to the plug.

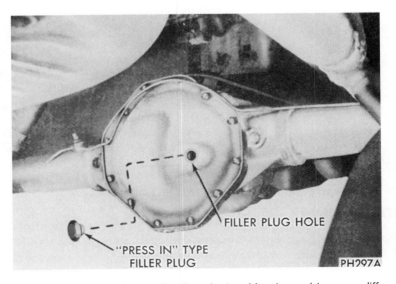

FILLER PLUG HOLE

"PRESS IN" TYPE FILLER PLUG   PH297A

Figure 14.22 A "press-in" plug made of synthetic rubber is used in some differentials (courtesy of Chrysler Corporation).

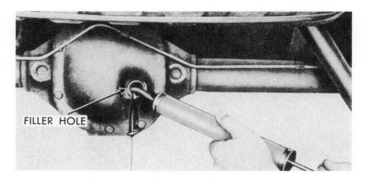

Figure 14.23 Using a suction gun to add lubricant to a differential (courtesy of Chrysler Corporation).

3. Check the level of the lubricant.

   Note: If you cannot insert your finger into the filler hole, fashion a small dipstick from a short length of wire.

4. Add the specified lubricant if the level is low. Use a suction gun to add lubricant, as shown in Figure 14.23. Allow excess lubricant to drain out.

   Note: Check to see if the differential is of the limited-slip type. Most limited-slip differentials require a special lubricant. Some limited-slip differentials are identified by a tag as shown in Figure 14.24. Others are identified by a code number or letter on the vehicle identification plate. Be sure that you add the correct lubricant.

5. Install the filler plug.

   Note: Tighten the plug with a short wrench to avoid overtightening. If the plug is of the press-in type, be sure it is fully seated in the axle cover.

6. Lower the car to the floor.

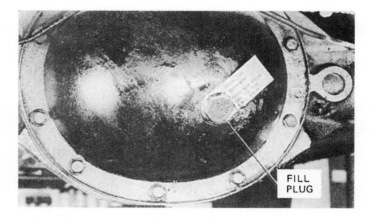

Figure 14.24 Limited-slip differential. Some limited-slip or locking-type differentials are identified by a tag or plate (courtesy of American Motors).

Universal Testing

Universal joints can wear out or become damaged. To look for universal joint damage, start the engine and put your foot on the brake. Open the door so you can hear better. Shift the transmission from reverse to drive and listen. A worn universal joint will make a loud clunk in the drive shaft area. Another method is to jack up the vehicle and place it on jack stands. When the wheels are turning, gently put your foot on the brake and let off. A worn-out universal joint will make a noise as the brakes are applied and released. A worn universal joint will show up on a road test as a vibration and a noise

Job 14A

CHECK AND ADJUST TRANSMISSION AND DIFFERENTIAL LEVELS

SATISFACTORY PERFORMANCE

A satisfactory performance on this job requires that you do the following:

1. Check and, if necessary, adjust the transmission and differential lubricant levels on the car assigned.
2. Following the steps in the "Performance Outline" and the procedures and specifications of the car manufacturer, complete the job within 30 minutes.
3. Fill in the blanks under "Information."

PERFORMANCE OUTLINE

1. Raise and support the car so that it is level.
2. Check the transmission lubricant level and adjust it if necessary.
3. Check the differential lubricant level and adjust it if necessary.
4. Lower the car to the floor.

INFORMATION

Vehicle identification _____

Reference used _____ Page(s) _____

Transmission lubricant specified _____

Transmission lubricant level was:

_____ Correct _____ Too low _____ Too high

If too low, was lubricant added? _____ Yes _____ No

If lubricant was added, indicate API classification and SAE viscosity _____

Differential type: _____ Standard _____ Limited-slip

Differential lubricant specified _____

Differential lubricant level was:

_____ Correct _____ Too low _____ Too high

If too low, was lubricant added? _____ Yes _____ No

If lubricant was added, indicate API classification and SAE viscosity _____

during acceleration and deceleration. A binding universal joint will cause a vibration but may not make a noise.

Differential Testing

The complexity of differentials presents more problems when troubleshooting for possible problems. Differentials should be checked for the following:

1. Leaks at the drain plugs, cover, and seal areas
2. Bearing damage and noise
3. Ring and pinion gear wear
4. Side gear damage or wear

When there are seal leaks, the differential lubricant usually drains out and makes a pattern on the tires. The brakes can be affected because the fluid leaks into the area where the brake shoes are located. The differential fluid on the linings will make them ineffective at stopping the vehicle. When only one wheel is affected, the other wheel will lock while the leaking wheel will not stop. A pinion shaft leak will let fluid drain out the front of the differential and under the housing toward the rear of the vehicle. Whenever there is a differential leak, always check to see if the differential has been overfilled. This will always cause leaks because the seals are not designed to hold back higher-than-normal fluid levels. If the level is correct, look for other problems, such as seal damage or gasket deterioration.

Bearing damage and noise will be felt and heard on a road test, or by driving the vehicle on jack stands. A loud grinding noise at either wheel usually indicates bearing damage or wear. *Note:* Certain brake problems can also make grinding noises at the wheels. Further investigation should be made to determine the source of any noise after it has been isolated to one of the wheels.

With differentials that are not positive traction, one wheel can be jacked up and the other left on the ground to listen for bearing damage and side gear noise. Check for side gear noise at each wheel by jacking up one wheel and driving the vehicle in place. Do the same for the other side. Listen for any unusual noise. *Never* try to drive in place with one wheel on the ground with a limited-slip or positive traction differential. *Never* drive the vehicle over 30 miles per hour because this translates to 60 miles per hour road speed. Multiply the speedometer speed by 2 to get the actual road speed when one wheel is stationary.

If the adjustment between the ring and pinion gear is too loose, the differential will make a noise on the road, or you may hear a clunk similar to a worn universal joint when moving the transmission selector from forward to reverse and back again.

VOCABULARY

Use the listed words in the blanks beside the sentences to complete the definitions. Either write out the words or place the letters in the blanks.

A. Drive shaft

B. Transaxle

C. Splines

D. Metal weights

E. Constant velocity

F. Grease fitting

G. Repack

H. Out of balance

I. Clip

J. Cross shaft

K. Cup

L. Vise

M. Torque

N. Differential

O. Drive pinion

P. Ring

Q. Side gear

R. Gear shaft

S. Dipstick

T. Wheel bearing

U. Drain plug

V. Positive traction

W. Race

X. Backlash

Y. Code number

_____ 1. Part used for lubrication

_____ 2. Removed to let fluid out

_____ 3. Transmits engine power to the wheels

_____ 4. Grooves cut in a shaft to prevent any turning between the parts

_____ 5. The part of the universal joint that fits over the ends of the cross shaft

_____ 6. Holds the universal joint in place in the yoke

_____ 7. Round gear that works with and is driven by the pinion gear

_____ 8. Space between the ring and pinion gear

_____ 9. To clean and lubricate a part

_____ 10. Tool that applies force to parts so they can be worked on

_____ 11. Special universal joint that reduces speed changes

_____ 12. The outside part of a wheel bearing that the roller bearings move against

_____ 13. Transmits engine power from the transmission to the differential

_____ 14. Contains balls or rollers used so shafts will have less friction

_____ 15. Parts identification numbers

_____ 16. Amount of twisting force applied to a shaft, nut, or bolt

_____ 17. More weight on one side of a shaft than the other causing a vibration

_____ 18. Part that drives the ring gear

_____ 19. Used to balance a drive shaft

_____ 20. Differential gears

_____ 21. Front wheel drive differential

_____ 22. Used to check fluid levels

_____ 23. Part that keeps the back wheels from spinning independently of each other

_____ 24. Center part of a universal joint

_____ 25. Part that the side gears rotate on

REVIEW QUESTIONS

The following questions will help you determine if you have accomplished the tasks stated at the beginning of this chapter. If you do not know many of the answers, go back and review the material before proceeding to the next chapter.

Lesson 14–1

1. What part connects the transmission to the differential in a rear wheel drive vehicle?
2. What part allows drive shaft parts to move independently of each other?
3. What part allows for distance changes between the transmission and differential?
4. What type of motion do universal joints allow?
5. What parts balance a drive shaft?
6. What is the advantage of a constant velocity universal joint over a standard one?
7. What additional part is needed if the distance between the transmission and the differential is large?
8. What is a spline?

Lesson 14–2

9. When is an excellent time to perform a drive shaft inspection?
10. What kind of universal joints may not have grease fittings?
11. What defect can be found by observing a rotating drive shaft?
12. What will the reverse and forward test reveal about a drive shaft?
13. What should be inspected on front wheel drive shafts?
14. What does a "clicking" noise indicate on a front wheel drive shaft?
15. Where is a seal located on a front wheel drive shaft system?

16. What type of lubricant is used on a universal joint that has grease fittings?
17. What parts have to slide on a center support bearing system to prevent damage?
18. What is the best procedure to use when making an accurate check of a drive shaft and universals?
19. Why should drive shaft parts be marked before disassembly?
20. What is the purpose of a clip or lock on a universal?
21. How are the universal joint cups removed from a drive shaft?
22. If after universal joint replacement a drive shaft vibrates, what is a possible problem?

Lesson 14–3
23. In a turn, which rear wheel rotates the fastest?
24. A differential does what two things?
25. What is attached to the forward end of the pinion shaft?
26. What part drives the ring gear?
27. What parts allow one wheel to move faster than another?
28. What parts are located on the outside of each rear axle?

Lesson 14–4
29. How many seals are located on a rear wheel drive differential?
30. What is a sign the rear wheel axle seals are leaking?
31. What other system may be damaged from a leaking axle seal?
32. How can a damaged bearing ruin a grease seal?
33. What kind of threads are on the drain and filler plug?
34. Where is RTV material used on a differential?
35. How often should differential fluid be changed?
36. What service should be done at each oil change to the differential fluid?
37. What should never be done to a positive traction differential?
38. How does a positive traction differential work?
39. How can standard differential axle bearings be checked?
40. What are two types of rear axle bearing systems used today?
41. On the type two system, what is usually damaged when the wheel bearings fail?
42. What happens to the ring and pinion gear adjustment when the parts are moved closer to each other?

Lesson 14–5
43. What are two causes of a drive shaft vibration?
44. How will a worn-out universal joint act during a forward and reverse test?
45. What will a binding universal joint cause?
46. What are four things to look for when checking a differential?
47. How will the brake system act if differential fluid is leaking out of one wheel into the brakes?
48. What is the first check to make if a differential is leaking at the seals?

ASE QUESTIONS

Each question or incomplete statement in this test is followed by four suggested answers or completions. In each case select the *one* that best answers the question or completes the statement.

1. There is a binding action and noise each time the rear wheels of a standard transmission vehicle go over a bump. Technician A says this could be a differential problem. Technician B says the sliding yoke is binding. Who is right?
   a. A only   b. B only
   c. Both A and B   d. Neither A nor B

2. The purpose of a universal joint is being discussed. Technician A says it allows side-to-side motion. Technician B says it allows up-and-down motion. Who is right?
   a. A only   b. B only
   c. Both A and B   d. Neither A nor B

3. Drive shaft operation is being discussed. Technician A says the drive shaft speed matches the engine speed. Technician B says the drive shaft speeds up and slows down independent of the engine speed. Who is right?
   a. A only   b. B only
   c. Both A and B   d. Neither A nor B

4. A vehicle has factory-installed universal joints. Technician A says this type of universal joint never needs lubrication. Technician B says this type of universal joint requires lubrication every 30,000 miles. Who is right?
   a. A only   b. B only
   c. Both A and B   d. Neither A nor B

5. A loud "clunk" is heard during a forward to reverse test. Technician A says the universal joints should be replaced. Technician B says the universal joints should be lubricated. Who is right?
   a. A only   b. B only
   c. Both A and B   d. Neither A nor B

6. A "clicking" noise is heard on a front wheel drive vehicle. This noise is in the front and louder when making a turn. Technician A says the universal joints should be replaced. Technician B says the universal joints should be repacked. Who is right?
   a. A only
   b. B only
   c. Both A and B
   d. Neither A nor B

7. A vibration is traced to the drive shaft. A visual inspection and driving in place test do not pinpoint the problem. Technician A says all parts should be lubricated to see if the problem goes away. Technician B says the drive shaft should be taken out and checked for wear and binding at the cups. Who is right?
   a. A only
   b. B only
   c. Both A and B
   d. Neither A nor B

8. A drive shaft universal joint has grease fittings. Technician A says chassis lubricant can be used. Technician B says wheel bearing grease can be used. Who is right?
   a. A only
   b. B only
   c. Both A and B
   d. Neither A nor B

9. A universal joint needs replacement. Technician A says that a hydraulic press is needed to remove the old parts and install new ones. Technician B says the old parts can be removed by placing the cross shaft on a vise and using a brass hammer to remove the cups. Who is right?
   a. A only
   b. B only
   c. Both A and B
   d. Neither A nor B

10. The new universal joint caps will not go onto the cross shaft far enough to get the locks in place. Technician A says a needle bearing has fallen inside the cup and has to be set back in place. Technician B says the universal joint is the wrong size for this application. Who is right?
    a. A only
    b. B only
    c. Both A and B
    d. Neither A nor B

11. Differential operation is being discussed. Technician A says the differential allows one wheel to rotate faster than the other while making a turn. Technician B says when one wheel spins no power is applied to the other wheel. Who is right?
    a. A only
    b. B only
    c. Both A and B
    d. Neither A nor B

12. A side gear in a rear wheel drive differential has damaged teeth. Technician A says the noise will be constant and only change with engine speed. Technician B says the noise will change in frequency on turns when the engine speed is constant. Who is right?
    a. A only
    b. B only
    c. Both A and B
    d. Neither A nor B

13. Grease is leaking at the axles and pinion shaft on a differential. Technician A says the differential was overfilled. Technician B says the grease seals are damaged and need to be replaced. Who is right?
    a. A only
    b. B only
    c. Both A and B
    d. Neither A nor B

14. A drive shaft is bent. Technician A says this can be verified more accurately by a road test. Technician B says this can be determined with a visual test and the vehicle run when jacked up. Who is right?
    a. A only
    b. B only
    c. Both A and B
    d. Neither A nor B

15. The backlash needs to be adjusted on a differential. Technician A says the backlash will get larger when the ring and pinion gears are brought closer together. Technician B says the backlash will get smaller when the gears are moved apart. Who is right?
    a. A only
    b. B only
    c. Both A and B
    d. Neither A nor B

16. The differential fluid in a rear wheel drive vehicle needs to be checked. Technician A says this can be done while the rear of the vehicle is jacked up and placed on jack stands. Technician B says the vehicle should be jacked up both front and rear and placed on jack stands. Who is right?
    a. A only
    b. B only
    c. Both A and B
    d. Neither A nor B

17. A seal is leaking at the end of one axle on a differential. Technician A says the bearing may be worn or damaged and should be replaced along with the seal. Technician B says the seal should be replaced and the brake system should be inspected for lining contamination. Who is right?
    a. A only
    b. B only
    c. Both A and B
    d. Neither A nor B

18. A positive traction differential is low on lubricant. Technician A says to use only the best quality regular gear oil. Technician B says to use a special lubricant made only for limited-slip differentials. Who is right?
    a. A only
    b. B only
    c. Both A and B
    d. Neither A nor B

15

Steering and Suspension System Maintenance

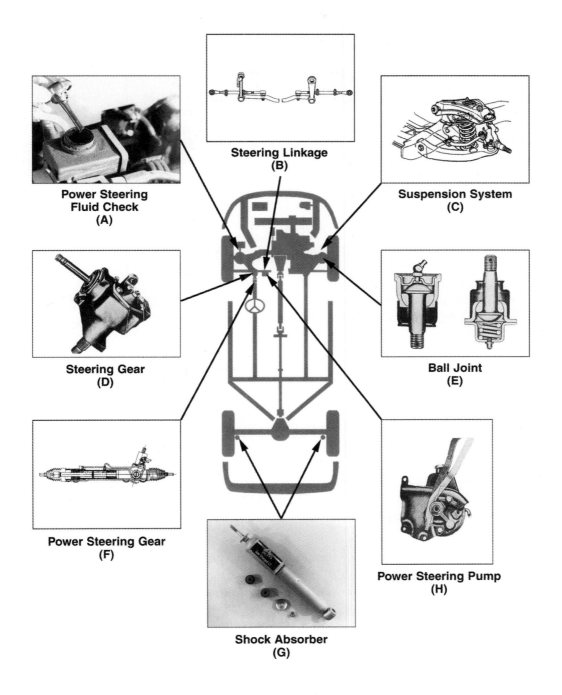

Power Steering
Fluid Check
(A)

Steering Linkage
(B)

Suspension System
(C)

Steering Gear
(D)

Ball Joint
(E)

Power Steering Gear
(F)

Power Steering Pump
(H)

Shock Absorber
(G)

The steering system (see Figure 15a, b, d, and f) allows the driver to control the vehicle and move it to the left or right as it goes down the road. The suspension system (see Figure 15c, e, and g) keeps the wheels on the surface of the road and at the same time allows the passengers to have a smooth comfortable ride. Bumps and road shocks are prevented from reaching the passengers when absorbed by the springs and shock absorbers. The trend is to move away from the need to lubricate the suspension system, but replacement parts often have grease fittings. These require chassis grease and regular maintenance.

Both steering and suspension systems do a lot of twisting, turning, bouncing, and vibrating. It is important to check these systems on a regular basis for damage and wear. When lubrication is required and applied, these units give many miles of service. The service technician should know how to check fluid levels and worn or damaged parts. Poorly serviced and maintained parts in these critical areas can result in serious accidents or loss of vehicle control.

Anyone studying to be an automotive technician should do a complete study of vehicle suspension and steering systems. You should know how to detect worn and damaged parts and how to replace these parts when needed. Use the correct lubrication materials in each unit as well as apply and maintain these materials.

TASKS

The following are six tasks to master before leaving this chapter:

Task 15-1.   Study the types of suspension systems and how they work.

Task 15-2.   Learn to service a suspension system.

Task 15-3.   Learn to troubleshoot a suspension system.

Task 15-4.   Study the parts that make up a steering system and how they work.

Task 15-5.   Learn to service a steering system.

Task 15-6.   Learn to troubleshoot a steering system.

LESSON 15-1   Suspension Systems

The suspension systems hold the wheels of a car in their proper relationship to the car and to the road. This relationship must be maintained regardless of the road surface, the direction of travel, or the speed of the car.

The steering system provides the link between the driver and the front wheels of the car. It must provide a sensitive but positive means of moving the wheels the exact distance required for steering.

Routine maintenance of the suspension and steering systems requires a knowledge of the parts in the systems and the function of those parts. Without suspension systems, a car could not be controlled at high speed. Road shock would bounce the wheels so much that the tires would lose contact with the road. Neither steering nor braking would be effective. In turning, the car would have a strong tendency to skid and even to roll over. The impact of each bump in the road would be passed on directly to the car and its passengers. Parts would break, and a comfortable ride would be impossible.

Many different suspension systems are in use. Most of them provide an acceptable degree of roadability and riding comfort. All use some sort of springs or other shock-absorbing devices. These systems are of two basic types: (1) *solid axle suspension systems*, and (2) *independent suspension systems*.

Solid Axle Suspension Systems

In solid axle systems, a wheel is mounted at each end of a solid, or undivided, axle or axle housing. This type of suspension system has the advantages of strength and low cost, but it provides less efficiency and comfort than independent systems. Where solid axle suspension systems are used in passenger cars, they are usually used only at the rear. A solid axle rear suspension system is shown in Figure 15.1. Solid axle front suspension systems are usually found only on heavy-duty vehicles and trucks. A solid axle front suspension system is shown in Figure 15.2

Because the axle connects both wheels, any condition that affects one wheel affects the other. Figure 15.3 shows that when one wheel is raised,

Figure 15.1 A solid rear axle suspension system used on a rear wheel drive car (courtesy of Chevrolet Motor Division, General Motors Corporation).

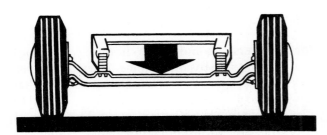

Figure 15.2 A solid axle front suspension (courtesy of Hunter Engineering Company, Bridgeton, MO).

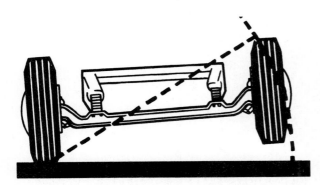

Figure 15.3 Axle-tilt effect. The tilt effect of a solid axle suspension system (courtesy of Hunter Engineering Company, Bridgeton, MO).

as it is by a bump in the road, the axle is tilted. Thus the motion of the raised wheel is passed to the other wheel, which tilts outward. Since the frame of the car is attached to the axle, the car body is also tilted.

Independent Suspension Systems

Independent suspension systems provide a separate mounting for each wheel. There is no connec-

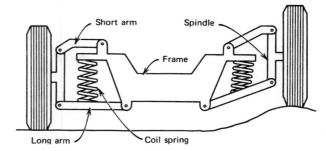

Figure 15.4 Independent front suspension. The action of a long and short arm independent front suspension system (courtesy of Ford Motor Company, Dearborn, MI).

tion between the wheels as there is with a solid axle. Therefore, the motion of one wheel is not transmitted to the other, and there is no tilting of an axle that, in turn, might tilt the entire car.

Long and Short Arm Suspension Systems

One type of independent suspension system commonly used on the front of rear wheel drive vehicles is referred to as the *long and short arm suspension system*. As shown in Figure 15.4, each wheel is mounted on a spindle. The spindle is attached to the frame of the car by a long arm on the bottom and a short arm on the top. These arms, called *control arms*, are pivoted at both ends. This permits the spindles to move up and down without moving the frame.

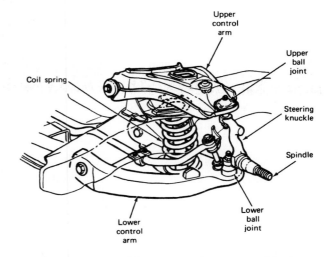

Figure 15.5 A typical front suspension system of the long and short arm type. Notice that the coil spring is mounted between the lower control arm and the frame (courtesy of Chevrolet Motor Division, General Motors Corporation).

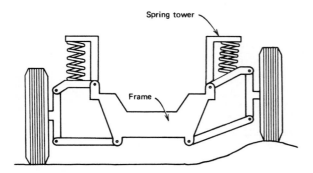

Figure 15.6 Upper spring mount. A long and short arm suspension system with the spring mounted between the upper control arm and a spring tower.

The length of the control arms and the placement of their pivot points are such that the point of contact between the tires and the road does not change as the wheels move up and down. This arrangement minimizes scuffing of the tires as the suspension system allows the wheels to rise and dip with the road surface.

Coil Springs.   The compact design of a coil spring makes it ideal for use in front suspen-

sion systems. Two types of coil spring mountings are commonly used in long and short arm suspension systems. In the first type, the spring is positioned between the frame and the lower control arm (refer to Figure 15.4). This mounting is most often used on cars with a conventional or partial front frame. Figure 15.5 shows this type of mounting as it actually appears on a car.

The second type of mounting is shown in Figure 15.6. In this mounting, the coil spring is positioned between the upper control arm and a spring tower formed in the inner section of the fender. This type of mounting is usually found on cars of unit body construction. Its actual appearance is shown in Figure 15.7.

Torsion Bars.   Some cars do not use coil springs in the front suspension systems. They use *torsion bars* instead. A torsion bar is a spring steel bar that is twisted to give spring action. It can be likened to a coil spring that has been unwound. The action of a torsion bar is shown in Figure 15.8.

In some systems, a torsion bar is mounted parallel to a side rail of the car frame. The forward

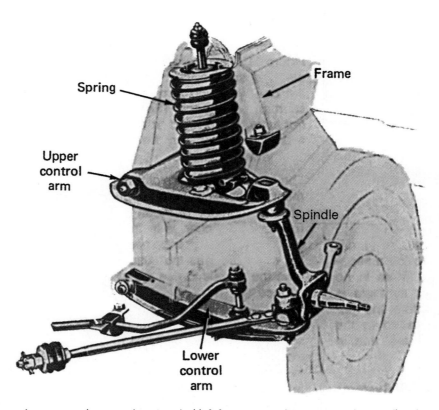

Figure 15.7 Upper-spring-mounted suspension. A typical left front suspension system using a coil spring mounted between the upper control arm and a spring tower (courtesy of Ford Motor Company, Dearborn, MI).

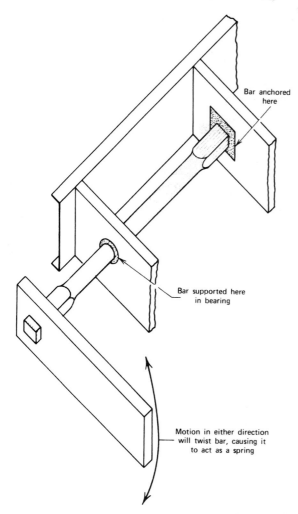

Figure 15.8 Torsion bar action. The action of a torsion bar is like a coil spring. Some manufacturers use the torsion bar in the place of a spring.

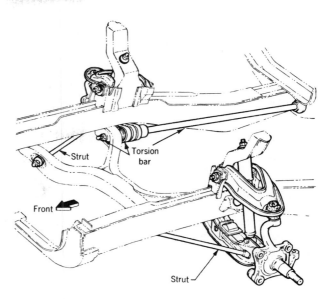

Figure 15.9 A front suspension system using torsion bars mounted parallel to the sides of the frame (courtesy of Chrysler Corporation).

end of the bar is connected to a lower control arm. The opposite end is connected to the frame. Figure 15.9 shows one type of torsion bar as it is mounted in a front suspension system. In some suspension systems, the torsion bar is mounted *transversely*, or across the frame, as shown in Figure 15.10.

Control Arms. The upper control arms are usually triangle-shaped (see Figure 15.11). The base of such an arm is fitted with a pivot shaft or bolts that allow the arm to swing up and down on bushings. The pivot shaft is attached to the car frame. The outer end of the arm is fitted with a *ball joint* that connects the upper arm to the spindle.

Lower control arms also may be triangle-shaped, as shown in Figure 15.12, or they may be straight, as shown in Figure 15.13. Both types are attached to the car frame by pivot shafts or bolts so they are free to swing up and down. The outer end of the lower control arm is also fitted with a ball joint. Lacking the broad, stable base provided by a triangle shape, a straight lower control arm tends to move back and forth. This movement is prevented by a brace called a *strut*. The strut is connected to the outer end of the lower control arm and to the frame (see Figure 15.14).

Spindles. Spindles are forged in one piece. They have a vertical brace that is attached to the ball joints of the control arms. Many car makers refer to spindles as *steering knuckles*. Both terms are commonly used. A typical spindle is shown in Figure 15.15.

Spindles perform many jobs. They connect the upper and lower control arms in the suspension system. Moved by the steering arms, they turn the front wheels. They also serve as mounts for the brake calipers and splash shields. On older cars with drum brakes at the front wheels, the spindles serve as mounts for the anchor pins and the backing plates. As you can see, spindles are part of the steering and brake systems as well as the suspension system.

To become familiar with the parts in typical long and short arm suspension systems, carefully study Figures 15.16 and 15.17.

Job 15A

IDENTIFY THE PARTS OF A LONG AND SHORT ARM INDEPENDENT FRONT SUSPENSION SYSTEM

SATISFACTORY PERFORMANCE
A satisfactory performance on this job requires that you do the following:

1. Identify the numbered parts on the drawing by placing each number in front of the correct part name.
2. Correctly identify all the parts within 15 minutes.

PERFORMANCE SITUATION

_____ Strut   _____ Strut bushings   _____ Stabilizer link bolt
_____ Upper ball Joint   _____ Spring insulator   _____ Upper control arm bushing
_____ Shock absorber   _____ Spindle   _____ Stabilizer bar
_____ Inner shaft   _____ Lower ball joint   _____ Coil spring
_____ Lower control arm   _____ Stabilizer link bolt spacer _____ Stabilizer bracket
_____ Upper control arm

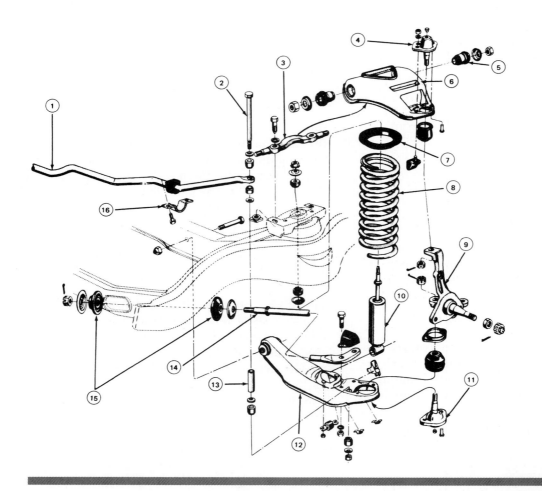

Chassis Lubrication

The suspension system, the steering system, and the drive train have many moving parts. Movement between parts in contact produces friction, which causes wear. Whenever there is motion between metal parts in contact, a lubricant must be used. The lubricant coats the parts, minimizing friction and wear.

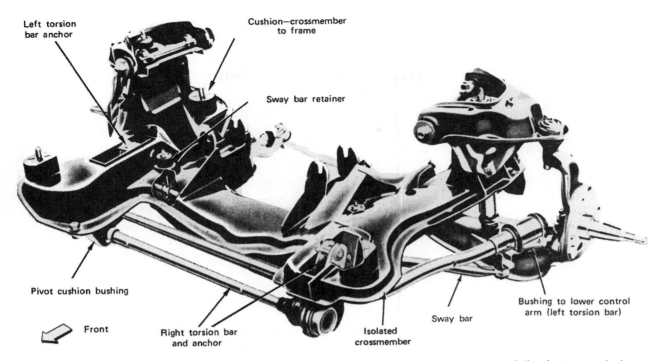

Figure 15.10 A front suspension system using torsion bars mounted across the frame (courtesy of Chrysler Corporation).

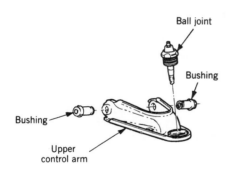

Figure 15.11 A typical upper control arm assembly (courtesy of Chrysler Corporation).

Figure 15.12 A triangle-shaped lower control arm (courtesy of General Motors Corporation).

Current trends have resulted in fewer lubrication points on front suspension and steering parts. This means inspection has become all-important. When lubricating the older system parts, the technician was making a point-to-point inspection of the entire suspension and steering system. This is no longer true. Inspect all suspension parts at each oil change interval.

Most chassis components on vehicles of current production are lubricated and sealed at the time of their manufacture. But there are millions of vehicles on the road with chassis parts that require lubrication at regular intervals. Depending on the particular car, lubrication intervals are specified from 6000 to 35,000 miles (9600 to 56,000 km).

Figure 15.13 A straight lower control arm (courtesy of Ford Motor Company, Dearborn, MI).

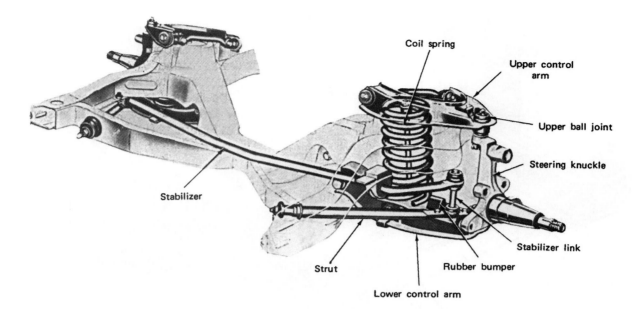

Figure 15.14 Strut-type front suspension. A front suspension system using a strut to control the movement of the straight lower control arm (courtesy of Buick Motor Division, General Motors Corporation).

Here again consult the car maker's manual for recommendations. The number of parts requiring lubrication also differs from one car to another. Figures 15.18 and 15.19 show the manner in which the various lubrication points are shown in some manuals.

The lubricant specified by most car makers is a semisolid, lithium-based, multipurpose grease. However, not all lubricants are compatible. If you use the wrong grease to lubricate a car, the new grease may react with the old grease to break down the lubricating properties of both. This may result in excessive wear. For this reason, always check the car maker's manual to determine the correct lubricant before attempting to lubricate chassis components. In most cases, a grease gun is used to force lubricant into parts through *grease fittings.* Figure 15.20 illustrates some of the many fittings

Figure 15.15 A typical spindle, or steering knuckle (courtesy of Ford Motor Company, Dearborn, MI).

Job 15B

LUBRICATE CHASSIS COMPONENTS

SATISFACTORY PERFORMANCE
A satisfactory performance on this job requires that you do the following:

1. Lubricate the chassis components on the car assigned.
2. Following the steps in the "Performance Outline" and the recommendations and specifications of the car manufacturer, complete the job within 30 minutes.
3. Fill in the blanks under "Information."

PERFORMANCE OUTLINE

1. Raise and support the car.
2. Locate and clean the lubricating points.
3. Lubricate the parts as specified by the manufacturer.
4. Check the transmission lubricant level. Adjust the level if necessary.
5. Check the differential lubricant level. Adjust the level if necessary.
6. Lubricate the other points specified by the manufacturer.
7. Lower the car to the floor.

INFORMATION

Vehicle identification _____
Reference used _____ Page(s) _____
Number of grease fittings on car _____
Transmission lube level: ____ OK ____ Lube added
Differential lube level: ____ OK ____ Lube added

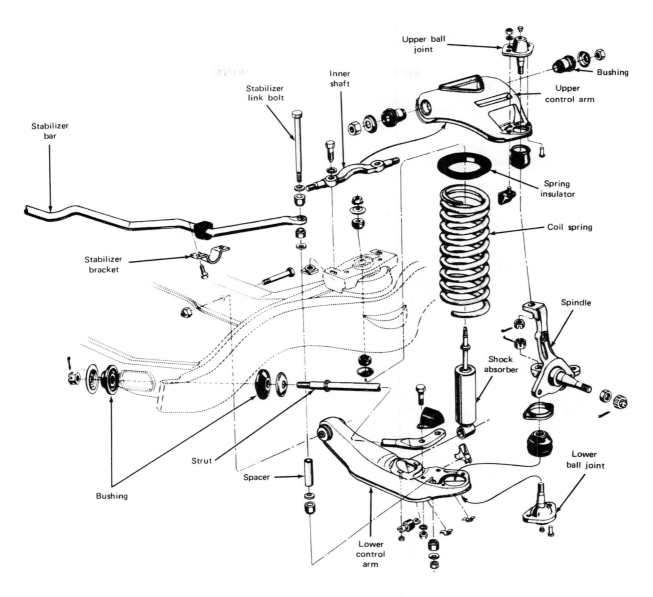

Figure 15.16 An exploded view of a left front independent suspension system using a straight lower control arm and a strut (courtesy of Ford Motor Company, Dearborn, MI).

used. Those fittings, sometimes called *Zerk fittings*, contain a check valve that allows grease to enter but closes to keep it from leaking out. The grease fittings are usually threaded into the parts as shown in Figure 15.21.

Although many shops have high-pressure grease guns operated by compressed air, the use of such guns is not recommended by most car makers. Hand-operated grease guns, similar to the one shown in Figure 15.22, develop sufficient pressure. They are also less likely to damage the seals and boots on the parts being lubricated. Various types

of seals and boots of the type shown in Figure 15.23 are used by most car makers to keep the lubricant inside the part and to keep out dirt and water.

The chassis parts on some cars are not fitted with grease fittings. Plugs are threaded into the holes where the grease fittings would normally be. The plugs are installed by the car maker after the parts have been lubricated during assembly. Those plugs discourage lubrication by persons who may not know the proper lubricant, the proper service interval, or about the damage that can be caused

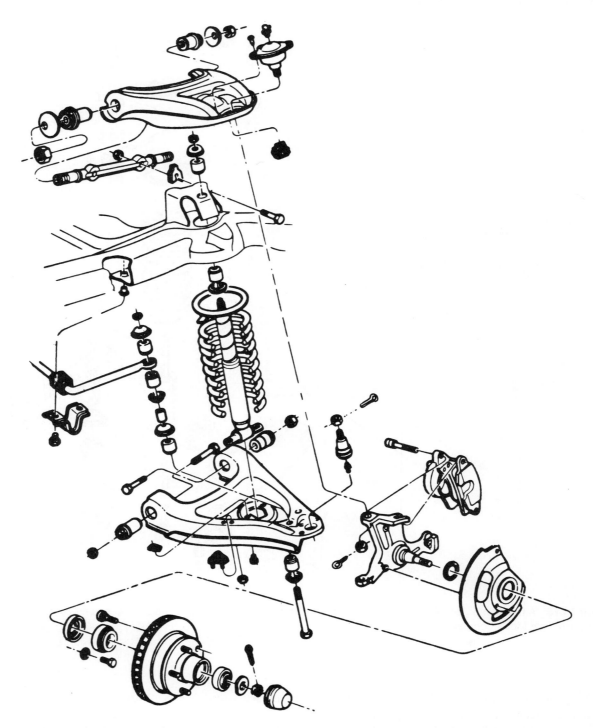

Figure 15.17 An exploded view of a left front independent suspension system using a triangular lower control arm (courtesy of Chevrolet Motor Division, General Motors Corporation).

by the use of high-pressure equipment. When those parts require lubrication, remove the plugs and install fittings. After the proper lubricant has been pumped in, the fittings should be removed and the plugs reinstalled. Some shops use adapters on their grease guns so that fittings do not have to be installed. These adapters fit into the threaded hole and allow you to pump lubricant directly into the part. An adapter of that type is shown in Figure 15.24.

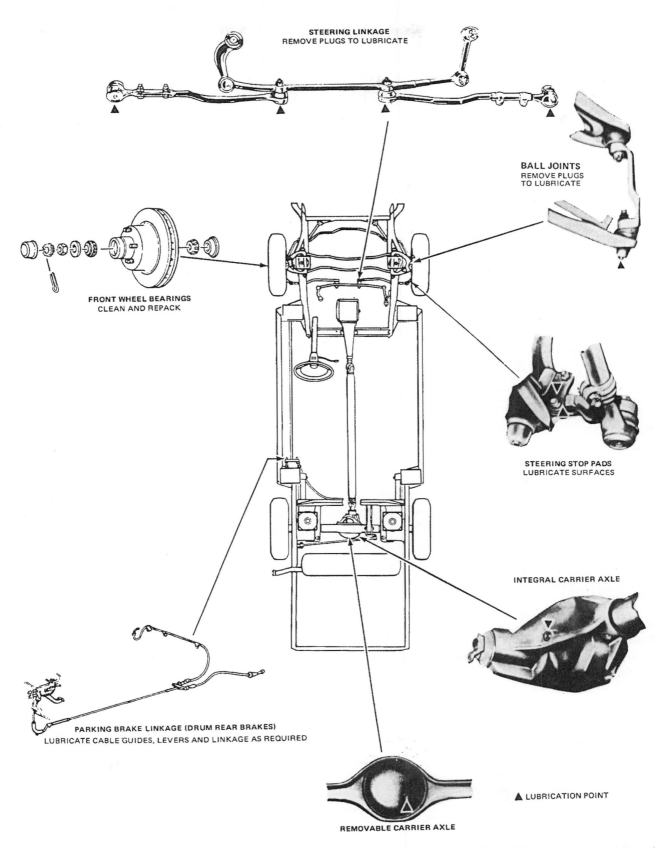

STEERING LINKAGE
REMOVE PLUGS TO LUBRICATE

BALL JOINTS
REMOVE PLUGS
TO LUBRICATE

FRONT WHEEL BEARINGS
CLEAN AND REPACK

STEERING STOP PADS
LUBRICATE SURFACES

INTEGRAL CARRIER AXLE

PARKING BRAKE LINKAGE (DRUM REAR BRAKES)
LUBRICATE CABLE GUIDES, LEVERS AND LINKAGE AS REQUIRED

▲ LUBRICATION POINT

REMOVABLE CARRIER AXLE

Figure 15.18 Chassis lubrication points. Typical chassis lubrication points are specified for each particular car (courtesy of Ford Motor Company, Dearborn, MI).

LUBRICATION POINTS
A-1   CHASSIS — See Maintenance Schedule
A-2   ENGINE OIL AND FILTER
A-4   COOLING SYSTEM
A-61 TRANSAXLE

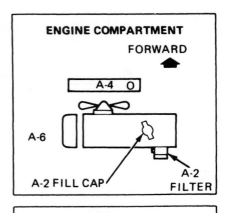

ENGINE COMPARTMENT

FORWARD

A-4   O

A-6

A-2 FILL CAP

A-2 FILTER

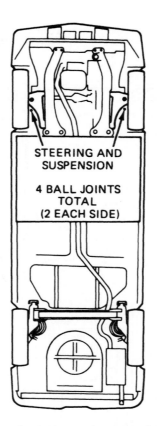

STEERING AND SUSPENSION

4 BALL JOINTS TOTAL
(2 EACH SIDE)

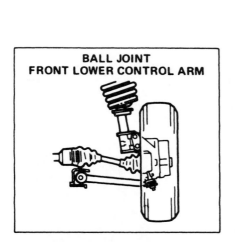

BALL JOINT
FRONT LOWER CONTROL ARM

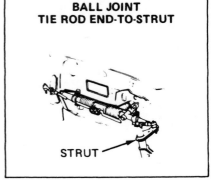

BALL JOINT
TIE ROD END-TO-STRUT

STRUT

Figure 15.19   Typical lubrication points on a front wheel drive car (courtesy of Chevrolet Motor Division, General Motors Corporation).

Some rubber bushings definitely show wear patterns when they have been turning and not flexing. Sometimes the parts have to be moved to check the condition of the rubber bushings. If there is a noise in the suspension system, take time to bounce the vehicle and both look and listen for rubber bushing failure.

Rubber Bushings. Where motion between metal parts is slight, rubber bushings are often used to eliminate metal-to-metal contact. Rubber bush-

ings of this type are shown in Figure 15.25. In most instances, rubber bushings are held tightly by the metal parts they separate. Thus the bushing *flexes*, or stretches, without moving. This means that there is no actual motion between the parts in contact and thus no friction. Rubber bushings require no lubrication. In fact, a petroleum-based lubricant applied to a rubber bushing could attack the rubber and destroy the part.

If a rubber bushing is noisy, it is moving in relation to one of the parts it separates. Noisy bushings should be replaced.

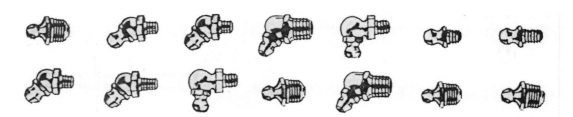

Figure 15.20   An assortment of grease fittings showing the various thread sizes and angles available (courtesy of Dorman Products, Inc.).

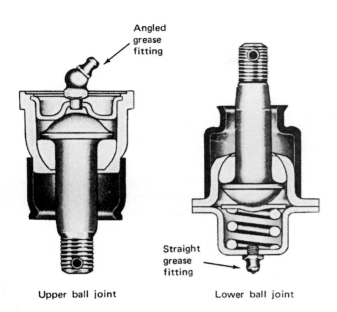

Figure 15.21 A pair of ball joints fitted with straight and angled grease fittings (courtesy of Buick Motor Division, General Motors Corporation).

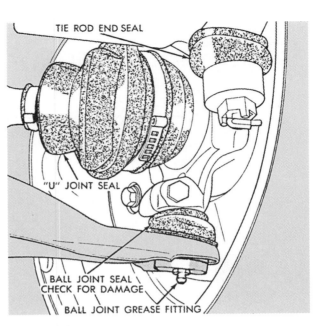

Figure 15.23 Seals and boots. An under-car view showing some of the many types of seals and boots used in a front wheel drive car (courtesy of Chrysler Corporation).

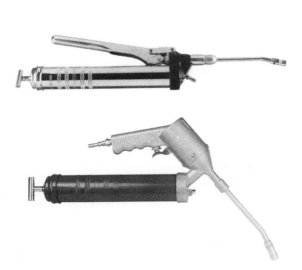

Figure 15.22 A typical hand-operated grease gun suitable for lubricating chassis components (courtesy of Lincoln St. Louis, Div. McNeil Corp., St. Louis, MO).

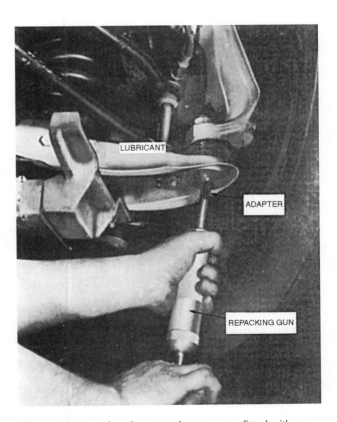

Figure 15.24 A hand-operated grease gun fitted with an adapter to allow lubrication through the plug hole without installing a fitting (courtesy of Cadillac Motor Car Division, General Motors Corporation).

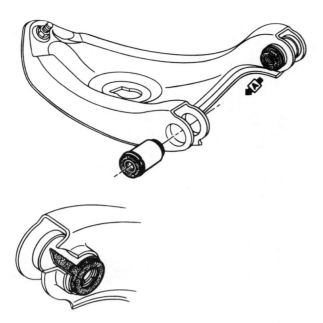

Figure 15.25 Lower control arm bushings. A lower control arm using rubber bushings. Note that the bushing is held between two metal sleeves (courtesy of Pontiac Motor Division, General Motors Corporation).

LESSON 15-2 Macpherson Strut Suspension Systems

Another independent front suspension system in common use is shown in Figure 15.27. Usually re-ferred to as a MacPherson strut system, it uses coil springs mounted on shock-absorbing struts. The struts are mounted between the steering knuckles and pockets formed in the upper fender wells as shown in Figure 15.28.

The upper mount of each strut contains a bearing as shown in Figure 15.29. The bearing allows the strut to turn in the mount. As shown in Figure 15.30, the lower end of each steering knuckle is connected to a control arm by a ball joint. The strut is firmly attached to the steering knuckle and, because of the bearing in the upper mount, turns with the steering knuckle when the wheels are turned.

MacPherson strut systems are ideally suited for cars of unit body design. Because those systems require no upper control arms, they offer savings in weight and allow more room in the engine compartment.

Steering Knuckles

In MacPherson strut systems used on rear wheel drive cars, the steering knuckles are similar to those used in long and short arm systems. Those steering knuckles are forged with spindles upon which the front hubs are mounted (refer to Figure 15.15). On cars with front wheel drive, the steering knuckles do not have spindles. On those cars, the end of the drive axle passes through a hole in the steering knuckle as shown in Figure 15.31.

LUBRICATING CHASSIS COMPONENTS	The steps that follow outline a typical procedure for lubricating chassis components. Obtain lubricant specifications and special procedures that may be necessary for the car on which you are working from an appropriate manual or lubrication chart:

1. Raise and support the car.
2. Locate the lubrication points.
3. Clean the grease fittings or plugs and the areas around them so dirt will not be forced into the part along with the grease.
4. Using a hand-operated grease gun, force grease through the fittings until the rubber boots on the parts start to expand or until grease leaks from a "bleed" hole provided in the boot.

   Note: If the parts are fitted with plugs, you must remove them. Install grease fittings or use an adapter on the grease gun. Reinstall the plugs after lubricating the parts.
5. Apply a dab of grease to each of the steering stops, as shown in Figure 15.26.

   Note: Some cars have protrusions on the lower control arms and on the steering arms. Those protrusions, called *steering stops*, limit the amount the front wheels can be turned in steering.
6. If the car is equipped with a manual transmission, check the lubricant level. Add lubricant if needed.
7. Check the level of the lubricant in the differential. Add the specified lubricant if needed.
8. Lower the car to the floor.

Figure 15.26 Steering stop lubrication points. Most manufacturers recommend that grease be applied to the steering stops during a chassis lubrication (courtesy of American Motors).

Control Arms

The control arms used in MacPherson strut systems can be either triangular or straight (refer to Figures 15.12 and 15.13). When straight control arms are used, a means of supporting the arm against fore-and-aft movement must be provided. On some cars, a strut is used (refer to Figure 15.14). On other cars, that function is handled by a special stabilizer bar as shown in Figure 15.32.

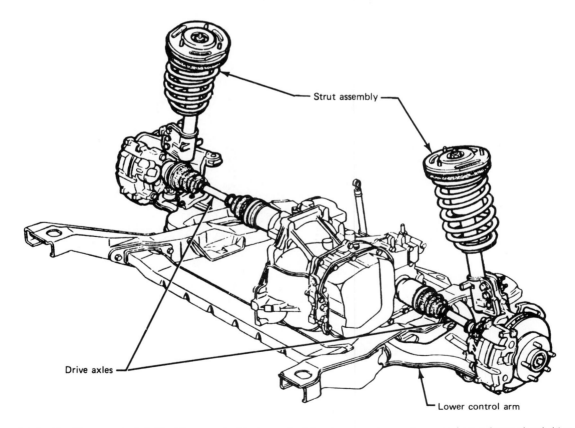

Figure 15.27 MacPherson strut. A MacPherson strut independent front suspension system used on a front wheel drive car (courtesy of Oldsmobile Motor Division, General Motors Corporation).

Job 15C

IDENTIFY THE PARTS OF A MacPHERSON STRUT INDEPENDENT FRONT SUSPENSION SYSTEM

SATISFACTORY PERFORMANCE

A satisfactory performance on this job requires that you do the following:

1. Identify the numbered parts on the drawing by placing the number of each part in front of the correct name of the part.
2. Correctly identify all the parts within 10 minutes.

PERFORMANCE SITUATION

_____ Upper control arm	_____ Lower control arm
_____ Upper mount	_____ Lower mount
_____ Strut assembly	_____ Bearing
_____ Spindle	_____ Steering knuckle
_____ Drive axles	_____ Ball joint

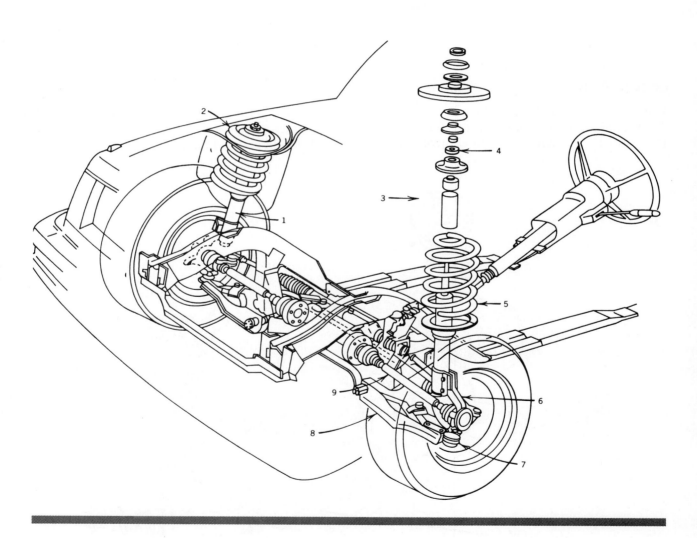

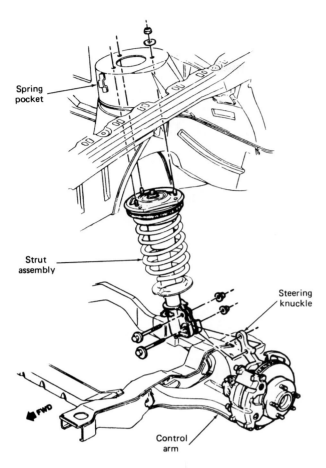

Figure 15.28 MacPherson strut mount. The strut is mounted between the steering knuckle and a pocket in the upper fender wall (courtesy of Oldsmobile Motor Division, General Motors Corporation).

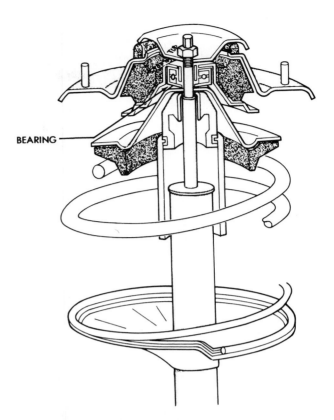

Figure 15.29 Upper MacPherson strut bearing. The upper strut mount contains a bearing so that the strut can turn with the steering knuckle when the wheels are turned (courtesy of Chrysler Corporation).

To become familiar with MacPherson strut suspension systems and their parts, study Figures 15.27 through 15.33.

Modified MacPherson Strut Suspension Systems

Some cars are built with suspension systems that are modifications of the MacPherson strut design. Some of those systems combine features of the long and short arm system with those of the MacPherson design. One of those systems in common use is shown in Figure 15.34. In that system, the coil springs are not mounted on the struts, but are positioned between the lower control arms and the frame.

LESSON 15-3 Ball Joints

Almost all independent front suspension systems use ball joints to connect the steering knuckles to the control arms. A *ball joint*, shown in Figure 15.35, is similar to the ball and socket joint in your shoulder. You can raise and lower your arm, move it forward and backward, twist it, or swing it. A ball joint allows movement in varying planes. Because of it, a steering knuckle or spindle can turn, even when the suspension system is moving up and down.

There are many different types of ball joints, but they all fit into two classifications: (1) *load-carrying ball joints* and (2) *nonload-carrying ball joints*.

Load-Carrying Ball Joints

A load-carrying ball joint is one that supports the weight of the car. That weight is transmitted through a spring or a torsion bar to a control arm. The control arm, in turn, transmits the weight to

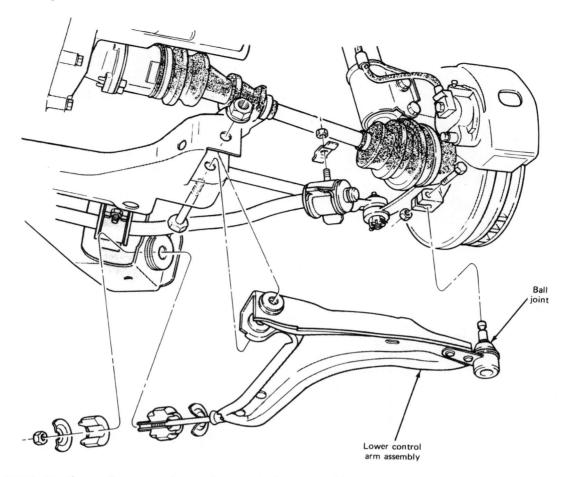

Figure 15.30 MacPherson lower control arm. A lower control arm assembly used in a MacPherson strut suspension system on a front wheel drive car (courtesy of Chrysler Corporation).

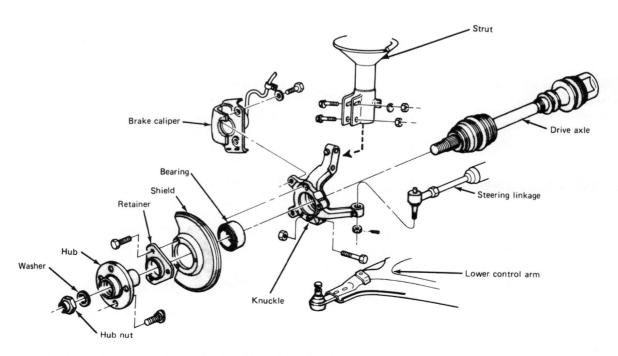

Figure 15.31 An exploded view of a steering knuckle and its related parts as used on a car with front wheel drive (courtesy of Chrysler Corporation).

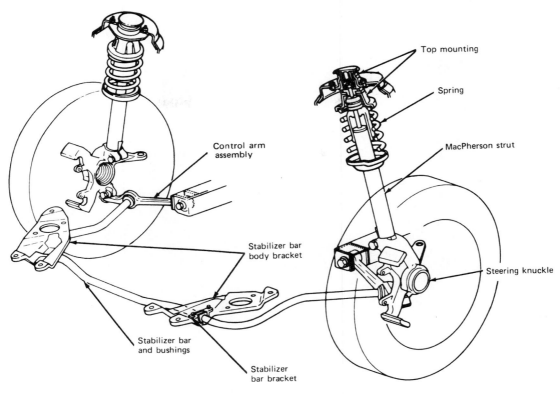

Figure 15.32 Straight control arm system. A MacPherson strut system that uses straight lower control arms. Notice that a stabilizer bar is used to control fore-and-aft movement of the arms (courtesy of Ford Motor Company, Dearborn, MI).

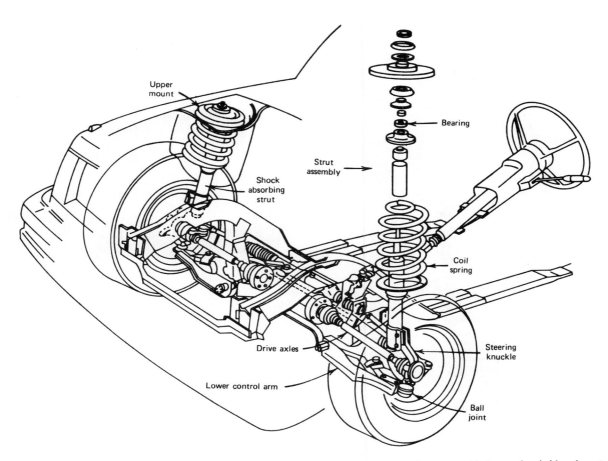

Figure 15.33 The major parts of a typical MacPherson strut suspension system used on cars with front wheel drive (courtesy of Chrysler Corporation).

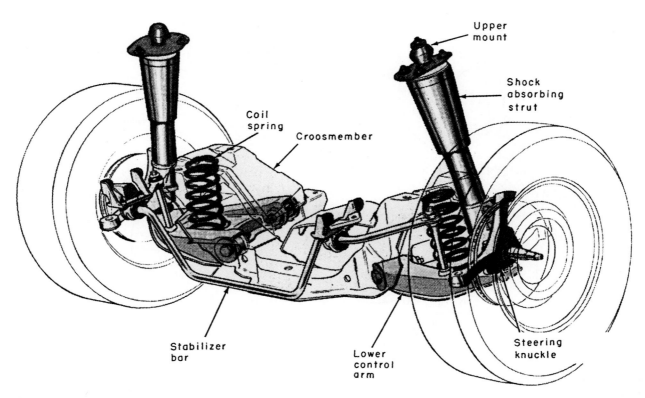

Figure 15.34 A modification of the MacPherson strut design. In this system, the coil springs are mounted between the lower control arms and the frame (courtesy of Ford Motor Company, Dearborn, MI).

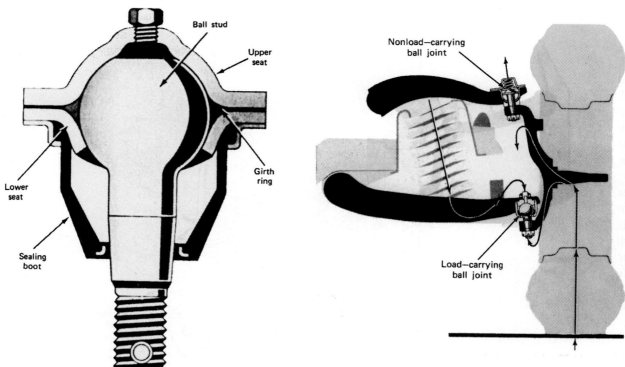

Figure 15.35 Typical ball joint. A ball joint allows movement of the parts up and down as the road acts on the vehicle suspension (courtesy of American Motors).

Figure 15.36 Long and short load-carrying ball joint. A long and short arm suspension system with the load-carrying ball joint at the lower control arm. Notice how the weight of the car is transmitted through the lower ball joint (courtesy of Moog Automotive, Inc.).

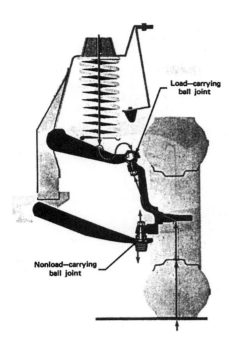

Figure 15.37 Upper control arm load-carrying ball joint. A long and short arm suspension system with the load-carrying ball joint at the upper control arm. Notice how the weight of the car is transmitted through the upper ball joint (courtesy of Moog Automotive, Inc.).

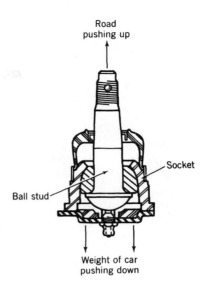

Figure 15.38 Typical load-carrying ball joint. The ball stud is kept tight in its socket by the weight of the car (courtesy of Chevrolet Motor Division, General Motors Corporation).

the spindle, or steering knuckle, through a ball joint. When the spring or torsion bar is positioned between the frame and the lower control arm, as shown in Figure 15.36, the lower ball joint is the load-carrying ball joint. When the spring is positioned between the frame and the upper control arm, as shown in Figure 15.37, the upper ball joint is the load-carrying ball joint.

Load-carrying ball joints are subject to considerable wear. Usually, they must be replaced before nonload-carrying ball joints. As shown in Figure 15.38, the weight of the car holds the ball stud tightly in its socket. Any wear on the ball or in the socket is not apparent under casual observation. Improper lubrication or the presence of water or dirt in the joint increases wear. This wear can result in a failure of the joint and a collapse of the suspension system.

There are two types of load-carrying ball joints. One design, shown in Figure 15.39, uses the weight of the car to pull the ball stud into its housing. This design is called a *tension-type ball joint*. The second design is called a *compression-type ball joint*. This design uses the weight of the car to push the ball stud into its housing, as shown in Figure 15.40.

Nonload-Carrying Ball Joints

Ball joints in MacPherson strut systems, and one of the ball joints in long and short arm systems, do not support any of the car's weight. They act to hold the other end of the spindle or steering knuckle in place and to maintain the proper steering axis angles. Nonload-carrying ball joints are often referred to as *follower joints, pilot joints,* and *friction*

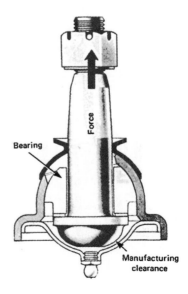

Figure 15.39 Tension-type ball joint. Notice how the weight of the car applies a force that pulls the ball stud into its socket (courtesy of TRW Inc., Cleveland, OH).

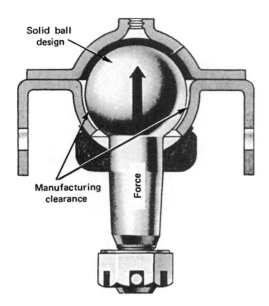

Figure 15.40   Compression-type ball joint. Notice how the weight of the car applies a force that pushes the ball stud into its socket (courtesy of TRW Inc., Cleveland, OH).

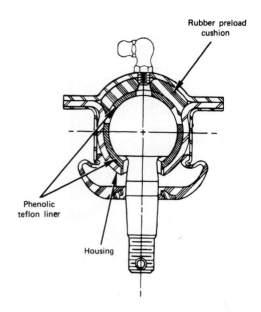

Figure 15.42   A nonload-carrying ball joint preloaded by a rubber ring (courtesy of Pontiac Motor Division, General Motors Corporation).

joints by different manufacturers. Most nonload-carrying ball joints are *preloaded*. This means that some method is used to hold the ball stud tight against its socket. In some cases, a spring is used to preload the ball joint, as shown in Figure 15.41. Other ball joints are preloaded by means of a rubber pressure ring, or cushion, as shown in Figure 15.42.

Ball joints are preloaded to provide a definite turning resistance. This turning resistance is deter-

mined by the car manufacturer to ensure proper handling and steering.

Unloading Ball Joints

A ball joint must move in its socket without excessive *play*, or looseness. The weight of the car holds load-carrying ball joints in compression or tension. Because of this, any looseness in the ball joint will not become apparent until the weight has been removed from the joint. Because of side thrust forces in the suspension system, even worn nonload-carrying ball joints may appear to be in good condition until the weight of the car is removed.

Routine maintenance of the suspension and steering systems require the frequent inspection of ball joints. Before ball joints can be effectively inspected, they must be *unloaded*. In other words, the car must be raised and supported so that the weight normally borne by the ball joints is held by a jack or car stands. The placement of the support depends on the location of the load-carrying ball joint.

On a long and short arm suspension system that uses a coil spring or a torsion bar between the frame and the lower control arm, the jack should be positioned under the lower control arm, as shown in Figure 15.43.

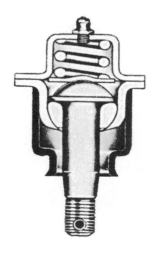

Figure 15.41   A nonload-carrying ball joint preloaded by a spring (courtesy of Buick Motor Division, General Motors Corporation).

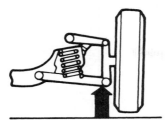

Figure 15.43 The jack position for checking ball joints of a long and short arm suspension system that uses coil springs or torsion bars between the frame and the lower control arms (courtesy of Ford Motor Company, Dearborn, MI).

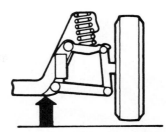

Figure 15.44 The jack position for checking ball joints of a long and short arm suspension system that uses coil springs between the frame and the upper control arms (courtesy of Ford Motor Company, Dearborn, MI).

On a long and short arm suspension system that uses coil springs between the frame and the upper control arms, the jack should be placed under the frame or underbody as shown in Figure 15.44.

Job 15D

IDENTIFY THE METHODS USED TO UNLOAD BALL JOINTS

SATISFACTORY PERFORMANCE

A satisfactory performance on this job requires that you do the following:

1. Identify the methods used to unload ball joints by matching each of the sentences below with one of the drawings showing jack placement.
2. Correctly match all the sentences with the drawings within 10 minutes.

PERFORMANCE SITUATION

_____ This drawing shows the proper jack placement when the lower ball joint is the load-carrying ball joint.

_____ This drawing shows the proper jack placement when a torsion bar is used between the frame and the lower control arm.

_____ This drawing shows the proper jack placement when the ball joint is used in a MacPherson strut system.

_____ This drawing shows the proper jack placement when the upper ball joint is the follower joint.

_____ This drawing shows the proper jack placement when the upper ball joint is the load-carrying joint.

_____ This drawing shows the proper jack placement on cars that require a support between the upper control arm and the frame.

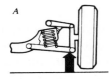
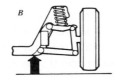

Often, a brace, or support, must be placed between the upper control arm and the frame, as shown in Figure 15.45. This brace is necessary to hold the spring in compression and to remove the load from the ball joint. On some cars, a block of wood can be used to provide this support (see Figure 15.46). Be sure to check the manufacturer's manual for specific unloading instructions.

Since the ball joints in most MacPherson strut suspension systems are nonload-carrying, they are not under any tension or compression forces. Because they are subjected to side thrust loads, most manufacturers suggest that those loads be removed by supporting the car by the frame or underbody as shown in Figure 15.47.

Figure 15.45 A steel support used to hold a coil spring in compression while checking ball joints (courtesy of Ford Motor Company, Dearborn, MI).

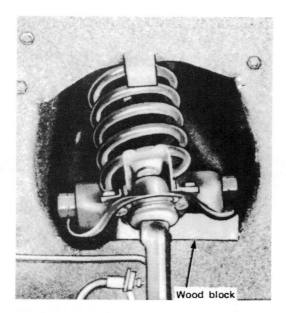

Figure 15.46 Wood block tool test. To completely unload the ball joints, a wood block can be used on some cars as shown (courtesy of Ford Motor Company, Dearborn, MI).

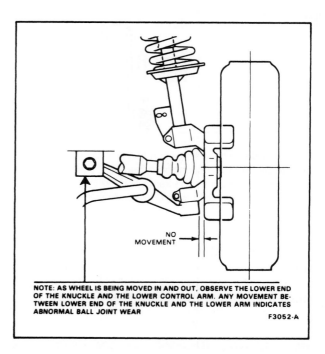

NOTE: AS WHEEL IS BEING MOVED IN AND OUT, OBSERVE THE LOWER END OF THE KNUCKLE AND THE LOWER CONTROL ARM. ANY MOVEMENT BE-TWEEN LOWER END OF THE KNUCKLE AND THE LOWER ARM INDICATES ABNORMAL BALL JOINT WEAR

F3052-A

Figure 15.47 The jack position for checking ball joints in a MacPherson strut suspension system (courtesy of Ford Motor Company, Dearborn, MI).

LESSON 15–4 Ball Joint Inspection

Ball joints should be inspected as a part of routine maintenance. They should also be inspected as a part of diagnosing any problems in the suspension and steering systems. Worn ball joints allow the spindles or steering knuckles to change position, which in turn changes the angles of wheel alignment. The latter change affects the handling of the car and causes abnormal tire wear. Excessively worn ball joints can fail and cause loss of car control. Most states that have compulsory motor vehicle inspections include ball joints on their list of parts to be checked.

Ball joint inspection should always include a check of wheel bearing adjustment. In most instances, worn or loose wheel bearings do not allow an accurate ball joint check. As you learned when you lubricated ball joints, each joint is fitted with a boot, or seal. These boots not only keep the grease in the ball joint, but they keep water and dirt out. If a boot is torn or otherwise damaged so that it cannot do its job, the ball joint should be replaced.

Wear-Indicating Ball Joints

Some cars are fitted with load-carrying ball joints that incorporate a visual wear indicator, as shown in Figure 15.48. The wear indicator usually consists of

a nipple about 1/2 in. (12.5 mm) in diameter that protrudes from the bottom of the ball joint. The nipple, often drilled and threaded for a grease fitting, extends 0.050 in. (1.27 mm) from the surface of the ball joint when the joint is new. Wear on the interior surfaces of the ball and its socket allows the nipple to retract, or move in. The amount of retraction is equal to the amount of wear in the joint. When the nipple is level with or lower than the surface of the joint, the joint has worn 0.050 in. (1.27 mm) or more, and it should be replaced.

Some wear-indicating ball joints are checked manually by grasping the grease fitting and attempting to move it as shown in Figure 15.49. If any movement is noted, the ball joint is worn and replacement is recommended.

Conventional Ball Joints

Each auto manufacturer sets the specifications for allowable wear in ball joints, and also sets the procedures for checking this wear. These specifications and procedures vary, even with different models from the same manufacturer. Therefore, consult an appropriate manual if you are to perform the inspection correctly. In most cases, conventional ball joints should be checked for *radial*, or side-to-side, movement. Some manufacturers provide

Steering and Suspension System Maintenance

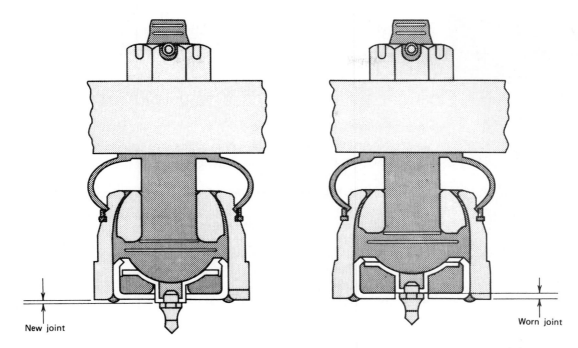

Figure 15.48 Ball joint wear indicator. A visual wear indicating ball joint of the type often used in long and short arm suspension systems. Notice how the nipple extends beyond the ball joint cover when new, but is flush with or below the cover when the ball joint is worn (courtesy of Buick Motor Division, General Motors Corporation).

specifications and procedures for checking *axial*, or up-and-down, movement.

When checking ball joints other than those with wear indicators, unload the joints. This ensures that the ball stud will be free to move in its socket and that any wear can be detected.

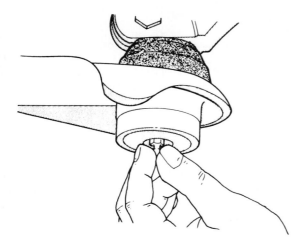

Figure 15.49 Grease fitting wear check. Wear in some ball joints can be detected by attempting to move the grease fitting. A loose fitting indicates that the joint has excessive wear (courtesy of Chrysler Corporation).

Job 15E

CHECK WEAR-INDICATING BALL JOINTS

SATISFACTORY PERFORMANCE
A satisfactory performance on this job requires that you do the following:

1. Check the wear-indicating ball joints on the car assigned.
2. Following the steps in the "Performance Outline" and the procedure and recommendations of the car manufacturer, complete the inspection within 15 minutes.
3. Fill in the blanks under "Information."

PERFORMANCE OUTLINE

1. Clean the ball joints.
2. Inspect the boots.
3. Check the protrusion of the nipples or the looseness of the grease fittings.

INFORMATION

Vehicle identification _____
Reference used _____ Page(s) _____
Condition of ball joints:
Left side ____ Serviceable ____ Unserviceable
Right side ____ Serviceable ____ Unserviceable
Recommendations _____

<table>
<tr><td>

CHECKING WEAR-INDICATING BALL JOINTS

</td><td>

The steps that follow outline a procedure for checking wear-indicating ball joints. Check an appropriate manual for specific instructions that may be necessary for the car on which you are working.

</td></tr>
</table>

Note: The wear indicators operate only when the ball joints are loaded as they would be when the car is on the floor. If it is necessary to raise the car, it should be supported so that the ball joints are not unloaded.

1. Check the condition of the ball joint boots.

Note: A ruptured, or torn, boot will require that the joint be replaced.

2. Clean the base of the ball joints, making sure the nipples and the grease fittings are free of all grease and dirt.

3. On ball joints that indicate wear by means of a protruding nipple, check the position of the nipples.

Note: If nipple protrusion cannot be seen, you might detect any existing protrusion with your fingernail, a small screwdriver, or the edge of a steel scale, as shown in Figure 15.50. If a nipple is even with, or below the surface of, a ball joint, the joint should be replaced. If even one ball joint has excessive wear, both joints should be replaced.

4. On ball joints that indicate wear by means of a loose-feeling grease fitting, attempt to move the fitting (refer to Figure 15.49). If the fitting can be moved, the ball joint should be replaced. If one ball joint requires replacement, it is advisable to replace both joints.

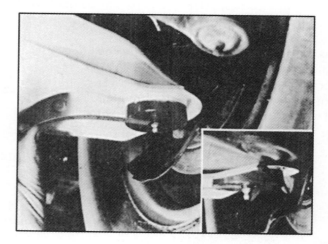

Figure 15.50   General Motors ball joint wear check. Checking the protrusion of the nipple on a wear-indicating ball joint (courtesy of Pontiac Motor Division, General Motors Corporation).

Radial Play

Radial play, or side-to-side movement, can be detected by grasping the tire at the top and at the bottom and by rocking the wheel in and out. Figures 15.51 and 15.52 show radial play at the load-carrying ball joints.

Load-carrying ball joints are constructed to allow for a certain amount of wear. If the allowable wear in a given joint is exceeded, the joint must be replaced. Any play found in a nonload-carrying ball joint indicates a loss of preload. Most car makers specify replacing nonload-carrying ball joints that have lost their preload.

The amount of play in ball joints can be accurately measured by several methods. The most accurate method requires the use of a *dial indicator.* A dial indicator, shown in Figure 15.53, is an instrument that measures movement

| CHECKING RADIAL PLAY IN BALL JOINTS | The steps that follow outline typical procedures for checking radial play in ball joints. Consult an appropriate manual for the exact procedures and specifications that may be necessary for the car on which you are working. |

Preliminary Steps

1. Raise and support the car so the ball joints are unloaded (refer to Figures 15.43, 15.44, and 15.47).
2. Check the adjustment of the front wheel bearings.
3. Adjust the wheel bearings if they are loose.
4. Check the condition of the ball joint boots.

   Note: A torn or ruptured boot requires that the joint be replaced.

Nonload-Carrying Ball Joints

1. Ask an assistant to grasp the tire at the top and bottom and to slowly rock the wheel in and out to obtain the movement shown in Figures 15.51 and 15.52.
2. While the assistant is rocking the wheel, carefully observe the nonload-carrying ball joint for any sign of movement.

   Note: Ignore any movement at the load-carrying ball joint.

3. Repeat steps 1 and 2 at the remaining wheel.

   Note: Most manufacturers recommend replacing nonload-carrying ball joints that show any evidence of radial play.

Load-Carrying Ball Joints

1. Attach a dial indicator to the control arm containing the load-carrying ball joint.
2. Position the indicator plunger so it contacts the inner side of the wheel rim next to the ball joint.
3. Zero the dial indicator.

   Note: This can be accomplished by turning the rim of the dial face.

4. Ask an assistant to grasp the tire at the top and bottom and to slowly rock the wheel in and out to obtain the movement shown in Figures 15.51 and 15.52.
5. Note the amount of movement shown by the dial indicator.
6. Repeat steps 1 through 5 at the remaining wheel.
7. Compare the readings obtained with the specifications for allowable play. If the movement exceeds the specifications, replace the ball joints.

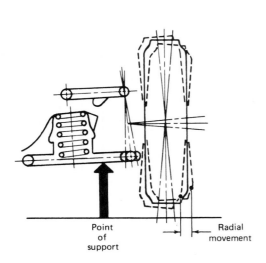

Figure 15.51 Radial play ball joint check. Radial play in a load-carrying lower ball joint (courtesy of Ford Motor Company, Dearborn, MI).

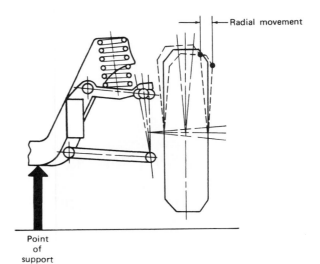

Figure 15.52 Upper ball joint radial play check. Radial play in a load-carrying upper ball joint (courtesy of Ford Motor Company, Dearborn, MI).

Figure 15.53 Typical dial indicator. The dial indicator allows the technician to make very accurate wear checks (courtesy of Chrysler Corporation).

in small increments, or additions. Most dial indicators measure movement in increments of 1 thousandth of 1 inch (0.001 in.). The movement is indicated by a pointer that moves on a dial face. Various means of anchoring the dial indicator are provided so the instrument can be positioned where desired.

Another method of measuring the amount of play in ball joints requires the use of a *ball joint checking gauge*. Such a gauge, shown in Figure 15.54, indicates movement by a pointer on a

Figure 15.54 Ball joint checking gauge. A ball joint checking gauge help's determine ball joint wear (courtesy of AMMCO Tools, Inc.).

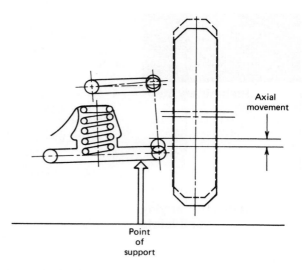

Figure 15.55 Axial play check. Axial play in a load-carrying lower ball joint (courtesy of Ford Motor Company, Dearborn, MI).

scale. It is usually graduated in increments of 1/32 in.

Axial Play

You can detect axial play by moving the wheel up and down. This is easily done by using a lever or a pry bar placed between the center of the tire and the floor. If the wheel is alternately raised and lowered, any axial movement in the ball joints can be observed. Axial movement is shown in Figures 15.55 and 15.56.

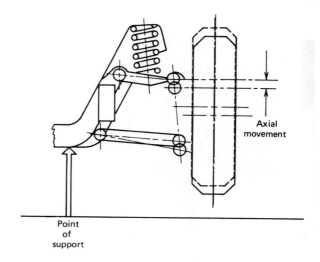

Figure 15.56 Upper ball joint axial play check. Axial play in a load-carrying upper ball joint (courtesy of Ford Motor Company, Dearborn, MI).

Job 15F

CHECK BALL JOINT PLAY

SATISFACTORY PERFORMANCE
A satisfactory performance on this job requires that you do the following:

1. Check the radial and axial play in the ball joints of the car assigned.
2. Following the steps in the "Performance Outline," complete the inspection within 60 minutes.
3. Fill in the blanks under "Information."

PERFORMANCE OUTLINE

1. Raise and support the car so that the ball joints are unloaded.
2. Inspect the wheel bearings and adjust them if they are loose.
3. Check the radial play in the nonload-carrying ball joints.
4. Check the radial play in the load-carrying ball joints.
5. Check the axial play in the load-carrying ball joints.
6. Lower the car to the floor.

INFORMATION

Vehicle identification _____
Reference used _____ Page(s) _____
Location of the load-carrying ball joints: _____ Upper _____ Lower

BALL JOINT	RADIAL PLAY FOUND	AMOUNT ALLOWABLE
Left upper	_____	_____
Left lower	_____	_____
Right upper	_____	_____
Right lower	_____	_____

BALL JOINT	AXIAL PLAY FOUND	AMOUNT ALLOWABLE
Left upper	_____	_____
Left lower	_____	_____
Right upper	_____	_____
Right lower	_____	_____

Recommendations _____
_____
_____

CHECKING AXIAL PLAY IN BALL JOINTS	The steps that follow outline a typical procedure for checking axial play in ball joints. However, consult an appropriate manual for the specific procedure and the specifications for the car on which you are working.
Preliminary Steps	1. Raise and support the car so that the ball joints are unloaded. 2. Check the adjustment of the front wheel bearings. 3. Adjust the front wheel bearings if they are loose. 4. Check the condition of the ball joint boots. *Note:* A torn or ruptured boot requires that the ball joint be replaced.
Measuring Axial Movement	1. Attach a dial indicator to the control arm near the load-carrying ball joint. 2. Position the plunger of the dial indicator so it contacts the spindle or the ball joint housing as shown in Figure 15.57. 3. Zero the dial indicator. *Note:* This can be accomplished by turning the rim of the dial face.

Figure 15.57 Axial play dial indicator check. A dial indicator positioned to measure axial play in a load-carrying lower ball joint (courtesy of Chrysler Corporation).

4. Have an assistant move the wheel up and down with a lever or pry bar to obtain the movement shown in Figures 15.55 and 15.56.
5. Note the movement indicated by the dial indicator.
6. Repeat steps 1 through 5 at the opposite wheel.
7. Compare the readings obtained with the specifications for allowable axial play.
   Note: If the movement exceeds specifications, the ball joints should be replaced.

LESSON 15-5 Shock Absorbers

When a wheel on a moving auto hits a bump in the road, the wheel is thrust upward. As it rises, the spring in its suspension system is *compressed,* or squeezed. By compressing, the spring absorbs some of the energy that would otherwise be transmitted to the frame of the car as a jolt or shock.

After the spring is compressed, it releases the stored energy by *rebounding,* or returning, to its original length and even beyond. In doing so, it forces the tire back down, actually bouncing it on the road. As the tire bounces, it rises again, and again it compresses the spring. This bouncing, shown in Figure 15.58, could continue, similar to the bouncing of a dropped ball.

The type of spring action just described is objectionable for several reasons:

1. When a tire bounces, it loses contact with the road. Because of this, the driver may lose control of the car. A tire can transmit driving, steering, and braking forces to the road only when it is in firm contact with the road.
2. The spring may *flex,* or bend, beyond the elastic limit of its material and then break.
3. The frame of the car moves in relation to the spring motion. Therefore, the driver and the passengers experience a wavy ride.

For the reasons that have been listed, all automobile suspension systems have *shock absorbers,* commonly called "shocks." Shock absorbers control spring action and therefore limit wheel bouncing.

A shock absorber is a hydraulic device consisting of a piston in an oil-filled cylinder. The cylinder is attached to the suspension system, and the piston is attached to the car frame, or underbody. As the suspension system moves up and down, the piston is pushed and pulled up and down in the cylinder. In order to move, the piston must displace the oil in the cylinder. Oil displacement is made possible by means of valves. By varying the size of the valves and the tension of the valve springs, a manufacturer can control the speed at which the piston moves. The piston speed, in turn, controls the speed at which the suspension system moves.

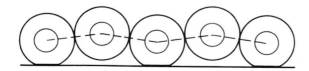

Figure 15.58 Shock absorber bounce pattern. Without a shock absorber to control the rebound of its spring, a wheel and tire assembly would tend to bounce.

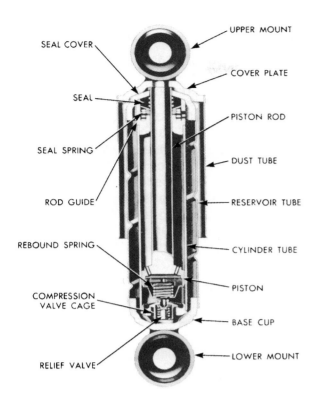

Figure 15.59 A typical direct action shock absorber (courtesy of Chevrolet Motor Division, General Motors Corporation).

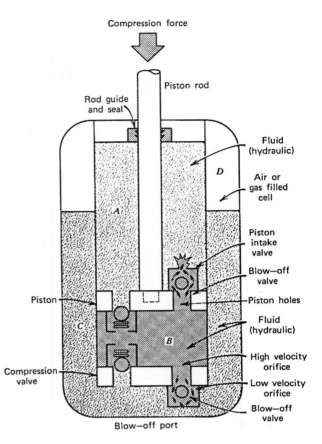

Figure 15.60 The operation of a shock absorber during the compression stroke (courtesy of Chevrolet Motor Division, General Motors Corporation).

Although there are many types of shock absorbers, the most commonly used are of the telescoping type, called *direct-action* shock absorbers. This type of shock absorber is pictured in Figure 15.59. It is called a direct-action shock absorber because it is installed directly between the suspension system and the car frame, or underbody. Most shocks of this type are also referred to as *double-action* shocks. They are given that name because they control the action between the car frame and the suspension system both when the spring is being compressed and when it rebounds. The operation of a double-action shock absorber is shown in Figures 15.60 and 15.61.

Most shock absorbers used as original equipment on cars cannot be adjusted, refilled, or repaired. If a shock is leaking or if testing reveals that it is weak, the shock must be replaced.

Testing Shock Absorbers

Shock absorbers can be tested by evaluating their effectiveness during a road test, but most techni-

cians perform (1) a bounce test, (2) a visual inspection, and (3) a manual inspection.

Bounce Test. The bounce test is quick, and simple to perform. Lift up and push down on one end of a bumper, bouncing one corner of the car. Continue until the maximum of movement is reached. Then let go of the bumper and watch the up-and-down motion. If the motion stops rather quickly, the shock absorber at that corner of the car can be considered to be in good condition. If the bouncing continues, the shock is defective.

After bouncing one corner of a car, bounce the opposite corner, using the other end of the same bumper. Compare the bounce at the corner with the bounce at the other corner. The bouncing motion should be the same at both sides. No comparison should be made between the bouncing at a front corner and the bouncing at a rear corner. The action of front shocks may be different from the action of rear shocks.

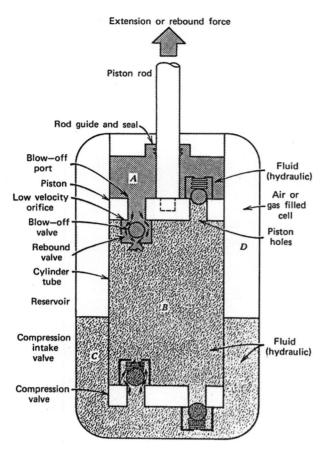

Extension or rebound force

Piston rod

Rod guide and seal

Blow–off port

Piston

Low velocity orifice

Blow–off valve

Rebound valve

Cylinder tube

Reservoir

Compression intake valve

Compression valve

Fluid (hydraulic)

Air or gas filled cell

Piston holes

Fluid (hydraulic)

Figure 15.61 The operation of a shock absorber during the rebound stroke (courtesy of Chevrolet Motor Division, General Motors Corporation).

Job 15G

TEST AND INSPECT SHOCK ABSORBERS

SATISFACTORY PERFORMANCE

A satisfactory performance on this job requires that you do the following:

1. Test and inspect the shock absorbers on the car assigned.
2. Following the steps in the "Performance Outline," complete the job within 30 minutes.
3. Fill in the blanks under "Information."

PERFORMANCE OUTLINE

1. Bounce test all four shocks.
2. Inspect the shock mountings.
3. Inspect the shocks for leakage.

INFORMATION

Vehicle identification _____

TEST AND INSPECTION RESULTS

LOCATION	BOUNCE TEST	MOUNTING	LEAKAGE
Left front	_____	_____	_____
Right front	_____	_____	_____
Left rear	_____	_____	_____
Right rear	_____	_____	_____

Recommendations _____

_____

VISUAL INSPECTION

A visual inspection may disclose a damaged shock, a leaking shock, or a loose shock mounting. The following steps will enable you to perform a thorough visual inspection:

1. Raise the car and support it by the suspension system so the shocks are not fully extended.
2. Check for worn or missing rubber bushings and for loose mounting bolts and nuts at the top and bottom of the shocks.
3. If the shocks are exposed and accessible, grasp and twist them to further check their mountings.
4. Check the shocks for fluid stains or wetness, which may indicate leakage.
5. Lower the car and raise it again, changing the position of the car stands so the car is supported by the frame or underbody. When the car is supported in this manner, the shocks are fully extended.
6. Check the seal cover area, shown in Figure 15.62, for leakage.

   Note: Slight traces of fluid around the seal cover area are normal. It does not require that the shock be replaced. The seal at the shock rod is designed to permit a slight seepage of fluid to lubricate the rod. Shocks are filled with sufficient fluid to compensate for this amount of leakage.

7. Lower the car to the floor.

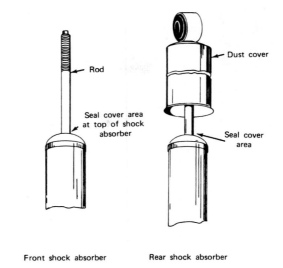

Front shock absorber   Rear shock absorber

Figure 15.62 Seal cover areas for front and rear shock absorbers (courtesy of Pontiac Motor Division, General Motors Corporation).

MANUAL INSPECTION

A manual inspection is sometimes the only way to detect a weak shock or a shock that is noisy. The following steps outline the procedure for a manual inspection:

1. Raise the car and support it by the suspension system so the shocks are not fully extended.
2. Disconnect the lower end of the shock.
3. Manually extend and compress the shock, feeling for any change in the resistance to its motion. The shock should offer a definite resistance to motion in both directions, and should have no "tight" or "loose" spots.

   Note: If you find you cannot get a good grip on the shock, attach a temporary handle to it, as shown in Figure 15.63.

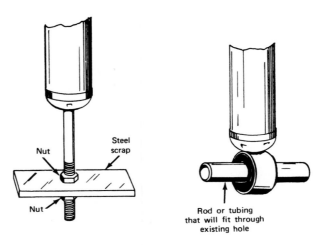

Figure 15.63 Manual shock absorber test. Temporary handles can be installed to manually operate shocks for testing (courtesy of Pontiac Motor Division, General Motors Corporation).

REMOVING AND INSTALLING SHOCK ABSORBERS

The following steps outline procedures for removing and installing shock absorbers. Check an appropriate manual for any specific procedure that may be necessary for the car on which you are working.

Testing and Expelling Air from Replacement Shock Absorbers

At times you will find that a replacement shock absorber has air trapped in the cylinder. Entrapped air can affect the operation of the shock. All replacement shocks should be tested for air entrapment. A shock is easily tested by holding it in its normal operating position and alternately extending and compressing it. If any "skipping" or lost motion is felt in either direction, it may be caused by entrapped air.

Air can usually be expelled from a shock in the following manner:

1. Hold the shock in its normal vertical position and fully extend it.
2. Invert the shock and slowly compress it (see Figure 15.64).

    Note: Do not extend the shock absorber while it is inverted.

3. Repeat steps 1 and 2 several times until the "skipping" and lost motion cannot be felt.

Removing Rear Shock Absorbers

1. Raise the rear of the car with a jack and support the car with car stands placed under the axle or axle housing.
2. Apply penetrating oil to the mounting bolts and nuts.
3. Remove the nut or bolt from the lower end of one of the shocks (see Figures 15.65 and 15.66).
4. Remove the attaching bolt(s) from the upper end of the shock (refer to Figures 15.65 and 15.66).
5. Remove the shock.
6. Repeat steps 3 through 5 to remove the remaining shock.

Installing Rear Shock Absorbers

1. Test the replacement shock and expell any entrapped air.
2. Hold the upper end of the shock in position, and install the attaching bolts and nuts.
3. Align the lower end of the shock and install the bolt or nut.
4. Tighten the attaching bolts and nuts to the manufacturer's torque specification.
5. Repeat steps 1 through 4 to install the remaining shock.
6. Lower the car to the floor.

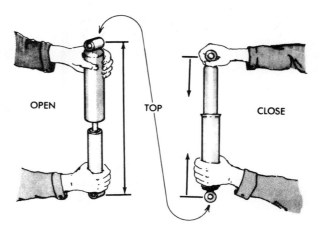

Figure 15.64 Shock absorber air removal. Entrapped air can be expelled from a shock by alternately extending it in its normal position, and compressing it while inverted (courtesy of Chrysler Corporation).

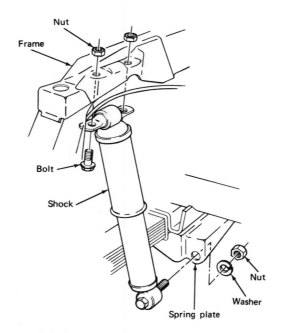

Figure 15.65   A typical rear shock absorber mounting on a rear wheel drive car (courtesy of Buick Motor Division, General Motors Corporation).

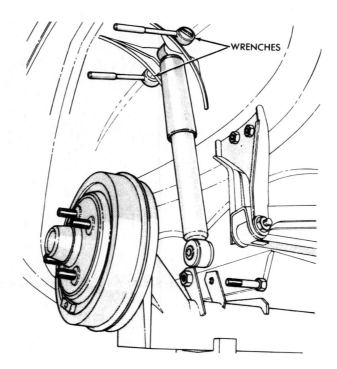

Figure 15.66   Removing a rear shock absorber from a front wheel drive vehicle (courtesy of Chrysler Corporation).

Removing Front Shock Absorbers

1. Raise the front of the car with a jack and support the car with car stands placed under the suspension system.

    Note: Position the car stands so they will not interfere with the removal of the shock.

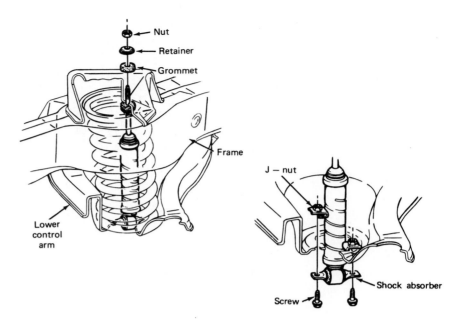

Figure 15.67   A typical method of mounting a front shock absorber in a rear wheel drive car. Notice the use of "J" nuts at the lower shock mounting in the lower control arm (courtesy of Buick Motor Division, General Motors Corporation).

2. Apply penetrating oil to the mounting bolts and nuts.
3. Remove the nut from the upper end of one shock (see Figure 15.67).
4. Remove the attaching screws at the lower end of the shock (refer to Figure 15.67).
5. Remove the shock by lowering it through the opening in the control arm.
6. Repeat steps 3 through 5 at the remaining shock.

Installing Front Shock Absorbers

1. Test the replacement shock and expell any entrapped air.
2. Extend the shock by pulling the piston rod out to its limit.
3. Install a retaining washer, with its concave (cupped) side up, on the piston rod, as shown in Figure 15.68.
4. Install a new rubber grommet on the piston rod (refer to Figure 15.68 for the correct placement).
5. Insert the shock up through the opening in the control arm, making sure that the piston rod enters its mounting hole in the frame.

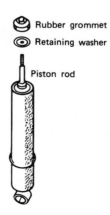

Figure 15.68   The correct positioning of the retaining washer and the grommet on a shock absorber piston rod.

6. Install the attaching screws to hold the lower end of the shock to the control arm.
7. Tighten the attaching screws to the manufacturer's torque specification.
8. Install a new rubber grommet on the end of the piston rod, as shown in Figure 15.69.
9. Install a retaining washer, concave side down, on the piston rod (refer to Figure 15.69).
10. Install the nut and tighten it to the manufacturer's torque specification.
11. Install the *Pal* nut, or lock nut, if provided.
12. Repeat steps 1 through 11 at the remaining shock.
13. Lower the car to the floor.

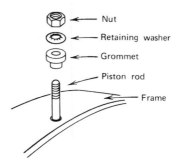

Figure 15.69 The correct positioning of the grommet, retaining washer, and nut on a shock absorber piston rod.

Job 15H

REPLACE SHOCK ABSORBERS

SATISFACTORY PERFORMANCE
A satisfactory performance on this job requires that you do the following:

1. Replace the designated shock absorbers on the car assigned.
2. Following the steps in the "Performance Outline" and the manufacturer's procedure and specifications, complete the job within 200% of the manufacturer's suggested time.
3. Fill in the blanks under "Information."

PERFORMANCE OUTLINE

1. Raise and support the car so the shocks are not extended.
2. Remove the designated shock absorbers.
3. Install the replacement shock absorbers.
4. Tighten all mountings to the manufacturer's torque specifications.
5. Lower the car to the floor.

INFORMATION

Vehicle identification _____
Reference used _____ Page(s) _____
Shock absorbers replaced:
_____ Left front   _____ Right front
_____ Left rear   _____ Right rear

LESSON 15–6 Steering Systems

In a steering system, the steering gear increases the steering effort of the driver. The steering linkage transmits this effort to the front wheels. During your work with chassis lubrication, you lubricated some of the parts in a steering system. Further work on steering systems requires that you know the names of the system parts and their functions.

Steering Linkage

The steering linkage transmits the movement of the steering gear to the front wheels. There are many different steering linkage designs. The *parallelogram type*, shown in Figure 15.70, is the most widely used, especially in rear wheel drive cars. This type is so named because if all the common pivot points on one side of the car are connected by lines to their corresponding points on the other side of the car, the lines will be parallel. This parallelism is shown in Figure 15.71.

The parallelogram design offers many advantages. It provides duplicate motion on both sides of a car. In addition, the placement of the pivot points can easily be aligned with the pivot points

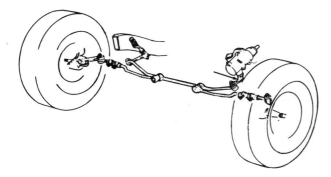

Figure 15.70   A parallelogram steering linkage system of the type used on most rear wheel drive cars (courtesy of Ford Motor Company. Dearborn, MI).

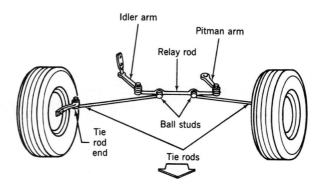

Figure 15.72   The location of the parts in a parallelogram steering linkage system (courtesy of Chevrolet Motor Division, General Motors Corporation).

of the suspension system. This allows the steering system to transmit the same motion to both front wheels regardless of their vertical position. Therefore, the steering motion at each front wheel is the same even when the suspension system on one side is up and the system on the other side is down.

All the parts in the steering linkage are subject to wear and damage and should be inspected at regular intervals. The names of these parts and their location in the system are shown in Figure 15.72. Their relationship to one another is shown in Figure 15.73.

Pitman Arm.   The Pitman arm is the first lever in the steering linkage. It changes the rotating motion at the steering gear to *linear*, or side-to-side, motion. The Pitman arm moves in an arc and pushes or pulls the *relay rod*, which is sometimes called a *center link*.

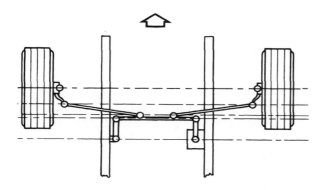

Figure 15.71   The alignment of the pivot points in a parallelogram steering linkage system. Notice that the lines connecting all common points are parallel (courtesy of Chevrolet Motor Division, General Motors Corporation).

Inspect and lubricate steering parts on a regular schedule. Replace worn or damaged parts immediately. Any failure of steering system parts is very serious and can result in loss of vehicle control and damage to the vehicle.

Relay Rod.   The relay rod is a rigid steel bar attached at one end to the Pitman arm by a *ball stud*. The ball stud is similar to a small ball joint in that it allows movement in many directions. The opposite end of the relay rod is supported by the *idler arm*. The relay rod moves back and forth across the bottom of the car as the steering wheel is turned. Two holes are drilled through the relay rod so that the tie rods can be attached, as shown in Figure 15.73.

Idler Arm.   The idler arm merely supports the end of the relay rod, but it is important because it keeps the relay rod aligned. As shown in Figure 15.73, the idler arm is constructed so it duplicates the Pitman arm. It is mounted on the frame or underbody so it moves in the same plane as the Pitman arm and thus parallels its motion.

Tie Rods.   The tie rods are steel bars that connect the relay rod to the *steering arms*. Movement at the relay rod is allowed by ball studs, usually formed in one end of the tie rods. The opposite end of each tie rod is threaded for *adjusting sleeves*. These adjusting sleeves provide a means of changing the length of the assembled tie rods. The adjustment is necessary to provide the correct *toe-in*, a function of wheel alignment.

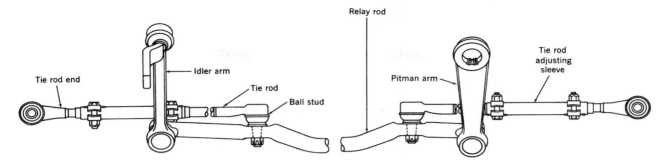

Figure 15.73 An assembled view of typical parallelogram steering linkage components (courtesy of Chevrolet Motor Division, General Motors Corporation).

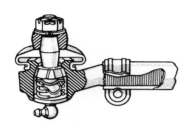

Figure 15.74 A cutaway view of a tie rod end (courtesy of Ford Motor Company, Dearborn, MI).

Tie Rod Ends. As shown in Figure 15.74, tie rod ends are ball and socket joints (ball studs) provided with threaded stems. The threaded stem fits into the tie rod adjusting sleeves, and the tapered stud fits into a matching hole in the steering arm.

The Steering Gear

The steering gear serves two functions. First, it converts the rotating motion of the steering wheel to lateral, or side-to-side, motion. Second, it multiplies the steering effort of the driver. The gear system that performs these tasks also minimizes the road shock that is passed back to the steering wheel. Two types of steering gear designs are in common use: (1) the recirculating ball type and (2) the rack and pinion type.

Recirculating Ball Steering Gear. Most rear wheel drive cars and some front wheel drive cars use a steering gear of this design, shown in Figure 15.75. The principle of operation is very simple. It can be likened to a nut that has been threaded on a bolt. When the bolt is turned, the nut moves up or down the thread of the bolt. The rotary motion of the bolt is converted to the lateral motion of the nut. Some steering gears of earlier design op-

erated in just this manner. But the friction between the moving parts required excessive steering effort and caused rapid wear.

In the recirculating ball steering gear, the bolt, called a *worm shaft*, and the nut, called a *ball nut*, never contact each other. They are separated by steel ball bearings, which roll and keep friction between the parts very low. As shown in Figure 15.76, the grooves on the worm shaft and in the

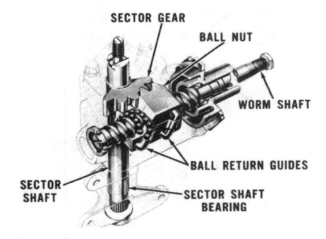

Figure 15.75 A recirculating ball steering gear (courtesy of Ford Motor Company, Dearborn, MI).

Figure 15.76 Ball and worm shaft disassembled. Notice the rounded threads in the nut and on the shaft (courtesy of Ford Motor Company, Dearborn, MI).

Job 15I

IDENTIFY STEERING LINKAGE PARTS

SATISFACTORY PERFORMANCE
A satisfactory performance on this job requires that you do the following:

1. Identify the numbered parts on the drawing by placing the number of each part in front of the correct part name.
2. Correctly identify all the parts within 15 minutes.

PERFORMANCE SITUATION

_____ Tie rod end   _____ Steering arm
_____ Idler arm bracket   _____ Relay rod
_____ Pitman arm   _____ Idler arm
_____ Strut   _____ Tie rod

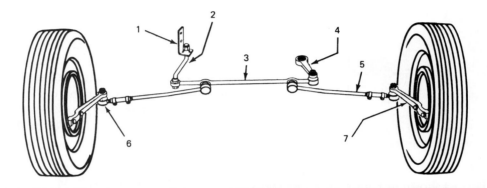

ball nut are in the form of threads. The steel balls fit into these threads. When the driver turns the steering wheel, the worm shaft turns. The ball nut moves up or down, and the balls roll in their grooves. Two loops of balls are usually used, as shown in Figure 15.77. To keep the balls from rolling out of the ends of the ball nut, *guides* are attached to the outside of the nut. When the balls reach the end of their *circuit*, or loop, they are directed back into the grooves at the other end of the nut. In this way, the balls are constantly recirculated.

As shown in Figure 15.75, the ball nut has teeth cut on one side. These teeth mesh with the teeth on the *sector shaft* gear. The sector shaft is sometimes called the *cross shaft*. As the ball nut moves up or down on the worm shaft, the sector shaft turns. Because the Pitman arm is attached to the end of the sector shaft, the steering linkage moves when the sector shaft is turned.

All the parts of the steering gear are contained in a cast housing, as shown in Figure 15.78. The housing is provided with mounting lugs, or "ears,"

so it can be bolted to the frame or underbody. Two adjusting devices are provided and, on some units, a filler hole is provided so the gear lubricant can be checked and replenished.

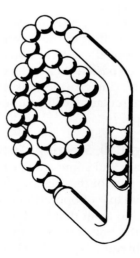

Figure 15.77 Typical ball circuit. Notice that the balls are recirculated through a guide (courtesy of Ford Motor Company, Dearborn, MI).

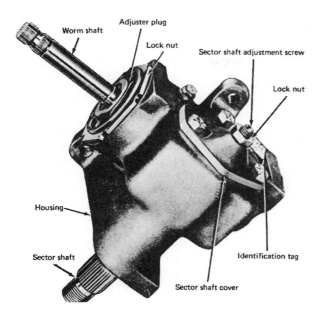

Figure 15.78 A manual recirculating ball steering gear (courtesy of Ford Motor Company, Dearborn, MI).

Rack and Pinion Steering Gear.

Rack and pinion steering gears of the types shown in Figures 15.79 and 15.80 offer some advantages over recirculating ball steering gears. They provide fast, sensitive steering, and they do not require extensive linkage systems. physical design and layout makes them especially suitable for use on front wheel drive cars. Rack and pinion steering gears also have certain disadvantages. Their basic design limits the

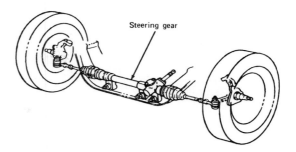

Figure 15.79 Typical rack and pinion system. Notice that the tie rods are connected directly to the steering gear (courtesy of Ford Motor Company, Dearborn, MI).

amount of steering effort reduction that can be provided. They also transmit more road shock back to the steering wheel than do recirculating ball types.

LESSON 15–7 Power Steering Systems

Cars that have power steering are fitted with a booster unit in the steering system. When the effort required to turn the steering wheel exceeds a certain limit, a hydraulic device boosts the effort of the driver. This booster unit provides most of the force required for steering. The hydraulic pressure is provided by a pump driven by the

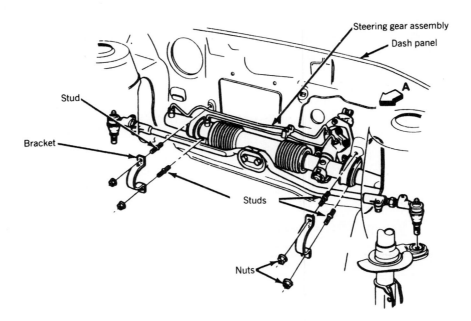

Figure 15.80 Power rack and pinion system. A power rack and pinion steering gear. In this installation, it is mounted on the dash panel behind the engine (courtesy of Chevrolet Motor Division, General Motors Corporation).

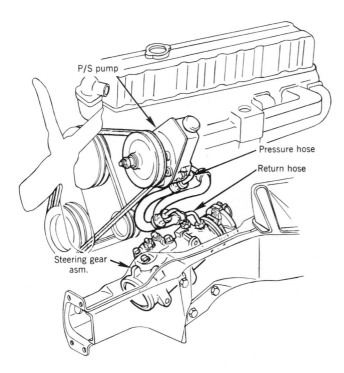

Figure 15.81 Power recirculating ball steering gear. The control valve and the power piston are contained in the steering gear assembly (courtesy of Chevrolet Motor Division, General Motors Corporation).

Job 15J

ADJUST A POWER STEERING PUMP BELT

SATISFACTORY PERFORMANCE

A satisfactory performance on this job requires that you do the following:

1. Adjust the power steering belt tension on the car assigned.
2. Following the steps in the "Performance Outline" and the manufacturer's procedure and specifications, complete the job within 200% of the manufacturer's suggested time.
3. Fill in the blanks under "Information."

PERFORMANCE OUTLINE

1. Measure the belt tension.
2. Compare the tension with the specification.
3. Loosen the adjusting bolts or nuts.
4. Adjust the belt tension to the specification.
5. Tighten the adjusting bolts and nuts to the torque specification.
6. Remove the gauge.

INFORMATION

Vehicle identification _____
Reference used _____ Page(s) _____
Belt tension at start of job _____
Belt tension specification _____
Belt tension at completion of job _____

engine. When the steering wheel is turned, a control valve directs the hydraulic pressure to one side of a piston. The piston then applies to the steering system a force that aids in turning the front wheels.

Three types of power steering systems are found. Two of these types are *integral.* In an integral system the control valve and the power piston are internal parts of the steering gear. Integral designs include the *power recirculating ball steering gear* and the *power rack and pinion steering gear* (see Figures 15.81 and 15.82).

The third type of power steering system is a *nonintegral system.* It is usually referred to as a *linkage-type* system. This type of system uses externally mounted components that are attached to the steering linkage. The control valve and the power piston are

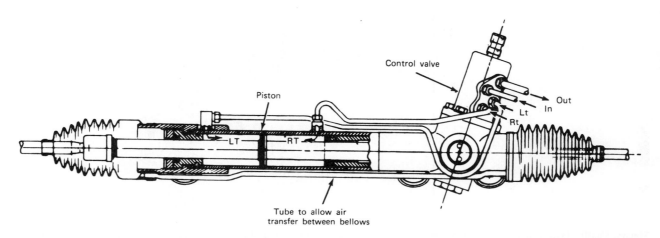

Figure 15.82 A typical integral power rack and pinion steering gear (courtesy of Ford Motor Company, Dearborn, MI).

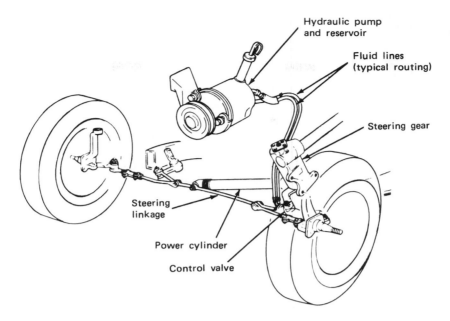

Figure 15.83 Typical linkage-type power steering. Notice that the control valve and the power cylinder are mounted separately on the steering linkage (courtesy of Ford Motor Company, Dearborn, MI).

connected by hoses or tubing. A typical linkage-type system is shown in Figure 15.83.

In most power steering systems, hydraulic pressure is provided by a pump mounted near the front of the engine. You are familiar with this location from your work in checking and adjusting the power steering fluid level. Typical pumps, shown in Figures 15.84 and 15.85, are driven by a belt from the crankshaft pulley. The pump is connected to

the control valve by means of two hoses. One hose delivers the hydraulic fluid to the control valve. The second hose returns the fluid to the reservoir.

> For a complete look at power steering fluids and how they should be checked, refer to Chapter 1.

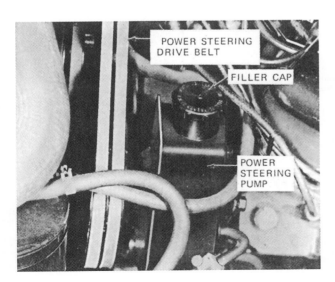

Figure 15.84 A typical power steering pump with dual drive belts (courtesy of Cadillac Motor Car Division, General Motors Corporation).

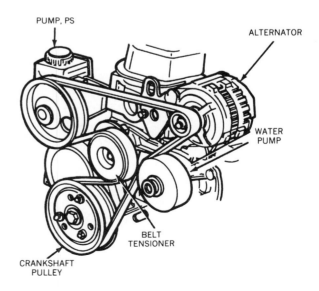

Figure 15.85 A power steering pump driven by a serpentine belt (courtesy of Chevrolet Motor Division, General Motors Corporation).

**ADJUSTING A
POWER STEERING
PUMP BELT**

Because most power steering pumps are driven by a belt, a failure of the belt usually results in a failure of the entire power steering system. Before any attempt is made to adjust a belt, the belt should be inspected.

As with a fan belt, a power steering belt should exhibit no cracks or glazing, and should not be oil-soaked. In most cases, an oil-soaked belt indicates that the seal on the pump shaft is leaking. The exact location of the leak must be found and the required repair performed. A belt with any of these defects should be replaced.

A loose belt cannot drive the pump properly. Therefore, a belt that is not cracked, glazed, or oil-soaked should be adjusted to increase its tension. Most manufacturers specify the tension to which the power steering belt on their cars should be adjusted. The belt tension gauge used to adjust a fan belt should also be used for this job (see Figure 15.86).

The steps that follow outline a typical procedure for adjusting a power steering pump drive belt. Consult an appropriate manual for the particular procedure and specifications necessary for the car on which you are working.

1. Position a belt tension gauge on the power steering belt (see Figure 15.87).

Figure 15.86 A typical belt tension gauge (courtesy of American Motors).

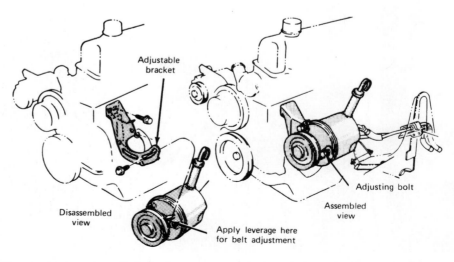

Figure 15.87 Using a belt tension gauge. Positioning a belt tension gauge on a power steering pump belt (courtesy of American Motors).

Figure 15.88 Power steering belt adjustment. Notice the slotted holes in the adjustment bracket (courtesy of Ford Motor Company, Dearborn, MI).

2. Loosen the adjustment bolts or nuts slightly so the pump can be moved in or out on its bracket (see Figure 15.88).
3. Carefully move the pump until the correct tension is indicated on the gauge.

   Note: Do not apply any force to the reservoir or filler neck. On some cars you must pry the pump out, as shown in Figures 15.89 and 15.90. The pry bar or special

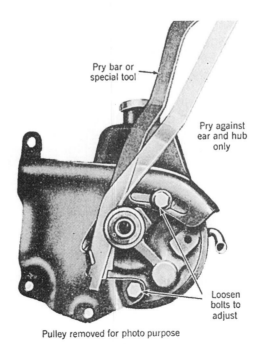

Figure 15.89 Power steering pump pry points. Typical prying points for adjusting power steering pump belts (courtesy of Oldsmobile Motor Division, General Motors Corporation).

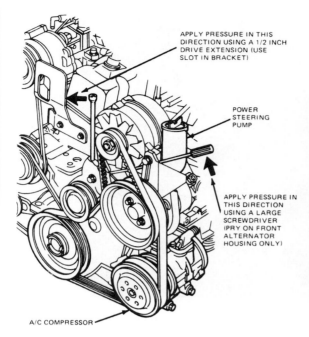

APPLY PRESSURE IN THIS
DIRECTION USING A 1/2 INCH
DRIVE EXTENSION (USE
SLOT IN BRACKET)

POWER
STEERING
PUMP

APPLY PRESSURE IN
THIS DIRECTION
USING A LARGE
SCREWDRIVER
(PRY ON FRONT
ALTERNATOR
HOUSING ONLY)

A/C COMPRESSOR

Figure 15.90 Serpentine belt adjustment. On this engine, the power steering pump is driven by a serpentine belt that is adjusted by means of an idler pulley (courtesy of Ford Motor Company, Dearborn, MI).

INSERT RATCHET
IN ADJUSTING LUG
OF BRACKET

Figure 15.91 Pump bracket leverage system. A power steering pump mounting bracket that allows the use of a ratchet handle to provide leverage for adjustment (courtesy of American Motors).

tool must be placed so it does not contact the reservoir. Any force applied to the reservoir could damage its thin metal or plastic housing and cause leakage. On some cars, a 1/2-inch square hole is provided in the pump bracket so a breaker bar or ratchet handle can be inserted and used as a lever. An adjustment feature of this type is shown in Figure 15.91.

4. Tighten the adjustment nuts or bolts to the torque specifications of the manufacturer while maintaining the correct tension.
5. Remove the belt tension gauge.

> The serpentine belt is very widely used. It has a built-in tension system. When the belt is at the right tension, indicator marks on the tensioner are aligned. Stretched belts and weak tensioner springs cause the indicators to move off their marks. Both sides of the belt are used, so look at both sides carefully for cuts, glazed spots, and cracks. Belts of this type often crack on the ribbed side first.

VOCABULARY

Use the listed words in the blanks beside the sentences to complete the definitions. Either write out the words or place the letters in the blanks.

A. Long arm
B. Pivot points
C. Coil spring
D. Transverse

E. Strut
F. Steering knuckles
G. Lithium based
H. Zerk fitting
I. Bushing
J. Gun adapter
K. Load carrying
L. Tension type

M. Compression type
N. Preloaded
O. Play
P. Unloaded
Q. Dial indicator
R. Rebound
S. Bounce
T. Direct-action
U. Flex
V. Pitman arm
W. Relay rod
X. Worm shaft
Y. Cross shaft

_____ 1. Slippery additive used in grease
_____ 2. Bending movement of a part and its return to normal without any turning motion
_____ 3. Top or bottom part going from the frame to the spindle and longer than the other
_____ 4. A part mounted across the frame from one side to the other
_____ 5. A part made for applying the grease to a suspension part
_____ 6. Loose motion in a part due to damage or wear
_____ 7. When a shock absorber is mounted between the suspension system and the car frame
_____ 8. A part that compresses and rebounds back to normal
_____ 9. Rubber part placed between parts to allow the parts to move but not rotate
_____ 10. Keeps the lower control arms from moving or shifting
_____ 11. When the vehicle weight is taken off a ball joint
_____ 12. A part where the spindles or drive axles are attached
_____ 13. Changes the rotating motion at the steering gear to linear motion
_____ 14. The bolt in a recirculating ball steering gear
_____ 15. Rigid steel bar attached to the Pitman arm by a ball stud
_____ 16. Places where the control arms move up and down
_____ 17. Rapid up-and-down motion of the suspension system

_____ 18. When a spring returns to its normal length
_____ 19. Used with a grease gun to lubricate special areas
_____ 20. Another name for the sector shaft
_____ 21. The ball joint that supports the weight of the vehicle
_____ 22. Tool used to check ball joint wear
_____ 23. Uses the weight of the vehicle to push the ball stud into its housing
_____ 24. Uses the weight of the vehicle to pull the ball stud into its housing
_____ 25. A method that holds the ball stud tight against its socket

REVIEW QUESTIONS

The following questions will help you determine if you have accomplished the tasks stated at the beginning of this chapter. If you do not know many of the answers, go back and review the material before proceeding to the next chapter.

Lesson 15–1
1. What is the main purpose of a suspension system?
2. What is the job of the steering wheel?
3. What are the advantages of a solid axle-type suspension system?
4. Where are the solid axle systems found on today's vehicles?
5. What is the disadvantage of a solid axle system when one wheel drops into a hole?
6. What is the advantage of the independent front suspension system?
7. What type of design keeps the point of contact between the tires and the road from changing?
8. The design of what part makes it ideal for use in front suspension systems?
9. What part takes the place of coil springs in some vehicles?
10. What does it mean when a part is transverse mounted?
11. What part is found on the outer end of a control arm?
12. What is the name of the part that prevents a straight lower control arm from movement?
13. What is another name for a spindle?
14. What are three jobs that a spindle performs?
15. On vehicles that require chassis lubrication, what is the lubrication interval range?
16. What happens when lubricants are not compatible?

17. What part allows the grease to enter the parts to be lubricated?
18. What happens when too much grease is forced into a part?
19. Why are plugs used instead of fittings in some vehicles?
20. What is the purpose of a rubber bushing?
21. Do rubber bushings require lubrication?
22. When should rubber bushings be replaced?

Lesson 15–2
23. How is a MacPherson strut system constructed?
24. What is at the top of the upper mount of a MacPherson system?
25. What is placed at the bottom of the lower part of a MacPherson system?
26. What is the difference between a front wheel drive MacPherson system and a rear wheel drive one?
27. What two types of control arms are used on a MacPherson system?
28. What part is used in the place of a strut on some MacPherson-equipped systems?

Lesson 15–3
29. What is a ball joint?
30. What are the two classifications of ball joints?
31. What is the name of the ball joint that supports the weight of the car?
32. What determines which ball joint will support the weight of the car?
33. What are two types of load-carrying ball joints?
34. Which ball joint wears out faster?
35. What type of ball joint is placed in a MacPherson system?
36. What are some other names for a nonload-carrying ball joint?
37. What is a preloaded ball joint?
38. Why are ball joints preloaded?
39. What must be done before checking the wear in a load-carrying ball joint?
40. Where should the jack be placed to check ball joint wear in a long and short arm suspension system?
41. Where should the jack be placed to check the wear in a MacPherson system ball joint?

Lesson 15–4
42. How can a worn ball joint change the wheel alignment angles?
43. What adjustment should be checked and corrected before a ball joint check?
44. How does a ball joint wear indicator work?

45. What is equal to the amount of wear in an indicator-type ball joint?
46. How will the indicator ball joint look when the wear reaches 0.050 in.?
47. How can a manual wear check be made on some ball joints?
48. What is a radial ball joint check and how is it performed?
49. What is an axial ball joint check and how is it performed?
50. What tool is used to make the most accurate ball joint wear test?

Lesson 15–5
51. What happens to a spring when the wheel is moved up against it?
52. What is it called when a spring returns to its original length?
53. What happens to a tire when it bounces?
54. What three things happen to a vehicle when the shock absorbers fail?
55. What is the purpose of a shock absorber?
56. Where is a direct-action shock absorber installed?
57. What do double-action shock absorbers control?
58. What three tests are used to check a shock absorber?
59. In a bounce test why can't the front shocks be compared with the rear?
60. What should you look for during a visual shock absorber check?

Lesson 15–6
61. What is the most widely used steering linkage design?
62. What are three advantages of the parallelogram design steering linkage system?
63. The Pitman arm changes rotating motion to what kind of motion?
64. What part does the Pitman arm push or pull?
65. What is a ball stud?
66. Between what two parts is the relay rod?
67. How are the tie rods attached to the relay rod?
68. What is the purpose of the idler arm?
69. What is the purpose of a tie rod?
70. What is the purpose of the tie rod adjusting sleeves?
71. What are two functions of a steering gear?
72. What are two types of steering gear systems?
73. In the recirculating ball steering gear, what separates the worm shaft from the ball nut?
74. What are the guides used for in the recirculating ball system?

75. What do the ball nut teeth mesh into?
76. What are the advantages and disadvantages of the rack and pinion gear system over the recirculating ball type?

Lesson 15–7
77. What are three types of power steering systems?
78. What provides the hydraulic pressure to operate the power steering system?
79. What types of fluid are used in the power steering system?
80. How is power steering fluid checked?

ASE QUESTIONS

Each question or incomplete statement in this test is followed by four suggested answers or completions. In each case select the *one* that best answers the question or completes the statement.

1. Different types of suspension systems are being discussed. Technician A says the solid axle suspension can have a problem called the "tilt effect." Technician B says the independent suspension systems can have the "tilt effect" problem. Who is right?
   a. A only
   b. B only
   c. Both A and B
   d. Neither A nor B

2. The long and short arm type of independent suspension system is being discussed. Technician A says the short arm is always on the bottom. Technician B says the short arm is always on the top. Who is right?
   a. A only
   b. B only
   c. Both A and B
   d. Neither A nor B

3. When the tires on a vehicle are inspected, point-of-contact scuffing is noticed on the tire treads. Technician A says this is normal on solid axle suspensions. Technician B says this is abnormal for a long and short arm suspension system. Who is right?
   a. A only
   b. B only
   c. Both A and B
   d. Neither A nor B

4. The coil spring is positioned between the frame and lower coil arm. Technician A says this system is often used on vehicles with a conventional or partial front frame. Technician B says this mounting is usually found on vehicles of unit body construction. Who is right?
   a. A only
   b. B only
   c. Both A and B
   d. Neither A nor B

5. A vehicle is equipped with a torsion bar. Technician A says this is used along with a coil spring.

Technician B says this is used in place of a coil spring. Who is right?
   a. A only
   b. B only
   c. Both A and B
   d. Neither A nor B

6. A vehicle has a control arm. Technician A says the base of each arm is mounted with a ball joint. Technician B says the outer end of the arm is mounted with a bushing. Who is right?
   a. A only
   b. B only
   c. Both A and B
   d. Neither A nor B

7. Spindles are being discussed. Technician A says they are attached to the control arms with ball joints. Technician B says they are moved by the steering arms to turn the front wheels. Who is right?
   a. A only
   b. B only
   c. Both A and B
   d. Neither A nor B

8. A vehicle needs a chassis lubrication. Technician A says the same grease that was used to lubricate the vehicle before should always be used. Technician B says a semisolid, lithium-based, multipurpose grease should be used. Who is right?
   a. A only
   b. B only
   c. Both A and B
   d. Neither A nor B

9. Grease plugs are found on a vehicle where lubricant should be applied. Technician A says the plugs should be removed and grease fittings installed and left. Technician B says that either an adapter should be used or fittings installed and after greasing the vehicle, the plugs should be placed back. Who is right?
   a. A only
   b. B only
   c. Both A and B
   d. Neither A nor B

10. Rubber bushings are being discussed. Technician A says the parts using rubber bushings should never rotate but just flex. Technician B says it is normal for rubber bushings to turn at their mounting points so the wear will be on the rubber and not the parts. Who is right?
    a. A only
    b. B only
    c. Both A and B
    d. Neither A nor B

11. The MacPherson suspension system is being discussed. Technician A says the system is mounted to the upper control arm by a ball joint. Technician B says this system is mounted to the lower control arm by a ball joint. Who is right?
    a. A only
    b. B only
    c. Both A and B
    d. Neither A nor B

12. A ball joint is being discussed. Technician A says it will allow up-and-down movement and some

twist. Technician B says it will allow side-to-side movement and some twist. Who is right?
a. A only
b. B only
c. Both A and B
d. Neither A nor B

13. A coil spring is positioned between the vehicle frame and the upper control arm. Technician A says the upper ball joint is the load-carrying one in this design. Technician B says the lower ball joint is the load-carrying one in this design. Who is right?
a. A only
b. B only
c. Both A and B
d. Neither A nor B

14. A vehicle has a load-carrying ball joint. Technician A says the weight of the vehicle is used to pull the ball stud into its housing on this joint. Technician B says the weight of the vehicle is used to push the ball stud into its housing. Who is right?
a. A only
b. B only
c. Both A and B
d. Neither A nor B

15. After an inspection it is found that a ball joint moves up and down in its socket. Technician A says this is normal and the vehicle weight will force the ball tight. Technician B says the ball joint has lost its preload. Who is right?
a. A only
b. B only
c. Both A and B
d. Neither A nor B

16. A vehicle was placed on a frame-type hydraulic lift with all the wheels suspended. A ball joint inspection was made and no problems were found. Technician A says the load-carrying ball joints must be unloaded for an accurate inspection. Technician B says all ball joints can be inspected with the wheels suspended. Who is right?
a. A only
b. B only
c. Both A and B
d. Neither A nor B

17. Ball joints on a vehicle are worn beyond acceptable limits. Technician A says this will affect the spindle and steering knuckle positions. Technician B says this will affect handling and cause abnormal tire wear. Who is right?
a. A only
b. B only
c. Both A and B
d. Neither A nor B

18. A ball joint is made with a visual wear indicator. Technician A says the indicator will retract as the ball joint wears. Technician B says the ball joint indicator will protrude as the ball joint wears. Who is right?
a. A only
b. B only
c. Both A and B
d. Neither A nor B

19. Ball joints should be checked for side-to-side movement and up-and-down movement. Technician A says up-and-down movement is radial wear. Technician B says side-to-side movement is axial wear. Who is right?
a. A only
b. B only
c. Both A and B
d. Neither A nor B

20. A vehicle shows some ball joint wear, but it is hard to determine how much. Technician A says the wear can be measured with a ball joint checking gauge. Technician B says the wear can be checked with a dial indicator. Who is right?
a. A only
b. B only
c. Both A and B
d. Neither A nor B

21. A shock absorber is mounted between the suspension system and the car frame. Technician A says this is called direct action. Technician B says this is called double action. Who is right?
a. A only
b. B only
c. Both A and B
d. Neither A nor B

22. A vehicle is given a bounce test to determine the shock absorber action and condition. Technician A says the test compares all the shocks with each other. Technician B says the test compares the front shocks with each other and the rear shocks with each other. Who is right?
a. A only
b. B only
c. Both A and B
d. Neither A nor B

23. Steering linkage systems are being discussed. Technician A says the parallelogram type system is the most commonly used. Technician B says the triangular type is the most commonly used. Who is right?
a. A only
b. B only
c. Both A and B
d. Neither A nor B

24. A Pitman arm operation is being discussed. Technician A says the Pitman arm pushes the relay rod. Technician B says the Pitman arm pulls the relay rod. Who is right?
a. A only
b. B only
c. Both A and B
d. Neither A nor B

25. A recirculating ball steering gear is being discussed. Technician A says the ball nut rides directly on the worm shaft. Technician B says the two parts never touch each other and are separated by a steel ball. Who is right?
a. A only
b. B only
c. Both A and B
d. Neither A nor B

26. A rack and pinion steering system is being discussed. Technician A says the design limits the amount of steering effort deduction that can be provided. Technician B says this design reduces the amount of road shock transmitted back to the steering wheel. Who is right?
    a. A only
    b. B only
    c. Both A and B
    d. Neither A nor B

27. A serpentine belt breaks on a moving vehicle. Technician A says the power steering system will continue to have hydraulic power to steer the vehicle. Technician B says all hydraulic power will stop and the steering will be manual. Who is right?
    a. A only
    b. B only
    c. Both A and B
    d. Neither A nor B

16 Tire, Wheel, and Hub System Maintenance

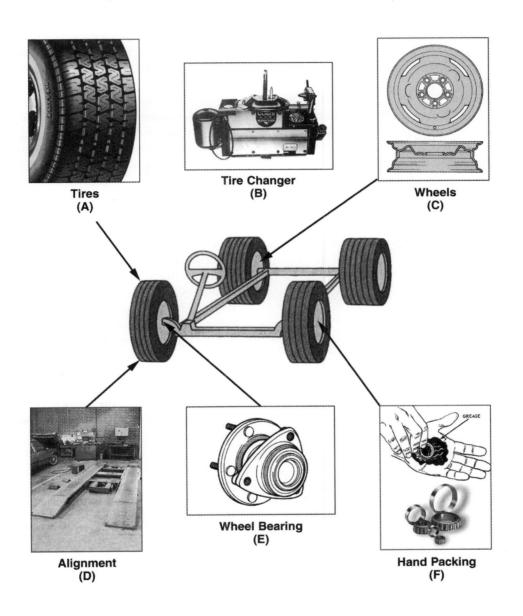

Tires
(A)

Tire Changer
(B)

Wheels
(C)

Alignment
(D)

Wheel Bearing
(E)

Hand Packing
(F)

Tires (see 16a) contact the road and provide the traction for the vehicle to move. They are mounted on wheels (see 16c) bolted to the hubs. Inside the hubs are the bearings (see 16f) that allow the tires and wheels to roll. These parts are constantly taking abuse from road hazards such as potholes. They have to be sealed from dirt and water. Tires must be trued, patched, and balanced. Hubs contain bearings and seals that must be serviced. Some brake knowledge is also required to disassemble the hubs for inspection and lubrication. Complicated machines are required to make sure the tires are aligned so the maximum mileage can be obtained from each tire (see Figure 16d).

Most service technicians can read tire tread wear and tell what needs attention on the vehicle to prevent further damage. Since tires are major indicators when something is wrong, learning to read abnormal tire wear patterns is a must. One of the major changes in the hub area is the introduction of antilock brake systems. This is covered in detail in Chapter 17.

TASKS

The following are nine tasks to master before leaving this chapter:

Task 16-1.   Learn the types of tires in use today and how are they identified.

Task 16-2.   Study how to service tires.

Task 16-3.   Study how to troubleshoot a tire for problems.

Task 16-4.   Learn the types of wheels in use today and the wheel parts.

Task 16-5.   Learn how to service a wheel.

Task 16-6.   Learn how to troubleshoot a wheel.

Task 16-7.   Study the types of hubs that are in use.

Task 16-8.   Learn how to service a hub.

Task 16-9.   Learn how to troubleshoot a hub.

LESSON 16–1   Tires

Four small areas of tire tread are the only contact between a car and the road. That frictional contact is very important. It allows the power developed by the engine to start a car in motion and keep it in motion. It allows the steering system to control a car's direction. And it allows the brakes to bring the car to a stop. Those four small areas of contact actually determine the roadability and handling qualities of a car.

In this chapter you will study the construction of various types of tires. You will become aware of the different systems used in tire measurement and identification. And you will learn how to interpret tire wear patterns. You will also dismount, mount, and repair tires. And you will perform other jobs related to tire maintenance.

Tires serve two basic functions. First, they act as primary shock absorbers, cushioning the car from the jarring effects of rough roads. Second, they provide the car's frictional contact with the road. This contact allows the driving wheels to start the car in motion and to keep it moving. It allows the front wheels to steer the car. And it allows the brakes to slow the car or bring it to a stop.

As shown in Figure 16.1, tires are made of layers of cords. Those layers are called *plies*. The cords are usually made of nylon, rayon, or polyester fiber. The layers of cords are impregnated with rubber. They are then placed over a donut-shaped form. Coils of steel wire are placed at the *beads*, or open edges of the tire. The rubber for the tread and sidewalls is laid on over the plies. The entire assembly is then placed in a special mold, where heat and pressure cause the rubber to flow. This process, called *vulcanizing*, bonds all the parts of the tire together. The mold also determines the sidewall and tread designs.

Tire Types

There are three types of tires in common use: (1) the radial ply, (2) the bias ply, and (3) the bias belted. Each type has a different construction.

Radial Ply Tires.   Radial ply tires have cords that run from bead to bead, crossing the tire centerline at a 90° angle, as shown in Figure 16.2. In effect, the cords radiate from the center point of the tire. Two or more "belts" are placed under the tread area, extending across the full width of the tread surface. These belts may be of steel mesh, fiberglass, or of the material used for the plies. Belts help make the tread more rigid than it would be without them. The greater rigidity reduces the amount of tread motion when the tread contacts the road. This construction not only prolongs tread life but also increases the flexibility of the sidewalls.

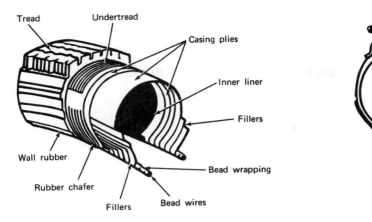

Figure 16.1   Cutaway views of a typical tubeless tire (courtesy of Chevrolet Motor Division, General Motors Corporation).

Bias Ply Tires.   Bias ply tires, sometimes called *cross-bias ply* tires or *diagonal bias ply* tires, usually have two or four plies. As shown in Figure 16.3, those plies crisscross the centerline of the tire at an angle of about 35°. The alternate plies cross at opposite angles and extend from bead to bead.

Bias Belted Tires.   Bias belted tires are bias ply tires that have two or more belts under the tread as shown in Figure 16.4. The belts provide greater tread rigidity and increase tread life.

Tire Sizes and Size Markings

As you know, tires come in many sizes. There are several methods of indicating tire sizes. However, all methods are based on two measurements. One is the rim diameter. The other is the cross-section width.

Rim Diameter.   Most cars use wheels that have a rim diameter of 13, 14, or 15 inches. Rim diameter is measured as shown in Figure 16.5. This measurement, in inches, is the last two-digit number in any given designation of tire size. For example, a tire

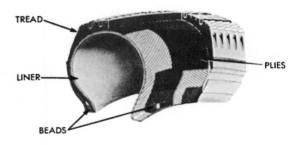

Figure 16.3   A sectioned view of a bias ply tire (courtesy of Chrysler Corporation).

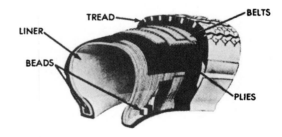

Figure 16.4   A sectioned view of a bias belted tire (courtesy of Chrysler Corporation).

marked P195/75R14 fits a wheel that has a rim diameter of 14 inches.

Cross-Section Width.   The cross-section width of a fully inflated tire, shown in Figure 16.6, can be given in several different ways. These include actual measurement in millimeters or inches, or as a ratio between the cross-section height and the cross-section width. This height-to-width ratio is often referred to as the *profile ratio*, or the *aspect ratio* (see Figure 16.7).

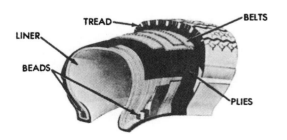

Figure 16.2   A sectioned view of a radial ply tire (courtesy of Chrysler Corporation).

Job 16A

IDENTIFY TIRE TYPES AND PARTS

SATISFACTORY PERFORMANCE
A satisfactory performance on this job requires that you do the following:

1. Identify each tire shown below by placing its identifying letter before the word or phrase that best describes the tire's construction.
2. Identify the parts of the tires shown by placing each part number in front of the correct part name.
3. Correctly identify all the tires and tire parts within 15 minutes.

PERFORMANCE SITUATION

_____ Beads		_____ Radial ply	
_____ Bias ply		_____ Tread	
_____ Liner		_____ Belts	
_____ Bias belted		_____ Break strip	
_____ Skirt		_____ Sidewall	
_____ Plies		_____ Rim	

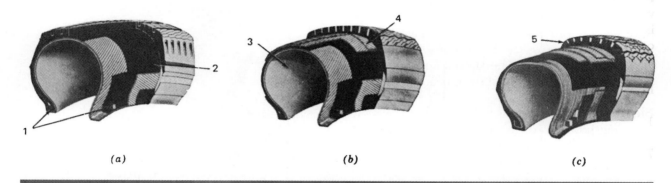

(a)   (b)   (c)

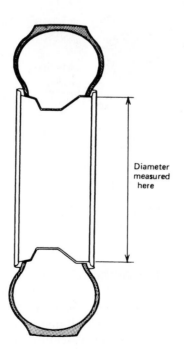

Figure 16.5 Wheel rim diameter. Measure the diameter through the center of the rim from one side to the other to determine the size of the rim.

Tire Size Designations

Several different systems are used to designate the sizes of passenger car tires. These systems are usually referred to as (1) P-Metric, (2) European Metric, (3) Alphanumeric, and (4) Numeric. In addition, there is a T Type Temporary

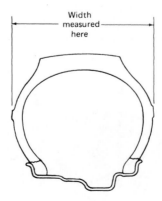

Figure 16.6 Tire cross-sectional width. The width of a tire is measured at the points shown (courtesy of Chevrolet Motor Division, General Motors Corporation).

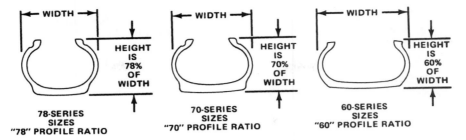

Figure 16.7 The determination of the height-to-width ratio (courtesy of American Motors).

Spare Tire designation, and additional light truck tire designations including LT-Metric and Flotation.

P-Metric. This is the latest method used to provide size information of passenger car tires. As it is based on international standards, it combines older American and European systems. A tire size of P195/75R14 is interpreted as follows:

P   Indicates that the tire is for passenger car use.

195   The measurement of the cross-section width in millimeters (refer to Figure 16.6).

75   The height-to-width ratio (refer to Figure 16.7).

R   The identification of the tire's construction (R—radial, B—belted, D—diagonal bias).

14   The rim diameter in inches.

European Metric. This is an older European system that may still be found in specifications for imported cars and on some imported tires. A European Metric tire sized 195R14 is similar to a 195/75R14, but only the following information is supplied in the size:

195   The measurement of the cross-section width in millimeters.

R   Indication of radial construction.

14   The rim diameter in inches.

Alphanumeric. This is the American system that has been replaced by the P-Metric system. The first symbol used in the size is a letter that indicates the load to size relationship of the tire. The lower the letter, the smaller the tire, and the smaller the load-carrying capacity. A tire with an Alphanumeric size of ER78-14 is similar to a P195/75R14, but the markings indicate the following.

E   The load to size relationship.

R   Indication of radial construction. (Tires of other than radial construction are not identified.)

78   The height-to-width ratio (refer to Figure 16.7).

14   The rim diameter in inches.

Numeric. Although the Numeric system can be considered obsolete, it is still used on tires built for antique and classic cars. A numeric-sized tire similar to a modern P195/75R14 would be identified as an 8.00-14. This size provides the following information:

8.00   The approximate measurement of the cross-section width in inches.

14   The rim diameter in inches.

Tire Sidewall Markings

The sidewalls of a tire contain a considerable amount of information in addition to the size, the name, and the maker of the tire. Some of that information is government mandated. An understanding of the markings can help you in determining the relative quality of different tires and in their selection for specific applications. The markings shown in Figure 16.8 are explained as follows:

DOT xxxxxxxx. The abbreviation DOT certifies that the tire complies with the safety standards of the Department of Transportation. This is followed by a "serial number" or identification number. The last three digits are numbers identifying the week and year of manufacture. For example, "376" means the 37th week of 1986; "248" means the 24th week of 1988. Other characters are the tire maker's code for size, type, and the plant where the tire was manufactured.

Figure 16.8 Typical tire sidewall markings (courtesy of the Rubber Manufacturers Association).

Tread 4 Plies - 2 xxxx Cord - 2 xxxx Cord - Sidewall 2 Plies xxxx Cord. This discloses the cord material, the number of plies, and the tire composition.

Radial. The word "radial" must be on the sidewall if the tire is of radial construction.

Tubeless. The tire must be marked either "tubeless" or "tube type."

Max Load 590 KG (1301 lbs) @ 240 kPa (35 PSI) Max Press. This specifies the load limit of the tire and the maximum cold inflation pressure. On P-Metric tires, this information is given in both metric and English units.

M/S. The letters M and S, in any combination, indicate that the tire meets the requirements of a Mud and Snow tire as defined by the Rubber Manufacturers Association (RMA).

Treadwear 160 Traction B Temperature A. These are quality grades required to be established by the tire maker in accordance with regulations of the Department of Transportation.

LESSON 16-2   Tire Inflation

Many car owners forget to maintain proper tire pressures. Their forgetfulness often leads to the need for repairs to the steering and suspension

Figure 16.9 A pocket-type tire pressure gauge. The one shown is calibrated to 50 pounds in 1-pound units (courtesy of H. B. Egan Manufacturing Co., Muskogee, OK).

systems and for the replacement of ruined tires. Routine maintenance should always include checking and adjusting the air pressure in all the tires. An accurate tire pressure gauge, similar to the one shown in Figure 16.9, is one of the most important instruments to have in your toolbox.

Many problems are caused by improper tire inflation. A properly inflated tire provides full contact with the road, as shown in Figure 16.10. The proper tire pressures for a car vary with the type and size of the tires on the car. They also vary with the loads the car is to carry. Proper tire pressures are listed in shop manuals, owner's manuals, and usually on a plate or decal affixed to the car. Figure 16.11 shows how tire inflation pressures are specified by one car manufacturer. Inflation pressures are usually given in pounds per square inch (psi). However, you will also find inflation pressures specified in *kilopascals* (kPa). A conversion chart for commonly used pressures is provided in Figure 16.12.

Underinflation

Normal air loss combined with owner neglect often results in tires that are underinflated. Underinflated tires not only bulge out excessively at the sidewalls but provide poor contact between the tread and the road surface. An underinflated tire is shown in Figure 16.13. Underinflated tires can cause the following problems:

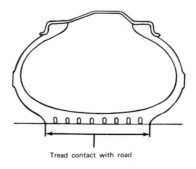

Tread contact with road

Figure 16.10 Properly inflated tire. Notice that the tread is in full contact with the road (courtesy of Chevrolet Motor Division, General Motors Corporation).

Chevrolet Nova	
Vehicle Capacity Weight (Lbs.) 850	
Designated Seating Capacity Total 5 (2 Front 3 Rear)	
Recommended Cold Tire Inflation Pressures (PSI)	
P155 80R 13	
Vehicle Load	
up to Vehicle Capacity Weight	Front 29 Rear 29
P175 70R 13	
Vehicle Load	
up to Vehicle Capacity Weight	Front 26 Rear 26
Recommended Tire Size	
P155/80R13 P175/70R13	
Compact Spare Tire	
Recommended Tire Size T115/70D14	
Recommended Cold Tire Inflation Pressure (PSI) 60	
*See Owner's Manual for additional information.	
	F10060–3E–5

Figure 16.11 An example of a tire label affixed to many new cars (courtesy of Chevrolet Motor Division, General Motors Corporation).

1. Increased steering effort and poor steering response
2. A tendency toward skidding and poor control on turns as the tire tread deflects and distorts with side thrust loads
3. Poor directional stability because of wander or pull in the steering
4. Early tire failure brought on by the heat generated by excessive flexing of the tire (see Figure 16.14)
5. Abnormal wear on the outer edges of the treads
6. Increased possibilities of tire and rim damage on impact with broken pavement (see Figures 16.15 and 16.16)
7. Erratic braking action
8. Increased fuel consumption because of increased friction and reduced rolling diameter

INFLATION PRESSURE CONVERSION CHART (KILOPASCALS TO PSI)

kPa	psi	kPa	psi
140	20	215	31
145	21	220	32
155	22	230	33
160	23	235	34
165	24	240	35
170	25	250	36
180	26	275	40
185	27	310	45
190	28	345	50
200	29	380	55
205	30	415	60

Conversion: 6.9 kPa = 1 psi

Figure 16.12 kPa to psi conversion chart (courtesy of Pontiac Motor Division, General Motors Corporation).

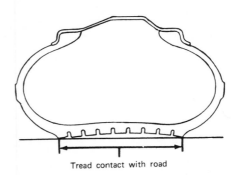

Tread contact with road

Figure 16.13 Underinflated tire. Notice that the center of the tread is not held in firm contact with the road surface (courtesy of Chevrolet Motor Division, General Motors Corporation).

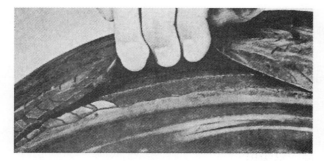

Figure 16.14 Damage caused by the heat produced while driving on an underinflated tire (courtesy of the Rubber Manufacturers Association).

Figure 16.15 Distortion of underinflated tire. An underinflated tire allows excessive distortion when broken pavement is encountered (courtesy of the Rubber Manufacturers Association).

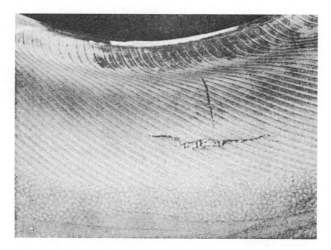

Figure 16.16 Underinflated impact damage. An underinflated tire is subject to impact damage of this type (courtesy of the Rubber Manufacturers Association).

Correct tire pressure is gauged by how the tread wears. If the wear is in the middle, the tire pressure is too high. Wear on the outside edges of the tread means too little pressure. The type of tire, size, weight on the tire, road conditions, and suspension condition all contribute to how much air is enough for a particular vehicle. After all these factors are used to determine the final pressure, a monitor of the tread wear is the final determining factor for the correct pressure. After this is calculated and the tread wear is right, keep the tires at this pressure unless something changes such as weight on the tire.

Overinflation

Overinflated tires are found less frequently than underinflated tires. An overinflated tire, shown in Figure 16.17, does not allow full tread contact with the road. Overinflated tires cause the following problems:

1. Decreased tread contact with the road surface
2. The transmission of excessive road shock to the steering and suspension systems
3. A less comfortable ride
4. Abnormal wear in the center of the tread

Checking and Adjusting Tire Pressures

Tire pressures should be checked when the tires are cool. The most accurate readings are obtained when the car has been parked for at least 3 hours or before it has been driven more than 3 miles. Tire temperatures increase as a car is being driven, and increased temperatures cause an increase in tire pressure.

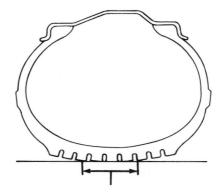

Figure 16.17 Overinflated tire. Notice that the edges of the tread do not contact the road surface (courtesy of Chevrolet Motor Division, General Motors Corporation).

Job 16B

CHECK AND ADJUST TIRE PRESSURES

SATISFACTORY PERFORMANCE
A satisfactory performance on this job requires that you do the following:

1. Check and adjust the pressures in the tires of the car assigned.
2. Following the steps in the "Performance Outline" and the specifications of the manufacturer, complete the job within 10 minutes.
3. Fill in the blanks under "Information."

PERFORMANCE OUTLINE

1. Determine the correct tire pressures for the front and rear tires.
2. Check the pressure in each tire, and add or release air to obtain the correct pressure.

INFORMATION

Vehicle identification _____
Reference used _____ Page(s) _____
Size of tires on vehicle _____
Tire pressure specified: Front ____ psi Rear ____ psi
Pressures at completion of job:
                Front ____ psi Rear ____ psi
Tires were: Cool ____ Hot ____
Are valve caps in place on all valve stems?
      Yes ____ No ____

Heavy loads, high road surface temperatures, and high-speed driving can raise tire pressures as much as 10 psi (70 kPa). This pressure buildup is normal. Therefore, no air should be released from a hot tire to lower the pressure.

Before you check tire pressures, always determine the pressures recommended by the car manufacturer. If the tire pressure specifications are not on a plate or decal on the car, check the owner's manual or an appropriate shop manual. Be sure to check the tire size. As mentioned earlier, proper tire pressures depend partially on tire size.

All tire valve stems contain valves similar to those shown in Figure 16.18. Those valves are designed to hold pressure during inflating and pressure checking operations. They are not designed to hold pressure indefinitely. All valve stems are threaded for valve caps similar to those shown in Figure 16.19. Valve caps provide a positive seal and keep dirt and water from entering the valve. After checking and adjusting the tire pressures, be sure all the valve stems are fitted with caps. If any caps are missing or damaged, install new caps.

Figure 16.18 Typical tire valves. The valve seals the opening in the stem where the tire can be inflated and deflated (courtesy of H. B. Egan Manufacturing Co., Muskogee, OK).

Figure 16.19 Typical tire valve caps. Tire valve caps keep dirt and water out of the valve (courtesy of H. B. Egan Manufacturing Co., Muskogee, OK).

LESSON 16–3 Tire Usage

Different types of tires impart different handling characteristics to a car. Certain combinations of different tire types on the same car can dangerously impair roadability. For that reason, tire usage should be governed by the following rules:

1. Except in an emergency, radial tires should not be used with bias ply or bias belted tires on the same car. If radial tires are to be used, they should be used on all four wheels (see Figure 16.20).

ALL FOUR TIRES SAME SIZE, SAME TYPE ON SAME VEHICLE
(Radial or non-radial)

(Front, Rear, or 4-Wheel Drive)

Figure 16.20 Radial tire use. Radial tires should not be mixed with other types of tires on the same axle (courtesy of the Rubber Manufacturers Association).

RADIALS AND NON-RADIALS ON SAME VEHICLE
(Front or Rear Wheel Drive)

- Same size and type on an axle.
- Radials on rear axle, non-radials on front axle.

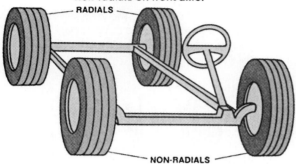

Figure 16.21 Radial tire and bias belted use. When radial tires and bias ply or bias belted tires must be used on the same car, the radial tires should be installed on the rear wheels (courtesy of the Rubber Manufacturers Association).

2. If radial tires must be used with bias ply or bias belted tires, they should be used in pairs on common axles. The radial tires should be installed on the rear wheels as shown in Figure 16.21. Radial tires should never be used on the front wheels when bias ply or bias belted tires are used on the rear wheels.

3. Bias ply and bias belted tires, also, may be used on the same car only in pairs on common axles. The bias belted tires should be used on the rear wheels.

DIFFERENT SERIES (PROFILE) ON SAME VEHICLE
(Front or Rear Wheel Drive)

- Same size and type on an axle.
- Place the lower series (profile) tires on rear.

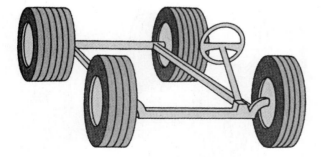

Figure 16.22 Wide/narrow tire use. When different series tires must be used on the same car, the widest tires should be installed on the rear wheels (courtesy of the Rubber Manufacturers Association).

4. Tires in different series sizes may be used on the same car only in pairs on common axles. Also, the tires on the front and those on the rear should be no more than one series apart. The widest tires should be placed on the rear wheels, as shown in Figure 16.22.

LESSON 16–4   Tire Maintenance

As mentioned earlier, the most important procedure in tire care is to maintain proper tire pressure. Other important procedures include tire rotation and tire inspection.

Try to rotate tires so an equal number of miles is placed on each tire in each position. If the tire warranty is for 40,000 miles, rotate the tires every 10,000 miles. This gives each tire a chance to be run in each position on the vehicle. Check the tread wear at the end of the fourth 10,000-mile rotation to see if an additional rotation is needed. Repeat the rotation interval until the tire treads are worn down to an unsafe level or the tread bars are showing. This means the tires will be placed back in their starting position. Never keep a tire that has a tread bar showing. In many states it is illegal to run a tire after the bar is visible on any place in the tread.

Tire Rotation

Most car makers recommend rotating tires at regular intervals of from 5000 to 10,000 miles (8000 to 16,000 km). Tires should be rotated so they will not remain in the same position throughout their lifetime.

Tire rotation equalizes wear and minimizes tire noise. Tires should be rotated in a definite pattern, and the same pattern should be followed each time they are rotated. All five tires should be rotated when possible. However, when the spare tire is in poor condition or when a "compact" or "stowaway" spare tire is used, only the four tires on the axles can be rotated.

Bias ply and bias belted tires should be rotated in a pattern similar to that shown in Figure 16.23.

Some manufacturers recommend that radial tires be rotated so they remain on one side of a car. They claim that the longest possible tread life for radial tires is obtained when the tires always revolve in the same direction. Figure 16.24 shows that preferred pattern for rotating radial tires.

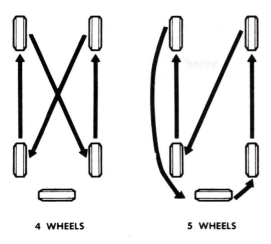

Figure 16.23 Bias ply and bias belted rotation. Typical tire rotation patterns for bias ply and bias belted tires (courtesy of Chevrolet Motor Division, General Motors Corporation).

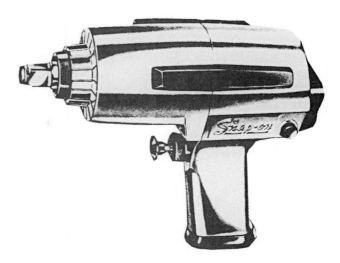

Figure 16.25 Typical impact wrench. The impact wrench uses high-pressure compressed air to operate and is very powerful and fast (courtesy of Snap-on Tools Corporation).

Removing Wheels. To rotate tires, you must remove the wheels from the car. Most shops use impact wrenches similar to the one shown in Figure 16.25 to remove the lug nuts that hold the wheels in place. Impact wrenches are like drill motors, but instead of spinning a drill bit they spin a socket wrench with a hammering action. Impact wrenches are great time savers, but they are not always available. In many instances you will have to use a muscle-powered *lug wrench*. A lug wrench is shown in Figure 16.26.

Have you ever tried to loosen a lug nut when the wheel is off the ground? You turn the wrench and the wheel turns. You can apply the parking

There are several times when it is ideal to have a vehicle aligned. One is when all four tires have been replaced. Look at the old tire wear patterns to determine what needs to be done to improve the tire wear. The other time is when the tires are to be rotated for the first time. Check the tire wear patterns on each tire and make a note of any abnormal patterns and on what axle they occurred. This is very good information to relay to the alignment specialist. Remember, alignment is not just for the front wheels. All four wheels should be checked and aligned. This is especially true if a tire is experiencing rapid wear at one position. Have the alignment checked and set if any front or rear suspension parts have just been replaced.

RADIAL TIRES

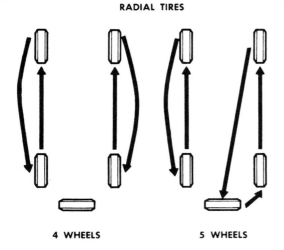

Figure 16.24 Typical tire rotation patterns recommended for radial tires (courtesy of Chevrolet Motor Division, General Motors Corporation).

Figure 16.26 A typical lug wrench. This is a four-way wrench with a different lug size on each end (courtesy of Snap-on Tools Corporation).

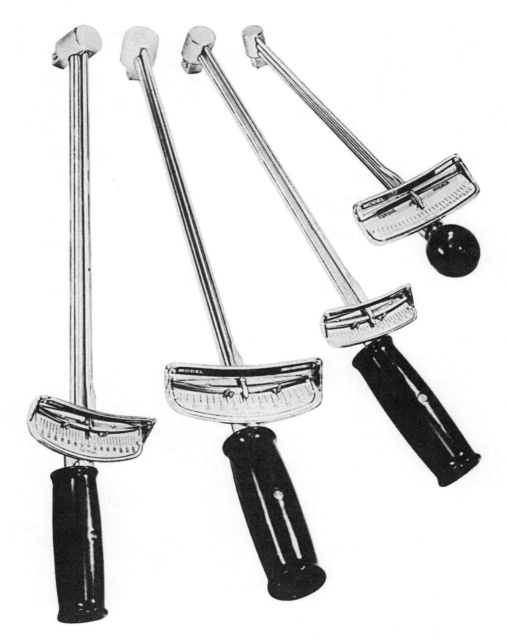

Figure 16.27   Four different beam-type torque wrenches (courtesy of AMMCO Tools, Inc.).

brakes, but on most cars they hold only the rear wheels. Maybe you can get a friend to sit in the car and press down on the brake pedal until you can loosen the nuts. But what if you are working alone?

If you are going to remove the wheels from a car, remove the wheel covers and loosen the lug nuts *before* you raise the car off the floor. This procedure is easy, and it requires far less energy than trying to loosen the lug nuts after the car is off the floor. Once the car is up in the air, you can spin the loosened nuts off with little effort.

Installing Wheels.   As a technician, you will find that many problems are caused by improper wheel installation. For example, if the lug nuts are left too loose, the wheel and the wheel studs may be damaged, and the wheel may come off. If the lug nuts are tightened too much, the wheel and the hub may be distorted. This distortion leads to vibrations in the steering system. In the brake system it can cause problems that become evident through pulsation of the brake pedal.

Lug nuts, then, should be tightened just enough to keep them from loosening, but not so much that

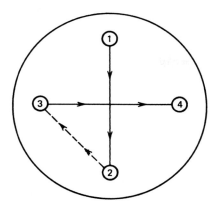

Figure 16.28 Four-lug tightening sequence. The "cross" pattern, recommended as the sequence for tightening lug nuts on a four-hole wheel.

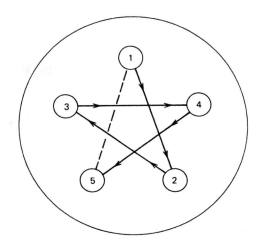

Figure 16.29 "Star" pattern tightening sequence. The "star" pattern, recommended as the sequence for tightening lug nuts on a five-hole wheel.

they will distort the wheel or hub. For that reason, lug nuts should be tightened to a torque specification. *Torque* can be defined as a turning or twisting effort. When you turn a wrench, you are applying torque to a bolt or nut. By measuring that torque, you can tell how much you are tightening it.

To measure torque, use a *torque wrench* whose handle indicates how much torque, or twisting effort, is being applied to a nut or bolt. There are many types of torque wrenches. Some have a wand, or pointer, that moves across a scale as you pull on the wrench. Some torque wrenches of that type are shown in Figure 16.27. Other torque wrenches indicate torque by means of a pointer on a dial, and some give off a loud click when a preset torque is reached.

Torque is measured in foot pounds (ft · lb) or in Newton-meters (N · m). Suppose you had a wrench that was 12 in. (30 cm) long, and you applied a force of 20 pounds (9 kg) to the handle. Then, the nut or bolt you were tightening would be tightened to 20 ft · lb (270 cm · kg) (27 N · m) of torque. There are hundreds of nuts and bolts on a car that must be tightened to a specified torque. This is one reason that the manufacturers' service manuals are so important to you. They contain the torque specifications you need to turn out a quality job.

Tightening the lug nuts to the right amount of torque is only half the job. The nuts must also be tightened in a sequence. The proper sequence for four-hole and five-hole wheels is shown by numerals and arrows in Figures 16.28 and 16.29. The proper sequence for four-hole wheels is represented by a "cross" pattern. For five-hole wheels it is represented by a "star" pattern.

If you used an impact wrench to remove the lug nuts, you can use it for installing them. Just

---

Job 16C

ROTATE TIRES

SATISFACTORY PERFORMANCE
A satisfactory performance on this job requires that you do the following:

1. Rotate the tires on the car assigned.
2. Following the steps in the "Performance Outline" and the recommendations and specifications of the manufacturer, complete the job within 60 minutes.
3. Fill in the blanks under "Information."

PERFORMANCE OUTLINE

1. Determine the rotation pattern to be used.
2. Rotate the tires to the new positions.
3. Tighten the lug nuts to the torque specification.
4. Check and adjust the tire pressures.

INFORMATION

Vehicle identification _____
Specified tire pressures: Front _____   Rear _____
Lug nut torque specification _____
Reference used _____   Page(s) _____
Indicate rotation pattern used.

← Front

ROTATING TIRES

The steps that follow outline a typical procedure for rotating tires:

1. Check all five tires and determine the rotation pattern to be used.
2. Remove the spare tire if it is to be used.
3. Remove the wheel covers and loosen the lug nuts.
4. Raise and support the car.
5. Remove the wheels and install them in their new locations.
6. Install the lug nuts.

   Note: Be sure you install the nuts with the tapered, or cone-shaped, end toward the wheel as shown in Figure 16.30.

7. Lower the car to the floor.
8. Tighten the lug nuts to the torque specification in the correct sequence.
9. Install the wheel covers.
10. Install the spare.
11. Check and adjust the tire pressures.

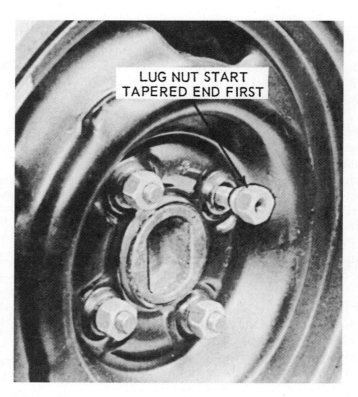

Figure 16.30 Lug nut installation. Lug nuts should be installed so that the tapered, or cone-shaped, end of the nut is toward the wheel (courtesy of Ford Motor Company, Dearborn, MI).

remember that it should be used only to run the nuts up snug. After you lower the car to the floor, use a torque wrench to tighten the nuts to specifications.

Tire Inspection

Tires should be inspected during each rotation and at regular intervals between rotations. Replace any tire that has a tread depth of less than 1/16 in. (1.6 mm). To aid you in determining when a tire requires replacement, tread wear indicators are molded into the tire when it is built. When the tread wears to a depth of less than 1/16 in. (1.6 mm), bands approximately 1/2 in. (13 mm) wide appear, as shown in Figure 16.31. When those indicators are visible in two or more adjacent tread grooves, the tire should be replaced.

Figure 16.31 A tread wear indicator strip (courtesy of Training Enterprises Company).

Tread wear should be evenly distributed across the entire tread. Any uneven wear should be considered abnormal, and its cause should be determined and corrected. A listing of the most commonly found abnormal wear patterns, their causes, and corrections is provided in Figure 16.32. Study those wear patterns so you will recognize them when you find them during a tire inspection.

> The most accurate way to determine if tires or the suspension needs service is to inspect the tire wear patterns. A tire cannot have a normal wear pattern if the suspension is worn out, the tire pressure is wrong, or the tire needs to be balanced.

LESSON 16–5 Tire Service

Tire service involves repairing punctures, balancing tires, rotating tires, and replacing tires. Removing and installing tires will be easier and safer if you understand certain facts about the design of wheels.

Job 16D

IDENTIFY THE CAUSES OF ABNORMAL TIRE WEAR

SATISFACTORY PERFORMANCE
A satisfactory performance on this job requires that you do the following:

1. Determine the cause of the abnormal wear patterns shown in the illustration below.
2. Place the letter of each wear pattern in front of its most probable cause in the list of causes provided.
3. Complete the job within 15 minutes.

PERFORMANCE SITUATION

____ Unbalanced wheel and tire
____ Underinflation
____ Incorrect caster
____ Worn suspension parts
____ Incorrect toe-in
____ Incorrect camber
____ Overinflation
____ Excessive speed

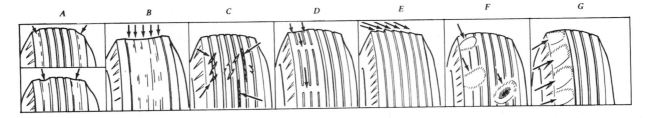

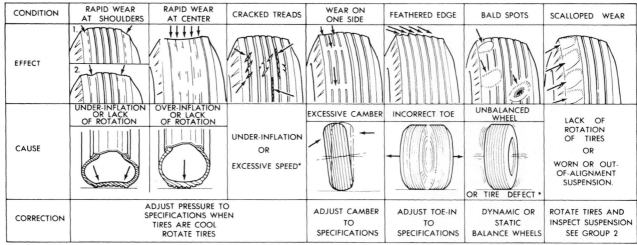

CONDITION	RAPID WEAR AT SHOULDERS	RAPID WEAR AT CENTER	CRACKED TREADS	WEAR ON ONE SIDE	FEATHERED EDGE	BALD SPOTS	SCALLOPED WEAR
EFFECT	1. 2.						
CAUSE	UNDER-INFLATION OR LACK OF ROTATION	OVER-INFLATION OR LACK OF ROTATION	UNDER-INFLATION OR EXCESSIVE SPEED*	EXCESSIVE CAMBER	INCORRECT TOE	UNBALANCED WHEEL OR TIRE DEFECT *	LACK OF ROTATION OF TIRES OR WORN OR OUT-OF-ALIGNMENT SUSPENSION.
CORRECTION	ADJUST PRESSURE TO SPECIFICATIONS WHEN TIRES ARE COOL ROTATE TIRES			ADJUST CAMBER TO SPECIFICATIONS	ADJUST TOE-IN TO SPECIFICATIONS	DYNAMIC OR STATIC BALANCE WHEELS	ROTATE TIRES AND INSPECT SUSPENSION SEE GROUP 2

*HAVE TIRE INSPECTED FOR FURTHER USE.

Figure 16.32 Typical tire wear patterns (courtesy of Chrysler Corporation).

Wheel Design

Most cars are fitted with steel wheels as standard equipment. A typical steel wheel is shown in Figure 16.33. Of two piece construction, the *spider,* or cen-ter section, of the wheel is electrically welded to the *rim.* The rim, shown in Figure 16.34, is made with a *dropped center.* This lowered area, or well, is necessary for tire installation and removal. One part of the tire bead can be held in the dropped center so the other part can be slipped over the rim flange. Most wheels incorporate small raised sections, or *safety ridges,* on the inner portion of the rim (see Figure 16.34). When the tire is inflated, the beads of the tire are forced over these ridges. The safety ridges serve two purposes: (1) They aid in preventing the beads from slipping inward during hard cornering. (2) They help hold the tire in position on the wheel in case of a tire failure.

Most manufacturers advise against any attempt to repair a damaged wheel. They suggest that wheels be replaced when any of the following conditions are found:

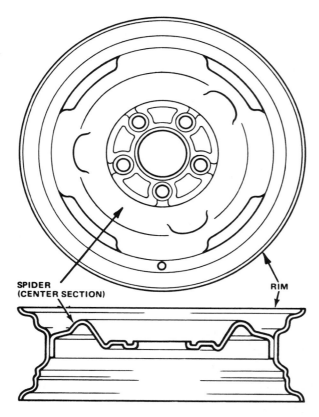

SPIDER (CENTER SECTION)

RIM

Figure 16.33 Typical construction of a standard steel wheel (courtesy of American Motors).

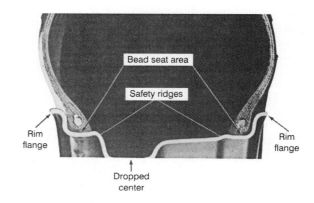

Bead seat area

Safety ridges

Rim flange

Rim flange

Dropped center

Figure 16.34 Wheel rim nomenclature (courtesy of Chrysler Corporation).

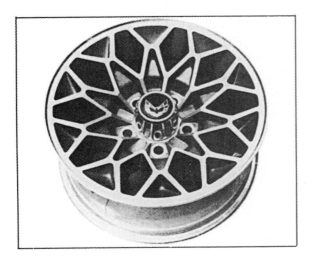

Figure 16.35 Cast aluminum alloy wheel (courtesy of Pontiac Motor Division, General Motors Corporation).

1. The wheel is bent or dented.
2. The wheel has excessive *runout* or "wobble."
3. Air is leaking through the welds.
4. The bolt holes are enlarged or elongated.
5. The wheel is heavily rusted.

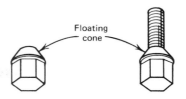

Figure 16.36 Special lug nuts and bolts are used with alloy wheels.

Some cars are fitted with wheels made of cast aluminum alloy as shown in Figure 16.35. As protection against corrosion, many of those alloy wheels are coated with clear lacquer. When working with alloy wheels, be careful not to scratch or chip that protective coating. Because the alloy is relatively soft, special lug nuts and lug bolts are usually used with alloy wheels. Some of those nuts and bolts have a steel sleeve or tube that fits into the hole in the wheel and protects it. Others, similar to the ones shown in Figure 16.36, have a cone-shaped end that is free to turn. Those special nuts and bolts prevent gouging and tearing the holes in the wheels as the nuts and bolts are tightened.

DISMOUNTING AND MOUNTING TIRES

In most shops, a tire machine similar to the one shown in Figure 16.37 is used to dismount and mount tires. Regardless of the type of machine that you use, the job will be much easier and you will minimize your chances of injury if you follow these basic precautions:

1. Remove the valve from the valve stem. (This will ensure that all the pressure is released from the tire.)
2. Mount the wheel and tire assembly on the machine so that the dropped center of the rim is facing up as shown in Figure 16.38. (This will allow the beads of the tire to slip easily over the rim flange.)
3. After breaking both beads loose from the rim, thoroughly lubricate the upper bead with rubber lubricant. (This decreases the friction between the bead and the rim flange. It also minimizes the possibility of bead damage.)
4. After removing the tire from the wheel, inspect the bead seat area of the rim. Use a wire brush, sandpaper, or coarse steel wool to clean the bead seat of all old lubricant, rubber deposits, and rust.
5. Before mounting the replacement tire, apply a liberal amount of rubber lubricant to both beads.
6. Do not stand or lean over the tire when inflating it. (There have been instances where bead wires have broken when the bead was forced over the safety ridge. This can cause you serious injury.)
7. Never exceed 40 psi (275 kPa) pressure when inflating a tire. (If a bead will not seat, deflate the tire, relubricate the beads, and reinflate the tire.)

The procedure you follow in dismounting and mounting tires is largely determined by the machine you have available. Study the instruction manual furnished with the tire machine before you attempt to dismount and mount tires. The procedure that follows can be considered typical.

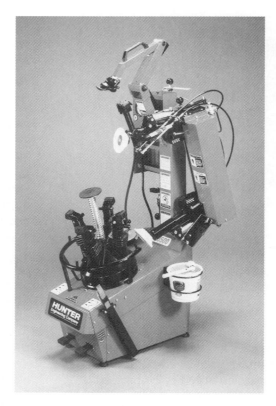

Figure 16.37   Tire changing machine. This type of machine is used to remove and replace tires on the rim (courtesy of Hunter Engineering Company).

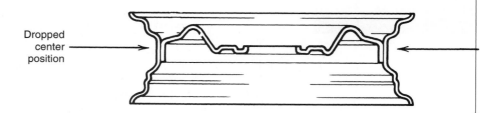

Dropped
center
position

Figure 16.38   Wheel position on a tire machine. When mounting a wheel and tire assembly on a tire machine, the dropped center of the wheel should be toward the top (courtesy of American Motors).

PUNCTURE REPAIRS

Tires punctured in the tread area shown in Figure 16.39 can be repaired if the puncture does not exceed 1/4 in. (6.4 mm) in diameter. Never attempt to repair a tire that has any of the following defects:

1. A sidewall puncture
2. Cuts or cracks extending into the tire fabric
3. Tread wear indicators showing, or tread depth of less than 1/16 in. (1.6 mm)
4. Loose cords
5. Evidence of ply separation
6. Tread separation
7. Broken or otherwise damaged bead wires

repairable area

Figure 16.39 Repairable area of tire. The repairable area of a tire (courtesy of the Rubber Manufacturers Association).

When the sidewalls of a tire are punctured, it is not repairable. Even if a patch is placed in the tire it will not be safe to run it. Tires in this condition should be replaced. Vandals sometimes slash tires. Since the tire is not repairable this is a vicious crime and causes much wasted time and money.

A permanent repair requires that you both plug the hole and patch the puncture. Both these operations should be done from the inside of the tire (see Figure 16.40). There are several methods of repair including chemical vulcanizing patching, hot vulcanizing patching, and the use of head-type plugs.

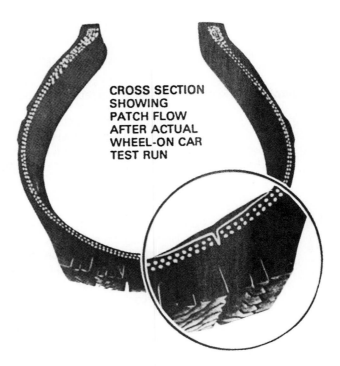

CROSS SECTION SHOWING PATCH FLOW AFTER ACTUAL WHEEL-ON CAR TEST RUN

Figure 16.40 Internal tire patch in place. A cross section of a punctured tire that has been repaired internally. Notice that the patch has flowed into the hole (courtesy of H. B. Egan Manufacturing Co., Muskogee, OK).

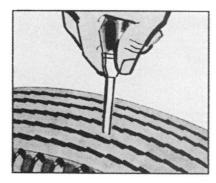

Figure 16.41   Using a tire probe. Probing a puncture to determine the extent of the damage and the direction of the hole (courtesy of the Rubber Manufacturers Association).

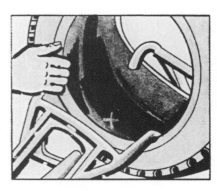

Figure 16.42   Internal inspection of a tire. An internal inspection of a tire is made easier by the use of a bead spreader (courtesy of the Rubber Manufacturers Association).

Figure 16.43   Marking area to be cleaned. With the patch centered over the hole, the area to be cleaned should be marked with chalk (courtesy of the Rubber Manufacturers Association).

Figure 16.44   The puncture and the surrounding area should be thoroughly cleaned (courtesy of the Rubber Manufacturers Association).

Preparation   Regardless of the type of repair you perform, take the following preparatory steps:

1. Locate and mark the puncture. Remove the puncturing object.
2. Dismount the tire from the wheel.
3. Using a blunt awl or similar tool, probe the puncture as shown in Figure 16.41 to determine the size and direction of the hole, and to clean the hole of any foreign material.
4. Spread the beads and inspect the inside of the tire for damage. Mark the puncture (see Figure 16.42).
5. Center the chosen patch over the hole as shown in Figure 16.43 and outline an area larger than the patch.
6. Clean the marked area with an appropriate chemical cleaner (see Figure 16.44).
7. Buff or otherwise roughen the area thoroughly to obtain a velvetlike surface. Although abrasive paper or cloth can be used, a power tire buffer, shown in Figure 16.45, is recommended for this operation.
8. Clean the dust from the inside of the tire.

Chemical Vulcanizing Repairs   The following steps outline a procedure for repairing a puncture with a chemical vulcanizing patch or "cold patch."

1. Coat the cleaned area with a thin, even coating of the appropriate cement as shown in Figure 16.46.

Figure 16.45 Buffing the area surrounding a puncture (courtesy of the Rubber Manufacturers Association).

Figure 16.46 Applying cement to the punctured area (courtesy of the Rubber Manufacturers Association).

Figure 16.47 Securing a patch with a stitching tool (courtesy of the Rubber Manufacturers Association).

Figure 16.48 A patch held in position by the pad of a vulcanizing clamp (courtesy of the Rubber Manufacturers Association).

Note: The cement must be allowed to dry thoroughly before the patch is applied.

2. Remove the protective backing from the patch and center it over the puncture, pressing it down firmly.
3. Secure the patch by "stitching" it with a stitching tool as shown in Figure 16.47, working from the center of the patch to the outer edges.

Hot Vulcanizing Repairs The following steps outline a basic procedure for repairing a puncture with a hot vulcanizing patch. The specific steps will be determined by the equipment you have available:

1. Coat the cleaned area with a thin, even coating of the appropriate cement (refer to Figure 16.46).

   Note: The cement must be allowed to dry thoroughly before the patch is applied.

2. Remove the protective backing from the patch and center it over the puncture, pressing it down firmly.
3. Clamp the patch firmly in place and vulcanize the repair by following the instructions furnished with the vulcanizing patches and equipment you have available (see Figure 16.48).

Head-Type Plug Repairs The steps that follow outline a procedure for repairing a puncture by using a head-type plug similar to the one shown in Figure 16.49.

1. Coat the cleaned area with a thin, even coating of the appropriate cement (refer to Figure 16.46).

   Note: The cement must be allowed to dry thoroughly before the plug is installed.

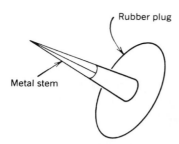

Figure 16.49 A head-type plug for repairing punctures. The metal stem enables you to insert the plug through the hole in the tire.

Figure 16.50 Pulling a head-type plug through a puncture (courtesy of the Rubber Manufacturers Association).

2. Remove the protective backing from the plug.
3. Push the metal stem of the plug through the puncture and, using a pair of pliers, pull the plug through the hole as shown in Figure 16.50. Discard the metal stem and trim the plug flush with the tire tread.
4. Secure the patch by "stitching" it with a stitching tool, working from the center of the patch to the outer edges (refer to Figure 16.47).

Job 16E

INTERNALLY REPAIR A PUNCTURED TUBELESS TIRE

SATISFACTORY PERFORMANCE
A satisfactory performance on this job requires that you do the following:

1. Repair a punctured tubeless tire by plugging and patching the puncture from the inside of the tire.
2. Following the steps in the "Performance Outline" and the instructions furnished by the maker of the patch used, complete the job within 30 minutes.
3. Fill in the blanks under "Information."

PERFORMANCE OUTLINE

1. Dismount the tire.
2. Prepare the puncture and its surrounding area for the repair.
3. Coat the prepared area with cement.
4. Install and secure the patch.
5. Mount the tire.
6. Inflate the tire and test the repair.

INFORMATION

Tire size and type _____
Type of patch used _____
Tire inflation pressure _____
Method used to test repair _____
Was the repair successful? Yes _____ No _____

RIVET-TYPE PLUG REPAIRS

Several tools are available that will allow you to seal a puncture without removing the tire from the wheel. One such tool is shown in Figure 16.51. This tool inserts a rivetlike rubber plug into a puncture from the outside of the tire. The following procedure outlines the steps to take when using a tool of this type:

1. Locate the puncture in the tire and remove the puncturing object if it is still present.
2. Dip the probing tool into vulcanizing cement.
3. Carefully push the prober into the puncture, feeling for the direction of the hole (see Figure 16.52).

   Note: Do not force the prober because you may cause another puncture.

4. Remove the prober. Repeat steps 2 and 3 several times so the hole will be well coated with cement. Leave the prober in the hole.
5. Remove the nozzle from the gun as shown in Figure 16.53.
6. Insert the stem of a lubricated plug into the gun as shown in Figure 16.54.

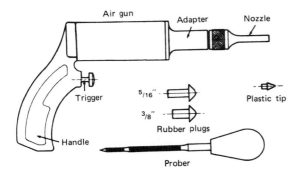

Figure 16.51   Tubeless tire air patch gun. A tubeless tire repair kit containing an air gun that installs rivetlike rubber plugs in punctures. Note the plugs, plastic tips, and the prober used with the gun (courtesy of Tyler Manufacturing Co., Inc., Hawthorne, CA).

Figure 16.52   Using a probe to locate the direction of the hole and to coat the hole with vulcanizing cement (courtesy of Tyler Manufacturing Co., Inc., Hawthorne, CA).

Figure 16.53   Removing the nozzle of the air gun to insert a plug (courtesy of Tyler Manufacturing Co., Inc., Hawthorne, CA).

Figure 16.54   Inserting the tire patch plug into the air gun (courtesy of Tyler Manufacturing Co., Inc., Hawthorne, CA).

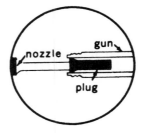

Figure 16.55   Using the reversed nozzle as a plunger to push the plug back into the gun (courtesy of Tyler Manufacturing Co., Inc., Hawthorne, CA).

Figure 16.56 Plastic tip installed. Installing a plastic tip on the nozzle of the air gun to make it easier to insert the nozzle into the tire (courtesy of Tyler Manufacturing Co., Inc., Hawthorne, CA).

Figure 16.57 Inserting and using plug gun. Inserting the nozzle of the gun into the puncture (courtesy of Tyler Manufacturing Co., Inc., Hawthorne, CA).

Note: The plugs are prelubricated, but if the lubricant has dried or has been removed, wet the plugs with the lubricant supplied with the repair kit.

7. Reverse the nozzle and, using it as a plunger as shown in Figure 16.55, push the head of the plug back into the gun.

Note: The flexible head of the plug will fold back, allowing the plug to enter the gun easily.

8. Install the nozzle on the gun.
9. Install a plastic tip on the nozzle of the gun (see Figure 16.56).
10. Remove the prober from the tire and insert the nozzle of the gun, following the direction of the puncture as determined with the prober (see Figure 16.57).
11. Press the trigger of the gun to fire the plug. Release the trigger.

Note: The trigger must be released before attempting to withdraw the gun. Failure to do so may stretch the stem of the plug and allow the repair to leak.

12. Withdraw the gun from the tire.
13. Cut off the protruding end of the plug to within 1/8 in. (3 mm) of the tread surface.
14. Inflate the tire to the pressure recommended by the manufacturer.
15. Test the repair for leakage.

String Plug Method   Another method of tire puncture repair is the string method. A string covered with sealant is inserted into the puncture from the outside and twisted so a knot is formed on the inside. The tool is then removed leaving the string in place. The string is coated and the edges of the tire puncture place enough pressure on the string to keep the puncture hole sealed. There are different strings for steel belted radial tires to keep the edges of the hole from cutting the string.

LESSON 16-6   Wheel and Tire Imbalance

When a car is in motion, its tires are subjected to many forces. Those forces vary with the weight the tire is carrying and with the speed at which the tire is rotating. These forces may cause a wheel and tire assembly to bounce up and down or to wobble from side to side. In most cases, these problems are caused by *imbalance,* the condition caused when the weight of the wheel and tire assembly is unevenly distributed. Most tires have some imbalance because of the variety of materials and the many operations used in their manufacture.

Static Balance

Static balance means "balance at rest." In a wheel and tire assembly it is the equal distribution of weight around the axis of rotation. A wheel and tire assembly that is in static balance has no tendency to rotate on its spindle, or axle, by itself. You will rarely find a wheel and tire assembly that is perfectly balanced. In most cases, the fault is in the tire. In the manufacture of a tire, the fabric and the rubber are sometimes unevenly distributed. This results in heavy spots and light spots in the tire. To bring the wheel and tire assembly into balance, attach weights to the wheel rim opposite any heavy spot in the tire. Typical wheel weights, shown in

Figure 16.58 Typical wheel weights. The steel clip holds the weight to the rim (courtesy of Ford Motor Company, Dearborn, MI).

Figure 16.58, are made of lead alloy. They are attached to the rim by a steel clip.

A wheel and tire assembly that is not in static balance causes *wheel tramp*. Wheel tramp is a vertical movement of the spindle as shown in Figure 16.59. Wheel tramp occurs when the heavy part of a tire moves up and down while the tire is rotating. This

motion causes a vibration as shown in Figure 16.60. This vibration annoys the driver and causes premature wear of the tire and of steering and suspension parts.

Static balance is easily obtained through the use of a *bubble balancer*. A bubble balancer is shown in

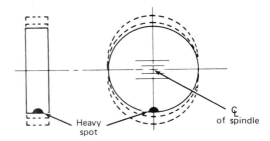

Figure 16.59 Wheel tramp. The heavy spot in the tire causes the spindle to move up and down as the wheel spins (courtesy of Pontiac Motor Division, General Motors Corporation).

Job 16F

EXTERNALLY REPAIR A PUNCTURED TUBELESS TIRE

SATISFACTORY PERFORMANCE

A satisfactory performance on this job requires that you do the following:

1. Repair a punctured tubeless tire by using a puncture repair gun to install a rubber plug.
2. Following the steps in the "Performance Outline" and the instructions furnished by the maker of the tool, complete the job within 15 minutes.
3. Fill in the blanks under "Information."

PERFORMANCE OUTLINE

1. Use a probing tool to locate the direction of the hole and coat the hole with cement.
2. Load the gun.
3. Fire the plug into the hole.
4. Cut off the excess plug.
5. Inflate the tire and test the repair.

INFORMATION

Tire size and type _____
Make of repair gun used _____
Size of rubber plug used _____
Tire inflation pressure _____
Method used to test repair _____
Was the repair successful?   Yes _____   No _____

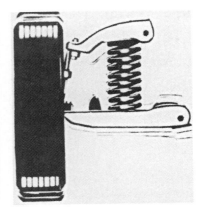

Figure 16.60 Wheel tramp vibration. The wheel will move up and down rapidly if there is a wheel tramp problem (courtesy of Ford Motor Company, Dearborn, MI).

Figure 16.61 Bubble balance. This type of wheel balancer uses a bubble system to tell when the tire is in balance (courtesy of AMMCO Tools, Inc.).

Figure 16.61. The wheel and tire assembly is placed horizontally on the balancer. Weights are placed on the wheel rim until the bubble level is centered. Figure 16.62 shows a typical bubble level.

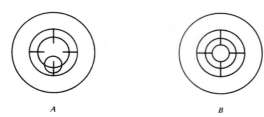

A   *B*

Figure 16.62 Bubble level reading. A bubble level typical of those used in static wheel balancers. (a) Shows the bubble off center, indicating an imbalance condition. (b) Shows the bubble centered, indicating perfect static balance.

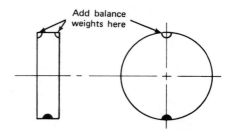

Figure 16.63 Static balance correction. Note that the amount of weight required to correct the imbalance is "split" and placed on both sides of the wheel (courtesy of Pontiac Motor Division, General Motors Corporation).

Although a bubble balancer can show you the location of the heavy portion of the tire, you have no way of knowing the exact location of the heavy spot. So you must assume it is directly under the tread. For this reason, the total amount of weight needed must be "split." Half the weight must be attached to the outside of the wheel, and half attached to the inside, as shown in Figure 16.63.

Dynamic Balance

Dynamic balance means "balance in motion." It requires that the wheel and tire assembly be in

Job 16G

STATIC BALANCE A WHEEL AND TIRE ASSEMBLY ON A BUBBLE BALANCER

SATISFACTORY PERFORMANCE
A satisfactory performance on this job requires that you do the following:

1. Static balance the wheel and tire assembly provided so the bubble is centered within the inner ring of the indicator.
2. Following the steps in the "Performance Outline" and the instructions of the balancer manufacturer, complete the job within 15 minutes.
3. Fill in the blanks under "Information."

PERFORMANCE OUTLINE

1. Clean the wheel and tire.
2. Zero the balancer.
3. Position the wheel and tire assembly.
4. Install the weights required.
5. Check that the proper balance was obtained.

INFORMATION

Total weight required _____
Amount attached to the outside of the wheel _____
Amount attached to the inside of the wheel _____

| **STATIC BALANCING** | The procedure that follows is typical for static balancing a wheel and tire assembly with a bubble balancer. Follow the procedure specified by the maker of the balancer you have available for zeroing the instrument and for positioning the weights. |

1. Remove all stones and dirt from between the tread ribs.
2. Remove all mud and dirt deposits from both sides of the wheel.
3. Zero the balancer as specified by the manufacturer.
4. Carefully place the wheel and tire assembly on the balancer so the centering cone enters the center hole in the wheel.
5. If the balancer has a locking lever, release the lock so the bubble is free to move.
6. Allow the bubble to come to rest. If the bubble is centered, the wheel and tire assembly is in static balance. If the bubble is not centered, remove the wheel and tire from the balancer and continue with step 7.
7. Remove any existing weights from the wheel.
8. Carefully place the wheel and tire assembly on the balancer so the centering cone enters the center hole in the wheel.
9. Release the lock (if necessary) and allow the bubble to come to rest.
10. Carefully place a weight on the rim in line with the bubble.
11. Continue to add weights until the bubble is centered.

    Note: You may have to shift the weights to either side to perfectly center the bubble.

12. With chalk, mark the position of the weight (the light spot) on the tire.
13. Determine the total amount of weight added to achieve balance.
14. Remove the wheel and tire assembly from the balancer.
15. Divide in half the amount of weight needed.

    Note: This determines the amount of weight you must install on each side of the wheel. For example, if 4 ounces of weight are required to balance the assembly, you will need two 2-ounce weights.

16. Install one weight on the outside wheel rim in line with the chalk mark on the tire.
17. Install the remaining weight on the inside rim in line with the outside weight (refer to Figure 16.63).

    Note: Some balancer manufacturers recommend the use of four weights spread out equally from the light spot. For the proper method, check the instruction manual for the balancer you are using.

18. Place the wheel and tire assembly back on the balancer and check that static balance has been obtained.

static balance. It also requires that the weight of the wheel and tire assembly be evenly distributed on both sides of the tire centerline. Figure 16.64 illustrates the condition that exists when a wheel and tire assembly is in static balance. The weight of the assembly is distributed evenly around the axis of rotation. Figure 16.65 illustrates the condition that exists when a wheel and tire assembly is in dynamic balance. The weight on both sides of the tire centerline must also be considered.

When you static balance a wheel and tire assembly on a bubble balancer, you must assume that the heavy spot of the tire is under the center of the tread. But in many cases it is under one of the sidewalls. A wheel and tire assembly may be in static balance but out of dynamic balance.

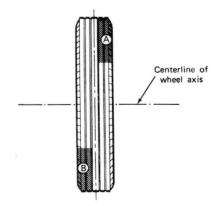

Figure 16.64 Tire in static balance. The weight on both sides of the axis centerline (positions *A* and *B*) is equal (courtesy of Ford Motor Company, Dearborn, MI).

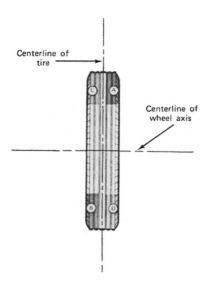

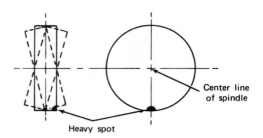

Figure 16.66 Shimmy. The heavy spot in the tire causes the wheel to shake or "wobble" as the wheel spins (courtesy of Pontiac Motor Division, General Motors Corporation).

A wheel and tire assembly that is not in dynamic balance will cause *shimmy*, a wobbling movement of the spindle as shown in Figure 16.66. This movement is caused by *centrifugal force*, a tendency of a rotating body to move away from its axis of rotation. When a wheel and tire assembly is rotating, the heavy parts of the tire tend to move outward and toward the centerline of tire. This movement is shown in Figure 16.67. Above certain car speeds,

Figure 16.65 Tire in dynamic balance. The total weight of positions *A* and *C* equals the total weight of positions *B* and *D*. Also, the weight at position *A* equals the weight at position *C*, and the weight at position *B* equals the weight at position *D* (courtesy of Ford Motor Company, Dearborn, MI).

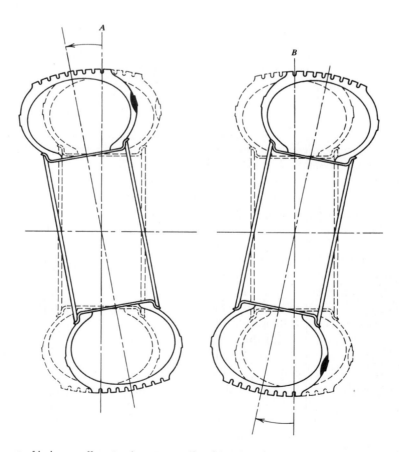

Figure 16.67 Dynamic out-of-balance effect. In view *A*, centrifugal force causes the heavy spot to move outward from the axis of rotation and toward the tire centerline. In this case the heavy spot tips to the left. View *B* shows the same tire after it has rotated 180°. Centrifugal force now causes the heavy spot to tip to the right. Centrifugal force increases with the speed of rotation. At high speeds dynamic imbalance causes severe vibration.

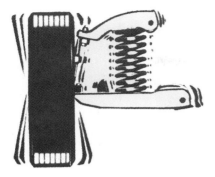

Figure 16.68 A vibration caused by shimmy (courtesy of Ford Motor Company, Dearborn, MI).

usually about 45 mph (72 km/h), this movement can cause a vibration, or shimmy, as shown in Figure 16.68. This vibration can cause violent shaking of the steering wheel and rapid wearing of steering and suspension parts.

As in the correction of static imbalance, dynamic imbalance is also corrected with weights. However, the amount of weight used and the position of the weights must be determined while the wheel and tire assembly is spinning. There are many types of dynamic balancers in use. Some require that you

Figure 16.69 Tire balancer. A tire is placed on this machine to check static and dynamic balance (while the tire is in motion). Weights are applied to the rim to correct any out-of-balance condition (courtesy of Hunter Engineering Company).

remove the wheel and tire assembly from the car. Others allow you to balance the assembly while it is on the car (see Figure 16.69).

> The dynamic balance method is preferred over the static method. Static balanced tires may still be out of dynamic balance and cause vibration at road speeds. The off-the-car dynamic balance method is preferred over the on-the-car static balance methods. After any method is used, road test the vehicle to see if there is any vibration. Remember, many things can cause a vibration other than tire balance. Look for improperly tightened wheel bearings, a bent wheel rim, and out-of-balance drums or rotors, to name a few possibilities.

LESSON 16–7 Wheel and Tire Alignment

As a vehicle moves along the highway, tire contact with the road causes tire wear. The ideal situation is to have the tire contact the road so wear is kept to a minimum. Since roads are not perfectly smooth, straight, and level, vehicle alignment has to be an average of road and driving conditions. Even load changes affect tire wear. For this reason, tires must be monitored and the alignment adjusted when tire wear is excessive. Tire wear will determine if you have reached the best alignment settings for the way the vehicle is being loaded and driven. We discuss next the wheel alignment angles that are set on a vehicle during an alignment job.

Wheel Alignment Angles

Camber. *Camber* is the amount of tire tilt away from or into the vehicle from a straight up (vertical) position (see Figure 16.70). A tire that tilts away from the car at the top has positive camber, and one that leans toward the vehicle at the top has negative camber. Since most roads have a slight crown, camber is usually set several degrees positive on both sides. Incorrect camber causes tire wear if not set right. Too much negative camber causes the inside edge of the tire to wear. Too much positive camber causes the outside edges of the tire to wear. Uneven camber causes the vehicle to steer toward the side with the most positive camber.

Caster. *Caster* is the fore and aft tilt of the ball joint axis at the tip from a vertical position (see Figure 16.71). With positive caster, the top leans toward the rear of the vehicle. Negative caster is

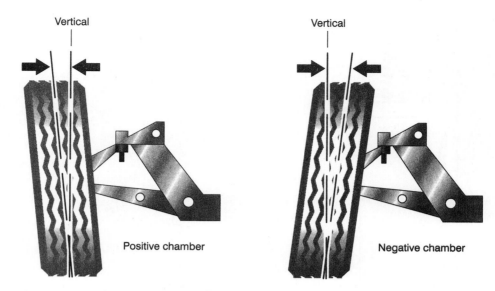

Figure 16.70   Camber. Positive camber is when the top of the tire tilts away from the vehicle. Negative camber is when the tire tilts in toward the vehicle (courtesy of Training Enterprises Company).

the reverse, when the top leans toward the front of the vehicle. Caster is a directional control setting. Negative caster makes steering the vehicle easier. Vehicles without power steering are often set with negative caster. Positive caster makes the wheels harder to turn. They tend to remain in a straight-ahead position. With power steering, a vehicle can have more positive caster, because the power steering will turn the wheels. Positive caster helps return the steering wheel to a straight-ahead position.

Too much caster will make the wheels wobble from side to side. This will cause cupping wear to appear on the tire tread. A vehicle with uneven caster will drift toward the side with the most negative caster. If caster is kept within the manufacturer's specifications, it does not cause tire wear. Positive caster on one wheel and negative on the other can cause a violent braking action to the side. Excessive positive caster can cause hard steering on a manual steering vehicle and wander or low-speed shimmy on a power steering vehicle.

Toe.   The distance between the front inside edge of the tires and the rear inside edge of the tires is called *toe* (see Figure 16.72). A toe-in condition exists when the front distance between the tires is smaller than the rear. The vehicle wheels tend to move out at the front when the vehicle is moving down the road. By setting a small amount of toe-in during alignment, the tires run straight when the vehicle is in motion. As steering parts wear, the wheels move toward a toe-out condition. Parts wear can be compensated for by alignment to some degree, but excessive wear means the parts should be replaced for safety. Wear should never mean that the toe be set out of the recommended specifications. Alignment technicians should always make sure that worn parts are replaced before an alignment job.

Excessive toe-in or toe-out causes a saw-toothed wear pattern on the tire tread.

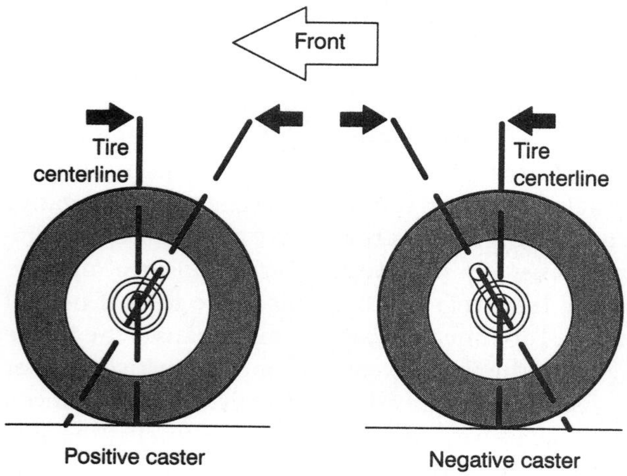

Figure 16.71   Caster. The fore-and-aft tilt of the ball joint axis at the top from a vertical position is called *caster*. With positive caster the tire leans toward the rear of the vehicle; with negative caster it leans toward the front (courtesy of Training Enterprises Company).

Toe-in
(B is larger than A)

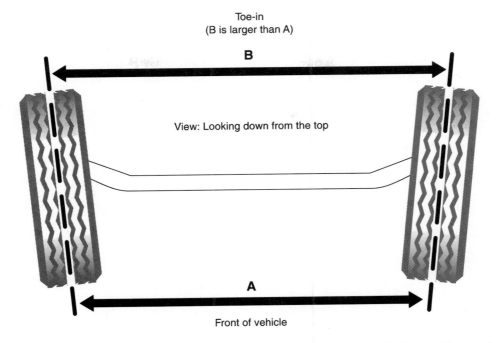

View: Looking down from the top

B

A

Front of vehicle

Figure 16.72 Toe. The *toe* is the measured difference between the inside front edge of the tires and the rear inside edge of the same tire. Toe-in occurs when the distance in the front is smaller than the distance in the rear (courtesy of Training Enterprises Company).

Alignment Machines. The machines needed to align a vehicle are expensive and highly specialized (see Figure 16.73). Alignment machines are run by technicians with extended training. Places where tires are sold and car dealerships are two businesses that have alignment machines. Some businesses do nothing but replace suspension parts and align tires.

Tire Alignment Problems and Wear

Whether the alignment is correct, and whether other problems exist, are determined by how the tires are wearing (see Figure 16.74 and refer to Figure 4.2). When the inside or outside edges of the tread wears faster than the center, look for a camber problem. A sawtooth pattern means the toe should be corrected. Cupping or dishing of the tread can be a caster problem if the caster is out of the normal specification range. Out-of-balance tires or steering system wear is the usual cause of cupping and dishing.

Excessive tread wear in the center or on both edges means the tire pressure needs to be set. Tire pressure set too high wears the tread in the center.

Alignment Settings

When a vehicle is first aligned, the tires should have good tread. Most alignment technicians have specifications or guidelines they use to set up a vehicle. After the vehicle is placed into service the tire wear should be monitored regularly. If wear develops,

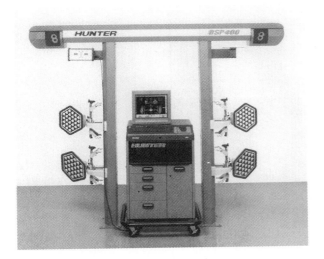

Figure 16.73 Alignment machine. This machine checks the alignment angles and guides the technician setting them. A final accuracy check is made before the machine is removed (courtesy of Hunter Engineering Company).

(a) Cupping

(b) Overinflation

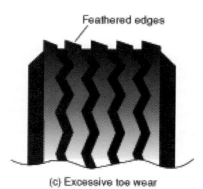

(d) Underinflation

Figure 16.74 Tire wear conditions. Use these illustrations to determine what is causing abnormal tire wear. Compare the tire wear pattern to those tires shown (courtesy of Training Enterprises Company).

this wear can help you fine-tune the alignment to compensate for this wear. At this point the total alignment may not have to be changed, just the side where wear is appearing. By aligning a vehicle in this manner, the vehicle can be set for the conditions under which it is driven. After several adjustments, the tire wear should be reduced to normal or below. While the alignment is being adjusted, the first set of tires may wear faster but the replacement set should get the recommended mileage. The vehicle driver should work with the alignment specialist to reduce abnormal tire wear. After the settings are reached that give the best results, save them as a permanent reference for this particular vehicle. The importance of this set of specifications becomes apparent when it may take at least one set of tires to obtain good wear patterns as time and mileage increase.

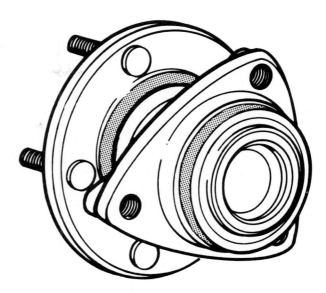

Figure 16.75 Typical sealed wheel bearing. A sealed wheel bearing cannot be lubricated, but needs to be checked on a regular basis (courtesy of Buick Motor Division, General Motors Corporation).

LESSON 16–8 Wheel Bearings

Wheel bearings should be serviced at intervals of from 20,000 to 40,000 miles (32,000 to 64,000 km) and as a part of every brake job. The specified service interval for any car is found in the manufacturer's manual for that car.

Worn or improperly adjusted wheel bearings can cause problems that may appear to be in the steering, suspension, or braking systems. The diagnosis of any problem in these systems should include a check of the wheel bearings. Wheel bearing service includes some simple but important jobs.

The front wheels of a car, and the rear wheels of most front wheel drive cars, are mounted on *hubs*. A hub provides the means for mounting a wheel and its brake drum or rotor so it will rotate on its spindle or axle. The hub is usually made of cast iron and contains two bearings. These bearings allow the hub to rotate freely, even with the weight of the car pressing down on the wheels.

Some hubs are assembled with their bearings lubricated, and then sealed at the time of their manufacture (see Figure 16.75). Those assemblies, usually called *sealed wheel bearings*, cannot be adjusted or disassembled for service. When the bearings become loose or noisy, the entire hub and bearing assembly must be replaced.

In other hubs, the bearings are adjustable and can be removed for service. Figure 16.76 shows a hub and drum assembly of that type. Study Figure 16.76 carefully. To perform the jobs in this chapter

correctly, you must be familiar with all the parts and their names.

> Use only a grease suitable and marked just for disc brake applications when repacking disc brake wheel bearings. The higher heat produced by these brake systems will cause the older greases to run away from the bearings and leave them without lubrication.

Wheel, Hub, and Drum Assembly Parts

Bearings. The bearings used in hubs are sometimes referred to as *antifriction* bearings. These bearings use balls or rollers to provide rolling friction. Rolling friction allows the wheel to rotate on the spindle very easily. The bearings in Figure 16.76 are *tapered roller bearings*. The rollers themselves are tapered, and they roll on a tapered *race*, or ring, which is also called a *cone*. The rollers are held in place on the cone by a *cage*, which is a metal band with a slot for each roller. The cage also keeps the rollers from contacting each other. The cone, rollers, and cage are assembled as a unit, as shown in Figure 16.77. This allows you to remove the bearing as an assembly without having to work with separate pieces.

There are two cone-and-roller assemblies in each hub. The inner assembly is installed from the rear of the hub. It is the larger of the two. The outer

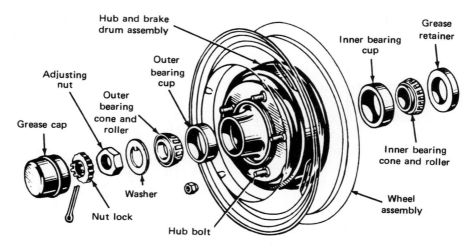

Figure 16.76 A typical hub and drum assembly showing all the component parts in the order of their assembly (courtesy of Ford Motor Company, Dearborn, MI).

Figure 16.77 Typical cone-and-roller assembly. A cone-and-roller assembly bearing needs to be cleaned and lubricated on a regular basis (courtesy of Ford Motor Company, Dearborn, MI).

Figure 16.79 Grease assembly or seal. A grease retainer, or grease seal, keeps the grease from contaminating the brake system (courtesy of Ford Motor Company, Dearborn, MI).

Figure 16.78 Typical bearing cup. A bearing cup needs to be changed if the bearing is defective (courtesy of Ford Motor Company, Dearborn, MI).

Figure 16.80 Spindle washer. Notice the tab, or key, that fits into the keyway on the spindle (courtesy of Ford Motor Company, Dearborn, MI).

cone-and-roller assembly is the smaller. It is accessible without removing the hub from the spindle. The cone-and-roller assemblies are easily removed.

Bearing Cups. The bearing *cups* provide a hard, smooth surface on which the rollers can roll. These cups form the outer race and are tapered to match the taper of the rollers. You can see one of these races in Figure 16.78. Even though these races are separate from the cone-and-roller assembly, they are actually a part of the bearing. They should be replaced whenever the cone-and-roller assembly is replaced.

Grease Retainer. The grease retainer, shown in Figure 16.79, is a seal that serves to keep the

wheel bearing grease from leaking out. Such leakage could contaminate the brake lining and cause braking problems. The grease retainer fits into the rear of the hub, behind the inner bearing assembly. Grease retainers should be replaced each time the wheel bearings are repacked with lubricant.

Washer. The washer, which is flat, fits near the end of the spindle or axle and is very important. In Figure 16.80, you will notice that the washer has a little *key*, or tab, on the inside. This key fits into a *keyway*, or groove, on the spindle and keeps the washer from turning. The washer separates the outer bearing assembly from the adjusting nut. If the bearing assembly were in contact with the nut, it could act to turn the nut.

Job 16H

IDENTIFY WHEEL BEARINGS AND RELATED PARTS

SATISFACTORY PERFORMANCE
A satisfactory performance on this job requires that you do the following:

1. Identify the numbered parts on the drawing by placing the number of each part in front of the correct part name.
2. Correctly identify all the parts within 15 minutes.

PERFORMANCE SITUATION

_____ Inner bearing cup   _____ Nut lock
_____ Cotter pin   _____ Adjusting nut
_____ Spindle shim   _____ Hub assembly
_____ Washer   _____ Grease retainer
_____ Outer bearing assembly   _____ Grease cap
_____ Outer bearing cup   _____ Inner bearing assembly

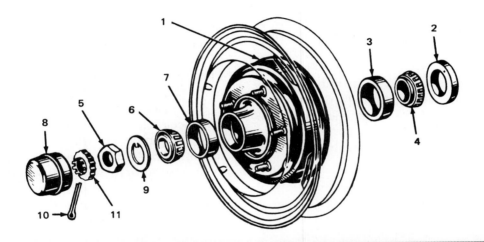

Adjusting Nut. The adjusting nut, pictured in Figure 16.81, holds the parts of the hub assembly on the spindle and in the proper position. Turning the nut right or left tightens or loosens the bearings in their cups.

Nut Lock. The nut lock is a pressed steel cover that fits over the adjusting nut. The nut lock has _castellations,_ or notches, as shown in Figure 16.82.

These castellations allow the nut to be locked in any desired position. You will find some cars that do not have nut locks. Since some adjusting nuts are castellated, they do not require additional locks. However, the nut lock is used by most manufacturers, and it allows you to obtain a more accurate wheel bearing adjustment than you can obtain with a castellated nut.

Figure 16.81 Adjusting nut. An adjusting nut is torqued to specifications and is kept from working loose by the nut lock (courtesy of Ford Motor Company, Dearborn, MI).

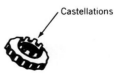

Figure 16.82 Nut lock. A nut lock is needed to keep the adjusting nut from loosening (courtesy of Ford Motor Company, Dearborn, MI).

Figure 16.83   Cotter pin. A cotter pin is an extremely important part that keeps the axle nut from turning off the axle (courtesy of Ford Motor Company, Dearborn, MI).

> Never allow a vehicle to be run without the grease cap. Dirt, dust, and water will destroy the bearing. Dirt in a bearing can cause the bearing to overheat and eventually lock up. This would either severely damage the hub and axle or cause an accident.

Cotter Pin.   The cotter pin, shown in Figure 16.83, is used to secure the nut lock. It passes through a hole drilled through the end of the spindle, and holds the nut lock by its castellations.

Grease Cap.   The grease cap, or hub cap, seals the open end of the hub. Although it does serve to keep grease in the hub, its primary job is to keep dirt and water out. A car should never be put into service without grease caps. Figure 16.84 shows a typical grease cap.

> Never allow a vehicle to be driven without the cotter pin in place holding the axle nut. If this is left out the nut can turn off the axle and let the wheel come off. This could happen when the vehicle is in motion. Use a new cotter pin each time the axle nut is removed and replaced.

LESSON 16–9   Bearing Loads

Wheel bearings are subjected to two major forces: radial loads and thrust loads. A *radial* load is a load that acts perpendicular, or at a right angle, to the axis of the wheel. The weight of the car pushes down on the road in a straight line from the spindle

Figure 16.84   Typical grease cap. A typical grease cap, or hub cap, is needed to keep dirt and water out of the bearings (courtesy of Ford Motor Company, Dearborn, MI).

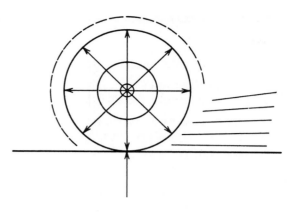

Figure 16.85   Radial load on a wheel. This load acts at right angles to the wheel.

to the road. When the wheel rotates, this load still pushes straight down, but the force is carried by another part of the wheel. If you could see these lines of force, they would look like spokes in a wheel. They would radiate from the spindle to the tread of the tire as shown in Figure 16.85.

A *thrust* load is one that acts parallel to the axis of the wheel. It tends to push the wheel off or further onto the spindle. The wheels of a car are subjected to considerable thrust loads, especially when cornering as shown in Figure 16.86. Because of these thrust loads, wheel bearings must do much more than spin freely and support the weight of the car. They must also keep the wheels from sliding in or out on their spindles.

Wheel bearings are designed to handle both radial and thrust loads. You may occasionally find ball bearings in the hubs of some cars, but tapered roller bearings are used in most. Tapered roller bearings have a long life and are capable of handling extreme loads. Figure 16.87 shows a view of a cone-and-roller assembly and a sectioned bearing cup. The arrows indicate where the thrust loads are

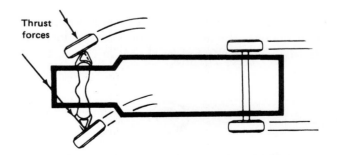

Figure 16.86   Side thrust forces on front wheels during cornering (courtesy of American Motors).

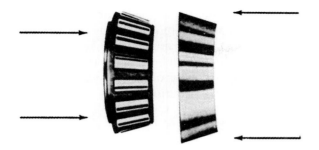

Figure 16.87 A view of a cone-and-roller assembly and a sectioned cup, showing where thrust loads are applied (courtesy of Pontiac Motor Division, General Motors Corporation).

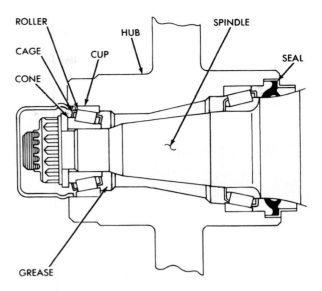

Figure 16.88 The wheel bearings and related parts assembled in a hub (courtesy of Chrysler Corporation).

applied. You can see that the tapered shape of the bearing assembly and its cup handle these loads.

When installed in a hub, the inner bearing handles the thrust loads that attempt to push the hub further into the spindle. The outer bearing handles the thrust loads that attempt to push the wheel off the spindle. The position of each bearing is shown in Figure 16.88.

Job 16I

IDENTIFY THE FUNCTION OF HUB PARTS

SATISFACTORY PERFORMANCE
A satisfactory performance on this job requires that you do the following:

1. Identify the function of the hub parts listed below by placing the part number in the space provided in front of the correct part function.
2. Complete the job by correctly identifying the function of all the parts within 15 minutes.

PERFORMANCE SITUATION

1. Grease retainer	6. Tapered roller bearing
2. Spindle nut	7. Bearing cup
3. Nut lock	8. Bearing cage
4. Bearing cone	9. Cotter pin
5. Spindle washer	10. Grease cap

_____ Handles both radial and thrust loads
_____ Secures the nut lock to the spindle
_____ Provides an inner race for the bearing
_____ Helps keep dirt and water from entering the hub
_____ Keeps the outer wheel bearing from turning the spindle nut
_____ Provides an outer race for the bearing
_____ Keeps the grease from contaminating the brake lining
_____ Secures the wheel to the hub
_____ Holds the rollers in place on the cone
_____ Provides a means of adjusting the bearings
_____ Provides a means of securing the adjustment

LESSON 16-10 Wheel Bearing Service

Wheel bearings should be serviced at regular intervals of from 20,000 to 40,000 miles (32,000 to 64,000 km) as a part of routine maintenance. The adjustment of the bearings should be checked as one of the first steps in diagnosing any problems in the steering, suspension, and brake systems. The condition of the wheel bearings is very important. Worn or loose bearings often cause a car to pull to one side or cause vibrations.

WHEEL BEARING ADJUSTMENT

On most rear wheel drive cars, the front wheel bearings are adjustable, as are the rear wheel bearings on certain front wheel drive cars.

Adjusting wheel bearings is a very simple, yet very important job. Tightening the adjusting nut forces the outer bearing in against its cup. The cup, in turn, pushes against the hub, which pushes the inner cup against its bearing. If the nut is overtightened, both bearings will be jammed against their cups. Jamming will increase the friction in the bearings and cause them to wear out very quickly. If the nut is left too loose, the bearings will not be in proper contact with their cups. Bearings that are too loose will also wear out fast. Moreover, they will allow the hub, and thus the wheel, to wobble.

The following adjustment procedure and specifications can be considered typical. However, such procedures and specifications vary with different car manufacturers. Therefore, consult the manufacturer's service manual before attempting the job.

1. Raise the wheel you are to adjust and support the car with car stands.
2. Remove the wheel cover from one of the wheels.
3. Remove the grease cap. A special pair of grease cap pliers similar to those shown in Figure 16.89 can be used for this task.

   Note: Lacking a pair of grease cap pliers, you can use a pair of Channellock pliers.

4. Using a pair of diagonal cutters, remove the cotter pin. First, straighten the legs of the pin. Then, grasp the head of the pin deep in the jaws of the pliers. By prying against the nut lock, you will pull the pin through the hole in the spindle.
5. Remove the nut lock.
6. Using a torque wrench, tighten the adjusting nut to between 17 and 25 foot-pounds (23 to 33 Nm) to seat the bearings. As shown in Figure 16.90 rotate the wheel while tightening the nut.
7. Place the nut lock over the adjusting nut so the castellations on the lock are aligned with the cotter pin hole in the spindle (see Figure 16.91).
8. Using a pair of Channellock pliers, back off on the nut and the nut lock together so the next castellation is aligned with the cotter pin hole.
9. Install a new cotter pin to lock the nut lock in this position.

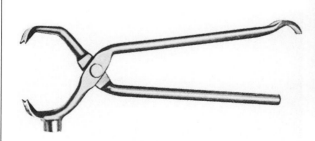

Figure 16.89 A pair of grease cap, or hub cap, pliers (courtesy of AMMCO Tools, Inc.).

TORQUE WRENCH

Figure 16.90 Torque to seat wheel bearings. Applying the initial torque to seat wheel bearings. Notice that the wheel is turning while this adjustment is made (courtesy of Ford Motor Company, Dearborn, MI).

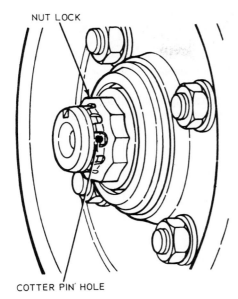

NUT LOCK

COTTER PIN HOLE

Figure 16.91 Nut lock position. The nut lock should be installed so the castellations are aligned with the hole for the cotter pin (courtesy of Ford Motor Company, Dearborn, MI).

Figure 16.92 A correctly installed cotter pin (courtesy of Ford Motor Company, Dearborn, MI).

Note: The cotter pin must fit the hole snugly and be tightly crimped over the nut lock. Figure 16.92 illustrates a correctly secured cotter pin.

10. Install the grease cap.
11. Install the wheel cover.
12. Repeat steps 2 through 11 at the remaining wheel.
13. Lower the car to the floor.

Job 16J

ADJUST WHEEL BEARINGS

SATISFACTORY PERFORMANCE
A satisfactory performance on this job requires that you do the following:

1. Adjust the wheel bearings on the car assigned.
2. Following the steps in the "Performance Outline" and the manufacturer's procedure and specifications, complete the job within 30 minutes.
3. Fill in the blanks under "Information."

PERFORMANCE OUTLINE

1. Raise and support the car.
2. Remove the cotter pins.
3. Adjust the bearings according to the car maker's procedure and specifications.
4. Install new cotter pins.
5. Install all parts removed to gain access to the cotter pin.
6. Lower the car to the floor.

INFORMATION

Vehicle identification _____
Reference used _____ Page(s) _____
Initial tightening torque specification _____
Amount backed off _____
Size of cotter pin used _____

Many front wheel drive cars have removable bearings in the hubs of the rear wheels (see Figure 16.93). On most of those cars, drum brakes are used, and the drums are attached to the hubs. Some older rear wheel drive cars have similar hubs and drums at the front wheels. Regardless of their location, the procedures for repacking the bearings are similar.

The steps of a typical procedure for repacking bearings follow, but consult an appropriate manual for the recommendations and specifications for the car on which you are working.

1. Remove the wheel covers.
2. Loosen the lug nuts holding the wheels to the hubs.
3. Raise the car and support it with car stands.
4. Remove the lug nuts from one of the wheels.
5. Remove the wheel.
6. Remove the grease cap.
7. Remove the cotter pin.
8. Remove the nut lock, the adjusting nut, the washer, and the outer bearing.

   Note: The outer wheel bearing can be easily removed by hitting the edge of the drum with the heel of your hand. This action usually causes the bearing to slide out on the spindle where it can be easily grasped.

9. Grasp the brake drum with both hands, and with a twisting motion, slide it off the spindle.

   Note: Never force a drum off if it will not slide off easily. Loosen the brake adjustment to provide more clearance between the drum and the brake shoes. (This procedure can be found in Chapter 17.)

   Note: The brake assembly and the inside of the brake drum may contain asbestos dust. Breathing asbestos dust may cause asbestosis and cancer. Wear an air-purifying respirator during all procedures where you may be exposed to asbestos dust.

10. Remove the grease retainer. Figure 16.94 shows how a puller may be used for this operation. Lacking such a puller, the inner bearing and the grease retainer may be removed together by means of a blunt punch, as shown in Figure 16.95.
11. Thoroughly wash all the parts (except the drum) in a suitable solvent such as Kleer-Flo or Agitene.
12. Dry all the parts.

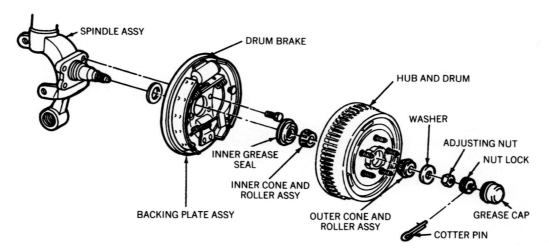

SPINDLE ASSY — DRUM BRAKE — HUB AND DRUM — WASHER — ADJUSTING NUT — NUT LOCK — GREASE CAP — COTTER PIN — OUTER CONE AND ROLLER ASSY — BACKING PLATE ASSY — INNER CONE AND ROLLER ASSY — INNER GREASE SEAL

Figure 16.93   A typical brake, drum, and hub assembly used at the rear wheels of a front wheel drive car (courtesy of Ford Motor Company, Dearborn, MI).

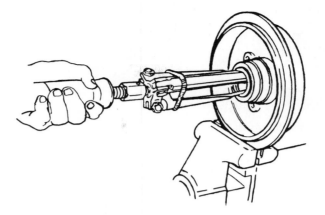

Figure 16.94   Removing a grease retainer with a puller (courtesy Ford Motor Company, Dearborn, MI).

Figure 16.95   Using a blunt punch to remove the inner bearing and the grease retainer (courtesy of Ford Motor Company, Dearborn, MI).

Note: If compressed air is used to dry the parts, be careful not to spin the bearings. Hold the bearings firmly and direct the air between the rollers at the small end of the bearing. This will dry the bearing and blow out all traces of old grease. Spinning the bearings with an air gun will cause damage to the bearings and may cause personal injury if a roller flies out of the cage.

13. Inspect the bearings (see Figures 16.96 and 16.97 for diagnosing bearing faults). Turn the cone and rollers so all the roller surfaces can be seen. Replace any bearing that shows signs of pitting, discoloration, or scoring. Also check for the presence of any metallic powder or flakes. They usually indicate a defective cone.

    Note: Whenever a bearing is replaced, the cup into which the bearing fits must also be replaced, even if it exhibits no apparent damage. Refer to Lesson 16–11, "Replacing Bearing Cups," for the procedure to follow.

14. Inspect the bearing cups (refer to Figures 16.96 and 16.97 for diagnosing bearing faults). Also check for the presence of any metallic powder or flakes. Replace any cups that exhibit those faults.

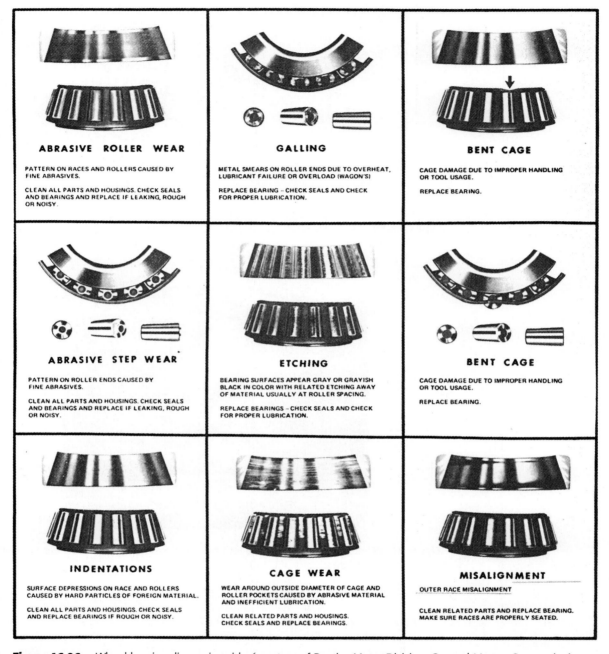

Figure 16.96   Wheel bearing diagnosis guide (courtesy of Pontiac Motor Division, General Motors Corporation).

Note: Whenever a bearing cup is replaced, its mating bearing must also be replaced, even if it exhibits no apparent damage. Refer to Lesson 16–11, "Replacing Bearing Cups," for the procedure to follow.

15. Repack the bearings. Many shops use a bearing packer similar to the one shown in Figure 16.98. Follow the instructions of the manufacturer if you use one of these devices. If a packing device is not available, the grease should be worked up between the rollers by drawing the bearing, large end down, across grease held in the palm of your hand. Figure 16.99 illustrates this method. Continue to push grease into the bearing in this manner until it oozes out at the small end.

Note: Be sure to use only grease that meets the specification stated in the manufacturer's service manual.

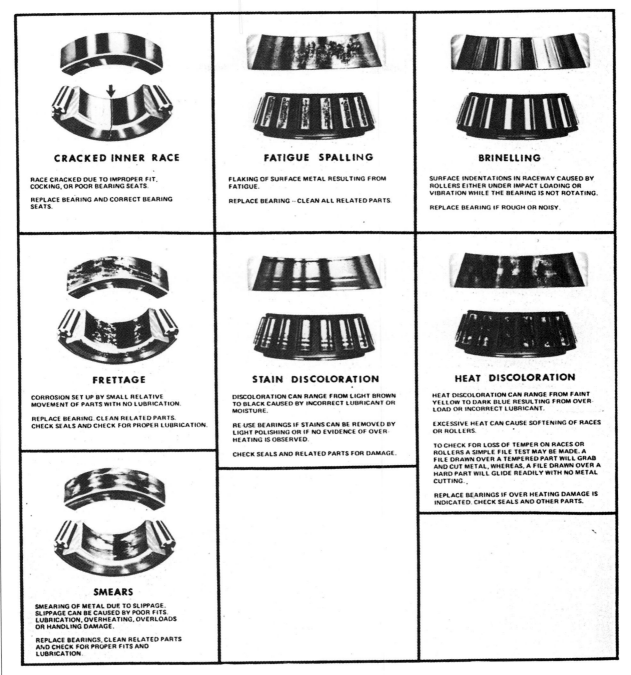

Figure 16.97 Diagnosis guide (continued). This is a continuation of the guide in Figure 16.96.

16. Place the inner (large) bearing in its cup.
17. Install a new grease retainer. The new grease retainer should be installed so that the sharp edge of the seal is facing in, as shown in Figure 16.100.

Note: An installing tool such as the one shown in Figure 16.101 enables you to drive the retainer in place without damaging it. Lacking an installing tool, you can carefully drive the retainer in place with a hammer and a block of wood, as shown in Figure 16.102. Most retainers should be driven in until their outer surface is flush with the surface of the hub.

Figure 16.98 A bearing packer is used to force the grease into the center of the bearing (courtesy of AMMCO Tools, Inc.).

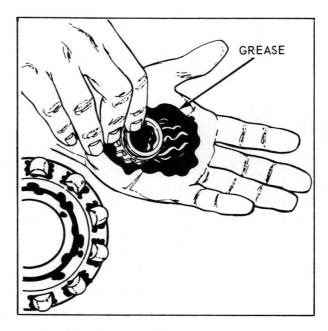

Figure 16.99 Hand packing a bearing. Packing grease between the rollers and cage of a wheel bearing (courtesy of Ford Motor Company, Dearborn, MI).

18. Check to see that there is no dirt, grease, or foreign matter on the inner surface of the drum. Carefully slide the hub in place over the spindle.

    Note: Use care to center the hub on the spindle. Otherwise, the threads on the spindle could damage the new retainer you just installed.

19. Install the outer bearing on the spindle, sliding it into its cup.

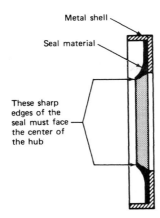

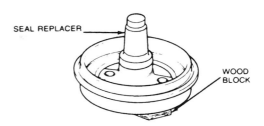

Figure 16.100 A crosssectional view of a typical grease retainer.

Figure 16.101 Seal replacer. A seal replacer positioned to drive in a grease retainer. Note that the hub is supported on a wood block (courtesy of Ford Motor Company, Dearborn, MI).

Figure 16.102 Block method to replace a seal. Lacking a seal replacer, a block of wood can be used to install a grease retainer (courtesy of Ford Motor Company, Dearborn, MI).

20. Install the washer and adjusting nut.
21. Adjust the bearings and install the nut lock and cotter pin in accordance with the procedure and specifications of the manufacturer.
22. Install the grease cap.
23. Install the wheel and run the lug nuts up snug.
24. Repeat steps 4 through 23 on the remaining wheel.
25. Lower the car to the floor.
26. Tighten the lug nuts to the torque specification in the sequence given by the manufacturer.
27. Install the wheel covers.

Job 16K

REPACK WHEEL BEARINGS: DRUM BRAKES

SATISFACTORY PERFORMANCE
A satisfactory performance on this job requires that you do the following:

1. Repack the wheel bearings on the car assigned.
2. Following the steps in the "Performance Outline" and the specifications of the car manufacturer, complete the job within 90 minutes.
3. Fill in the blanks under "Information."

PERFORMANCE OUTLINE

1. Raise and support the car.
2. Remove the wheels.
3. Remove a hub assembly.
4. Clean and inspect all parts.
5. Repack the bearings.
6. Assemble the parts and install the hub on the spindle.
7. Adjust the bearings to the manufacturer's specifications.
8. Install the cotter pin and the grease cap.
9. Repeat steps 3 through 8 on the remaining wheel.
10. Install the wheels and lower the car to the floor. Torque the lug nuts and install the wheel covers.

INFORMATION

Vehicle identification _____
Reference used _____ Page(s) _____
Wheel bearing repacked: _____ Front _____ Rear
Size of cotter pin used _____
Wheel bearing initial torque specification _____
Wheel lug nut torque specification _____

REPACKING WHEEL BEARINGS: DISC BRAKES

Most rear wheel drive cars have disc brakes on the front wheels. The bearings used in the hubs of those cars are the same as the bearings used in drum brakes. The procedure for repacking them, however, is more involved. This is because the disc brake caliper must be removed before the rotor, or disc, can be removed from the spindle. There are many different types of calipers in use. Because of this, refer to the manufacturer's manual for the specific removal and installation procedures required for the car on which you are working.

Cars Fitted with Delco-Moraine–Type Single-Piston Calipers

The following procedure can be used on cars equipped with Delco-Moraine–type single-piston calipers. A caliper of this type is shown in Figure 16.103.

1. Remove the wheel covers.
2. Loosen the lug nuts holding the wheels.
3. Raise the car and support it with car stands.
4. Remove the lug nuts from one of the wheels.
5. Remove the wheel.

   Note: The caliper assembly and the disc brake rotor may be coated with asbestos dust. Breathing asbestos dust may cause asbestosis and cancer. Wear an air-purifying respirator during all procedures where you may be exposed to asbestos dust.

6. Push the caliper piston back into the caliper a slight distance to separate the brake shoes from the rotor. This will make the caliper easier to remove. The piston can be pushed back by (1) slowly prying the caliper outward with a prybar positioned

Figure 16.103 Single-piston caliper disc brake. A Delco-Moraine single-piston caliper disc brake used at the front wheels of some rear wheel drive cars (courtesy of Oldsmobile Division, General Motors Corporation).

as shown in Figure 16.104, or (3) by using a "C" clamp positioned over the caliper with the pad of the clamp against the back of the outboard brake shoe as shown in Figure 16.105.

Note: When using either method, move the caliper only enough to allow the rotor to spin freely.

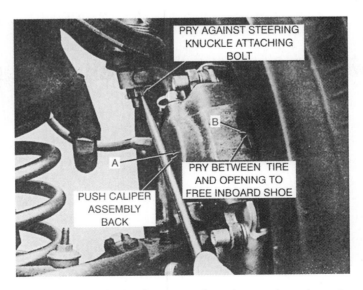

Figure 16.104 Moving disc brake shoes away from the rotor by prying outward on the caliper (courtesy of Chevrolet Motor Division, General Motors Corporation).

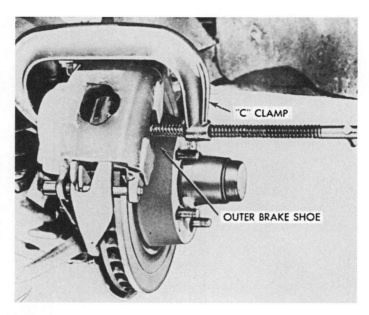

Figure 16.105   Using a "C" clamp to push a caliper piston back in its bore (courtesy of Chevrolet Motor Division, General Motors Corporation).

7. Using a suitable wrench or socket, remove the mounting bolts as shown in Figure 16.106.
8. Lift the caliper up and off the rotor. Support the caliper by trying it securely to a part of the suspension system as shown in Figure 16.107.

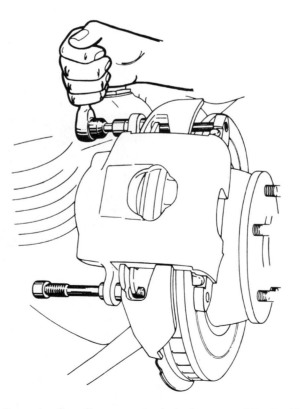

Figure 16.106   Removing the caliper mounting bolts (courtesy of Pontiac Motor Division, General Motors Corporation).

Figure 16.107 Caliper storage after removal. A caliper wired to a part of the front suspension system. A caliper should never be allowed to hang from the brake hose (courtesy of Pontiac Motor Division, General Motors Corporation).

Note: Never allow a caliper to hang by the brake hose. To do so could weaken the hose.

9. Remove the grease cap from the hub.
10. Remove the cotter pin.
11. Remove the nut lock, the adjusting nut, the washer, and the outer bearing.

Note: The outer bearing can be easily removed by hitting the edge of the rotor with the heel of your hand. This action usually causes the bearing to slide out on the spindle where it can be easily grasped.

12. Grasp the rotor with both hands, and carefully slide it off the spindle.
13. Lay the rotor on a bench covered with clean paper. This will protect the inner surface of the rotor from damage and contamination.
14. Remove the grease retainer and the inner bearing (refer to Figures 16.94 and 16.95).
15. Thoroughly wash and clean all the parts (except the rotor) in a suitable solvent such as Kleer-Flo or Agitene.
16. Dry all the parts.

Note: If compressed air is used to dry the parts, be careful not to spin the bearings. Hold the bearings firmly and direct the air between the rollers at the small end of the bearing. This will dry the bearing and will blow out all traces of old grease. Spinning the bearing with an air gun will cause damage to the bearing and may cause personal injury if a roller flies out of the cage.

17. Inspect the bearings (refer to Figures 16.96 and 16.97 for diagnosing bearing faults). Turn the cone and rollers so all the roller surfaces can be seen. Replace any bearing that shows signs of pitting, discoloration, or scoring. Also check for the presence of any metallic powder or flakes. They usually indicate a defective cone.

Note: Whenever a bearing is replaced, the cup into which the bearing fits must also be replaced, even if it exhibits no apparent damage: Refer to Lesson 16–11, "Replacing Bearing Cups," for the procedure to follow.

18. Carefully clean all traces of grease from the inside of the hub. Inspect the bearing cups (refer to Figures 16.96 and 16.97). Also check for the presence of any metallic powder or flakes. Replace any cups that exhibit these faults.

Note: Whenever a bearing cup is replaced, its mating bearing must also be replaced, even if it exhibits no apparent damage. Refer to Lesson 16–11, "Replacing Bearing Cups," for the procedure to follow.

19. Repack the bearings. Many shops use a bearing packer for this operation (refer to Figure 16.98). Follow the instructions of the manufacturer if you use one of these devices. If a packing device is not available, the grease should be worked up between the rollers by drawing the bearing, large end down, across grease held in the palm of your hand (refer to Figure 16.99). Continue to push grease into the bearing in this manner until it oozes out at the small end.

    Note: Be sure to use only grease that meets the specifications of the car manufacturer.

> Checking and replacing damaged wheel bearings is just as important as repacking them. Never repack a damaged bearing and place it back in service. Once a bearing has been damaged, grease will not improve it. Instead the heat buildup from the damaged bearing will cause the grease to thin out. The thinned grease will leave the bearing and it will be without lubrication. An out-of-balance tire can damage wheel bearings. Wheel tramp and shimmy are very hard on wheel bearings because they contain hardened steel parts and should not be shocked or jarred constantly.

20. Place the inner (large) bearing in its cup.
21. Install a new grease retainer. The new grease retainer should be installed so the sharp edge of the seal is facing in (refer to Figure 16.100).

    Note: An installing tool should be used if available. An installing tool, shown in Figure 16.108, enables you to drive the retainer in place without danger of damaging it. Lacking an installing tool, you can carefully drive the retainer in place with a hammer and a block of wood (refer to Figure 16.107). Most retainers should be driven in until their outer surface is flush with the surface of the hub.

22. Check to see there is no dirt, grease, or foreign matter on the surfaces of the rotor. Carefully slide the hub in place over the spindle.

    Note: Use care to center the hub on the spindle. Otherwise, the threads on the spindle could damage the new retainer you just installed.

23. Install the outer bearing on the spindle, sliding it into its cup.
24. Install the washer and the adjusting nut.
25. Adjust the bearings and install the nut lock and cotter pin in accordance with the procedure and specifications of the car manufacturer.
26. Install the grease cap.
27. Push the caliper down over the rotor, and align the holes in the caliper with the holes in the mounting.

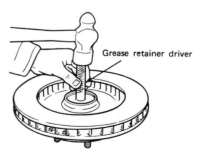

Figure 16.108   Installing a grease retainer. Using a grease retainer driver, or seal replacer, to install a grease retainer in the hub of a rotor (courtesy of Ford Motor Company, Dearborn, MI).

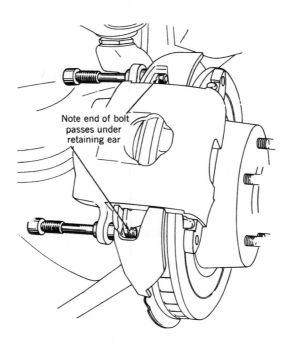

Figure 16.109 Installing the caliper mounting bolts (courtesy of Chevrolet Motor Division, General Motors Corporation).

28. Push the mounting bolts through the caliper and through the mount, as shown in Figure 16.109. Make sure the bolts pass under the ears of the inboard shoe.
29. Push the bolts through the holes in the outboard shoe and through the holes in the outer caliper ears. Thread the bolts into the mounting bracket, starting the threads by hand to avoid cross-threading.
30. Tighten the bolts to the torque specification of the manufacturer.
31. Pump the brake pedal several times to position the piston and the caliper.

    Note: Do not remove the caliper at the remaining wheel until the caliper you just installed has been repositioned.

32. Repeat steps 4 through 31 at the remaining wheel.
33. Install the wheels and run the lug nuts up snug.
34. Lower the car to the floor.
35. Tighten the lug nuts to the torque specification in the sequence given by the manufacturer.
36. Install the wheel covers.

Cars Fitted with Ford-Type Single-Piston Calipers

The following procedure can be used on cars equipped with Ford-type single-piston calipers. A caliper of this type is shown in Figure 16.110.

1. Remove the wheel covers.
2. Loosen the lug nuts holding the wheels.
3. Raise the car and support it with car stands.
4. Remove the lug nuts from one of the wheels.
5. Remove the wheel.

   Note: The caliper assembly and the disc brake rotor may be coated with asbestos dust. Breathing asbestos dust may cause asbestosis and cancer. Wear an air-purifying respirator during all procedures where you may be exposed to asbestos dust.

6. Push the caliper piston back into the caliper a slight distance to separate the brake shoes from the rotor. This will make the caliper easier to remove. The piston can be pushed back by (1) prying the piston back with a screwdriver as shown in

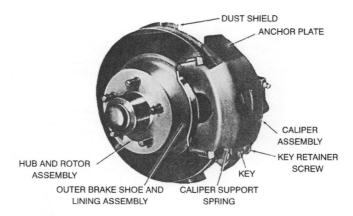

Figure 16.110   Ford disc brake. A Ford-type, single-piston caliper disc brake assembly used on the front wheels of some rear wheel drive vehicles (courtesy of Ford Motor Company, Dearborn, MI).

Figure 16.111   Prying a caliper piston back into its bore by using a screwdriver inserted between the piston and the inboard shoe (courtesy of American Motors).

Figure 16.111, or (2) by using a "C" clamp positioned over the caliper with the pad of the clamp against the outboard shoe (refer to Figure 16.105).

Note: When using either method, move the caliper only enough to allow the rotor to spin freely.

7. Remove the screw holding the caliper retaining key as shown in Figure 16.112.
8. Carefully drive the retaining key and its support spring from the key slot as shown in Figure 16.113.
9. Lift the caliper off the rotor and out of its mounting. To do this, push the caliper downward, then tip the caliper outward as shown in Figure 16.114.

   Note: On disc brakes of this type, the inboard shoe will remain in its mounting behind the rotor. The outboard shoe will remain in place in the caliper as shown in Figure 16.115

10. Support the caliper by placing it securely on a part of the suspension system, or tie it up in place with a piece of wire (refer to Figure 16.107).

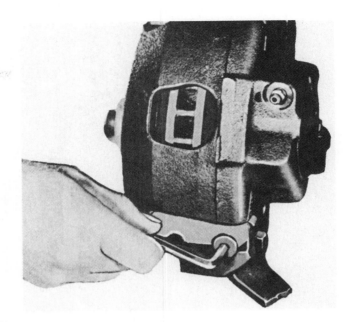

Figure 16.112   Removing the screw that holds the caliper retaining key (courtesy of Ford Motor Company, Dearborn, MI).

Figure 16.113   Driving out the caliper retaining key (courtesy of Ford Motor Company, Dearborn, MI).

Note: Never allow a caliper to hang by its brake hose. To do so could weaken the hose.

11. Remove the grease cap.
12. Remove the cotter pin.
13. Remove the nut lock, the adjusting nut, the washer, and the outer bearing.

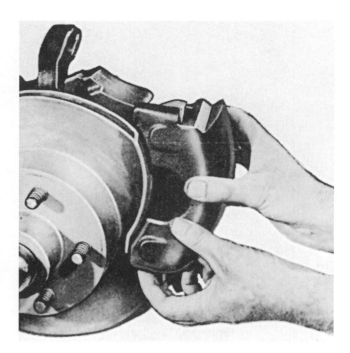

Figure 16.114   Lifting the caliper out of its mounting (courtesy of Ford Motor Company, Dearborn, MI).

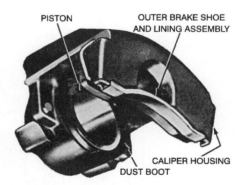

PISTON   OUTER BRAKE SHOE
AND LINING ASSEMBLY

CALIPER HOUSING
DUST BOOT

Figure 16.115   A removed caliper with the outboard shoe in place (courtesy of Ford Motor Company, Dearborn, MI).

Note: The outer bearing can be easily removed by hitting the edge of the rotor with the heel of your hand. This action usually causes the bearing to slide out on the spindle where it can be easily grasped.

14. Grasp the rotor with both hands, and carefully slide it off the spindle.
15. Lay the rotor on a bench covered with clean paper. This will protect the inner surface of the rotor from damage and contamination.
16. Remove the grease retainer and the inner bearing (refer to Figures 16.94 and 16.95).
17. Thoroughly wash all the parts (except the rotor) in a suitable solvent such as Kleer-Flo or Agitene.
18. Dry all the parts.

Note: If compressed air is used to dry the parts, be careful not to spin the bearings. Hold the bearings firmly and direct the air between the rollers at the small end of the bearing. This will dry the bearing and will blow out all traces of old grease.

Spinning the bearing with an air gun will cause damage to the bearing and may cause personal injury if a roller flies out of the cage.

19. Inspect the bearings (refer to Figures 16.96 and 16.97). Turn the cone and rollers so all the roller surfaces can be seen. Replace any bearing that shows signs of pitting, discoloration, or scoring. Also check for the presence of any metallic powder or flakes. They usually indicate a defective cone.

    Note: Whenever a bearing is replaced, the cup into which the bearing fits must also be replaced, even if it exhibits no apparent wear or damage. Refer to Lesson 16–11, "Replacing Bearing Cups," for the procedure to follow.

20. Carefully clean all traces of grease from the inside of the hub. Inspect the bearing cups (refer to Figures 16.96 and 16.97). Also check for the presence of any metallic powder or flakes. Replace any cups that exhibit these faults.

    Note: Whenever a bearing cup is replaced, its matching bearing must also be replaced, even if it exhibits no apparent wear or damage. Refer to Lesson 16–11, "Replacing Bearing Cups," for the procedure to follow.

21. Repack the bearings. Many shops use a bearing packer for this operation (refer to Figure 16.98). Follow the instructions of the manufacturer if you use one of these devices. If a packing device is not available, the grease should be worked up between the rollers by drawing the bearing, large end down, across grease held in the palm of your hand (refer to Figure 16.99). Continue to push grease into the bearing in this manner until it oozes out at the small end.

    Note: Be sure to use only grease that meets the car maker's specifications.

22. Place the inner (large) bearing in its cup.
23. Install a new grease retainer. The new retainer should be installed so the sharp edge of the seal is facing in (refer to Figure 16.100).

    Note: An installing tool should be used if available. An installing tool will allow you to drive the retainer in place without damaging it (refer to Figure 16.101). Lacking an installing tool, you can carefully drive the retainer in place with a hammer and a block of wood (refer to Figure 16.102). Most retainers should be driven in until their outer surface is flush with the surface of the hub.

24. Check to see there is no dirt, grease, or foreign matter on the surfaces of the rotor. Carefully slide the hub in place over the spindle.

    Note: Use care to center the hub on the spindle. Otherwise the threads on the spindle could damage the new retainer you just installed.

25. Install the outer bearing on the spindle, sliding it into its cup.
26. Install the washer and the adjusting nut.
27. Adjust the bearings and install the nut lock and cotter pin in accordance with the procedure and specifications of the manufacturer.
28. Install the grease cap.
29. Position the caliper over the rotor so the lower mounting groove on the caliper rests on the mounting, or anchor plate (see Figure 16.116).
30. Pivot the caliper upward and inward toward the rotor until the edge of the dust boot is about 1/4 in. (6 mm) away from the edge of the inboard shoe (see Figure 16.117).
31. Place a piece of lightweight cardboard between the lower half of the dust boot and the shoe as shown in Figure 16.118. (This prevents the dust boot from getting caught between the piston and the shoe.)
32. Pivot the caliper toward the rotor. When you feel a slight resistance, pull the cardboard down toward the center of the rotor while pushing the caliper over the rotor. This step is shown in Figure 16.119.
33. Remove the cardboard, and push the caliper all the way down over the rotor as shown in Figure 16.120.
34. Slide the caliper up against the machined surface of the upper part of the mounting, or anchor, as shown in Figure 16.121.

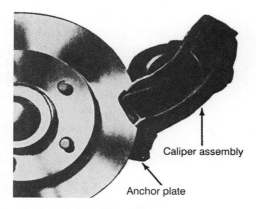

Figure 16.116 First step in caliper installation. Notice that the lower mounting groove on the caliper is resting on the anchor plate (courtesy of Ford Motor Company, Dearborn, MI).

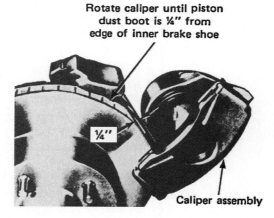

Figure 16.117 The second step in caliper installation (courtesy of Ford Motor Company, Dearborn, MI).

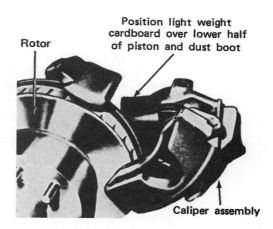

Figure 16.118 Third step in caliper installation. A piece of light cardboard such as a parts tag is used to protect the dust boot (courtesy of Ford Motor Company, Dearborn, MI).

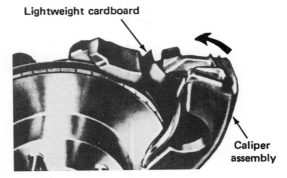

Figure 16.119 The fourth step in caliper installation (courtesy of Ford Motor Company, Dearborn, MI).

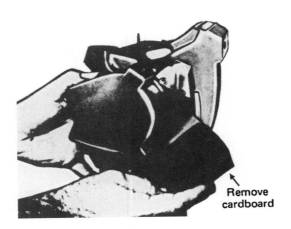

Figure 16.120 Fifth step in caliper installation. The caliper is in place over the rotor and the cardboard is removed (courtesy of Ford Motor Company, Dearborn, MI).

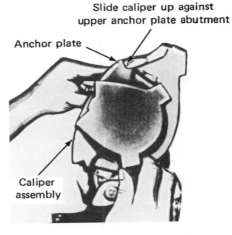

Figure 16.121 A caliper being slid into place against the upper part of its mounting (courtesy of Ford Motor Company, Dearborn, MI).

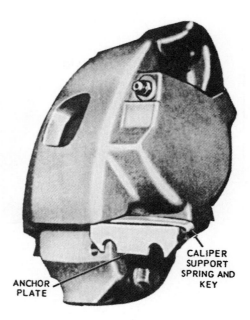

ANCHOR
PLATE

CALIPER
SUPPORT
SPRING AND
KEY

Figure 16.122 Installing the caliper retaining key and support spring (courtesy of Ford Motor Company, Dearborn, MI).

35. Position the lower part of the caliper so the retaining key and its support spring can be inserted into the opening between the caliper and the anchor plate as shown in Figure 16.122.
36. Carefully drive the retaining key and its support spring into the slot until the notch on the key aligns with the threaded hole in the anchor plate.
37. Install the retaining screw and tighten it to the manufacturer's torque specification.
38. Pump the brake pedal several times to position the piston and the caliper.

    Note: Do not remove the caliper at the remaining wheel until the caliper you just installed has been positioned.

39. Repeat steps 4 through 38 at the remaining wheel.
40. Install the wheels and run the lug nuts up snug.
41. Lower the car to the floor.
42. Tighten the lug nuts to the torque specifications and sequence given by the manufacturer.
43. Install the wheel covers.

LESSON 16–11 Replacing Bearing Cups

Because the rollers of a wheel bearing roll inside their cup, any wear on one part affects the other. If a worn bearing is replaced without replacing its cup, the new bearing will have a short life. Bearing cups, or *races,* are fitted very tightly in the hub. This prevents them from turning with the bearing. If you find a cup that is loose in its hub, the hub must be replaced. This is because the cup is made of very hard steel and the hub is made of cast iron. If the cup turns in the hub, the relatively soft cast iron

will wear and thus it will not provide a tight fit for a new cup.

Some manufacturers recommend the use of special pullers to remove bearing cups. These pullers have hooklike fingers or *jaws* that grab the inner edges of the cup. The jaws are expanded until they have a firm grip on the cup. Then the tool and the cup are pulled out together (see Figures 16.123 and 16.124).

Lacking special pullers, you can remove a bearing cup by carefully driving it out with a punch. The inner edge of the cup is raised a little above the inner surface of the hub. Some hubs have notches

Job 16L

REPACK WHEEL BEARINGS: DISC BRAKES

SATISFACTORY PERFORMANCE
A satisfactory performance on this job requires that you do the following:

1. Repack the wheel bearings of the car assigned.
2. Following the steps in the "Performance Outline" and the specifications of the car manufacturer, complete the job within 120 minutes.
3. Fill in the blanks under "Information."

PERFORMANCE OUTLINE

1. Raise and support the car.
2. Remove a wheel.
3. Remove a disc brake caliper.
4. Remove the hub and rotor assembly.
5. Clean and inspect all the parts.
6. Repack the bearings.
7. Assemble the parts and install the hub and rotor assembly.
8. Adjust the bearings to the manufacturer's specifications.
9. Install the cotter pin and grease cap.
10. Install the caliper.
11. Repeat steps 2 through 10 on the remaining wheel.
12. Install the wheels and lower the car to the floor.
13. Torque the lug nuts and install the wheel covers.

INFORMATION

Vehicle identification _____
Reference used _____ Page(s) _____
Type of caliper _____
Size of cotter pin used _____
Wheel bearing initial torque specification _____
Wheel lug nut torque specification _____

Figure 16.123 Removing an inner bearing cup from the hub of a rotor by using a puller (courtesy of Ford Motor Company, Dearborn, MI).

that expose portions of the edge of the cup. A punch with a flat end can be used to drive the cup out. The edge of the punch is placed against the inner edge of the cup and struck with a hammer. The punch is then shifted to the other side of the cup and struck again. This eases the cup out of the hub. Do not try to drive the cup out too fast. You must move it slowly and keep it as straight as possible. By shifting the punch back and forth, you will not cock the cup in its bore. If the cup is cocked, it may damage the hub.

After the cup has been removed, clean the hub carefully. Special cup drivers are available to drive the new cup in place. These tools are shown in Figure 16.125. The use of cup drivers is recommended because they make the job easier, and they guard the cup against damage.

Because all shops do not have cup drivers, you can use a brass punch to install the cups. When you

install a new cup, be sure it is facing the correct way. The thickest edge of the cup always goes into the hub first. Because the outer edge of the cup is much thinner than the inner edge, it is sometimes difficult to keep the punch from slipping. If you keep the corners of your punch ground or filed square, the punch will be less likely to slip.

Another method of installing a new cup is to use the old cup as a driver. Hold the old cup, thick

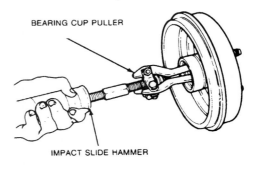

Figure 16.124 Removing an inner bearing cup from the hub of a drum by using a slide hammer puller (courtesy of Ford Motor Company, Dearborn, MI).

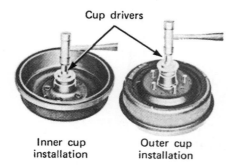

Figure 16.125 Installing wheel bearing cups by using cup drivers (courtesy of Ford Motor Company, Dearborn, MI).

side down, against the new cup. The new cup must be driven all the way down into its bore. You will know when it hits bottom by the different sound you hear when you hit the punch or old cup with your hammer. If you use the old cup as a driver, you may have to drive it out after the new cup is all the way in. To do this, turn the drum or rotor around and drive the old cup out again. It will come out easily if you remembered to place the thick side down.

Job 16M

REPLACE A BEARING CUP

SATISFACTORY PERFORMANCE
A satisfactory performance on this job requires that you do the following:

1. Replace a wheel bearing cup in the hub assigned.
2. Following the steps in the "Performance Outline," complete the job within 30 minutes. At the completion of the job, the cup should be bottomed in the bore, and the hub and the cup should exhibit no damage.
3. Fill in the blanks under "Information."

PERFORMANCE OUTLINE

1. Remove the assigned bearing cup.
2. Clean and inspect the hub.
3. Install the replacement bearing cup.
4. Present the hub for inspection.

INFORMATION

Vehicle or hub identification _____
Bearing cup(s) replaced: _____ Inner _____ Outer
Method used to remove cup(s):
_____ Puller _____ Punch
Method used to install cup(s):
_____ Driver _____ Punch _____ Old cup

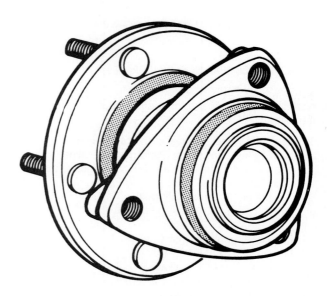

Figure 16.126 A typical sealed hub and bearing assembly (courtesy of Buick Motor Division, General Motors Corporation).

LESSON 16–12 Sealed Wheel Bearings

Many front wheel drive cars are equipped with sealed wheel bearings similar to the one shown in Figure 16.126. As shown in Figure 16.127, some of those cars use sealed wheel bearings at the rear wheels as well as at the front wheels. As previously mentioned, sealed wheel bearings cannot be adjusted or repacked. If a sealed wheel bearing is found to be noisy or loose, the entire hub and bearing assembly must be replaced. Before you

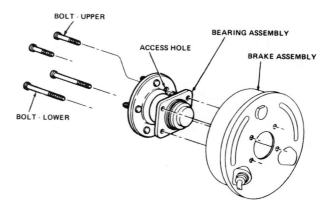

Figure 16.127 Sealed wheel bearing (Buick). A sealed wheel bearing used at the rear wheels of certain front wheel drive cars (courtesy of Buick Motor Division, General Motors Corporation).

attempt to replace a sealed wheel bearing, determine if the part is defective, or if the noise or looseness is caused by other reasons.

Preliminary Checks for Sealed Wheel Bearing Noise and Looseness

Noise attributed to wheel bearings may be caused by many factors. These include tire tread design, incorrect tire pressures, and uneven tread wear patterns. In addition, loose or damaged wheels, and tires that are out of round or out of balance can cause vibration and road noise that may be blamed on wheel bearings. If a road test indicates that a wheel bearing may be noisy, perform the following checks:

1. Using an accurate tire gauge, check to see that the tires are inflated to the manufacturer's rec-

ommended pressures. Adjust the pressures as necessary.
2. Using a torque wrench, check to see that the wheel lug nuts are tightened to specifications.
3. Check the tire treads for abnormal wear patterns. Rotate or replace tires as necessary.
4. Raise and support each wheel and check for out-of-round tires, bent wheels, and any imbalance condition. Listen for noise and feel for roughness while turning each wheel.

> Damaged wheel bearings make a noise that will get louder as the damage gets more severe. It is never wise to run a vehicle that has a wheel bearing noise. Damaged bearings can destroy themselves, and continued running will damage the axle and hub. This can increase the cost of the repair and is a safety risk.

DIAGNOSIS OF WHEEL BEARING NOISE	If noise or roughness is suspected after performing the preliminary checks, the following diagnostic procedure will enable you to verify your findings.

Note: This procedure should *not* be used on any vehicle equipped with a limited-slip differential.

Driving Wheels

1. Raise the wheel with the suspected defective bearing and support the car so the wheel remains about 3 in. (75 mm) off the floor.

   Note: Be sure the car is supported in accordance with the manufacturer's specifications.

2. Apply the parking brake if it locks the nondriving wheels. Block the three wheels remaining on the floor so the car cannot roll.

3. Start the engine. Place the transmission selector in DRIVE or HIGH and allow the engine to drive the wheel that is raised from the floor.

   Note: If the car is equipped with an automatic transmission, accelerate slowly to allow the transmission to upshift. NEVER EXCEED AN INDICATED SPEED OF 30 MPH. Since one wheel is on the floor, the differential will drive the free wheel at double the speed indicated on the speedometer.

4. Listen for noise or roughness that indicates a defective bearing.

   Note: It may be helpful to check both driving wheels in the same manner so the difference in noise levels can be determined.

Nondriving Wheels

1. Raise the wheel with the suspected defective bearing and support the car so the wheel remains about 3 in. (75 mm) off the floor.

   Note: Be sure the car is supported in accordance with the manufacturer's specifications.

2. Apply the parking brake if it locks the driving wheels. Block the three wheels remaining on the floor so the car cannot roll.

3. Using a wheel spinner similar to the one shown in Figure 16.128, spin the wheel.

4. Listen for noise or roughness that indicates a defective bearing.

   Note: It may be helpful to check both nondriving wheels in the same manner so the difference in noise levels can be determined.

Figure 16.128 A typical wheel spinner (courtesy of Hunter Engineering Company, Bridgeton, MO).

DIAGNOSIS OF SEALED WHEEL BEARING LOOSENESS

Even though a sealed wheel bearing may not be noisy, it must be replaced if it is too loose. Most manufacturers provide a specification for maximum *lateral* (in-and-out) movement. Although this specification varies on different cars, any movement over 0.005 in. (0.1270 mm) can be considered excessive. Movement in the bearing assembly can be accurately measured by means of a *dial indicator* similar to the one shown in Figure 16.129. A dial indicator is an instrument that measures in small increments, or additions. Most dial indicators measure increments of one-thousandth of 1 inch (0.001 in.). The movement is indicated by a pointer that moves on a dial face. Various means of anchoring the dial indicator are possible so the instrument can be positioned where desired.

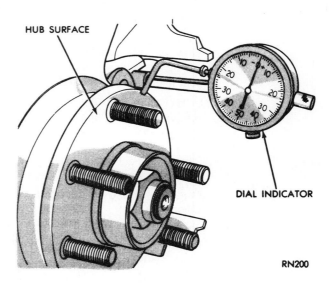

HUB SURFACE

DIAL INDICATOR

RN200

Figure 16.129 A typical dial indicator mounted to measure movement in a hub. Notice that the dial has been set to zero (courtesy of Chrysler Corporation).

The following steps outline procedures for measuring looseness in sealed wheel bearings.

Drum Brakes
1. Raise and support the car.
2. Remove the wheel.
3. Remove the drum.
4. Mount a dial indicator so the plunger contacts the face of the bearing hub flange (see Figure 16.130).
5. Zero the dial indicator.
6. Grasp the flange and note the movement indicated by the dial indicator while pushing and pulling the flange in and out.
7. Compare the indicated movement with the manufacturer's specification. Movement in excess of the specification indicates that the bearing assembly must be replaced.

Disc Brakes
1. Raise and support the car.
2. Remove the wheel.
3. Secure the rotor to the hub flange with two or three lug nuts.
4. Push the caliper piston back into the caliper so the brake shoes do not contact the rotor (refer to Figures 16.104, 16.105, and 16.111 for suggested methods).
5. Mount a dial indicator so the plunger contacts the hub flange (see Figure 16.131).
6. Zero the dial indicator.
7. Grasp the rotor and note the movement indicated by the dial indicator while pushing and pulling the rotor in and out.
8. Compare the indicated movement with the manufacturer's specification. Movement in excess of the specification indicates that the bearing assembly must be replaced.

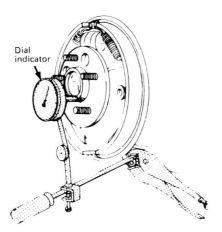

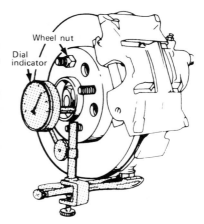

Figure 16.130 Indicator check of bearing movement. A dial indicator mounted to measure sealed wheel bearing looseness on a car with drum brakes. Notice that a screwdriver and a pair of gripping pliers are used to mount the dial indicator (courtesy of buick Motor Division, General Motors Corporation).

Figure 16.131 Indicator check of disc brake movement. A dial indicator mounted to measure sealed wheel bearing looseness on a car with disc brakes. Notice that the dial indicator is mounted on a pair of gripping pliers (courtesy of Buick Motor Division, General Motors Corporation).

Job 16N

DIAGNOSE SEALED WHEEL BEARING NOISE AND LOOSENESS

SATISFACTORY PERFORMANCE
A satisfactory performance on this job requires that you do the following:

1. Perform diagnostic checks for noise and looseness of the sealed wheel bearings on the car assigned.
2. Following the steps in the "Performance Outline" and the manufacturer's procedure and specifications, complete the job within 200% the manufacturer's suggested time.
3. Fill in the blanks under "Information."

PERFORMANCE OUTLINE

1. Check the tire pressure and wheel lug nut torque.
2. Check for abnormal tire tread wear patterns.
3. Check for out-of-round tires and bent wheels.
4. Check for bearing noise and roughness.
5. Check for lateral play in the bearing assemblies.

INFORMATION

Vehicle identification _____

Reference used _____ Page(s) _____

Tire pressure specifications: Front _____   Rear _____

Were tire pressures adjusted to specifications?   _____ Yes _____ No

Wheel lug nut torque specification _____

Were lug nuts tightened to the specification?   _____ Yes _____ No

Tire tread wear patterns:

	NORMAL	ABNORMAL
Left front	_____	_____
Right front	_____	_____
Left rear	_____	_____
Right rear	_____	_____

Identification of abnormal wear patterns _____
_____

Tire condition:

	ROUND	OUT OF ROUND
Left front	_____	_____
Right front	_____	_____
Left rear	_____	_____
Right rear	_____	_____

Wheel condition:

	OK	BENT
Left front	_____	_____
Right front	_____	_____
Left rear	_____	_____
Right rear	_____	_____

Bearing noise or roughness:

	OK	NOISY OR ROUGH
Left front	_____	_____
Right front	_____	_____
Left rear	_____	_____
Right rear	_____	_____

Was a wheel spinner used?   _____ Yes _____ No

Job 160

REPLACE A SEALED WHEEL BEARING ASSEMBLY

SATISFACTORY PERFORMANCE
A satisfactory performance on this job requires that you do the following:

1. Replace the designated wheel bearing on the car assigned.
2. Following the steps in the "Performance Outline" and the manufacturer's procedure and specifications, complete the job within 200% of the manufacturer's suggested time.
3. Fill in the blanks under "Information."

PERFORMANCE OUTLINE

1. Loosen the lug nuts.
2. Raise and support the car.
3. Remove the wheel and other parts necessary to gain access to the bearing assembly.
4. Remove the wheel bearing assembly.
5. Clean the bearing mounting surfaces.
6. Install the replacement bearing.
7. Install the parts removed to gain access to the bearing.
8. Install the wheel.
9. Lower the car to the floor.
10. Tighten the lug nuts to the manufacturer's torque specification.

INFORMATION

Vehicle identification _____
Location of bearing replaced:
_____ LF _____ LR _____ RF _____ RR
Reference used _____ Page(s) _____
Torque specification for bearing mounting bolts or nuts _____

_____

Torque specification for wheel lug nuts_____

VOCABULARY

Use the listed words in the blanks beside the sentences to complete the definitions. Either write out the words or place the letters in the blanks.

A. Tread
B. Aspect ratio
C. Plies
D. Radial
E. kPa
F. Overinflation
G. Valve stem
H. Lug nut
I. Torque wrench
J. Tread wear indicator
K. Wheel tramp
L. Wheel weight
M. Static balance
N. Dynamic balance
O. Shimmy
P. Camber
Q. Caster
R. Toe
S. Adjusting nut
T. Cone
U. Grease retainer
V. Nut lock
W. Radial load
X. Thrust load
Y. Dial indicator

_____ 1. Metric term for pressure
_____ 2. Tool used to check for loose parts
_____ 3. Layers of cords
_____ 4. Tool used to measure force placed on a nut or bolt
_____ 5. Clipped to a rim to correct imbalance
_____ 6. Part of a tire that makes contact with the road
_____ 7. Amount of tilt inward or outward from a vertical position of the tire at the top
_____ 8. Part that holds the tire rim on the hub
_____ 9. Acts at right angles to the spindle or axis
_____ 10. Place where air is added or removed from a tire
_____ 11. Tire with cords that run from bead to bead at a 90° angle to the center
_____ 12. Part that keeps the axle nut from loosening
_____ 13. Tire height-to-width ratio
_____ 14. Can be seen when the tire tread gets thin
_____ 15. A condition where there is too much air in a tire
_____ 16. Balance of a tire when in motion
_____ 17. A condition that shows when the dynamic balance of a tire is incorrect

_____ 18. Front and rear tilt of the ball joint axis from a vertical position

_____ 19. A condition that shows up when the static balance of a tire is incorrect

_____ 20. The roller bearings and cage plus the inner part of a tapered roller bearing

_____ 21. Balance of a tire when stationary

_____ 22. A part that prevents grease from leaking out of the hub

_____ 23. A force that acts parallel to the axis of the wheel

_____ 24. Distance between the front inside edge of the tires and the rear inside edge

_____ 25. Holds the parts of the hub assembly on the spindle

REVIEW QUESTIONS

The following questions will help you determine if you have accomplished the tasks stated at the beginning of this chapter. If you do not know many of the answers, go back and review the material before proceeding to the next chapter.

Lesson 16–1

1. How much of a vehicle tire is effective for power development and steering?
2. What are two basic functions of an automotive tire?
3. What is the name for the layers of tire cords?
4. What is the name of the process where heat and pressure mold the tire?
5. Name three types of tires.
6. What materials are used for tire belts?
7. What two methods are used to indicate tire sizes?
8. What position means rim diameter in the tire size designation molded on the tire sidewall?
9. What is another name for profile ratio?
10. How is the profile ratio figured?
11. How is rim diameter figured?
12. In the tire size P195/75R14, what does the "P" and "R" stand for?
13. When DOT is molded on the tire sidewall, what does it mean?
14. What must always be molded on the tire sidewall of a radial tire?
15. What does M/S molded on a tire sidewall mean?

Lesson 16–2

16. What are three things that must be considered to inflate a tire properly?
17. List at least four problems caused by an underinflated tire.
18. List at least four problems caused by an overinflated tire.
19. What should be the temperature of a tire to get an accurate tire pressure check?
20. What happens to the tire pressure as the vehicle is driven?
21. What are some things that cause tire temperature to rise?
22. Why is the use of a valve cap important?
23. How does a tire valve work?
24. Where are general tire pressure recommendations found in a vehicle?

Lesson 16–3

25. What is the safety rule about mixing bias ply and bias belted tires on the same vehicle?
26. Where should radial tires never be used when bias ply or bias belted tires are used?
27. Can tires in different series sizes be used on the same vehicle?
28. If a tire is wider than the others, where should it be placed?

Lesson 16–4

29. Why is tire rotation necessary?
30. Give two reasons why a five-tire rotation may not be possible.
31. When considering tire rotation how can the longest possible tread life be obtained?
32. What is the most common wrench used to remove tires?
33. When using a lug wrench, how should the wheels be positioned to loosen the lugs?
34. What is the definition of *torque*?
35. What are two types of torque wrench?
36. How is torque measured?
37. What is the "cross" pattern for tightening lug nuts and in how many steps is it used?
38. What is the "star" pattern for tightening lug nuts and when is it used?
39. What is tread replacement depth?
40. What is a tread wear indicator?
41. List at least four abnormal tire wear patterns and tell what problems they indicate.

Lesson 16–5

42. What is a dropped center rim?

43. What two purposes does the safety ridge serve?
44. What are five conditions that require the rim to be replaced?
45. What is the purpose of the floating cone lug nut?
46. Where should the dropped center part of a rim be placed when using a tire machine?
47. What is considered the repairable area of a tire?
48. What is the purpose of a tire spreader?

Lesson 16–6
49. What is tire imbalance and what causes it?
50. What is static imbalance?
51. What is the primary cause of static imbalance?
52. What is the name of the condition caused by static imbalance?
53. What is the name of the machine used to correct static balance?
54. What conditions must be met for a tire to be in correct dynamic balance?
55. What is the name of the condition caused by dynamic imbalance?
56. What part is used to correct both dynamic and static balance?

Lesson 16–7
57. What two things are averaged to accomplish correct wheel alignment?
58. What is *camber*?
59. How is camber set to correct for road crown?
60. What will be the result if too much negative camber is set on the wheel?
61. How will a vehicle steer if the camber is uneven between the wheels?
62. What is *caster*?
63. Where is the tire in relation to the vehicle if the caster is set positive?
64. How can caster be set to make the vehicle steer more easily?
65. What is the result of more positive caster?
66. Should power steering vehicles have more positive or negative camber?
67. What is the result of too much caster?
68. To which side will a vehicle drift if the caster is uneven?
69. What will be the result of positive caster on one wheel and negative caster on the other?
70. What kind of caster can cause wander on a power steering vehicle?
71. What is *toe*?
72. What is a toe-in condition?

73. Where does the toe move normally when the vehicle is in motion?
74. As vehicle parts wear, what happens to the toe setting?
75. What should never be done when setting toe?
76. What will be the result of excessive toe-in or toe-out?
77. If the inside or outside edges of the tires wear, what alignment angle should be checked?
78. What misalignment problems cause cupping or dishing of the tire tread?
79. What problems other than alignment cause cupping and dishing of the tire tread?
80. What should be done before a tire is aligned?
81. Why should tire wear be monitored after the first alignment?

Lesson 16–8
82. What is the recommended mileage service interval for wheel bearing service?
83. What kind of problems does an improperly adjusted wheel bearing cause?
84. Which type of hub cannot be lubricated?
85. What holds the roller bearings in place on the cone?
86. What is the name of the part that provides the surface where roller bearings roll?
87. What is the name of the part that keeps grease from leaking out of a wheel bearing?
88. Which part allows the most accurate setting, a nut lock or castellated nut?
89. What is the name of the part that keeps the castellated nut from turning?
90. What is the purpose of a grease cup?

Lesson 16–9
91. What is a radial wheel bearing load?
92. What is a wheel bearing thrust load?
93. In a hub, what thrust load does the inner bearing handle?
94. In a hub, what thrust load does the outer bearing handle?

Lesson 16–10
95. What are some of the problems that loose or worn wheel bearings cause?
96. What is the name of the tool made to remove grease cups?
97. What tool is commonly used to remove the cotter key?
98. What are seven wheel bearing problems found on a diagnostic chart?

99. How are the sharp edges of a grease seal placed during installation?

Lesson 16–11

100. For a longer part life, what must be replaced along with the wheel bearing?
101. What bearing defect causes a hub to be replaced?
102. What method other than a puller can be used to replace a bearing cup?
103. What method is used to install a bearing cup in the hub?

Lesson 16–12

104. How can a noisy or loose sealed wheel bearing be repaired?
105. If a sealed wheel bearing is loose but not noisy, how can it be repaired?

ASE QUESTIONS

Each question or incomplete statement in this test is followed by four suggested answers or completions. In each case select the *one* that best answers the question or completes the statement.

1. Automotive tire functions are being discussed by two technicians. Technician A says they act as shock absorbers and cushion the vehicle from road shock. Technician B says they provide the vehicles frictional contact with the road. Who is right?
   a. A only   b. B only
   c. Both A and B   d. Neither A nor B

2. Two basic measurements are used to indicate tire size. Technician A says one is rim circumference. Technician B says the other is cross-sectional width. Who is right?
   a. A only   b. B only
   c. Both A and B   d. Neither A nor B

3. One of the markings on a tire is the number 78. Technician A says this number represents 78% of the width. Technician B says this number represents 78% of the height. Who is right?
   a. A only   b. B only
   c. Both A and B   d. Neither A nor B

4. The markings on a tire read as follows: P195/75 R14. Technician A says the R means rim. Technician B says the R means radial. Who is right?
   a. A only   b. B only
   c. Both A and B   d. Neither A nor B

5. A tire is wearing more rapidly in the center. Technician A says the toe alignment is incorrect. Technician B says the camber is incorrect. Who is right?
   a. A only   b. B only
   c. Both A and B   d. Neither A nor B

6. Two radial tires are mixed with two bias belted tires on the same vehicle. Technician A says the bias belted tires or the radials should be exchanged so all the same type tires are on all four wheels. Technician B says the radial tires should be on the front and the bias ply on the rear. Who is right?
   a. A only   b. B only
   c. Both A and B   d. Neither A nor B

7. Tires in different sizes are to be used on a vehicle. Technician A says they may be used only in pairs on common axles. Technician B says the tires on the front and those on the rear should be no more than one size apart. Who is right?
   a. A only   b. B only
   c. Both A and B   d. Neither A nor B

8. Tire rotation is to be performed on a vehicle that has a space saver spare. Technician A says the right rear tire should be placed on the left front. Technician B says the left rear should be placed on the left front. Who is right?
   a. A only   b. B only
   c. Both A and B   d. Neither A nor B

9. Tires are being installed on a vehicle with an air wrench. Technician A says a torque wrench should be used to install the tires and an air wrench can be used to remove them. Technician B says the air wrench can be used to both install and remove the tires. Who is right?
   a. A only   b. B only
   c. Both A and B   d. Neither A nor B

10. The lug nuts are being tightened on a five-hole wheel. Technician A says a "star" pattern sequence should be used in three steps. Technician B says a "cross" pattern should be used in three steps. Who is right?
    a. A only   b. B only
    c. Both A and B   d. Neither A nor B

11. A wheel and tire are mounted on a tire machine. Technician A says the dropped center should be toward the bottom of the machine. Technician B says the dropped center should be toward the top of the machine. Who is right?
    a. A only   b. B only
    c. Both A and B   d. Neither A nor B

12. A tire has received a puncture in the sidewall area of the tire. Technician A says it can be

repaired with a patch. Technician B says it can be repaired with a plug. Who is right?
a. A only   b. B only
c. Both A and B   d. Neither A nor B

13. A tire on a vehicle is making a wheel tramp motion (moving up and down) when the vehicle is driven on a smooth road. Technician A says the wheel is out of dynamic balance. Technician B says the wheel is out of static balance. Who is right?
a. A only   b. B only
c. Both A and B   d. Neither A nor B

14. A tire is experiencing camber wear. Technician A says too much negative camber will wear the outside edge of the tire. Technician B says too much positive camber will wear the inside edge of the tire. Who is right?
a. A only   b. B only
c. Both A and B   d. Neither A nor B

15. A tire is wearing in a saw-toothed pattern on the tread. Technician A says this is an indication of too much camber. Technician B says this is a sign of incorrect toe adjustment. Who is right?
a. A only   b. B only
c. Both A and B   d. Neither A nor B

16. The wheel bearings on a vehicle are not adjusted properly and are too loose. Technician A says this can cause symptoms just like a suspension problem. Technician B says this can cause symptoms just like brake problems. Who is right?

a. A only   b. B only
c. Both A and B   d. Neither A nor B

17. Two technicians are discussing the type of forces placed on wheel bearings when the vehicle is moving. Technician A says they have radial loads placed on them. Technician B says they have thrust loads placed on them. Who is right?
a. A only   b. B only
c. Both A and B   d. Neither A nor B

18. A tapered roller wheel bearing is being adjusted. Technician A says the bearing should be left with a preload. Technician B says the bearing should be finger tight with no preload. Who is right?
a. A only   b. B only
c. Both A and B   d. Neither A nor B

19. A bearing cup is being inspected. It is found to move slightly in the hub. Technician A says this is normal. Technician B says it should be tight in the hub and made with a press or interference fit. Who is right?
a. A only   b. B only
c. Both A and B   d. Neither A nor B

20. A sealed wheel bearing is inspected and rotated. It is noisy and loose. Technician A says the bearing can be replaced. Technician B says the hub and bearing must be replaced. Who is right?
a. A only   b. B only
c. Both A and B   d. Neither A nor B

17

Standard, Power, Antilock and Parking Brake System Maintenance

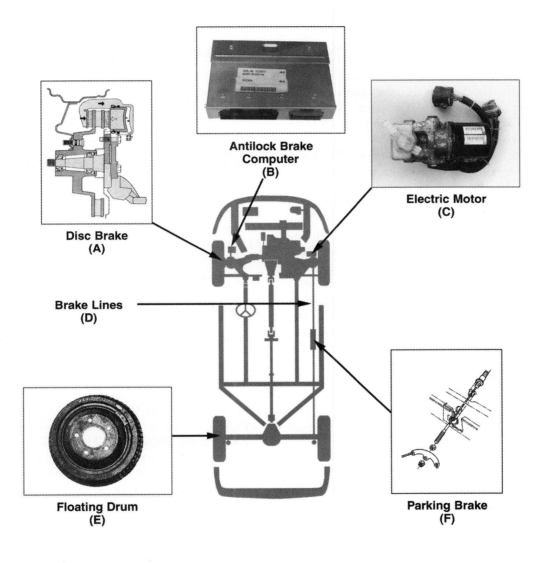

Disc Brake
(A)

Antilock Brake
Computer
(B)

Electric Motor
(C)

Brake Lines
(D)

Floating Drum
(E)

Parking Brake
(F)

We trust our life to our brakes. The brake system is probably the most important system in the automobile. It would be hard to imagine what driving would be like without dependable brakes. A failure in the brake system can cause property damage, serious injury, and even death. The front brakes do more to stop the vehicle than the rear brakes. The weight of the car moves forward when the brakes are applied. This adds force to the front wheels and causes the front brakes to work harder. Disc brakes are found on the front of the vehicle for cooler and better stopping power. Drum brakes are placed on the rear. Most parking brakes work with the drum brakes at the rear of the vehicle. The recent trend is all-wheel disc brakes along with an antilocking system. The parking brake is still made into the system, usually on the rear brakes.

The brake system works under extreme heat, which becomes more of a problem in the summer. In the winter the system is expected not to freeze. The brake system is expected to work well through mud, dust, water, heat, and cold. Although there are many parts to a brake system it is very reliable when maintained (see Figure 17). Now the technician must learn how to service all the old types of brake systems and the new antilock brake systems as well. This requires constant study, but the customer expects the brakes to work every time the pedal is depressed. This is a large responsibility, so study the lessons in this chapter well.

TASKS

The following are twelve tasks to master before leaving this chapter:

Task 17-1.   Study the parts of a standard brake system.

Task 17-2.   Learn the correct procedures used to service a standard brake system.

Task 17-3.   Learn how to troubleshoot a standard brake system.

Task 17-4.   Study the parts of a power brake system.

Task 17-5.   Learn the correct procedures used to service a power brake system.

Task 17-6.   Learn how to troubleshoot a power brake system.

Task 17-7.   Learn what parts make up an antilock brake system.

Task 17-8.   Study the correct service procedures to keep an antilock brake system working correctly.

Task 17-9.   Learn how to troubleshoot an antilock brake system.

Task 17-10.   Study the parts of a parking brake system.

Task 17-11.   Learn how to service a parking brake system.

Task 17-12.   Study how to troubleshoot a parking brake system.

LESSON 17–1   Brake System Maintenance

The hydraulic brake system is a closed system and should not let brake fluid leak to the ground. The fluid in the master cylinder reservoir becomes lower as the disc brake pads wear. The piston moves out to compensate for the wear and the brake fluid runs into the area behind the caliper piston. Fluid leaks, unusual brake pedal feel, brake lights on the dash lighting, or unusual noises should be investigated. These are some of the many trouble signs.

Brake Inspection

Start by removing the cover to the brake master cylinder reservoir. The fluid level should be about 1/4 in. from the top (see Figure 17.1). Check the fluid quality. Clean brake fluid is amber in color.

Look for fluid leaks at the master cylinder, and along the entire length of the brake system lines from front to rear. Inspect the inside of each tire for fluid marks. Check all flex lines at the front or rear wheels for cracks or cuts.

Most vehicles in production today use DOT 3 brake fluid. DOT 4 brake fluid is produced but not widely recommended. DOT 5 brake fluid has a silicone base and is used in some special applications. Check the manufacturer's recommendations and always be sure what type fluid is being used before adding any type brake fluid. Use only recommended fluids.

Look at all hydraulic pressure lines. They are made out of steel lines and rubber hose. These

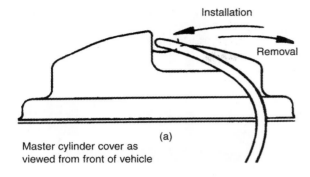

Installation

Removal

(a)

Master cylinder cover as
viewed from front of vehicle

$\frac{1"}{4}$

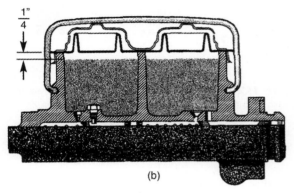

(b)

Figure 17.1 Checking master cylinder. A master cylinder should have fluid up to 1/4 in. from the top in both the front and rear reservoir. The fluid should not appear dirty or contain other contaminates (courtesy of Chevrolet Motor Division, General Motors Corporation).

can deteriorate with age by rust and heat cracking. Look for dents, as these can restrict fluid flow.

Push the brake pedal down hard. It should move about 2 in. and feel solid. A spongy pedal means that air is in the system. A pedal that moves almost to the floor and becomes solid indicates either a front or rear hydraulic failure. The system is divided into two parts, with two wheels on each system. When one side fails, the other can still stop the vehicle. Immediate repair is indicated because the stopping distance of the vehicle is greatly increased and if the remaining side fails, the vehicle will not have brakes.

Look to see if the brake lights come "on" in the rear of the vehicle when the pedal is depressed. Check to see that both sides light. Usually it is a bulb failure if only one side lights. No brake light on either side could be a problem with the "hot" wire, both bulbs, or the ground circuit.

Turn the ignition switch to the ON position. Look on the instrument panel to see if the brake warning light is lit. No light means a burned-out bulb or circuit failure. This light comes "on" when

the parking brake has been set or there is a failure in one side of the hydraulic brake system.

Checking a Power Assist. Before starting the engine, a vehicle power assist can be tested. Follow these steps:

1. Depress the brake pedal several times before starting the engine.
2. Depress and hold the brake pedal down.
3. Start the engine.
4. The brake pedal should immediately move away from your foot as the power assist takes over. No movement means the power assist is not working and the system should be checked. Check the vacuum source first. If that is normal, look for problems in the power assist such as a leaking diaphragm.

Vehicle Brake Test Drive. Look for pulling to the right or left when the brakes are applied. Listen for single wheel lockup. This wheel will slide while the others roll. If there are any unusual noises when the brakes are applied, investigate further when back at the shop. Any pedal that does not feel normal or any brake reaction that is slow when the pedal is applied should be checked out later.

We have gone over some of the more common brake problems. Space will not permit going into detail on each system in use. Consult the manufacturer's repair manuals for other conditions to check.

Common Disc Brake Conditions

Condition 1. No braking or excessive pedal travel. *Look for:* A system hydraulic failure.

Condition 2. Heavy pedal effort needed to stop. *Look for:* Contaminated or worn out pads. Frozen caliper pistons.

Condition 3. Pedal vibrates or moves when applied and held. *Look for:* Warped rotors or bad wheel bearings.

Condition 4. The vehicle drives to the right or left when the brakes are applied. *Look for:* Improper alignment, uneven tire pressure, wrong diameter tires on the front or rear, and frozen hydraulic parts on one side.

Condition 5. Leaks at cylinders or calipers. *Look for:* Worn-out caliper seals, scored caliper bore, or damaged bleeder screw.

Condition 6. Brakes make noises such as chatter, scraping, rattle, or squeal. *Look for:* Worn out friction materials, lack of lubrication, or damaged parts at individual wheels.

Condition 7. Brakes produce too much heat or fail to let go. *Look for:* Frozen wheel cylinders, parking brake adjustment too tight, weak return springs.

LESSON 17–2   Brake Systems

Because of the importance of the brake system, routine maintenance is a necessity. The importance of your work can be measured only in terms of safety.

Different types of brake systems are used on different cars. This lesson will acquaint you with some of those systems. It will provide you with the means to gain the knowledge and to develop the diagnostic and repair skills necessary to perform the routine services required.

Every car has two brake systems. One system is used to slow or stop a car when it is moving. This system is called the *service brake system.* The other system is used to hold a stopped car in place. This system, which is not intended to stop a moving car, is called the *parking brake system.*

> The service brake is a dual system. If one side fails, the other side should be enough to stop the vehicle. The stopping distance will be a lot longer and the pedal will move down more than normal before the brakes are applied. When this happens the vehicle should be immediately brought in for repair. Never recommend running a vehicle in this condition except to get it to the repair shop. Failure of the front brakes is more critical than the rear. A higher percentage of the stopping power is in the front.

The Service Brake System

The service brakes are applied by pushing down on the service brake pedal. This action causes brake shoes at all four wheels to be forced against *rotors* or *drums* behind the wheels. The contact of the shoes against the rotors or drums creates friction, which stops the wheels from turning.

The force a driver applies to the brake pedal is carried to each wheel by a *hydraulic system,* as shown in Figure 17.2. A hydraulic system is one that transmits pressure by means of a fluid.

Disc Brakes.   In a disc brake, two brake pads are forced against opposite sides of a rotor. The action

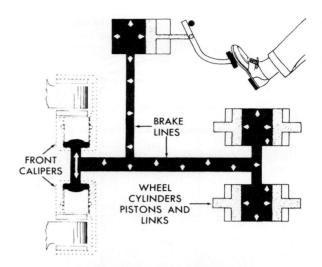

Figure 17.2   Brake hydraulic system. A hydraulic system transmits the driver's effort to the brakes at the wheels (courtesy of Chevrolet Motor Division, General Motors Corporation).

of a disc brake is shown in Figure 17.3. A rotor is a disc attached to the inside of a wheel that rotates with it. The brake pads squeeze the rotor between them. The friction between the pads and the rotor causes the rotor to slow down and stop turning. Because the wheel is bolted to the rotor, the wheel stops turning.

Drum Brakes.   In a drum brake, the brake shoes are forced against the inside surface of a drum. The action of a drum brake is shown in Figure 17.4. A drum is a ring attached to the inside of a wheel that rotates with it. The friction between the brake shoes and the drum causes the drum to slow down

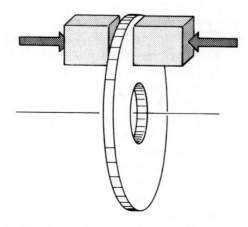

Figure 17.3   Disc brake action. Two pads move together to contact the surfaces of a rotor or disc (courtesy of Management and Marketing Institute).

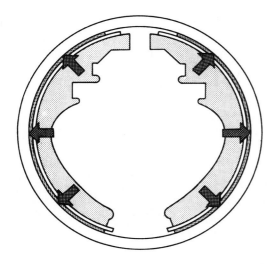

Figure 17.4 Drum brake action. Two shoes move outward to contact the inner surface of a drum (courtesy of Management and Marketing Institute).

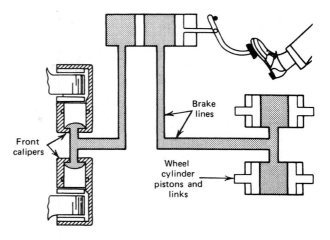

Figure 17.5 Front/rear hydraulic system. A dual hydraulic brake system. One system operates the front brakes, the other operates the rear brakes.

and stop turning. Because the wheel is bolted to the drum, the wheel stops rolling.

Combination Brake Systems. Most cars have combination brake systems. A combination brake system uses disc brakes on the front wheels and drum brakes on the rear wheels. Each type of brake has certain braking characteristics, including some advantages, that the other does not have. Combining the two types of brakes enables the manufacturer to take advantage of both types.

> More vehicles are being produced with four-wheel disc brakes. Eventually the drum brake technology will be phased out. But as long as there are vehicles with combination brakes being produced and used, it will be many years before drum brake technology is not needed. In fact, the combination systems are presently at the stage where they have enough mileage to need brake service. If the manufacturers could find better and cheaper ways to make parking brakes, the drum brake systems would have been changed for this system long ago.

Dual Hydraulic Systems. All cars in current production have dual hydraulic systems. When you worked with master cylinders, you found that they had dual reservoirs. Each reservoir stores fluid for a separate system. On some cars, a separate hydraulic system is provided for the front brakes and another for the rear brakes. This arrangement is shown in Figure 17.5. On other cars, the hydraulic systems are arranged so each system serves one front brake

and the opposite rear brake. A system of that type is shown in Figure 17.6.

Although one of the dual braking systems can stop the car if the other system fails, the stopping distance is increased. Consequently, there is an increased possibility of an accident. There are two indications that one of the systems has failed. First, the driver notices increased pedal travel and a need to apply greater effort to the pedal. Second, a warning light in the instrument panel turns on. Stopping distances increase.

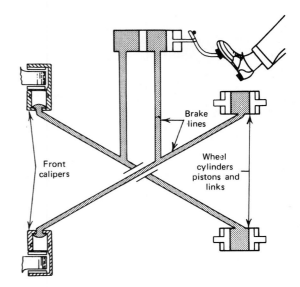

Figure 17.6 Cross-action hydraulic system. A dual hydraulic brake system. One system operates the left front brake and the right rear brake. The other system operates the right front brake and the left rear brake (courtesy of General Motors Corporation).

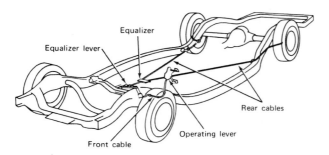

Figure 17.7 Typical parking brake system. Note that the system is entirely mechanical and uses cables and levers (courtesy of Ford Motor Company, Dearborn, MI).

The Parking Brake System

The parking brake system is entirely mechanical. The driver applies the parking brakes by pulling a lever or by stepping on a pedal. The parking brakes generally operate on the rear wheels only. They use cables pulled by levers to carry the driver-applied force to the wheels. The hydraulic system is not used. Parking brakes normally use the same brake shoes that the service brakes use on the rear wheels. A typical parking brake system is shown in Figure 17.7.

If a vehicle is driven with the parking brake applied, a large volume of heat is produced that can damage the rear shoes, lining, and drum. If driven far enough, the heat can cause a fire in the rear wheels. This can damage wheel bearings and seals as well as the brake system. Periodic checks of the brake warning light can detect a burned-out bulb. The bulb can be tested along with all the other warning system bulbs with the ignition key in the on, start, or run position. This will reduce the chance of operating the vehicle with the parking brake engaged and a burned-out bulb in the brake warning light system.

Brake Shoes and Lining

Most rotors and drums are made of cast iron, and most brake shoes are made of steel. Since the forcing of steel shoes against cast iron rotors or drums would provide poor braking and excessive wear, the shoes must be covered, or *lined*. That lining must provide the right amount of friction when pushed against cast iron.

Many compounds have been formulated for use as brake lining. Some contain asbestos. Asbestos provides just about the right amount of friction when used with cast iron rotors and drums. As-

bestos is often used for another reason. The friction of braking produces a great amount of heat. Actually, the energy of the moving car must be converted to heat energy to bring the car to a stop. Asbestos withstands very high temperatures without burning or failing.

Although asbestos may be ideal for use in brake lining, it creates a serious health hazard.

> **!** **Warning:** Breathing asbestos dust may cause asbestosis and cancer. During brake servicing, an air-purifying respirator should be worn during all procedures, starting with the removal of the wheels and including reassembly.

Two methods are used to hold the lining to the shoe. One method is to use *rivets*. The other is to use a *bonding* agent, or cement. Linings held to their shoes by each method are shown in Figure 17.8.

The brake shoes, or *pads*, used with disc brakes consist of flat metal plates with pieces of lining riveted or bonded to them. A typical pair of disc brake shoes is shown in Figure 17.9. Some shoes have retaining tabs to hold the shoes in position in the caliper. Others have holes or slots for positioning pins or bolts. In some instances, the shoes have an extra tab or spring that acts as a wear-sensing device. As shown in Figure 17.10, wear-sensing tabs touch the rotor when the lining wears to a predetermined thinness. The

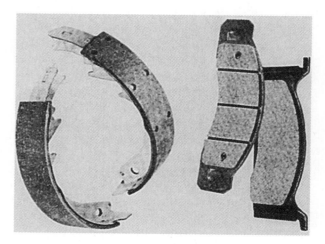

Figure 17.8 Types of brake lining. Various types of brake lining attached to brake shoes by bonding and riveting (courtesy of Brake Systems, Inc., manufacturers of Raybestos brake products).

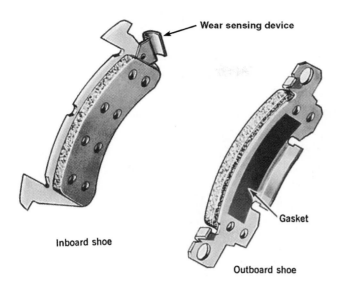

Figure 17.9 Disc brake shoes. Note that the inboard shoe has a wear-sensing device (courtesy of Oldsmobile Motor Division, General Motors Corporation).

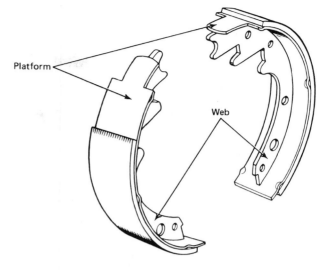

Figure 17.11 A pair of brake shoes showing the platform and the web (courtesy of Chrysler Corporation).

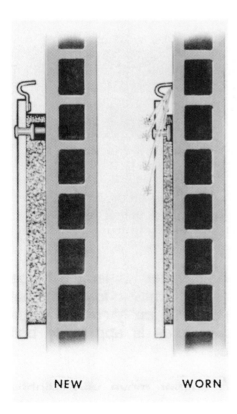

Figure 17.10 Wear sensor operation. When the lining wears to a predetermined thinness, the spring or tab contacts the rotor and causes a squeal (courtesy of Oldsmobile Motor Division, General Motors Corporation).

resulting noise warns the driver that the shoes require replacement.

> When the pads are worn down to where the wear sensor (not on every vehicle) contacts the surface of the rotor, a scratching noise will first be heard when turning corners. Cornering puts added pressure on the brake pads and allows the wear gauge to scrape. Any time a squeal or scratching sound is heard at the wheels, it is time for an inspection and pad replacement. Running the vehicle further will damage more expensive parts like the rotor.

The brake shoes used with drum brakes are usually made of two pieces of stamped steel welded together. These pieces, called the *platform* and the *web*, are shown in Figure 17.11. The web is made of heavy gauge metal and is shaped and drilled so the various springs and adjusting mechanisms can be anchored to it. The platform is formed to the desired curve, centered on the web, and welded to it. The platform provides the surface to which the lining is attached.

LESSON 17-3 Disc Brakes

The most commonly used disc brake uses brake shoes held in a hydraulically operated *caliper*, or clamp. The caliper bridges the rotor like a vise. Applying the brakes causes the caliper to squeeze the shoes together. The shoes grasp the rotor and slow or stop its motion. Figure 17.12 provides a

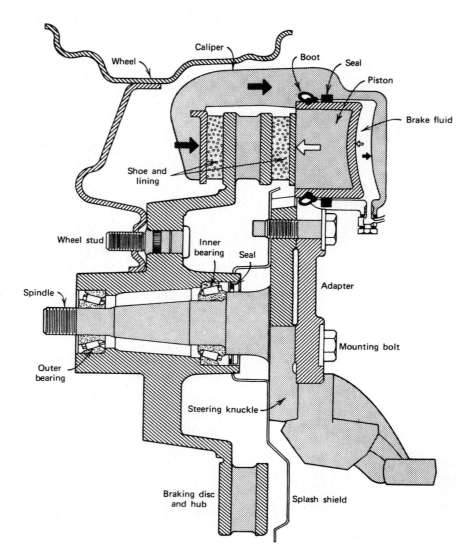

Figure 17.12 A front sectional view of a single piston disc brake assembly (courtesy of Chrysler Corporation).

sectional view of a complete disc brake assembly. Study that drawing to become familiar with the parts and their location.

Disc Brake Parts

The rotor of a disc brake is often made in one piece with the hub. On other cars, the rotor is a separate part and is held to the hub by the wheel studs. Some small, light cars use solid rotors of the type shown in Figure 17.13. Rotors used on heavy or fast cars are usually ventilated. As shown in Figure 17.14, a ventilated rotor is made with cooling fins between the friction surfaces. This design allows the rotor to act as its own cooling fan. As the rotor turns, the fins pull air in from the inner edge and discharge it at the outer edge. One advantage of disc brakes is

that a rotor can pass off the heat developed during braking much faster than a drum.

There are calipers with one, two, or four pistons. But the type with one piston is most common. The

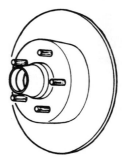

Figure 17.13 Solid rotor. Rotors of this type are found on small, light cars.

Job 17A

IDENTIFY THE PARTS OF A TYPICAL DISC BRAKE ASSEMBLY

SATISFACTORY PERFORMANCE
A satisfactory performance on this job requires that you do the following:

1. Identify the numbered parts on the drawing on page 563 by placing the number of each part in front of the correct part name listed below.
2. Correctly identify 13 of the 17 parts within 15 minutes.

PERFORMANCE SITUATION

_____	Caliper	_____	Piston seal
_____	Spindle	_____	Wheel stud
_____	Steering knuckle	_____	Pads and lining
_____	Rotor-and-hub assembly	_____	Adapter or mount
_____	Wheel	_____	Outer bearing
_____	Inner bearing	_____	Guide plate
_____	Backing plate	_____	Splash shield
_____	Mounting bolt	_____	Grease retainer
_____	Brake fluid	_____	Piston
_____	Dust boot	_____	Reaction arm

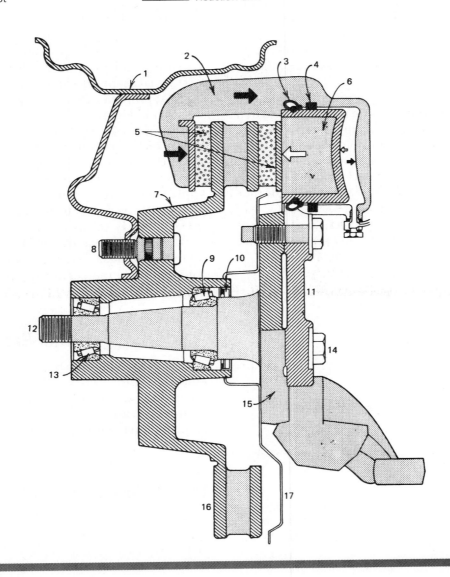

Figure 17.14 Ventilated rotor. Rotors of this type are used on heavy, fast cars (courtesy of Chevrolet Motor Division, General Motors Corporation).

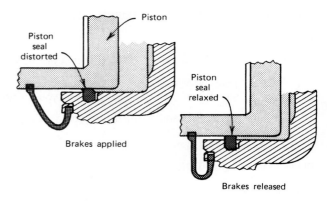

Figure 17.16 The action of the piston seal in retracting the piston. The distance the piston actually moves is exaggerated in this drawing for emphasis (courtesy of Ford Motor Company, Dearborn, MI).

operation of a single piston caliper is shown in Figure 17.15. When the brake pedal is depressed, hydraulic pressure acts equally against the bottom of the piston and the bottom of the cylinder. The pressure applied to the piston pushes the piston outward and forces the inboard pad against the inner surface of the rotor. The pressure applied to the bottom of the cylinder causes the caliper to slide inward. This movement forces the outboard pad against the outer surface of the rotor. Thus equal force is applied to both sides of the rotor.

The piston and caliper move very slightly. When the brakes are released, the caliper relaxes, but the pads do not move away from the rotor. There are no springs present to pull the pads away from the rotor or to push the piston back into the cylinder. Even so, the pads do not drag on the rotor. If they did, they would quickly wear out.

Two factors act to establish a slight but sufficient clearance between the pads and the rotor. One

is the slight amount of rotor *runout*, or wobble. It pushes the pads away from the rotor surfaces. The other is the action of the *piston seal* fitted into the cylinder wall. The outward movement of the piston during brake application distorts the seal. When the brakes are released, the seal returns to its original shape and thus returns the piston to its original position. This function of the piston seal is shown in Figure 17.16.

Both the construction of the caliper and the action of the piston seal automatically compensate for lining wear. As the linings wear, the piston moves farther out in its cylinder bore on brake applications. The piston slips through the seal far enough to compensate for the wear. When the brake pedal is released, the piston returns only as far as the seal was distorted. This action makes up for lining wear, maintains the correct lining-to-rotor clearance, and eliminates the need for brake adjustment.

LESSON 17–4   Drum Brakes

Two basic types of drum brakes are in common use. One type is the *self-energizing duo-servo brake*. The other is the *non-servo brake*. With slight variations, both designs are used at the rear wheels of cars with combination brake systems, and they are used at all four wheels of older cars.

The Self-Energizing Duo-Servo Brake

Except for slight changes to enable different self-adjuster parts to be fitted, many cars use a brake of this type (see Figure 17.17). All the parts are

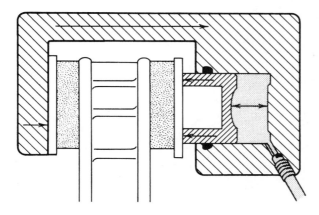

Figure 17.15 Single-caliper piston operation. Note that because the pressure is equal, the forces pushing the shoes against the rotor are equal (courtesy of Ford Motor Company, Dearborn, MI).

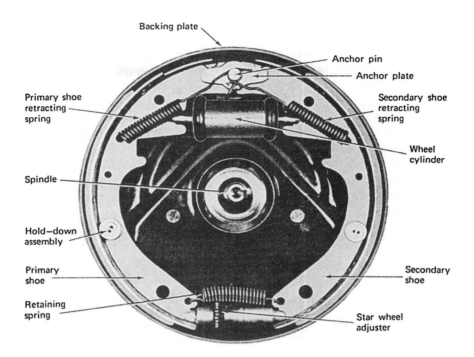

Figure 17.17 Duo-servo drum brake. A typical self-energizing duo-servo drum brake assembly. The assembly is shown without any self-adjusting mechanism (courtesy of Brake Systems, Inc., manufacturers of Raybestos brake products).

mounted on a steel *backing plate,* which is attached to the car. An *anchor pin* is located at the top of the backing plate. The anchor pin takes the full load of the braking forces and must be securely attached. Spring-loaded *hold-down assemblies* hold the shoes against the backing plate. The *retaining spring* holds the bottom of the shoes in contact with the *star wheel adjuster.*

Self-adjusting brakes, now found mostly in the rear, adjust or expand the shoes when the vehicle is backing up and the brakes applied. If a vehicle is parked where it seldom or never has to be backed up, over a period of time it may be necessary to adjust the brakes. One way to tell they need adjusting is the way the pedal travel increases before the brakes are applied. To adjust the brakes, find a place where the vehicle can be backed up for a long distance. As the vehicle is being backed, sharply apply and release the brakes. Stop when the brake pedal returns to its normal operating position. If this doesn't work, the brakes will have to be inspected for self-adjuster problems or worn-out brake shoes.

The star wheel adjuster is a threaded device that can be expanded to push the brake shoes farther apart as the lining wears. This adjustment maintains the correct drum-to-lining clearance and correct pedal height. Depending on the make and

model of the car, *self-adjusting mechanisms* of various designs are added to the brake assembly to operate the star wheel adjusters (see Figure 17.18).

The *wheel cylinder,* mounted near the top of the backing plate, is a hydraulic device (refer to Figure 17.17). It contains two pistons that move outward

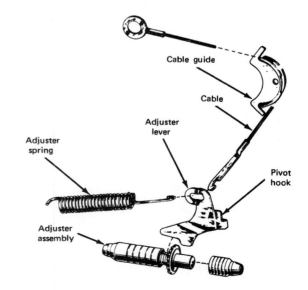

Figure 17.18 The parts of a typical self-adjusting brake mechanism. Installed in the brake assembly, these parts adjust the brakes to compensate for lining wear (courtesy of American Motors).

when the driver steps on the brake pedal. This outward movement pushes the brake shoes against the brake drum. The *retracting springs* pull the shoes away from the drum and push the pistons back in the cylinder when the driver releases the brake pedal.

In studying Figure 17.17, you probably noticed that the brake shoes are labeled *primary* and *secondary*. Both shoes are designed in the same way, but the linings attached to them are quite different. This is because the shoes are subjected to different forces in braking. Therefore, each lining must provide a different coefficient of friction with the brake drum.

Operation of the Self-Energizing Duo-Servo Brake

When brakes are applied to a wheel in motion, the friction between the rotating drum and the brake lining tries to pull the shoes around with the drum. The anchor pin prevents the shoes from rotating and causes the pulling effort to tug the shoes out into tighter contact with the drum. The positions of the anchor pin and the star wheel adjuster determine the ease with which the shoes yield to this pulling action. By carefully positioning these parts, the manufacturer can obtain high braking forces without requiring the driver to exert much effort on the brake pedal. This is the *self-energizing* feature of this design. It uses friction together with the placement of parts to increase the force holding the shoes against the drum.

The motion of the rotating drum jams the secondary shoe against the anchor pin. The same motion of the drum pulls the primary shoe away from

the anchor pin and forces it against the star wheel adjuster. The star wheel adjuster passes this push along to the bottom of the secondary shoe. This extra push adds to the force holding the secondary shoe against the drum. In this manner the primary shoe "serves" the secondary shoe. This *servo action* is shown in Figure 17.19.

When a car is moving backward, the drum rotation is reversed. The function of the shoes is also reversed. The secondary shoe is pulled away from the anchor pin and is forced against the star wheel adjuster. The push is then passed along to the primary shoe. This action adds to the force holding the primary shoe against the drum.

As you can see, a brake of this type provides servo action regardless of the direction of wheel rotation. This means that the brake is as effective in stopping a vehicle moving backward as it is in stopping one moving forward. Since servo action is provided in both directions, the brake is termed *duo-servo*.

The Non-Servo Brake

This type of drum brake is used at the rear wheels of many small cars. Although there are many variations of this brake, they are all alike in that they do not have any type of movable link between the shoes. The anchor pin over the wheel cylinder is replaced by an *anchor block* or *anchor plate* located between the shoes opposite the wheel cylinder. Two different non-servo brakes are shown in Figures 17.20 and 17.21.

The parts in a non-servo brake are similar to the parts in the duo-servo brake. The shoes used in a non-servo brake are usually referred to as "forward" or "leading" shoes and "reverse" or "trailing"

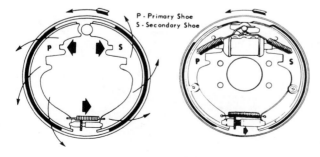

Figure 17.19 Servo action when brakes are applied to a drum moving counterclockwise. Note that the primary shoe is pulled away from the anchor pin and that the secondary shoe is pushed against the anchor pin. Because of this servo action, both shoes are energized.

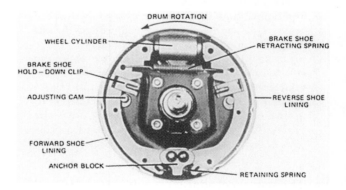

Figure 17.20 A basic non-servo drum brake assembly (courtesy of Brake Systems, Inc., manufacturers of Raybestos brake products).

Job 17B

IDENTIFY THE PARTS OF A DUO-SERVO BRAKE

SATISFACTORY PERFORMANCE
A satisfactory performance on this job requires that you do the following:

1. Identify the numbered parts on the drawing by placing the number of each part in front of the correct part name listed below.
2. Correctly identify all the parts within 15 minutes.

PERFORMANCE SITUATION

____ Backing plate
____ Secondary shoe retracting spring
____ Secondary shoe
____ Star wheel adjuster
____ Wheel cylinder
____ Cam plate
____ Primary shoe
____ Primary shoe retracting spring
____ Anchor pin
____ Retaining spring
____ Hold-down assembly
____ Anchor plate

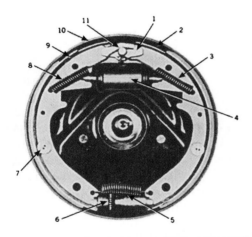

Job 17C

IDENTIFY THE FUNCTION OF PARTS IN A DUO-SERVO BRAKE

SATISFACTORY PERFORMANCE
A satisfactory performance on this job requires that you do the following:

1. Identify the function of the following listed brake parts by placing the number of each part in front of the term that best describes its function.
2. Correctly identify the function of all the parts within 15 minutes.

PERFORMANCE SITUATION

1. Holddown assembly
2. Brake shoe
3. Retracting spring
4. Star wheel adjuster
5. Anchor pin
6. Brake lining
7. Retaining spring
8. Wheel cylinder

____ Provides a means of expanding the assembled brake shoes
____ Holds the shoes together at the star wheel adjuster
____ Provides the proper coefficient of friction with the drum
____ Pulls the shoes away from the drum when the brakes are released
____ Keeps the shoes from turning with the brake drum
____ Holds the shoes flat against the backing plate
____ Provides a mounting for the brake lining
____ Holds the wheel cylinder against the anchor pin
____ Pushes the brake shoes into contact with the drum

shoes. This change in terminology is because of the operation of the brake. Since the anchor block is secured to the backing plate, one shoe cannot push or "serve" the other shoe. Therefore, no servo action is obtained. During a stop while the car is moving forward, the forward shoe is energized, but the reverse shoe is deenergized and provides little braking effort. When stopping while the car is moving in reverse, the reverse shoe is energized and the forward shoe is deenergized. This action is shown in Figure 17.22.

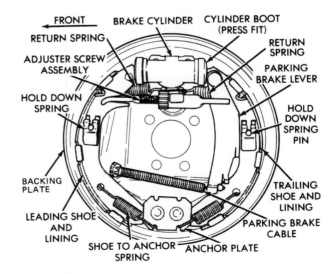

Figure 17.21 A non-servo drum brake design used at the rear wheels of a front wheel drive car (courtesy of Chrysler Corporation).

Job 17D

IDENTIFY THE PARTS OF A NON-SERVO BRAKE

SATISFACTORY PERFORMANCE
A satisfactory performance on this job requires that you do the following:

1. Identify the numbered parts on the drawing by placing the number for each part in front of the correct part name listed below.
2. Correctly identify all the parts within 15 minutes.

PERFORMANCE SITUATION

____ Backing plate
____ Retracting spring
____ Reverse shoe
____ Retaining spring
____ Hold-down assembly
____ Forward shoe
____ Star wheel adjuster
____ Wheel cylinder
____ Adjusting cam
____ Anchor block

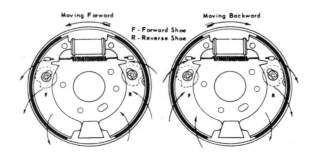

Figure 17.22 Non-servo brake action. Note that the forward shoe is energized when the brakes are applied to a forward-moving drum. When the brakes are applied while the drum is moving in the reverse direction, the reverse shoe is energized.

LESSON 17–5 Brake Lining

Each time the brakes are applied on a moving car, a slight amount of brake lining is worn away. Depending on the type of use to which the car is subjected and the skills of the driver, brake lining life averages from 20,000 to 40,000 miles (32,000 to 64,000 km). The inspection of brake lining is an important part of routine maintenance. Worn lining can decrease the effectiveness of braking and may cause an accident. Worn lining is not only dangerous, but it can cause excessive rotor and drum wear, requiring the replacement of those expensive parts.

When a car has been driven over 20,000 miles (32,000 km), the brake lining should be inspected. Because the front wheels of a car do most of the braking, the front brakes are subjected to the most wear. Because of road crown, the right front brake lining usually wears faster than the lining at the left front. But because this is not always the case, always check both front brakes. Many technicians combine a brake inspection with a wheel bearing repack. By combining these jobs you can save a great amount of time.

Riveted Lining

Riveted lining should be replaced if it is worn to less than 1/32 in. (about 1 mm) over the heads of the rivets. This measurement is shown in Figure 17.23. If the lining is allowed to wear down to the rivets, the rivets can damage the rotor or drum. Because brake lining does not always wear evenly, check all the rivet holes. You will often find that the lining on disc brake shoes is worn more on the trailing edge than on the leading edge. As shown in Figure 17.24, this is caused by the higher temperatures at the trailing edge of the shoe. In drum brakes, the center section of the lining on the secondary

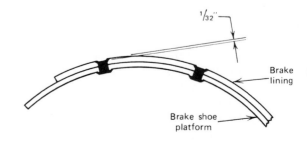

Figure 17.23 Worn riveted brake lining. Riveted brake lining worn to less than 1/32 in. over the heads of the rivets should be replaced.

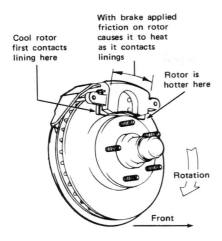

Figure 17.24 Disc brake heat pattern. The heat pattern in an operating disc brake. This can cause excessive wear at the trailing edge of the pads (courtesy of Pontiac Motor Division, General Motors Corporation).

shoe normally shows the greatest wear. This area is shown in Figure 17.25.

Bonded Lining

Because bonded lining has no rivets, it usually has a longer service life. Bonded lining should be replaced when it is worn to less than 1/16 in. (about 2 mm) in thickness. This measurement is shown in Figure 17.26. As with riveted lining, bonded lining does not always wear out evenly.

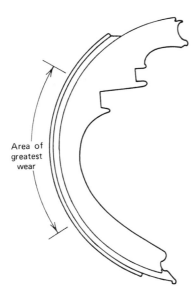

Figure 17.25 Greatest lining wear area. In a drum brake, the greatest amount of lining wear usually occurs in the center of the secondary shoe.

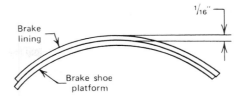

Figure 17.26 Worn bonded lining. Bonded lining worn to less than 1/16 in. in thickness should be replaced.

Worn linings are not the only ones that should be replaced. Recommend replacement of any lining that is contaminated by grease or brake fluid. In addition, the cause of the contamination must be determined and repaired. If the brake lining at one wheel requires replacement, the lining at the opposite wheel should also be replaced, even if it appears to be in good condition. Replacing lining at only one wheel almost always results in a pull to one side when the brakes are applied.

LESSON 17–6 Brake Lining Inspection

Usually, the thickness of the lining remaining on disc brake shoes can be observed when the wheel is removed. Most calipers have an *inspection port*, or hole, as shown in Figure 17.27. As shown in Figure 17.28, the lining on the inboard shoe can usually be seen through this port. The lining on the

Figure 17.27 The location of the inspection port in a caliper (courtesy of American Motors).

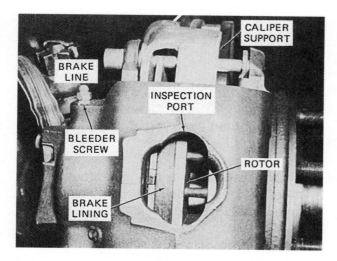

Figure 17.28 Lining inspection. The lining on the inboard shoe can easily be seen through the inspection port (courtesy of American Motors).

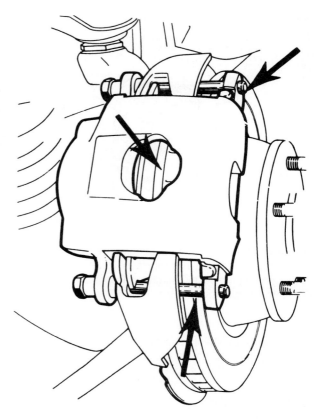

Figure 17.29 GM lining inspection. Lining inspection on a typical disc brake assembly (courtesy of Pontiac Motor Division, General Motors Corporation).

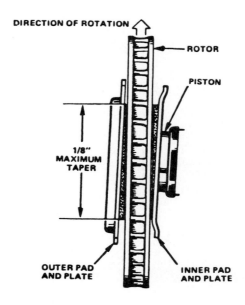

Figure 17.30 Twisted caliper. The twist of a caliper during braking can cause tapered shoe wear (courtesy of the Bendix Corporation).

outboard shoe should be checked at both the leading and trailing edges. These are the points where the greatest wear occurs. Lining inspection points are shown in Figure 17.29. Because the lining is somewhat difficult to see, always perform the inspection with the aid of a flashlight or a drop light. Inspecting the lining may expose you to asbestos dust, so be sure to wear a respirator.

When you check the leading and trailing edges of the shoes, you will often find that the lining is worn unevenly. This is called a *tapered wear pattern*. In most cases it can be considered normal (refer to Figure 17.24). Sometimes you will find that the lining is worn more at the leading edge of the inner shoe and at the trailing edge of the outer shoe, as shown in Figure 17.30. This wear pattern is caused by the design of the caliper mounting, which allows the caliper to twist slightly on brake applications. Because of the various wear patterns possible, always check the leading and trailing edges of both shoes. One edge could appear safe, but the other edge could be dangerously worn.

Not only do disc brake shoes sometimes wear unevenly, but they do not always wear at the same rate. The type and rate of wear vary considerably with different cars under different driving conditions. Brake shoes should be replaced when the lining is worn to the minimal thickness allowed by the manufacturer. This specification depends on the type of brakes fitted and whether bonded or riveted lining is used. Always check an appropriate manual for this specification. Allowing lining to wear beyond this point could cause rotor damage.

INSPECTING DISC BRAKE LINING	The following steps outline a procedure for inspecting the lining in disc brakes. Consult an appropriate manual for the specific procedure and specifications that apply to the car on which you are working.

1. Remove the front wheel covers and loosen the lug nuts on both front wheels.
2. Raise the front of the car and support it with car stands.
3. Remove one front wheel.
4. With the aid of a flashlight or a drop light, inspect the lining on the inboard and outboard shoes. Be sure to inspect both the leading and trailing edges (refer to Figure 17.30). (Be sure to wear a respirator.)
5. Install the wheel and run the lug nuts up snug.
6. Repeat steps 3 through 5 at the remaining wheel.
7. Lower the car to the floor.
8. Tighten the lug nuts to the torque specification of the manufacturer.
9. Install the wheel covers.

Job 17E

INSPECT DRUM BRAKE LINING

SATISFACTORY PERFORMANCE

A satisfactory performance on this job requires that you do the following:

1. Inspect the brake lining at the designated wheels of the car assigned.
2. Following the steps in the "Performance Outline" and the procedure and specifications of the manufacturer, complete the job within 60 minutes.
3. Fill in the blanks under "Information."

PERFORMANCE OUTLINE

1. Raise and support the car.
2. Remove the wheels.
3. Remove the drums.
4. Inspect the drums and lining.
5. Install all parts removed.
6. Lower the car to the floor.
7. Tighten the lug nuts to the manufacturer's torque specifications.

INFORMATION

Vehicle identification _____
Reference used _____ Page(s) _____
Type of lining: _____ Riveted _____ Bonded
Was the lining contaminated? _____ Yes _____ No
Minimum lining thickness found:
    Riveted lining _____ over rivet heads
    Bonded lining _____ over shoe platform

INSPECTING DRUM BRAKE LINING	Most cars have drum brakes at the rear wheels, and some older cars have drum brakes at all four wheels. To inspect the lining in those brakes, the drums must be removed. Since there are different types of brake drums, there are different drum removal procedures.
Hubbed Drums	You became familiar with hubbed drums from your work in Chapter 16 (see Figure 17.31). The procedure for removal and installation is the same that you followed when you repacked bearings.

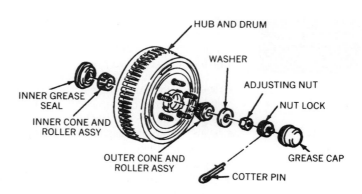

Figure 17.31   A typical hubbed drum (courtesy of Ford Motor Company, Dearborn, MI).

Floating Drums   Some cars have floating drums of the type shown in Figure 17.32. A floating drum has no hub. When used on the rear wheels of a rear wheel drive car, the drums are mounted on *flanges* at the ends of the rear axle shafts, as shown in Figure 17.33. When used on the rear wheels of some front wheel drive cars, floating drums are mounted on separate hubs (see Figure 17.34).

Most floating drums are held in place by the wheel. When some cars are built, two or three pressed steel nuts, called *Tinnerman nuts*, are often installed on the rear wheel studs after the drums are installed. These nuts are needed only to keep the drums in place during storage, shipping, and assembly. They serve no purpose after the wheels have been installed. Some car makers do not use Tinnerman nuts, but use small screws to hold the drums. If you find those nuts or screws in place after you remove a wheel, you must remove them before the drum will come off (see Figure 17.35).

Figure 17.32   Typical floating drum. Note that the drum has no hub (courtesy of Oldsmobile Motor Division, General Motors Corporation).

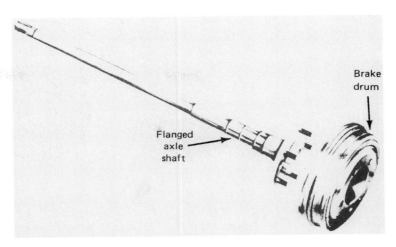

Figure 17.33 Floating drum and axle shaft. A view of a floating drum and a flanged axle shaft of the type used on rear wheel drive cars (courtesy of American Motors).

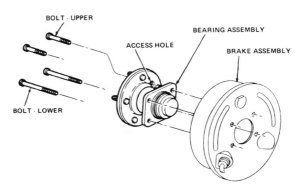

Figure 17.34 Hub and brake assembly. A hub and brake assembly used at the rear wheels of certain front wheel drive cars (courtesy of Buick Motor Division, General Motors Corporation).

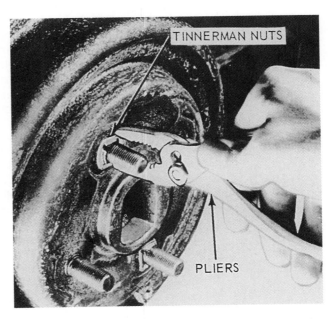

Figure 17.35 Removing Tinnerman nuts. Removing Tinnerman nuts so that a rear drum can be removed (courtesy of Ford Motor Company, Dearborn, MI).

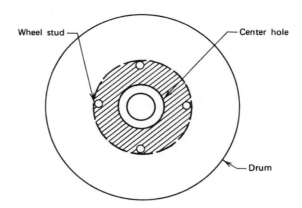

Figure 17.36 Applying heat to a drum. The shaded area represents the proper place to apply heat to a brake drum that is "frozen" to an axle flange or bearing.

You will sometimes find drums that will not come off the axle flange or spindle. Because of the damage you may cause, never force a drum off. There are three reasons why a drum may not come off:

1. The parking brake may still be applied. If the drum will not come off, check the parking brake to be sure it is released. If the brake is released, the drum should turn freely.
2. The brake shoes may have been expanded or adjusted into a badly worn or scored drum. If the drum will not come off and the parking brake is not applied, you may have to release or back off on the brake adjustment. Because of the many different adjusting mechanisms in use, that procedure is best obtained from a manual that covers the car on which you are working.
3. A floating drum may be "frozen" on the axle flange or hub. The center hole in the drum fits snugly on a round protrusion on the flange or hub. Sometimes rust forms between the drum and the flange, causing the drum to resist normal efforts to remove it. The easiest way of removing a frozen drum is to apply heat to the drum around the center hole. An acetylene torch works best. The heat expands the drum so it releases its grip on the axle flange. Figure 17.36 shows where heat should be applied to release a frozen drum.

Be sure to clean all traces of rust from the center hole of a floating drum and from the hub or axle flange before you put the drum back on. A light coating of brake lubricant or similar light grease at the center hole will keep the trouble from recurring.

The following steps outline a procedure for inspecting the lining of drum brakes using floating drums. Consult an appropriate manual for the specific procedure that may be necessary for the car on which you are working.

1. Remove the wheel covers and loosen the lug nuts on both wheels.
2. Raise the car and support it with car stands.
3. Check to see that the parking brake is released.
4. Remove the wheels.
5. Remove the Tinnerman nuts or small screws that hold the drum (refer to Figure 17.35).
6. Rotate the drums to determine if the parking brake is fully released.
7. Removed the drums. (*Note:* Be sure to wear a respirator.)
8. Inspect the inner surfaces of the drums for scoring. A badly scored drum may require machining or replacement.
9. Inspect the linings for wear (refer to Figures 17.23, 17.25, and 17.26).
10. Inspect the linings for grease or brake fluid contamination. Contaminated linings should be replaced and the cause of the contamination should be located and repaired.

11. Clean and lubricate the center hole in the drums.
12. Install the drums.
13. Install the wheels and run the lug nuts up snug.
14. Lower the car to the floor.
15. Tighten the lug nuts on both wheels to the torque specifications of the manufacturer.
16. Install the wheel covers.

Job 17F

INSPECT DISC BRAKE LINING

SATISFACTORY PERFORMANCE

A satisfactory performance on this job requires that you do the following:

1. Inspect the disc brake lining of the car assigned.
2. Following the steps in the "Performance Outline" and the procedure and specifications of the manufacturer, complete the job within 60 minutes.
3. Fill in the blanks under "information."

PERFORMANCE OUTLINE

1. Raise and support the car.
2. Remove the wheels.
3. Inspect the brake lining.
4. Install the wheels.
5. Lower the car to the floor.
6. Tighten the lug nuts to the manufacturer's specification.

INFORMATION

Vehicle identification _____
Reference used _____ Page(s) _____
Type of lining: _____ Riveted _____ Bonded
Minimum lining thickness specification _____
Minimum lining thickness found _____
Should the lining be replaced? _____ Yes _____ No
Wheel lug torque specification _____

LESSON 17-7   Parking Brakes

The parking brake system used by most manufacturers is a mechanical system that expands the rear shoes inside their drums. When the driver of a car applies the parking brake, that motion is transmitted to the rear brake shoes by cables. Levers in the system multiply the physical effort of the driver enough to force the shoes into tight contact with the drums. A typical parking brake cable and lever system is shown in Figure 17.37.

Compared with service brake systems, parking brake systems are relatively inefficient. The force with which they are applied depends on the

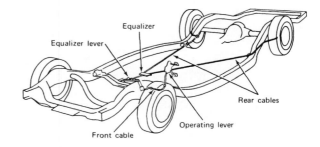

Figure 17.37   A typical parking brake cable-and-lever system (courtesy of Ford Motor Company, Dearborn, MI).

strength of the driver. Always remember this fact when diagnosing problems that involve slipping parking brakes. A parking brake system in good operating condition may fail to hold a parked car if the brakes are improperly applied. The service brakes should be applied before the parking brakes are applied. This action allows the more efficient hydraulic system to force the shoes into contact with the drums. The less efficient mechanical system, then, merely holds them in place.

Parking Brake Operation

Most parking brake systems use three levers to multiply the physical effort of the driver. The first lever is the operating lever (refer to Figure 17.37). When the operating lever is moved, the driver's effort is multiplied and used to pull the front cable. The front cable, in turn, pulls the equalizer lever.

The equalizer lever multiplies the effort of the operating lever and pulls the rear cables. This pulling effort passes through an equalizer, which ensures equal pull on both rear cables. The equalizer functions by allowing the rear brake cables to slip slightly so as to balance out small differences in cable length or adjustment. The rear cables, in turn, pull the *parking brake levers*.

On most cars, the parking brake levers are attached to the secondary or reverse shoes in the rear drum brakes. A parking brake lever and its related

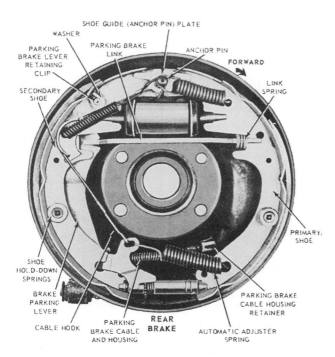

SHOE GUIDE (ANCHOR PIN) PLATE
WASHER
PARKING BRAKE LEVER RETAINING CLIP
PARKING BRAKE LINK
ANCHOR PIN
FORWARD
SECONDARY SHOE
LINK SPRING
SHOE HOLD-DOWN SPRINGS
BRAKE PARKING LEVER
CABLE HOOK
PARKING BRAKE CABLE AND HOUSING
REAR BRAKE
PARKING BRAKE CABLE HOUSING RETAINER
AUTOMATIC ADJUSTER SPRING
PRIMARY SHOE

Figure 17.38   A rear drum brake assembly showing the parking brake lever, link, and spring (courtesy of Ford Motor Company, Dearborn, MI).

parts are shown in Figure 17.38. When the parking brake lever is pulled forward, it forces the link against the link spring, compressing the spring. The link continues to move, forcing the primary or forward shoe against the brake drum. When the primary or forward shoe contacts the drum, the motion of the link is stopped. The parking brake lever then pivots on the end of the link, and the top of the lever forces the secondary or reverse shoe against the drum. The action of the parking brake lever again multiplies the driver's effort.

Because of the placement of the *fulcrums*, or pivot points, on the parking brake lever, drum-type parking brakes are self-energizing. In servo-type brakes, they also provide servo action, but only when the car is moving or trying to move forward, as it does when facing downhill. For this reason, drum-type parking brakes in servo-type systems are not as efficient when the car is facing uphill as they are when it is facing downhill.

Job 17G

IDENTIFY PARKING BRAKE SYSTEM PARTS

SATISFACTORY PERFORMANCE
A satisfactory performance on this job requires that you do the following:

1. Identify the parts of a cable-and-lever parking brake system by matching the numbered parts on the drawing with a list of part names.
2. Correctly identify all the numbered parts within 10 minutes.

PERFORMANCE SITUATION

_____ Equalizer	_____ Front cable	_____ Operating lever
_____ Link	_____ Equalizer lever	_____ Rear cables

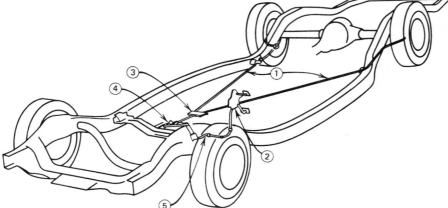

Job 17H

IDENTIFY THE FUNCTION OF PARKING BRAKE PARTS

SATISFACTORY PERFORMANCE
A satisfactory performance on this job requires that you do the following:

1. Identify the function of the listed parking brake parts by inserting the number of each part in the space provided in front of a list of part functions.
2. Identify the function of all the parts within 15 minutes.

PERFORMANCE SITUATION

1. Operating lever
2. Equalizer
3. Parking brake lever
4. Link

5. Secondary shoe
6. Front cable
7. Rear cables
8. Equalizer lever

_____ Provides an even pull on both rear cables
_____ Pulls the parking brake levers
_____ Pulls the front cable
_____ Transmits the movement of the parking brake lever to the primary shoe
_____ Pivots on the secondary shoe
_____ Pulls the rear cables
_____ Pulls the equalizer lever
_____ Provides a mounting point for the parking brake lever

| **PARKING BRAKE ADJUSTMENT** | A parking brake is considered adjusted when it meets the following criteria: |

1. The parking brakes are fully applied and holding after the pedal or lever has been moved through less than half its possible travel.
2. The brakes are fully released when the pedal or lever is in the released position.

Since the parking brakes actuate the rear brake shoes, the service brakes should be in good condition and in proper adjustment. In most instances parking brake adjustment consists of shortening the length of one or more of the cables to remove unnecessary slack. The adjustment is usually made by means of an adjusting nut at the equalizer (see Figure 17.39). This nut is easy to reach once the car has been raised.

Parking brake adjustment, however, involves more than just turning the adjusting nut until you obtain the desired braking action. The operation of certain self-adjusting mechanisms can be affected by an improperly adjusted parking brake cable. Most manufacturers have established specific procedures for adjusting the parking brakes on their various models. Therefore, always consult an appropriate manual for the specific procedure that may be necessary for the car on which you are working.

Here is a typical procedure:

1. Raise the car and support it by the suspension systems.
2. Place the transmission selector in NEUTRAL.
3. Place the parking brake lever in the released position.
4. Loosen the lock nut on the brake cable adjustment (refer to Figure 17.39).
5. Tighten the adjusting nut until the brakes barely start to drag.
6. Loosen the adjusting nut until the brakes are fully released.
7. Tighten the lock nut.
8. Check the operation of the parking brake.
9. Lower the car to the floor.

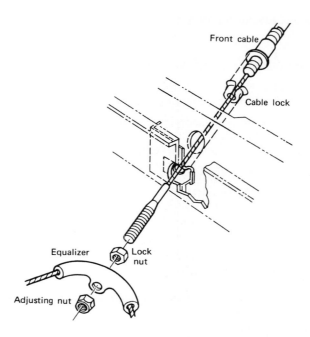

Figure 17.39 Typical provision for parking brake cable adjustment at the equalizer (courtesy of Chrysler Corporation).

Job 17I

ADJUST A PARKING BRAKE

SATISFACTORY PERFORMANCE
A satisfactory performance on this job requires that you do the following:

1. Adjust the parking brake on the car assigned.
2. Following the steps in the "Performance Outline" and the manufacturer's procedure and specifications, complete the job within 150% of the manufacturer's suggested time.
3. Fill in the blanks under "information."

PERFORMANCE OUTLINE

1. Raise and support the car.
2. Set the transmission selector and the parking brake lever in their proper positions.
3. Adjust the parking brake.
4. Check the parking brake operation.
5. Lower the car to the floor.

INFORMATION

Vehicle identification _____
Reference used _____ Page(s) _____
Location of adjustment _____
Wrench size of adjusting nut _____

LESSON 17-8 Antilock Brakes

Automotive manufacturers are constantly improving all the systems on their vehicles. Brakes are no exception, and have gone from all-drum systems to disc brakes on the front and drum brakes on the rear. The newest development is antilock brakes (ABS), which change the way vehicle brakes are applied during hard stops. Wheel sensors tell a computer whether the brakes have locked the wheel or whether the wheel is still rotating. A locked wheel will cause loss of control and lengthen the time it takes to stop. By regulating the pressure to the calipers and wheel cylinders, the computer will not let the wheel lock up. We describe here the parts that make up an antilock system.

Antilock Brake System Parts

Electronic Control Unit (ECM). This is the "brains" of the antilock system (see Figure 17.40). The wheel sensors send signals to the ECM to tell the unit how fast the wheel is turning. A built-in program in the ECM compares the speed of the wheel

Figure 17.40 ECM control. Sensors transmit information to the ECM control. This information is used to apply the brakes and prevent wheel lockup (courtesy of Training Enterprises Company).

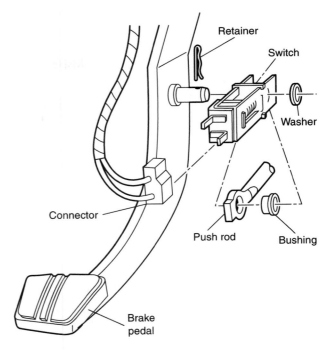

Figure 17.41 Brake light switch. This switch turns the brake lights on when the brakes are applied and signals the ECM computer that the brakes are being applied (courtesy of Ford Motor Company, Dearborn, MI).

with the speed of the vehicle and determines if the wheel is about to lock up. If the computer detects a lockup condition, it sends a signal to a hydraulic accumulator.

Hydraulic Accumulator. This unit is controlled by the ECM. Its purpose is to control the hydraulic brake pressure to the calipers and wheel cylinders (see Figure 17.40). This pressure is rapidly released and applied and keeps the wheel rotating during hard stops. The hydraulic accumulator can turn the pressure off and on up to ten times a second. This is enough to prevent wheel lockup.

Brake Light Switch. On a regular system this switch operates the brake lights. On an antilock brake system the switch also signals the computer that the brake pedal is applied (see Figure 17.41). This warns the system that it may have to regulate brake pressure.

Wheel Speed Sensors. To work, the antilock system needs to know the speed of each wheel as the brakes are applied. A current generating device called a *wheel sensor* is located at the wheels (see Figure 17.42). The speed of the alternating current cycles increases and decreases with the speed of the wheel. A *reluctor*, a tooth-shaped ring, revolves near a permanent magnet and coil. As each tooth on the reluctor passes the magnet, an alternating current is produced. As the wheel speed changes, the length of time to complete one cycle of the alternating current changes. The computer takes this information and determines if the wheel speed is nearing lockup. If this is the case, a signal is sent

from the computer to the hydraulic accumulator to control the brake pressure and prevent loss of wheel rotation.

Electric Motor and Pump. Brake fluid must be pumped to the calipers and wheel cylinders and back to the master cylinder for this system to work. It is the job of an electric pump to supply the pressure to circulate the brake fluid (see Figure 17.43).

Accumulator. Cylinders charged with nitrogen gas are used to put heavy pressure on the hydraulic fluid to operate the system. In case of a brake system failure, this pressure is used as an emergency pressure source. One safety precaution that all technicians must follow is to not open a bleeder screw or loosen a line fitting if the ABS system is applied. The nitrogen cylinder will immediately place the fluid under a very high pressure.

Antilock Warning Light. If the system fails, a light warns the operator that the system has a problem and needs to be serviced. Some systems use the old red brake warning light that warned of hydraulic pressure failure or that the parking brake is on. Other systems have an amber light that is

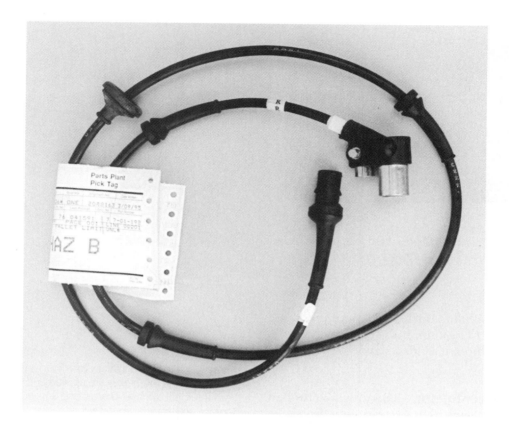

Figure 17.42   Wheel sensor. The computer must know the speed of each wheel when the brakes are applied. The wheel sensor sends the computer information about the speed of each wheel (courtesy of Training Enterprises Company).

Figure 17.43   Electric motor and pump. This unit is used to circulate the brake fluid between the calipers or wheel cylinders and the master cylinder (courtesy of Training Enterprises Company).

separate and used only for the antilock brake system. The control module has the ability to evaluate failure situations and send a code. This code is read at the warning light by looking at the number of times the light blinks on and off. Five blinks followed by a short pause and three more blinks would be read as a 5-3 code. Consult a repair manual for the particular system being serviced to read the codes and interpret the results.

LESSON 17–9 Troubleshooting

Brake Hydraulics

The hydraulic system on a brake system is a closed system. Brake fluid should never leave the system. On disc brake systems, hydraulic fluid replaces worn pad linings as the caliper piston moves out to compensate for the wear. This is indicated by a drop in the master cylinder reservoir level that supplies brake fluid to the front calipers. Look for leaks around the master cylinder, brake lines, and at each wheel. If there is a change in the pedal "feel," such as a spongy pedal or a larger pedal movement before the brakes are applied, check this abnormal condition. A spongy pedal means air is trapped in the lines and the system needs to be bled to release all air. Larger pedal movement, as well as the brake light coming on, means one side of the hydraulic system has developed a leak. It will be on the side where all the fluid leaves the master cylinder reservoir.

Any time a brake hydraulic system is opened for repair, all the air has to be removed from the system before it will work properly. This is called *bleeding*. Bleeder screws are located at each wheel and sometimes at the master cylinder. Bleeding the system sometimes requires a pressure bleeder. Most systems can be bled by using the master cylinder pressure. Learning how to bleed all the different types of brake systems is an essential part of brake service. Antilock brake systems require special bleeding techniques because they can become pressurized by the nitrogen gas cylinders.

Brake Mechanical Parts

Brake drums can get out of round or scored, or may develop hard spots (see Figure 17.44). These conditions will result in brake noise or pedal pulsation as the brakes are applied. Always investigate brake

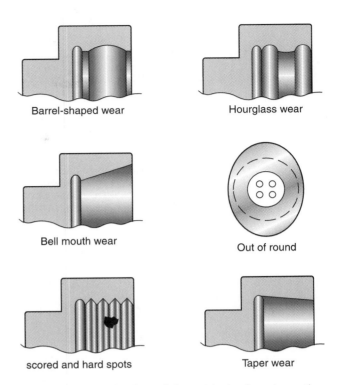

Barrel-shaped wear

Hourglass wear

Bell mouth wear

Out of round

scored and hard spots

Taper wear

Figure 17.44 Brake drum defects. A brake drum inspection should include checks for out of round, scoring, hard spots, barrel shapes, hourglass shapes, and cracks (courtesy of Training Enterprises Company).

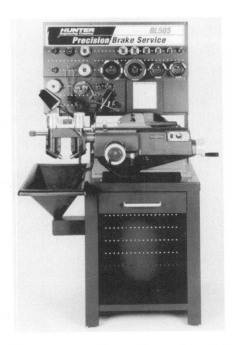

Figure 17.45 Drum and disc turning machine. This machine turns brake drums and discs. Brake shoes and pads produce wear patterns in both parts. To restore them back to factory standards, these patterns have to be removed (courtesy of Hunter Engineering Company).

Brake Warning Light	
ON	**OFF**
When there is any front system hydraulic failure.	When there is equal pressure on all the hydraulic lines.
When there is any rear system hydraulic failure.	When the bulb is burned out or there is a wiring problem in the bulb circuit.
When the parking brake is applied.	When the parking brake is released.
During the "check light" phase when the ignition key is turned to START.	After the ignition key is released to the ON position if the parking brake is OFF and if there is not a brake pressure problem.

Figure 17.46 Brake warning light. The warning light will come on when there is a loss of hydraulic pressure in either side of the system. The light should also be on when the parking brake is set. Always check the system if the light is on when it should be off (courtesy of Training Enterprises Company).

noises, as they usually mean pads, drums, rotors, and shoes are worn out.

The parking brake should be adjusted if the lever or pedal does not lock the wheels when fully applied. When the parking brake is applied, the brake warning light should light.

When a drum or rotor is scored from use, it can be reconditioned on a brake lathe. Cutting tools take off enough metal on the brake surface to restore the surface back to factory standards (see Figure 17.45).

Brake drum defects (see Figure 17.44) require turning the drum on a special brake machine to correct (see Figure 17.45). After turning the drum be sure to torque the lug nuts or bolts to the correct specification. Uneven nut or bolt torque can cause the drum to be warped and result in brake pedal pulsation. The drums will have to be turned again to correct the problem. There are only so many times brake drums can be turned before they have to be replaced. Any time tires are rotated or replaced the lug nuts should always be torqued rather than tightened with an air wrench. This is just good professional service. Vehicle owners should not have new problems in their brake system as a result of improper repair techniques.

Brake Electrical Parts

There is a brake switch that operates the rear brake lights as the brakes are applied check all brake

lights for burned out bulbs. The brake warning light will come on if the hydraulic pressure of either the front or rear drops to zero. This light is also used to warn the driver if the parking brake is applied. In antilock brakes, an additional duty of the brake warning light switch is to signal the computer when the brakes are applied. Replace bulbs when needed and make sure the brake switch is adjusted properly (see Figure 17.46). Always stop and check the hydraulic system if the warning light comes on. Be sure to make a warning light bulb test.

Inspecting and Troubleshooting Antilock Brakes

Make all the regular brake hydraulic, mechanical, and electrical checks first. Check each wheel to see that the sensor cables are connected and that there is not a damaged cable. Road test the vehicle and check for the correct stopping distance and for balance between each wheel. Locking wheels or pulling to one side should be investigated further.

Most antilock systems require the use of a special tester to hook into the system and read codes or sensor operation. Ford uses a breakout box; General Motors uses a Kent Moore ABS Tester. All systems use high-pressure fluid gauges to check brake hydraulic pressure in the lines (see Figure 17.47).

When the ABS warning light comes on, hook up a tester and make the necessary tests.

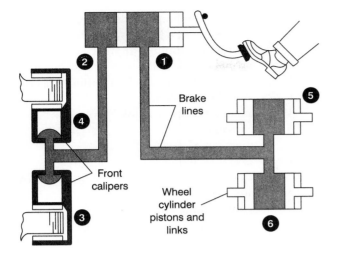

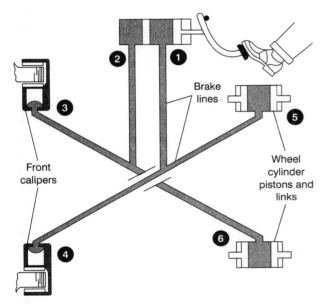

Figure 17.47 Brake fluid pressure gauge points. Restricted or damaged brake lines can reduce the pressure going to the brakes at that wheel. High-pressure fluid gauges can be installed and used to check pressure problems. Install the gauges at the pressure points as numbered in this figure. Compare the gauge readings with the manufacturer's specifications (courtesy of Training Enterprises Company).

VOCABULARY

Use the listed words in the blanks beside the sentences to complete the definitions. Either write out the words or place the letters in the blanks.

A. Master cylinder

B. Rotor

C. Drum

D. Hydraulic system

E. Cast iron

F. Asbestos

G. Rivets

H. Bonding

I. Pads

J. Shoes

K. Caliper

L. Friction

M. Piston seal

N. Self-energizing

O. Equalizer

P. Retracting springs

Q. Primary shoe

R. Servo action

S. Inspection port

T. Parking brake lever

U. ABS

V. Accumulator

W. Code

X. Bell mouth

Y. Barrel-shaped

_____ 1. A large metal disc for the friction pads to work against to stop the vehicle

_____ 2. Openings in a caliper used to evaluate the condition of the pads and rotor

_____ 3. When numbers are set in the computer indicating there may be a problem

_____ 4. Parts that rub against the brake drum

_____ 5. When the lining is glued to the shoe

_____ 6. Happens when two parts rub together

_____ 7. Caliper part that goes between the piston and the cylinder

_____ 8. Brake shoe located toward the front

_____ 9. Part that applies the service brake

_____ 10. When a brake drum is worn wider on the outside and tapers down smaller on the inside

_____ 11. Material used to make the lining on pads and shoes

_____ 12. Part that provides fluid pressure to apply the brakes

_____ 13. Antilock brake system

_____ 14. When a brake drum has no wear on the outside and inside but is worn in the middle

_____ 15. A part located at the wheel that applies the brakes

_____ 16. Material from which brake drums and wheel cylinders are made

_____ 17. Uses brake fluid to operate pistons and calipers and apply the brakes

_____ 18. Metal parts that hold brake lining to the shoes

_____ 19. Parts used to return the brake shoes back to their starting position

_____ 20. When the force supplied by one brake shoe is used to apply the other shoe

_____ 21. The part brake shoes rub against to stop the vehicle

_____ 22. Uses nitrogen gas to operate the brakes

_____ 23. The friction parts working against the rotor to stop the vehicle

_____ 24. A part that multiplies the effort of the operating lever to pull the rear cables

_____ 25. When the effort of one brake shoe is used to push on the other brake shoe and increase braking

REVIEW QUESTIONS

The following questions will help you determine if you have accomplished the tasks stated at the beginning of this chapter. If you do not know many of the answers, go back and review the material before proceeding to the next chapter.

Lesson 17–1

1. Why does the fluid level in a dual master cylinder drop in level on the disc brake side when there is not a leak in the system?
2. How far from the top should a master cylinder be filled?
3. What DOT value brake fluid do most vehicles use?
4. How far down, in inches, should the brake pedal move before the brakes are applied?
5. Why is a vehicle brake system divided into two parts?
6. What three things could be at fault if the brake lights do not come on?
7. How is the brake warning light bulb checked?

8. What are the four steps to use when checking the power assist on a brake system?
9. What should be looked at in a condition 1 brake problem?
10. What items should be checked if there is a condition 7 brake problem?
11. What are some things to look for in a condition 4 brake problem?

Lesson 17–2

12. Name the two types of brake systems used on an automobile.
13. What is a hydraulic system?
14. How does a disc brake system work?
15. How does a drum brake system work?
16. What is applied by each side of a dual master cylinder?
17. What are the indications that one part of a dual hydraulic brake system has failed?
18. What type of system is the parking brake?
19. What part of the service brake is used by the parking brake?
20. What material is used to make rotors and drums?
21. What material is used in the lining of brake shoes?
22. What is the warning about the material used in brake shoes?
23. What are two methods used to fasten brake lining to brake shoes?
24. What will be the result if a vehicle is driven very far with the parking brake applied?
25. What system uses brake pads?
26. How and when does the brake pad warning sensor work?
27. What is the platform and the web?

Lesson 17–3

28. What is the function of a caliper?
29. Where is the ventilated rotor primarily used?
30. What is the advantage of the disc brake system over the drum brake system?
31. What type of caliper piston arrangements are currently being used?
32. Why are springs not needed to retract the pads in a disc brake system?
33. Define rotor runout.
34. How does the piston seal return the piston to its original position?

Lesson 17–4

35. What are the two basic types of drum brake systems in use today?
36. What is the purpose of a backing plate?

37. What is the purpose of the anchor pin?
38. Describe what the star wheel adjuster does.
39. What is the purpose of a wheel cylinder?
40. What is the purpose of a retracting spring?
41. What is the front brake shoe called and what is the rear brake shoe called on the same axle?
42. Why are the front and rear brake shoes on each axle different on self-energizing systems?
43. Describe how the self-energizing feature works.
44. In the forward direction, which shoe "serves" the other?
45. What is meant by the term *duo-servo*?
46. Which shoe provides little brake action in a non-servo system?

Lesson 17–5
47. What is the expected brake system life in miles before it should be serviced?
48. Which front brake system, left or right, usually wears quicker and why?
49. What other repair operation is usually combined with a brake system repair?
50. At what wear point should riveted brake lining be replaced?
51. What part can be damaged if brake lining is used down to the rivets?
52. When inspecting disc brake pads, which edge can be expected to wear faster?
53. When should bonded brake lining be replaced?
54. What are some reasons other than wear that require brake lining replacement?
55. What will be the result if just the brake lining on one wheel is replaced?
56. On which brake shoe and where can most wear be expected?

Lesson 17–6
57. What is meant by a tapered lining wear pattern?
58. What causes a tapered wear pattern?
59. When should disc brake pads be replaced?
60. What does the factory use to hold brake drums in place during vehicle assembly?
61. What are three reasons a brake drum may not be easy to remove?
62. Where should heat be applied to the brake drum for removal when "frozen"?

Lesson 17–7
63. What kind of system is a parking brake?
64. What does the force that applies the parking brake depend on?
65. What are the steps to follow when applying the parking brake?

66. How does a parking brake equalizer work?
67. What three parking brake levers multiply the physical effort of the driver?
68. Which shoe does the parking brake activate in the rear drum system?
69. Is the action of the parking brake self-energizing in a self-energizing system?
70. When are drum-type parking brakes in servo-type systems not efficient?
71. What two tests must a parking brake pass to be considered correctly adjusted?

Lesson 17–8
72. How does an antilock brake system work?
73. What does the ECM do in an antilock brake system?
74. What does the hydraulic accumulator do in an antilock brake system?
75. What two functions does the brake light switch perform in an antilock brake system?
76. What does the wheel speed sensor do in an antilock brake system?
77. How does the reluctor tell the computer the wheel speed is changing?
78. What keeps brake fluid circulating to the calipers and wheel cylinders and back to the master cylinder in an antilock brake system?
79. What is the emergency power source in an antilock brake system?
80. What safety precaution should the technician follow when bleeding antilock brakes?
81. What indicates to the driver there is a problem in the antilock brake system?

Lesson 17–9
82. Is it normal to find the disc brake side of the master cylinder needs brake fluid if there is no leak?
83. What does it mean when the brake pedal feels spongy when applied?
84. When the brake system warning light is on and the brake pedal travel is excessive, what should be inspected?
85. What are six defects that can happen to a brake drum?
86. When are four times the brake warning light should come on?
87. When are four times the brake warning light should be off?
88. What mechanical operation will cause a brake drum defect if it is not done right?
89. What is meant by "bleeding" the system?
90. What is a breakout box and when is it used?

ASE QUESTIONS

Each question or incomplete statement in this test is followed by four suggested answers or completions. In each case select the *one* that best answers the question or completes the statement.

1. The brake fluid level has dropped in the disc brake side of the master cylinder. Technician A says the fluid level should never drop in a brake system because it is a closed system. Technician B says this is normal. Check for leaks and if none are found, add the correct amount of brake fluid. Who is right?
   a. A only
   b. B only
   c. Both A and B
   d. Neither A nor B

2. A brake pedal feels "spongy" when applied. Technician A says there is air in the hydraulic parts. Technician B says the brake lines are expanding due to the hydraulic force. Who is right?
   a. A only
   b. B only
   c. Both A and B
   d. Neither A nor B

3. A brake power assist is being checked. Technician A says to start the engine with your foot on the pedal. Technician B says the power assist can only be checked with the engine running because it requires a vacuum to operate. Who is right?
   a. A only
   b. B only
   c. Both A and B
   d. Neither A nor B

4. A vehicle on a test run drives to the right when the brakes are applied. Technician A says this could be improper alignment. Technician B says this could be frozen hydraulic parts on the left side. Who is right?
   a. A only
   b. B only
   c. Both A and B
   d. Neither A nor B

5. Brake theory is being discussed. Technician A says friction stops the vehicle. Technician B says hydraulic pressure stops the vehicle. Who is right?
   a. A only
   b. B only
   c. Both A and B
   d. Neither A nor B

6. A brake pedal moves further than normal when the brakes are applied. A red brake warning light is lit at the dash. Technician A says there is a failure in either the front or rear brake system. Technician B says there is a leak in the hydraulic system. Who is right?
   a. A only
   b. B only
   c. Both A and B
   d. Neither A nor B

7. A dual hydraulic brake system is being discussed. Technician A says the front and rear are on separate systems. Technician B says the left front and right rear are on one system and the right front and left rear on the other. Who is right?
   a. A only
   b. B only
   c. Both A and B
   d. Neither A nor B

8. A drum-type rear brake system is being cleaned and repaired. Technician A says compressed air is the best way to get all the dust out of the system. Technician B says brake dust could be harmful if it gets in the air. Who is right?
   a. A only
   b. B only
   c. Both A and B
   d. Neither A nor B

9. A vehicle was driven with the parking brake applied. Technician A says there should have been a red warning light on the dash. Technician B says the system would have produced heat and smoke that could have been seen. Who is right?
   a. A only
   b. B only
   c. Both A and B
   d. Neither A nor B

10. A scratching noise is heard each time a disc brake equipped vehicle makes a turn. Technician A says the noise is a warning signal that the pads are worn out. Technician B says worn-out wheel bearings are causing the wheel to rub. Who is right?
    a. A only
    b. B only
    c. Both A and B
    d. Neither A nor B

11. The differences between drum brake systems and disc brake systems are being discussed. Technician A says both systems use retracting springs to move the pads or shoes back to normal. Technician B says the front brake shoe and the rear brake shoe in a drum system are the same and can be reversed. Who is right?
    a. A only
    b. B only
    c. Both A and B
    d. Neither A nor B

12. One side of a rear drum brake system does not brake with the same force as the other. Technician A says the wheel cylinder may be sticking. Technician B says the lining may be contaminated. Who is right?
    a. A only
    b. B only
    c. Both A and B
    d. Neither A nor B

13. A non-servo brake system is being discussed. Technician A says when the vehicle is moving forward and the brakes are applied, the forward shoe does most of the braking.

Technician B says both shoes provide equal braking. Who is right?

a. A only
b. B only
c. Both A and B
d. Neither A nor B

14. Brake lining wear is being discussed. Technician A says the right front will wear faster than the left front. Technician B says the front lining will wear faster than the rear. Who is right?

a. A only
b. B only
c. Both A and B
d. Neither A nor B

15. A right rear wheel grease seal is leaking and has contaminated the brake lining. Technician A says only the lining and seal on this wheel should be replaced. Technician B says the lining on both wheels should be replaced. Who is right?

a. A only
b. B only
c. Both A and B
d. Neither A nor B

16. The worn pads on a disc brake job are being inspected after they were replaced. The leading edge of the inner pad and the training edge of the outer pad show a tapered wear pattern. Technician A says the caliper is warped and should be replaced. Technician B says the wear pattern is normal.

a. A only
b. B only
c. Both A and B
d. Neither A nor B

17. Some Tinnerman nuts are found locking the brake drum in place after the tire has been removed. Technician A says they do not need to be replaced and can be discarded. Technician B says they are needed to keep the drum in place. Who is right?

a. A only
b. B only
c. Both A and B
d. Neither A nor B

18. A parking brake is set on a vehicle facing uphill. Technician A says the parking brake is not as efficient when the vehicle is facing this direction. Technician B says the parking brake works equally well no matter how the vehicle is parked. Who is right?

a. A only
b. B only
c. Both A and B
d. Neither A nor B

19. The function of the brake light switch on a vehicle with an antilock brake system is being discussed. Technician A says it operates the brake lights only. Technician B says it operates the brake lights and is part of the antilock brake system. Who is right?

a. A only
b. B only
c. Both A and B
d. Neither A nor B

20. A computer has set a problem code indicating a failure in the antilock brake system. Technician A says the code will be 63. Technician B says the code will be 72. Who is right?

a. A only
b. B only
c. Both A and B
d. Neither A nor B

21. A brake drum shows wear on the inside of the shoe surface and the outside of the shoe surface but no wear in the center. Technician A says this a typical barrel-shaped wear pattern. Technician B says this is a typical hourglass wear pattern. Who is right?

a. A only
b. B only
c. Both A and B
d. Neither A nor B

22. An antilock brake system has air in the hydraulic system. Technician A says the procedure of bleeding the system should start in the rear and move toward the front. Technician B says this type of system requires a different bleeding technique to avoid setting off the nitrogen gas cylinders. Who is right?

a. A only
b. B only
c. Both A and B
d. Neither A nor B

18

Electrical Circuits and Light System Maintenance

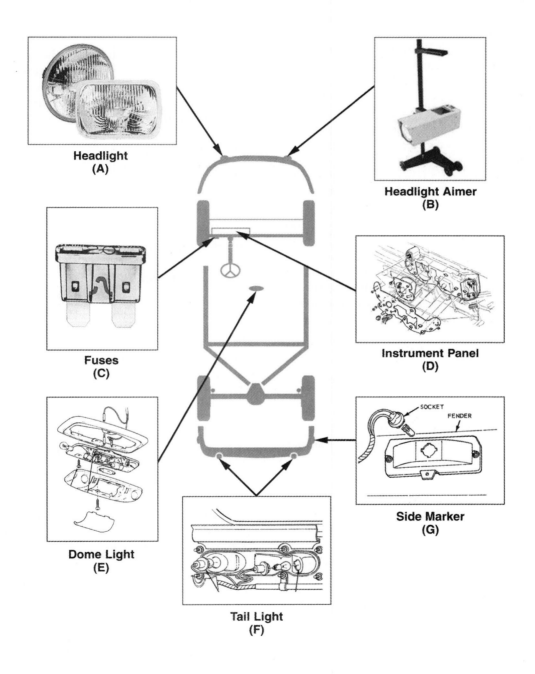

Headlight
(A)

Headlight Aimer
(B)

Fuses
(C)

Instrument Panel
(D)

Dome Light
(E)

Tail Light
(F)

Side Marker
(G)

SOCKET

FENDER

Knowledge of wires, lights, relays, fuses, and bulbs are just a few of the many things that are very important when servicing the electrical circuits. Lights are used behind colored lenses to make our vehicle more visible and tell others our intentions. Our vehicle headlights light the way and allow us to travel along dark roads. Circuits control everything in the vehicle such as the horn and the wipers. The headlights have to be correctly aligned or we will cause oncoming drivers to be blinded. Circuits in automobiles contain miles of wire. All this mileage can become a problem if it separates or shorts. A service technician must be able to read wiring diagrams and identify standard electrical symbols to solve electrical problems in modern vehicles.

Sometimes replacing a burned-out bulb can be very hard if it is in the instrument panel. Electricity cannot be seen, which means the technician must understand how it works in order to solve problems. Test equipment such as voltmeters, ammeters, and ohmmeters are standard electrical tools that must be used correctly to enable the technician to solve electrical problems. This chapter should guide the service technician toward solving most of the common electrical problems (see Figure 18).

TASKS

The following are five tasks to master before leaving this chapter:

Task 18-1. Study basic electrical circuitry to learn how electrical voltage, resistance, and amperage react in the different types of circuits.

Task 18-2. Learn how to use electrical test equipment to find problems in electrical circuits. Since electricity cannot be seen, learn to rely on testers to solve electrical problems.

Task 18-3. Study electrical circuit protection and controls. Fuses and circuit breakers are used to prevent damage to electrical wires. When these fail you have to determine the cause and replace them.

Task 18-4. Learn how to test and replace parts in electrical circuits.

Task 18-5. Learn how to set and adjust headlights. This requires the use of headlight adjusting equipment and knowledge of how to adjust the various types of headlights on the market today.

LESSON 18–1   Basic Electrical Circuitry

The electrical energy available from the battery is used in many systems. The starting system uses electrical energy to crank the engine. The ignition system uses electrical energy to ignite the fuel and air mixture in the engine. And the lighting system uses electrical energy to illuminate the road, to signal the driver's intent to stop and turn, and to light the car so it can be seen by other drivers. Although all these systems are important, for safety reasons the lighting system is the most important.

Routine maintenance of the lighting system requires that you perform certain services in many different circuits. In this chapter you will learn about basic circuitry, circuit control, and circuit protection. With this knowledge, you will gain an understanding of how these circuits operate. You will then learn about various circuit components and develop skills in testing and replacing those components.

From your work with batteries, you know that a battery converts chemical energy to electrical energy. Electrical energy can be converted to other forms of energy such as light, heat, and motion. Before the electrical energy of a battery can be put to work, the battery must be connected in a circuit.

Circuits

A circuit is nothing more than a path for electricity. Before electricity will flow in a circuit, the circuit must be *closed*, or complete. This means that the path must be continuous. It must provide a route for the current to flow from the battery. And it must also provide a route for the current to return to the battery.

The ground circuit is just as important as the power circuit. This is especially true when repairs are made. Ground straps are sometimes left disconnected, and with all the plastic and rubber products used in vehicle construction, these straps are needed to make good electrical paths back to the battery. Ground path problems of this type are very hard to find because the ground may not be completely open but just have higher resistance.

A circuit must have a minimum of three components.

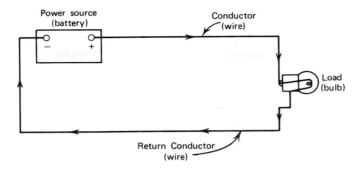

Figure 18.1 Simple circuit. Current flows from the battery through a wire to the bulb. After flowing through the filament of the bulb, the current flows back to the battery through the return wire.

1. *A power source.* This can be the battery or, when the engine is running, the generator.
2. *Conductors.* These can be wires and the metal parts of the automobile.
3. *A load.* This can be a light, motor, or other device that converts electrical energy to another form of energy.

Figure 18.1 shows how those components can be connected to form a simple lighting circuit. In this circuit, a wire conducts current to a bulb. The current flows through the *filament* of the bulb. The filament is a fine wire that gets white hot, or *incandescent*, when current flows through it. After passing through the filament, the current flows back to the battery through the return wire. The electrical energy of the battery is converted to light energy because the circuit is closed.

All electrical circuits follow Ohm's law. Here is Ohm's law written in three different ways:

Voltage = Current Times Resistance
Current = Voltage Divided by Resistance
Resistance = Voltage Divided by Current

Another useful formula is that for wattage:

Watts = Current Times Voltage

Current is measured in *amperes*, resistance is measured in *ohms*, and voltage is measured in *volts*. By placing two values in these formulas the other value can be figured (two values have to be known to get the third). The automotive technician uses test instruments such as an ohmmeter, voltmeter, or ammeter to measure the circuits. All the technician has to know is what value should be obtained at each test point. If this value is not obtained, further tests and repairs are indicated.

Circuit Control. The circuit shown in Figure 18.1 has several disadvantages. One is that the circuit cannot be controlled. The light will continue to burn until all the electrical energy is converted to light energy. By adding a control that will *open*, or break, the circuit, the light can be turned on and off. A control that opens and closes a circuit is called a *switch*. Figure 18.2 shows how a switch can be installed in a circuit.

Ground Return. Another disadvantage of the circuit shown in Figure 18.1 is that it requires too much wire. Figure 18.3 shows how most of the return wire can be eliminated. Because the frame and body of the car are made of metal, these parts can form the return conductor. When the metal parts of a car form the return conductor, that part of the circuit is referred to as the *ground*. Most automotive circuits use the frame as a return conductor. If an automobile had only a few circuits, a few extra lengths of wire would be of no concern. However, an automobile has hundreds of separate circuits. If the frame was not used as the return conductor, the amount of wire used in an automobile would be doubled.

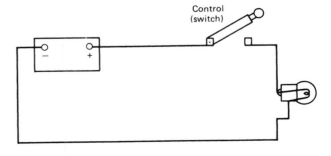

Figure 18.2 A simple circuit with a switch as a control. Opening the switch opens the circuit and stops the flow of current.

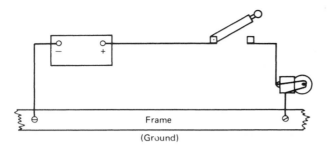

Figure 18.3 A simple circuit using the automobile frame and body as the return conductor.

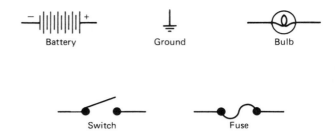

Figure 18.5 Symbols used in wiring diagrams. Symbols like these are used in wiring diagrams to make the drawing simpler and easier to follow.

Circuit Protection.

Another disadvantage of the circuit shown in Figure 18.1 is that it has no protection against overload. If the load in the circuit is increased, or if an additional load is added, the wires and switch may be unable to carry the extra current required. The wires and switch will overheat and be damaged. The heat may also cause an electrical fire.

One method of providing circuit protection is to install a *fuse* in the circuit. A fuse is a "sacrifice" conductor which will *blow*, or burn out, when the current that flows through it exceeds a certain limit. Because a fuse protects only those parts of the circuit "downstream" from its location, a fuse is usually located as close as possible to the power source. Figure 18.4 shows how a fuse is placed in a circuit.

> Never disable a fuse system by using a piece of metal in the place of the correct fuse. If there is a problem in the circuit such as a short, the wires may burn out or cause a fire. The battery is capable of producing heavy amperage that can easily burn any wire apart. Replace the fuse with the right size, and if the fuse blows again repair the circuit.

Symbols.

The circuits shown in Figure 18.1 through 18.4 are in pictorial form. The parts of the circuit are drawn to resemble the actual parts. This method is often used for simple circuits with few parts. But it has limited usage in showing automotive circuits.

Most automotive circuits are shown by *wiring diagrams*. The parts in those drawings are often represented by *symbols*. Symbols are codes or signs that have been adopted by the automotive industry to indicate certain parts and conditions. Symbols are part of the written language of the automotive trades. Figure 18.5 shows some of the most commonly used symbols. These symbols are used in Figure 18.6 to diagram the same circuit shown in Figure 18.4. Compare those two illustrations. You will see that a diagram with symbols is not difficult to understand.

Types of Circuits

There are only two major types of circuits—*series circuits* and *parallel circuits*. Both types are used in automotive electrical systems. At times, both are combined. A circuit of this type is called a *series-parallel circuit*.

Series Circuits.

The simple circuit that was developed in Figure 18.1 through 18.6 is a series circuit. When a circuit contains only one load and one power source, it can only be a series circuit.

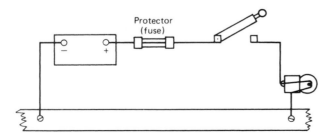

Figure 18.4 A simple circuit protected by a fuse. Note that the fuse is placed "first" in the circuit directly after the power source.

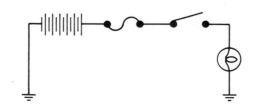

Figure 18.6 A wiring diagram for a simple circuit.

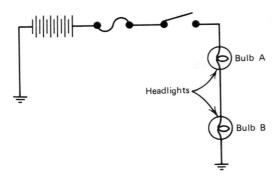

Figure 18.7 A pair of headlights connected in a series circuit. If either bulb "A" or bulb "B" burns out, it will break the circuit. The remaining bulb then cannot operate.

A series circuit has one continuous path for the flow of current. Therefore, current flows through all the parts of a series circuit. If any of the parts fail, or if the circuit is broken at any point, current stops flowing in the entire circuit. Some examples of series circuits used in automobiles include the starter circuit and the primary circuit of breaker point ignition systems.

A series circuit provides only one path for the flow of current. Therefore, it is seldom used for a lighting circuit containing two or more loads. Figure 18.7 shows a pair of headlights connected in a series circuit. As shown, the failure of one headlight would result in an open circuit. Current flow would stop and the other headlight would go out.

> The skill of being able to read and follow wiring diagrams is the single most important key to the success of an electrical and electronics technician. This type of work involves some very complicated circuits, sensors, and test equipment. The trend is toward more of this with greater use of electronics. The automotive repair industry is just on the edge of the electronics and computer age.

Series circuits have other disadvantages that relate to voltage and current flow. Most cars have a

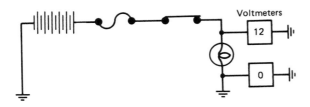

Figure 18.8 Voltage in series circuit. Two voltmeters connected as shown will indicate that full voltage is present before the load, and that there is no voltage after the load.

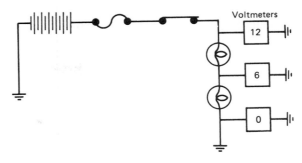

Figure 18.9 Voltage in a circuit with two loads in series. The voltmeters show the effect of the increased resistance.

12-volt battery. The voltage is a unit of electrical pressure. A 12-volt battery provides a 12-volt pressure to push current through a circuit. The load in the circuit is designed to operate at that pressure. The load is built so its resistance allows a pressure of 12 volts to push sufficient current through the load so it functions properly. In effect, the load "uses up" the voltage in the circuit as it converts electrical energy to energy of another form. Assuming no losses through bad connections, the voltage in a circuit just before the load is the full circuit voltage. The voltage just after the load is zero. This can be proven by using a voltmeter, as shown in Figure 18.8.

If a second similar load were placed in the circuit, the resistance of the circuit would be doubled. The 12-volt pressure from the battery would be insufficient to make both loads operate correctly. This voltage would push only half as much current through the loads. A voltmeter test in a circuit of this type would reveal the results shown in Figure 18.9.

Adding a third similar load to the circuit as shown in Figure 18.10 further increases the

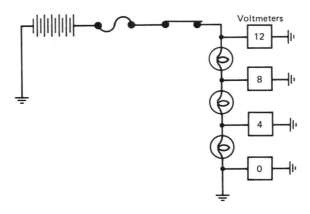

Figure 18.10 Voltage in a circuit with three loads in series. The voltmeters show the further effects of the increased resistance.

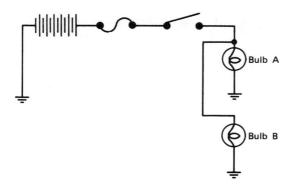

Figure 18.11   A pair of headlights connected in a parallel circuit. If either bulb "A" or bulb "B" burns out, the remaining bulb will not be affected.

resistance. This causes a greater drop in voltage and in current flow. As you can see, series circuits containing two or more loads do not allow efficient use of electrical energy.

Following are basic series circuit rules:

1. Current measured at any point in the circuit will be the same.
2. Adding together each individual load or resistance in the circuit gives the total resistance for the circuit.
3. The voltage drops or gets lower across each load or resistance. The sum of all voltage drops will equal the source or battery voltage.
4. When any resistance or load becomes open (no path in the wire), the circuit can no longer work. There must be a complete path from one post of the battery to the other for anything in the circuit to work.

Parallel Circuits.   A parallel circuit is one where two or more loads are connected so each is provided with its own return path to the power source. Figure 18.11 shows a pair of headlights connected in a parallel circuit. Compare that illustration with the one shown in Figure 18.7. When a pair of headlights are wired in a parallel circuit, the failure of either bulb will not affect the operation of the remaining bulb. This is one reason that automotive lighting systems use parallel circuits.

A parallel circuit offers another advantage. Each load receives full system voltage as shown in Figure 18.12. Also, when loads are connected in parallel, the total circuit resistance drops because of the additional return paths provided. Therefore, more current can flow in the circuit and the loads can operate at full efficiency. This is another reason

Job 18A

IDENTIFY CIRCUIT PARTS AND THEIR DEFINITIONS

SATISFACTORY PERFORMANCE

A satisfactory performance on this job requires that you do the following:

1. Identify the symbolized circuit parts in the diagram below by placing the number of each part in front of the correct part name.
2. Identify the definition of each part by placing the number of each part in front of its correct definition.
3. Correctly identify all the parts and their definitions within 15 minutes.

PERFORMANCE SITUATION

____ Fuse	____ Switch
____ Ground	____ In-line fuse
____ Bulb	____ Battery

____ a connection to the metal parts of a car
____ a power source
____ a device that boosts voltage in a circuit
____ a control device that opens and closes a circuit
____ a device that converts electrical energy to light energy
____ a "sacrifice" part that protects a circuit

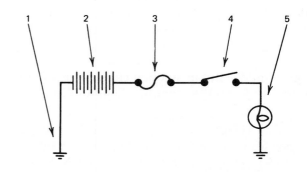

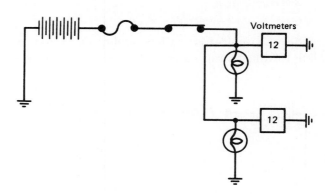

Figure 18.12   Voltage in a parallel circuit. Two voltmeters connected as shown will indicate that full voltage is present before each load.

that parallel circuits are used in automotive lighting systems.

Following are basic parallel circuit rules:

1. The voltage is the same across each path or branch of a parallel circuit.
2. Adding together each individual branch current gives the total for all the current used in the circuit.
3. The total resistance in a parallel circuit will be less than the resistance value of the branch with the smallest resistance.
4. When any one load becomes open (broken wire), the other loads and resistances will still operate. The circuit will still have a path from one battery terminal to the other. The load and resistance in the open branch will not work.

LESSON 18–2 Circuit Protection and Control

Basic maintenance of the lighting system includes the replacement of various components. Before you attempt to replace any component, check to determine that the suspected component is defec-

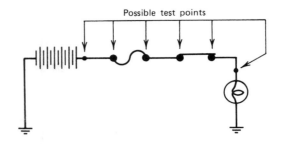

Figure 18.14 Using a test light. A test light glows when connected between ground and any of the test points shown.

tive. Replacing a part that does not require replacement is not only time consuming but embarrassing. Simple diagnosis of electrical problems requires (1) a knowledge of basic circuitry and (2) a *test light*.

The Test Light

In most instances, a simple test light of the type shown in Figure 18.13 can be used to determine the cause of a problem in a lighting circuit. A test light consists of a bulb wired to a sharp steel probe and to a length of wire fitted with an alligator clip. For convenience, the bulb is usually enclosed in a plastic handle to which the probe is attached.

When the alligator clip is attached to ground, the bulb will light when the probe is touched to any current-carrying conductor not on the ground side of the load in a circuit. Figure 18.14 shows some test points in a simple circuit.

Fuses

A blown fuse is one of the most common causes of circuit failure. As you know, a fuse is a "sacrifice" part that blows, or burns out, when too much current flows through it. When a fuse blows, it opens its

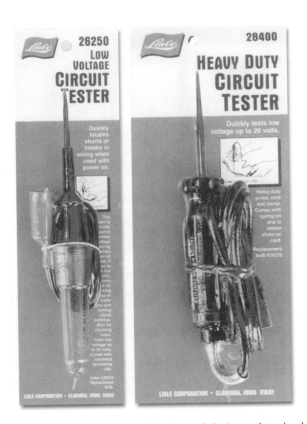

Figure 18.13 Simple test light. A test light is used to check for open wires and circuits (courtesy of American Motors).

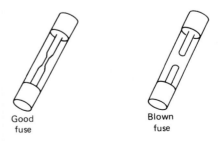

Figure 18.15 A typical glass cartridge fuse of the type used in automotive electrical systems. The one on the right is defective and will not allow current flow.

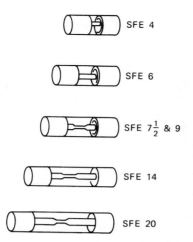

SFE 4

SFE 6

SFE 7$\frac{1}{2}$ & 9

SFE 14

SFE 20

Figure 18.16   A few of the more popular glass fuse sizes and ratings.

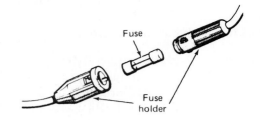

Fuse

Fuse holder

Figure 18.18   In-line fuse holder. Fuse holders of this type are often used in accessory circuits (courtesy of Ford Motor Company, Dearborn, MI).

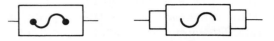

Figure 18.19   Two symbols commonly used to represent an-in-line fuse.

circuit and thus protects all the other circuit parts from damage.

Glass Cartridge Fuses. The most commonly used fuse consists of a strip of metal that has a low melting point. The strip is enclosed in a glass tube and is connected to a metal cap at each end. The metal strip is designed to handle a limited amount of current. When the current flowing through the fuse exceeds that limit, the strip melts. Figure 18.15 shows a good glass cartridge fuse and one that has blown.

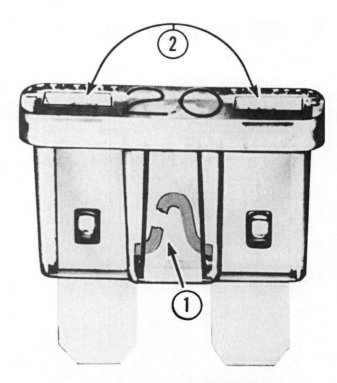

TO TEST FOR BLOWN MINI-FUSE:

①   PULL FUSE OUT AND CHECK VISUALLY.

②   WITH THE CIRCUIT ACTIVATED, USE A TEST LIGHT ACROSS THE POINTS SHOWN.

MINI-FUSE COLOR CODES

RATING	COLOR
5 AMP	TAN
10 AMP	RED
20 AMP	YELLOW
25 AMP	WHITE

Figure 18.20   An enlarged view of a miniaturized fuse. Note that the fuse is blown (courtesy of Pontiac Motor Division, general Motors Corporation).

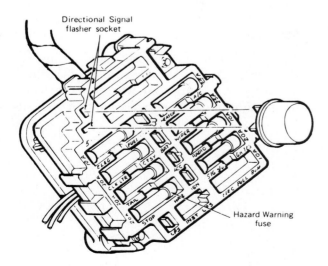

Directional Signal flasher socket

Hazard Warning fuse

Figure 18.17   Fuse block. Some automobiles have a fuse block of this type mounted beneath the instrument panel. Note that the fuses, when installed, are recessed below the surface of the fuse block (courtesy of Chevrolet Motor Division, General Motors Corporation).

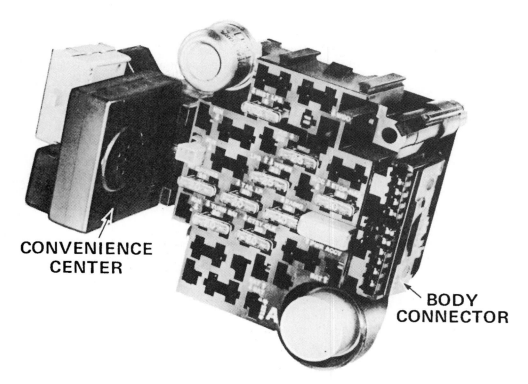

CONVENIENCE
CENTER

BODY
CONNECTOR

Figure 18.21   A miniaturized fuse block (courtesy of Pontiac Motor Division, General Motors Corporation).

Glass cartridge fuses are available in many sizes and ratings. Figure 18.16 shows some of the more commonly used sizes and ratings. A replacement fuse should always be of the same rating and size as the one removed. If you install a fuse with a lower rating, it may not be able to handle the normal current flow in the circuit. If you install a fuse with a higher rating, it will allow too much current to flow in the circuit. The excess current could damage other components.

> A resettable circuit breaker is a very useful tester tool. It should be wired so it can be put in the place of a fuse. The technician can repair problems and check the circuit without having the cost of a fuse if the problem is not completely solved. This cycle can be repeated as many times as necessary until the circuit is restored. Then the correct fuse can be installed.

Most cars have a *fuse block* located under the instrument panel. A fuse block provides a convenient, single location for most, if not all, of the fuses in a car. Figure 18.17 shows a fuse block for glass cartridge fuses. At times, a particular circuit will not have its fuse located in the fuse block. These circuits use an *in-line fuse holder* of the type shown in Figure 18.18. In wiring diagrams, an in-line fuse

holder is usually symbolized as shown in Figure 18.19. In-line fuse holders are often used in the wiring of accessories that have been added to a car. Those accessories include radios, tape decks, and special auxiliary lights.

Miniaturized Fuses.   Most late model cars use a miniaturized fuse, or *mini-fuse*, as shown in Figure 18.20. These fuses also use a strip of metal that melts. Mini-fuses plug into special fuse blocks and cannot be interchanged with glass cartridge fuses. A mini-fuse block is shown in Figure 18.21.

> When any electrical system does not work, always check the fuse to that circuit first. Fuses can fail even if the circuit does not have a problem. Remember, they are supposed to be the weakest link in the circuit. If the fuse passes a continuity test, check the wiring and circuits next. Motors can be checked by connecting a jumper wire directly to a battery source.

As with glass cartridge fuses, mini-fuses should be replaced only with fuses of the same rating. The rating of a mini-fuse is indicated by number and by color code (refer to Figure 18.20).

TESTING FUSES

When it is suspected that a fuse is blown, it is easier to test the fuse in the circuit than to remove it for testing. You can make the job even easier by using an appropriate manual. The manual will tell you where the fuse block is located. It will also show you the location of each fuse and the correct fuse rating. Figures 18.22 and 18.23 show how that information is given.

Glass Cartridge Fuses

Glass cartridge fuses can often be checked visually. With the aid of a flashlight you can usually see if the fuse is blown (refer to Figure 18.15). A positive test can be made by using a test light in the following manner:

1. Check the operation of the test light by connecting it across the terminals of a battery.
2. Turn ON the circuit that you wish to test.
3. Connect the test light alligator clip to a good ground.
4. Touch the probe of the test light to each end of the suspected fuse. Three results are possible:
   a. The test light glows when touched to either end of the fuse. This means that the fuse is good.
   b. The test light glows only when touched to one end of the fuse. This means that the fuse is blown or defective.
   c. The test light does not glow when touched to either end of the fuse. This means that the circuit is not turned ON, or that the circuit is broken between the fuse and the power source. It can also mean that you have a bad ground connection at the alligator clip.

Mini-Fuses

It is almost impossible to see if a mini-fuse is blown without removing it from the fuse block. Mini-fuses can easily be checked by using a test light in the following manner:

1. Check the operation of the test light by connecting it across the terminals of a battery.
2. Turn ON the circuit that you wish to test.

FUSES

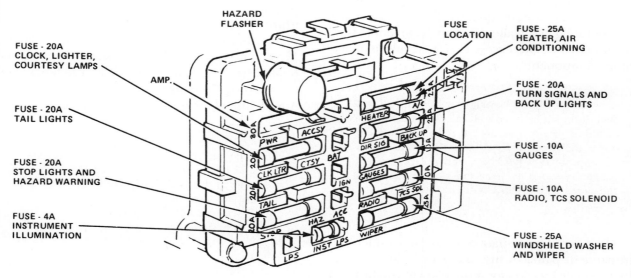

DO NOT USE   FUSES OF HIGHER AMPERAGE RATING THAN THOSE SPECIFIED

Figure 18.22   Fuse locations and specifications as found in a typical manufacturer's service manual (courtesy of Buick Motor Division, General Motors Corporation).

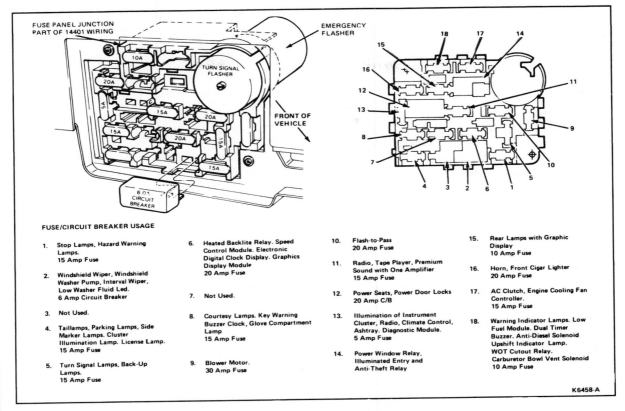

FUSE/CIRCUIT BREAKER USAGE

1. Stop Lamps, Hazard Warning Lamps.
   15 Amp Fuse

2. Windshield Wiper, Windshield Washer Pump, Interval Wiper, Low Washer Fluid Led.
   6 Amp Circuit Breaker

3. Not Used.

4. Taillamps, Parking Lamps, Side Marker Lamps. Cluster Illumination Lamp. License Lamp.
   15 Amp Fuse

5. Turn Signal Lamps, Back-Up Lamps.
   15 Amp Fuse

6. Heated Backlite Relay. Speed Control Module. Electronic Digital Clock Display. Graphics Display Module.
   20 Amp Fuse

7. Not Used.

8. Courtesy Lamps. Key Warning Buzzer Clock, Glove Compartment Lamp.
   15 Amp Fuse

9. Blower Motor.
   30 Amp Fuse

10. Flash-to-Pass
    20 Amp Fuse

11. Radio, Tape Player, Premium Sound with One Amplifier
    15 Amp Fuse

12. Power Seats, Power Door Locks
    20 Amp C/B

13. Illumination of Instrument Cluster, Radio, Climate Control, Ashtray. Diagnostic Module.
    5 Amp Fuse

14. Power Window Relay. Illuminated Entry and Anti-Theft Relay

15. Rear Lamps with Graphic Display
    10 Amp Fuse

16. Horn, Front Cigar Lighter
    20 Amp Fuse

17. AC Clutch, Engine Cooling Fan Controller.
    15 Amp Fuse

18. Warning Indicator Lamps. Low Fuel Module. Dual Timer Buzzer. Anti-Diesel Solenoid Upshift Indicator Lamp. WOT Cutout Relay. Carburetor Bowl Vent Solenoid
    10 Amp Fuse

Figure 18.23 Views of a typical fuse panel and the usage and locations of the fuses, circuit breakers, and flasher as provided in one manufacturer's service manual. Notice that the turn signal flasher and the hazard warning flasher are mounted back to back (courtesy of Ford Motor Company, Dearborn, MI).

3. Connect the test light alligator clip to a good ground.
4. Touch the probe of the test light to each of the test points exposed on the top of the fuse (refer to Figure 18.20). Three results are possible:

   a. The test light glows when touched to either of the test points. This means that the fuse is good.
   b. The test light glows only when touched to one of the test points. This means that the fuse is blown or defective.
   c. The test light does not glow when touched to either of the test points. This means that the circuit is not turned ON, or that the circuit is broken between the fuse and the power source. It can also mean that you have a bad ground connection at the alligator clip.

Replacing Fuses. When a glass cartridge fuse is mounted in a fuse block, it is almost impossible to remove it with your fingers. A hook made of stiff wire such as welding rod or coat hanger wire should be used. You can make that tool by following the sketch in Figure 18.24. The replacement fuse is easily pushed in place with your fingertips (refer to Figure 18.17).

Fuses contained inside in-line fuse holders are removed by grasping the ends of the fuse holder,

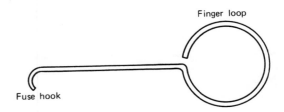

Figure 18.24 Fuse hook. A piece of stiff wire bent to the shape shown will enable you to remove fuses from a fuse block.

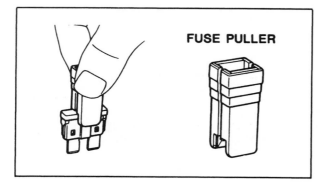

FUSE PULLER

Figure 18.25   Fuse puller. To avoid damaging the terminals in the fuse block, most manufacturers recommend the use of a fuse puller to remove mini-fuses (courtesy of Chevrolet Motor Division, General Motors Corporation).

pushing them together, and twisting the ends counterclockwise. The locking lugs will release and the ends can be pulled apart. After the replacement fuse is inserted, the ends are pushed together and twisted clockwise.

Although mini-fuses can often be removed by grasping them with your fingernails, most manufacturers recommend the use of a mini-fuse puller as shown in Figure 18.25. The use of a puller minimizes the possibility of damaging the terminals in the fuse block.

> Never replace a blown fuse with one of a higher amperage rating. The fuse should always be weaker than any component in the circuit. A higher fuse changes this, and something else in the circuit may be the weakest link. This can cause damage to components in the circuit if something happens to increase the amperage in the circuit.

Testing Removed Fuses.   Testing fuses that have been removed from a circuit is easily done with a *continuity tester*. A continuity tester, shown in Figure 18.26, is a test light that contains its own battery. Lacking a continuity tester, you can use a

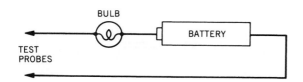

Figure 18.26   Continuity tester. A continuity tester, or self-powered test light, contains a small flashlight battery and a bulb. When continuity, or a complete circuit, is made between the test probes, the bulb will light.

Job 18B

REPLACE A FUSE

SATISFACTORY PERFORMANCE

A satisfactory performance on this job requires that you do the following:

1. Check the fuses in the vehicle assigned and replace the defective fuse.
2. Following the steps in the "Performance Outline" and the procedure and specifications of the manufacturer, complete the job within 15 minutes.
3. Fill in the blanks under "Information."

PERFORMANCE OUTLINE

1. Locate the fuse block or fuse holder.
2. Locate the defective fuse.
3. Install a replacement fuse.
4. Test the fused circuit.

INFORMATION

Vehicle identification _____
Reference used _____ Page(s) _____
Circuit in which defective fuse was found _____
Location of fuse:
____ Fuse block   ____ In-line fuse holder
Type of fuse:
____ Glass cartridge fuse   ____ Mini-fuse
Fuse identification and rating _____
Did the circuit operate properly after the fuse was replaced?
____ Yes   ____ No

---

test light and a battery as shown in Figure 18.27. When the test light glows, it indicates continuity, or a complete circuit, through the fuse.

Circuit Breakers

Although fuses provide a simple method of circuit protection, they are not always desirable. Some circuits are normally subjected to temporary over-

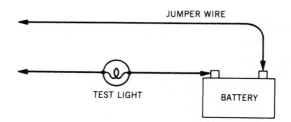

Figure 18.27   Test light and jumper wire. A test light and a jumper wire connected to a battery are often used to check for continuity.

Figure 18.28 A typical plug-in circuit breaker.

Figure 18.29 Fuse clip circuit breaker. Breakers of this type often are used to replace fuses because they can be plugged into standard cartridge fuse clips.

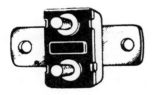

Figure 18.30 Stud circuit breaker. Breakers of this type often are used to protect window and seat motor circuits.

loads. As an example, the switches that control the motors for windows and seats are often inadvertently held in the ON position after the window or seat has moved to the limit of its travel. When that occurs, the motor stalls and the current flow in the circuit increases. If those circuits were pro-

tected by fuses, the fuses would require frequent replacement.

Another example of where the use of a fuse is not practical is in the headlight circuit. If a headlight circuit was protected by a fuse, a short that occurred in that circuit would blow the fuse. This would cause the headlights to go out and remain out until the short was eliminated and the fuse replaced. A headlight failure of that type could be the cause of an accident.

What is needed is a device that will open the circuit when current flow exceeds a certain limit, but will close the circuit again after a short length of time. Such a device is called a *circuit breaker*. Typical circuit breakers are shown in Figures 18.28 to 18.30. A circuit breaker is wired in a circuit in series, as if it were a fuse. Like a fuse, a circuit breaker is sensitive to heat and is rated by the amperage, or amount of current, that can flow through it. The current that passes through a circuit breaker flows through a special *bimetallic* conductor. That conductor is termed bimetallic because it is made of two strips of different metals bonded together. When heated, as by excessive current flow, the different metals expand at different rates, causing the conductor to bend as shown in Figure 18.31. That motion opens a set of switch contacts and breaks the circuit. Since the flow of current stops, the bimetallic conductor cools and returns to its original shape. That motion closes the switch contacts and the cycle is repeated. Operating in this manner, a circuit breaker provides the necessary protection, yet does not require replacement each time it is subjected to an overload.

In a headlight circuit, a circuit breaker usually turns the lights off and then on, alternating until the short or other cause of excessive current flow is located and eliminated.

Some circuit breakers are designed so they do not reset themselves automatically. As shown in

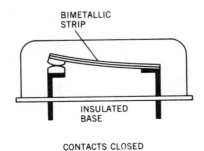

Figure 18.31 Circuit breaker operation. When excessive current flows through the bimetallic strip, the strip is heated, causing it to bend and open the contact points. When the strip cools, the points close.

Figure 18.32 Resettable circuit breaker. Note that the breaker is rated at 30 amperes and is for use in both 12- and 24-volt systems (courtesy of Chevrolet Motor Division, General Motors Corporation).

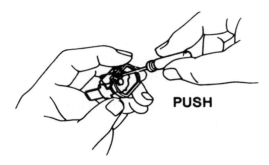

Figure 18.33 Resetting a circuit breaker (courtesy of Chevrolet Motor Division, General Motors Corporation).

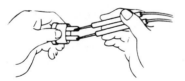

Figure 18.34 Testing a circuit breaker. With the test prods held to the terminals, a good circuit breaker should indicate continuity by causing a continuity tester to light (courtesy of Chevrolet Motor Division, General Motors Corporation).

Figures 18.32 and 18.33, they must be reset manually by inserting a probe or a piece of stiff wire in a reset hole.

Testing Circuit Breakers. Circuit breakers rarely fail, but when they are suspected of causing trouble, they can be checked easily. The easiest way to test a circuit breaker is by substitution. A replacement breaker known to be good is substituted for the one suspected of being bad. If the problem is eliminated, the breaker was bad. A circuit breaker removed from a circuit can be tested with a continuity tester in the same manner you tested fuses. Connected as shown in Figure 18.34, a good circuit breaker should have continuity.

Job 18C

REPLACE A CIRCUIT BREAKER

SATISFACTORY PERFORMANCE

A satisfactory performance on this job requires that you do the following:

1. Replace the designated circuit breaker on the car assigned.
2. Following the steps in the "Performance Outline" and the manufacturer's procedure and specifications, complete the job within 15 minutes.
3. Fill in the blanks under "Information."

PERFORMANCE OUTLINE

1. Determine the location of the designated circuit breaker.
2. Remove the old circuit breaker.
3. Install the replacement circuit breaker.
4. Test the operation of the circuit.

INFORMATION

Vehicle identification _____
Circuit breaker replaced _____
Reference used _____ Page(s) _____
Circuit breaker location _____
Circuit breaker rating _____
Was the circuit working properly after the breaker was replaced? ____ Yes ____ No

Replacing Circuit Breakers. Replacing a circuit breaker is a simple job. On most cars, the circuit breakers are located on the fuse block as shown in Figure 18.35. They are removed by unplugging them from their socket, and the replacement breaker is merely plugged in. At times,

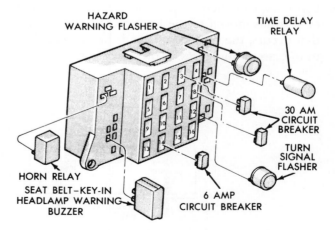

Figure 18.35 A fuse block for mini-fuses combined with a center for flashers, relays, circuit breakers, and a buzzer. An assembly of this type is called a *fuse block and relay module* (courtesy of Chrysler Corporation).

circuit breakers are placed in other locations. These locations vary with different makes and models of cars and can best be found with the aid of the car maker's service manual.

On many cars, stud-type circuit breakers (refer to Figure 18.30) are mounted on the firewall in the engine compartment. Some window and seat motors are protected by circuit breakers at their ground wires. Those breakers are located near the motors in the doors and under the seats. On many cars, the circuit breaker for the headlight circuit is built inside the headlight switch. The breaker is not serviced as a separate part, and the headlight switch must be replaced if the breaker fails.

Flashers

Most automotive lighting systems contain two flashers. The directional signal circuit includes one flasher. The hazard warning circuit contains the other. Flashers are controls, or switches, that automatically open and close a circuit. Because they are switches, flashers are placed in series in a circuit. This means that all the current which flows in the circuit passes through the flasher. Any failure of the flasher will affect the entire circuit.

As shown in Figure 18.36, a flasher is similar to a circuit breaker in that it is operated by heat. The current in the circuit flows through a bimetallic conductor that bends and opens a set of switch contacts. The contacts close when the conductor cools. The bimetallic conductor used in a flasher is selected to bend when the normal current for the circuit flows through it.

Most flashers are heat operated, but some electronic flashers are also found. Figure 18.37 shows a flasher of that type and its mounting.

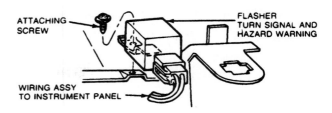

Figure 18.37 Electronic flasher. One some cars, a single electronic flasher is used to perform the functions of two heat-operated flashers (courtesy of Ford Motor Company, Dearborn, MI).

Testing a Flasher. The easiest way to test a flasher is by substitution. A replacement flasher known to be good is substituted for the one suspected of being bad.

Replacing a Flasher. Replacing a flasher is easy. In fact, at times it is more difficult to locate a flasher than it is to replace it. Because of this, the easiest method of replacing a flasher is to use an appropriate manual to find where the flasher is located.

Flashers are usually mounted under the instrument panel, but the exact locations vary, even among cars built by the same manufacturer. On some cars, both flashers are located on the fuse block (refer to Figure 18.21). On other cars, only one flasher will be found on the fuse block (refer to Figure 18.22). The remaining flasher is mounted in some other location. Figure 18.38 shows the location chosen by one car maker to mount both flashers in one model car. On some

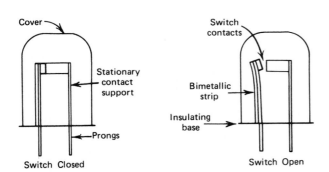

Figure 18.36 Flasher operation. Current flowing through the bimetallic strip causes the strip to bend, opening the contacts. When the strip cools, it returns and the contacts close.

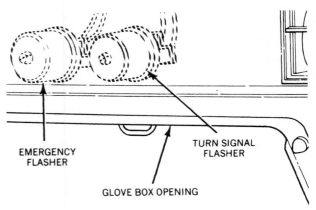

Figure 18.38 Flasher locations vary with each model car. On this model they are mounted above the glove box (courtesy of Ford Motor Company, Dearborn, MI).

Job 18D

REPLACE A FLASHER

SATISFACTORY PERFORMANCE
A satisfactory performance on this job requires that you do the following:

1. Replace the designated flasher on the car assigned.
2. Following the steps in the "Performance Outline" and the manufacturer's procedure and specifications, complete the job within 15 minutes.
3. Fill in the blanks under "Information."

PERFORMANCE OUTLINE

1. Determine the location of the designated flasher.
2. Remove the old flasher.
3. Install the correct replacement flasher.
4. If necessary, secure the replacement flasher.
5. Test the operation of the circuit.

INFORMATION

Vehicle identification _____
Reference used _____ Page(s) _____
Flasher replaced: Directional signal ____
                     Hazard warning ____
                     Combination ____
Flasher location _____
Was circuit working properly after the flasher was replaced?

_____

cars, one of the flashers is taped to part of the wiring harness.

Most flashers have two prongs as shown in Figure 18.39. Unplugging the old flasher and

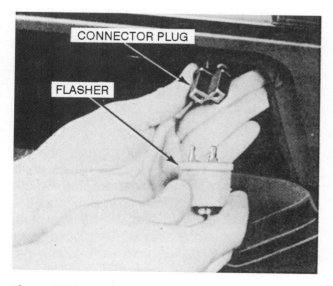

Figure 18.39 Replacing a flasher. Note that the flasher has two prongs that plug into a socket or quick disconnect (courtesy of Ford Motor Company, Dearborn, MI).

plugging in the replacement is usually all that is required.

> When the turn signal panel indicator light comes on but does not blink, look for a burned-out bulb in either the front or rear on the side that doesn't flash. Correct this problem immediately because other drivers will not know the vehicle is getting ready to make a turn.

Switches

Every car has a variety of switches that open and close the different lighting circuits. Some of these switches, including the headlight switch and the turn signal switch, are operated manually. Other switches, such as those that control the stop lights and the backup lights, are operated remotely.

Replacing Switches. The following replacement procedures are typical for the switches listed. Many variations of switch design and mounting are used. So obtain the replacement procedure for a specific switch on a particular car from the manufacturer's manual.

Dimmer Switches. On may cars, the headlight dimmer switch is located on the steering column where it can be controlled by the left hand. The switch is activated by lifting up on the end of the turn signal switch arm. To repair or replace this switch requires a knowledge of how to remove the steering wheel parts covering the switch (see Figure 18.40).

Headlight Switches. In most instances, headlight switches are removed from behind the instrument panel. Before you attempt to remove a headlight switch, disconnect the ground cable from the battery. This will eliminate the possibility of a short and fire in the wiring (see Figure 18.41).

The headlight switch on older cars is held to the instrument panel by a nut. Before that nut can be removed, the knob or the knob and shaft assembly must be removed.

On these cars, the shaft is released by pushing a release button located on the switch. The switch must be in the ON position while the release button is pushed. On some cars, the knob is held to the shaft by a spring clip. This clip can be released by using a stiff wire hook, as shown in Figure 18.42.

After the knob or the knob and shaft assembly have been removed, the retaining nut can be

Figure 18.40 Combination switch. Switches like this are used for a combination of uses such as wiper, cruise control, headlight dimmer, and windshield washer (courtesy of Training Enterprises Company).

Figure 18.41 Headlight switch. A typical headlight and parking light switch. These switches are turned on by pushing on the end of the switch button (courtesy of Training Enterprises Company).

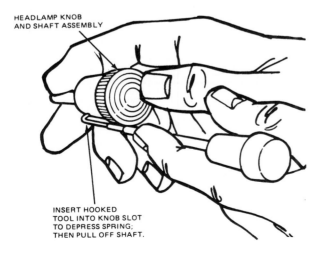

Figure 18.42 Removing a knob from the shaft of a headlight switch (courtesy of Ford Motor Company, Dearborn, MI).

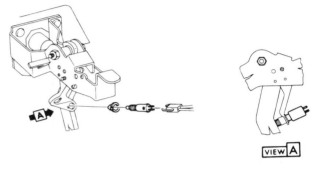

Figure 18.43 A typical stoplight switch installation. When the brake pedal is depressed, the spring-loaded plunger moves outward, turning the switch on (courtesy of Chevrolet Motor Division, General Motors Corporation).

removed. The switch is then lowered and unplugged from its socket on the end of the wiring harness. The replacement switch is installed by reversing the procedure.

Stoplight Switches. The stoplight switch on most cars is located under the instrument panel and above the brake pedal. Some of those switches are similar to the one shown in Figure 18.43. The switch fits into a hole in a mounting bracket and is secured with a lock nut. Prongs on the back of the switch plug into a socket on the wires. The switch is removed by disconnecting the wires and removing the lock nut. The replacement switch is installed by reversing those steps. The switch should be adjusted so it closes the stoplight circuit when the brake pedal is depressed about 1/4 in. (6 mm) to 5/8 in. (15 mm) from its fully released position. On some cars, the bracket is adjustable (refer to Figure 18.43). On other cars, the hole in the mounting bracket is threaded. Turning the switch in or out provides the adjustment.

Figure 18.44 shows another type of stoplight switch in common use. A switch of this type fits on the pin that connects the brake pedal to the master cylinder push rod. Switches of this type are nonadjustable. The switch closes the stoplight

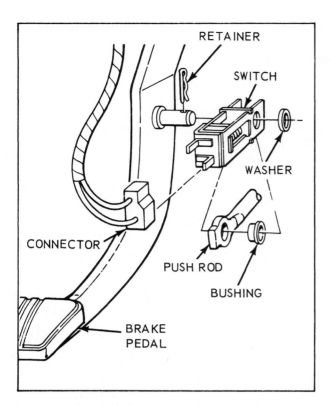

Figure 18.44   A stoplight switch that is mounted on the brake pedal linkage (courtesy of Ford Motor Company, Dearborn, MI).

Job 18E

REPLACE A SWITCH

SATISFACTORY PERFORMANCE

A satisfactory performance on this job requires that you do the following:

1. Replace the designated switch on the car assigned.
2. Following the steps in the "Performance Outline" and the procedure and specifications of the manufacturer complete the job within 200% of the manufacturer's suggested time.
3. Fill in the blanks under "Information."

PERFORMANCE OUTLINE

1. Remove the designated switch.
2. Install the replacement switch.
3. Check the operation of the circuit.

INFORMATION

Vehicle identification _____

Switch replaced _____

Reference used _____ Page(s) _____

circuit when the pedal is moved the small distance allowed by the oversize hole in the eye of the push rod. The operation of the switch is shown in Figure 18.45.

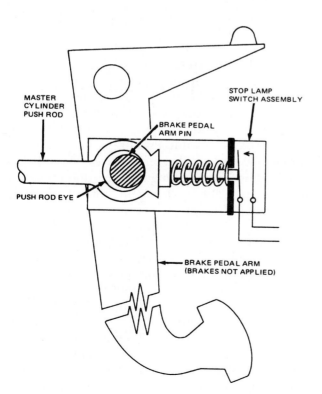

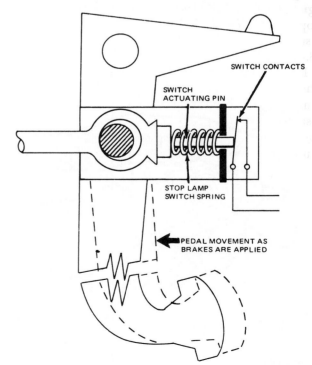

Figure 18.45   The operation of a linkage-mounted stoplight switch. The switch is operated by the movement allowed by the oversize hole in the push rod eye (courtesy of Ford Motor Company, Dearborn, MI).

To remove a switch of this type, unplug the wire connector. Then pull out the hairpin-shaped retainer and slide the switch and the push rod off the pedal pin. The replacement switch is aligned with the push rod, the bushing, and the washer, and slipped over the pin. Installing the retainer and connecting the wires completes the installation (refer to Figure 18.44).

LESSON 18–3 Lights

Small Bulbs

A small bulb consists of a filament enclosed in a ball-shaped glass envelope. To prevent the filament from burning out, the air is evacuated from the bulb and it is sealed. Most automotive bulbs have a metal base that fits into a socket. That base is referred to as a *bayonet base* because it usually has lugs, or pins, on its side that engage with locking slots in the socket. Bulbs with threaded bases are not used in automobiles because they tend to become loose with vibration. The construction of a typical small bulb is shown in Figure 18.46.

Some bulbs contain two filaments. These bulbs are used where one light must serve two functions. An example of where a bulb of this type is used is in a parking light that is also used as a directional signal. On many cars, the function of taillights and stoplights is served by bulbs of this construction. A small bulb with two filaments is shown in Figure 18.47.

Dozens of small bulbs are used in every car. These bulbs are of many different designs. They range from the wedge type used to illuminate the instruments to the double filament designs used in parking lights and taillights. Bulbs are identified by a universal numbering system, used by all American

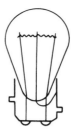

Figure 18.47 A sectioned view of a bulb with two filaments. Note that the center wire is attached to the metal base and forms a common ground for both filaments.

car manufacturers. Figure 18.48 shows some of the more commonly used bulb types.

> Bulbs can be checked with a 12-volt tester or connected to a battery (see Figure 18.49). A double filament bulb has to be checked on both filaments in order to pass the test.

Testing Small Bulbs. In most instances, a bulb can be checked visually. If the filament is broken or missing, the bulb is defective. A bulb can be tested by using a jumper wire as shown in Figure 18.49 to connect it across the terminals of a battery. But, because the bulb must be removed for testing, it is usually easier to test it by substitution. Just install a replacement bulb known to be good and turn on the circuit. If the replacement bulb lights, you can assume the old bulb was defective.

Replacing Small Bulbs in Exterior Lights. Before you can replace a bulb, you must gain access to it. On most cars, the designs of the parking lights, taillights, and marker lights change annually with the styling of the car. These changes often require a change in service procedure. The correct procedure for any particular car can be found in the manufacturer's service manual.

> The best place to check bulbs is in a shaded area. Check the intensity of each bulb. Sometimes one bulb will be intense and another in the same circuit will be very weak. This is largely due to the condition of the socket and differences in circuit resistance. Clean the socket and check the intensity again. Low intensity may mean the socket needs to be replaced.

In general, you can gain access to a bulb in one of two ways. You can remove the lens, or you can remove the socket. As shown in Figure 18.50, the lens on some lamp assemblies is secured by screws.

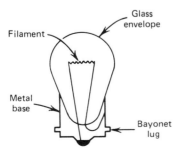

Figure 18.46 A sectioned view of a typical small bulb. The air is evacuated from the glass envelope so the filament can glow white-hot without burning.

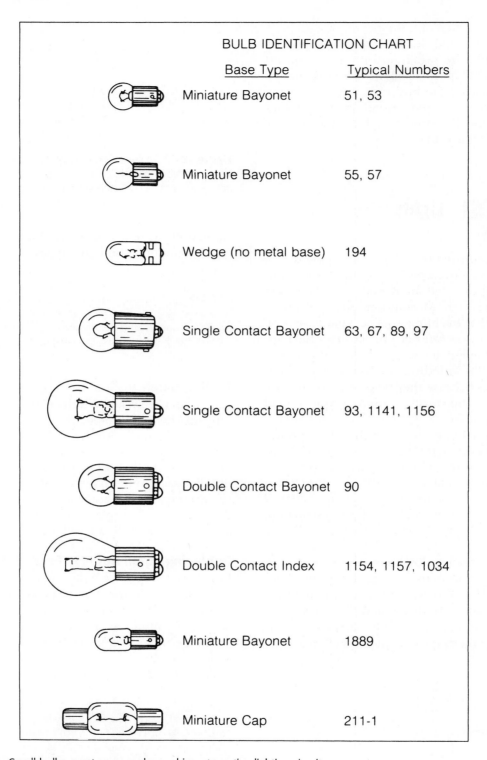

Figure 18.48 Small bulbs most commonly used in automotive lighting circuits.

Removing those screws will allow you to remove the lens. On some cars, the space between the bulb and the sides of the reflector is very limited and it is hard to get a grip on the bulb. In such instances, and where the bulb may be tight in its socket, you may find it helpful to use a pair of bulb-gripping pliers of the type shown in Figure 18.51. Another similar pair of pliers, shown in Figure 18.52, can be used to remove the base of a broken bulb. Those tools can help you to avoid cuts from broken bulbs.

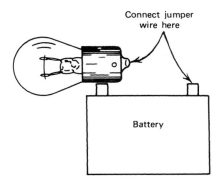

Connect jumper
wire here

Battery

Figure 18.49 Small bulb test. A small bulb can be tested by using a jumper wire to connect the bulb across the terminals of a battery.

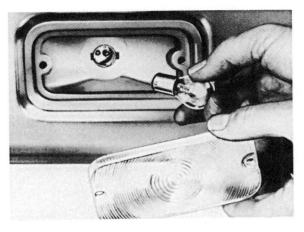

Figure 18.50 Bulb replacement. On some cars, the bulbs in some of the exterior lights can be reached by removing the lens (courtesy of Ford Motor Company, Dearborn, MI).

Figure 18.51 A pair of pliers designed for removing bulbs. The soft, plastic-coated jaws grip the bulb securely and minimize breakage (courtesy of KD Tools, Lancaster, PA 17604).

On other cars, you must remove the socket from the rear of the reflector. Figure 18.53 shows two different types of removable sockets. Both types must be pushed in and turned counter clockwise for removal. Sockets of these types usually have locating keys or tabs that allow installation in only one posi-

Figure 18.52 A pair of pliers designed for removing the bases of broken bulbs (courtesy of KD Tools, Lancaster, PA).

tion. When installing these sockets, align the tabs, push the socket in, and turn clockwise to lock it. Access to those sockets may be from inside the trunk, or luggage compartment, behind the grill, behind the bumper, or inside a fender. Figures 18.54 to 18.56 show some of those locations.

Replacing Small Bulbs in Interior Lights. The bulbs used inside a car quite often outnumber those used for exterior lighting. Bulbs used to

Job 18F

REPLACE A SMALL BULB

SATISFACTORY PERFORMANCE
A satisfactory performance on this job requires that you do the following:

1. Replace the designated bulb on the car assigned.
2. Following the steps in the "Performance Outline" and the procedure and specifications of the manufacturer, complete the job within 200% of the manufacturer's suggested time.
3. Fill in the blanks under "Information."

PERFORMANCE OUTLINE

1. Remove any parts necessary to gain access to the bulb.
2. Remove the defective bulb.
3. Install the replacement bulb.
4. Install any parts removed to gain access.
5. Test the operation of the bulb.

INFORMATION

Vehicle identification _____
Location of bulb replaced _____
Number of bulb replaced _____
Reference used _____ Page(s) _____
Bulb was replaced by removing:
_____ lens _____ socket
Was the light working correctly after the bulb was replaced?
_____ Yes _____ No

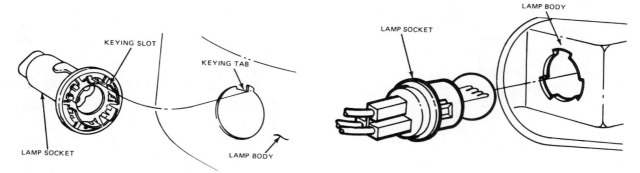

Figure 18.53   Sockets. Different sockets have different types of alignment and locking keys (courtesy of Ford Motor Company, Dearborn, MI).

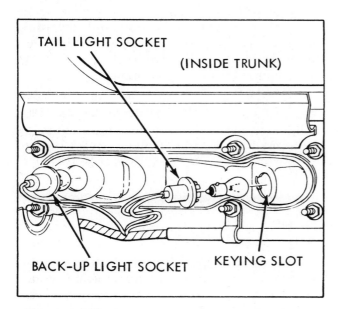

Figure 18.54   Inside trunk bulb replacement system. On many cars, the bulbs in the rear lights are accessible from inside the trunk (courtesy of Ford Motor Company, Dearborn, MI).

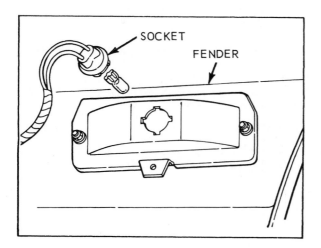

Figure 18.55   Side marker bulbs. Access to the bulbs in side marker lights is usually obtained from inside the fenders (courtesy of Ford Motor Company, Dearborn, MI).

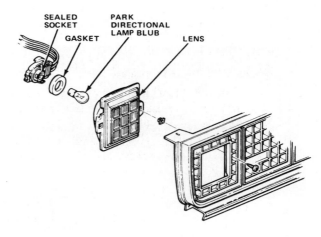

Figure 18.56   Parking lamp bulb. Access to the bulb in this parking lamp is from behind the grill (courtesy of American Motors).

illuminate the passenger compartment will be found with all types of bases (refer to Figure 18.48). In most instances, the lens of the lamp must be removed to replace the bulb. The lenses in some cars are retained by screws, as shown in Figure 18.57. On other cars, the lens snaps into place and is removed by squeezing the lens or by prying it loose as shown in Figure 18.58. Since many different lamp designs are used, consult the car maker's manual for the correct replacement procedure.

Figures 18.59 and 18.60 show the location of the bulbs used in typical instrument panels. Bulbs used to illuminate instruments and bulbs used in the various warning lights are usually of the wedge type. The bulb is pushed into a plastic socket fitted with bayonet lugs. The socket in turn is installed in the back of the instrument panel with the same push-and-twist motion used to install bayonet base bulbs. On some cars, the bulbs are accessible by reaching under the instrument panel. On most cars, however, the instrument panel must be partially or completely removed in order to change a bulb.

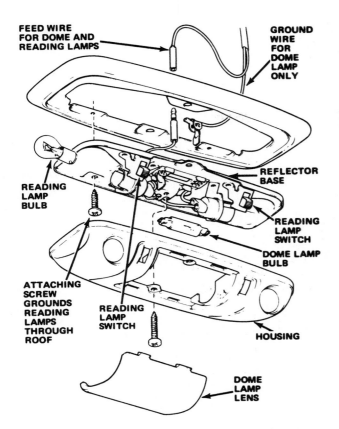

Figure 18.57 Dome light assembly. The dome lamp lens can be pried off to change the bulb in this assembly, but the screws holding the housing must be removed to change the reading lamp bulbs (courtesy of American Motors).

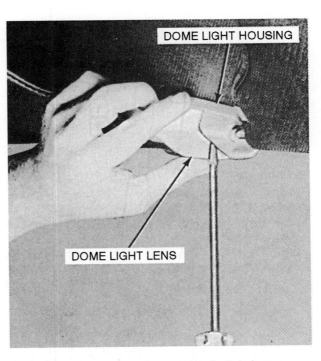

Figure 18.58 Interior lights. Some interior light lenses are removed by carefully prying the lens loose from its housing (courtesy of Ford Motor Company, Dearborn, MI).

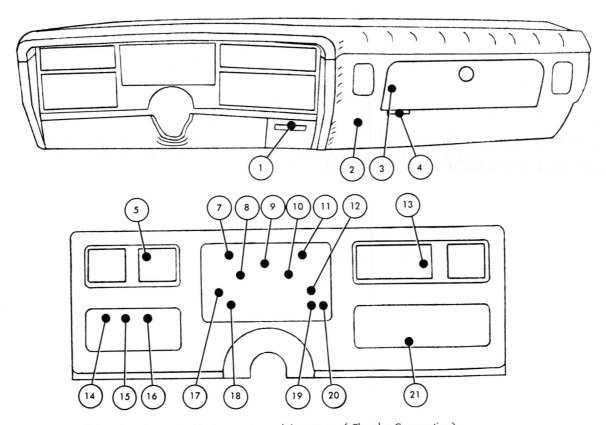

Figure 18.59 Bulb locations in a typical instrument panel (courtesy of Chrysler Corporation).

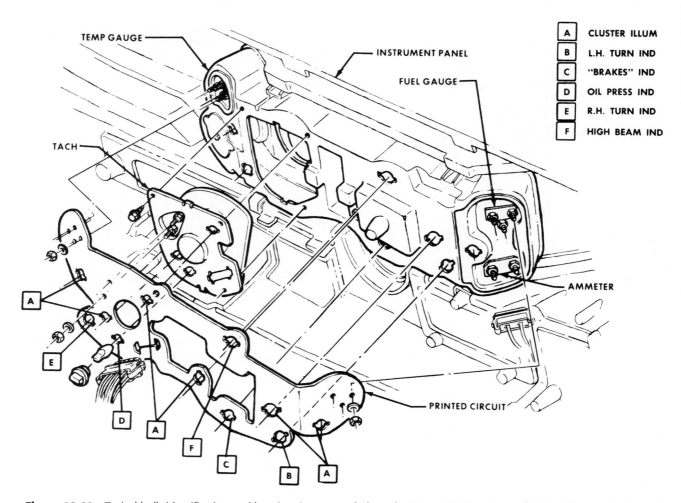

Figure 18.60 Typical bulb identification and location (courtesy of Chevrolet Motor Division, General Motors Corporation).

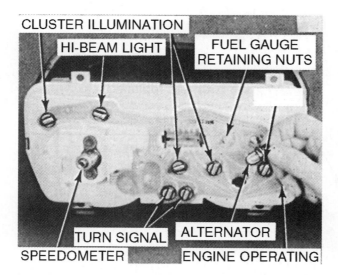

Figure 18.61 Instrument cluster bulbs. The rear of an instrument cluster that has been removed from an instrument panel. Notice the plastic caps that hold the wedge-type bulbs (courtesy of Ford Motor Company, Dearborn, MI).

Figure 18.61 shows the bulb locations in an instrument cluster that has been removed. The procedure for removing the instrument cluster varies greatly from car to car. Obtain the specific procedure for a particular car from the manufacturer's manual.

Bulb Service

A sealed beam bulb is actually an assembly of a bulb, a lens, and a reflector. In a true sealed beam bulb, the lens and the reflector are fused together into one unit. The filament is mounted in the reflector and positioned so the light is most effectively reflected. Since the unit is sealed and all air evacuated from it, the thin glass envelope used on small bulbs is not needed. The lens has small prisms molded on its inner surface. Those prisms bend the light rays so the desired beam shape is projected. Typical sealed beam bulbs are shown in Figures 18.62 and 18.63.

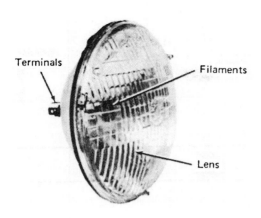

Figure 18.62 A typical round sealed beam headlight bulb (courtesy of Guide Lamp Division, General Motors Corporation).

Some sealed beam bulbs have two filaments. One filament provides a *high beam* that projects a concentrated, high-intensity beam of light straight ahead. The high beam is intended for use only when it cannot interfere with the vision of the drivers of oncoming cars. The remaining filament provides a *low beam.* The low beam provides a less concentrated distribution of light that is aimed slightly downward and toward the right. The low beam is intended for use in traffic and at other times when the high beam could disturb other drivers. Sealed beam bulbs with two filaments have three prongs, or terminals, projecting from the rear of the reflector.

Some sealed beam bulbs have only one filament. That filament is used as a high beam only. Bulbs of that type are used as the inner or lower bulbs in *dual headlight systems,* systems that use four headlights. Since they have only one filament, they require only two prongs, or terminals.

Sealed beam bulbs used as automotive headlights are built in two shapes, round and rectangular. Two sizes are available in each shape. The larger bulbs are for use in systems that have two headlights. The smaller bulbs are for use in dual systems. A number/letter code, usually molded into the lens, has been adopted to identify the most commonly used sealed beam bulbs. The number indicates the number of filaments, and the letter indicates the size and shape of the bulb. Figure 18.64 lists those bulbs and their codes.

Many cars are fitted with halogen headlight bulbs. In most instances those units are physically similar to conventional sealed beam bulbs, but they are more efficient and provide more light. Although conventional and halogen sealed beam bulbs are interchangeable in most instances, they should never be mixed. All of the headlights on a car should be of the same type—all conventional or all halogen.

Some cars have headlights that are not of the sealed beam type. As shown in Figure 18.65, those headlights contain a small, replaceable halogen bulb. In most instances, those small bulbs may be replaced without removing or disturbing the headlight assembly.

Aiming Headlights. To provide effective lighting, headlights must be aimed. Proper

Figure 18.63 A typical rectangular sealed beam bulb (courtesy of Wagner Division, Cooper Industries, Inc.).

SHAPE	SIZE	NUMBER OF FILAMENTS	FUNCTION	CODE
Round	7" (178 mm) diameter	2	High-Low	2D
Round	5¾" (146 mm) diameter	2	High-Low	2C
Round	5¾" (146 mm) diameter	1	High Only	1C
Rectangular	5.6" x 7.9" (142 x 200 mm)	2	High-Low	2B
Rectangular	4" x 6.5" (100 x 165 mm)	2	High-Low	2A
Rectangular	4" x 6.5" (100 x 165 mm)	1	High-Only	1A

Figure 18.64 Identification chart for the six most commonly used automotive sealed beam headlight bulbs. The code usually is molded into the lens.

Figure 18.65 A replaceable halogen bulb used in certain headlights (courtesy of Ford Motor Company, Dearborn, MI).

maintenance of any vehicle should include checking the aim of the headlights. In many states, motor vehicle inspection laws require that headlight aim be checked and adjusted periodically. The aim of the headlights can be changed by road shock, minor accidents, and changes in suspension height. Most car makers suggest that headlight aim be checked at least once each year and after the replacement of a sealed beam bulb.

Most shops use headlight aiming devices to obtain the proper adjustment. Lacking those devices, headlights can be aimed by observing the spots of light projected on a wall chart or on a marked wall.

REPLACING SEALED BEAM BULBS

The following steps outline a typical procedure for replacing a sealed beam headlight bulb. Consult an appropriate manual for alternate procedures that may be necessary on some cars.

1. Remove the screws holding the headlight door or trim (see Figures 18.66 and 18.67).

   Note: A Phillips screwdriver will remove the screws holding the headlight doors on some cars, and others have special screws requiring tools of the type shown in Figure 18.68.

2. Remove the headlight door.
3. Remove the small screws holding the headlight retainer. Do not loosen or disturb the adjusting screws (see Figures 18.69 and 18.70).

   Note: Some cars have a spring that holds one side of the retainer. That spring can easily be disconnected by using the tool you made to remove fuses (refer to Figure 18.24).

4. Remove the retainer.

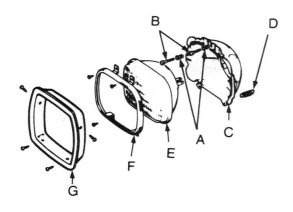

A. Plastic Adjuster
   Nut(s)
B. Adjusting Screw(s)
C. Headlamp Bucket

D. Adjusting Spring
E. Headlamp
F. Retaining Ring
G. Trim Ring

Figure 18.66 A typical headlamp assembly (courtesy of American Motors).

Figure 18.67 A headlight door and its attaching screws. On most cars, the door, or trim, must be removed to gain access to the sealed beam retainer (courtesy of American Motors).

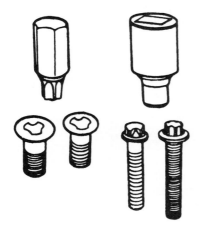

Figure 18.68 Headlight screws. The headlight doors and trim on some cars are secured with special screws and bolts that require special screwdriver bits and sockets (courtesy of Chevrolet Motor Division, General Motors Corporation).

Figure 18.69 Retainer screw removal. After the headlight door has been removed, the screws holding the retainer are removed (courtesy of American Motors).

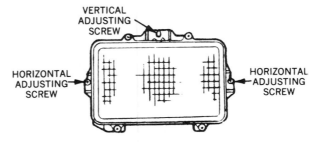

Figure 18.70 Headlight adjusting screws. The vertical adjusting screw usually is located at the top, but the horizontal adjusting screw may be found on either side (courtesy of Chevrolet Motor Division, General Motors Corporation).

Some vehicles have a built-in headlight aiming system. The vehicle has to be level and the vertical and horizontal screws adjusted so the headlamp-adjusting bubbles are right. Loads in the trunk and weight in the passenger compartment all affect the headlight beam direction. If the driver notices that oncoming drivers are annoyed by headlight beams in their eyes, the headlights should be adjusted.

5. Carefully pull the sealed beam bulb forward and disconnect the wiring harness plug by pulling it straight off.
6. Align the prongs of the replacement bulb with the wiring harness plug and push the parts together so the prongs are fully seated.
7. Position the bulb in the adjustment ring so the alignment tabs on the rear edge of the bulb fit into the slots in the ring.

   Note: The alignment tabs are located so the bulb will fit properly in only one position.

8. Install the retainer.

   Note: The screw holes in the edge of the retainer are usually located so the retainer will fit properly in only one position.

9. Check the operation of the bulb.
10. Install the headlight door.

REPLACING SMALL HALOGEN BULBS

Although different methods of bulb retention may be found, the following steps outline a typical procedure for the removal and installation of replaceable bulbs in headlight assemblies:

> **! WARNING:**   Replaceable halogen headlight bulbs contain gas under pressure. Those bulbs may shatter if the glass envelope is scratched or if they are dropped. Handle these bulbs very carefully, holding them only by their plastic base.

1. Check to be sure the headlight switch is in the OFF position.
2. Unplug the electrical connector from the rear of the bulb (see Figure 18.71).
3. Unlock the bulb retaining ring by turning it counterclockwise, and remove it from the base of the bulb.

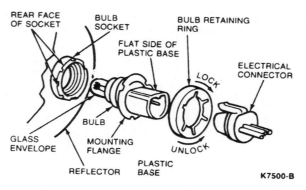

Figure 18.71   A typical installation of a small halogen headlight bulb (courtesy of Ford Motor Company, Dearborn, MI).

4. Carefully remove the bulb from its socket by pulling it straight out.
5. Insert the replacement bulb in the socket, aligning the mounting flange.
6. Install the bulb retaining ring, rotating it clockwise until it locks.
7. Plug the electrical connector into the base of the bulb.
8. Check the operation of the headlights.

Job 18G

REPLACE A HEADLIGHT BULB

SATISFACTORY PERFORMANCE

A satisfactory performance on this job requires that you do the following:

1. Replace the designated headlight bulb(s) on the car assigned.
2. Following the steps in the "Performance Outline" and the procedure and specifications of the manufacturer, complete the job within 200% of the manufacturer's suggested time.
3. Fill in the blanks under "Information."

PERFORMANCE OUTLINE

1. Remove any parts necessary to gain access to the headlight bulb.
2. Remove the bulb.
3. Install the replacement bulb.
4. Install parts removed to gain access.
5. Check bulb operation.

INFORMATION

Vehicle identification _____

Location of bulb(s) replaced:

_____ Right side   _____ Left side
_____ Upper   _____ Upper
_____ Lower   _____ Lower
_____ Inner   _____ Inner
_____ Outer   _____ Outer

Number marked on bulb(s) replaced _____

Were the lights working correctly after the bulb(s) were replaced? _____ Yes _____ No

| AIMING HEADLIGHTS BY USING MECHANICAL AIMERS | The following steps outline a procedure for aiming headlights by using mechanical aimers. The aiming device used, shown in Figure 18.72, is the type recommended by most car manufacturers. If the aiming device you have available is not of that type, consult the manual furnished with the aimers you have available. |

Adjusting the Aimers   The aimers are furnished with calibration fixtures that enable you to adjust the aimers to compensate for any slight slope in the floor.

1. Park the vehicle in an area that appears to be level.
2. Check to see that the tires are properly inflated.
3. Attach the calibration fixtures to the aimers as shown in Figure 18.73.

   Note: The calibration fixtures snap into place when properly aligned.

4. Stand the aimers on the floor next to the right side of the car as shown in Figure 18.74. Aimer A must be aligned with the center of the rear wheel. Aimer B must be aligned with the center of the front wheel. The adjusting knobs must face outward and the targets must face each other.

Figure 18.72 A typical mechanical headlight aiming kit. Note the various adapters furnished so the aimers can be used on all types and sizes of bulbs (courtesy of American Motors).

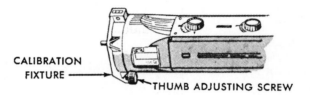

CALIBRATION FIXTURE

THUMB ADJUSTING SCREW

Figure 18.73 A calibration fixture attached to a headlight aimer (courtesy of Chrysler Corporation).

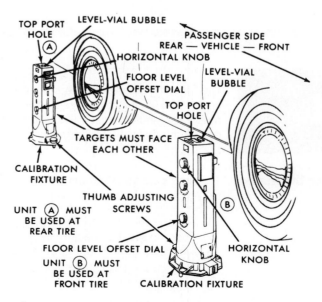

TOP PORT HOLE (A)   LEVEL-VIAL BUBBLE   PASSENGER SIDE REAR — VEHICLE — FRONT   HORIZONTAL KNOB   FLOOR LEVEL OFFSET DIAL   LEVEL-VIAL BUBBLE   TOP PORT HOLE   TARGETS MUST FACE EACH OTHER   CALIBRATION FIXTURE   THUMB ADJUSTING SCREWS   (B)   UNIT (A) MUST BE USED AT REAR TIRE   FLOOR LEVEL OFFSET DIAL   UNIT (B) MUST BE USED AT FRONT TIRE   CALIBRATION FIXTURE   HORIZONTAL KNOB

Figure 18.74 Slope compensation. Any slope of the floor can be compensated for by measurements taken with the aimers positioned at the front and rear wheels of the car (courtesy of Chrysler Corporation).

Figure 18.75 Reading the bubbles. Bubble levels are used to adjust the level of the aimers (courtesy of Chrysler Corporation).

Mark out a special spot in the shop to position each vehicle prior to setting the headlights. If this is done, the aimers will not have to be calibrated each time they are used. Leave the aimers on this setting and drive each vehicle to this spot. Do a calibration check once a month to see if anything has happened to the aimers.

When finished aiming a set of headlights, the high-beam pattern should be pointed straight ahead and should drop 2 inches at a 20-foot distance. The dimmer light pattern is built into the bulb. When the lights are set on dim, the light beam pattern should move left and down.

5. Adjust the level of each aimer by turning the thumb adjusting screw on each calibration fixture (refer to Figure 18.73). The adjustment is correct when the bubble in the top level vial is centered as shown in Figure 18.75.

6. Look down into the top port hole in aimer A (refer to Figure 18.74). You should see an image similar to those shown in Figure 18.76.

   Note: Moving your head from side to side will enable you to locate the image. At times, you will have to rotate one or both of the aimers slightly to correct their alignment.

7. While watching the image, turn the horizontal knob back and forth slowly until the split image is aligned (refer to Figure 18.76).

8. Lift aimer A and observe the plus (+) or minus (−) reading indicated on the horizontal dial.

9. Adjust the floor level dials on both aimers to the reading found on the horizontal dial (see Figure 18.77).

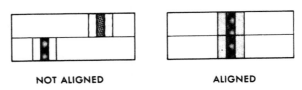

Figure 18.76 Reading the split image. The "split image" is aligned by turning the horizontal knob (courtesy of Chrysler Corporation).

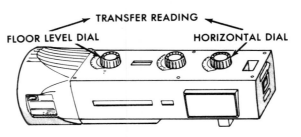

Figure 18.77 Reading the headlight aimer. The reading obtained at the horizontal dial must be transferred to the floor level dial. This adjusts the aimer to compensate for any slope in the floor (courtesy of Chrysler Corporation).

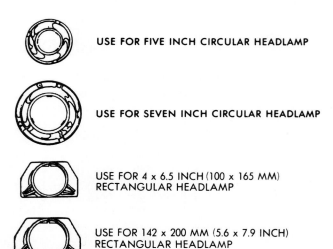

USE FOR FIVE INCH CIRCULAR HEADLAMP

USE FOR SEVEN INCH CIRCULAR HEADLAMP

USE FOR 4 x 6.5 INCH (100 x 165 MM)
RECTANGULAR HEADLAMP

USE FOR 142 x 200 MM (5.6 x 7.9 INCH)
RECTANGULAR HEADLAMP

Figure 18.78 Some of the more commonly used headlight aimer adapters and their application (courtesy of Chrysler Corporation).

Note: The floor level dials are self-locking. They must be pushed in slightly before they can be turned.

10. Remove the calibration fixtures from the aimers.

Mounting the Aimers

The aimers must be fitted with adapters before they can be mounted on the headlights.

1. Clean the headlight lenses with a wet paper towel.

   Note: The suction cups in the aimers will not hold on dirty lenses.

2. Select the adapters required to fit the headlights and install them on the aimers. Figure 18.78 shows the various adapters and their applications.

3. Check the accessibility of the adjusting screws. Remove the headlight doors if necessary.

   Note: On some cars, the headlight doors are notched as shown in Figure 18.79. Those notches enable you to reach the adjusting screws without removing the doors.

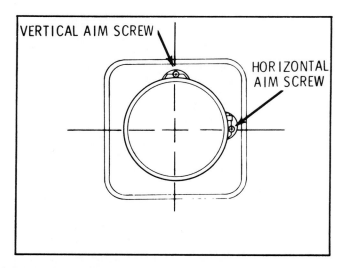

Figure 18.79 Adjusting screw locations. Some headlight doors are notched or drilled for access to the adjusting screws (courtesy of Chevrolet Motor Division, General Motors Corporation).

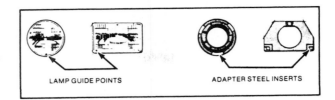

Figure 18.80 Lamp guide posts. All sealed beam headlight bulbs have guide points molded into the edge of the lens. The steel inserts in the adapters must contact those points when the aimers are installed (courtesy of Pontiac Motor Division, General Motors Corporation).

4. Position aimer A on the left (driver's side) headlight. Check to see that the steel inserts in the adapter are in contact with the guide points that project from the edge of the lens (see Figure 18.80).
5. Holding the aimer in position, push the piston handle on the bottom of the aimer forward to force the suction cup against the lens. Pull the handle back immediately until it locks in place (see Figure 18.81). The aimer should now be mounted on the lens.
6. Repeat steps 4 and 5 to mount aimer B on the right-side headlight.

Horizontal Adjustment

1. Adjust the horizontal dial on aimer A to zero (0) (see Figure 18.82).
2. Look down into the viewing port on aimer A. You should see the split image lines (refer to Figure 18.76).

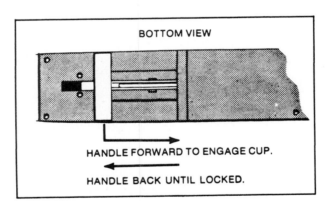

Figure 18.81 The operation of the piston handle on the headlight aimer (courtesy of Pontiac Motor Division, General Motors Corporation).

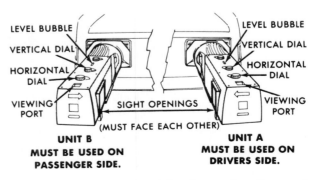

Figure 18.82 The location of the parts of the aimers when they are installed on the headlights (courtesy of Chrysler Corporation).

Figure 18.83   Horizontal adjusting screw. The horizontal adjusting screw in the headlight assembly is turned to align the split image (courtesy of Chrysler Corporation).

Note: If the lines are not visible, you may have to rotate one or both of the aimers slightly to shift the position of the sight openings.

3. Using a screwdriver, slowly turn the horizontal adjusting screw located at the side of the headlight (refer to Figures 18.69 and 18.70). Turn the screw in or out as required until the split image is aligned (see Figure 18.83).
4. Repeat steps 1 through 3 at the opposite headlight.

Vertical Adjustment

1. Set the vertical dial knob on aimer A to zero (0). (Refer to Figure 18.82).
   Note: The motor vehicle laws of your state may require a different setting.
2. Using a screwdriver, slowly turn the vertical adjusting screw located at the top (or bottom) of the headlight (refer to Figures 18.69 and 18.70). Turn the screw in or out as required until the bubble in the level is centered (see Figure 18.84).
3. Repeat steps 1 and 2 at the opposite headlight.
4. Check the alignment of the split images at both aimers.
   Note: A slight readjustment at one or both lights may be necessary.
5. Remove the aimers by holding them securely and pressing the vacuum release button on the piston handle (see Figure 18.85).

If the car is equipped with dual headlights, the steps listed under "Mounting the Aimers," "Horizontal Adjustment," and "Vertical Adjustment" must be performed on the second pair of headlights.

Figure 18.84   Vertical adjusting screw. The vertical adjusting screw in the headlamp assembly is turned to center the bubble (courtesy of Chrysler Corporation).

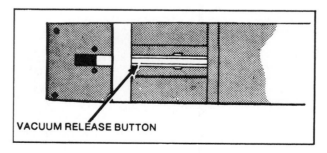

Figure 18.85   Vacuum release. The vacuum release button is used to release the suction cup from the headlight lens (courtesy of Pontiac Motor Division, General Motors Corporation).

AIMING HEADLIGHTS BY OBSERVING THE PROJECTED LIGHT

Headlights can be aimed by observing the location of the high-intensity areas of projected light. This method often is used when aiming devices are not available. A special chart can be used, or lines can be taped on a light-colored wall. A typical procedure follows:

Preparation

Since the horizontal and vertical centerlines of the headlights on various cars differ, certain measurements are used to locate lines on a chart or on a wall, as shown in Figure 18.86.

1. Position the car on a level floor so that it squarely faces a vertical wall or chart.
2. Adjust the position of the car so that the headlights are 25 feet (750 cm) from the chart or wall.
3. Tape a vertical line in alignment with the centerline of the car (refer to Figure 18.86).

   Note: The centerline of the car can be determined by standing behind the car and carefully sighting through the rear window at the chart or wall. The window trim moulding, the rear view mirror, and the hood ornament can be used as sighting aids.

4. Measure the distance between the centers of the headlights.
5. Transfer that measurement to the chart or wall and tape vertical lines representing the vertical centerlines of the headlights (refer to Figure 18.86).

   Note: If the car is equipped with dual headlights, two sets of vertical centerlines must be marked.

6. Measure the distance from the floor to the center of the headlights.
7. Transfer that measurement to the chart or wall and tape a centerline to represent the horizontal centerline of the headlights (refer to Figure 18.86).

Adjustment of Bulbs with Two Filaments

Bulbs with two filaments should be adjusted with the low beams on.

1. Turn the vertical adjusting screws (refer to Figures 18.69 and 18.70) so the high-intensity areas are located just below the horizontal centerline, as shown in Figure 18.87.
2. Turn the horizontal adjusting screws (refer to Figures 18.69 and 18.70) so the high-intensity areas are located just to the right of the vertical centerlines (refer to Figure 18.87).

Adjustment of Bulbs with One Filament

Bulbs with one filament should be adjusted with the high beams on. Bulbs with two filaments used in the system should be covered while adjusting the single filament bulbs.

1. Turn the vertical adjusting screws so the high-intensity areas are centered on the horizontal centerline, as shown in Figure 18.88.
2. Turn the horizontal adjusting screws so the high-intensity areas are centered on the vertical centerlines (refer to Figure 18.88).

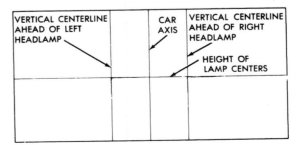

Figure 18.86 Headlight wall chart. The lines that must be marked on a chart or on a wall to aim headlights. The locations of the lines must be determined by measurements made on the particular car (courtesy of Chrysler Corporation).

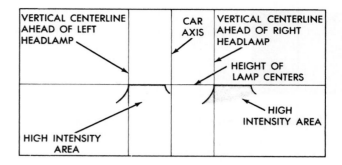

Figure 18.87   The correct low-beam pattern for sealed beam bulbs with two filaments (courtesy of Chrysler Corporation).

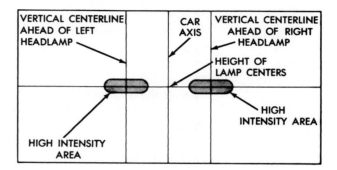

Figure 18.88   The correct high-beam pattern for headlight bulbs with one filament (courtesy of Chrysler Corporation).

Job 18H

ADJUST HEADLIGHT AIM

SATISFACTORY PERFORMANCE
A satisfactory performance on this job requires that you do the following:

1. Adjust the aim of the headlights of the car assigned.
2. Following the steps in the "Performance Outline" and the procedure and specifications of the manufacturer, complete the job within 45 minutes.
3. Fill in the blanks under "Information."

PERFORMANCE OUTLINE

1. Prepare for adjustment.
2. Adjust the horizontal and vertical aim.

INFORMATION

Vehicle identification _____

Headlight system: _____ Single   _____ Dual

Reference used _____ Page(s) _____

Method used to adjust aim: _____ Mechanical aimers
                             _____ Projected light

Identification of instrument used _____

Was car positioned on a level floor?   _____ Yes _____ No

Was instrument adjusted for floor slope?   _____ Yes _____ No

Bulbs with two filaments were adjusted on: _____ High beam   _____ Low beam

Bulbs with one filament were adjusted on: _____ High beam   _____ Low beam

VOCABULARY

Use the listed words in the blanks beside the sentences to complete the definitions. Either write out the words or place the letters in the blanks.

A. Circuit
B. Closed
C. Power source
D. Conductor
E. Load
F. Filament
G. Incandescent
H. Amperes
I. Open
J. Switch
K. Resistance
L. Ground
M. Series
N. Parallel
O. Fuse block
P. Rating
Q. Continuity tester
R. Bimetallic
S. Hazard warning circuit
T. Bayonet base
U. Double filament
V. High beam
W. Halogen
X. Vertical
Y. Split image

_____ 1. A part in a bulb that when hooked to a power source glows and produces light
_____ 2. The way the bubbles look in a headlight aimer when the bulbs are out of adjustment
_____ 3. Term for the path that electricity can take from the power source and back
_____ 4. Device that opens and closes a circuit
_____ 5. Another term for the return path to the power source such as the frame of the vehicle
_____ 6. Tool used to check a circuit to see if the path is complete
_____ 7. A part containing a large number of fuses
_____ 8. One bulb with two separate paths each producing light
_____ 9. A circuit containing one power source and one load
_____ 10. An amperage system used for fuses
_____ 11. Another term for the bright lights on a vehicle
_____ 12. Another term for a battery or generator
_____ 13. An uninterrupted path for the current to flow from the power source and back
_____ 14. A brighter more intense bulb used in headlight applications
_____ 15. A bulb with a cone-shaped base with the outside the ground and the inside the positive
_____ 16. A part that moves as it heats up and cools down inside a flasher
_____ 17. When the filament gets white-hot and produces light
_____ 18. A circuit using a flasher to blink both the front and rear turn signal lights
_____ 19. Another term for a wire
_____ 20. What happens when a circuit has been cut and is not complete
_____ 21. Direction the headlight beams are set when moved up and down
_____ 22. Another name for current
_____ 23. Another name for a light or motor
_____ 24. Anything that makes it hard for electricity to travel in a circuit
_____ 25. A circuit made with more than one path between the power source and the return

REVIEW QUESTIONS

The following questions will help you determine if you have accomplished the tasks stated at the beginning of this chapter. If you do not know many of the answers, go back and review the material before proceeding to the next chapter.

Lesson 18–1
1. What is a circuit?
2. What three components must a circuit have to be complete?
3. What is a filament?

4. What is voltage equal to in Ohm's law?

5. How is resistance defined by Ohm's law?

6. How are watts defined?

7. How is current measured?

8. How is resistance measured?

9. What is the name for a control that opens and closes a circuit?

10. What other than wire is used to make a ground path?

11. What is the purpose of a fuse?

12. How are most automotive circuits shown?

13. What is the purpose of a symbol?

14. What are three types of circuits used in an automobile?

15. Why should a fuse never be disabled by a piece of wire or metal?

16. Why are headlights not wired in series?

17. What happens to the lights in a series circuit when more lights are added?

18. How is total resistance figured in a series circuit?

19. What is the rule about how voltage acts in a series circuit?

20. What happens if there is a break in the path of a series circuit?

Lesson 18–2

21. How does the test light work?

22. What causes a fuse to blow out?

23. What is one common type of fuse in automotive use today?

24. How are fuses rated?

25. What is a fuse block?

26. Where are most in-line fuses found?

27. What makes a good tester for circuits where fuses are constantly blowing?

28. What should be the first thing to inspect when an electrical system does not work?

29. What will be the amperage rating of a red-colored mini-fuse?

30. What is a fuse hook?

31. What is the instrument often used to test fuses?

32. Where would the use of a fuse not be practical in a vehicle?

33. How does a circuit breaker work?

34. What is the purpose of the bimetallic strip in a circuit breaker?

35. How is a circuit breaker superior to a fuse?

36. What is the easiest way to be sure a circuit breaker is defective?

37. How can a circuit breaker be tested?

38. Name two circuits where flashers are used.

39. What is another type of flasher that is not heat operated?

40. How are flashers removed from their connectors?

41. What is the usual problem when a turn signal instrument arrow lights but does not flash?

42. What knowledge is required to repair a defect in a handle-mounted headlight dimmer switch?

43. Where is the brake light switch found on most vehicles?

Lesson 18–3

44. What prevents a bulb filament from instantly burning out?

45. What is a bayonet base?

46. Where are some two-filament bulbs located?

47. How can a jumper wire be used to check a bulb?

48. What is the quickest way to check a bulb, socket, and current to the bulb without a tester?

49. What are two common ways to access a bulb to replace it?

50. What three parts make up a sealed beam bulb?

51. In a system that used four headlights in a row, where are the high beams located?

52. What is the rule about using halogen lights with other types?

53. Where is the vertical aim screw located on a headlight bulb?

54. Where is the horizontal aim screw located on a headlight bulb?

55. How can some vehicles provide an accurate headlight adjustment procedure without machines or the lights turned on?

56. What are the guidepoints used for on a headlight bulb?

ASE QUESTIONS

Each question or incomplete statement in this test is followed by four suggested answers or completions. In each case select the *one* that best answers the question or completes the statement.

1. Which of the following does a circuit not need to work?
   a. Power source   b. Conductor
   c. Load   d. Filament

2. Using Ohm's law, what is the current value in a circuit with a 12-volt power source and a total resistance of 22 ohms?
   a. 0.45 amps   b. 0.55 amps
   c. 0.65 amps   d. 0.35 amps

3. No current is flowing in a series circuit. Technician A says the circuit is open. Techni-

cian B says the circuit is shorted. Who is right?
a. A only   b. B only
c. Both A and B   d. Neither A nor B

4. Fuses and their function is a topic of discussion between two technicians. Technician A says the fuse should be stronger than the weakest part of the circuit. Technician B says a fuse should be weaker than any other part of the circuit. Who is right?
a. A only   b. B only
c. Both A and B   d. Neither A nor B

5. A circuit has a blown fuse. Technician A says a piece of wire can be substituted for the fuse. Technician B says a circuit breaker can be used in place of the fuse. Who is right?
a. A only   b. B only
c. Both A and B   d. Neither A nor B

6. The headlights do not burn when the switch is turned on. Technician A says vehicle headlights are hooked in series and when one doesn't work the other won't either. Technician B says headlights are hooked in parallel and when one won't light the other is not affected. Who is right?
a. A only   b. B only
c. Both A and B   d. Neither A nor B

7. A series circuit is being tested. Technician A says the current should be the same in all parts of the circuit. Technician B says the resistance in all parts of the circuit is added together to get total resistance. Who is right?
a. A only   b. B only
c. Both A and B   d. Neither A nor B

8. A parallel circuit is being tested. Technician A says the voltage will be the same in all parts of the circuit. Technician B says the current will be the same in all parts of the circuit. Who is right?
a. A only   b. B only
c. Both A and B   d. Neither A nor B

9. A 10-amp mini-fuse has blown in a vehicle. Technician A says it should be replaced with a fuse color coded yellow. Technician B says it should be replaced with a fuse color coded red. Who is right?
a. A only   b. B only
c. Both A and B   d. Neither A nor B

10. A fuse that has just been removed from a fuse block is to be tested to see if it is defective. Technician A says to use a voltmeter. Techni-

cian B says to use a self-powered test light. Who is right?
a. A only   b. B only
c. Both A and B   d. Neither A nor B

11. Vehicle headlight circuit protection is being discussed. Technician A says the manufacturers use a circuit breaker. Technician B says the manufacturers use an in-line fuse. Who is right?
a. A only   b. B only
c. Both A and B   d. Neither A nor B

12. A vehicle circuit breaker has tripped due to a circuit overload. Technician A says the circuit breaker will set itself after it cools. Technician B says the circuit breaker must be set each time it trips. Who is right?
a. A only   b. B only
c. Both A and B   d. Neither A nor B

13. A circuit breaker is suspected to be causing trouble in a circuit. Technician A says it can be tested with a continuity tester. Technician B says it can be tested by the substitution method. Who is right?
a. A only   b. B only
c. Both A and B   d. Neither A nor B

14. Vehicle flasher construction is being discussed by two technicians. Technician A says a flasher is made like a circuit breaker but operates at normal current for the circuit. Technician B says a circuit breaker will only operate when the current is above normal for the circuit.
a. A only   b. B only
c. Both A and B   d. Neither A nor B

15. The bulbs on a vehicle are being checked. Technician A says any time a bulb lights it passes the test. Technician B says some bulbs have to be checked twice. Who is right?
a. A only   b. B only
c. Both A and B   d. Neither A nor B

16. A bulb does not shine as bright or with the intensity it should. Technician A says this could be the ground connection. Technician B says this could be a defective socket. Who is right?
a. A only   b. B only
c. Both A and B   d. Neither A nor B

17. A sealed headlight beam has the code 1C on the glass. Technician A says it can be used as either a high or low beam. Technician B says it only replaces a low-beam headlight. Who is right?
a. A only   b. B only
c. Both A and B   d. Neither A nor B

18. Three molded tips extend from the outside glass on a sealed beam headlight. Technician A says these are the result of having to fill the headlight with gas. Technician B says these are used to aim the bulb. Who is right?
    a. A only
    b. B only
    c. Both A and B
    d. Neither A nor B

19. The headlights on a vehicle need to be adjusted. Headlight aimers will be used. Technician A says all headlights are to be aimed 2 inches to the left and level. Technician B says all headlights should be aimed straight ahead and down 2 inches in 20 feet.
    a. A only
    b. B only
    c. Both A and B
    d. Neither A nor B

Air Conditioning and Heating System Maintenance

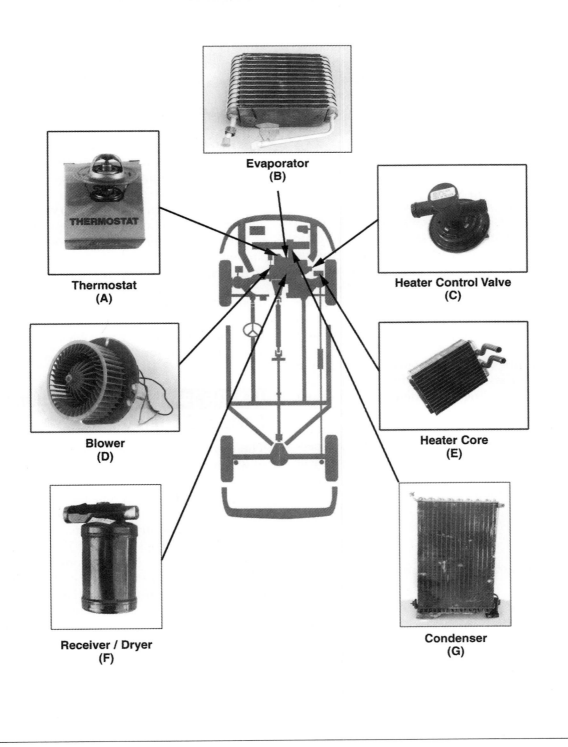

Evaporator
(B)

Thermostat
(A)

Heater Control Valve
(C)

Blower
(D)

Heater Core
(E)

Receiver / Dryer
(F)

Condenser
(G)

There was a time when an air conditioner was considered a luxury item and heaters were optional. Those days are gone forever. It is now hard to sell an automobile that does not have an air conditioner. All this is not without an environmental impact, however. We have a crisis developing from the discharge into the atmosphere of refrigerant R-12, used in automotive air conditioners, and R-22, used in household air conditioners. R-12 is a chemical compound used to conduct the heat from the passenger compartment to a heat exchanger, where it is cooled by the outside air. When R-12 escapes to the outside air, it rises to the upper atmosphere and oxidizes the protective layer of ozone. Without ozone, people develop skin cancer from the unfiltered rays of the sun.

A special license is required to work on an air conditioning system. Refrigerant is now recycled by saving it, filtering out the impurities, and using it again. The skills needed to work on the systems have understandably increased, and the price of the recovery machines has made servicing air conditioners very expensive. The danger to our planet has made air conditioning maintenance a very important automotive skill. The new vehicles now have R-134a installed at the factory to replace the older systems that used R-12. Figure 19 shows some of the parts of a typical air conditioner and heater system.

Heaters work off the hot coolant found in the engine cooling system. The condition of the radiator and engine cooling system determines how well the heater will work.

Good passenger comfort is a very important maintenance responsibility and one each prospective maintenance technician should study. Vehicle owners rarely travel without heat in the winter and cool air in the summer.

TASKS

The following are six tasks to master before leaving this chapter:

Task 19-1. Study what component parts are found in an air conditioner system and their purpose. In order to service an air conditioning system it is important to know what each part is and its purpose for being in the system. Then, if the part fails, you can check the part and replace or repair it if necessary. Lesson 19–1 provides the information to complete this task.

Task 19-2. Learn to test and service an air conditioner. An important part of keeping an air conditioner working is to perform maintenance service on it. In air conditioner work this means checking refrigerant levels, adjusting belts, replacing filters, cleaning condenser and evaporator fins, and replacing refrigerant oil. For a complete list, refer to Lesson 19–2.

Task 19-3. Learn to troubleshoot an air conditioning system. When the system fails, the technician must be able to use tests and procedures to discover the problems and solve them.

Task 19-4. Study what parts make up a typical passenger heater system. Some parts in the heater and air conditioner share the same parts such as the blower and ducts. Lesson 19–4 provides the information to complete this task.

Task 19-5. Learn to test and service a passenger heater system. In Lesson 19–5, the text details how to keep a passenger car heater providing the right amount of heat when needed. It also explains how to prevent heater failure or reduced performance.

Task 19-6. Learn to troubleshoot a heater system. When the heater fails you will need this information to pinpoint the problem and return the system back to normal.

LESSON 19–1   Air Conditioning Parts and Components

There are many parts in an air conditioner, some of which are very complex. This offers a great opportunity to technicians because the average car owner cannot service or repair an air conditioning system. Special and expensive pieces of equipment are needed to conduct many repair and service operations. Some shops specialize in nothing but air conditioning repair. New environmental concerns require a new license for anyone who works on air conditioning systems. A technician that studies the material presented in this chapter will find the path to a license easier. The following parts are located in the air conditioning system:

1. *Compressor.* The compressor is a belt-driven, piston component that compresses the refrigerant gas, which increases the temperature (see Figure 19.1). The result is a high-pressure gas with pressures from 100 to 400 pounds per

A.

B.

Figure 19.1 Compressor. This unit raises the refrigerant pressure starting at 100 psi and sometimes reaching 400 psi depending on outside temperature and humidity (courtesy of Training Enterprises Company).

Figure 19.2 Condenser. The condenser takes the compressed hot refrigerant and removes most of the heat (courtesy of Training Enterprises Company).

square inch (psi), depending on the outside air temperature.

2. *Condenser.* A high-pressure hose conducts the pressurized, heated refrigerant to the condenser, which is located in front of the radiator. The condenser is just a heat exchanger (see Figure 19.2). The compressed gas flows into the condenser tubes as ram air flows around these tubes from the movement of the vehicle down the road or from the coolant fan. The heat from the refrigerant is transferred into the outside air. At this point the refrigerant is condensed back from a gas to a liquid and travels by hose to the receiver/dryer.

3. *Receiver/dryer.* When the liquid and gas leave the condenser, they are stored in the receiver/dryer (see Figure 19.3). Here they are separated so only the liquid is passed on. Desiccant in the receiver/dryer removes moisture in the refrigerant. A filter prevents any

Figure 19.3 Receiver/dryer. This part stores some of the refrigerant and has a desiccant that removes moisture. There is also a filter in most units (courtesy of Training Enterprises Company).

Figure 19.4 Expansion valve. This part is placed between the high- and low-pressure sides of the air conditioner. It regulates the pressure and maintains the correct pressure differential between the two sides (courtesy of Training Enterprises Company).

Figure 19.5 Evaporator. Inside passenger air flows over the coils of this unit. The heat is absorbed into the refrigerant (courtesy of Training Enterprises Company).

metal particles or debris from circulating in the hoses and components. Any excess refrigerant needed to run the system is stored in the receiver/dryer. From the receiver/dryer the refrigerant goes by hose to the expansion valve.

4. *Expansion valve.* The expansion valve (see Figure 19.4) is the separation point between the high-pressure and low-pressure sides of the air conditioning system. This valve restricts the flow of refrigerant so only liquid is allowed into the next component, the evaporator (see Figure 19.5). An opening or orifice is placed in the line to let the high pressure build up on one side and low pressure stay on the other. The size of the opening is regulated so the pressure remains right for the system to work.

5. *Evaporator.* This unit is also a heat exchanger like the condenser (see Figure 19.5). Passenger compartment hot air is circulated by blower through the evaporator. Refrigerant in the tubes of the evaporator absorbs this heat. The heated refrigerant is then carried by hose back to the compressor. This side of the system is considered the low-pressure side and has pressures from 22 to 40 psi gauge.

We have described the major parts of an air conditioning system. There are other parts such as filters, temperature controls, air passageways, and electrical controls. We go into detail with these parts in the next lesson.

LESSON 19-2   Air Conditioning Service

Service of the air conditioning system is year round because the system is used in the winter to dry the air that is forced on the windshield in order to defrost it. We cover most of the service items in this lesson.

Service Items

Belt Tension and Adjustment. The belt that drives the air conditioner compressor has a big job to do. It takes a lot of horsepower to run the compressor. Two types of belt systems are used. The single belt system is a V belt, which has to be at the correct tension so it will not slip. The tension is adjusted by moving the compressor out against the belt (refer to Figures 10.60 to 10.67). Loosen the bolts so the compressor can rotate. Rotate it out against the belt until the correct tension is achieved, and tighten the bolts. Check the tension by pushing down on the belt halfway between the pulleys. The belt should not move more than 1/2 inch. If you have a belt tension gauge, use it to get the exact tension.

The other type of belt system is the serpentine system, in which only one multigrooved belt is used to drive all the units on the engine. This belt should be inspected regularly and replaced every

Figure 19.6 Service gauges. The high- and low-pressure gauges are connected to an air conditioner. Pressure checks determine if the system is operating as it should (courtesy of Training Enterprises Company).

four years or 50,000 miles. This belt has a spring-loaded tension device that should be checked periodically to ensure it is correctly loading the belt to avoid premature wear from slipping.

> The serpentine belt tensioner arm has a built-in tension check on some systems. An index mark on the arm should stay inside some marks on the bracket. If the belt tension is not correct, the tension has to be corrected. Either the spring has to be adjusted or the system has to be replaced.

Service Gauges. Figure 19.6 shows a typical service gauge. The gauge on the left is used for the low-pressure side and is color coded blue. This gauge is also a compound gauge used to measure the vacuum placed on the system by a vacuum pump. It measures vacuum from 0 to 30 in. of mercury. The high-side gauge is on the right and is color coded red. It measures pressures up to about 500 psi. Most systems do not exceed 400 psi or dip below 100 psi unless there is a problem. The center hose is for servicing the system and is either white or yellow.

Both gauges can be closed off by valves. The gauges are attached to service ports on the low and high side of the air conditioner. Refrigerant and refrigerant oil are dispensed through the center hose into the system. Refrigerant is never put into a system on the high side. Use the low side only to install new refrigerant into a system. A vacuum pump is used to dry out the moisture in the system when needed and it, too, is attached to the center hose.

Compressor Oil. The compressor requires oil for the bearings and other moving parts. Refrigerant oil for an R-12 air conditioner is a mineral-based oil. (see Figure 19.9c) The R-134a system uses a synthetic polyalkylene glycol (PAG) oil (see Figure 19.7a and b). *Do not* mix or interchange the two lubrication products. Using either lubricant in the wrong system will cause internal damage and compressor failure. Consult the manufacturer's recommendations before using any oil. Use only approved oil in each system, and use only the amount recommended. Overfilling can result in system damage. Insufficient oil can result in compressor damage.

> Use separate tools and gauges for R-12 and R-134a systems. If an R-12 system fails it should be converted over to the newer R-134a refrigerant. R-12 is getting harder to find and more expensive because it is not good for the environment and the R-134a systems are made as a replacement. Once the system is changed over, R-134a has to be used to service it and R-12 would no longer work. This should be noted in the owner's manual, and stickers should be placed near the service ports so those servicing the system will know the change was made.

Refrigerant. R-12 or R-134a is added to the air conditioning system by using the service gauges (refer to Figure 19.6). The most common refrigerant is R-12 (dichlorodifluoromethane) but this is changing rapidly. All new systems are being manufactured with R-134a in them and some of the older R-12 systems are being changed over (retrofitted) with the new refrigerant. The 1-pound can, which actually contains 14 ounces, is the usual way automotive air conditioners have been serviced. It takes from three to four cans to fill most systems. R-134a systems now use recovery systems and the 30-pound cylinders. Refrigerant is dangerous if it strikes an open flame and causes blindness by freezing the eyes if sprayed into them. A system low on refrigerant has a low reading on both the high- and low-pressure gauges. If the pressure is too low the compressor clutch will not engage. When the gauges are installed, look at the pressure on both before the engine is started and the compressor clutch engaged. Low pressure means the clutch will have to be connected to the car battery with a jumper wire before more freon can be added.

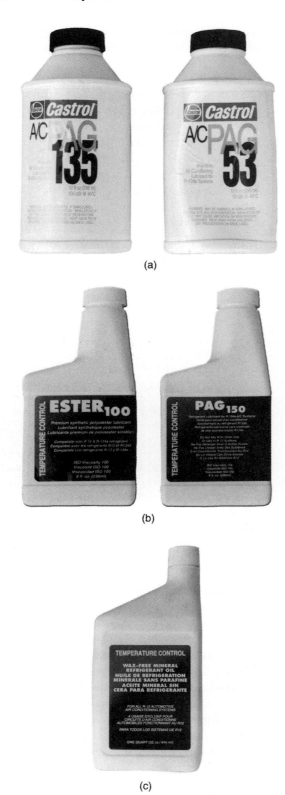

(a)

(b)

(c)

Figure 19.7 Compressor lubricants. A and B are synthetic oils to be used with R-134a systems according to the manufacturer's specifications. The oil pictured in C is only to be used in the older R-12 systems (courtesy of Training Enterprises Company).

Figure 19.8 Compressor clutch. This clutch connects the compressor shaft with the belt driving the compressor. An electromagnet is activated and locks the compressor friction disk so belt power can turn the compressor pulley (courtesy of Training Enterprises Company).

Compressor Clutch. For the engine to drive the compressor, the compressor pulley must be locked to the compressor shaft. A clutch is used, activated by an electromagnet powered by the battery (see Figure 19.8). The magnet gets its power from the battery. The clutch is constantly being turned on and off to keep the high and low pressure in a certain range. On many air conditioning systems, the distance between the clutch facing and the matching surface can be adjusted. There is a low-pressure switch, which does not let the clutch engage unless the system has enough pressure. Low pressure usually means the refrigerant is low. The compressor depends on oil circulating with the refrigerant for lubrication and can become damaged without good oil circulation. This switch has to be bypassed when more freon needs to be added. See Figure 19.9 for a troubleshooting chart.

Condenser. Condenser service involves keeping the front of the core free from debris so outside air can flow through the coils and fins. Without good air flow, heat cannot be removed from the freon in the condenser tubes. Check all line fittings for tightness. A loose fitting can sometimes be identified by dirt around the fitting. Dirt will stick to the compressor oil at the leak site. Use tubing nut wrenches to tighten air conditioning fittings.

LOW OR NO SYSTEM PRESSURE	
Step one	Compressor will not operate. Check fuses and wiring.
Recommendation	Replace burned-out fuses and repair faulty wiring.
Step two	Check compressor belt for condition and tension.
Recommendation	Adjust or replace the compressor belt.
Step three	Install gauges and check both high and low system pressure.
Recommendation	Add refrigerant when the system has below normal low- and high-side pressure.
Step four	Use a jumper wire, as the refrigerant is added, to start the compressor until the low-pressure switch lets the system operate without the jumper.
Recommendation	Look for leaks and check system condition after the refrigerant is added and gauge pressures are normal.

Figure 19.9 Low of no system pressure. When the refrigerant gets low in an air conditioner, the compressor oil cannot circulate and lubricate the compressor. A low-pressure switch opens and will not let the compressor clutch operate. The system will not cool until more refrigerant is added (courtesy of Training Enterprises Company).

Evaporator. The evaporator is also a heat exchanger (refer to Figure 19.5). Air in the passenger compartment is moved over the coils in the evaporator and heat is transferred to the freon in the coils. Under the coils is a drip pan that collects moisture draining off the coils. One end of the pan has a drain. This drain should be kept open so the moisture collected in the pan will drain to the road.

Blower and Controls. When the air conditioner switch is turned on, several things are supposed to happen. The air conditioner clutch coil is activated so the clutch can lock and the engine will drive the compressor. The blower motor is turned on to circulate the hot air over the evaporator coils (see Figure 19.10). Ducts are opened to direct the air flow where it is needed. The ducts are vacuum or mechanically operated. There is a filter located

Figure 19.10 Blower and controls. The blower circulates the passenger air through the evaporator core. The compressor clutch should be turned on and the ducts or air passages should direct the air over the coils (courtesy of Training Enterprises Company).

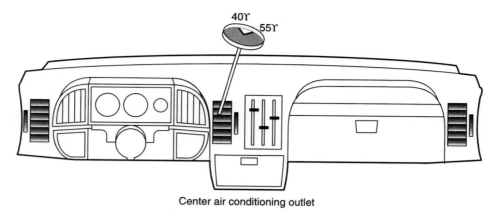

Center air conditioning outlet

Figure 19.11   Temperature checking. When the air conditioning system is operating correctly there should be a center duct temperature of between 40° and 55°F. This is affected by outside temperature and humidity (courtesy of Training Enterprises Company).

in the blower ducts. This filter keeps dirt from entering the blower and prevents circulation of dirt in the air going to the passengers. This filter has to be serviced when it gets clogged. Consult the owner's manual or service manuals for information on specific makes and models.

Temperature Checking.   You can easily make one very important check of an air conditioning system by sticking a thermometer into the center duct (see Figure 19.11). Determine if the compressor clutch and the blower are working by turning on the air conditioner controls and observing the clutch and listening for the blower motor. If the air is cool, cool-warm, or warm, the next step is to road test the system. Place a thermometer in the center duct and drive the vehicle with the air conditioner on. The temperature of a correctly operating system will be in a range from 40° to 55°F. Outside air temperature (ambient air) and humidity make a difference in how cool and efficiently an air conditioner operates. As the blower exhaust temperature gets higher, air goes from feeling cold to feeling cool. This is felt around 60°F. Cool-warm, the next stage, is around 65°F, and warm is 70°F and higher. At these temperatures there will be no difference between the air going into the blower and the air coming out. The vehicle operator would complain that the system was not cooling. Seventy degrees (70°F) would make a difference in the passenger compartment only when the outside temperature was above 90°F. This indicates a system problem and should be investigated. When a problem is suspected, install gauges and perform full air conditioner tests on the high- and low-side system pres-

sures. If there is a sight glass in the system, inspect it to see if there are many bubbles in the refrigerant flow (refer to Figure 1.18). Bubbles mean the system does not have enough charge, or has air, moisture, or a high-side restriction. Low pressure on both the low- and high-pressure gauges or bubbles in the sight glass mean the system refrigerant charge is low.

Air conditioners should be checked with the service gauges at least once a year. Check both high and low pressures and take a temperature reading at the center duct in the passenger compartment. Adjust the readings for ambient temperature and humidity. If the readings are abnormal, further service will be required. The vehicle owner may only discover a problem when the outside (ambient) temperature gets hotter and the system does not cool the inside of the passenger compartment. Temperature testing the system will indicate when more refrigerant is needed and when defective parts should be replaced.

Leak Detection.   Usually a leak is found when the system gets so low on refrigerant that the pressure switch does not let the compressor clutch operate. Leaks usually leave marks at the place where the refrigerant and compressor oil escapes. Dirt collects around the leak. Examine each fitting and part to see if there are signs of leaks. Repair all leaks. If the leak is hidden, use an electronic leak detector to find it. Instruments of this type are very sensitive and sound an alarm if any refrigerant leak is present (see Figure 19.12). The system may be so low on refrigerant that the compressor clutch low-pressure switch has to be bypassed to get the

Figure 19.13 Hoses and clamps. Heater, radiator, gasoline, and vacuum are common types of hoses (courtesy of Training Enterprises Company).

Figure 19.12 Leak detector. An electronic leak detector will make a noise if there is any refrigerant leaving a system. Be sure to use the detector under the dash where the evaporator is located. This is a common leak area that is hidden from sight (courtesy of Training Enterprises Company).

compressor to operate. The compressor has to be running to add refrigerant.

LESSON 19-3 Heater Parts and Components

The heater uses many of the same parts as the air conditioner system. Both systems use some of the same ducts and the blower. The heater takes the hot coolant from the engine cooling system and circulates it through a heat exchanger. Air from the passenger compartment is directed around the fins in the heater core and collects heat from the coolant. This hot air is then directed back into the passenger compartment to heat the space.

1. *Hoses.* One heater hose carries the heated coolant to the heater core and another carries the coolant back to the engine cooling system. The engine water pump circulates the coolant. Service of hoses requires an inspection to see if they are cracked, spongy, or leaking. Hoses get brittle when exposed to heat for long periods of time. They get spongy when constantly exposed to oil and gas. It is recommended that all hoses be replaced every four years. Hardened hoses should be replaced when found. Hoses are sealed with clamps (see Figure 19.13). If an inspection finds a leak around the ends of heater hoses, first try to stop the leak by tightening the clamp. Replace rusty and damaged clamps at the same time the hoses are replaced.

> The new radiator coolants have a longer mileage and yearly life before they need to be changed. Do not mix these coolants with the older coolants or the longer mileage will be reduced and you will have to replace the coolant and flush the radiators on the older coolant plan. Look to see what coolant is being used and only add the same type to each system.

2. *Thermostat.* Since the heat produced by the heater depends on the engine coolant temperature, the thermostat directly controls the heater efficiency (see Figure 19.14). Thermostats come in several different temperature ratings. The lower the rating, the cooler the maintained engine temperature. A thermostat that has been removed or that is stuck open will result in low coolant temperature and a correspondingly low heater output. If the heater is not hot enough, look at the thermostat and the

Figure 19.14   Thermostat. This part is used to control the coolant flow through the radiator. Thermostats maintain an even engine temperature (courtesy of Training Enterprises Company).

Figure 19.16   Coolant sealers. When a radiator or heater core develops a leak, chemicals can be added to the coolant to seal the leak. One of these products is shown (courtesy of Training Enterprises Company).

engine temperature first. Thermostats are replaced when they no longer control the engine temperature as they should.

3. *Controls.* The heater controls operate the blower and the control valve, which lets coolant flow through the heater core. In some systems the blower air for the heater also goes through the air conditioner evaporator core. This is not a problem because the air conditioner compressor is not operating. Sometimes the air conditioner is used with the heater to dry the

air as it goes onto the windshield to reduce fogging in cold weather. Some systems blend heated and air conditioned air to get the correct temperature the driver desires. Many systems do this automatically. All one has to do is set the desired temperature.

4. *Heater core.* The heater core is a heat exchanger (see Figure 19.15). A good flow of air has to go through the outside tubes and fins and a good flow of engine coolant has to go through the inside of the tubes. In time, heater cores become clogged and spring leaks. A clogged core can sometimes be opened by chemical cleaners placed in the coolant. Leaks require removal of the core and repair by soldering. There are some products on the market that can be placed in the coolant to repair minor leaks. The material hardens when it comes to a leak and contacts the outside air (see Figure 19.16). Try one of these products first before going to the trouble and expense of removing the heater core when coolant is leaking from the heater core.

Figure 19.15   Heater core. Hot engine coolant flows through the heater core. Passenger compartment air is passed through the core and heated, maintaining passenger compartment heat temperature (courtesy of Training Enterprises Company).

LESSON 19–4   Air Conditioning and Heater Troubleshooting

We look at some of the common heater and air conditioning problems in this lesson and suggest solutions. Consult the specific repair manuals on individual systems for more in-depth problem and solution advice.

Air Conditioning Troubleshooting

1. *No cooling.* The temperature of the air exiting the inside air ducts is hot. First check to see if the compressor clutch is engaging. If it is, install gauges and check the high- and low side pressures. Low pressure on both sides usually means the coolant is low.

2. *Cycling.* If the compressor is running for short periods of time and then stopping, it usually means the refrigerant is getting low. Install pressure gauges and check the high- and low-side pressures. Install more coolant as required until the pressures are normal and the sight glass clears (refer to Figure 1.18).

3. *Leaks.* No refrigerant in the system indicates a major leak. If the coolant pressure drops over a short period of time, it indicates a slow leak. Add leak detect dye and trace where the dye is staining the system. Repair the leak and recharge the system (see Figure 19.17).

4. *Blower.* The blower should change speed when the system switch is turned to different speed selections. Check the blower fuse if the blower motor does not come on at any speed setting. Inspect for objects jammed into the blower fan, keeping it from turning. Check the blower switch and any electrical controls with a multimeter.

5. *Ducts.* When the air is not being directed where it should, the ducts or controls could be at fault.

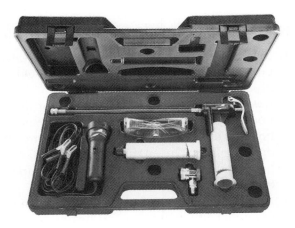

Figure 19.17 Leak detectors. The propane detector can determine where leaks are in the system. Run the hose or probe around the systems to discover any leaks (courtesy of Training Enterprises Company).

Check the vacuum controls and mechanical controls. Look for duct doors that are warped or stuck, preventing complete sealing. Sometimes duct flex pipes become disconnected.

6. *Heater and A/C both on at same time.* Both the air conditioner and the heater use the same blower. Both the heater and evaporator are heat exchangers and require air flow to work. The heater coolant flow is shut off when the heater is turned off. Look for a faulty heater coolant control valve if the heater stays on during air conditioning operation, especially if there is not a problem with the air conditioner (see Figure 19.18).

7. *Gauges.* Gauge pressure on both the low and high side of an air conditioner will be high, low, or normal. If the pressures are too high or too low, find the problem and use the pressure gauges again to see if the problem is solved. The sight glass is another way to tell if the system is normal. A system that has been started and stabilized should have a clear sight glass. Bubbles indicate a problem (refer to Figure 1.18 in chapter one).

8. *Belts.* Inspect belts for damage, wear, and incorrect tension. A slipping belt results in poor output and may make a noise. A belt that is too tight may do some damage to the pulley bearings (refer to Figures 10.60 to 10.67).

9. *Clutch problems.* The clutch requires 12 volts to work. Friction material can wear to the point where the clutch will slip. Before damage starts, the gap between the friction material and the clutch face should be checked and adjusted if the gap is too large (see Figure 19.19). A worn-out clutch (one with too little friction material) should be replaced. A burned-out electromagnet should have the coil replaced.

10. *Moisture in the system.* Moisture in the system is usually removed by the desiccant in the receiver/dryer or as part of the operation of a coolant recovery system (see Figure 19.20). When gauge pressures are normal, but there are bubbles in the sight glass, the system has too much moisture. The receiver/dryer should be removed and the moisture vacuumed out. A new receiver/dryer should be used.

11. *Compressor problems.* Compressors receive the most damage when the compressor oil is too low. The oil is circulated in the freon and keeps the internal parts of the compressor lubricated. If the system has never had a leak it should never need compressor oil. Compressor oil leaks with freon at a leak site. When a leak is discovered, check the compressor oil level

Figure 19.18   Heater coolant control valves. Engine coolant to the heater is controlled by either a mechanical or a vacuum-operated valve. If the valve lets hot coolant into the heater when the air conditioner is in operation, the two systems will cancel each other out. Replace or repair faulty valves and replace vacuum hoses when cracked (courtesy of Training Enterprises Company).

before placing the system back into operation. The system has to be evacuated to check the oil level. When components are replaced, oil must be added to compensate for the oil trapped in the old component. Oil can be added, if it is suspected that some has left at a leak, by getting a can of oil charge and adding it at the service hose of the gauges (see Figure 19.21).

12. *Blocked hoses and filters.* The system has several restricted areas where metal and other materi-

als can plug the hoses and restrict refrigerant flow. When both gauges read low or the low-side gauge reads low and the high-side gauge reads high, there could be an orifice tube restriction or a high-side restriction. The side where the system filter is located may also get blocked. This system filter should be changed every 50,000 miles. This requires a complete evacuation of the system. The receiver/dryer should also be replaced at this time. Most drivers do not know about this filter and drive the system until reduced oil flow damages the compressor (see Figure 19.22).

Heater Troubleshooting

1. *No heat.* Check the heater coolant control valve. Look for blockage in the heater core or the hoses.
2. *Not enough heat.* Check the blower motor speed. Look for restrictions in the heater core or the hoses. The heater control valve may not be opening fully. The engine thermostat may not be maintaining the correct coolant temperature (see Figure 19.23).
3. *Leaks.* A coolant leak inside the vehicle on the floor mat usually means the heater core has a hole in it. Look for cracked heater hoses. Make sure the heater hose clamps are tight (see Figure 19.24).

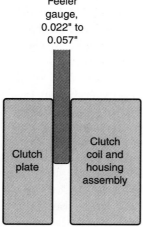

Figure 19.19   Electromagnetic clutch gap. Check the electromagnetic clutch wear with a feeler gauge. Adjust the gap if the friction material is all right. Replace the clutch if it is not (courtesy of Training Enterprises Company).

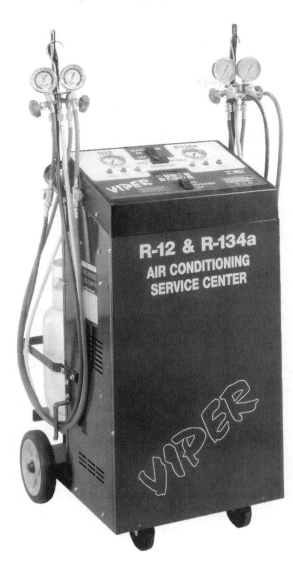

Figure 19.20 Coolant recovery station. This equipment removes coolant from the system, removes impurities, and replaces the coolant without allowing any harmful refrigerant to be released into the atmosphere (courtesy of Century Manufacturing Co.).

Figure 19.21 Oil charge. When oil has leaked out of a system due to refrigerant loss, it can be added by using oil charge cans. The oil is mixed with the refrigerant and is added just like a regular refrigerant (courtesy of Training Enterprises Company).

A heater core can become clogged just like a radiator core. When using a radiator flush, run the heater so the cleaner and flush can act inside the heater core as well as the radiator. During the flush and neutralizer phase, be sure all the cleaner is flushed out of the heater core. Again, do all flushing operations with the heater on. Be sure to let the vehicle warm up enough so the thermostat will open up to allow a good flow through the heater core. The flush chemicals need to be neutralized before the antifreeze is added to the system. The extended-life coolants require only a water flush unless the radiator and heater cores are clogged.

4. *Blower problems.* Check the blower motor fuse. Look for something caught in the blower fan. Check the blower switch and power going to the motor (see Figure 19.25).
5. *Duct problems.* Check the mechanical and vacuum controls to the duct passages. Look for something caught in the duct doors. See whether the duct hoses are disconnected. The blower motor draws air into the heater and air conditioning passages. When cool air is needed, it is directed over the evaporator core. For heat, the air flows through the heater core. On automatic heating and cooling systems, the outside temperature is measured and either heat or cold is used to maintain the temperature to the thermostat setting. Doors are opened or closed in the system to direct the blower air where it is needed.

Figure 19.22 Air conditioner filter. Air conditioners have a filter in the lines to prevent trash from entering and locking up the compressor. The filter has to be changed when it gets plugged (courtesy of Training Enterprises Company).

THERMOSTAT PROBLEMS

Problem	Engine temperature stays above normal.
Probable causes	Thermostat not opening fully. Radiator clogged. Hoses collapsing. Wrong thermostat.
Problem	Engine temperature below normal.
Probable causes	Thermostat has been removed. Thermostat sticking in the open position.
Problem	Intermittent high and low engine temperature.
Probable causes	Thermostat slow to open and close or sticking. Hoses collapsing. Dirt in the system affecting the opening and closing of the thermostat.

Figure 19.23 Thermostat problems. When the engine temperature is not being maintained or the engine is overheating, the thermostat usually is the problem. Replace a faulty thermostat (courtesy of Training Enterprises Company).

HEATER CORE LEAK

Problem	Coolant level drops but the leak is not obvious.
Probable causes	Bad hoses, holes in the radiator or heater core, water pump, head gasket, radiator cap, coolant recovery system, block expansion plugs, internal or external engine cracks.
Solution	Find the leak by pressure testing the system. Repair or replace all defective parts.
Problem	Floor mat on the passenger's side is damp and has a coolant smell and color.
Probable causes	Heater core has a leak, heater hoses either split or the clamps are loose.
Solution	Tighten hose clamps, replace any split hoses. Presssure test the system and look for leaks. Either remove and repair the heater core or put material in the coolant to stop the leak.

Figure 19.24 Heater core leak. Look for a heater core leak every time the floor mat is damp with coolant. To make sure, pressure test the system and see if coolant is running onto the floor mat (courtesy of Training Enterprises Company).

BLOWER SWITCH

Problem	Blower motor does not turn.
Probable causes	Fuse, motor bearings locked up, open circuit, bad switch.
Problem	Blower motor does not change speeds.
Probable cause	Blower motor switch bad.

Figure 19.25 Blower switch. When the blower does not change speeds or turn on, check the control switch, fuse, and blower motor (courtesy of Training Enterprises Company).

These doors are either mechanically or vacuum operated. On vacuum-operated doors, hoses and diaphragms should be checked and changed when they become brittle or leak. Doors may stick or be blocked by trash. Check and clean the system when it does not operate as it should. Switches and sensors may become defective on the automatic systems. These can be checked with a digital ohmmeter and voltmeter.

VOCABULARY

Use the listed words in the blanks beside the sentences to complete the definitions. Either write out the words or place the letters in the blanks.

A. License

B. Compressor

C. Condenser

D. Receiver/dryer

E. Evaporator

F. PSI

G. V-belt

H. Belt tension gauge

I. High side

J. Low side

K. Vacuum pump

L. R-12

M. R-234a

N. Low pressure switch

O. Clutch

P. Cool-warm

Q. Fins

R. Thermostat

S. Control valve

T. Clamp

U. Coolant sealer

V. Ducts

W. Service gauge

X. Leak detector

Y. Pressure test

_____ 1. Tool used to check a belt for correct pressure and installation

_____ 2. The latest refrigerant used to replace all obsolete ones

_____ 3. Thin materials that air can flow over to remove heat from a liquid

_____ 4. Applies pressure to a hose and prevents the hose from leaking

_____ 5. Tool used to check for coolant leaks in an engine cooling system

_____ 6. Pressures ranging from 20 to 30 psi

_____ 7. What must be obtained to work on automotive air conditioners

_____ 8. The old-type refrigerant that has now been replaced with another type

_____ 9. A device that regulates the temperature of the cooling system

_____ 10. Placed in a radiator to seal minor leaks in the system

_____ 11. Helps pinpoint leaks in an air conditioning system

_____ 12. A measure of pressure of both air and fluid

_____ 13. Part that releases heat from air conditioner freon to the outside air

_____ 14. A part used to drive an air conditioner compressor

_____ 15. When the inside air is about 65°F

_____ 16. Controls the flow of coolant to the heater core

_____ 17. Tool used to pressure test an air conditioning system

_____ 18. Machine used to dry the moisture out of the inside of an air conditioner

_____ 19. A storage place for refrigerant inside the air conditioning system

_____ 20. Can reach pressures of up to 400 pounds psi

_____ 21. Air conditioner heat exchanger used inside the passenger compartment

_____ 22. Used to shut off the current to an air conditioner compressor clutch if pressure is low

_____ 23. Parts that go from the fan to the outlets in the passenger compartment

_____ 24. Operated by an electromagnet and locks up to drive the air conditioner compressor

_____ 25. Part that raises the pressure and temperature of the refrigerant

REVIEW QUESTIONS

The following questions will help you determine if you have accomplished the tasks stated at the beginning of this chapter. If you do not know many of the answers, go back and review the material before proceeding to the next chapter.

Lesson 19–1

1. What proof of ability must a technician have to work on an automotive air conditioner?
2. What is the purpose of the compressor?
3. What is the high-pressure range for refrigerant?
4. What is the purpose of a condenser?

5. What causes the air to flow through the condenser?
6. Where does the heat from the condenser go?
7. What happens to the refrigerant when the heat leaves?
8. What is the purpose of the receiver dryer?
9. What removes moisture from the refrigerant at the receiver dryer?
10. What prevents metal particles from circulating in the system?
11. What is the purpose of the expansion valve?
12. In what state is the refrigerant when it leaves the expansion valve?
13. What is the purpose of the expansion valve orifice?
14. What is the purpose of the evaporator?
15. How is air circulated through the evaporator?
16. What is the pressure range for refrigerant in the evaporator?

Lesson 19–2

17. How is the tension checked on the belt that drives the compressor?
18. How is the tension maintained on a serpentine belt?
19. What two things is the left gauge used for on the service gauge set?
20. What is the color of the high-side gauge?
21. How much pressure does the high-side gauge measure?
22. What is the center hose on the gauge set used for?
23. What is used to remove moisture from an air conditioning system?
24. What operates the air conditioner ducts?
25. What prevents circulation of dust and dirt into the passenger compartment by the air conditioning system?
26. What temperature is considered cool? Cool-warm? Warm?
27. What is the best method to use when checking air conditioner problems?
28. How does a sight glass look when the system is defective?
29. How can some refrigerant leaks be detected without equipment?
30. What tool is used to find refrigerant leaks?

Lesson 19–3

31. What parts of the air conditioner system are shared by the heater system?
32. What supplies the heat used by a heater?
33. What is the purpose of a heater core?

34. What is the purpose of the two hoses going to the heater core?
35. What circulates the coolant through the heater core?
36. What are three common heater hose problems that require replacement to correct?
37. How often should heater hoses be replaced?
38. What is the purpose of a clamp?
39. What does the thermostat do in the cooling system?
40. What happens to the engine temperature if a lower rating thermostat is used?
41. What happens to the heater system when a thermostat sticks open?
42. What are two things controlled in a heater system?
43. What is the purpose of the heater control valve?
44. When is the air conditioner used with the heater?
45. What two things have to flow well for a heater core to work?
46. What can be used to open a clogged heater core?
47. What can sometimes be used to fix a heater core leak?

Lesson 19–4

48. What are some items to check if the air conditioner is not cooling?
49. What is the usual cause of cycling?
50. What can be used in the refrigerant to find leaks?
51. What is the first item to check if the blower does not operate?
52. What are two methods used to operate duct doors?
53. What problem can let the heater and air conditioner on at the same time when only the air conditioner is needed?
54. Gauge pressures are found in what three ranges?
55. How does a sight glass look if the system is normal?
56. What type of service is required on a air conditioner clutch?
57. How is moisture removed from an air conditioner?
58. What circulates the oil needed to lubricate the compressor?
59. What has to be done before the compressor oil can be checked for level?
60. When a component is replaced, how does this affect the oil level in the system?

61. How do the high- and low-side gauges react when there is a system blockage?
62. How often should the internal air conditioner filter be changed?
63. What two problems can be the cause of no heat from the heater?
64. What two tools are used to check heater switches and sensors?

ASE QUESTIONS

Each question or incomplete statement in this test is followed by four suggested answers or completions. In each case select the *one* that best answers the question or completes the statement.

1. An air conditioning system is not cooling properly due to moisture in the system. Technician A says it is the job of the receiver dryer to remove moisture from the refrigerant. Technician B says it is the job of the condenser to remove moisture from the refrigerant. Who is right?
   a. A only   b. B only
   c. Both A and B   d. Neither A nor B

2. A serpentine belt is slipping and must be tightened for the air conditioning compressor to work properly. Technician A says this can be corrected by loosening the compressor and placing more tension on the belt. Technician B says the belt tension spring may need to be adjusted or replaced. Who is right?
   a. A only   b. B only
   c. Both A and B   d. Neither A nor B

3. A service gauge set is to be hooked to an air conditioning system to check the system pressure. Technician A says the left gauge should be hooked to the high-pressure side. Technician B says the right gauge should be hooked to the high-pressure side. Who is right?
   a. A only   b. B only
   c. Both A and B   d. Neither A nor B

4. An R-134a air conditioner system needs to have some refrigerant oil added. Technician A says that only PAG oil should be used. Technician B says only a mineral-based oil should be used. Who is right?
   a. A only   b. B only
   c. Both A and B   d. Neither A nor B

5. An air conditioner using R-12 refrigerant is low and needs to have some refrigerant added. Technician A says the new R-134a refrigerant can be used. Technician B says only R-12 refrigerant can be used. Who is right?
   a. A only   b. B only
   c. Both A and B   d. Neither A nor B

6. A gauge set has determined the refrigerant is low in an air conditioning system. Technician A says it should be added on the low-pressure side. Technician B says it can be added on either the low or the high side. Who is right?
   a. A only   b. B only
   c. Both A and B   d. Neither A nor B

7. Dirt has formed around the fitting on a condenser. Technician A says this is normal and should be wiped off. Technician B says this could indicate a leak and the fitting should be checked. Who is right?
   a. A only   b. B only
   c. Both A and B   d. Neither A nor B

8. A compressor clutch is cycling (turning on and off rapidly). Technician A says the refrigerant may be low. Technician B says the magnetic clutch needs to be adjusted. Who is right?
   a. A only   b. B only
   c. Both A and B   d. Neither A nor B

9. A shop uses two gauge sets for checking air conditioner system pressures. Technician A says they both can be used for either R-12 or R-134a. Technician B says one should be used only for R-12 and the other for R-134a. Who is right?
   a. A only   b. B only
   c. Both A and B   d. Neither A nor B

10. A thermometer is placed in the blower outlet of a vehicle air conditioner. The temperature is measured at 65°F. In air conditioner terms, what is this temperature called?
    a. Cool   b. Cool-warm
    c. Warm   d. Hot

11. When a thermometer is used to measure the temperature of a correctly operating air conditioner system, what will be the range in degrees Fahrenheit?
    a. 38° to 50°   b. 40° to 55°
    c. 45° to 60°   d. 35° to 45°

12. When the sight glass of a normal and correctly operating air conditioner is examined, how should it look?
    a. Clear   b. Small bubble flow
    c. Large bubble flow d. Solid flow

13. The low- and high-side readings of an air conditioning system are recorded. Technician A says to be accurate they must be adjusted for ambient temperature. Technician B says to be

accurate they must be adjusted for humidity. Who is right?

a. A only
b. B only
c. Both A and B
d. Neither A nor B

14. A heater system does not provide enough heat. Technician A says the fault could be the cooling system thermostat stuck in the open position. Technician B says the fault could be in the heater control valve stuck in the closed position. Who is right?

a. A only
b. B only
c. Both A and B
d. Neither A nor B

15. An air conditioning system has a leak in a place that is hard to spot. Technician A says an electronic leak detector can find the leak. Technician B says a colored dye can be added to the refrigerant to find the leak. Who is right?

a. A only
b. B only
c. Both A and B
d. Neither A nor B

16. An air conditioning system has to be disassembled to add a new receiver dryer and to change the filter. Technician A says the pressure can be released through the gauge set center hose. Technician B says only a coolant recovery system must be used. Who is right?

a. A only
b. B only
c. Both A and B
d. Neither A nor B

17. The engine temperature stays above normal during regular use of the vehicle. Technician A says the thermostat may not be opening fully. Technician B says the radiator may need cleaning. Who is right?

a. A only
b. B only
c. Both A and B
d. Neither A nor B

Glossary

AC Alternating current.

Accelerator prop Telescopic rod used to hold the accelerator pedal depressed.

Accelerator pump Small pump in the carburetor that forces an additional amount of fuel into the fuel and air mixture when the accelerator pedal is pushed down.

Access slots Openings in the backing plates or brake drums that allow access to the star wheel adjusters.

Accumulator Chamber in a hydraulically operated brake booster unit that stores a small quantity of fluid under pressure.

Ackerman principle Geometric principle used to provide toe-out on turns. The ends of the steering arms are angled so the inside wheel turns more than the outside wheel when a car is making a turn.

Active material Material used to coat the grids of the plates in a lead-acid battery. See **Lead peroxide** and **Sponge lead.**

Additive Anything added to a product in an attempt to improve the product.

Advance (spark) To change the ignition timing so that the spark occurs earlier.

Aerated When air becomes mixed with the liquid.

Air cleaner Device that removes dirt and dust from the air.

Air horn Upper portion of a carburetor. Usually contains the choke.

Air spring Air-filled device, usually a rubber bag, that is pressurized to provide spring action.

Align To bring into position. To adjust to a specification.

Alignment Adjustment of components to bring them into a predetermined position. Usually considered a combination of camber, caster, and toe-in adjustments.

Allen wrench Hex-shaped tool or bit that fits into a hex-shaped hole in the head of a bolt or screw.

Alternating current Electrical current that alternately changes polarity.

Alternator Device that converts mechanical energy to electrical energy in the form of alternating current.

Ammeter Instrument that measures current flow in amperes.

Ampere Unit of measurement of electrical current flow. With a pressure of 1 volt, 1 ampere flows in a circuit that has a resistance of 1 ohm.

Ampere-hour capacity Measurement of a battery's ability to deliver a specified amount of current for a specified time.

Anchor pin Steel pin, or stud, mounted on the backing plate. The anchor pin keeps the brake shoes from turning with the drum.

Antifreeze Chemical added to water to lower its freezing point.

API American Petroleum Institute.

Arbor Rotating shaft of a lathe on which a drum or rotor is mounted for machining.

Arbor press Piece of equipment used to apply pressure through leverage.

Arcing Spark formed when electricity jumps a gap. Arcing usually occurs when a circuit is broken.

Armature Rotating part in a motor or generator. The movable arm in a relay.

Asbestos Nonflammable, heat-resistant mineral used in making some brake linings and clutch facings.

ATDC After top dead center.

Atmospheric pressure Pressure exerted by the weight of the atmosphere; 14.7 psi at sea level.

Atomize To disperse fuel into a fine spray and mix with air.

Available voltage Maximum voltage produced by the ignition system. The voltage available at a load.

AWG American Wire Gauge.

Axial play Movement that is parallel to the axis of rotation.

Axle, front (front wheel drive) Shaft that transmits the driving force from the differential to a front wheel.

Axle, front (rear wheel drive) Crossbeam designed to support the weight of the front of the car. Steerable spindles are mounted at each end.

Axle, rear (front wheel drive)   Crossbeam designed to support the weight of the rear of the car. Spindles are mounted at each end.

Axle, rear (rear wheel drive)   Shaft that transmits the driving force from the differential to a rear wheel.

Backing plate   Pressed-steel plate on which the brake shoes, wheel cylinder, and anchor pin are mounted.

Backlash   Amount of space between the ring and pinion gear teeth in a differential.

Bail   Spring-wire loop used to secure the cover on some master cylinders.

Ball bearing   Antifriction bearing that uses a series of steel balls held between the inner and outer bearing races.

Ball guides   Curved tubes that recirculate the balls in a recirculating ball steering gear.

Ball joint   Joint, or connection, where a ball moves within a socket to allow rotary motion while the angle of the axis of rotation changes.

Ball joint inclination   See **Steering axis inclination.**

Ball joint press   Tool used to remove and install ball joints that are pressed into control arms.

Ball nut   Gear with internal teeth or grooves that mesh with the teeth or grooves of a worm shaft by means of a series of ball bearings.

Barrel shape   Brake drum defect caused by excessive wear at the center of the friction surface.

Battery   Electrochemical device that converts electrical energy to chemical energy while charging, and converts chemical energy to electrical energy while discharging.

Bayonet base bulb   Bulb with a metal base that has pins or lugs on its side that engage in locking slots in a socket.

BCI   Battery Council International.

BDC   Bottom dead center.

Bead   Part of a tire that contacts the rim of a wheel.

Bearing   Device that acts to reduce friction between two moving parts.

Bearing clearance   Space allowed for the lubricating film between a bearing and a shaft or journal.

Bearing cone   Inner race for a ball or roller bearing.

Bearing cup   Outer race for a ball or roller bearing.

Bearing race   Inner or outer ring that provides the smooth, hard contact surface for the balls or rollers in a bearing.

Bell housing   Cover at the rear of an engine that encloses the flywheel and the torque converter or clutch assembly.

Bell mouth   Brake drum defect caused by excessive wear, expansion, or both at the open end of a brake drum.

Bellows   Movable cover or seal, usually of a rubberlike material, that is pleated or folded like an accordion to allow for expansion and contraction.

Bellows seal   Expanding diaphragm used as a seal between the master cylinder reservoir and the reservoir cover. It prevents air from contacting the fluid, yet it allows the fluid to change in volume.

Belt tension gauge   Tool used to measure the tension of drive belts.

Bench bleeding   Method of purging air from a master cylinder prior to the installation of the cylinder.

BHP   Brake horsepower.

Bias belted tire   Bias ply tire that has reinforcing strips or belts placed over the plies at the tread section.

Bias ply tire   Tire constructed of alternate plies positioned so the cords cross the centerline of the tire at an angle of about 35°.

Bimetallic   Made of two different metals.

Bleeder hose   Length of rubber tubing used in bleeding brakes.

Bleeder jar   Glass or transparent plastic container used to detect the escape of air while bleeding brakes.

Bleeder screw   See **Bleeder valve.**

Bleedertank   See **Pressure bleeder.**

Bleeder tubes   Short, curved pieces of tubing used to facilitate the bleeding of master cylinders.

Bleeder valve   Valve placed in a hydraulic system where it can be opened to allow the release of air.

Bleeder wrench   Tool used to open bleeder valves.

Bleeding   Procedure by which air is purged from a hydraulic system.

Block   See **Cylinder block.**

Blow-by   Leakage of compression and combustion pressure past the piston rings.

Blower   Supercharger.

Blue tag   Colored tag affixed to a machine that is defective and needs repair.

Body roll   Tipping of a car body to one side, usually in a turn.

Boiling point   Exact temperature at which a liquid begins to turn to a vapor.

Bonded lining   Brake lining attached to a brake shoe by an adhesive.

Bonding agent   Cement used to secure bonded lining to a brake shoe.

Booster (brake)   Power brake unit.

Booster battery   Auxiliary battery used to start the engine of a car that has a discharged battery.

Booster cables   See **Jumper cables.**

Boot   Flexible rubber or plastic cover used over the open ends of master cylinders, wheel cylinders, and various steering and suspension parts to keep out water and other foreign matter.

Bore   Walls of a cylinder. Also used to refer to the diameter of a cylinder.

Bore diameter   Diameter of a cylinder.

Brake drum   Ring-shaped housing that rotates around fixed brake shoes and is slowed or stopped when the shoes are expanded.

Brake drum lathe   Machine used to refinish the inner surface of a brake drum.

Brake fade   Loss of braking friction caused by excessive heat.

Brake feel   Feeling transmitted from the brake system back to the driver during braking.

Brake fluid   Special fluid used in hydraulic brake systems.

Brake hose   Flexible tubing used to transmit pressure in the hydraulic part of a brake system.

Brake line   Special rigid steel tubing used to transmit pressure in the hydraulic part of a brake system.

Brake lining   Friction material fastened to the brake shoes.

Brake shoe   Metal form to which the brake lining is attached.

Brake spoon   Tool used to turn star wheel adjusters and thus to adjust the brake lining-to-drum clearance.

Breaker arm   Movable part of a pair of ignition breaker points.

Breaker points   Pair of contact points that are opened and closed by the action of a cam.

Brush   Electrical conductor that contacts a commutator or a slip ring.

BTDC   Before top dead center.

Bubble balancer   Instrument used to static balance wheel and tire assemblies.

Bushing   Liner or separator between parts. Usually made of soft metal, plastic, or rubber, it is used to reduce friction and wear between parts.

Bypass port   Cooling system passage that allows coolant to go around the thermostat.

Caliper (brake)   Actuating device of a disc brake. A hydraulically actuated clamp that forces brake shoes into contact with a disc brake rotor.

Caliper (tool)   Adjustable measuring device.

Cam angle   See **Dwell.**

Camber   Inward or outward tilt of a wheel. The angle formed by the centerline of the wheel and the true vertical.

Camber roll   Inherent characteristic of independent front suspension systems to change camber angles when cornering.

Camber wear   Wear on one side of a tire tread caused by the angle at which the tire tread contacts the road surface.

Cam bolt   Bolt fitted with an eccentric that causes parts to change position when the bolt is turned.

Camshaft   Shaft machined to have a series of cam lobes. The rotation of a camshaft opens the valves in an engine.

Canister   Container of activated charcoal used to absorb and store fuel evaporation emissions.

Capacitor   See **Condenser.**

Carbon monoxide (CO)   Harmful gas produced by automotive engine combustion.

Carbon pile   Variable resistance unit used to perform certain electrical tests.

Carburetor   Device that measures and mixes fuel and air.

Car stands   Pedestal-type supports for holding up a car once the car has been raised.

Case hardened   Hardening of the outside layer of a tool or part.

Castellated nut   Nut that has slots through which a cotter pin may be passed to secure the nut to its bolt or stud.

Caster   Forward or backward tilt of the steering axis centerline. The angle formed by the centerline of the steering axis and the true vertical when viewed from the side.

Catalytic converter   Chamber in an exhaust system that contains a catalyst. The catalyst decreases the amount of unburned hydrocarbons in the exhaust gases by increasing their rate of oxidation.

Cell   One unit or compartment of a battery.

Celsius or centigrade (C)   System of measurement used to measure heat and cold.

Center bolt   Bolt that maintains the alignment of the leaves in a leaf spring. It also maintains the position of the axle housing on the spring.

Center link   See **Relay rod.**

Center of gravity   Point about which the weight of a car is evenly distributed. The point of balance.

Centrifugal advance   System that uses centrifugal force to advance spark timing as engine speed increases.

Centrifugal force   Outward force from the center of a rotating object.

Cetane number   Used to designate how well a diesel fuel reacts or burns.

Charging rate   Current flow, measured in amperes, from the generator or charger to the battery.

Chassis   Frame, suspension systems, engine, and drive train of a vehicle. The assembled parts of an automobile without the body.

Check valve   Valve that opens to allow passage in one direction but closes to prohibit flow in a reverse direction.

Choke   Valve used to reduce the amount of air that enters a carburetor.

CID   Cubic inch displacement.

Circuit   Connection of conductors that provides a complete path for current to flow from a power source, through a load, and return to the power source.

Circuit breaker   Circuit protection device that opens the circuit when current flow exceeds a predetermined amount.

Closed circuit   Complete circuit.

Clutch   Friction device used to connect and disconnect the engine and the transmission.

Clutch cover assembly   Assembly of the pressure plate, springs, and release levers that acts to engage and disengage a clutch.

Clutch disc   Driven member in an automotive clutch.

Clutch fork   Lever that holds and moves the clutch release bearing.

Clutch housing   See **Bell housing.**

Clutch pedal play   Distance a clutch pedal can be depressed before the release bearing contacts the levers of the cover assembly.

Clutch pressure plate   Spring-loaded part of a clutch assembly that holds the clutch disc against the flywheel.

Clutch release bearing   Bearing that contacts the levers or fingers of a clutch cover assembly.

Coefficient of friction   Relative measurement of the friction developed between two objects in contact with each other.

Coil (ignition)   Transformer that multiplies battery voltage to a voltage sufficient to push current across the gap of a spark plug.

Coil spring   Length of spring-steel wire wound in the shape of a spiral.

Coil spring compressor   Tool for compressing a coil spring to allow its removal and installation.

Cold cranking rating   Measurement of the amount of current a battery can supply for 30 seconds at 0°F (−18°C) without the voltage of any cell dropping below 1.2 volts.

Color code   Color markings used to identify wires in a circuit.

Combination brake system   Dual brake system that uses disc brakes at the front wheels and drum brakes at the rear wheels.

Combination valve   Valve used in combination brake systems that combines two or more valves in a common housing. A combination valve may contain a pressure differential valve, a proportioning valve, and a metering valve.

Combustion   Rapid burning.

Combustion chamber   Area provided for combustion to occur above the top of a piston.

Commutator   Series of metal bars or segments that are connected to the windings of an armature.

Compensating port   Small hole connecting the master cylinder reservoir with the master cylinder bore. The compensating port is open while the brakes are released, and it provides a means for allowing for expansion and contraction of the brake fluid.

Compression   Application of pressure to a gas.

Compression (springs)   Loading, or storing of energy, in a spring.

Compression gauge   Instrument used to measure the compression in the cylinders of an engine.

Compression ratio   Ratio between the volume of a combustion chamber and a cylinder when the piston is at BDC, and the volume of the combustion chamber when the piston is at TDC.

Compression test   Comparison of the compression measured in all the cylinders of an engine.

Concentric   Having the same center.

Condensation   Conversion of a vapor to a liquid.

Condenser   Electrical device that can absorb and store surges of current.

Conductor   Any material that allows the flow of current.

Connecting rod   Link between a piston and the crankshaft.

Contact area   Portion of a tire that contacts the road at any given time.

Continuity   Continuous, unbroken path for current flow. A closed or complete circuit.

Control arms, front   Horizontal arms that connect the front wheel to the car and support the weight of the front of the car.

Control arms, rear   Horizontal arms that connect the rear axle housing to the frame when coil springs are used in the rear suspension system. The arms maintain axle alignment and handle the driving and torque loads.

Control circuit   Used to operate the starting circuit of an engine.

Coolant   Mixture of water and antifreeze used in a cooling system.

Coolant recovery system   Captures automotive coolant and returns it to the radiator.

Corbin hose clamp   Self-tightening spring clamp used to seal a hose.

Core (radiator)   Tubular section of a radiator where the coolant transfers its heat to the air.

Cotter pin   Round locking pin formed by a folded semicircular steel wire. The pin is locked by spreading the paired ends of the wire.

CPR   Cardiopulmonary resuscitation. A life-saving technique.

Crankcase   Lower housing of an engine. The crankcase houses the crankshaft.

Cranking voltage   Battery voltage valve when the starter is cranking an engine.

Crankshaft   Offset or cranklike shaft by which an engine delivers power. By means of connecting rods, the crankshaft converts the reciprocating motion of the pistons to rotating motion.

Crossmember   Structural part of a frame that connects the side rans.

Cross shaft   See **Sector shaft.**

Crowfoot wrench   Short open end wrench that can be attached to a handle or to an extension.

Curb weight   Weight of a vehicle with a full supply of fuel, oil, and coolant but with no driver, passengers, or luggage.

Current   Flow of electrons through a conductor.

Cylinder   Hole in which a piston moves.

Cylinder block   Engine casting that contains cylinders.

Cylinder head   Upper casting of an engine. The combustion chambers are usually formed in the cylinder head.

Cylinder hone   Rotating tool that uses abrasive stones to remove minor imperfections and to polish the bore of a cylinder.

DC   Direct current.

Decibel   Measure of sound intensity.

Deflection   See **Distortion.**

Deflection, tire   Difference between the free diameter and the rolling diameter of a tire.

Degree   Unit used to measure angles. It is 1/360 of a circle. Usually abbreviated by the symbol ° placed behind a number.

Desiccant   Material used to remove moisture in an air conditioning system.

Detonation   Violent combustion of the fuel and air mixture in a cylinder.

Diagnosis   Scientific process of determining the causes of problems.

Dial indicator   Precision instrument that indicates linear measurement on a dial face.

Diaphragm   Flexible membrane that separates two chambers and yet allows the volume of each chamber to change.

Die (thread)   Tool for cutting threads on a shaft.

Differential   Gear device that allows the driving wheels on a common axle to rotate at different speeds.

Dimmer switch   Two-way switch, usually SPDT, used to select the high beams or the low beams of the headlights.

Diode   Solid state electronic device that allows current to flow in only one direction.

Dipstick   Device that measures the fluid level in an automotive unit. It dips into the fluid and has markings to indicate how much fluid is present.

Direct current   Electrical current that maintains a constant polarity.

Directional stability   Ability of a car to travel in a straight line with a minimum of driver control.

Disc   See **Rotor.**

Disc brake   Brake system that utilizes a disc, or rotor, attached to the wheel. The car is slowed or stopped when brake shoes, or pads, grasp the rotor with a clamping action.

Displacement   See **Piston displacement.**

Dissipate   To dry and evaporate a liquid.

Distilled water   Water with all the impurities removed.

Distortion   Twisting or bending condition.

Distributor (ignition)   Rotating switching device that opens and closes the primary circuit and distributes the secondary circuit voltage to the spark plugs.

DOHC   Double overhead camshafts.

DOT   Department of Transportation.

Double flare   Expanded end of tubing that is folded back to provide a double thickness.

Drag link   See **Relay rod.**

Drain plug   Plug that when removed allows fluid to escape from an automotive part.

Drift   See **Pull.**

Drive (starter)   Movable gear and clutch assembly that enables the starter motor to turn the flywheel.

Drive shaft   Shaft connecting the transmission to the driving axle.

Drive train   System of parts that transmits power from the engine to the driving wheels.

Drop center rim   Common wheel design in which the center of the rim is lower than the edges, or flanges.

Dropped center   Lowered area in the center section of a wheel rim.

Drum brake   Brake system that uses curved shoes which are expanded to contact the inside of a rotating drum or ring.

Dual brake system   Brake system that utilizes two separate hydraulic systems.

Dual master cylinder   Master cylinder that has two reservoirs and two pistons, usually in tandem. Dual master cylinders are used in dual brake systems.

Duo-servo   Brake design that provides servo action regardless of the direction of drum rotation.

Dust covers   Small plugs made of rubber or metal, used to cover the access holes in backing plates and drums.

Dwell   Amount of time, measured in degrees of distributor shaft rotation, that current flows in the primary circuit.

Dwell meter   Instrument that measures dwell.

Dynamic balance   Balance in motion. The balance of a wheel while it is rotating. The total weight distributed evenly over both the axis of rotation and the centerline of the wheel.

Eccentric   Off-center.

Eccentric bolt   See **Cam bolt.**

Electricity   Directed movement of electrons.

Electrochemical action   Chemical action that takes place between the plates and the electrolyte in a battery.

Electrode   Center and outside parts of a spark plug where electricity flows to jump a gap.

Electrolyte   Mixture of sulfuric acid and water used in a lead/acid battery.

Electromagnet   Nonpermanent magnet consisting of a coil of wire wrapped around a soft iron core. Magnetism is present only while current flows through the coil.

Electromotive force   Electrical pressure. Voltage.

Electronic ignition system   System that uses solid state electronic components in the primary circuit to eliminate the need for breaker points.

Element (battery)   Group of positive plates and a group of negative plates assembled with separators.

Emergency disconnect   Switch used to cut off the power to a machine.

End play   See **Axial play.**

Energy   Ability to do work.

Energy absorbing steering column   Steering column designed to collapse, or telescope, at a controlled rate in the event of a frontal collision.

Energy conserving   Term found in labeling of an oil container to indicate the oil has additives that reduce enough friction to conserve fuel. Used on synthetic oil products.

Engine   Device that converts heat energy to mechanical energy.

Engine displacement   Total displacement of all the cylinders in an engine.

Equalizer   Device used in parking brake systems to equalize the pull of both brake cables.

Ethylene glycol   Chemical compound used as the major ingredient in permanent antifreeze.

Evaporation   Conversion of a liquid to a vapor.

Exhaust manifold   System of passages that connects each cylinder of an engine to the exhaust pipe.

Exhaust pipe   Pipe connecting the exhaust manifold to the muffler.

Exhaust stroke   That stroke of a four-stroke cycle during which the burnt gases are forced from the cylinder.

Extreme pressure (EP)   Designates a grease that can withstand high pressure.

Eye wash station   Device used to put distilled water into the eyes when chemicals have been splashed in them.

Feather-edge wear pattern   See **Sawtooth wear pattern.**

Feeler gauge   Thin strip of metal of known thickness used to measure the clearance between two parts.

Field   Area of magnetic force that surrounds a magnet.

Filament   Wire conductor in a bulb. The filament glows to produce light.

Filler port   Large hole connecting the master cylinder reservoir with the master cylinder bore. The filler port permits fluid to flow from the reservoir into the hydraulic system.

Filter   Straining device that removes foreign matter from a liquid or from a gas.

Firewall   Body panel that separates the engine compartment from the passenger compartment.

Firing order   Sequence in which the cylinders of an engine fire.

Flameproof cabinet   Air-tight cabinet used to store flammable liquids.

Flare   Expanded, funnel-shaped end of a piece of tubing.

Flare nut wrench   See **Tubing wrench.**

Flaring tool   Tool used to give the ends of tubing a flared shape.

Flasher   Rapidly operating circuit breaker used to alternately make and break a circuit. Usually used in turn signals and emergency light circuits.

Floating caliper   Single-piston caliper positioned by pins, bolts, or ways.

Flushing   Method of cleaning a system by pumping a liquid through the system to wash away foreign matter.

Flux   Compound used to remove traces of surface oxidation and prevent additional oxidation during soldering.

Flywheel   Heavy wheel attached to a crankshaft. The flywheel smooths out the rotation between power strokes through its momentum.

Focal colors   Safety colors used around edges of tables and machines.

Foot-pound   Unit of measurement for torque. In tightening a nut or bolt, 1 foot-pound is the torque obtained by a pulling force of 1 pound applied to a wrench handle 12 inches long.

Force   Pulling or pushing effort measured in pounds.

Fouled   When a spark plug is shorted across the electrodes with oil and carbon.

Four-stroke cycle   Term used to describe the operation of a particular type of internal combustion engine. The strokes indicate the action that occurs with each movement of the piston: (1) intake, (2) compression, (3) power, and (4) exhaust.

Frame   Foundation of an automobile. The steel structure to which the body is attached.

Free diameter   Outer diameter of a tire that is not under load.

Friction   Resistance to motion between two objects in contact with each other.

Fuel pump   Device that pulls fuel from the fuel tank and forces it to the carburetor or injector pump.

Fuse   Electrical safety device. A fuse allows a limited amount of current to flow through it. If the current flow exceeds that limit, the fuse melts, or "blows," breaking the circuit.

Fuse block   Assembly of fuse holders for various circuits.

Fusible link   Length of fuse wire used in a circuit to protect the circuit from excess current.

Gallery   Oil passage in an engine block.

Gap   Air space between two electrodes or contacts.

Gasket   Liner or packing sandwiched between two parts to obtain a leakproof joint.

Generator   Device that converts mechanical energy to electrical energy.

Glazed   When the sides of a belt become slick and no longer transmit power to the unit being driven.

Gravity bleeding   Method of purging air from a hydraulic system by allowing the fluid to force air out of an opened bleeder valve by its own weight.

Grid   Meshlike framework of a plate in a lead-acid battery.

Ground   Common return route in electrical circuits. The metal parts of a car are usually used as a ground to provide a return path to the negative (−) battery terminal.

Ground cable   Cable connecting the battery to the engine or to the frame of a vehicle.

Halogen light   Gas-filled bulb that produces strong light.

Headlight aimers   Machine used to set vehicle headlights so the light pattern will be correct.

Heat dissipation   Transfer of heat, usually to the surrounding air.

Heat exchanger   Device used to remove heat from automatic transmission fluid.

Heat range   Operating temperature range of a spark plug.

Heat riser   Part of an intake manifold heated by exhaust gases to aid vaporization while the engine is cold.

Heel   End of a brake shoe nearest the anchor.

Heimlich maneuver   Technique used to save a person from choking.

High pedal   Condition in which the brakes are applied when the brake pedal is depressed only a slight amount.

High-rate discharge test   See **Load test.**

High tension wires   See **Secondary wires.**

Hold-down (battery)   Clamp that holds a battery in its tray or mount.

Hold-down (brake shoe)   Device that uses spring tension to hold a brake shoe against a backing plate.

Hone   To remove metal with a fine abrasive stone.

Horses   See **Car stands.**

Hotchkiss drive   Rear axle suspension system in which the driving force and axle torque are handled by leaf springs.

Hub   Central part of a wheel. The housing for the bearings on which the wheel rotates around a spindle.

Hubbed drum   Brake drum mounted on a hub.

Hubbed rotor   Rotor mounted on a hub.

Hydraulic   Using fluids to transmit force and motion.

Hydraulic brakes   Brakes actuated by hydraulic pressure.

Hydraulics   Science of the use of fluids to transmit force and motion.

Hydrocarbon   Chemical compound made up of hydrogen and carbon.

Hydrometer   Instrument used to measure the specific gravity of a liquid.

Hydroscopic   Tendency to absorb water.

ID   Inside diameter.

Idler arm   Arm or lever that can rotate about its support and is used to support one end of a relay rod. Usually duplicates the motion of the Pitman arm.

Idler pulley   Pulley that can be moved to adjust the tension of a belt in a belt drive system.

Idle speed   Slowest engine operating speed.

Ignition system   System that boosts battery voltage and distributes it to each spark plug at the proper time.

ILSAC   International Lubrication Standardization and Approval Committee.

Impact puller   Tool designed to loosen or separate parts by impact. One part is struck to cause sudden movement.

Impact wrench   Power tool that turns nuts and bolts by means of a series of blows.

Incandescent   Glowing white-hot. Light is produced by the incandescence of the filament in a bulb.

Included angle   Sum of the angles of camber and steering axis inclination.

Independent suspension   Suspension systems by which a wheel on one side of a car can move, vertically without affecting the wheel on the other side of the car.

Induction   Transfer of electricity by means of magnetism.

Inertia   Tendency of a body at rest to remain at rest, and the tendency of a body in motion to remain in motion.

Infinity   Ohmmeter reading that indicates an open circuit or an infinite resistance.

In-line engine   Engine whose cylinders are arranged in a single row.

Insulation   Any material used to prevent the flow of current or heat.

Intake manifold   System of passages that connects the carburetor of air intake system to each of the cylinders in an engine.

Intake stroke   That stroke in a four-stroke cycle during which the fuel and air mixture enters the cylinder.

Integral   Made in one piece. A combination of two or more parts made as one unit.

Interleaf friction   Friction between the leaves of a leaf spring.

Intermediate link   See **Relay rod.**

Jack   Device for raising a car.

Jack stands   See **Car stands.**

Jam nut (Jamb nut)   See **Lock nut.**

Journal   That part of a shaft which contacts a bearing.

Jumper cables   Cables used to start a car that has a discharged battery.

Jumper wires   Tools used to temporarily reroute current by bridging or bypassing components for test purposes.

Jump start   When another battery or charger is used to start a vehicle.

Kilopascal (kPa)   Unit used to measure pressure.

Kinetic balance   Balance of the radial forces on a spinning tire. Determined by an electronic balancer.

Kinetic energy   Energy of a mass in motion.

Kingpin   Pin or shaft on which the steering spindle assembly rotates.

Kingpin inclination   See **Steering axis inclination.**

Knock-off puller   Type of impact puller consisting of an internally threaded cap that is installed on a threaded shaft. The cap is struck with a hammer until the impact loosens the fit between the shaft and its adjacent part.

KPI   Kingpin inclination.

Lash   Movement, or play, between parts. The clearance between moving parts, such as meshing gear teeth.

Lateral   Side.

Lateral runout   Wobble, or side-to-side movement, of a rotating wheel or of a rotating wheel and tire assembly.

Lead   Slight pull to one side.

Lead-acid battery   Battery that operates through the electrochemical action of lead, lead peroxide, and sulfuric acid.

Lead peroxide   Active material used to form the positive plates of a lead-acid battery.

Leaf spring   Spring made of individual strips, or leaves, of flat spring steel.

Leak detect dye   Used in an air conditioning system to detect leaks.

Lean mixture   When there is not enough fuel mixed with the air for proper combustion.

Limited-slip differential   Differential that utilizes a clutch device to deliver power to either driving wheel when the opposite wheel is spinning.

Lines of force   Lines by which a magnetic field can be visualized.

Linkage   System of rods and levers used to transmit motion or force.

Lithium   Material added to grease to reduce friction.

Load (electrical)   Any device that converts electrical energy to another form of energy.

Load range   Alphabetic system used to identify the service limitations of a tire.

Load test   Measurement of battery voltage taken while the battery is delivering a specified amount of current.

Lock nut   Second nut threaded on a bolt or stud. The lock nut is tightened against the nut which secures the bolt or stud and locks that nut in place.

Lock washer   Washer designed to prevent a nut or a bolt from loosening.

Long and short arm suspension   Independent suspension system that utilizes short upper control arms and long lower control arms.

Low pedal   Condition in which the brake pedal must travel very far or very close to the floor before the brakes are applied.

Low-profile tire   Tire designed with less height and a wider cross section than conventional tires.

Lubricant   Any material, usually liquid or semiliquid, that reduces friction when placed between two moving parts.

MacPherson strut   Suspension unit comprised of a coil spring mounted around a telescopic shock absorbing strut. When used in front suspension systems, the unit is usually mounted between a lower control arm and the frame, eliminating the need for an upper control arm.

Magnetic field   Area surrounding a magnet that is made up of lines of magnetic force.

Magnetic poles   Points where magnetic lines of force enter and leave a magnet.

Magnetism   Ability of a substance to attract iron.

Main leaf   Longest leaf in a leaf spring. The leaf in a leaf spring that has its ends rolled into eyes.

Manual bleeding   Method of purging air from a hydraulic brake system by manually operating the brake pedal.

Master cylinder   Part of the hydraulic system that converts the force of the driver to hydraulic pressure.

Mechanical advance   See **Centrifugal advance.**

Mechanical brakes   Brake system that is actuated mechanically, usually by rods or cables.

Mesothelioma   Cancer of the lining of the chest or abdominal cavity.

Metering valve   Valve used in combination brake systems that shuts off the flow of fluid to the front calipers during light pedal applications. It acts to delay the operation of the front brakes until the rear brakes have started to apply.

Micrometer   Precision instrument for linear measurement.

Millimeter   Metric unit of measurement equal to 0.039370 inch. Usually found abbreviated as mm, as in 1 mm.

Minute   Angle measure equal to 1/60 of 1°. Usually found abbreviated as ' following a number, as in 30'.

Molded   Term used to describe hoses made in curved shapes.

Molybdenum disulfide   Additive that helps grease withstand heat and pressure.

Motor   Device that converts electrical energy to mechanical energy.

Motor circuit   Circuit that runs the starter and supplies battery power to the starter.

MSDS   Material Safety Data Sheets. Supply safety data about a product.

Muffler   Device used to silence the noise of engine exhaust gases.

Multiviscosity   Term used to describe oils and greases that cover a range of viscosities.

Mushroom edges   When the edges of a tool are rounded over and deformed.

Needle bearing   Antifriction bearing that utilizes a series of very thin steel rollers.

Negative (NEG)   Used to label the ground side of a battery.

Neutralizer   Water or a chemical used to neutralize an acid.

Neutral start (safety) switch   Switch operated by the transmission operated by the transmission selector lever that prevents the starter motor from operating unless the transmission is placed in PARK or NEUTRAL.

NIASE   National Institute for Automotive Service Excellence.

Nitrogen oxides (NOx)   Fuel combustion by-product gases that contribute to air pollution.

Octane rating   Measurement of the ability of fuel to resist detonation.

OD   Outside diameter.

Ohm   Unit of measurement of resistance. A pressure of 1 volt is required to push a current of 1 ampere through a resistance of 1 ohm.

Ohmmeter   Instrument that measures resistance in ohms.

Oil filter   Straining device that removes foreign matter from oil.

Oil pan   On most engines, the lower part of the crankcase.

One-way clutch   See **Overrunning clutch.**

Open circuit   Circuit in which a break prevents the flow of current.

Orifice   Measured opening or hole that allows fluid flow in controlled amounts.

Oscillate   To move back and forth.

Out-of-round (brakes)   Drum defect in which the friction surface is not round, but has worn or warped into an oval or elliptical shape.

Out-of-round (journal)   Defect on a shaft where the journal has worn to an oval or elliptical shape.

Out-of-round (wheel and tire)   Defect in which the wheel or tire is not round.

Overcharge   When the battery is receiving more voltage and amperage than it needs.

Overinflation   Condition of a tire that is inflated to more than the recommended pressure.

Overrunning clutch   Clutch that transmits torque when turned in one direction, but slips when turned in the opposite direction.

Oversteer   Tendency of a car to turn more sharply than the driver intends while negotiating a turn.

Oxidation   When the battery terminals corrode due to air and moisture.

Oxygen sensor   Device that tells the computer how much oxygen is in the exhaust flow.

Ozone layer   Layer in the atmosphere that prevents solar ultraviolet rays from harming life on earth.

Pad   Common term for a brake shoe used in disc brakes.

PAG   Polyalkylene glycol. Used to lubricate air conditioner compressors.

Parallel circuit   Electrical circuit that provides a separate path for current flow to and return from each of two or more loads.

Parallelism   Parallel alignment of the two surfaces of a disc brake rotor.

Parallelogram steering linkage   Commonly used steering linkage system that utilizes a relay rod or center link to connect the Pitman arm to an idler arm which duplicates the Pitman arm's length and motion. Separate tie rods connect the steering arms to the relay rod. The assembled linkage resembles a parallelogram in shape, and the centerlines of the pivot points are parallel.

Parking brake   Mechanical brake system used to keep a parked car from moving.

Pascal's law   Basic law of hydraulics: "When pressure is exerted on a confined fluid, the pressure is transmitted equally and in all directions."

Patch area   See **Contact area.**

Pattern   Image that appears on an oscilloscope during testing.

PCV   Positive crankcase ventilation.

Pedal reserve   See **High pedal.**

Penetrating oil   Very thin oil used to penetrate rust and corrosion and to free rusted parts.

Permanent magnet   Piece of steel or alloy that acts as a magnet without the need for an electric current to create a magnetic field.

Petcock   Drain valve.

Phosgene gas   Deadly gas created when refrigerant is burned.

Pinging   Metallic knocking caused by detonation.

Pinion angle   Angle between the centerline of the drive shaft and the centerline of the differential pinion gear.

Piston   Movable plug that fits in a cylinder.

Piston cup   Rubber cup-shaped part that seals a brake cylinder and eliminates leakage between the piston and the cylinder walls.

Piston displacement   Volume displaced by a piston when it moves from BDC to TDC.

Piston pin   Pin that connects the piston to the connecting rod.

Piston rings   Expanding metal rings that fit in grooves cut around a piston. The rings provide a tight seal against the cylinder walls.

Piston skirt   Part of a piston below the piston rings.

Piston stops (brakes)   Tabs, or protrusions, on a backing plate positioned to prevent the wheel cylinder pistons from leaving the wheel cylinder.

Pitman arm   Arm connected to the steering gear sector shaft that transforms the rotating motion of the shaft to lateral motion at the relay rod.

Pitman shaft   See **Sector shaft.**

Pits   Holes or roughness left on a surface as a result of rust or corrosion.

Plates   Metal grids in a battery. Positive plates are composed of lead peroxide. Negative plates are composed of sponge lead.

Play   Movement between parts.

Plies   Layers of cord that make up the carcass, or body, of a tire.

Ply rating   Method of indicating relative tire strength. The ply rating usually does not indicate the actual number of plies.

Point gap   Distance between breaker points when they are held open by the highest part of a cam lobe.

Point resistance   Resistance to current flow between breaker points.

Polarity   Having poles, such as the north and south poles of a magnet, or the positive and negative terminals of an electrical power source or of a load. Polarity determines the direction of a magnetic field or the direction of current flow.

Pole shoes   Iron cores of the electromagnets that form the fields in a motor or in a DC generator.

Positive (POS)   Used to label the positive battery post and cable. The "hot" side.

Positive crankcase ventilation   Emission control system that pulls fumes from the crankcase and burns them in the engine.

Pour point depressants   Oil additives that improve the flow of the oil when cold and thicken the oil when hot.

Power brakes   Hydraulic brake system that utilizes engine manifold vacuum or an external hydraulic power source to boost the braking effort of the driver.

Power steering   Steering system that utilizes hydraulic pressure to boost the steering effort of the driver.

Power stroke   That stroke in a four-stroke cycle during which the fuel and air mixture burns.

Pre-ignition   Ignition of the fuel and air mixture before the spark jumps the plug gap.

Preload   Thrust load applied to bearings that support a rotating part to eliminate axial play or movement.

Pressure   Amount of force applied to a definite area. It is measured in pounds per square inch.

Pressure bleeder   Tank that stores brake fluid under pressure. When connected to the master cylinder, the fluid is forced through the system and facilitates bleeding.

Pressure bleeding   Method of purging air from a hydraulic system by forcing fluid through the system by means of a pressure bleeder.

Pressure cap   Radiator cap designed to hold in some of the pressure exerted by expanded coolant.

Pressure differential valve   Spool-type valve used in dual brake systems to detect any difference in pressure between the systems.

Pressure sender   Variable resistor actuated by pressure change.

Pressure sensitive switch   Switch actuated by a change in pressure.

Primary brake shoe   In self-energizing brakes, the primary shoe is the one that is pulled away from the anchor by the rotation of the drum. Usually it is the forward shoe.

Primary circuit   Circuit in the ignition system that creates the magnetic field in the coil.

Primary winding   Winding in an ignition coil that uses battery current to create a magnetic field.

Primary wires   Wires that form the conductors in the primary circuit.

Production option code (POC)   Code placed on a sticker to tell technicians what options have been placed in the vehicle. This is used to order parts.

Propeller shaft   See **Driveshaft.**

Proportioning valve   Valve used in dual brake systems that decreases the pressure at the rear brakes in proportion to pedal force.

psi   Pounds per square inch.

Pull   Tendency of a car to veer to one side.

Puller   Tool used to remove parts from a shaft or from a hole.

Pulley   Wheel, usually with a V-shaped groove or grooves, that drives or is driven by a belt.

Pushrod (master cylinder)   Rod that transmits the movement and force of the driver from the brake pedal lever to the master cylinder piston.

Pushrod (valve)   Rod that transmits the movement of the valve lifter to the rocker arm.

Pushrod (wheel cylinder)   Rod that transmits the movement and force of the wheel cylinder piston to the brake shoe.

R-12, R-134a   Refrigerants used in automotive air conditioners.

Race   See **Bearing race.**

Rack and pinion steering gear   Steering gear design that utilizes a small pinion gear attached to the steering shaft to move a long toothed bar, called the rack gear. The ends of the rack gear are attached to the steering arms by means of tie rods.

Radial force variation   Difference in stiffness at two or more points on a tire.

Radial load   Load applied at 90° to an axis of rotation.

Radial play   Movement at 90° to an axis of rotation.

Radial ply tire   Tire constructed of alternative plies positioned so the cords cross the tire centerline at an angle of 90°.

Radial runout   Variation in the radius of a wheel or a wheel and tire assembly. Out of round.

Radiator   Heat exchanger that allows the heat in the coolant to be passed off into the air.

Rag joint   Flexible coupling that contains a rubberized fabric disc or wafer. Usually found in steering systems.

Rate   Softness or stiffness of a spring. The load required to cause a spring to deflect 1 inch.

Reach   Distance between the firing end of a spark plug and its seat.

Rebound   Motion of a spring when suddenly released after compression. The release of energy from a compressed spring.

Recirculating ball steering gear   Commonly used steering gear design that utilizes a series of ball bearings to connect the worm gear to the ball nut. The balls, recirculated through tubes, provide rolling friction between the worm gear and the ball nut.

Rectifier   Device used to change AC to DC.

Regulator (alternator)   Device used to control output voltage.

Relay   Electromagnetic switch.

Relay rod   Part of a steering linkage that connects the Pitman arm to the idler arm.

Required voltage   Voltage necessary to force current across the gap of a spark plug.

Reserve capacity rating   Battery rating based on the amount of time that a battery at 80°F (27°C) can deliver 25 amperes without the voltage of any cell dropping below 1.75 volts.

Reservoir   Storage area.

Residual magnetism   Magnetism remaining in a material after the current flow that produces the magnetism is stopped.

Residual pressure   Slight pressure that remains in a hydraulic system after the brake pedal has been released.

Residual pressure (check) valve   Valve which is in the master cylinder and that acts to maintain a slight pressure in the system at all times.

Resistance   Ability of a conductor to restrict the flow of current.

Resonator   Exhaust system part that reduces engine noise.

Retaining spring   Spring used to connect the lower ends of a pair of brake shoes and hold them in contact with an anchor or a star wheel adjuster.

Retard (spark)   To change the ignition timing so the spark occurs later.

Retracting spring   Spring used to pull the brake shoes away from the drum when the brake pedal is released. Retracting springs also push the wheel cylinder pistons back into their bores and thus return the brake fluid to the master cylinder.

Reverse bleeding   Method of purging air from a hydraulic system by forcing fluid into the system at a bleeder valve and by allowing the air to escape at the master cylinder.

Rheostat   Variable resistor.

Rich mixture   When there is more fuel mixed with the air than the engine needs.

Riding height   See **Suspension height.**

Rim diameter   Diameter of a wheel measured at the base of the rim flange.

Ring gear (flywheel)   Gear fitted around the circumference of a flywheel so the starter motor drive gear can mesh with it and crank the engine.

Rivet   Fastening device used to secure lining to a brake shoe. A headed pin that is placed through holes in two or more objects. The end opposite the head is expanded to secure the pin.

Road crown   Slope, or pitch, of a road from its center to the curbs or shoulders.

Road feel   Feeling transmitted back to the steering wheel by the wheels of the car.

Road shock   Shock or movement transmitted from the road surface to the steering wheel through the steering gear and linkage.

Rocker arm   Lever that transmits the movement of a pushrod or a cam to a valve.

Roller bearing   Antifriction bearing that uses a series of steel rollers held between inner and outer bearing races.

Rotor (alternator)   Rotating field coil that creates a moving magnetic field.

Rotor (brake)   Disc attached to a wheel or hub to provide a friction surface for a brake system.

Rotor (distributor)   Rotating switch contact that distributes the high voltage produced in the coil to each of the spark plug wires.

Rotor lathe   Machine used to refinish the surfaces of a brake rotor.

rpm   Revolutions per minute.

RTV   Room temperature vulcanizing sealer used as a gasket material between parts.

Runout   Any variation in the movement of the surface of a rotating object.

Saddle   That portion of an axle housing which mounts on a leaf spring.

SAE   Society of Automotive Engineers.

Safe range   Area on a dipstick that indicates the correct fluid operating range.

Safety colors   Colors used to alert shop workers about possible safety hazards.

Safety rim   Wheel design in which the rim has two ridges inside the flanged edges. The bead of the tire is held between the flange and the ridge and restrained from slipping into the dropped center in the event of a blowout.

Sawtooth wear pattern   Tire wear pattern in which the tread ribs wear more on one side than on the other side. Usually caused by incorrect toe-in.

Schematic   See **Wiring diagram.**

Score   Scratch or groove. Commonly found on cylinder walls and on the friction surfaces of brake drums, brake rotors, and flywheels.

Scrub radius   Distance between the extended centerline of the steering axis and the centerline of the tire at the point where the tire contacts the road.

Scrub rib   Protective rib, or ridge, on the sidewall of a tire. Designed to protect the sidewall when the tire comes in contact with a curb.

Sealed beam bulb   Unitized bulb consisting of a lens, reflector, and a filament.

Sealed bearing   Bearing that has been lubricated and sealed at the time of its manufacture.

Secondary brake shoe   In self-energizing brakes, the brake shoe that is pushed into contact with an anchor by the rotation of the drum. Usually the rear shoe.

Secondary circuit   Ignition system circuit that transmits the high voltage from the coil to the spark plugs.

Sector (gear)   Segment of a gear with two or more teeth.

Sector shaft   Shaft to which the sector (gear) is attached. The output shaft of a steering gear.

Self-adjusting brake   Brake that automatically maintains the proper lining-to-drum clearance.

Self-discharge   Chemical action in a battery that causes it to slowly discharge.

Self-energizing brake   Brake design in which the brake shoes, through leverage and wedging action, are applied with a greater force than that furnished by the wheel cylinder.

Semielliptical spring   Leaf spring that is formed in the shape of one-half an ellipse.

Separators   Insulators in a battery that prevent the plates from contacting each other.

Series circuit   Electrical circuit that provides only one path for the flow of current through two or more loads.

Series-parallel circuit   Circuit that has some components in series with the power source and some components in parallel with each other and with the power source.

Serpentine   Name given to a belt that drives all the accessories.

Serrations   Grooves, or teeth, formed in parts so they do not shift positions when they are tightened together.

Service classification   Two-letter method used to designate oil quality.

Servo action   Braking action in which one shoe serves to add to the application force of another. This action provides a high brake application force without requiring high pedal effort on the part of the driver.

Shackle   Movable link used to attach one end of a leaf spring to the frame while allowing it to change in length.

Shim   Spacer used to adjust the distance between two parts.

Shimmy   Rapid oscillation, or wobble, of a wheel and tire assembly about the steering axis.

Shock absorber   Device used to dampen the oscillations of a spring.

Shoe   Part used in a drum brake system that applies friction to the drum, stopping the vehicle.

Short circuit   Defect in an electrical circuit that allows current to return to the power source before passing through the load.

Side rails   Structural members that comprise the sides of a frame.

Sight glass   Used in an air conditioner system to look at refrigerant flow.

Single-wire system   Circuit using a single wire to conduct current to a load and using the metal frame and body of the car as the return conductor or ground.

Slave cylinder   Used in hydraulic clutches to operate the pressure plate.

Sleeves   See **Tie rod sleeves.**

Sliding caliper   Single piston caliper positioned by machined surfaces on its anchor plate.

Sliding yoke   Allows a drive shaft to expand and contract.

Slip angle   Angle between the true centerline of the tire and the actual path followed by the tire while rounding a turn.

Slip ring   Part of an alternator rotor contacted by a brush.

Snap ring   Split ring held in a groove by its own tension. Internal snap rings are used in grooves cut around the bore of a hole. External snap rings are used in grooves cut around a shaft.

Soft pedal   Soft, springy feeling detected when the brake pedal is depressed and when air is present in the hydraulic system.

Solenoid   Electromagnet with a movable core.

Solid-axle suspension   Suspension system in which the wheels are mounted at each end of a solid, or undivided, axle or axle housing.

Spanner   A wrench. Tool designed to turn a nut or threaded ring by means of holes or notches in the part.

Spark knock   When the fuel in the combustion chamber burns incorrectly.

Spark plug   Device that provides a fixed air gap across which current jumps to provide a spark.

Spark timing   See **Timing.**

Specifications   Measurements recommended by the manufacturer.

Specific gravity   Weight of a substance compared with the weight of an equal volume of water.

Spindle   That part of a suspension system about which a wheel rotates. A shaft or pin about which another part rotates.

Spindle bolt   See **King pin.**

Spinner   Electrically driven drum or roller used to spin a wheel and tire assembly on the car to check for imbalance.

Splash shield   Metal deflector used to protect a disc brake rotor from road splash.

Splice   To join together.

Spline   Tooth or serration cut on a shaft or in a hole. Used where a part must fit on a shaft without turning.

Sponge lead   Type of battery plate material.

Spongy pedal   See **Soft pedal.**

Spontaneous combustion   When gasoline-soaked materials catch fire due to excess heat buildup.

Spoon   See **Brake spoon.**

Spring bolt   Bolt used to attach the fixed end of a leaf spring to the car frame.

Spring clips   Clamps or straps used on leaf springs to prevent the ends of the leaves from separating when the spring rebounds.

Spring hanger   Mounting to which the fixed end of a leaf spring is attached by the spring bolt.

Spring liners   Strips of soft metal or plastic used to separate the leaves in a leaf spring.

Spring pockets   Formed sections of a frame designed to retain one end of a coil spring.

Spring seats   See **Spring pockets.**

Spring steel   Type of steel which has properties that allow it to withstand a great amount of deflection and still return to its original shape.

Spring wind-up   Deflection of a leaf spring during acceleration and deceleration.

Sprung weight   Total weight of all the parts of a car supported by the springs.

Stability   Property of a body that causes it, when disturbed from a condition of equilibrium or steady motion, to develop forces or tendencies to restore it to its original condition.

Stabilizer   Device that uses the torsional resistance of a steel bar to reduce the roll of a car and to prevent too great a difference in the spring action at the wheels on a common axle.

Stake   To secure a part by burring or distorting adjacent surfaces.

Star wheel adjuster   Threaded device used to expand the brake shoes to obtain the proper lining-to-drum clearance.

Static   At rest. Stationary.

Static balance   Balance at rest. A distribution of weight around the axis of rotation so a wheel has no tendency to rotate by itself, regardless of its position.

Static pressure   See **Residual pressure.**

Stator (alternator)   Stationary winding in which current is induced by a moving magnetic field.

Steering angle   See **Toe-out on turns.**

Steering arms   Arms that transmit the steering motion from the tie rods to the steering knuckles.

Steering axis inclination   Tilt of the centerline of the steering axis toward the centerline of the car. The angle formed by the centerline of the steering axis and the true vertical when viewed from the front of the car.

Steering column   Support for the steering wheel. It includes the mast jacket, steering shaft, and shift tube. It also serves as a mounting for other controls.

Steering gear   Device made of gears to transmit steering effort to the steering linkage.

Steering geometry   Term used to describe the relationships of the various measurements and angles in the steering and suspension systems.

Steering knuckle   Forging consisting of a spindle and its mounting. It is mounted between the upper and lower ball joints and pivots for steering.

Steering linkage   System of links, rods, and levers used to transmit motion from the steering gear to the steering knuckles.

Steering shaft   Steel rod that connects the steering wheel to the steering gear.

Steering system   Combination of the steering gear, steering wheel, and steering linkage, which enables the driver to turn the front wheels.

Steering wheel play   Any movement of the steering wheel that does not produce movement of the front wheels.

Straddle mounted   Method of mounting a rotating part on bearings so the part is supported on two sides.

Striker plate   Part of a vehicle door latch that locks the door closed.

Stroke   Distance a piston travels as it moves from TDC to BDC.

Strut   Brace used between a control arm and the frame.

Stud   Headless bolt that is threaded on both ends.

Sulfated   Condition of a lead-acid battery when the composition of the plates has changed to lead sulfate.

Supercharger   Device that forces the fuel and air mixture into the intake manifold.

Support yoke   Part of a rack and pinion steering gear that braces the pinion against the reaction force of the rack.

Surface charge   When the battery voltage is higher than normal due to a recent charge being placed on the battery. This charge has to be removed to test the battery.

Suspension arms   See **Control arms.**

Suspension height   Distance from a specified point on a car to the road surface when the car is at curb weight.

Switch   Control device used to open and close an electrical circuit.

Synchronizer   Standard transmission parts that cause the gears to run at the same speed and make shifting easier.

Tach-Dwell meter   Instrument that measures both engine speed and ignition system dwell.

Tachometer   Instrument for measuring engine speed.

Tailpipe   Outlet pipe from a muffler.

Tap (thread)   Tool used to cut threads in a hole.

Taper   Lack of parallelism. A cylinder defect in which one end of a cylinder has a larger diameter than the opposite end. A drum defect in which the diameter of the outer edge is different from the diameter at the inner edge.

Tapered roller bearing   Antifriction bearing that uses a series of tapered steel rollers held between tapered inner and outer races.

TDC   Top dead center.

Temperature sender   Variable resistor actuated by temperature change.

Temperature-sensitive switch   Switch actuated by a change in temperature.

Tensile cord breakage   When the cords of a drive belt break and cause the belt to fail.

Test lamp   Bulb with wires attached to it so it can be inserted in a circuit to confirm the presence of voltage.

Thermal switch   See **Temperature-sensitive switch.**

Thermistor   Resistor whose resistance decreases as its temperature increases.

Thermostat   Temperature operated valve that controls the flow of coolant in a cooling system.

Throttle   Valve in the carburetor that controls the flow of fuel and air mixture into the intake manifold.

Thrust load   Load applied in line with an axis of rotation.

Tie rod   Rod used to connect the relay rod or rack gear to a steering arm.

Tie rod end   Ball-and-socket joint at the end of a tie rod.

Tie rod fork   Fork-shaped wedge used to remove a ball stud from its mounting hole.

Tie rod sleeves   Tubes or pipes with internal threads into which the tie rods and tie rod ends are threaded. Turning the sleeves extends or retracts the tie rod, changing its length.

Timing (ignition)   Timing of the firing of the spark plug in relation to the position of the piston.

Timing belt   Cogged belt that connects the crankshaft to the camshaft.

Timing chain   Chain that connects the crankshaft to the camshaft.

Timing gears   Gears that connect the crankshaft to the camshaft.

Timing light   Strobe light used to "stop" the motion of a crankshaft pulley or flywheel so the alignment of the timing marks can be observed.

Timing marks   Marks, usually on the crankshaft pulley or flywheel and on the engine, used to indicate the position of the crankshaft.

Tire bead   See **Bead.**

Tire casing   Body of a tire exclusive of its tread.

Tire print   Pattern made by the tire at the point of road contact.

Tire problem detector (TPD)   Instrument that measures the radial force variation of a mounted tire.

Tire rotation   System by which wheel and tire assemblies are moved to different locations at regular intervals. Tire rotation often equalizes wear and thus extends tire life.

Tire sidewall   Portion of the tire between the bead and the tread.

Tire tread   Portion of a tire that contacts the road surface.

Tire wear pattern   Characteristics of the wear shown by the tread of a tire.

Toe (alignment)   Difference between the measurements taken between the front and the rear of the tires mounted on a common axle.

Toe (brakes)   End of a brake shoe that is not adjacent to its anchor.

Toe-in   Condition in which the front of the wheels on a common axle are closer together than the rear of the wheels.

Toe-out   Condition in which the front of the wheels on a common axle are farther apart than the rear of the wheels.

Toe-out on turns   Difference between the turning angle of the inside wheel and the outside wheel during a turn. The angle is usually measured while the inner wheel is turned 20°.

Tolerance   Permissible variation, usually stated as extremes of a specification.

Tool bit   Hardened steel or carbide blade that cuts away metal during machining.

Torque   Force that tends to produce a twisting or turning motion.

Torque sequence   Order in which a series of bolts or nuts should be tightened.

Torque wrench   Wrench or handle that indicates the amount of torque applied to a bolt or nut. A tool used to tighten bolts and nuts to a specified torque.

Torsion bar   Spring steel bar that is supported and anchored at one end, whereas the other end is supported but allowed to twist. The bar's resistance to any torque or twisting effort provides spring action.

Torsion bar suspension   Suspension system that utilizes torsion bars in place of springs.

Tracking   Relationship of the paths taken by the front wheels and the rear wheels. The alignment of the center of the tread distance of the front wheels with the center of the tread distance of the rear wheels.

Tramp   See **Wheel tramp.**

Transistor   Semiconductor device used in electronic circuits.

Transmission   Device used to adjust engine speed and torque to particular driving situations.

Transmission cooler   Device placed in the hydraulic flow of an automatic transmission to reduce heat. This is added when vehicles are used to tow trailers.

Transverse torsion bars   Torsion bars mounted so they extend across the frame.

Tread (alignment)   Distance between the centerlines of the wheels on a common axle.

Tread wear indicators   Ridges molded into the grooves between the ribs of a tire tread. The indicators become visible when the tread is worn to a depth of less than 1/16 inch (1.6 mm).

Trouble codes   When the computer detects a part failure these codes are set and tell the technician what has failed in the system.

Tubes (steering)   See **Tie rod sleeves.**

Tubing bender   Tool used to bend tubing without kinking or deforming its walls.

Tubing cutter   Tool used to cut tubing. In operation, the tubing is held between a pair of rollers and a sharp wheel. The tool is moved around the tubing, and the wheel cuts the tubing cleanly and without distortion.

Tubing wrench   Wrench used to turn fittings on tubing. A tubing wrench distributes the turning forces evenly around the fitting, and thus minimizes the possibility of damage.

Turbocharger   Supercharger driven by the pressure of exhaust gasses.

Turning angle   See **Toe-out on turns.**

Turning radius   Usually given as the diameter of the smallest circle in which a car can travel.

U-bolt   A steel shaft, threaded at both ends, that is bent 180° (U shaped). Used to attach an axle housing to a leaf spring.

Underinflation   Condition of a tire that is inflated to less than the recommended pressure.

Understeer   Tendency of a car to turn less sharply than the driver intends while negotiating a turn.

Unibody   Car design that does not use a frame. The body of the car, reinforced at appropriate points, provides the mounting for the suspension systems.

Unit body   See **Unibody.**

Universal joint   Connection that allows torque to be transmitted through an angle.

Unsprung weight   Weight of the parts in the suspension and steering systems that are not supported by the springs.

Vacuum   Pressure less than atmospheric pressure.

Vacuum advance   System that utilizes engine manifold vacuum to advance spark timing as engine load decreases.

Valve (engine)   Movable plug or door that opens and closes a port in the combustion chamber. Most engines have two valves for each cylinder. An intake valve opens to let the fuel and air mixture in, and an exhaust valve opens to let the burned gases out.

Valve lifter   Part moved by the lobe on a camshaft. A cam follower.

Valve spring   Spring that closes a valve and holds it closed.

Vaporize   To change a liquid to a gas. Fuel is vaporized so it mixes better with air and burns cleaner.

Ventilated rotor   Disc brake rotor that is formed with cooling fins cast between its friction surfaces.

VIN   Vehicle identification number. Used to identify the vehicle and help technicians get the right parts and use correct specifications.

Viscosity   Measurement of the ability of a liquid to flow.

Viscosity index improver   Oil additive that helps the oil flow better when cold and thicken when hot.

Volt   Unit of measurement of electrical pressure. A pressure of 1 volt is required to push 1 ampere of current through a resistance of 1 ohm.

Voltage   Electrical pressure that causes current to flow in a circuit.

Voltage drop   Loss in electrical pressure as it pushes current through resistance.

Voltmeter   Instrument that measures electrical pressure in volts.

Vulcanizing   Process used to bond rubber by means of chemical action under heat and pressure.

Waddle   Side-to-side movement of a car. Usually caused by a tire that has a belt which has been installed crookedly.

Wander   Tendency of a car to veer, or drift, to either side from a straight path.

Water jacket   Hollow areas surrounding the cylinders and combustion chambers of an engine. Coolant flows through the water jackets to carry off excess heat.

Water pump   Device in the cooling system that circulates the coolant through the system.

Watt   Unit of measurement of electrical power. Volts times amperes equals watts.

Watts rating   Battery rating obtained by multiplying the current flow from a battery by the battery voltage of 0°F (−18°C).

Wear indicator bar   Area in the tread pattern of a tire that tells the technician when the tire is worn out. If the bar is visible across the tread the tire is not legal or safe to run.

Weave   See **Wander.**

Wedge bulb   Bulb that has no metal base.

Wheel alignment   See **Alignment.**

Wheel alignment rack   Equipment that supports and positions a car so accurate measurements can be made of the relationships of parts in the steering and suspension systems.

Wheel balancer   Machine used to check and correct the balance of a wheel and tire assembly.

Wheelbase   Distance between the centers of the front and rear wheels.

Wheel cylinder   Output cylinder in a hydraulic brake system.

Wheel tramp   Vertical movement of a spindle caused by static imbalance.

Wheel weights   Weights made of lead alloy. They are attached to a wheel rim to balance a wheel and tire assembly.

Wire gauge   Wire size numbers based on the cross-section area of the conductor.

Wiring diagram   Drawing of the components and conductors in a circuit.

Working device   See **Load.**

Worm and sector steering   Steering gear design which utilizes a worm shaft that engages a sector shaft.

Worm shaft (gear)   Shaft that has a spiraled tooth in the shape of a very coarse thread. Normally used to engage a ball nut or a sector gear.

Zerk fitting   Grease fitting.

Index